1812

1812

War with America

JON LATIMER

THE BELKNAP PRESS OF
HARVARD UNIVERSITY PRESS
Cambridge, Massachusetts
London, England
2007

Printed in the United States of America

Library of Congress Cataloging-in-Publication Data

Latimer, Jon.
1812: war with America / Jon Latimer.
p. cm.
Includes bibliographical references and index.
ISBN-13: 978-0-674-02584-4 (alk. paper)
ISBN-10: 0-674-02584-9 (alk. paper)
1. United States—History—War of 1812. 2. United States—History—War of 1812—Participation, British. 3. United States—History—War of 1812—Campaigns. 4. Great Britain—History, Military—1789–1820. 5. Napoleonic Wars, 1800–1815. I. Title.
E354.L36 2007
973.5'2—dc22 2007005075

To John McHugh (1962–2006)
a dear friend

Acknowledgements

This book represents the first comprehensive history of the American War of 1812 to be written from the British perspective since Reginald Horsman's work in 1968. It necessarily relies on the research of numerous American and Canadian scholars to whom I am greatly indebted. Foremost among these is Ernest Cruikshank, whose work in compiling and publishing contemporary documents and in writing accounts of so many aspects of the war along the American-Canadian border underpins most of the scholarship of the war to this day. Particular mention must also be made of Donald E. Graves, whose unparalleled knowledge of the Canadian archives enabled his reverse engineering of J. Mackay Hitsman's excellent *Incredible War of 1812* and the addition of extensive notes; and whose own works on the battles of Crysler's Farm and Lundy's Lane are models of historical reportage, as are Robert Malcomson's accounts of Queenston Heights and study of the struggle on Lake Ontario. On the American side the way has been led by John K. Mahon and Donald R. Hickey on political and economic matters and by John C. Fredriksen, John R. Elting, and Robert Quimby on military ones, while William S. Dudley and Michael J. Crawford have performed an invaluable service in compiling original documents concerning the naval war. Among the many other scholars and writers who have examined aspects of the war in detail and to whom I am greatly indebted, I would like to thank whoever was responsible for putting on the Internet both the *Annals of Congress* and the entire contents of the thirty-eight volumes of *American State Papers* covering 1789 to 1838, thus making a foreign-based historian's work much easier.

I owe thanks as well to John Hall of the University of Wales, Swansea, for his support and encouragement; to Professor John France of the History

Department and Drs. Duncan Campbell and Steve McVeigh in American Studies; and to the library staffs at UW Swansea, Swansea Central Library, Carmarthen and Llanelli Libraries, the British Library, the National Army Museum and National Maritime Museum reading rooms. Personal thanks also to Floyd Rudmin of the Psychology Department, University of Tromsø; Dr. Elizabeth Greenhalgh of the University of New South Wales, joint editor of *War & Society;* Maia Armaleo of *American Heritage;* Cindy Bianconcini of Filson Historical Society, Louisville, Kentucky; Romaine Ahlstrom and Jean-Robert Durbin at the Huntington Library, San Marino, California; Ulrike Livingston of the History Department at the University of Maine; Suzanne Hahn and Susan Fletcher of the Indiana Historical Society, Indianapolis, and in particular to Greg Chaplin; Bob Murphy of the Vermont Historical Society, Barre; Daisy Benson and Prudence Doherty of the Reference Desk at Bailey/Howe Library, University of Vermont; Peter Furtado, editor of *History Today;* Allison Wareham and Sue Goodger at the Royal Naval Museum, Portsmouth; Matt Little at the Royal Marines Museum, Southsea; Mark Smith, Matthew Buck, and Paul Evans of Firepower: The Royal Artillery Museum, Woolwich; David Murphy of The Royal Scots Regimental Museum, Edinburgh; Loraine Chesters of the Museum of Liverpool Life; Lieutenant-Colonel David Eliot of the Light Infantry Office, Taunton; Major (Ret.) Bob Prophet at Regimental Headquarters, The Worcestershire and Sherwood Foresters Regiment, Worcester; Amanda Moreno of The Royal Irish Fusiliers Museum, Armagh; Terry F. Mackenzie of Low Parks Museum, Hamilton; Paul Robinson of Northampton Museum and Art Gallery; Ian Hook of Chelmsford Museum; Peter Donnelly, The King's Own Royal Regiment Museum, Lancaster; David Hopkins, Tameside Museum Service, Ashton-Under-Lyne; Major Willie Shaw, M.B.E., of The Royal Highland Fusiliers Museum, Glasgow; P. E. Kingham at The Light Dragoons Museum, Newcastle; Finn Wheatley and Hayley Caves of The Keep Military Museum, Dorchester; Dr. Stephen Bull at the Museum of Lancashire, Preston; Major (Ret.) Jack Dunlop of The Inniskillings Museum, Enniskillen; Gordon Calhoun at Hampton Roads Naval Museum, Virginia; Anthony Staunton of the Military History Society of Australia, Sydney; Nick Mercer, formerly of 52 (Niagara) Battery, Royal Artillery; William Furry at the Illinois State Historical Society, Springfield; James V. Bredeson at the Wisconsin Historical Society, Madison; Peter Czaly at Upper Canada Village, Morrisburg, Ontario; Peter Harrington, curator of the Anne S. K. Brown Military Collection at Brown University; Laura Waayers at the Naval Historical Center, Washington (D.C.) Navy Yard; Renée Klish, Army Art Curator, U.S.

Army Center of Military History, Fort Leslie J. McNair, Washington, D.C.; Geneviève Viens at Musée du Château Ramezay, Montreal; Pierre Beaulieu at Bibliothèque et Archives Nationales du Québec, Montreal; Mariam Touba at New York Historical Society, New York City; Librarian Claudia Jew of the Mariner's Museum, Newport News, Virginia; Celina Bak at Library and Archives Canada, Ottawa; Kenneth Johnson at the Library of Congress; and special thanks to Peter Rindlisbacher for use of his superb artwork.

Thanks also to Simon Brett, Lucasta Miller, Don Paterson, Munro Price, and Barbara Trapido of the Authors' Foundation; to Dorothy Sym of the Society of Authors, for a grant in aid of travel to North America; to Bob Farquharson, Steve Pitt, and Marianne Fedunkiw in Toronto; to Ms. Alex Thomson, archivist at the United Church of Canada/Victoria University Archives; to Dr. Elizabeth Kaegi and George Dutton for their hospitality; to Ray Hobbs, Professor Emeritus of McMaster University, and Tom Fournier, both of the 41st Regiment (Military Living History Group); and to fellow former Territorial John Dart of The Welch Regiment Museum at Cardiff Castle. For the maps I am greatly indebted to my old friend Leslie Evans of Doc Penfro; and thanks also to Ann Hawthorne for her excellent editing, to Kathleen McDermott, Kathleen Drummy, and Susan Abel at Harvard, and, of course, to my agent, Andrew Lownie.

Contents

CONTENTS

Maps and Illustrations

Maps

Illustrations

Note on Place-Names and Currency

Where variations occur in place-names, the modern spelling has been chosen—for example, Sackets Harbor over the many earlier permutations of Sacket's, Sackett's, Sacketts, and Harbour found in sources. According to Donald R. Hickey, in his *War of 1812,* the rate of exchange for currency during the period remained steady, at around $4.40 = £1. The latter comprises 20 shillings, each itself consisting of 12 pence (d).

1812

Introduction

> In reading the history of nations, we find that, like individuals, they have their whims and their peculiarities; their seasons of excitement and recklessness, when they care not what they do . . . We see one nation suddenly seized, from its highest to its lowest members, with a fierce desire of military glory; another as suddenly becoming crazed upon a religious scruple, and neither of them recovering its senses until it has shed rivers of blood and sowed a harvest of groans and tears.
>
> —Charles Mackay, *Memoirs of Extraordinary Popular Delusions*

As the Canadian historian William Kingsford observed more than a century ago, events in North America between 1812 and 1815 were not forgotten in Britain, "for they have never been known there."[1] Even today most Britons remain unaware that a British force burned the White House in 1814, and indeed most Americans would admit to knowing little more about the conflict than the fact of the battle of New Orleans and the fact that the national anthem was composed at the time.

It has been said that the British consult history and, when necessary, invent it; but an examination of the War of 1812 shows that this is by no means an exclusively British trait. Following Andrew Jackson's defensive victory at New Orleans, which placed him firmly on the road to the presidency—giving him and his supporters grounds to mythologize it into the greatest military engagement of the war—the entire conflict was conflated into a stunning American triumph, a version of events effectively carved in stone by George Bancroft in his multivolume *History of the United States* (1834–1873). This was substantially echoed by Henry Adams in his *History of the United States* (1889–1891), and in some respects all subsequent histories of the conflict remain in the shadow of Bancroft's interpretation.[2] The war has often been portrayed as being forced on a peaceable America by continuous provocation by an arrogant Britain. But there is little evidence for such a claim. In particular, there has been a failure to root it clearly in the French Revolutionary and Napoleonic Wars, known to the Victorians as the "Great War." As President James Madison later admitted, the United States would not have entered the conflict had the defeat of Napoleon Bonaparte been foreseen.[3]

The basis of the antagonism that led to war was America's desire to continue its overseas trade undisturbed by events in Europe. But while British encroachments on American rights were real and serious, they were not the result of simple arrogance, as many American writers have assumed. Britain's sole objective throughout the period was the defeat of France, and all its actions must be seen through the prism of a twenty-two-year struggle whose scope threatened its continued existence as a pre-eminent world power.[4] Consequently Britain was prepared to go to any lengths to deny neutral trade with France; the Royal Navy blockaded the French coast and restricted neutral trade with French colonies, strictly defined contraband and stopped neutral vessels to search for it, seized British deserters, and impressed seamen they believed to be British. The extent of the impressment of American seamen, both illegal in principle and unjust in practice, has often been exaggerated; it was also a sign of weakness in desperate times. All of this British activity seriously angered Americans, whose memories of their erstwhile colonial masters remained vivid and bitter. They were engaged in a great republican experiment designed to demonstrate how a country could live peacefully in freedom and prosperity, firmly guided by Enlightenment principles, and they resented a nation they regarded as weighed down under tyrannical monarchy and corrupt aristocracy.

All nations rely on myths to create their self-images. In Canada a myth grew up that "Spartan bands of Canadian Loyalist volunteers aided by a few hundred" British troops "repelled the Persian thousands of democratic American invaders and marinated the virgin soil of Canada unpolluted by the foot of the plundering invader."[5] The origins of Canada's "militia myth" may be traced to a sermon given by the Reverend John Strachan at York (Toronto) in 1812, who was confident that future historians would promote the line that Upper Canada (modern Ontario), "without the assistance of men or arms, except a handful of regular troops, repelled its invaders, slew or took them all prisoners, and captured from its enemies the greater part of the arms by which it was defended."[6] Strachan's prediction came true; many subsequent accounts, especially Canadian ones, embellished the myth. But it was completely false; the defence of Canada owed everything to British Army regulars, although that fact cannot and should not detract from the vital role Canadians played in their own defence.[7]

The war's heroes and heroines have generally been North American, and the myths created die hard. Subsequent mythologizing cannot detract from the victories won by the United States Navy (USN) or from the real shock and embarrassment that Jackson's crushing victory inflicted upon Britain, but nor does it justify such triumphalism as Anthony S. Pitch's claim that the British "would never be so humiliated on the field of battle."[8] But then, few Americans have heard of Majuba Hill or Maiwand, to name but two, and the domination of the historiography of the war by American writers has particularly affected coverage of its naval aspect. Historians have generally accepted either the outspoken anti-American view presented by the one major British chronicler of the war, William James, or the American version promulgated by Theodore Roosevelt and Alfred Thayer Mahan, which makes little effort to take into account British policy and strategy. Neither is satisfactory. The naval war was not simply a series of single-ship engagements, important though these were to public opinion; the blockade of the American coast was far more significant. Nor, despite American victories, is there any evidence of a decline in the effectiveness of the Royal Navy after the victory at Trafalgar in 1805. British defects were the same as those evident in naval engagements against France ever since 1793, the result of the colossal pressures under which the Royal Navy was operating in fighting a world war.[9]

Occurring in an era before "unconditional surrender" and zero-sum games, in which victory for one side means clear and absolute defeat for the other, the outcome of the war may appear obscure. In America the twin myths immediately grew up that it had been a glorious victory and a second war of independence; myths which suited the political establishment and the aspirations of former officers and generals seeking to forge political careers, and which persist to this day.[10] Certainly, in America the conflict helped create a national sense of unity and pride, but it was by no means a "second war of independence"; nor was it a war that "both sides won." It was fundamentally a failed war of conquest. American desire to possess British North America dated back to the earliest days of the Revolution and the ill-fated attack on Quebec of 31 December 1775.[11] For the United States in 1812 the goal was to conquer Canada, and for more than two and a half years it tried and repeatedly failed to do so.[12] If the war had one concrete result, it was the guarantee of Canada's existence as a separate nation. But American desire for Canada did not end with the war, and its repercussions were felt well into the twentieth century, riding on an enduring legacy of anglophobia. By the war's end U.S. trade had been strangled to practically nothing, and the nation's capital city lay in ashes. In contrast, Canadian territorial integrity was intact; Britain controlled northern Maine, parts of New York, and a huge area west of Lake Michigan; and it had made no concessions whatsoever on the crucial issues of trade or impressment for which America ostensibly went to war. For Britain the French Revolutionary and Napoleonic Wars were wars of national survival and the war in America an irritating distraction. Britain was content to settle for the 1812 status quo, and that is what Britain got. The United States, in contrast, achieved none of its war aims, and in these terms, the War of 1812 must be seen as a British victory, however marginal. It is therefore unsurprising that distance in time and lack of tangible success have helped to make it, as Donald R. Hickey has noted, America's "most obscure war."[13]

Britain, on the other hand, went on to spend the nineteenth century engaged in innumerable obscure wars, although a frequently repeated misconception is that the American War received scant notice at the time. In fact, British newspapers followed events in North America closely despite the long delays necessarily involved in transmitting news, especially from the western frontier.[14] But the end of the American War was immediately overshadowed by the towering figure who was indirectly responsible for it in the first place: Bonaparte.[15] Within six months of signing the treaty that ended the war the former self-styled emperor had returned from exile on Elba, retaken his throne, and marched against the Allied armies in what is now Belgium, only to be decisively defeated near a small village south of Brussels. In the years since it was fought, the battle of Waterloo has probably been more closely examined than any other battle in history, and it defined the end of the era. With the final defeat of Bonaparte Britain gained control of Malta, Ceylon, Tobago and St. Lucia, and the Cape in South Africa, the strategic building blocks that would enable the spread of the British Empire across Asia and Africa. The conflict in America rapidly faded from view as Britain set about the serious postwar business of making money.

The end of the Seven Years' War in 1763 marked the true beginning of Great Britain's empire as its people looked forward excitedly to exploiting the riches secured by Robert Clive's great victory in Bengal, with the West Indies and Greenland fisheries also forming important strands in plans for national prosperity. This colonial system was mercantile rather than imperial: merchant shipping tonnage then available amounted to some 500,000 tons. The new ships built for the East India trade were much larger: strong three-deckers capable of running around the Cape of Good Hope to Bengal and China. War had expanded the merchant marine, and there was no intention of allowing this extra capacity to become redundant in a postwar slump. This end was to be secured by the Navigation Laws, which formed the heart of the mercantilist system, an obvious element being national security in time of war. Thus commodities would be moved in British vessels to guarantee the supply of British seamen for both the Royal Navy and the merchant marine. British interest in Newfoundland is a striking example: throughout the eighteenth century nobody was permitted to settle there permanently. Rather, it was to be a base for West Country fishermen for the drying of nets and the salting and packing of fish, and regarded as part of the naval service, a fact clearly attested by the rotating presence of naval officers as governors of the outpost. Exploration by Captain James Cook and others was encouraged in the search for harbours and storage points that would open up additional markets.

Before the loss of the thirteen American colonies North America was still regarded as a vital part of the whole, and a revived Board of Trade oversaw an increase in shipping between 1774 and 1784 from 701,000 tons (including American ships) to 869,000 tons (excluding American ships).[16] By the end of the century British trade was funding industrial development and creating the capital necessary to open up new markets. At the same time, the United States steadily increased its role as a commercial rival to Britain, especially while the latter's gaze was diverted to chronic warfare against France.[17]

During the thirty years between the end of the American Revolutionary War and the War of 1812, unremitting mutual hostility between Britain and the United States prompted recurring threats of open conflict. War almost came in 1794, 1807, and 1808, yet diplomacy always managed to lance the boil of resentment. Nor was war in 1812 an inevitability, except in the Tolstoyan sense that everything is inevitable because it happened. "Never before in the history of enlightened nations," declared one nineteenth-century American historian, "did such . . . an absurd issue result in war."[18] But by 1812 rationalism was beginning to give way to romanticism, and war was promoted by people who saw it as a form of glory, not as a bloody reality. Thus European wars entrapped the young United States as surely as would the world wars of the twentieth century.[19]

By 1812, apart from a pro-British Federalist minority, there was little to moderate the passionate anti-British traditions of the War for Independence. Meanwhile, in Britain, there was positive dislike for the upstart former colonists;

the pro-American *Monthly Review* agreed in March 1808 with an anonymous pamphleteer that "hatred of America seems a prevailing sentiment in this country."[20] Between 1807 and 1812 Britain was awash with anti-American feeling, fed by patriotic fervour from the war against France, commercial jealousy, and anger at perceived American support for Bonaparte.[21] But above all else Britain had to maintain naval superiority over France. Although technically enlistment in the Royal Navy was voluntary, conditions of service were harsh, and in wartime few men came forward, desertion was rife, and gaps had to be filled by impressment.[22]

One reason was the superior conditions and pay on American ships; perhaps a quarter of the seamen in American service were in fact British.[23] Sailors were extremely skilled, and therefore a precious resource, and impressment was a form of selective conscription in a state that successfully mobilized huge manpower resources without recourse to any other form of compulsion. In 1809 the army had mobilized over 300,000 men and the navy 141,000; this total represented somewhere between 11 and 14 percent of the adult male population, a figure three times higher than the share of Bonaparte's available manpower raised through conscription.[24]

The harshness of maritime service is often overstated. Throughout the period of the Great War, flogging was accepted by virtually everybody as normal—it was even more prevalent in the army—and only from the 1830s onwards, when radical politicians in both Britain and America found in it a convenient shorthand for numerous social and political themes, did it become a feature of polemical books and pamphlets describing attitudes that were alien before 1815. Seamen understood flogging and did not object to it if it was not overused.[25] The young U.S. Navy flogged at least twice as much and, unlike the Royal Navy, had not abolished "starting"—the practice of chasing men to their work with a rope or cane's end.[26] With surprising unanimity seamen accepted impressment, even though they resented its corollary, not being trusted with occasional liberty. Indeed, though impressment had no supporters, least of all among officers, it was regarded by all as a necessary evil.[27]

Bonaparte, in boastful reminiscences to his biographer, said it was he "who developed the measures which compelled America to fight England in 1812."[28] But this was a characteristic overstatement. In fact, instead of encouraging American trade, which would have benefitted France and perhaps led more quickly to war between Britain and America, he restricted it and subjected America's ministers in Paris to constant humiliation.[29] Yet he successfully turned American bellicosity away from France and towards Britain.

That France was an old ally and Britain a former oppressor encouraged those who favoured war with the latter.[30] Other factors may also have encouraged a warlike attitude. At the turn of the nineteenth century, America was in the grip of a Great Revival of self-assertive Christianity, a crusading spirit and righteous outpouring of largely Protestant zeal. Both Federalists and Republicans sought to claim Christ's support for their economic interests, regional bias, and moral outlook, and, later, their stance on the war.[31] The United States was already engaged in aggressive westward expansion against the Indian nations of the Old Northwest, and was seeking to expand in the south-west as well, but most historians assert that the war's primary causes were maritime.[32] Others have called the conflict "Madison's War" and "Clay's War," after the president and the leader of the "War Hawks" in Congress. But whether the reasons included land hunger, wounded national pride, or fear for the republican experiment, as Albert Z. Carr succinctly put it: "Where there are so many explanations, nothing is explained. Static analysis of history can no more reveal the causes of the war phenomenon than dissection of a suicide's body can reveal his despair."[33] One of the few certainties is that, like most wars, it lasted longer and cost far more in both blood and treasure than its instigators expected, for "[wars] rarely achieve the political goals that might justify the risks, the cost and the pain."[34]

BEFORE considering the history of the war, it is useful to survey briefly the apparatus of early nineteenth-century warfare. First is the naval component. Warships were categorized according to a system devised by the Royal Navy into three broad types and six "rates" by the number of guns they carried. A ship-of-the-line was ship-rigged with two or more covered gun-decks; a frigate was similar but with only one covered gun-deck designed for scouting, reconnaissance, and detached tasks; the third type comprised all other craft, mainly schooners, sloops, and brigs, to provide patrol craft, conduct convoy duties, and carry despatches. A "first rate" carried 100 guns or more; a "second rate," 90–100; a "third rate," 60–90; and a "fourth rate," 50–60, although by this period this category was considered too weak to fight in the line, and there were very few left. Frigates of 30–44 guns were officially "fifth rate," and smaller vessels warranting the command of a "post-captain" were "sixth rate." But the advent of the short-barrelled carronade in the 1780s rendered the rating system obsolescent, since more guns could be carried and higher up, so that most ships carried more than their official listing.[35] A "ship" rig had three masts, fore, main, and mizzen, running from bow to stern, each carrying four-sided "square" sails suspended on horizontal yards. Other sails could be deployed between the masts and forward along the protruding bowsprit. On the mizzen could also be deployed a "spanker" or "driver" "fore-and-aft" sail rigged from a boom and gaff pivoting aft of the mast. A brig was a vessel with two masts, both carrying square sails and a spanker; a brigantine had square sails on the foremast and was rigged fore-and-aft on the main mast. A schooner was a vessel with usually two masts (more became common later), all carrying fore-and-aft sails, and possibly some square sails at the mastheads. A sloop was a single-masted vessel with a fore-and-aft sail, and possibly a square sail above. Sixth-rate warships were also termed "sloops of war" even though very few had sloop rigs; such small vessels were usually unrated. The British also employed bomb ketches with two masts, one central and one in the mizzen position, leaving the forward part of the boat free to mount a mortar or rocket launchers.[36]

In the British Army the regiment of foot—infantry—was an administrative organization, with the principal tactical unit being the battalion. Each regiment was nominally headed by a colonel, but he was not required to be present in the field. A regiment might comprise one or more battalions, each commanded in the field by a lieutenant-colonel. Two or more battalions (usually three, and usually drawn from different regiments) formed a brigade. Two or more brigades were then grouped to form divisions, although in North America such large formations were never available until almost the very end. Battalions were divided into ten companies of around 100 men each. Two of these companies were designated "elite" or "flank" companies; one of these, the "grenadier" company, traditionally comprised robust veterans or the most imposing men, armed with hand grenades, although these were seldom used any more, and formed up on the right side of the battalion when deployed in line of battle. The second would be a "light" company of skilled individual soldiers who formed up on the left but who could also operate as a skirmish screen in front of the line to direct individual fire at enemy formations and help disrupt them, and to protect the line from enemy skirmishers. (Some regiments were designated and trained entirely as light infantry.) Between these stood eight "line" or "battalion" companies. Generally speaking, American regiments were organized along the same lines as a British battalion, consisting of eight companies; but in the spring of 1812 the U.S. Army raised a number of two-battalion regiments, and although this organization was quickly dispensed with, some retained this shape until 1813.[37] Adding to the confusion, the Americans also used the term "battalion" in two other ways: it could refer either to an ad hoc grouping of two or more companies from different regiments commanded by an officer of at least field rank (major), or to an order "to form battalion," meaning to form a line.

Land warfare of the period was dominated by massed ranks of infantry armed with smooth-bore muskets.[38] Loading and firing involved biting the tip of a greased paper cartridge and pouring a small amount of powder into the pan of the firing mechanism, which was then snapped shut, and the lock—or hammer—was pulled back to half-cock. The remaining contents of the cartridge were then poured and rammed down the barrel with a rod housed in the wooden stock of the weapon. When this procedure had been completed the weapon was fully cocked, brought to the shoulder, and pointed towards the enemy—most muskets had no sights—and on the appropriate word of command the soldier pulled the trigger, which threw the lock sharply forward, so that the flint it carried struck the vertical arm of the pan and caused a spark that ignited the powder, which was carried through the touch hole to fire the main charge in the base of the barrel. The effective range of such weapons was never more than 200 yards, and as the black-powder propellant generated vast billowing clouds of white smoke, this range was soon dramatically reduced.

With weaponry slow to fire, inaccurate, and tending (sometimes as much as 25 percent) to misfire, effective firepower was generated through volley fire, either simultaneously by entire battalions, or by companies or by platoons within the companies to create a rolling effect. Although an individual rate of five rounds per minute was not unheard of among veteran British units fighting the French in the Iberian Peninsula, a rate of two or three rounds per minute was more usual. If firepower alone was not enough to carry the day, the infantryman could use a socket bayonet, some 15–17 inches long, that fitted around the muzzle of his weapon, turning it into a mini-pike and enabling the battalion to present a fearsome row of tipped steel.[39] It was essential for defence against cavalry—an arm that found little opportunity for employment in North America because of the difficulties of supplying forage for horses—and could put a wavering enemy to flight, since occasions when two sides used it at the same time were extremely rare. Cavalry were employed only in small detachments as couriers and scouts.

In order to manoeuvre lines of men perhaps 500 yards long on the battlefield, to operate as a coordinated whole, and to use all the permutations necessary to gain maximum advantage from their massed musketry, a high standard of disciplined drill was necessary, achieved only through endless practice. The British Army believed it took three years for an infantryman to be fully trained and dependable in battle. Before the war the 41st Regiment of Foot was observed exercising at Montreal, "continually on parade, marching, forming, filling etc. . . . They made a very fine appearance."[40] And appearance was important: it helped instil pride in one's unit that would carry the soldier through the horrors of the battlefield, and at best it made an impression on the enemy that caused him to falter and run. However, British troops seldom looked very smart in the field: their red coats took on a decidedly muddy hue in rainy weather. But their training showed, and that gave them an edge, at least early in the war, before the Americans caught up; the well-trained British regulars could fire and reload their muskets much more quickly than the Americans, performing complex drills even when under fire themselves. The battalion in line stood two deep to maximize firepower, whereas until 1814 the Americans tended to prefer the continental style of three-deep lines.

The Americans' drill was largely modelled on continental patterns, but they lacked a firm template and used a variety of extemporized manuals.[41] The Americans also emphasized accuracy over the British preference for fire discipline and rate of fire—the 13th U.S. Infantry was taught to aim using rail fences as a substitute for an enemy line—and, as in the Revolutionary War, Americans tended to pick off British officers.[42] In one respect the Americans had a distinct advantage, having a long tradition of use of the rifle. Rifled weapons, with a spiralling groove running the length of the barrel, were inherently more accurate, since they imparted spin to the bullet, making it more stable in flight. A regiment of riflemen was raised by the U.S. Army in 1808, and during the war the Americans deployed numerous militia and volunteer rifle units, which were ideally suited to the skirmishing role and to fighting in woods and other difficult terrain. But increased accuracy came at a cost: the rate of fire was less, and got progressively slower as the weapon fouled, so that in a stand-up fight the advantage would lie with musket-armed troops, who could fire faster. The U.S. Navy armed its marine sharpshooters with rifles, but to little advantage, since naval warfare usually took place at short ranges to maximize the effectiveness of the smooth-barrelled naval guns, thus negating the long-range accuracy of rifles over quicker-firing muskets.

The artillery that armed ships and supported the infantry was operated along similar principles. Guns, or cannon as they were sometimes referred to at sea or in American parlance on land, were essentially smooth-bore barrels on wheeled wooden mountings suitable for their element, down which a charge and a round were placed and rammed tight. Before the 1780s the Royal

Navy referred to its ordnance only as "guns" but picked up the word *canon* from the French, and "cannon" and "gun" became synonymous. The Royal Artillery, however, regarded the term "cannon" as vague and incorrect, and its use in the smooth-bore period can be correctly used only of ship-borne weapons. On ships the charge was often ignited through a flintlock system similar to that of a musket; in field guns on land, through a simple touch hole ignited by a taper. They usually fired solid iron shot—the weight of the shot giving the weapon its designation—that would smash the hull or rigging of a ship, and the bodies of any men in the way. Solid shot could cut a swathe through the ranks of infantry, although they might lie down to avoid the worst effects. The range of these weapons varied according to their size and deployment: on land the largest pieces achieved a maximum of around 2,000 yards; at sea, where the movement of water necessarily limited accuracy, ranges were usually kept as short as possible. In such situations, carronades came into their own, usually firing a heavier weight of shot than the ship's main armament despite having a shorter range.[43] Guns also fired different ammunition at short range: case or canister (often mistakenly called grape shot, a naval ammunition) was a tin filled with bullets to create a shotgun effect and was used by field guns at ranges of 300 yards and less; both grape shot and chain shot were naval specialities for attacking an adversary's rigging.

On land the larger calibres (barrel widths) of guns (18-pounders and above) were generally too heavy to make effective field artillery and were restricted to siege trains or fixed emplacements, often on naval-style carriages. Another type of gun found on land was the howitzer, a short-barrelled weapon that permitted shooting at a higher elevation to lob the favoured round, a shell, a metal sphere filled with powder and fitted with a wooden fuse ignited in the process of firing. If skilfully trimmed by the gunners it exploded above the enemy, showering them with fragments. Howitzers were designated by calibre rather than by the weight of their rounds, as were mortars, a stubby version usually employed in or against fortifications. The British also possessed a most effective explosive round called spherical case, invented by Henry Shrapnel, by whose name it became more commonly known.[44] This was a cross between shell and canister enabling an explosive round filled with bullets to be fired a great distance. The British also deployed rockets, named after their inventor, Sir William Congreve; these were wildly unpredictable and often caused more consternation to friendly troops than damage to the enemy.[45]

Artillery on land was organized into "brigades" or batteries of five guns and a howitzer, but in North America it tended to be deployed in ad hoc units comprising whatever guns and gunners were available. Guns were towed by teams of horses, and in the British Army the drivers were from different units—often locally raised—from those manning the guns. The gun was hitched to a limber that carried its ammunition, and was preferably deployed to the flanks of the infantry to engage the enemy's infantry rather than other guns. The standard rate of fire was about one round per minute for light and field pieces and one round per two minutes for heavier guns.[46] The gunners were vulnerable to sharpshooters and skirmishers, and if they were about to be overrun and were unable to limber up, or drag their guns away, they had to resort to "spiking" them by hammering a headless nail into the touch hole.[47]

Finally, it is necessary to note two factors that irretrievably limit our retrospective knowledge. The matter of timing in nineteenth-century battles is fraught with difficulty, as Arthur Wellesley, Duke of Wellington, noted when he discouraged John Wilson Croker from writing an account of the battle of Waterloo: "No individual can recollect the order in which, or the exact moment at which [events] occurred, which makes all the difference to their value or importance."[48] This difficulty remains true even of accounts of modern battles, which have the benefit of logs, war diaries, and synchronized watches; but in this period there was no standardized time, and all timings given by witnesses must be regarded as no more than estimations; any history that does otherwise should be treated with healthy scepticism.[49] For similar reasons, troop figures are generally rounded because even precise figures given in contemporary documents are not always reliable measures of troop numbers actually taking part. Memoirs written for publication are also suspect, being often highly imaginative and sometimes drenched in malice, distortion, and self-aggrandizement. Thus nothing is ever clear, even to a participant.

1

"Canada! Canada! Canada!"

Whilome in Albion's isle there dwelt a youth
Who ne in Virtue's ways did take delight;
But spent his days in riot most uncouth,
And vexed with mirth the drowsy ear of Night.
Ah me! In sooth he was a shameless wight,
Sore given to revel and ungodly glee;
Few earthly things found favour in his sight
Save concubines and carnal companie,
And flaunting wassailers of high and low degree.

—George Gordon, Lord Byron, *Childe Harold's Pilgrimage*

When Lord Byron's autobiographical poem *Childe Harold* was published in March 1812, it sold out the first 500 folio copies in three days and made him an instant star: "I awoke one morning and found myself famous," said the lion of literary London.[1] Byron was a phenomenon, a proto-celebrity; the subject of conversation in salons, noted Elizabeth, Duchess of Devonshire, "of curiosity, of enthusiasm almost, one might say, of the moment, is not Spain or Portugal, Warriors or Patriots, but Lord Byron!"[2] But as the summer arrived, the continuing war with France commanded most Britons' interest, so that when news came that the United States had declared war on Britain, the editor of the *Leicester Journal* fulminated that President James Madison's war message was "the most laboured, peevish, canting, petulant, querulous and weak effusion, that ever issued from a man assuming the character of a statesman and the President, or elective quadrennial King, of a professedly Republican country."[3]

He expressed a sense of shock felt throughout the country that the United States should seemingly choose to throw in its lot with Bonaparte, whose boundless ambition depended, politically and socially, on continuous warfare, and demanded war to finance itself.[4] Both in France and abroad, Bonaparte used his self-styled empire as a bloody racket to sustain his own despotism and the military aristocracy that supported it; at home he stifled free speech and purged political opponents.[5] By 1812 resistance, first to the Revolutionary regime and then to "the Atheist Emperor and his infidel advisers" that replaced it, had already consumed the people of Britain for nineteen years.[6]

Throughout that time Americans regarded Europe's troubles as none of their business. Until 1793 the United States was sympathetic to France's revolution, but the excesses of the Terror diluted this support, and Britain's prime minister, William Pitt, actively pursued rapprochement with the former colonies. But when war broke out in Europe, Anglo-American relations were already strained by Britain's failure to evacuate the posts around the Great Lakes as agreed in 1783, and American merchants soon developed a major interest in shipping the produce of the French, Dutch, and Spanish West Indies to Europe, circumventing the British blockade. Britain's invocation of the Rule of 1756 against neutral trade then led to the seizure of some 250 American vessels carrying goods from the French West Indies to France.[7] The British government operated by two clear principles: first, a belligerent had a right to seize contraband of war going to an enemy port; second, no neutral could carry on a trade in time of war which had been closed to it in peace—this had been the rule of war in 1756. Consequently, an executive Order in Council issued in 1794 authorized the seizure of *any* vessel sailing from the French West Indies to Europe, and *any* French-owned goods from the West Indies regardless of their destination. In response the United States demanded that American ships remain free from interference, regarding a neutral flag as covering whatever they carried, French or not. President George Washington, conscious that the young republic could not afford war, sent John Jay to London to negotiate a settlement, concluded in November 1794, and war was duly avoided.[8]

In 1796 an exhausted Washington declined to stand for a third presidential term. His Federalist party, drawing its main support from commercial interests in New England and the mid-Atlantic states, chose John Adams as its candidate. The Democratic-Republicans, who derived strength largely from agricultural interests, especially in the south, chose Thomas Jefferson.[9] Adams won and soon faced a new French government in the Directory that seized over 300 American ships carrying British cargoes, forcing the Americans into de facto alliance with Britain and an undeclared naval war with France from

1798 to 1800. A Navy Department was created on 30 April 1798, and the infant U.S. Navy performed well in a series of single-ship engagements during the "Quasi-War," taking 80 French privateers.[10] Lacking effective naval forces to impose a blockade, France accepted the American doctrine of freedom of the seas in 1800 in the interest of ensuring peace between the two nations. When the presidential election came later that year, schism within the Federalist party saw Adams isolated, and in due course defeated, by Jefferson.[11]

The new Treasury secretary, Albert Gallatin, set about eliminating debt by implementing severe expenditure cuts; the army was reduced from 4,000 to 2,500 men, and several warships were sold or laid up.[12] Paradoxically, the administration founded the United States Military Academy at West Point in 1802, and in order to protect American shipping in the Mediterranean and combat the Barbary pirates of North Africa, Jefferson was forced to recommission a number of ships, earning valuable naval experience.[13] But Jefferson's greatest triumph was the Louisiana Purchase from France, encompassing the vast territory west of the Mississippi River to the Rockies, an excellent deal that included New Orleans.[14] All western trade from Indiana, Illinois, Ohio, and western Pennsylvania, through Tennessee to the Gulf of Mexico, depended on the Mississippi, and the city at its mouth was the vital key. It earned Bonaparte Jefferson's warmest gratitude and 54 million francs, earmarked for one purpose: a renewed war of expansion in Europe with at least one-third reserved for an invasion of Britain.[15] In December 1803 the territory was formally handed over to the United States, and the popularity of this measure ensured resounding success across the board for Republicans in the 1804 elections.

With the Anglo-French Peace of Amiens in 1801 there followed a brief period of calm between the United States and Britain.[16] But William Cobbett's new and widely read *Political Register* was among many papers which denounced the peace as a French plan in conjunction with the United States to ensure Britain's commercial ruin, since America's commerce ranked second only to Britain's and was expanding rapidly.[17] European war had brought a boom to the American shipping industry. Between 1790 and 1802 the number of American vessels on transatlantic trade tripled to over 1,000 ships or nearly 250,000 tons; the total grew from 558,000 tons in 1802 to 981,000 tons in 1810, while British shipping declined and undercut exports from the British West Indies between 1802 and 1806 by 50 percent, and the collapse of sugar prices created a powerful lobby group in Parliament.[18] As the American historian J. B. McMaster noted, it was ships under the American flag that "filled the warehouses at Cadiz and Antwerp to overflowing. They glutted the markets of Emden, Lisbon, Hamburg and Copenhagen with the produce of the West Indies and the fabrics of the East, and, bringing back the products of the looms and forges of Germany to the New World, drove out the manufactures of Yorkshire, Manchester and Birmingham."[19] While Britain's population (excluding Ireland) rose from 8 to 10 million between 1780 and 1805, America's doubled, to some 7 million, and its national psychology changed from a colonial to an increasingly independent one: its land area quintupled, and production of agricultural commodities expanded enormously. Britain, facing mortal peril from a France twice its size, could ill afford to alienate a young country still resentful of British attitudes and practices. Three areas of contention remained. The first was static: money owed to private British citizens since the American Revolution. The other two were potentially explosive.[20]

Renewed hostilities between Britain and France in 1803 saw the press gangs go into action with unparalleled speed, secrecy, and efficiency. On the Thames nearly 1,000 seamen were taken in a single night, and large hauls were made at Plymouth, Portsmouth, and elsewhere. The Royal Navy, having grown from 16,000 in 1792 to 145,000 by 1812, was constantly short of men, and neutral ships were boarded and searched for deserters and other British seamen, all of whom were liable to impressment.[21] Although it took years to train seamen—who had different manners, dress, and language from the rest of society—the Royal Navy itself provided little training; instead it relied on impressing experienced men from the merchant marine, who then suffered all the disadvantages of long service with none of the advantages of belonging permanently to the organization. Bounties might lure some men into service, but only impressment could secure the numbers needed.[22] At the same time there was a rise in desertions; even the ship carrying the British minister Anthony Merry to Washington in 1803 lost 14 men, and the return of Pitt as prime minister saw Anglo-American tensions rise as the twin problems of desertion and impressment became acute.[23] But the problem of desertion was not simply, as is often portrayed, related to the harshness of conditions aboard His Majesty's ships.

As Adam Smith noted, with war forcing between 40,000 and 50,000 seamen from the merchant service into that of the Crown, "the demand for sailors for merchant ships necessarily rises with their scarcity, and their wages commonly rise from a guinea [21s] to 27s to 40s and £3 per month."[24] Service in the Royal Navy prevented seamen from sharing in this bonanza, particularly since it was indefinite: once enlisted, a man might serve for years with no end in sight, at least as long as war with France continued. They often lost rank on transfer from one ship to another, while back pay and prize money might take years to catch up with them; and even when awaiting transfer the men were accommodated in hulks and not permitted ashore. The problem came to a head when men claimed to be American, for the British government refused to accept the easy naturalization laws of the United States.[25] An American in British law was anyone residing there before 1783 or born there since; federal American law after 1802 demanded residence in the United States for five years—a difficult requirement for anyone following the ashore-today-afloat-tomorrow life of a sailor, so that few if any British-born sailors could claim genuine American nationality.[26]

At the end of 1803 Madison, then secretary of state, complained to Congress about Royal Navy impressment, saying that forty-three Americans had been taken, twelve of whom carried "proof of citizenship." Yet although the process was necessarily slow, the Royal Navy took great pains to investigate and repatriate genuine cases.[27] Uriah P. Levy was impressed in 1808 and released by Rear-Admiral Alexander Cochrane, who "on inspecting my protection and the duplicate of my indentures which were fortunately in my possession, ordered me released and to be paid for my services."[28] Nonetheless many men loudly proclaiming American nationality were swept into the anonymity of the Royal Navy, since documentary "proof" was freely available to all and sundry, and many men carried false "protections" obtained from American notaries, consuls, and customs officers.[29] The last, besides being entitled to a 25¢ fee for putting a custom-house stamp on a notary's protection, sometimes issued the protection itself. British seamen could always find shysters to supply them, such as the New Orleans notary who ignored Robert Clark's Edinburgh accent and received $4.25 for stamping Clark's papers; or the New York customs officer who asked no questions of Thomas Brown of Falmouth, Cornwall, but gave him his protection on the say-so of "Deborah Ann . . . a woman I then lived with."[30] William Lyman, as U.S. consul in London, provided a form for Richard Chadwick, captain of the *Wareham,* stating that Chadwick had "Personally appeared before me and made the Oath" regarding the nominal roll of his ship's company; except that by the time the form was taken from him and forwarded to the Admiralty, instead of containing "the Names of all the Officers and Crew . . . together with their Places of Birth and Residence," Chadwick had yet to fill it in. Lyman also received "many hundreds" of half-crowns (2/6d) from British seamen for papers, providing "convincing proof of the irregularity of these documents, and the extensive deceit which they are calculated to shield."[31]

Despite their impressive appearance, with the republic's arms and "United States of America" printed across the top, the papers gave only a cursory physical description of the holder—height and age. With no central registry there was nothing to prevent Daniel Robertson, a Cockney from Stepney, instead of Jonathan from Delaware ("Jonathan" was the British nickname for an American person or ship), from visiting a series of notaries over a few days in New York and obtaining dozens of protections to sell to other men of similar height and age, for anything up to £5.[32] Thus it was hardly surprising that British captains ignored such papers and pressed "any likely-looking lad who had the slightest trace of an Irish or British accent."[33] Because ultimately Britain could not afford to allow her seamen to desert to America with impunity: she would sooner go to war with the United States than do so, and by the summer of 1804 HMS *Leander* was operating with considerable aggression in the waters off New York.[34] Congress began discussing protecting American sailors by force if necessary and wanted Madison to renegotiate the commercial terms of the Jay Treaty, which was soon due to expire; and this issue touched on a second, kindred one: the freedom of the seas.

One of the defining strategic themes of the Revolutionary and Napoleonic Wars was economic warfare. From the outbreak in 1793 the French Directory government actively tried to damage British commerce; Britain exported to the Continent its own manufactures, raw materials, and colonial produce. In 1798 France issued instructions that neutral ships would be seized if they called at a British port; yet France also needed this material, and these early restrictions were so ineffective that in the decade to 1800 British exports doubled, while its imports increased by 64 percent.[35] Besides objecting to America's role in the carrying trade between the French West Indies and Europe, Britain was also in commercial rivalry with the United States over its own trade with the British West Indies, which swarmed with American ships and, far more galling, with many French and Spanish ones now "American" after taking American captains, crews, and papers, and flying the Stars and Stripes.[36] Bonaparte was glad to see no shortage of imported commodities in Europe, while James Monroe, the American minister in London, was able to report that "our commerce never enjoyed in any war, as much freedom, and indeed favor from this govt. as it now does."[37] But in Britain relaxation of the Navigation system was seen as a mistake, weakening the economy and guaranteeing the loss of a major source of British seamen. In the spring of 1805 the Lords Commissioners of Appeals handed down the *Essex* decision, which sharply checked the system of "broken voyages" that enabled American ships to import goods to Europe by travelling via the United States. A product of the total war now being waged against France, it was also an important factor in the deterioration of Anglo-American relations.[38]

THE STRAIN of war and threat of invasion loomed large in British minds. Bonaparte, the "ogre of Europe," could watch its coast from Boulogne, where he assembled a grand fleet of invasion barges. In what was known as the "Time of Terror," a blazing haystack mistaken for a beacon brought to arms the volunteers of Derbyshire and Yorkshire, and wicked children were warned:

> Baby, baby, naughty baby,
> Hush you squalling thing I say;
> Hush your squalling, or it may be,
> Bonaparte may pass this way.[39]

Although Bonaparte abandoned ideas of invasion in August 1805 and Vice-Admiral Lord Horatio Nelson's stunning victory at Trafalgar in October brought relief from the threat of invasion, contrary to popular belief, this respite was only temporary.[40]

In the same month an anti-slavery lawyer, James Stephen—brother-in-law to William Wilberforce—published an influential pamphlet called *War in Disguise, or, the Frauds of the Neutral Flags,* which within three months appeared in three British and two American editions. It closely argued that since 1793 the Americans had taken every opportunity to build their commerce at the expense of Britain, and concluded that "the neutral powers can subsist without this newly acquired commerce; but Great Britain cannot long exist as a nation, if left bereft of her ancient means of offensive maritime war."[41] Stephen believed Americans could not fail to see that Britain's defeat would "be fatal to the last hope of liberty in Europe," and that not even the Atlantic would protect them should Britain fail.[42] Yet soon all continental Europe was under Bonapartist control. Following the battles of Austerlitz, Jena, and Auerstadt in 1806, and then Eylau and Friedland in 1807, Austria, Prussia, and Russia were successively forced to bow before *le petit caporal.* This development heralded a period of sustained economic warfare, and it is here that the roots of the War of 1812 lie. To defeat France, Britain must ignore neutral opinion; yet successive U.S. governments formulated policy as if the British government was sensitive to American actions.[43] Not that relations were helped by another incident involving *Leander* on 25 April 1806. Attempting to stop the American sloop *Delaware,* she fired a shot that killed the latter's helmsman, prompting riotous protests in New York.[44] That British ships were empowered to stop American ships off the American coast was a constant source of irritation and affront to American pride. But things were becoming progressively worse for the British. Early that year the Admiralty reported that "the demands for men have been beyond all imagination, and the want of them hampers every operation considerably."[45]

The brief thirteen months of the "Ministry of All the Talents" was the only Whig-led administration between 1783 and 1830, and offered an opportunity for compromise. But the problem of desertion remained crucial, as the pro-American Henry Fox and William Eden, Lords Holland and Auckland, negotiating a new treaty with America's James Monroe and William Pinkney, noted in a statement: "If it were admitted that our Sea Faring people might transfer themselves with impunity to the American Service, our homeward bound fleets would be returned manned by foreigners at the commencement of every War, and our Navy might be confined to Port for want of hands."[46] The ensuing Monroe-Pinkney Treaty was in many ways more generous to the United States than the Jay Treaty had been.[47] But the prosperity of the U.S. government depended on customs revenues generated by shipping, and as no agreement could maintain foreign subjects in American service against their sovereign's wishes, an agreement had to be avoided, and Jefferson refused to send it to Congress for fear it might pass.[48] Unwilling and unable to go to war, Jefferson imposed trade restrictions, and Republicans would later claim that the United States faced a choice of "War, Embargo or nothing." But Jefferson reportedly told a friend, "I do not wish any treaty with Great Britain," and in sidestepping the Monroe-Pinkney agreement he "missed an opportunity to substitute peace and prosperity for commercial restrictions and war."[49] To compound Anglo-American differences and effectively annul the treaty before it could be ratified, following the defeat of Prussia Bonaparte issued the Berlin Decree on 21 November 1806, establishing what became known as the Continental System with the purpose of destroying British trade, and declaring that the British Isles were now in a state of blockade: no vessel coming directly from Britain or its colonies, including American ships, would be received at ports under his control.[50]

In reply Spencer Perceval, chancellor of the Exchequer in the Duke of Portland's new Tory administration, introduced legislation in March 1807 through Orders in Council to confine Europe's trade with neutrals.[51] The Tories, with the hardline George Canning as foreign minister, were sure the best means of answering the French decree was a total prohibition of neutral carrying trade between the West Indies and Europe, a retaliation that would have the side-effect of protecting British trade from American competition.[52] Then in June another impressment incident occurred that could have sparked war immediately. While awaiting two French ships in Chesapeake Bay, a British squadron suffered from serious desertion, several of the sailors enlisting in the American frigate USS *Chesapeake.* When the *Chesapeake* put to sea, flying the pennant of Commodore James Barron but under the command of Master Commandant Charles Gordon, she was intercepted by HMS *Leopard* under Captain Salusbury Humphreys of the Royal Navy (RN).[53] When a man went aboard to request the return of the deserters Barron refused, whereupon Humphreys, on orders from Vice-Admiral George Berkeley, who commanded the North American Station, opened fire, killing three Americans and wounding eighteen, and forcing the *Chesapeake* to strike her colours. Four men were taken off, including Jenkin Ratford, a notorious British deserter who was later hanged. The other three were Americans, two of whom had volunteered for the Royal Navy in 1806 and taken the bounty before absconding, of which written records were kept, and there were no legal or diplomatic grounds for releasing them from a bargain made of their own volition.[54] But the return of the *Chesapeake* to Hampton Roads produced immediate demands for vengeance at New York and Norfolk, and the incident much embarrassed the British government, which had to apologize and disavow Berkeley. Jefferson managed to defuse the anger by sending USS *Revenge* to Britain to seek redress, and by the time she returned in the autumn, war fever had subsided as American domestic political factors intervened.[55]

News that Bonaparte was implementing the Berlin Decree came with that of the Treaty of Tilsit, bringing Russia into the Bonapartist system and renewing the invasion threat with a massive fleet of the combined nations of Europe. Jefferson knew that Britain could not yield on impressment; it was immaterial that desertion was not a problem of America's making, yet to expect Britain to allow the collapse of its navy was unreasonable, so Jefferson sought an adjustment to the controversy. However, the new Tory government was hard-nosed and determined, and 1807 provided graphic evidence of what a neutral might expect if it pushed Britain too hard: the brutal assault on Copenhagen.[56] The government would appease nobody—certainly not neutrals—while at war with France. Perceval was a man of few ideas, but those he had he fought for: his idea now was to turn Stephen's *War in Disguise* into British policy, and he designed new and harsh Orders in Council stressing the right of retaliation against Bonaparte but also restricting neutral trade. Supported by the combined West Indies and shipping interests, though opposed by the manufacturing and financial interests represented by the weak Whig opposition, the orders were passed on 11 November 1807.[57] In turn, Bonaparte on 23 November issued the Milan Decrees, which stated that all ships touching British ports would have their goods confiscated. Thus neutrals obeying British Orders in Council were punished by the French, the most seriously affected being Americans.[58]

In the same month the French invasion of Portugal began the conflict in the Iberian Peninsula that would dominate British strategy for the rest of the war, although the threat of invasion remained as Bonaparte's massive shipbuilding programme took shape.[59] By year's end the United States could expect no respite from the cold winds of economic warfare blowing from Europe, and Anglo-American relations were in deadlock; Britain had placed America in a position in which it could do no harm, and its aim was to maintain this position. In America the Non-Importation Act of 1806 was followed by an Embargo Act in the spring of 1808 that proved worse than useless, particularly along the Canadian frontier, where smuggling was rife and violence to customs officers common.[60] This situation culminated in the Enforcement Act of 1809, which gave the army and navy extensive powers to act against smuggling. Yet during the embargo the quantity of goods reaching Canada may actually have doubled, according to contemporary observers; smuggling became such good business that a special "Embargo Road" was hacked through northern New York to facilitate it, and shots were exchanged with troops in the "Potash Rebellion."[61] But as shipping became idle the greatest sufferers were seamen, and from New Hampshire came a bitter song:

> Our ships all in motion once whitened the ocean;
> They sailed and returned with a cargo.
> Now doomed they decay, they are fallen a prey
> To Jefferson, worms and EMBARGO.[62]

To avoid the embargo, ship-owners, for the most part Federalists anyway, sent their vessels to Canada or Florida and continued trading illegally, a strategy which did nothing to dispose the Republican administration to make particular efforts on their behalf.[63]

Britain's control of the seas ensured that American resentment of its role in the economic battle was greater than resentment against France: so complete was it that Lloyd's insurance rates halved, from 12 percent to 6, between 1806 and 1810.[64] Yet when Bonaparte seized all the American ships in European ports he insisted that he acted out of friendship for the United States. After all, he reasoned, since the embargo forbade sailing from American ports they must be British ships in disguise, or had "denationalized" themselves by paying licence money to Britain; to relieve America of these troublemakers was, said the crafty hypocrite, the least he could do for a friendly power. In fact, Bonaparte was relentlessly hostile to American commerce, and his actions were certainly more cynical than Britain's.[65]

During 1808 Britain's economic situation deteriorated badly, with exports sharply declining; frequent and violent strikes affected Manchester cotton mills, and the loss of Baltic timber led to a desperate search for replacement sources, chiefly in British North America. And although America's embargo had little impact on the powers that decreed the Orders in Council, it was far from painless: Yorkshire wool was hit hard, and although the iron industry was not directly affected, nail manufacturers in south Staffordshire and Birmingham and cutlers in Sheffield were laid off.[66] The merchant navy suffered the most; its consumption of material in 1810 was reduced to five-ninths of the level of six years previously. However, what hardship the embargo caused in Britain was firmly blamed on money-grubbing America, and Britain sought other markets in the Mediterranean, where exports quadrupled between 1805 and 1811. Furthermore, despite American objections, British sales to South America increased from £8 million to £20 million in 1808, a substantial crutch in times of crisis. When Bonaparte then tried to enforce his blockade with a coup d'état in Spain in the same year, the diversion of British trade to South America became both safer and more respectable. But despite these developments, the view from the Board of Trade in 1808 remained bleak.[67]

As his presidency drew to a close that year, Jefferson's policy of coercion through trade restrictions had plainly failed; yet this remained the policy of his successor, so that throughout the period, first as secretary of state then as president, it fell to Madison to respond to British attacks on the American maritime economy. But his negotiations were doomed to failure because he insisted, with dedicated myopia, on treating Britain and France as though they would be equally affected by these measures.[68] A conscientious but passionless Republican, Madison was solemn and humourless. His actions were dominated by a concern for the republican system of government and the Republican party; to accept British impositions entailed national humiliation and was potentially fatal to the party, and like Jefferson he could see none but the American point of view.[69] Madison briefly threatened to go to war if the Orders in Council were not revoked, but instead in March 1809 he replaced embargo with another weak economic measure, the Non-Intercourse Act.[70] The hawkish Canning was delighted, noting that the "the Yankees have been obliged to give way," but Madison would soon face a new ministry in London: in August Perceval became prime minister after Portland suffered a stroke, and Marquis Richard Wellesley became foreign secretary after Robert Stewart, Viscount Castlereagh, fought a duel with Canning, in which Canning was wounded.[71]

Although renewed war with Austria distracted Bonaparte from his blockade during 1809, the greatest strain on his Continental System of economic warfare was that imposed on French customs receipts and particularly on those of his vassal states. Life without sugar, coffee, cotton, and soda was not only miserable but uneconomic; grape sugar and linen made poor substitutes, and in the autumn of 1809, when British fortunes were at their lowest ebb both militarily and economically, Bonaparte made a decision which as surely as any army helped to wreck his empire. He yielded to the increasingly desperate pleas of his tradesmen and treasury and permitted "trade by exception" in imitation of Perceval's licensing system. Permits would be sold to neutral ships to sell food to Britain, albeit at high prices and in specie. With this device he hoped to drain Britain of hard cash, but instead he produced a rash of flags never seen before or since as nominally neutral land-locked German states such as Pappenberg, Tönningen, and Varel suddenly discovered they had merchant navies. Holland opened its ports to American ships provided that imports were stored in government-controlled warehouses under French supervision. The black market and smuggling had long flourished, but once the dike was breached the system was impossible to maintain. By 1810 Frankfurt was full of British colonial produce, Leipzig was a distribution centre for British trade throughout central Europe, and Bonaparte had to sack his brother Louis as king of Holland.[72] Far worse, however, by breaking his own Continental System Bonaparte broke Tsar Alexander's support for it, and for him. Increasingly Russian ports were opened to neutral shipping, and war began to loom on the eastern horizon.[73]

THE ISSUE of overseas markets was of paramount importance to the agricultural producers of the western and southern United States, who felt the pinch of depression between 1808 and 1812, when prices collapsed. They blamed foreign trade restrictions, especially the Orders in Council, while New England shipping continued to make a tidy profit in spite of them.[74] But while the main pressures leading to war were unquestionably those of trade and impressment, another factor would tip the scales into war: expansionism. Western nationalism had been a factor behind the War for Independence, and southerners wanted new land because they believed that slavery must expand or it would shrivel and die.[75] After Major-General Anthony Wayne's victory over the Indians at Fallen Timbers in 1794, and the Treaty of Greenville the following year, American settlers poured into the Old Northwest—Ohio, Kentucky, Illinois, and Indiana. The Indians prepared to fight for their lands and looked to the British for assistance, although at first the British were not interested, seeing no need to pursue Indian favours.[76]

When news of the *Chesapeake* affair brought war looming in June 1807, however, the British Indian Department began to make overtures to enlist Indian help in the event of an American invasion of Canada. The British knew that an American war would necessarily involve an invasion of Canada, openly advocated in the south that year.[77] The captain-general and governor-in-chief of British North America, Lieutenant-General Sir James Craig, therefore authorized the Indian agent at Fort Malden/Amherstburg to begin negotiations with Indian leaders, notably a mystical prophet called Tenskwatawa ("The Open Door," also known as "Loud Mouth") and his brother Tecumseh ("The Shooting Star" or "Leaping Panther").[78] But this was hardly Bismarckian scheming: in the days before telephone and telegraph a great deal had to be left to the discretion of the man on the ground, who from February 1808 was a seventy-odd-year-old Irishman called Matthew Elliott.[79] The Prophet preached separation from white people, but his speaking against the Americans and not the British was bitterly resented by leading War Hawks, including Henry Clay of Kentucky, the thirty-one-year-old spokesman for the growing war party, although as Elliott's predecessor, Thomas McKee, noted the year before, the "discontent of the Indians arises principally from the unfair purchases of their lands [by the United States, but] the Americans ascribe it to the machinations of our government."[80]

War could just as easily have been undertaken against France as against Britain, but there was no enthusiasm for such a course in the United States, even though America would thus have gained not only unfettered trade with Britain and her colonies, but also protection for American ships trading with Europe. Instead Jefferson wrote to Madison in August 1809 that "should Bonaparte have the wisdom to correct his injustice towards us I consider war with England as inevitable."[81] Bonaparte had only to provide a chimera of conciliation in order to give America the excuse to pick a fight with Britain. Like Jefferson before him, Madison tolerated French offences that would have provoked righteous wrath coming from the British, and Henry Clay wrote in August 1810: "I scarcely know of an injury that France could do to us, short of an actual invasion of our Territory, that would induce me to go to War with her, while the injuries we have received from Great Britain remain unredressed."[82] He went on to tell Congress that the conquest of Canada "was in your power," and summoned the spirit of '76: "I cannot subscribe to British slavery upon the water, that we may escape French subjugation on land."[83] However, this belligerency could not gain currency so long as the defeatist Eleventh Congress remained in session. It would not face reelection until the autumn of 1810 or be superseded until 1811, and in the meantime on 10 May 1810 it brought forth another watery measure of economic coercion—Macon's Bill No. 2.

In Britain this toothless bill was hailed by Tories as vindication for taking a harsh stance towards America: it appeared a few weeks after Bonaparte's Rambouillet Decree, which ordered seizure of all American ships in French ports to a value of $10 million. Then respite for America appeared to come on 5 August 1810, when French Foreign Minister Jean Champagny, duc de Cadore, informed the American minister in Paris, John Armstrong, that the Berlin and Milan Decrees might be considered revoked as of 1 November. Bonaparte was playing a very cunning game: that same night in the Trianon Decree he ordered that all American ships in European ports be seized and that others wishing to enter be prevented from leaving. Americans did not learn of this decree until 1821, when Albert Gallatin, then minister to France, discovered it among some old documents. He sent it to the White House with the interesting comment that "no one can suppose that if it had been communicated or published at the same time [as the Cadore letter] the United States would have taken the ground which ultimately led to war with Great Britain."[84] But Madison chose to accept the Cadore letter at face value when Armstrong forwarded it without comment, believing that he could persuade the British to lift the Orders in Council and that if instead events led to war, it would be with Britain only—the ancient enemy. Jefferson's dream of acquiring the Floridas also strongly influenced his relationship with Bonaparte, since aligning with France might further this aim; it also meant aligning against Britain's ally, Spain.[85]

The refusal of the United States to recognize the regency established for Ferdinand VII, the rightful king of Spain following the usurpation of the throne by Joseph Bonaparte in 1808, provided America with the pretext to apply pressure on the Floridas: the Treaty of Versailles in 1783 had confirmed West Florida to Spain, but the boundaries were vaguely defined. In 1803 the United States claimed Mobile Bay as part of the Louisiana Purchase, but Spanish garrisons remained in possession. Aggressive American settlers in West Florida formed a Committee of Public Safety headed by John Rhea, who asked the United States for annexation on 25 July 1810 and a loan to finance the committee's government. When Madison refused, the committee unilaterally declared the Republic of West Florida and formally applied for statehood. This move was annoying to Madison because it threatened his ongoing negotiations to take all of Spanish Florida. Though troubled by "constitutional qualms," Madison was not inclined to let these divert him from grasping an attractive geopolitical prize; without clear legislative or constitutional authority he acted on the grounds that "a crisis has at length arrived subversive of the order of things under the Spanish authorities."[86] On 27 October he authorized the governor of Orleans Territory to take possession of West Florida, although the governor's forces occupied only Baton Rouge and the area between the Mississippi and Pearl Rivers.[87]

Meanwhile, in Europe Bonaparte reserved his greatest energy for a drive against smuggling, and in 1811 the economic war reached a second peak, leading to a rash of bankruptcies all over Europe and prompting allies and vassals to revolt against him.[88] Amid accusations from Federalists that Madison had been duped by Bonaparte and demands for proof of his revocation of the Berlin and Milan Decrees, Congress affirmed the Non-Intercourse Act in May 1811, which coincided with the worst time for Britain economically. Sweden had joined the Continental System, and exports to northern Europe were reduced to only 20 percent of those in 1810; exports to South America also declined by 65 percent and to the United States by 76 percent; Lancashire was working a three-day week, and in Nottinghamshire workers responded by smashing machinery. Unrest soon spread and could be controlled only by military repression, and these woes were compounded by wartime inflation as gold payments to Europe, especially to Spain and Portugal, led to further depreciation of the pound and a drain on Bank of England reserves.[89]

On 16 May the frigate USS *President* fired broadsides into His Majesty's Sloop *Lille Belt* (a Danish prize widely known as *Little Belt* in Royal Navy circles), killing eleven men and wounding twenty-one. The incident delighted Americans as revenge for the *Chesapeake* but provoked howls of rage in the British press.[90] Yet by November the *Chesapeake* affair had finally been

1.1. John Bull at the frontier. *A Scene on the Frontiers . . .*, etching by William Charles. *Source:* Library of Congress, Prints and Photographs Division.

resolved by the new British minister in Washington, Augustus Foster, son of the Duchess of Devonshire and a young man who left behind a broken romance with the girl who later married Byron.[91] And the economic crisis of confidence also passed; the government secured further loans, and Bonaparte failed to capitalize on Britain's problems. After two years of poor harvests, food shortages could have caused greater stress, yet imports from Europe were actively encouraged—paid for in gold—since by the autumn it was clear that France was suffering as much as Britain from the trade war. In November the tension eased with the granting of new licences on both sides of the English Channel, a move that increased their number from 1,600 in 1807 to over 18,000. Britain had survived this first attempt to defeat it through economic dislocation, one not repeated until the U-boat menace of the twentieth century.[92]

Although it was now clear that Bonaparte had failed to abide by the Cadore "agreement," Madison believed this outcome was due to his lack of faith in America's promise to break off intercourse with Britain. Armstrong resigned as minister to France as a consequence of the affair; he favoured war with France, and with a presidential election imminent, he briefly offered a political alternative within the Republican party.[93] At the same time Governor William Henry Harrison of Indiana provoked a quarrel with Tecumseh by violating a treaty signed two years earlier. Harrison was an ambitious professional politician, the first governor of Indiana Territory in 1802 at just twenty-seven: he was close to land speculators and determined to raise Indiana to statehood through white settlement. In November he advanced against Prophetstown, where Tenskwatawa held court, and fought the battle of Tippecanoe on 7 November 1811, involving about 900 Americans and 500 Indians.[94] "ANGLO-SAVAGE WAR," shrieked the frontier press; "the SCALPING KNIFE and TOMAHAWK of British savages, is now, again devastating our frontiers."[95] Senator Andrew Jackson, who had long been convinced that the British were responsible for Indian depredations, was not alone in demanding that "the blood of our murdered heroes must be revenged!"[96]

In the deep south the Creek Indians also stood against the United States. The Creek (or Muskogee) Confederacy spanned most of what is today Alabama. Many half-breeds lived among the Creek, and American agents encouraged white ways in an advanced Indian culture: owning slaves, manufacturing cloth for market, practicing agriculture, and raising livestock to supplement hunting, combined with an effective form of tribal government.[97] But like tribal peoples to the north, the Creeks had long-standing grievances about

American encroachment on their lands. Tecumseh visited them in 1811 to persuade them to join his confederacy, and found willing listeners among a group called the "Red Sticks" from their practice of carrying wands painted red, a traditional south-eastern colour denoting war.[98]

In early 1812 angry Creeks killed several whites, and in May a Red Sticks party returning from visiting Tenskwatawa at Prophetstown massacred a family of seven near the Duck River south of Nashville, including five children, and seized a woman prisoner—Martha Crawley. In the south "the fire of the militia was up" against the Creeks, as Andrew Jackson informed Willie Blount, governor of Tennessee. "They burn for revenge, and now is the time to give the Creeks the fatal blow."[99] Tennesseans found no difficulty forming a picture of Indian barbarity and British complicity. The first account of Crawley's capture published in the *Knoxville Gazette* came under the headline "Indians and British Depredations," accompanied by a string of correspondence from the Northwest suggesting British involvement, although no evidence of any such involvement was offered.[100]

Other papers across the nation made the same assumptions as Jackson. Hezekiah Niles's *Weekly Register* insisted that the cause of these horrible murders "arises from our good friends at Amherstburg and [Fort] Malden in Upper Canada."[101] Once they were unleashed, Madison found he could not restrain the expansionists. When the Twelfth Congress assembled three days after Tippecanoe, the War Hawks, who represented a loose grouping rather than a distinct faction coming mainly from the new western states or frontier regions of the lower south, seized the initiative.[102] Henry Clay gained the key position of Speaker of the House of Representatives and packed important committees with war supporters, like John C. Calhoun of South Carolina and Felix Grundy of Tennessee—too young to remember the horrors of the last war and eager to risk another. Peter B. Porter, who had key business interests in expansionist road projects in the Niagara region, became chairman of the Foreign Affairs Committee; together they pushed Madison for a breach with Britain, and Porter's committee duly reported that it was necessary to go to war. Only the desperate need to raise forces prevented immediate hostilities.[103]

The most obvious way to prosecute a war was an invasion of Upper Canada: this would hurt the British and cut them off from the Indians of the Old Northwest. War would also, it was believed, destroy British fishery controls on the northern shore and shatter British control of American trade with the West Indies.[104] Madison consciously linked Bonaparte's impending invasion of Russia with the assumption that Britain would not be able to support

Canada, and that French co-belligerence would allow the United States to exploit French bases in the maritime war.[105] And, as with every other matter, religion was invoked to support both sides. Although pro-war Christians were less literate than their opponents, they were absolutely convinced of the righteousness of their policy; most were loyal not only to the Republican party but personally to Madison himself, and they were adept at matching anti-war Christians prophecy for prophecy, apocalypse for apocalypse, as both parties predicted imminent armageddon in Europe. Foremost among the war churches were the Baptists, with their deep-rooted resentment of Anglicanism and Congregationalism; most Methodists supported it too, while religious opposition was led by Quakers, Congregationalists, and, to a lesser extent, Presbyterians.[106] And just as patriotism could be strengthened by faith, so inter-denominational ire could be inflamed by the sure knowledge that one's opponents were traitors.

During subsequent congressional debate, the weakness of the moral case for war forced the War Hawks to fall back on the unanswerable mystique of expansionism bolstered by anglophobia, and linking Indian depredations to British subterfuge added fuel to their fiery demands. For westerners the easiest way to end the Indian threat was to drive the British from Canada; they were indispensable in driving the war party, while southerners saw backing an invasion as providing a lever to support their claims to the Floridas.[107] But John Randolph, the lone wolf of the Republican party, a shrill, madcap Virginian whom many believed deranged, sneered on those whose real purpose was "a scuffle and scramble for plunder." War was nothing but a cover for a land grab. "Ever since the report of the Committee on Foreign Relations came into the House," he said, "we have heard but one word—like the whip-poor-will, but one monotonous tone—Canada! Canada! Canada!" Let the nation beware, he warned; conquest of Canada would strengthen anti-slavery elements and force the south to secede.[108] Joseph Desha of Kentucky argued that nothing the United States could do would succeed as long as "the British have Canada or a Nova Scotia on the continent of America."[109] And William R. King of North Carolina insisted that it was not a war of conquest, then went on to say that if Britain did not yield, "we shall take Canada. Yes sir, by force."[110] However, "Canada was not the end but the means," Henry Clay would later claim, "the object of the War being the redress of injuries, and Canada being the instrument by which that redress was to be obtained."[111]

In January 1812 Madison produced a shoddy report on impressment that claimed a total of 6,257 cases of alleged Americans "impressed and held in bondage"; many names were duplicated, and some were recorded three or four times.[112] But as a Foreign Office minute noted in February, American seamen now sold so many citizenship certificates to British sailors that "it not infrequently happens that a man with a fair complexion, produces a certificate describing him as half-caste, and the West Indian Mulatto, is not infrequently described with blue eyes and long sandy hair."[113] By 1812 the Admiralty believed that no fewer than 20,000 Britons were serving in the American merchant marine, and even Gallatin estimated that 9,000 seamen, or about half the seamen in America's foreign trade, were British even by U.S. definition.[114] However, by rhetorically connecting impressment with slavery and linking it with Algerian despotism—something that both fascinated and appalled American readers—the War Hawks and their press supporters like Niles created a powerful tool in favour of action.[115] To assist matters, Madison produced letters in March provided by Comte Edouard de Crillon between John Henry, an Irishman living in New England, and Sir James Craig. For a while Federalists squirmed, and "Henryism" became a derisive term for pro-British feeling, even though the letters—which cost a cool $50,000—revealed only the intrigues Boston Federalists had *not* had with the British government.[116] But the furor died two weeks later, when French warships seized and burned two American ships licensed to carry grain to Spain for British troops.

Ironically, here had been an opportunity for Madison to exert exactly the sort of economic pressure he needed. The British Army in the Iberian Peninsula relied heavily on American grain, shipments of which rose from 80,000 bushels in 1807 to 835,000 in 1811—coinciding with the poor harvest in Europe—and to over 900,000 in 1812.[117] In January Jonathan Russell, the American *chargé d'affaires* in London, wrote that Britain would repeal the Orders in Council "from fear of an *immediate* embargo or war which would cut off our supplies from the armies in Spain and Portugal"; and in April a British observer in Lisbon noted that "provisions were plentiful, but principally from America . . . and if it was not for the supplies from America, the army here could not be maintained."[118] Yet Madison never attempted to use this lever, fearing an outcry from grain producers in the mid-Atlantic states. Augustus Foster demanded once more to see official proof that Bonaparte had revoked the Berlin and Milan Decrees, which alone, he said, would justify revoking the Orders in Council.[119] Then came a letter from Joel Barlow, a writer and sometime diplomat in Paris, that gave all Washington, outside the president's circle, a great laugh. Monsieur le comte de Crillon was an experienced rogue called Paul Emile Soubiron, an agent of Joseph Fouché's French secret police.[120]

On 17 March 1812 American "Patriots" under Major-General Thomas Pinckney and Colonel Thomas Smith declared East Florida to be U.S. territory and occupied Fernandina; but confusing messages from Washington gave no clear indication of what official support they enjoyed. On 12 April Smith's force occupied Fort Moosa, near St. Augustine, but was forced to pull back after the Spanish and their free black allies attacked Smith's camp.[121] By mid-spring, Madison was seemingly groping for a way out of his dilemma without war, and without losing the presidency, and he agreed to send a peace mission to Britain. But he also approved a ninety-day embargo designed to get the majority of the American merchant fleet home before a declaration of war was made.[122] Then on 12 or 13 April Henry Clay led a group of "hot-headed violent men" to the Executive Mansion. Officially they represented the Republican caucus, on whom Madison's nomination for reelection depended. According to Senator Thomas Worthington, Clay told Madison that "nothing less than open and direct war" with Britain would satisfy the committee; otherwise "they would forsake him and be opposed to him." Although doubts have been cast on this version, Clay undoubtedly delivered a strong message reaffirming his earlier advice that America would not prepare properly for war until she was at war: therefore, declare war and then prepare for it.[123]

Yet even as voices in Congress demanded war, voices in Parliament were straining to avoid it. The Whig opposition, led by Henry Brougham, made another concerted effort to have the Orders in Council revoked.[124] Although this was defeated, five great centres of opposition had emerged: the Birmingham hardware district, Staffordshire potteries, cutlers of Sheffield, and Lancashire and Yorkshire cotton centres. Worcester's porcelain and glass manufacturers and Leicester's framework-knitters added their voices to the appeals, as did Scottish manufacturers in Glasgow, Dunfermline, and Paisley and the shipping interest of Liverpool, all now doing business on an unprecedented scale, the heralds of free trade.[125] But in response to this opposition *The Times* demanded no let-up, arguing that with France "We are engaged in a war—a war of no common description—a war of system against system, in which no choice is left to us, but victory or extirpation."[126]

Throughout the spring the clamour against the Orders grew so loud that it seemed the government must relent. Then, on 11 May, John Bellingham assassinated Spencer Perceval—inspired by personal rather than political motives—an act which produced savage joy among hungry northern workers.[127] For almost a month, until the appointment on 8 June of another Tory, Robert Banks Jenkinson, second earl of Liverpool, as prime minister, there was no effective government.[128] But with the author of the controversial Orders in Council dead and the country in increasingly vocal opposition, revocation soon followed, on 23 June. The news brought rejoicing throughout Britain, with "ringing of bells, Bonfires, Roasting Sheep, Processions, Public Meetings, Votes of Thanks" in honour of Brougham.[129] As late as 3 August *Aris' Birmingham Gazette* recalled a public dinner to celebrate at which a toast was given: "May the Revocation of the Orders in Council be the means of establishing permanent friendship between Great Britain and the United States."[130] Alas, the same paper contained news of the declaration of war.

While Bonaparte's Grande Armée massed for its ill-fated invasion of Russia, it enforced control of the north German ports; but when it departed towards the eastern steppes the smugglers reappeared: the Continental System and Bonaparte's avarice for conquest had become a vicious circle. When Madison set out the grievances supposedly necessitating war in a secret message to Congress on 1 June, he did so under five headings. The first four dealt with maritime quarrels. Yet those groups most affected by blockade, impressment, and search opposed war: they were doing fine evading the rules and supplying the deficiency of British shipping. On these four points the American case was strong in law but carried little heartfelt conviction. Madison's fifth point, however, was "the warfare just renewed by the savages on our extensive frontiers . . . among tribes in constant intercourse with British traders and garrisons."[131] Here the law was weak, but the power to stir hearts was strong, with outraged pride at stake. "We are going to fight," said Jackson, "for the reestablishment of our national character, misunderstood and vilified at home and abroad."[132] After much wrangling the House of Representatives voted on 3 June by seventy-nine to forty-nine for war against Britain; the Senate agreed two weeks later by nineteen to thirteen, making it the war bill receiving the least support in American history. The votes also reflected strong regional divisions: congressmen and senators from New York northwards voted for peace, and those from Pennsylvania southwards for war.[133] In the same week that the Anglo-Portuguese Army under Arthur Wellesley, recently created earl of Wellington, crossed the Agueda River into Spain, heading for victory at Salamanca; and on the same day—18 June—that Bonaparte's Grand Armée crossed the Niemen heading for destruction in Russia, Madison led the United States across a North American Rubicon.

2

Soldiers, Sailors, Immigrants, and Indians

After a peace of thirty years, and entirely engrossed in trade, every means had been neglected to prepare for war. Our treasury poor, our arsenals empty, fortifications in ruin, our Navy neglected, Military Science unknown, our Army nominally 6000 men, the country divided in opinion . . .

—Lieutenant Isaac Roach, 2nd U.S. Artillery

John Wilson Croker, secretary of the Admiralty, expressed the sense of sadness and betrayal felt in Britain at the folly in which America had indulged.

> There are now two free nations . . . Great Britain and America—let the latter beware how she raises her parricidal hand against the parent country; her trade and liberty cannot long survive the downfall of British commerce and British freedom. If the citadel which now encloses and protects all that remains of European liberty be stormed, what shall defend the American union from the inroads of the despot?[1]

But for the British government the American War was, in truth, little more than an annoying distraction, albeit at a time when it could ill afford one.[2]

The Cabinet now in place under Lord Liverpool was an experienced and capable group of men. Since February the foreign secretary had been the immensely able Castlereagh; specific naval and military matters fell to Robert Saunders Dundas, second viscount Melville, as first lord of the Admiralty—although Croker was of greater significance to the operational conduct of the

American War—and to Henry Bathurst, third earl Bathurst, the secretary of state for war and the colonies.[3] As a matter of protocol all matters were referred to George, Prince of Wales, appointed Prince Regent in February to act in place of King George III after the court physicians pronounced the old king's insanity to be incurable. Widely known derisively as "Prinny," he managed simultaneously to be a national scandal, a national disaster, a national achievement, and a national entertainment.[4] Strategically there were two options: America possessed neither fleet nor army, but because of its increasing rivalry in trade some voices claimed it would benefit Britain to strike preemptively, free the slaves, and force it to return Louisiana to Spain.[5] But these voices were few, and many others urged caution. France would welcome any such distraction, and France remained the principal enemy; no resources should be diverted from the struggle against Bonaparte.[6] With attention firmly focused on the Iberian Peninsula, Canada would have to look to its own means for defence, which lay primarily with the Royal Navy based on Halifax and the West Indies, and the small regular army garrison.[7]

Following the brief peace in 1803, authority was given to raise fencible regiments in Newfoundland, New Brunswick, Nova Scotia, and Canada. These were regular units but limited to service in defence of their home area, in this case North America (including Bermuda).[8] When Brigadier-General Martin Hunter realized he would not be able to recruit locally more than 200 of the 1,100-man establishment for His Majesty's New Brunswick Regiment of Fencible Infantry, he sought recruits in the Scottish Highlands. Eventually the unit reached some 800, including another 400 men found in Upper and Lower Canada, but other units struggled; the Nova Scotia Fencibles raised only 312 men by 1 January 1805, and as late as 1806 the Canadian Fencibles had only 124 men, insufficient to be employable.[9] In the same year Colonel Isaac Brock of the 49th (Hertfordshire) Regiment of Foot noted that the wide dispersal of the regular garrisons combined with the dull life of garrison duty was undermining morale, and this situation was exacerbated by the apparent wealth of the local population, leading to desertion. Drunkenness—long the bane of the British Army—was a another chronic problem, and Brock wrote to Frederick, Duke of York, the commander-in-chief, that experience

> has taught me that no regular regiment, however high its claims to discipline can occupy the frontier posts of Lower and Upper Canada without suffering materially in its numbers. It might have been otherwise some years ago; but now that the country, particularly the opposite shore

> [United States], is chiefly inhabited by the vilest characters, who have an interest in debauching the soldier from his duty, since roads are opened from the interior of the States which facilitates desertion, it is impossible to avoid the contagion.[10]

Brock was born on 6 October 1769 at Guernsey in the Channel Islands and commissioned in the 8th (The King's) Regiment aged 15. He took command of the 49th Regiment at age twenty-eight and led it during the expedition in 1799 to the Low Countries, where a young Lieutenant Thomas Pearson was serving with the 23rd. Brock distinguished himself at the battle of Egmont-op-Zee, and the 49th served as marines with Nelson's assault on Copenhagen in 1801, before arriving in Canada the following year. Over the next three years the regiment provided garrisons at York, Montreal, Fort George, and Quebec, and the young officer gained vital frontier experience; but after serving so long away from active fronts, he was becoming impatient.[11] Brock advised that the vital heart of the defence of Canada was Quebec and that it should have the main concentration of the regular garrison, while a veteran battalion of old soldiers should man the frontier. Nine such battalions of long-service men of good character were already on the Army List, and on 25 December 1806 the 10th Royal Veteran Battalion was formed for North America, its 650 volunteers drawn from existing veteran battalions, men discharged from line regiments but fit for garrison duties, or time-expired men who wished to continue serving.[12] Promoted to full colonel and acting commander of the forces in late 1805, Brock requested Mr. Thomas Dunn, the elderly administrator of Lower Canada in the temporary absence of a governor, to call out sufficient militia to repair the crumbling defences of Quebec and to train for an emergency.

Militia service was a long tradition in North America, and all fit males aged sixteen to sixty were expected to take part unless exempted through government employment or as essential workers, such as millers and ferrymen. Normally militia service involved little more than an annual muster for training or the provision of men for tasks such as the transport of supplies by boat, cart, or sleigh, providing labour for building fortifications, guarding prisoners, and providing mounted couriers—tasks that required little formal military training and are nowadays performed by the service support branches of the army.[13] It was usually achieved through ballot or lot whenever insufficient volunteers came forward, and those who served were normally excused from further service until the balance of the unit had been balloted. But as such duties usually involved arduous physical labour in return for the pitiful wages paid to British soldiers, the better off would hire substitutes to perform their service for them. Equally, the requirement to supply one's own musket and ammunition was honoured more often in the breach than in compliance.[14]

When the *Chesapeake* war scare was at its height, Lieutenant-Governor Francis Gore of Upper Canada came to Montreal to consult with Brock, who informed him of the parlous state of the militia in his district, which was practically without arms.[15] Gore wrote to Castlereagh, then secretary of state for war, that he was refraining from calling out any part of the militia, so that "the Americans may not be made acquainted with our weakness."[16] Sir James Craig had arrived at Quebec on 18 October 1807 to take up the long-vacant posts of captain-general and governor-in-chief of British North America, and the 10th Royal Veteran Battalion had arrived a few weeks earlier. The Quebec garrison was further strengthened by the 98th Regiment and the Royal Newfoundland Regiment of Fencible Infantry from Halifax, but not until 20 August 1808 did Dunn finally agree on a limited call-out. The *Quebec Mercury* declared that "never, on a similar occasion, could there be manifested more cheerful alacrity and zeal, as were shown on these occasions, as well by the Canadians as by the British . . . Too much praise cannot be given to the animating language of the field officers and others, in their speeches, addressed to the different battalions and companies, on the occasion. The whole has been attended with much festivity and hilarity."[17] Not that Brock was laughing: having previously reported to his brother in disgust that the men were scattered along a line of some 500 miles, "unarmed and totally unacquainted with anything military, without officers capable of giving them instructions," he lamented that considerable time would be necessary to bring them to a state of discipline.[18] Gore was confident of the loyalty of inhabitants from Kingston to Lower Canada, less sure of those around York, Niagara, and Lake Erie. But, he continued, "I have also to observe that excepting the Inhabitants of Glengarry and those Persons who have served in the American War and their Descendants, which form a considerable body of men, the residue of the Inhabitants of this colony consist chiefly of Persons who have emigrated from the States of America and of consequence, retain those ideas of equality and insubordination much to the prejudice of this government, so prevalent in that country."[19] By now Upper Canada was very much a North American hybrid; tied to the British Crown but strongly influenced by the United States on everything from agriculture to education, and with a population around the Great Lakes some 80 percent of which had been born in the United States.

In 1792 the lieutenant-governors of the newly separated Lower and Upper Canadas issued proclamations offering land grants in exchange for good farms with loyalty requirements by no means onerous. British policy was to encourage immigration from the United States to balance the growing francophone population of Lower Canada, which had almost doubled since 1759, and the political reliability of such immigrants was, at first, not regarded as posing a problem.[20] Thus whatever their position might have been during the War for Independence, and some at least had fought against the Crown, all were now happy to "promise and declare that I will maintain and defend to the utmost of my power the authority of the King in His Parliament as the supreme Legislature in this Province."[21] Many were Quakers, Mennonites, and Dunkers who made sober citizens and good farmers, but as conscientious objectors were not expected to serve in the militia. Others would have little objection to military service, if not much enthusiasm.[22] But Gore would not have to face the problem: it would fall to Brock. On 9 October 1811 the newly promoted major-general was appointed administrator as well as military commander of Upper Canada while Gore was granted leave to attend to business in Britain. Brock had long chafed at the poor prospects for advancement in North America and badly wanted posting to a more active theatre. But family financial difficulties forced him to stay, and in early 1812, when the Horse Guards granted a request for leave in Britain, he turned it down.[23]

His commander, Lieutenant-General Sir George Prevost, had taken over as the new governor-in-chief less than a month earlier, on 13 September, while commanding in Lower Canada since 1810 was the vastly experienced Major-General Francis Baron de Rottenburg.[24] Prevost was born on 19 May 1767 in New Jersey, the son of French-speaking Swiss Protestants; he was educated in England and on the Continent and commissioned in 1783 into the 60th (Royal American) Regiment, and when war broke out ten years later was commanding the 3rd Battalion on Antigua. He was twice wounded fighting the French on St. Vincent in 1796, and after promotion to colonel was appointed governor of St. Lucia until it was returned to France by the Treaty of Amiens. He successfully defended Dominica against French assault during the winter of 1803, gaining promotion to major-general, a baronetcy, and a short tour of duty in England. In 1808 he was appointed lieutenant-governor of Nova Scotia and for three years had provided pragmatic leadership that reconciled Catholics and Presbyterians.[25]

One of Prevost's first tasks as governor-in-chief was to placate the francophone inhabitants of Lower Canada, who were now in solid opposition to the

Lake Superior
SAULT Ste. MARIE
St. Joseph Island
INDIANA TERRITORY
FORT St. JOSEPH
FORT MICHILIMACKINAC
MACKINAC ISLAND
Area Controlled by British 1814
Lake Michigan
Lake Huron
MISSOURI TERRITORY
ILLINOIS TERRITORY
MICHIGAN TERRITORY
Wisconsin
Ft. SHELBY
McKay
PRAIRIE DU CHIEN
St. Clair River
Lake Sinclair
DETROIT
FORT SHELBY
SPRING WELLS
MAGUAGA
BROWNSTOWN
FRENCHTOWN
FORT MALDEN
Raisin River
Put-in-Bay
FORT DEARBORN
CAMPBELL'S ISLAND
SAUKENUK
ROCK ISLAND RAPIDS
FORT MEIGS
Maumee River
FORT STEPHENSON
MISSISSINEWA
PROPHETSTOWN
FORT MADISON
Des Moines R.
Mississippi
Illinois R.
INDIANA TERRITORY
TIPPECANOE
URBANA
OHIO
SINK HOLE
Missouri
St. Louis
FORT HARRISON
CINCINNATI

UPPER CANADA
and the GREAT LAKES
QUEBEC
LOWER
St. Lawrence River
CANADA
MONTREAL
Ottawa River
Richelieu R.
FORT CHAMBLY
FORT St. JOHN
La COLLE MILL
ISLE-AUX-NOIX
CORNWALL
CHATEAUGUAY
Chateauguay R.
CRYSLER'S FARM
Lake Champlain
PRESCOTT
OGDENSBURG
GANANOQUE
BURLINGTON
UPPER CANADA
Nottawasaga Bay
AMHERSTVIEW
KINGSTON
Lake George
Lake Simcoe
Bay of Quinte
Prince Edward Pen
SACKETS HARBOR
YORK
(TORONTO)
Lake Ontario
VERMONT
OSWEGO
Oswego R.
Burlington Bay
STONEY CREEK
NIAGARA FALLS
BRADDOCK BAY
Mohawk River
Oneida Lake
BUFFALO
Genesee R.
ALBANY
PORT DOVER
LONG POINT
NEW YORK
ERIE
(PRESQUE ISLE)
New York
PENNSYLVANIA
PITTSBURGH
Atlantic Ocean
0
50
100
150
200
Scale of Miles

anglophone commercial oligarchy, or *Château Clique*. Craig had been firmly convinced of the need to govern the province in the interests of this group, a position that brought him into conflict with the *parti Canadien* and created conflict with the Legislative Assembly and powerful Catholic clergy; he went so far as to suppress the radical newspaper *Le Canadien* and to imprison its editors without trial. Prevost made a number of appointments to appease the francophone community, although his placatory moves towards the Catholic bishop Joseph-Octave Plessis earned him the undying enmity of the Anglican bishop of Quebec, Jacob Mountain.[26] But it was military preparations that claimed most of Prevost's attention. He visited Montreal in October and inspected the forts at Chambly, St. John's, and Sorel (or William Henry), and in case reinforcements needed to move from Halifax to Quebec he ordered two officers to reconnoitre the canoe and portage route on the lower St. Lawrence, across New Brunswick to Rivière du Loup.[27]

During this period British North America was compared to a tree, with the Canadas forming the upper branches, the lakes and 1,000 miles of the mighty St. Lawrence River forming the trunk, and its tap-roots at Halifax stretching across the Atlantic to Britain.[28] The maritime provinces were less vulnerable to attack with the Royal Navy in support, but preparations for war everywhere were rudimentary in the extreme: there was no staff in the modern sense, and since all paperwork had to be written out in long-hand it was kept to a bare minimum. In the army, staff duties were usually combined with other tasks, and Prevost's adjutant-general, Colonel Edward Baynes, along with his military secretary, Captain Noah Freer, often undertook to act as chief of staff.[29] Medical and hospital provision was primitive, even by contemporary standards, and the supply and transport organization was equally so. For not only lack of manpower hampered British defence preparations, especially in Upper Canada. The province was economically primitive, with a white population of just 77,000 (New York City alone had 96,000) and a vulnerable line of communications 1,200 miles long from Quebec to its most westerly post at Fort St. Joseph on an island in the St. Mary's River on the north shore of Lake Huron. With the bulk of the Canadian population engaged in transportation and agriculture, the country could neither defend itself nor feed the necessary British forces; Wellington later characterized it as "all frontier and nothing else."[30]

Everything was in short supply—provisions, clothes, specie, medicines, weapons, and ammunition—especially in the far west at Forts Malden and St. Joseph; but also pens, paper, pencils, penknives, and sealing wax for sending dispatches.[31] At least the true pioneer era was finally ending in the Canadas, with log cabins replaced by fine buildings and settlements coalescing. A military traveller along the road between Montreal and Kingston, Upper Canada's principal military base, which mostly followed the line of the St. Lawrence River, noted that the "streets of Cornwall were wide and straight. It has a church, a court house, a jail and neat houses, all built of wood." However, although he noted that the "roads are good enough," from Cornwall westward the woods began, and the roads were then "unpleasant; long stretches of corduroy [logs] bridge the swamps and low grounds . . . span creeks and fairly wide rivers."[32] The wet weather of autumn and spring could soon make such roads impassable; it was always much easier to send dispatches or to transport supplies and men by boat. Water transport was six times faster and correspondingly cheaper, except in winter when icebound for several months and replaced by horse-drawn sleigh; and besides waggons and draught animals were in desperately short supply.[33] Indeed, every item of war would have to come from Britain across the Atlantic—prey for privateers—to Quebec, a journey taking about eight weeks. Then it would have to be transhipped to schooners or to brewer John Molson's steamboats, *Malsham* and *Swiftsure*, the latter of which could carry 400 men or light stores, to reach Montreal.[34] There it would be transhipped again to *bateaux*—a term covering a wide variety of river craft, but particularly double-ended flat-bottomed rowing boats about 40 feet long, capable of carrying 3–5 tons of stores or three dozen men—for Kingston some 175 miles away. This enterprise involved moving around three sets of rapids, necessitating arduous, backbreaking portering; then shipment across Lake Ontario, portaging around Niagara Falls, and shipment across Lake Erie. Between Montreal and Amherstburg the Quartermaster-General's Department in conjunction with the Commissariat Department operated nearly 190 *bateaux*, and these formed a critical element in keeping the supply line free to move on the lakes almost with impunity during the first year of the war. Nevertheless, it took four to six months between ordering an item and receiving it, a fact that necessitated particular foresight on the part of British commanders.[35]

The defence of Canada was divided into zones; the Left Division was closest to the citadel of Quebec and included the St. Lawrence as far as Kingston. The Centre Division enclosed York and Niagara, and the Right Division encompassed the area to the west. Prevost's strategy was to hold on as long as possible until help could arrive, and the key, as he saw it, was the "only permanent Fortress" in the country, Quebec City. Since any approaching American force would have first to take Montreal, he stationed the bulk of his forces to protect it, and he was quite prepared, if necessary, to abandon everything to the west, especially Upper Canada. Thanks to American newspapers he was well acquainted with both political and military developments in the United States and the unpopularity of the war in New England, and he resolved not to attack American territory where such action might create "the least tendency to unite the people of America," since while disunion prevailed "their attempts on the British American provinces will be feeble."[36] He received permission from London to improve the fortifications started by Craig and requested a further 10,000 muskets and equipment for the militia, plus sabres and equipment for 200 cavalry. He also discovered that a considerable part of the garrison's provisions normally came from the United States.[37]

Fortunately, when it came to movement of supplies across the Great Lakes the army-run Provincial Marine, though ossified, enjoyed considerable superiority over U.S. forces, who had nothing to match the brig *Queen Charlotte* (16 guns) and the schooner *General Hunter* (6) on the upper lakes, while on Lake Ontario the U.S. Navy's brig *Oneida* (18), built in 1809 and commanded by Lieutenant Melancthon T. Woolsey USN based at American Sackets Harbor, was outclassed by the *Royal George* (22)—a ship-rigged mini-frigate supported by the brig *Earl of Moira* (14) and the elderly 6-gun schooner *Duke of Gloucester*, whose replacement *Prince Regent* (8) was launched in July 1812.[38] And when news of war reached Halifax on 29 June, it came with the heartening news that New England wished to continue normal trading. Major-General Sir John Coape Sherbrooke, commanding the Atlantic provinces, issued a proclamation on 3 July officially sanctioning the arrangement permitting unarmed American ships to sail. Sherbrooke believed the American need for manufactures would ensure the continued supply of provisions and specie to Nova Scotia, and that the Royal Navy should not interfere with trade.[39] As the New Brunswick assembly was renewing the expiring militia law and making £10,000—twice the province's annual expenditure—available for defence, the chairman of the Committee of Public Safety for Eastport, Maine, wrote to the mayor of St. John that his fellow citizens had unanimously agreed "to preserve a good understanding with the Inhabitants of New Brunswick, and to discountenance all depredations on the Property of each other," and the city of Saint John reciprocated. Following consultations, their supplies greatly benefited New Brunswick, which depended for its very sustenance on New England, being very short of food, especially salt pork.[40]

WITH THE WAR against France dominating policy, the Canadas could expect no reinforcement for the foreseeable future. Its garrison comprised some 450 gunners of the Royal Artillery in four companies, 1st Battalion, the 8th, 41st, 49th, and 100th (Prince Regent's County of Dublin) Regiments and the 10th Royal Veteran Battalion; a total of around 5,600 effectives.[41] Both the 41st and 49th Regiments were due to return to Britain after lengthy tours of duty, but in the event of war Prevost was authorized to retain them and to treat their replacements as reinforcements (a 2nd Battalion of the 41st was ordered to be raised on 25 August 1812).[42] In addition there were the Royal Newfoundland Regiment and the Canadian Regiment of Fencible Infantry, but the total garrison of Upper Canada was only some 1,200 men scattered in small garrisons. And besides, neither the Royal Artillery nor his four Royal Engineers officers were entirely under Prevost's command, being also answerable to the Board of Ordnance in far-away London. And until Prevost's request for a company of Royal Military Artificers was answered, the sapper officers would have to rely on local civilian or militia labour for any tasks they might undertake. Sherbrooke's subordinate command of "Nova Scotia and its Dependencies" covered New Brunswick, Cape Breton, Newfoundland, and Bermuda and included three Royal Artillery companies and one of Royal Military Artificers, along with the 104th (New Brunswick) Regiment (with companies detached to Cape Breton and Prince Edward Island),[43] the 2nd/8th and 98th Regiments (the latter about 300 men in Bermuda), the 99th (Prince of Wales's Tipperary) Regiment in Nova Scotia, and the Nova Scotia Fencibles, who were in Newfoundland.[44]

Prevost decided to revive the proposal to raise a fencible corps in Glengarry County of Upper Canada, and without waiting for permission from London sent Captain (brevet, or temporary, Major) "Red" George Macdonell of the 8th Regiment to raise a small unit of 376 men armed with rifles to operate in green after the fashion of the 95th Rifles who were proving so effective in the Peninsula. Starting in February 1812, Macdonell sought assistance from a kinsman, Father Alexander Macdonell, who had previously been chaplain to the Glengarry Fencibles in Scotland and had been responsible for bringing many of the discharged men to Canada.[45] The captains and all but two of the lieutenants were from regular and fencible regiments serving in North America and were to recruit 30 and 15 men each, respectively, but francophones and men recently arrived from the United States were to be referred to the Canadian Fencibles. Soon afterwards Prevost agreed to the formation of another two companies, which helped to bring the overall strength of the unit up to

600 and made a colonelcy necessary. This Prevost gave to Baynes, his adjutant-general, and the lieutenant-colonelcy went to Major Francis Battersby of the 8th Regiment, while Macdonell had to be satisfied with having his majority confirmed.[46] Promised a £4 bounty and a grant of 100 acres of land after the war, recruits were eventually found from Scottish communities all over North America, including Prince Edward Island and Nova Scotia, so that Prevost admitted, "not a sufficient portion has been raised in Glengarry to give the Corps claim to bear that name"; but Prevost had too many important things to worry about to find another, and by May the Glengarry Regiment of Light Infantry Fencibles was concentrated for training at Trois-Rivières.[47]

At the same time, Prevost was trying to placate the Assembly of Lower Canada, which, although it refused a temporary suspension of habeas corpus, did agree to a new militia act on 4 April that allowed for 2,000 men aged eighteen to twenty-five, and selected by lot, to be embodied at regular pay rates for up to two years in the case of war, although half should be replaced annually. Along with this Select Embodied Militia, £12,000 would be provided for immediate measures and another £30,000 should war break out, although Prevost regarded this force as "a mere posse, ill arm'd and without discipline."[48] With this accomplished, Prevost decided to raise a Provincial Corps of Light Infantry, or Voltigeurs Canadiens, under the terms of the new act. This task was given to another Captain (brevet Major) Charles Michel de Salaberry of the 60th Regiment, a member of a well-known francophone family who in turn selected his officers from other prominent families.[49] They would be junior to all regular and fencible officers of the same rank, would have no claim to back-pay, and would receive their commissions once they achieved their quotas for recruits (36 men for captains, 16 for lieutenants), who would receive a £4 bounty and a 50-acre land grant on discharge; but by 9 June only 309 from 538 authorized junior ranks had been enlisted.[50] In contrast to Prevost's successful dealings with the Assembly of Lower Canada, Brock in Upper Canada met resistance to defence measures, including militia training.[51] Fortunately he was a man who commanded respect, standing 6 feet 3 or 4 inches tall. Lieutenant William H. Merritt of the Niagara Light Horse recalled that he had "a peculiar habit of attaching all parties and people to his person: in short, he infused the most unbounded confidence in all ranks and descriptions of men under his command."[52] He would certainly need that quality over the coming months. The defence of Upper Canada presented the British with a logistical nightmare, requiring the projection of military power into the Canadian heartland, an extended and very vulnerable flank. In an appreciation, Captain Noah Freer reasoned that it would be dangerous to assume a defensive posture, as this would soon expose York, "where it is presumed the last stand will be made."[53]

In the west, Canadian fur traders suffering from American competition as war approached were very willing to enlist Indian help in repelling any invasion of their territory.[54] Following Jay's Treaty, blood ties with Indians linked Montreal to the western outposts of Michilimackinac, Prairie du Chien, Grand Portage, and Fond du Lac, creating an informal empire south of the treaty line. In late 1811 and early 1812, discussions were entered into with the great fur trading companies, the North West and the South West, to enlist their help in case of war.[55] They would, it was reported to Prevost, "enter with zeal into any measure of Defence, *or even offence,* that may be proposed to them."[56] The two companies promised definite aid in men: the South West—or Michilimackinac Company, as it was also known—promised 100 Britons and Canadians and 300 Indians; the North West promised some 250 employees and up to 500 Indians.[57] The Nor'Westers feared that American forces would cut them off at Sault Ste. Marie and offered the War Department use of all their Great Lakes vessels, including one of 120 tons capable of carrying six guns on Lake Superior and one of 60 tons that could run the falls at St. Mary's and Sault Ste. Marie for use on Lakes Huron and Michigan. There were also at Moy, or Sandwich, the schooners *Caledonia* and *Nancy,* each capable of carrying four guns and companies of traders.[58]

Besides, it was necessary to sustain the policy of Indian alliance, as Tecumseh reminded the British in November 1811, when he presented the Great Wampum, a symbolic belt given to the tribes following the Seven Years' War.[59] In 1812 Tecumseh was forty-three, a singularly impressive and charismatic man. At some 5 feet 10 inches, he was well built and athletic despite a slight limp, the result of a hunting accident. He was a man of great humanity with commanding and forceful speech.[60] According to John McDonald, who saw him address an assembly at Ohio's then capital, Chillicothe, in 1807, he was "the most dignified man I ever beheld. While this orator of nature was speaking the vast crowd preserved the most profound silence."[61] But in the period since that appearance, Tecumseh had become increasingly frustrated by the "Big Knives,"[62] as the Indians referred to the Americans, who were constantly encroaching on Indian lands. Often deals to buy land were made with one group that were invalid in Tecumseh's eyes, who believed the land was held in common by all Indians. His attempts to create an Indian confederacy were not the first, but he assembled a broad following from among his own Shawnees together with Kickapoos, Ojibwas, Potawatomis, Winnebagos, and others.

The Treaty of Fort Wayne in 1809 proved the last straw for Tecumseh and many other Indians. Tecumseh was determined to fight the Americans whether the British helped him or not, although following the battle of Tippecanoe he had little choice but to seek British assistance, however little he trusted them. Yet during the first half of 1812, despite American accusations, he received no shot and considerably less powder from the British than previously.[63] Also of considerable importance among the Indians, particularly those of the upper Mississippi Valley and around Lakes Superior and Michigan was the burly, bearded, Dumfriesshire-born fur trader Robert Dickson, known to the Dakota Sioux as Mascotapah—"the Red-Haired Man."[64] During the winter of 1811–12 he induced many starving Indians to favour the British by providing them with his entire stock of supplies, and made promises to them that went far beyond the official ones of His Majesty's government.[65] His efforts posed a potentially greater threat to the United States than did Tecumseh, since the tribes under his influence could mobilize more warriors and were equipped with war canoes capable of wreaking havoc around Lake Huron.[66]

Brock disliked the idea of abandoning Upper Canada and proposed measures to hold it to Prevost in December 1811, since if the western Indians could be persuaded to take British supplies and make war, no American force could then invade. "The reduction of Detroit and Michilimackinac must convince people, who conceive themselves to have been sacrificed, in 1794 [at Fallen Timbers], to our policy, that we are earnestly engaged in the war."[67] However, Prevost had recently received explicit instructions expressly forbidding minor offensive actions, and although he agreed with Brock that an attack against Detroit and Mackinac might be effective while they remained weakly held, there remained serious doubts about American intentions.[68] As war approached, the British continued to be cautious in their approach to Tecumseh, who was preparing to launch his war with the United States at the same time as the United States was preparing to launch one against Britain. In mid-June he was holding final talks with American officials at Fort Wayne when he learned that William Hull, the fifty-nine-year-old governor of Michigan Territory, had begun blazing a trail on 11 June known as Hull's Trace north from Urbana, Ohio, leading a force to reinforce Detroit, which news Tecumseh brought to the British at Fort Malden at the end of the month.[69]

Meanwhile, on 15 May Prevost learned that he could expect no immediate assistance from Europe, and before he had a chance to inspect Upper Canada and discuss matters personally with Brock, he received a letter from Bathurst requesting a detailed appreciation of the situation, to which he replied three days later.[70] He described various small isolated and exposed detachments across Upper Canada and along the Niagara, the navigation of which would require the capture of Fort Niagara on the American shore that had been relinquished under Jay's Treaty. In the event of war, Prevost considered that Montreal would be the "first object of attack"; its garrison consisted of the 49th Regiment and a field battery of artillery, the only one in the Canadas, with five 6-pounders and a 5.5-inch howitzer. It was up to strength in gunners but had only 30 drivers for its teams, and thus was not entirely mobile. The only permanent garrison in the Canadas was at Quebec with 2,300 regulars, although its fortifications needed improving.

> I have considered the preservation of Quebec as the first object, and to which all others must be subordinate: Defective as Quebec is, it is the only post that can be considered as tenable for a moment, the preservation of it being of the utmost to the Canadas, as the door of Entry for that Force the King's Government, might find it expedient to send for the recovery of both, or either of these Provinces.[71]

When Frederick Marryat arrived at Quebec in June 1812, he was impressed with its romantic appearance. "The houses and churches are generally covered in tin," he noted, "to prevent conflagration, to which this place was remarkably subject . . . When the rays of the sun lay on the buildings, they had the appearance of being covered in silver."[72]

News reached Quebec on 24 June that war had been declared, and Prevost immediately cancelled the planned moves of the 41st and 49th Regiments back to Britain, and of the 100th to Halifax, and concentrated most of the battalion companies of these units forward of Montreal. The 1st Battalion, 1st Regiment (The Royal Scots), was already en route to Canada, and he also sent Brock 300 recruits for the 41st who had arrived the previous autumn with six companies of the Royal Newfoundland Regiment.[73] Command at Quebec went to Major-General George Glasgow, who Prevost agreed might remain in Canada, where he had been for twenty-three years without the chance of active service, rather than return to a desk job with the Board of Ordnance.[74] Prevost was short of experienced officers and wherever possible put regulars in command of posts and detachments. They and fencible officers were senior to militia officers of the same rank, and most militia units were commanded

2.1. The *Lord Nelson* leaving the Niagara River, with Fort Niagara on the left. *Harbour at Niagara, Summer, 1811*, painting by Peter Rindlisbacher.

by regulars with a higher local rank where necessary. Consequently, most companies of the 41st and 49th Regiments were commanded by lieutenants, as the captains and majors were serving elsewhere, while five captains of the 49th were on leave in Britain awaiting the return of their unit there. Brock was not impressed and complained that the 41st in particular was "wretchedly officered," a charge later strongly refuted by John Richardson, who was at the time a fifteen-year-old "gentleman volunteer," or officer cadet.[75] Later Dr. William "Tiger" Dunlop, assistant surgeon with the 2nd/89th Regiment, asserted that "we got the rubbish of every department in the army. Any man whom the Duke [of Wellington] deemed unfit for the Peninsula was considered as quite good enough for the Canadian market."[76] In fact, despite earlier warnings to Prevost that no help could be expected from Europe, Dunlop's unit was dispatched from Ireland in August as soon as news arrived of war; it arrived at Halifax on 13 October.[77]

Brock knew he would not have time or resources to train his 13,500 militia in the early months of 1812, so he passed a bill authorizing the establishment of volunteer flank companies from each regiment; this step proved immediately popular, with 700 names on the rolls by the end of April and more added weekly. In addition, the Niagara Light Horse was raised together with volunteer artillery and driver units.[78] He also enlisted the support of the Mohawk chief Teyoninhokarawen ("The Snipe"), better known as John Norton. Norton's father was Cherokee and his mother Scottish, and in 1811 he was planning to move to the American south-west, being fed up with Upper Canada, until Brock persuaded him to stay.[79] His Six Nations of the Grand River formed an Indian element distinct from the western nations under Tecumseh, being largely drawn from the Iroquois nations (Mohawks, Oneidas, Onondagas, Cayugas, Senecas, and Tuscaroras), plus other groups that had joined them in the eighteenth century.[80] When news of war came in June, not only did Brock mobilize his militia but 100 Grand River warriors soon joined him at a camp near Fort George. And although doubts remained about their reliability, the sight of these warriors roaming the banks of the Niagara sowed fear in the minds of American settlers and militia.[81]

THE AMERICANS might also have had Indian auxiliaries had they chosen to; but Erastus Granger, the Indian agent in the Niagara region, informed the local Iroquois that the U.S. Army was so strong that it had no need for them.[82] In those days war did not seem so serious: American strategy was uncomplicated;

the easy conquest of Canada and speedy starvation of the British West Indies were articles of faith among Americans. Jefferson considered the conquest of Canada at least as far as the walls of Quebec an almost costless exercise, and during the scare of 1807 one of his young supporters argued that enlistment should be for the duration rather than a twelve-month period, since this would be shorter.[83] Now Andrew Jackson appealed to the youth of Tennessee to seize the opportunity to join him in a visit to Niagara Falls and Quebec, and perform "a military *promenade.*"[84]

Most Republicans were delighted at the declaration of war, and many celebrated openly, agreeing with Jefferson that the conquest of Canada was but "a mere matter of marching."[85] Federalists were dejected, having failed to limit conflict to a naval campaign, even though the war slogan "Free Trade and Sailors' Rights" appeared to be so much hokum to Federalists and the shipping business in general.[86] In the boom-town of Baltimore—the only strongly Republican town on the east coast, with strong ties to France—an article on 20 June strongly opposing war in a spirited Federalist newspaper, the *Federal Republican,* led to a riot that destroyed the paper's offices. Afterwards mobs held sway all over town.[87] Eventually the paper reestablished itself and printed another condemnation of the war on 27 July, but this only provoked the mob to greater fury. It tried to storm the new offices while the militia, under Brigadier-General John Stricker, refused to enforce order.[88] Stricker urged the paper's staff to surrender and accept protective custody, but the mob stormed the gaol and attacked and brutally tortured those they could lay hands on, leaving them for dead. Among the victims was Henry "Light Horse Harry" Lee, the Revolutionary War hero and father of Civil War general Robert E. Lee, who never recovered his health and died three years later.[89] Elsewhere Republican mobs drove the Federalist *American Patriot* of Savannah and the *Herald* of Norristown, Pennsylvania, out of business, so that the *Connecticut Courant* claimed the war, "pretendedly for freedom of the seas, is valiantly waged against freedom of the press."[90] Republican papers tried to blame Federalists for expressing obnoxious opinions, but the violence rebounded on the war party and only served to strengthen anti-war feeling elsewhere, particularly in New England, but also in Maryland and New York, where the riots helped Federalists to election victories in the autumn. Many Federalists now felt that the war threatened their basic liberties and consequently would actively oppose it throughout.[91]

If British preparations seemed painfully feeble as war approached, the British were at least unsure it was coming; the American authorities had no such excuses. Both Madison and William Eustis, the secretary of war, seemed satisfied with the plan first submitted in April, to launch operations simultaneously against Montreal, Kingston, and across the Niagara River from the Northern Department.[92] Quebec was considered too strongly fortified, and besides, any attack in that direction would pass through increasingly uncooperative New England.[93] The attack on Montreal was therefore supposed to form the main effort; but mismanagement at every level left other operations assuming greater importance. A march on Montreal could not be attempted, Madison later wrote, "without sacrificing the Western and N. W. Frontier, threatened with an inundation of savages under the influence of the British establishment."[94] American leadership was characterized by a lack of will to dominate the decisive moments and of understanding of the administrative complexities of war; it overreached itself by trying to seize all of Canada without the means to hold part of it. Such a failure was unsurprising given that the officer corps expanded from 191 during Jefferson's administration to 3,145 by 1814, many men being commissioned direct from civilian life with no prior military experience or training.[95] In contrast, most British officers were reasonably well trained and experienced; the notorious system of officer promotion by "purchase," "with which wealth and influence are everything, and merit nothing," had long been effectively in abeyance.[96]

Then as now, the president was titular commander-in-chief, and the secretary of war and secretary of the navy were civilian members of his cabinet. But there were no equivalents to the chiefs of staff to offer professional advice, nor any staff officers in Washington to make plans. The 1800 election had seen the beginning of a struggle between proponents of a professional military and the traditional republican defence system of citizen militia. The subsequent decade of parsimony and retrenchment made preparation for war difficult; an almost total reliance on customs revenues meant a serious reduction in income whenever trade restrictions or war interfered with them, while abolition of internal taxes destroyed a potentially broad tax base. Cuts to the armed services were extreme: in 1806 the navy—regarded as symbolic of Federalist involvement in foreign quarrels at the behest of nonagricultural interests—had only one frigate on active service. Far more republican, far cheaper, thought Jefferson, were gunboats manned by skeleton crews until sea militia could spring to arms in an emergency.[97] While the frigate USS *Constitution* cost $300,000, a gunboat cost only $10,000–14,000. Jefferson built some 200 of these "miserable vessels," which "lay about in harbors in various conditions of uselessness"—a macabre monument to his ignorance of such matters.[98]

By 1812 there were only five frigates in commission, with another five laid up in need of overhaul; seven brigs and sixty-two of the practically useless gunboats. These were manned by some 4,000 sailors while the U.S. Marine Corps comprised some 1,800 men. Leadership was lacking too: though an advocate of preparedness, the secretary of the navy, Paul Hamilton, was usually drunk by noon.[99] His request for a navy of twelve 74-gun ships of the line and twenty frigates was rejected by Congress in favour of repairing the laid-up frigates and the purchase of timber for unspecified construction at some indefinite point in the future. Ironically, it was the War Hawks who opposed the creation of a blue-water navy that alone could hope to counter the Royal Navy in the long term.[100] With no officer more senior than a captain, the navy lacked a professional head and had no guiding doctrine. However, any war against Canada involved control of the Great Lakes, and John Armstrong recommended in January 1812 that resting, "as the line of Canadian defences does, in its whole extent on navigable lakes and rivers, no time should be lost in getting a naval ascendancy on both"; but nothing happened.[101] On 21 May Hamilton asked Captains John Rodgers and Stephen Decatur USN to submit plans to confront the Royal Navy. He received opposing suggestions then and later, from Captain William Bainbridge USN, who happened to be in Washington some weeks afterwards, all of which went nowhere to solving the problem of what to actually do when war came.[102]

The matter of immediate war funding also provoked fierce debate. A belligerent Congress saw the seizure of Canada as a way of gaining the lands of the Old Northwest but failed to vote for the funds necessary to achieve it; Republicans disagreed with and defeated the bills to support war preparations, and to build either a navy or an army to fight it.[103] Treasury Secretary Gallatin was authorized to borrow $11 million, but the thorny question of higher taxes was put off until later, and little was done to expand the War Department. Eustis was also quartermaster-general, commissary-general, Indian commissioner, commissioner of pensions, and commissioner of public lands, for which posts he had a staff of only about a dozen, and he was preoccupied with petty details.[104] The Commissary and Quartermaster Departments having been closed in 1802, a new Quartermaster Department under former Federalist New York governor Morgan Lewis was officially set up on 28 March, but the staffing and organization took many weeks to complete, and the new commissary-general, Callender Irvine, was not appointed until August. However, newly appointed officers could achieve efficiency only with time, and time was not available.[105] To set the necessary preparations in train would require an efficient and well-funded military administration, and the U.S. government was anything but efficient and well funded. The Jeffersonians would soon discover that rejection of standing forces left the country badly unprepared for war against a professional army, however small; and an unforeseen result of Indian participation on the British side was the reduction in the effectiveness of the militia, as American whites were reluctant to leave their homes.[106]

Officials found themselves working without instructions from above while under severe pressure from regiments forming below. Everything was scarce; blue-dyed woollen cloth for uniforms was replaced by whatever was available, including grey, black, brown, and "drab," a sort of dirty beige; but even then production lagged far behind demand, and delivery was hampered by the War Department's inability to locate units and detachments and match them to requirements, and by chronic lack of transport.[107] Having decided to try to conquer Canada without first securing Lakes Erie and Ontario, American forces had to rely on tenuous overland trails while the British would be supplied over water.[108] Feeding the troops was based on private contract in order to save money, but contractors were so bent on making it that quality and quantity were continually undermined; many units were still not properly dressed or equipped by the autumn as making a profit took higher priority than providing suitable shoes, clothes, blankets, camp equipment, or rations. Complaints from units would multiply as the war progressed, with sickness and many deaths blamed on the system.[109] Since medical science was in its infancy, doctors were incapable of dealing with the ravages of epidemic diseases that took hold in the crowded camps amid unsanitary conditions; by the war's end, generals would complain that money-grubbing contractors were responsible for far greater casualties than enemy action.[110]

Madison's senior soldier responsible for the April plan, Henry Dearborn, was a sixty-one-year-old who had distinguished himself during the War for Independence but had since devoted himself to politics.[111] He was described by Augustus Foster as having "apparently accepted his appointment with great reluctance, having hesitated till within a few days. His military reputation does not stand very high."[112] Nevertheless, on 27 January 1812 he was appointed major-general in command of the Northern Department while sixty-three-year-old Thomas Pinckney, another Revolutionary veteran, was appointed major-general to command the Southern Department. At the same time, William Hull, who had served only in junior capacities during the Revolutionary War, had very reluctantly agreed to Madison's request to accept a commission as brigadier-general in command of a North Western Command separate from Dearborn. Hull had not aged well, having already suffered a stroke, but was the only candidate for the post.[113] Before the declaration of war he received orders to march to Fort Detroit, which would entail cutting a road through the wilderness, and in early summer he gathered a force of 2,000 regulars and militia, some of whom wore caps bearing the motto "Conquer or Die."[114] He was promised that diversionary operations would take place in the north-east, but there was no coordination with Dearborn. From late June, Eustis assumed that preparations were under way for three columns moving into Canada and virtually abdicated responsibility to Dearborn; between them everything dissolved into muddle.[115]

Nor were more junior ranks better prepared than the high command: there were only twenty-nine field officers (majors and colonels) in the entire regular army, and many of these were either too old for active service, or had been too rusted by the grinding inactivity of garrison life to provide competent command at regimental level. As Winfield Scott, a twenty-six-year-old newly appointed lieutenant-colonel who would go on to become general-in-chief of the U.S. Army, retiring in 1861, and whose youthful energy set him apart from his peers, noted, the majority were "swaggerers, dependants, decayed gentlemen . . . *utterly unfit for any military purpose whatever.*"[116] In 1811 the army had an establishment of 10,000 but numbered less than 5,500 in seven regiments of infantry and one each of rifles, dragoons, artillery, and light artillery, with a small engineers corps.[117] American regular army pay of five dollars a month was never going to entice large numbers of men to sign up for five years when a day labourer could earn perhaps twice that amount.[118] To begin with, the bounty to join was $31 and 160 acres of land on discharge, but with recruiting sluggish this was gradually raised to $124 and 320 acres, and recruiting picked up, although the ranks were never filled. On 11 January 1812 Congress agreed to the establishment of an army 35,603 strong, although nobody seriously expected sufficient recruits to materialize.[119] And as late as 6 June the regular army had only 6,744 officers and men on establishment—a force no stronger than total British forces but spread over a far wider area—and around 5,000 on newly authorized establishments whose officers were as wholly inexperienced as their men.[120]

According to a report in February 1811, the states had over 700,000 men on their militia rolls. Therefore on 6 February Congress had given Madison power to accept 30,000 militia volunteers on one-year terms, although whether these volunteers could be compelled to serve outside the United States, or even outside their own states, remained unresolved. Only six such regiments were ever raised, described by one officer as little better than organized bandits engaged in "desertion robbery [and] disorderly & Mutinous Conduct."[121] On 8 April Madison was authorized to accept 50,000 further short enlistments of eighteen months' duration for the regular army, and two days later he was empowered to give each state governor a quota to prepare a total of 100,000 militia who, if called into federal service, were to serve between three and six months.[122] But the militia was everywhere in disarray—inefficient, unreliable, and expensive; every state had its own administrative system, most of which quickly broke down. As the *National Intelligencer* noted: "There seems to be a deplorable supineness and local jealousy that act as a dead weight against every attempt that is made for amelioration of the militia service."[123] Importantly, and unlike the British Army, militia officers were to have sole command of militia units, however inexperienced; and although time would eventually make militia officers much better fighting soldiers than most company level regular officers, time was not available.

Then on 22 June the Federalist governors of Massachusetts, Connecticut, and Rhode Island refused to comply with an order from Dearborn to call out companies that would release regulars for service at the frontier, both to protest against the war and to retain control over state forces. Madison condemned the decision but did not press it, hoping the militia would turn out voluntarily: none did. In the run-up to war, the people of border states had let it be known in Lower Canada that they wished to continue normal trading, providing the British Army with vital ration supplies. Even most of those who did enlist assumed that Madison's call-up order was to guard the borders.[124]

In fact, most states maintained "uniform" companies of the most enthusiastic citizen-soldiers, men who actually took some pride in their role, and the legislation worked on the basis that these bodies would be willing to operate under federal control. Yet the number of these volunteers was no more encouraging than that of regulars: the inducement of a 160-acre grant to the family of those who fell in active service proved no such thing; why should a man turn up and get himself killed for a modest cash bounty and 160 acres of land, wondered one potential recruit, who wished "every member of Congress had 160 acres of land stuffed up his [arse] instead of receiving $6 per day."[125] Although the regular army gained many individual recruits from New England, and enthusiasm in the west produced troops in that region, it was not possible to inflict a decisive blow against Canada from the Mississippi Valley, so that the lack of uniform support for war meant American strategy was hamstrung by domestic opposition, forcing it to delay operations towards Montreal in favour of those in the west.[126]

New York had already been asked to furnish militia along the Niagara frontier and Ohio to reinforce the regular garrison of Detroit. In New York State there were mixed feelings about the declaration of war. Governor Daniel D. Tompkins was an energetic and forceful Republican who had been active in preparing his state, with little help from the War Department, ever since the war scare of 1807.[127] Now, as preparations became urgent with volunteer militia companies dispatched to guard the frontier, Tompkins wrote to Eustis asking for supplies and information, little of which were forthcoming, and forcing him to rely on his state quartermaster-general, Peter B. Porter. Porter's initial enthusiasm for war had waned when he realized New York's vulnerability to attack, as he had written to Eustis in April.[128] Dearborn established a military camp at Greenbush near Albany in early May, but he showed no urgency, and his instructions from Eustis on 26 June did not demand haste.[129] He then announced he was going to Boston to confer with the Federalist governors refusing to activate militia and stayed away until 26 July.[130] Thus the defence of New York fell entirely on Tompkins and his staff, the first task being to raise the 13,500 militia quota for the state as detached regiments within the existing framework, although only 1,600 were to be deployed initially. Supply problems were legion: there were no blankets, tents, or camp kettles—a problem that also affected the Canadian militia, who Brock complained were especially short of clothing.[131]

At the frontier the Americans had no tools for improving defences, and what small amounts of equipment were available could not be distributed without orders from Eustis. But when rumours arrived that the Lower Canada militia was reluctant to take up arms, Tompkins predicted the same would happen in the Upper province, and claimed: "we shall make ourselves masters of Canada by militia only."[132] In a sharp move he proposed a political rival for command at Niagara: forty-seven-year-old Stephen Van Rensselaer, a man with "no training beyond the sanguinary prognosis of a dress parade, or a night attack on the café of the Fort Orange Hotel at Albany."[133] But Van Rensselaer's command was expected to be only temporary; he was not expected to be responsible for a major invasion of Upper Canada when his appointment was formally announced on 13 July. And Van Rensselaer was no fool; he knew his military limitations and to offset them ensured that he had two good men close to hand—Major John Lovett and his second cousin, Lieutenant-Colonel Solomon Van Rensselaer.[134] Throughout July, men and stores trickled north; Dearborn's absence exacerbated the command problems, and arrangements were left to inexperienced militia officers. Indeed, defeat was practically guaranteed from the moment Madison and Congress stepped onto the warpath with risible preparations that undercooked the navy and put a half-baked army in the field: America would have to go to war with the army it had, not the army it might want, or wish it had.

3

Brock—Saviour of Canada

Upon the heights of Queenston one dark October day,
Invading foes were marshalled in battle's dread array,
Brave Brock looked up the rugged steep and planned a bold attack;
"No foreign flag shall float," said he, "above the Union Jack."
. . .
Each true Canadian soldier laments the death of Brock;
His country told his sorrow in monumental rock;
And if a foe should e'er invade our land in future years,
His dying words will guide us still: "Push on, brave Volunteers!"
—James L. Hughes, "The Battle of Queenston Heights"

LIEUTENANT Archer Galloway of the New York militia claimed to have fired the first shot of the war when, acting against orders as soon as news arrived of its declaration, his small battery at Lewiston engaged a British party on the far side of the Niagara River. "When one of our officers made inquiries who had disobeyed orders, no one knew anything about it," he said. "They did not try very hard to find out."[1] Ten days after the declaration Jefferson announced that "upon the whole, I have known no war entered into under more favorable auspices. Our present enemy will have the sea to herself, while we shall be equally predominant on land, and shall strip her of all her possessions on this continent."[2]

When news of war reached Montreal on 24 June, the authorities made immediate preparations to meet and resist invasion, and their worst fears appeared to be confirmed when a mob formed as the militia was being embodied in villages around Montreal, and the Light Company of the 49th Regiment opened fire, killing one rioter. This was the reaction among *Canadiens* (French Canadians) that the Americans had hoped for, but it would prove an isolated incident, and with order restored the following day, over 400 militia joined the regular troops to march through the area.[3] Elsewhere minor clashes occurred along the border: the Americans seized four soldier caretakers at the former British naval base on Carleton Island; the British captured two American schooners trying to make a dash upriver to Sackets Harbor, forcing eleven others to seek shelter in Ogdensburg. On 19 July Kingston's Provincial Marine squadron tried to shoot up the naturally well-protected Sackets Harbor, but was driven off, and a few days later Brigadier-General Jacob Brown's militia brigade defending this vital post was reinforced by Captain Benjamin Forsyth's company of grey-clad riflemen, the first regular troops to reach northern New York State.[4]

The American capture of the schooner *Julia* on Lake Ontario, failure at Ogdensburg, and the poor state of the militia in Upper Canada, including a number of inhabitants in Leeds County who refused to take the oath of allegiance, caused Colonel Robert Lethbridge, the inspecting officer of militia at Kingston, "to confess I have had a most fatiguing week."[5] In contrast Hull was confident that his North Western Army would be welcomed by the inhabitants of Upper Canada, and on 24 June Eustis sent him instructions to cross the Detroit River and take Fort Malden and nearby Amherstburg with its important Provincial Marine dockyard, although he noted there were insufficient forces on the Niagara front to create any sort of diversion.[6] Hull was still slowly cutting a road towards Detroit, struggling through rain across swampland and woods, attacked by black flies and mosquitoes. He commanded some 400 regulars, including the 4th U.S. Infantry, veterans of Tippecanoe, and 1,200 men in the 1st, 2nd, and 3rd Regiments of Ohio Volunteers, whose clique of colonels—Duncan McArthur, James Findlay, and Lewis Cass (a future secretary of state)—outranked a resentful Lieutenant-Colonel James Miller commanding the regulars, who had not been paid and were becoming fractious.[7]

Hull reached the Maumee (Miami) River at the end of June, and on 1 July, still unaware of the declaration of war, he chartered the schooner *Cuyahoga* to carry his heavy baggage, sick men, and official papers to Detroit.[8] Shortly afterwards he learned of the declaration and sent horsemen to try to overtake the schooner, but thanks to a warning letter sent by Brock on 25 June the British were waiting, and she was promptly taken by six soldiers in a *bateau* under Lieutenant Charles Frederick Rolette RN, veteran of the Nile and Trafalgar. Having boarded and ordered her into Amherstburg, Rolette made the American musicians on board play a rousing "God Save the King."[9] More importantly, vital papers were captured, and consequently Brock informed Prevost that until now "I had no idea General Hull was advancing with so large a force."[10] Hull reached Detroit on 6 July, and, knowing that the Provincial Marine could interdict his supply columns on the road running close by Lake Erie, he wrote to Eustis that his force was not strong enough to take Amherstburg.[11]

Nevertheless, on 12 July Hull crossed the Detroit River, a sight that inspired Detroit resident John Hunt: "My blood thrilled with delight when I saw from Detroit that beautiful morning the march of that fine army, with drums beating and colors flying, with the gleaming of bright muskets."[12] But the people of Ohio and Michigan knew how exposed they were in the event of war, and already 188 Ohio militiamen had refused to cross the border, being legally liable to serve only in-state; and the rest were reluctant to undertake the rigorous training they clearly needed.[13] The crossing was unopposed, and Sandwich village was occupied, whence Hull issued a florid proclamation designed to appeal to recently arrived American settlers:

> Had I any doubt of our eventual success I might ask your assistance, but I do not. I come prepared for every contingency. I have a force which will look down any opposition and that force is but a vanguard of much greater. If, contrary to your own interest & the just expectation of my country, you should take part in the approaching contest, you will be considered and treated as enemies, and the horrors and calamities of war will stalk you.

But Hull's abject fear of Indians was expressed by the bloodthirsty declaration: "No white man found fighting by the side of an Indian will be taken prisoner. Instant destruction will be his lot."[14]

Some fifty mounted local men were recruited to lead foraging parties against their neighbours, and many militia deserted and returned to their farms, leaving Lieutenant-Colonel Thomas Bligh St. George of the 41st Regiment, who was in local command with some 450 men under arms.[15] Thus he could rely only on his 300 regulars from the Royal Artillery, 41st Regiment, and Royal Newfoundland Regiment, with some 400 warriors under Tecumseh. Brock expected Amherstburg to fall quickly but sent Colonel Henry Proctor of the 41st Regiment to assume command there; yet Hull sat still, wondering what to do next.[16] Between Sandwich and Amherstburg flowed the Aux Canards stream; on 16 July 280 Americans under Cass approached the small bridge, whose British advance piquet under Lieutenant John Chernow withdrew, apart from Privates John Dean and James Hancock, who refused to surrender to the impossible odds. Dean was killed and Hancock wounded and captured, and the incident was later held up by Brock in general orders as an example of "heroism, self-devotion, firmness and intrepidity."[17] But Ensign James Cochran was less impressed, pointing out that Dean and Hancock "were both drunk and asleep when the advancing enemy drove in the picket and in their stupid surprise, offered useless resistance when roused by the Americans."[18] Cass then left a forty-man detachment near the bridge and marched 5 miles upstream to a ford, returning along the far bank to drive off the fifty British defenders under Captain Joseph Tallon before darkness halted the pursuit.[19]

Thus fell the only defensible position before Fort Malden, which now lay open; the majority of Indians remained neutral, and had Hull reacted quickly he might have taken Amherstburg.[20] William K. Beall, Hull's quartermaster-general held prisoner there after being taken on the *Cuyahoga,* told his diary that the British position was "very weak," and "at one leap I could get into the fort."[21] But Hull preferred to await the repair of his artillery carriages, and next morning the British, with Indian support, found the bridge abandoned and tore it up. At this stage Hull's force amounted to around 450 regulars and some 1,400 militia with 200 Michiganders, but as Major James Denny informed his wife, he was "losing all the confidence he had in the army. H[ull] holds a council of war every day, and nothing can be done—and councils again. The result is still the same."[22] On 26 July Proctor arrived and took command, but not until 7 August were Hull's guns mounted in anticipation of an attack on the fort. Then dramatic news came from Fort Mackinac (now pronounced *mac-i-naw,* though often *mac-i-nac* at the time) in the north.[23]

While the 61 men of the American garrison remained unaware of the declaration of war, news reached Captain Charles Roberts, commanding Fort St. Joseph's 45-man garrison from the 10th Royal Veteran Battalion, on 8 July.[24] In a series of dispatches from Brock and Prevost, Roberts received conflicting instructions, and was eventually told by Brock on 15 July to use his discretion.[25] With some 180 Nor'Westers and over 400 Indians from various tribes under Robert Dickson, Roberts knew that his blockhouse was far harder to defend than the American one and decided not to wait for them to attack him. On 16 July he got as many men as he could onto the North West Company schooner *Caledonia* and a few canoes, and they landed on Mackinac Island the following day. They set up a 6-pounder and summoned Lieutenant Porter Hanks, commanding the U.S. garrison, to surrender. Not wishing to risk the wrath of the Indians, Hanks agreed, and his men were paroled—the civilized practice that meant they would not be allowed to serve again until formally exchanged for British troops elsewhere—and a great quantity of stores was also secured.[26] In fact, possession of this small post would prove one of the most significant acts of the opening weeks of war, continually distracting American attention from the main theatre of operations around Lake Ontario.[27] But Roberts remained cautious; not only about his relations with the Indians, some of whom were distinctly unreliable, but also about his relations with his own men, who were, he wrote, "so debilitated and worn down by unconquerable drunkenness that neither fear of punishment, the love of fame or the honor of their country can animate them to extraordinary exertions."[28]

On 29 July the news reached Brock, who was struggling to persuade the Legislative Assembly of Upper Canada at York to adopt measures necessary to pursue the war, but whose members were more interested in a school bill.

> A full belief possesses them all that this province must inevitably succumb. This prepossession is fatal to every exertion. Legislators, magistrates, militia officers, all have imbibed the idea, and are so sluggish and indifferent to their respective offices . . . Most of the people have lost all confidence. I, however, speak loud and look big.[29]

In disgust he prorogued the assembly on 5 August and set off to take a relief force to Amherstburg from volunteer flank companies of the York militia.[30] Meanwhile, Hull learned of the loss of Mackinac, and, fearing that all the Indians of the north-west would now join the British unless he could restore American prestige by the quick capture of Fort Malden, he begged the governors of Ohio and Kentucky for reinforcements, having already warned Eustis that he might have to retreat. Portly, with a shock of white hair, long past the youthful vigour of his Revolutionary exploits, Hull was a mass of self-doubt and fears, especially of what the Indians might do; these were magnified after a second skirmish on the Aux Canards.[31] Then, on 2 and 3 August Tecumseh and about 100 British regulars and Canadian militia under Captain Adam Muir of the 41st Regiment crossed the Detroit River near the Indian villages of Maguaga, Blue Jacket's Town, and Brownstown, where 300 Wyandots and Shawnees were encamped, and persuaded them to defect to the British side, adding another 70 warriors to Tecumseh's band.[32] This move cut Hull's line of communications with Ohio, and the next day he wrote to Eustis about his fear of being surrounded by thousands of Indians.[33] Earlier the rations contractor, Augustus Porter, wrote that he could not deliver food by water because of British vessels, while land transport was hazardous because the woods were infested with Indians.[34] A hastily organized supply train under Captain Henry Brush with 300 cattle and 70 pack-horses laden with flour halted at the Raisin River, some 35 miles away, but on 5 August Tecumseh ambushed a force of 150 men under Major Thomas Van Horne sent to Brownstown to support Brush, killing and then scalping 17, and capturing the mail in the opposite direction.[35] Hull—now called the "Old Lady" by his officers—ordered the abandonment of the indefensible Fort Dearborn (site of present-day Chicago), and on 8 August, after learning that Brock was on his way to Amherstburg, he recrossed the Detroit River with most of his force.[36] He wanted to withdraw to re-form his severed supply line, but the Ohio colonels and their men fiercely opposed such a move. Instead, a 600-strong force under Miller, with a 6-pounder but only two days' rations, was sent to protect the Raisin convoy; "the best troops in the army," according to Hull. Miller urged them to "Remember Tippecanoe."[37]

At around 4 P.M. on 9 August near Maguaga, 14 miles south of Detroit, this force blundered into an ambush by 200 British and Canadians under Muir, who had marched rapidly up from Brownstown, and 200 Indians under Tecumseh. The Americans reacted fiercely and drove off the smaller British force on the right with a bayonet charge, but Van Horne on the left was engaged by Indians from within woods and called for assistance. The break enabled Muir to retire to another well-organized position having lost 6 dead, 21 wounded (including himself twice), and 2 men prisoners, and the Indians 11 dead, while the Americans lost 18 dead and 64 wounded.[38] But instead of continuing on to meet their supply train, the Americans halted without shelter and in pouring rain, to spend a hungry night before returning to Detroit the next morning, harassed all the way by gunfire from the *Queen Charlotte* and *General Hunter*.[39]

On 11 August Hull ordered the small detachment still at Sandwich to retire to Detroit while the Ohioans circulated petitions requesting his arrest or removal. Shortly before midnight on 13 August, Brock reached Amherstburg with 50 regulars of the 41st Regiment, 250 militia, and a 6-pounder, and met Tecumseh for the first time.[40] The meeting of these two imposing men produced mutual respect and admiration. Although Brock "found the judicious arrangement which had been adopted immediately upon the arrival of Colonel Henry Proctor, had compelled the enemy to retreat and take shelter under the guns of his Fort," Proctor had been acting too cautiously for the Indians' taste.[41] The arrival of the bold commander of all the Redcoats in Upper Canada made an immense impression on them. Built by the French in 1701, Detroit was home to around 700 people in 160 houses and surrounded by a palisade; but Fort Detroit was on high ground beyond the town, and its line of fire was thus impeded.[42] Brock knew from captured dispatches that Hull's position was precarious unless quickly reinforced, and he swiftly formed a plan to bluff Hull, using his fear of the Indians, and if that failed, to draw him out of Detroit for a fight in the open, a plan which he explained to his officers and the enthusiastic Indians, who prepared with a war dance.[43]

Hull was only too pleased to get rid of the scheming Cass and McArthur on 14 August in another move to secure his supply lines with some 400 men to meet Brush, but next morning a battery at Sandwich mounting an 18-pounder, two 12-pounders, and two 5.5-inch mortars manned by men belonging to the battery of Captain William Holcroft of the Royal Artillery (RA), commenced firing; the bombardment lasted seven hours.[44] Brock sent a note to Hull demanding surrender, adding that "you must be aware, that the numerous body of Indians who have attached themselves to my troops will be beyond all control the moment the contest commences."[45] Hull was naturally alarmed but refused, being more worried by the continued absence of the 400 Ohioans sent to meet the supply column at the Raisin River. McArthur and Cass, who had been among those plotting and demanding that Hull step down, made no hurry to return, and despite camping only 3 miles away failed to inform Hull of their whereabouts.[46] Hull deployed the remaining militia around the town as protection against night attack by the Indians and placed his regulars in the fort. But this step left nobody to cover the obvious crossing point at Spring Wells, 3 miles south of town.

During the night 600 Indians crossed under Matthew Elliott's direction, and early on a pleasant and sunny 16 August Brock formed his 300 regulars and 400 militia into three groups under regular officers; two each of 50 regulars and 200 militia, and one of 200 men of the 41st Regiment under Proctor with a small battery of three 6-pounders and two 3-pounder guns served by Holcroft's 30 gunners.[47] Brock crossed the river covered by the Sandwich battery, which recommenced firing at dawn, now worked by the Provincial Marine. Mrs. M. MacCarty, a young mother in Detroit, described the bombardment: "Hour after hour how I passed thus alone, listening to the booming cannon and the startling and shrieking as a ball whizzed by the house, sometimes feeling almost sure that it was a mark for the enemy and thinking perhaps the next shot should terminate my existence."[48] Brock soon learned from locals of the absence of the Ohioans and, abandoning his plan to fight in front of the town, immediately advanced in order to storm it. As many of the Canadian militia wore old redcoats from Fort Malden, and the sections moved with double the normal distance between them, they made an impressive sight, as Brock appreciated: "Your thought of clothing the militia in the 41st cast off clothing proved a most happy one," he later wrote to his aide, Major Thomas Evans of the 8th Regiment, "it having more than doubled our own regular force in the enemy's eye."[49] Hull soon began to doubt the chances of a successful defence, and as governor of Michigan Territory, the lives of the civilian population were his responsibility.[50]

The crisis was about to break, with Indians appearing nearby and the Michigan militia deserting their posts, when an 18-pounder shot fired from Sandwich hit the officers' mess, killing four including Lieutenant Porter Hanks.[51] "The British troops filed into a ravine," recounted Ensign James Cochran of the 41st Regiment, "about 700 yards from the fort, and made every disposition for an immediate assault, but at this moment a white flag displayed by the enemy arrested the advance, a capitulation was, after some discussion, agreed to by which the fort, town, were surrendered to the British arms."[52] At about 10 A.M. a British Union flag that had been carried around the body of a sailor was fluttering above Fort Detroit, prompting Captain Josiah Snelling of the 4th U.S. Infantry to despair of the utter incompetence surrounding Hull's command: "I affirm that at least six hours elapsed between the summons and delivering the answer and that the panic was spread among the citizens by him and the members of his family had completely paralyzed them."[53] The national colour of the 4th U.S. Infantry was surrendered to Lieutenant Richard Bullock of the 41st Regiment by Captain Cook, who said: "Sir, the fortune of war has placed these in your hands. They are yours." Bullock simply bowed and withdrew.[54] Neither Cass or McArthur made any attempt to contact Hull that morning and instead sent two men to reconnoitre who reported that Detroit had already fallen; they retreated a few miles, then allowed their men to kill and roast an ox. Brigadier-General James Taylor of the Kentucky militia later declared to Madison: "I think the whole course of proceedings the most weak, cowardly and imbecile that ever came to my notice."[55] Indeed, the episode at Detroit represents the only time a white flag was unfurled over an American city before a foreign foe, and although Hull later defended his decision by claiming he had only one day's supply of powder and a few days' provisions, this claim was denied by both his own officers and the British, who found 5,000 pounds of powder after capturing the fort.[56]

After the surrender Cass and McArthur sent an officer under a flag of truce to the fort as a British officer came the other way carrying Hull's orders for them to return. Seething with indignation at their interpretation of Hull's surrender and vowing revenge, they too laid down their arms. Some 1,606 Ohio militia were paroled to their homes and escorted beyond possible danger from the Indians. But Hull and the 582 regulars began the long ignominious journey to Quebec. Alec Gilpin concluded that Hull "surrendered for the sake of humanity, but lost his good name because of the Administration [which] required a scapegoat to bear its responsibility for the disastrous blow to American arms and pride."[57] But though he surrendered for humanitarian reasons, his failure was a colossal disaster for the United States: in one blow its strategic plans were shattered, and the whole middle western frontier was now open to Indian depredations far worse than might have occurred at Detroit, as several previously neutral tribes now took up the tomahawk. Cass and McArthur, ever the politicians, refused to bear any responsibility for their part in the disaster.[58] In another example of Ohio insubordination, Brush's 194 men absconded without surrendering their weapons, but their names were entered on the prisoners' roll, so they were forbidden to serve again until formally exchanged.[59]

Captain Charles Askin regarded the prisoners as "ill-dressed and few of them appeared healthy or well, indeed, they seemed to me to be the poorest looking set of men I have seen for a long time."[60] Both sides were reluctant to hold prisoners because of the cost involved, and would seek to parole or exchange them whenever possible. But those taken included twenty-three British-born and British Army deserters, who were to be sent for trial in Britain and thus faced death for treason, the start of a long and bitter wrangle.[61] Also captured were thirty-nine guns, including nine 24-pounders and four brass pieces—captured from Major-General John Burgoyne's army at the Battle of Bennington, Vermont, on 16 August 1777—2,500 muskets, and a considerable quantity of military stores; and the new brig *Adams,* renamed *Detroit* by the Provincial Marine.[62] Proctor was established as governor of Michigan, although he remained at Fort Malden, which was a better defensive position, while Brock hurried back to the Niagara front. Ironically, Brock's victory and his subsequent act of detaching Michigan Territory from the United States virtually guaranteed the war would continue; just as Britain was seeking a peaceful solution, Brock's success removed any chance of a diplomatic breakthrough.[63] On hearing the news as he was leaving Washington to escape the summer heat, Madison immediately returned and convened only the second full cabinet meeting of his presidency. Two important decisions were taken: the United States would set about gaining control of the lakes, and another army would be sent to recover Detroit.[64] But first came more immediate tragedy.

Acting on Hull's orders to evacuate Fort Dearborn on 14 August, 54 regulars, 12 militia, with 9 women and 18 children under Captain Nathan Heald, accompanied by 30 Miami warriors and Indian agent William Wells, were attacked by 500 local Potawatomi Indians under Blackbird, who had heard of the British success at Mackinac.[65] The Miamis quickly fled, and all the militia, 26 regulars, 2 women, and 12 children were killed in the ensuing massacre, which fur trader John Kinzie described as "one of the most shocking scenes of butchery perhaps ever witnessed . . . the tomahawk & knife performed their work without distinctions of age or condition."[66] Wells died dressed in full Indian regalia with his face painted black—a Miami custom signifying certain death—and the few survivors surrendered, Heald having been twice wounded and his wife seven times, and were later ransomed to the British.[67] Fortunately for American spirits, Captain Zachary Taylor led a stout defence of Fort Harrison in Indiana Territory against Indian attack on the night of 4–5 September. The Indians then resorted to trying to starve the defenders out, but a relief force arrived two days later and they gave up soon after.[68] Efforts to drive away settlers also failed; many left, but others retired to blockhouses, and only one devastating attack was recorded at Pigeon Roost, Indiana, where 24 people were killed, including 21 women and children.[69]

On 5 September Winnebagos and Sacs (or Sauks) attacked Fort Madison on the Mississippi (Iowa) and destroyed some property outside, but failed to set the post itself on fire. At Fort Wayne a similar story unfolded; a party of 150 men of the 41st Regiment plus an artillery detachment under Adam Muir set out towards it on 14 September, but following disagreements with the Indians Muir retired to the decrepit Fort Miami on the 30th.[70] In two attacks launched by the Indians only 4 Americans were killed, although no thanks to the fort's commander, Captain James Rhea, who was, according to Ensign Daniel Curtis, "as drunk as a fool all night and had not yet come to his perfect senses if he had any."[71] On 15 September in northern Ohio Indians attacked the Copus family, who were accompanied by 9 soldiers from Beam's Mill, killing James Copus and 6 of the soldiers, and wounding Copus' ten-year-old daughter in what became known as the Copus massacre.[72] Though brilliant guerrilla fighters, the Indians faced enormous military difficulties, being restricted by

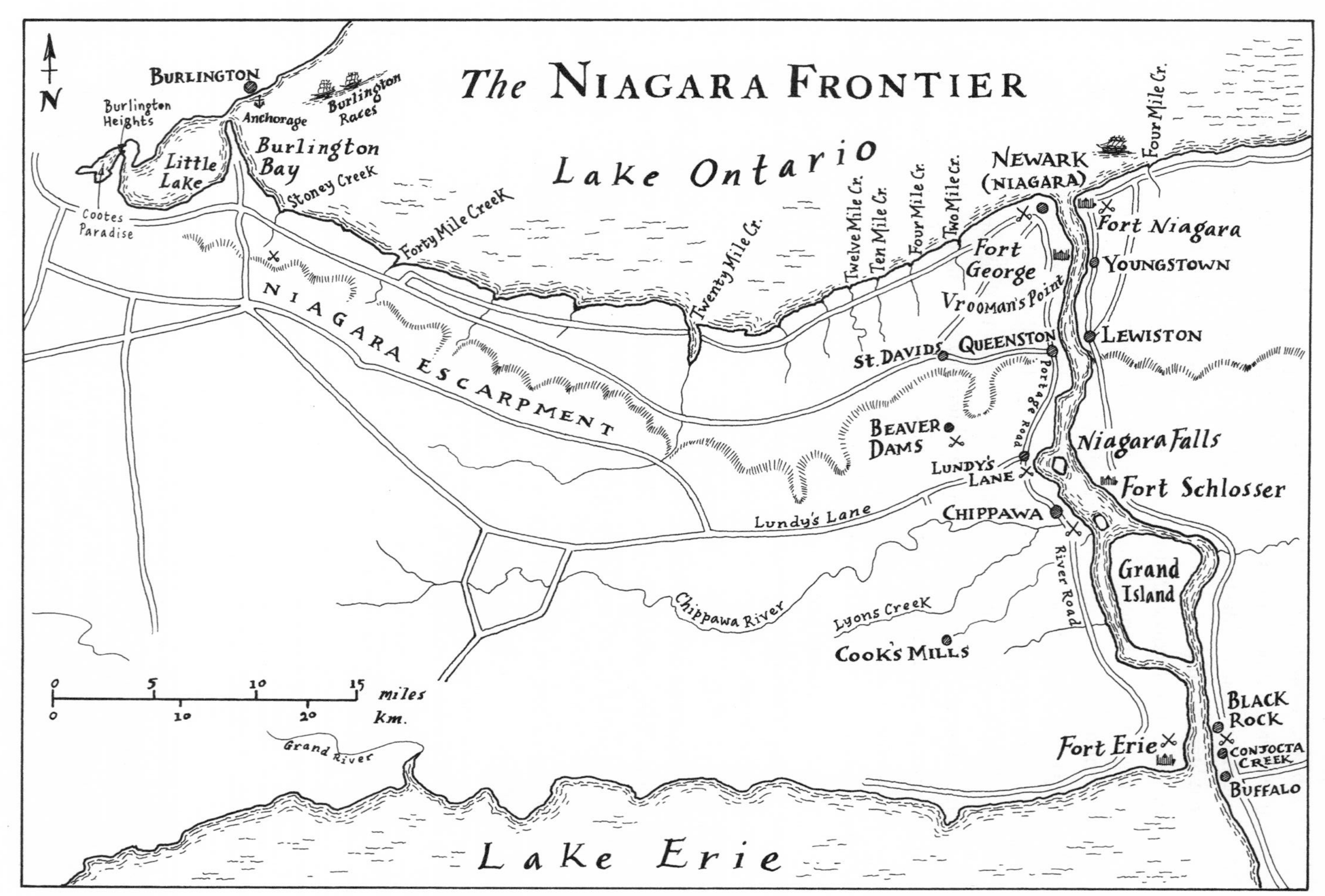
The Niagara Frontier
N
Burlington
Burlington Heights
Anchorage
Burlington Races
Little Lake
Burlington Bay
Cootes Paradise
Stoney Creek
Forty Mile Creek
Lake Ontario
Twenty Mile Cr.
Twelve Mile Cr.
Ten Mile Cr.
Four Mile Cr.
Two Mile Cr.
Newark (Niagara)
Four Mile Cr.
Fort Niagara
Fort George
Youngstown
Vrooman's Point
Niagara Escarpment
St. Davids
Queenston
Lewiston
Portage Road
Beaver Dams
Niagara Falls
Lundy's Lane
Fort Schlosser
Lundy's Lane
Chippawa
Grand Island
River Road
Chippawa River
Lyons Creek
Cook's Mills
0 5 10 15 miles
0 10 20 km.
Grand River
Fort Erie
Black Rock
Conjocta Creek
Buffalo
Lake Erie

a shortage of powder and faced with formidable American defences. With no artillery to breach posts physically, their own food supplies were too fragile to sustain sieges for any length of time, and unless they could take a careless or unwary post by surprise their attacks on forts usually failed.

Brock warned Prevost, and Prevost in turn warned the government in London of the need to support the Indians: the idea of an Indian "barrier state" was resurrected, but it would require maintaining their position, not an easy prospect.[73] In the vast expanses of the far west the war would be a spring-to-autumn phenomenon of dread and fear of British and Indian danger, but once it became clear to the settlers that they could expect no help from central government, they raised their own defences.[74] Meanwhile news of victory at Detroit lifted the pressure on the British government. "After the strong representations which I had received of the inadequacy of the force in those American settlements," wrote Bathurst to Wellington, "I know not how I should have withstood the attacks against me for having sent reinforcements to Spain instead of sending them to the defence of British possessions."[75]

WHEN DEARBORN eventually returned to Albany on 26 July, there were only 1,200 men there, unorganized, untrained, and without equipment. Despite being the architect of the invasion strategy and having received explicit instructions, "Granny," as he was known to his troops, inquired of Eustis two days later: "Who is to have command of the operations in Upper Canada; I take it for granted that my command does not extend to that distant quarter."[76] On 1 August news reached Quebec of the repeal of the Orders in Council and that the erstwhile British minister to Washington was trying to open negotiations with the American government from Halifax. Prevost immediately sent Colonel Baynes to Dearborn under a flag of truce to try to arrange an armistice. Dearborn felt sure that the United States would not wish to continue a pointless war, but he did not have the authority to agree to a proper armistice. He was, however, prepared to give orders confining his officers to defensive measures until he had word of his government's wishes, after which four days' notice would be given before hostilities were resumed.

This arrangement suited both Dearborn and Prevost: the former was unaware of events at Detroit, but there was little chance of early offensive operations on the Niagara front. Prevost's strategy was already entirely defensive, and while Brock chafed at the bit to take offensive action, Prevost repeatedly urged caution. Besides, he could spare Brock no reinforcements;

his aim was to reinforce south-west Upper Canada, and to do so required open waterways. Prevost has since been widely criticized, but the directives he received from Bathurst on 10 August were quite clear.[77] Bathurst concurred with Prevost's defensive strategy centred on Quebec and maintaining trade connections with New England, but, apart from two battalions en route to Montreal and Halifax with 15,000 stands of arms, the worldwide danger facing the British Empire meant that no reinforcements or specie would be forthcoming in the foreseeable future, and significantly he told Prevost to pay the "strictest and most unremitting attention to Economy."[78] Not that Prevost needed telling: to cover the chronic lack of specie to pay his military costs in mid-July he had resorted to government-backed paper army bills in Lower Canada, later extended to Upper Canada. Citizens were mistrustful of them and accepted them only on the recommendation of Bishop Plessis, justifying Prevost's cultivation of the Catholic Church.[79] Madison, however, unreservedly condemned Dearborn. One American grievance had been addressed, but, more importantly, Madison and his supporters would lose all face if they called off the war at this stage. Both he and Eustis doubted that Dearborn had the resources to implement the plan of attacking Montreal and Kingston and crossing the Niagara River simultaneously, so Dearborn was instructed to seize the latter two and at least make a feint against Montreal to concentrate Prevost's attention. But Dearborn's lassitude went beyond his instructions from Washington: he was at a loss over arrangements within New York State.

Fortunately Navy Secretary Hamilton understood the urgent need to contest control of Lakes Erie and Ontario, on which the Provincial Marine freely roamed. On 23 September he ordered Captain Isaac Chauncey USN to supersede Woolsey and create the necessary naval squadrons, "and to use every exertion to obtain control of them this fall."[80] Chauncey was widely considered the most efficient and versatile officer in the service and had experience in the undeclared war against France and against the Barbary pirates of Tripoli. He had commanded at the New York dockyard for the previous four years, essential experience for his task; but although 170 sailors, 140 ship's carpenters, and large quantities of guns and stores had gone before him, travel proved difficult, and he did not arrive at Sackets Harbor until 6 October.[81] In the meantime Stephen Van Rensselaer arrived at Ogdensburg on 16 July to find the town under apparent threat of attack: the *Duke of Gloucester* and *Earl of Moira* were anchored across the river, where militia were assembling. Solomon Van Rensselaer proposed an immediate cutting-out operation, only to find that all but 63 of the 400 militia assembled for the task refused when the appointed hour came. The general and his entourage stayed at Ogdensburg until 29 July before setting out for Niagara with a two-week ride ahead of them; a delay that exacerbated the problems of equipping and training the force he was to command.

On 17 August Brock set sail from Amherstburg but was delayed by contrary winds and did not reach Fort Erie until six days later, where he learned that Stephen Van Rensselaer had finally set up his headquarters at Lewiston, and that Major-General Roger Hale Sheaffe, commanding at Niagara, had made his own supplementary arrangement with Van Rensselaer.[82] This arrangement, which Sheaffe regarded himself as clever in making because he knew of Detroit but Van Rensselaer did not, involved an understanding that no men or stores were to be sent forward. But Solomon Van Rensselaer had outwitted Sheaffe in the negotiations on 20 August by ensuring that water transport was permitted, enabling the Americans to bring up heavy ordnance from Oswego and to allow their schooners, previously chased into Ogdensburg, to reach Sackets Harbor. The largest and best of these were purchased by the U.S. Navy for use as warships or as transports, a development which further threatened the security of the St. Lawrence water route along which *bateau* convoys vital to the support of Upper Canada were organized by the Corps of Canadian Voyageurs, formed from the North West Company.[83] In a demonstration of their vulnerability, one of these convoys was ambushed, albeit unsuccessfully, by American militia as it passed Toussaint Island on 16 September, and five days later Captain Forsyth made a successful raid on Gananoque, a staging post in the heart of the Thousand Islands.[84]

Prevost had at least received reinforcements: the 1st Royal Scots and the 103rd Regiment, about 1,100 and 750 strong respectively, although the former came from the disease-riddled West Indies and would need their health restored, and the 103rd were mostly very young men and boys. Now Colonel John Vincent at Kingston was able to send a steady stream of reinforcements westwards; six companies of the 49th Regiment, the flank companies of the Royal Newfoundland Fencibles, and 50 men of the 10th Royal Veterans, although Prevost blamed these unauthorized movements for exposing his position at Prescott to the predations of Forsyth's riflemen.[85] Brock was glad to find his old regiment at hand, for even if it had been in the country for ten years "drinking rum without bounds, it is still respectable, and apparently ardent for an opportunity to acquire distinction."[86] Brock sent the Newfoundlanders to Amherstburg and half the Veterans to Mackinac. Proctor sent a detachment to destroy American forts on the Maumee River while remaining at Detroit to protect American civilians from Tecumseh's vengeful warriors, as it would take almost two months to ship the captured stores and ordnance to Fort Erie. Eventually Dearborn informed Prevost that from 4 September the armistice was off, and that night Brock sailed from Kingston to take personal command of the Niagara front, whence Sheaffe's gloomy reports of an American build-up suggested an imminent attack. On arrival, however, Brock found American preparations almost entirely defensive. Indeed, the state of their troops made little else practical, and even prominent War Hawks knew that the demands of agriculture would also draw men away. Most of the militia on both sides remained destitute of the necessities of war, and were soon clamouring to return to their farms for the harvest. Pinckney had been authorized to reduce the numbers of militia on service in the Southern Department and to man garrisons with regulars, but this step prevented their transfer north as originally planned.[87]

The Niagara River is 35 miles long, carrying the waters of Lake Erie to Lake Ontario via the famous falls beyond which the river roars up a 7-mile gorge before forming a wide stream with many backflows and eddies between Queenston on the Canadian side and Lewiston on the New York side, where Van Rensselaer's force was concentrated. Queenston was deemed a good spot by the British Army to build a post in 1791, and a detachment of Queen's Rangers gave the village that grew up there its name. It was dominated by the adjoining Queenston Heights, where the British had emplaced an 18-pounder and a mortar in a redan (an earthwork with two faces forming a salient angle), and the river ran swiftly between high banks but was only 250 yards across. At the northern end of the river on the Canadian side the local capital, Newark (modern Niagara-on-the-Lake), with nearby Fort George, the main British headquarters, sat opposite the American post of Fort Niagara.[88] On arriving at Lewiston, Van Rensselaer found less than 1,000 men, many shoeless, all ill-equipped, and badly in arrears of pay. There was hardly any artillery, tents, camp equipment, or medicines, and, unsurprisingly, he thought the men insubordinate, unreliable, and undisciplined. He instituted a routine and training, but most of the men found camp life tedious and exhausting.[89] News of defeat at Detroit was a blow soon made manifest: the majority of the American force along the Niagara saw the prisoners—many destitute, without even jackets or shoes—marching along River Road from Fort Erie to Niagara town amid "insinuations that Gen. Van Rensselaer would do the like": allow his army to be *"Hulled."*[90]

At least reinforcements were finally being sent up from Greenbush, where Dearborn was showing some administrative energy at last, and the general gloom was raised when news arrived of the victory of USS *Constitution* over HMS *Guerrière,* achieved by Captain Isaac Hull USN, nephew of the disgraced general. At least the term "Hulled" could now be interpreted in both ways. But reports reached the British of high levels of sickness on the American side, and Brock interviewed two deserters who complained of "bad usage, bad and scanty food, and a total want of pay," who said their company numbers were already halved and half the rest were planning to desert.[91] As a hot and humid summer turned into a windy, rainy autumn, conditions deteriorated and the number of courts-martial for desertion, drunkenness, and indiscipline rose. Lack of supplies was blamed on Peter B. Porter and almost provoked a duel with Solomon Van Rensselaer.[92] But at least reinforcements were also arriving; elements of the 5th, 12th, 13th, and 14th U.S. Infantry and 2nd U.S. Artillery Regiments were followed at Buffalo by the arrival of Brigadier-General Alexander Smyth on 29 September, bringing the total in theatre to the 6,000 men that Major-Generals Dearborn and Van Rensselaer insisted were necessary for an advance into Upper Canada. Dearborn stressed to Stephen Van Rensselaer: "At all events, we must calculate on possessing Upper Canada before winter sets in."[93] But if Van Rensselaer hoped for support from Smyth at Buffalo, he was to be sadly disappointed.

The forty-seven-year-old Smyth was an arrogant man soon known to his men as "Van Bladder."[94] A former lawyer who had forsaken politics to take command of the rifle regiment added to the U.S. Army in 1808, he had no serious military experience; but he was not going to take orders from a New York militia general, and he refused to attend Van Rensselaer's regular councils of war. Consequently, Van Rensselaer went forward with his own scheme, since the forces available to him at Lewiston were greater than Brock's guarding the whole river line, though he acknowledged that his "best troops are raw; many of them dejected by the distress their families suffer by their absence, and many have not necessary clothing."[95] Brock was convinced that a major attack would soon occur, but his difficulty was not knowing precisely where a blow might fall. At least he was pleased to note that in two months he had not lost a single man on the Niagara from wound or disease, "certainly something singular."[96] His main deployments were at Fort Erie in the south and Chippawa in the centre above the Falls, where a crossing would be easiest. At Queenston there were only the flank companies of the 49th Regiment and an equal number of militia. Besides the redan on the Heights, a 12-pounder and an 18-pounder carronade were mounted at Vrooman's Point about a mile downriver, and a single 9-pounder in the village.

An abortive raid was made on Ogdensburg on Sunday, 4 October, in retaliation for American attacks on the St. Lawrence, when the boats carrying two companies of Glengarry Light Infantry Fencibles and 600 militia were driven off by American shore batteries.[97] On 8 October, however, Lieutenant Jesse D. Elliott USN proposed a daring raid on Fort Erie from Black Rock to cut out the Provincial Marine's *Caledonia* and the recently captured *Detroit,* since with these vessels, "added to those which I have purchased and am fitting out," he wrote, "I should be able to meet the remainder of the British force on the Upper Lakes."[98] This was a baptism of fire for Lieutenant-Colonel Winfield Scott and two companies of 2nd U.S. Artillery, who had arrived at Buffalo two days earlier. When he demanded volunteers from his 160 men to take four paces forward, none stood still. As Lieutenant Isaac Roach, who was to command 50 of them, walked along the line, "every face was pushed forward with 'can I go, Sir?' 'I'm a Philadelphia Boy'; 'don't forget McGee.' "[99] That night two boats carrying over 100 men slipped through the darkness and carried away the thinly manned prizes, although the *Detroit* ran aground and later had to be burned. Brock was deeply annoyed by the raid but most worried that the Americans now had four vessels fitting out for service on Lake Erie. "This event is particularly unfortunate," he said, "and may reduce us to incalculable distress."[100]

American forces at Lewiston had been reinforced to about 2,300 regulars and 4,000 militia, while in the British line were some 1,200 regulars, 800 militia, and 300 Grand River warriors.[101] This superiority, coupled with Elliott's success, added impetus to Van Rensselaer's plans at his daily councils of war. On 10 October Van Rensselaer instructed Smyth to strike camp immediately and march all his troops to join him at Lewiston, which Smyth proceeded to do; elsewhere similar instructions were being issued, and soldiers were marching towards the embarkation point where 13 *bateaux* had been assembled, 12 capable of carrying about 30 men each and one larger. But rainfall increasingly worsened the roads, and few troops reached the assembly area. After half a day and a night Smyth turned round in disgust to trudge back for another 10 or 12 hours through the sucking, ankle-deep mud. Later on the morning of 11 October he received a note from Van Rensselaer to say the operation had been postponed until Tuesday, 13 October. Smyth refused to take part before the 14th, saying his troops needed time to rest and clean up.[102]

On 12 October Brock sent Major Thomas Evans to deal with a drunken and mutinous incident amongst the 49th's Grenadier Company at Queenston and to treat with Van Rensselaer for the exchange of prisoners taken in Elliott's raid. But the apparent imminence of an American attack prevented him from dealing with the indiscipline immediately; he reported to Brock at Fort George that he kept being put off until "the day after tomorrow" and had heard that the American force had been swelled "by a horde of half-savage troops from Kentucky, Ohio and Tennessee."[103] Van Rensselaer was in a hurry: "On the morning of the 12th," he later wrote, "such was the pressure upon me from all quarters, that I became satisfied that my refusal to act might involve me in suspicion, and the service in disgrace."[104] But not only were the American troops who had struggled through the mud not given proper time to recover; he failed to coordinate his action with Chauncey on Lake Erie or Brigadier-General William Henry Harrison—appointed by Madison to replace Hull as commander in the north-west—and hastily pressed on.[105] Command throughout the American force was as muddy as the roads, through absenteeism, refusals, and arguments; and ammunition was in as short supply as order.

At 3 A.M. on 13 October 300 regulars climbed into 13 *bateaux* and set out to cross the river under the direct command of Solomon Van Rensselaer, covered by an artillery bombardment from two 18-pounders in Fort Grey on the heights above Lewiston and a mortar in the woods nearby. Each wave was supposed to be mixed regulars and militia, but staff work was woefully inadequate, and not only were the 13 *bateaux* available insufficient to mount an effective assault in one wave—another 39 were left lying idly at nearby Fort Schlosser—but confusion reigned at the embarkation point and the regulars simply clambered in first.[106] A weary Lieutenant George Ridout of the Canadian 3rd York Militia was on his fifth consecutive night of guard duty when he heard gunfire. "I went down to our battery from whence the view was truly tremendous, the darkness of the night, interrupted by the flash of the guns and small-arms."[107] Beneath him the first wave of American attackers was struggling with the current; 3 boats went too far downstream and eventually returned to the embarkation point, but the others landed above Queenston as planned, where they came under fire from the 49th's Grenadiers and the militia. After a sharp firefight some 160 men of the 13th U.S. Infantry—known as the "Snorters" because Colonel Robert Chrystie insisted that they all wear moustaches—led by Captain John E. Wool managed to drive the defenders off towards Queenston, although both Wool and Solomon Van Rensselaer were severely wounded. Wool stayed on his feet and asked Van Rensselaer

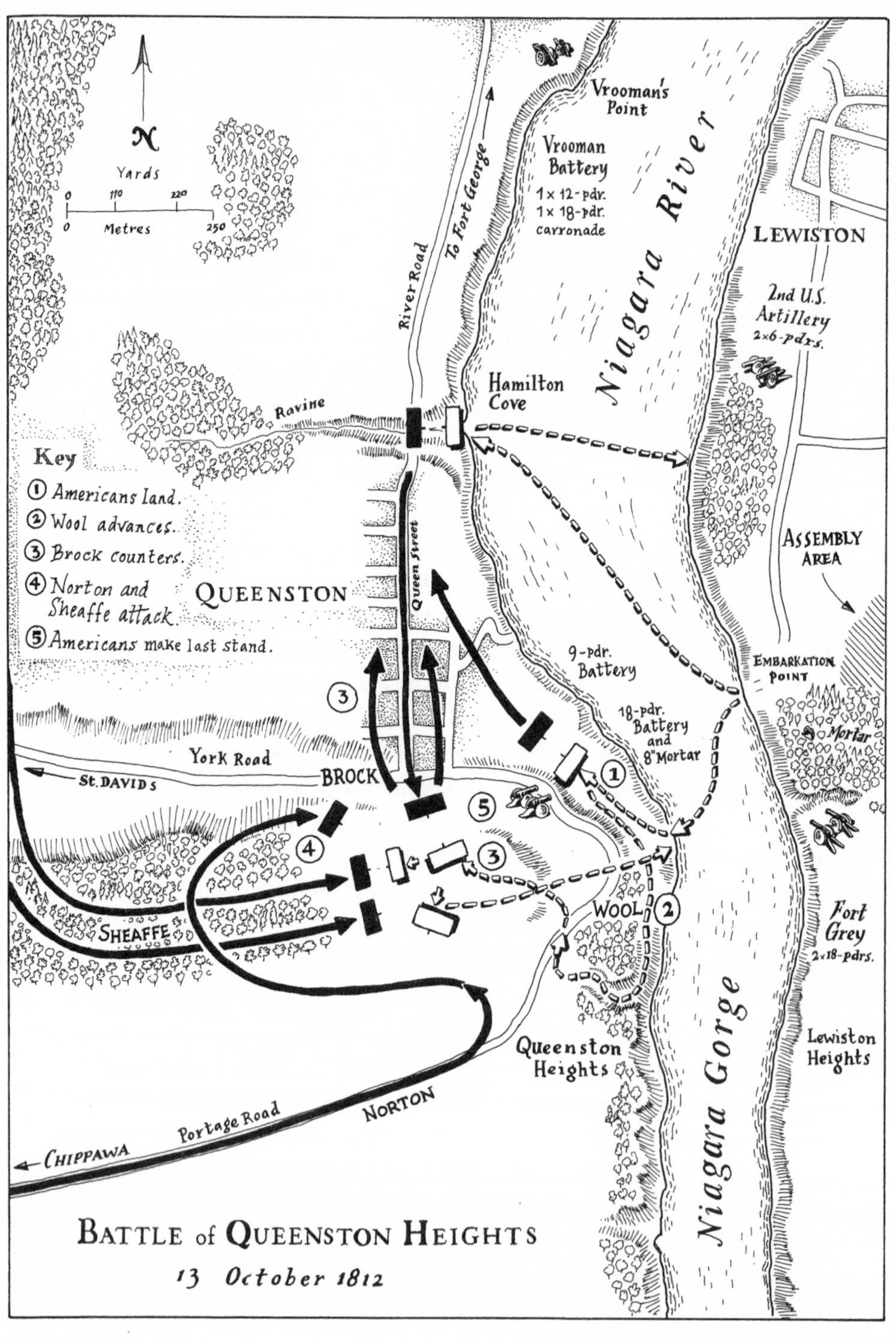

N
Yards
0
110
220
0
Metres
250
Vrooman's Point
Vrooman Battery
1 × 12-pdr.
1 × 18-pdr. carronade
Niagara River
LEWISTON
2nd U.S. Artillery
2×6-pdrs.
River Road
To Fort George
Hamilton Cove
Ravine
Key
1 Americans land.
2 Wool advances.
3 Brock counters.
4 Norton and Sheaffe attack.
5 Americans make last stand.
QUEENSTON
Queen Street
ASSEMBLY AREA
9-pdr. Battery
EMBARKATION POINT
18-pdr. Battery and 8" Mortar
Mortar
York Road
St. DAVIDS
BROCK
WOOL
SHEAFFE
Fort Grey
2×18-pdrs.
Queenston Heights
Lewiston Heights
Niagara Gorge
Portage Road
NORTON
CHIPPAWA
BATTLE of QUEENSTON HEIGHTS
13 October 1812

what could be done: Van Rensselaer said he knew of nothing unless they could take Queenston Heights.[108]

From Fort George, Brock rushed straight to the scene. Another wave of American attackers in four boats had been taken by the current downriver to Hamilton's Point just north of the village. They landed only to be met by a withering fire from the 49th's Light Company, which had been ordered down from the Heights to support the grenadiers in the village, nobody suspecting the enemy would find the steep path to the Heights in the half-light. The Americans were shot to pieces, and most of those not cut down surrendered, only one boat making good its escape. At Fort George, Ensign John Smith of the 41st Regiment saw some of the boats drift past "with six or 7 corpses in them who had been destroyed by the shot from our batteries."[109] Lieutenant John Beverley Robinson of the 3rd York Militia witnessed the dejected survivors marching under guard from Queenston: "The road was lined with miserable wretches suffering from wounds of all descriptions and crawling to our houses for protection and comfort."[110]

Meanwhile, leaving Van Rensselaer to be evacuated by returning boat, Wool found a winding pathway leading 350 feet up to the Heights just to the south of the redan. The 18-pounder and the mortar there had located the American embarkation point and were plastering it with shot and shrapnel, creating "a scene of confusion hardly to be described."[111] Wool and his men reached the summit covered by woods and quickly overran the redan as the gunners made off. Brock's aide-de-camp, Lieutenant-Colonel John Macdonell, launched an attack with two companies of militia and drove the Americans back.[112] But they received reinforcements from below and Macdonell was fatally wounded, and once more the Redcoats and militia retreated down the hill. Realizing his mistake in withdrawing the Light Company from the Heights, Brock immediately got all the men available in the village into line and advanced up the hill. It was now about 7 A.M., and there was no mistaking him in his red uniform with gold epaulettes and the decorative scarf given to him by Tecumseh after Detroit: he fell shot through the left breast, just three days after his appointment to Knight Commander of the Bath as reward for Detroit. Legend has the dying Brock urging the York Militia to "Push on, brave York Volunteers!"[113] But according to George Jarvis, a fifteen-year-old gentleman volunteer who was with the 49th's Light Company close by, "our gallant General fell on his left side, within a few feet of where I stood. Running up to him I enquired, 'Are you much hurt, Sir?' He placed his hand on his breast and made no reply and slowly sunk down."[114] Militia Private John

3.1. *Attack on Hamilton Cove, Queenston, 1812,* painting by Peter Rindlisbacher.

Birney also saw Brock fall, and "with the help of others he was laid on the grass and the surgeon called out, but he was past human aid and never moved or spoke."[115] With Brock's death and sustained fire from the Americans, the attack petered out at about 7:30 A.M.

Captain John Williams of the 49th's Light Company now tried to manoeuvre and attack from the west along the line of the Heights with about 80 men from the 41st and 49th Regiments and militia. By now the Americans had gathered some 400 men on the Heights, and although put under severe pressure by this move, so that somebody spiked the 18-pounder, they fought the British off, with Williams so severely wounded in the head that he appeared scalped. The Americans captured 21 of their attackers, including young Jarvis, who was unscathed, and the British withdrew to the north, abandoning the village at around 9 A.M. The river was now clear for crossing, and reinforcements arrived, including a 6-pounder, but shortage of *bateaux* slowed the Americans while other men sloped off to plunder the village or to return to the American bank, having seen enough of war. Equally, many among the militia were reluctant to cross, now remembering that they were liable only to serve in defence of their state; eventually some 700 did cross with 600 regulars by noon.[116]

By now the remainder of the British defences were also fully alert, and while Stephen Van Rensselaer at Lewiston was at a loss for what to do without Solomon's guidance, American command on the Heights was also in disarray, with militia and regular officers at odds. By contrast, Sheaffe had quickly taken control on the British side; he sent the 41st's Light Company under Captain William Derenzy, a composite artillery battery of two 6-pounders and a 5.5-inch howitzer under Holcroft, and about 160 of John Norton's Grand River warriors from Fort George towards Queenston. At about the same time the American guns at Fort Niagara and in the Salt Battery—built where earth had been heaped on hundreds of salt barrels—opened a furious bombardment on Fort George and Newark, which Van Rensselaer had ordered to start as soon as there was sufficient light. They were served by a shot oven to heat the rounds, and soon the court house, gaol, brewery, and several houses were alight, causing panic. But the British put all hands to work and controlled the fires, and replied effectively via the dozen heavy pieces at Fort George, which soon quietened though never entirely silenced the Americans. It was during this duel that news arrived from Queenston of Brock's death, and Sheaffe set out for the main battle, followed soon after by another 140 men of the 41st Regiment, with some additional militia including Captain Robert Runchey's "Company of Coloured Men," also known as The Corps of Artificers (Coloured Corps).[117]

At about 11 A.M. came the first sure signs of a British reaction, when the rifle company deployed as flank guard to the American line was attacked "by a party of Indian Devils"; these "savages, greedy for plunder and thirsting for blood," swiftly routed the riflemen. Lieutenant Jared Willson "thought hell had broken loose and let her dogs of war upon us . . . I expected every moment to be made a 'cold Yankee' as the soldiers say." He was deeply embittered by the militia's refusal to fight: "The Indian war whoop even echoed through their camp and still they could not be prevailed upon to mingle with their associates in arms to oppose the inhuman foe."[118] Norton's men worked their way to the south of the American position, where they proceeded to harass and attack the Americans as best they could, although they suffered in turn and many left the fight after they came too close to the American line, now commanded by Winfield Scott. When he ordered a charge, it was "executed with great bravery by our soldiers," and the Indians fled.[119] But the Americans were becoming tired, having had no food and with ammunition running low. Stephen Van Rensselaer briefly went to confer with his officers in Canada before returning to organize more reinforcements, but when he reached his boat many American soldiers suddenly appeared, jumped in, and shoved off, and ran away as soon as it landed on American soil—a process that was repeated throughout the afternoon.[120]

Sheaffe reached Vrooman's Point at about noon and established his headquarters nearby, where he gathered men together. Ahead of him Derenzy's 41st Light Company had flushed the looters out of the village and enabled Holcroft to set up his guns to engage the American embarkation point, where Holcroft noted enthusiastically "our spherical case was of great use."[121] At around 1 P.M. Sheaffe was satisfied that every available man was to hand, some 650 regulars and militia, and decided to attack the Americans from the south-west, necessitating a roundabout approach march much as Norton's warriors had made. But although he had a reputation as an overbearing perfectionist in matters of drill, he managed to get the column mixed up with itself so that it seemed to Scott that the British "approached with an awful tediousness," although he did not attempt to interfere with it while it was vulnerable, later claiming there were only 139 regulars and 250 militia remaining to defend the Heights.[122] Shortly after 3 P.M. the British advanced and a firefight developed; "the discharge of small-arms, the whizzing of the balls and yells that issued from all quarters exceed all description," noted George Ridout.[123] Some American officers were already counselling retreat, with Indians rushing about willing to finish off any unfortunates; some Americans jumped over the cliff, and others threw down their arms and ran for the landing. The British closed in, and after a final stand Jared Willson recalled "we were forced to lay down our arms."[124] Not that this was easy: it took three attempts with a flag of truce to gain the attention of someone in authority, and as desperate Americans tried to swim the river, British and Indians took pot-shots until around 4 P.M., when a single repeated bugle call ended the firing. The British had suffered 20 dead, 85 wounded, and 22 taken prisoner. Accurate numbers of American dead and wounded have never been recorded, although in a letter to Dearborn Stephen Van Rensselaer stated 60 were killed and 170 wounded. Once they had been rooted out of all the hiding holes they had found for themselves two days later, the total number of American prisoners came to 925 (436 regulars and 489 militia).[125] There was also a large booty, including a 6-pounder, muskets and ammunition, and a stand of New York militia colours, which were sent to Britain for display. Once more the militia were paroled while the regulars were sent to Quebec, a most unpleasant experience as Scott later recalled.[126]

The death of Brock soon gave rise to a personality cult in Upper Canada that eventually saw his name gracing streets, towns, and a university.[127] More immediately, Sheaffe assumed command and received a baronetcy as reward for his victory. He arranged an armistice with Van Rensselaer to deal with the prisoners and wounded, and when this expired it was extended, then extended again until 20 November, all of which gave him time to attend his civic duties in York and effect repairs and improvements in defences.[128] But this delay was unpopular among the militia, who were now keen to attack Fort Niagara, and it also displeased Prevost, who, despite his normal caution, later wrote that Sheaffe had "lost a glorious opportunity of crossing the Niagara River during the confusion and dismay which then prevailed, for the purpose of destroying Fort Niagara, by which the command of the Niagara River would have been secured to us during the war."[129] For the war was far from over, and the American army was in disarray all along the frontier. Men who had enlisted five months before had received no pay and "absolutely refused to march" until they did.[130]

4

Frigates and Privateers

A crash,—as when some swollen cloud
Cracks o'er the tangled trees!
With side to side, and spar to spar,
Whose smoking decks are these?
I know Saint George's blood-red cross.
Thou mistress of the Seas,—
But what is she whose streaming bars
Roll out before the breeze?
Ah, well her iron ribs are knit,
Whose thunders strive to quell
The bellowing throats, the blazing lips,
That pealed the Armada's knell!
The mist was cleared,—a wreath of stars
Rose o'er the crimsoned swell,
And, wavering from its haughty peak,
The cross of England fell!

—Oliver Wendell Holmes, "The Pilgrim's Vision"

AFTER twenty years of almost continuous victories the Royal Navy was prone to a superiority complex easily extended to a U.S. Navy that amounted to little more than a squadron of 20 ships—8 frigates and 12 sloops—only 17 of which were available for sea service.[1] The Royal Navy's 584 ships included 102 ships-of-the-line and 124 frigates: the force that had recently taken Java—4 ships-of-the-line and 14 frigates—was three times stronger than the entire U.S. Navy.[2] But the latter certainly comprised excellent human material: the north-eastern states in particular produced a race of hardy and skilful seamen, and it was almost unique in the world in that it did not require any form of conscription to man its ships in wartime, although this fact had less to do with patriotism than with good conditions. Men enlisted for two years with two to four months' advance wages at $8–10 per month for an ordinary seaman and $12 for an able seaman, rates that compared very favourably with pay in merchant ships. But although some British authorities suggested that the U.S. Navy relied on British deserters in its ranks, a realistic estimate puts British-born sailors at between 5 and 10 percent, although many American-born sailors had also served in the Royal Navy at some point.[3]

However, Theodore Roosevelt's claim that the average American sailor was superior to a British one is false.[4] It ignores the fact that the Royal Navy's power lay in her battle fleets and that the line-of-battle ships had first claim on men and equipment. Despite the current concentration on power projection, two decades of expansion had drained the pool so much that on a man-per-ton basis Royal Navy crews were the smallest among all the maritime powers. Thus in comparing American frigates and sloops to British ones, Roosevelt compares the best and second-best American units to the second- and third-best British ones; and hitherto peaceful American waters did not require deployment of the best of these.[5] Furthermore, the Royal Navy concentrated on squadron actions, demanding rapid changes of formation via signals from the flagship, at which it excelled; but this emphasis on coordinated action greatly reduced the significance of aimed gunnery in favour of rapid fire and coordination. During its early development the U.S. Navy, with no record to sustain it and aware of its numerical inferiority, learned to excel at sailing and gunnery—matters enhanced by its all-volunteer crews—which would improve their chances in single-ship actions.[6]

Far more significant was the superiority of American warships class for class. The warnings of Dr. James Gregory in 1808 that the Americans were "building long 46-gun frigates, which really carry 56 or 60 guns," were dismissed. Nobody believed an Edinburgh physician on naval matters. But his warning would return to haunt the naysayers: "when our 44s come to meet them," he warned, "you will hear something new of these days."[7] Indeed, American frigates were superior to any other frigates afloat. The United States possessed boundless forests of fine quality, so that only the very best wood was selected; no need to scrimp and save. And every American warship had an experienced captain on hand throughout construction, so that class-for-class they were guaranteed to be of the highest possible quality. Yet the Americans were not satisfied with a class-for-class advantage; they wanted something superior at every level, and were well served by their chief constructor, Joshua Humphreys.[8] In 1797 the *United States* and the *Constitution* were launched,

LOWER CANADA and the MARITIMES
0 50 100 150 200
Scale of Miles
N
LOWER CANADA
QUEBEC CITY
TROIS-RIVIÈRES
MONTREAL
CORNWALL
RIVIÈRE DU LOUP
OVERLAND ROUTE
St. Lawrence River
Anticosti Island
Gulf of St. Lawrence
NEWFOUNDLAND
St. John's
Cabot Strait
Prince Edward Island
Cape Breton Island
NEW BRUNSWICK
FREDERICTON
St. John River
SAINT JOHN
Bay of Fundy
NOVA SCOTIA
HALIFAX
Passamaquoddy Bay
EASTPORT
MACHIAS
CASTINE
BANGOR
HAMPDEN
BELFAST
Penobscot River
Kennebec River
MAINE
PORTLAND
PORTSMOUTH
NEW HAMPSHIRE
VERMONT
Connecticut River
Lake Champlain
PLATTSBURGH
BURLINGTON
Lake Ontario
NEW YORK
ALBANY
Hudson River
MASSACHUSETTS
WORCESTER
BOSTON
HARTFORD
CONNECTICUT
NEW LONDON
NEW YORK
Long Island Sound
Block Island
Shannon vs. Chesapeake
PROVINCETOWN
Cape Cod
MARTHA'S VINEYARD
NANTUCKET
Atlantic Ocean

both rated as 44s. In 1798 two more 44s were built—the *President* at New York and *Philadelphia* at that city, lighter and with better sailing ability, but still bigger and far more powerful than any other frigate in the world. These "44s" mounted a battery of 30 long 24-pounders and 18 42-pounder carronades on the quarter-deck, with six more carronades on the forecastle and two more long 24s, totaling 56 guns firing a broadside of 768 pounds.[9] By American standards they displaced 1,444 tons (1,533 by British measure), and with their great length and sail-power, carrying large crews of over 450 men to work sails and guns and provide boarding parties, they were the fastest warships in the world and by far the most powerful of their class.[10]

With slow communications making it difficult to inform ships at sea of a declaration of war, the side declaring it had a marked advantage. A strong American squadron set sail from New York on 21 June comprising *President* and *United States;* another frigate, *Congress* (38); and two brigs—*Hornet* (18) and *Argus* (16)—all under John Rodgers, now carrying the honourary rank of commodore. Rodgers was enacting his own plan, evolved with little help from the government, which remained divided over the best way to employ the U.S. Navy.[11] Without awaiting specific orders, Rodgers put to sea before orders arrived to divide his squadron in halves; one to operate off Chesapeake and one off New York. But the Royal Navy was, in any case, too busy with defensive measures to take offensive action at this point. Vice-Admiral Herbert Sawyer at Halifax, whose command stretched to Bermuda, had only 25 ships, including *Africa* (64), 8 frigates, and 7 sloops.[12] The French, Spanish, and Dutch islands of the West Indies having been occupied by the end of 1810, the fleet operating there—divided into two commands based on Jamaica and the Leeward Islands—had been reduced by 1812 to 27 vessels, including one ship-of-the-line, 5 frigates, and 13 sloops. And with Bonaparte rebuilding his fleet and the need to supply the army in Spain, the British were reluctant to divert shipping to American waters.[13]

When on 1 July the *Nova Scotia Royal Gazette* announced that "the madness which has for many years pervaded the European continent, has at length reached this Hemisphere," Sawyer was very glad to grant licences such as this one:

> Whereas Mr. Andrew Allen, his Majesty's consul at Boston, has recommended to me Mr. Robert Elwell, a merchant of that place and well inclined towards the British interest, who is desirous of sending provisions to Spain and Portugal, for the use of the allied armies in the Peninsula;

> and whereas I think it fit and necessary that encouragement and protection should be afforded him in so doing . . .[14]

Nothing was to be allowed to interfere with the grand objective of defeating Bonaparte, and certainly not war with America. By the third week in August 180 licences had been issued to American, Swedish, Portuguese, and Spanish vessels to carry American provisions to Wellington's army in Spain.[15] Congress had chosen not to end the vital trade on which not only Wellington's army but also American farmers relied, and Madison's attempts to restrict or limit it were thwarted.[16] Republicans generally wanted Bonaparte to succeed in Russia but not for Europe to succumb so completely that British armies then in the Peninsula might end up diverted to Canada. Such reflections enabled Secretary of State James Monroe to rationalize the continued American trade with the Peninsula despite French objections.[17] Similarly, the enemy trade act adopted shortly after the declaration of war should have ended trade with Canada and the West Indies, but there was no shortage of Americans more interested in earning good money supplying British forces; Federalist ports provided Halifax and the Royal Navy offshore with everything they needed through the licence system.[18] British licences were known, after the authorities granting them, as "Sidmouths" (one of the principal secretaries at the Board of Trade) or "Prince Regents." They were extremely valuable, regularly forged, and openly hawked around American cities for up to $5,000.[19]

Admiralty instructions were that the southern states that supported war were to feel its harsh effects while the north-eastern states should be encouraged to continue as before; the British government was also anxious not to ruin manufacturing exports to the United States worth £5 million annually.[20] But Sawyer operated at a distinct disadvantage at the start of the war: British licences prevented an effective blockade had he even possessed sufficient ships and men to mount one, but initially he was also forbidden by Admiralty orders to sail within 15 leagues (45 miles) of the coast or to board ships flying the American flag.[21] Thus the large frigates were able to leave New York at the commencement of war without interference, although the U.S. Navy would fail to engage British maritime commerce effectively, taking only fifty merchantmen in 1812. That task fell to what Republican John Binns called "our cheapest and best navy"—privateers.[22] George Little, who shipped on the privateer *George Washington,* noted the atmosphere in July in Baltimore, where he "found the most active preparations were in progress to prosecute the war. A number of privateers were fitting out and everywhere the American flag might be seen flying, denoting the places of rendezvous; in a word, the most intense excitement prevailed throughout the city."[23]

From the moment war seemed likely, American ship-owners turned their thoughts to privateering, and on 26 June Congress passed an "Act Concerning Letters of Marque [the certificate licensing a privateer], Prizes and Prize Goods."[24] Some owners were aware of the true weakness of the British position off the American coast and hurried to exploit it while it lasted, hastily arming ships to make an early profit; others took the longer view that a time would come when prizes were less forthcoming, and sought earnestly to equip ships for these eventualities.[25] Conferences were held to discuss the relative merits of long guns over carronades or fore-and-aft as opposed to square rigs. Speed and handiness were recognized as essential, both to take prizes and to avoid capture, and a fore-and-aft rig would certainly bear closer to the wind but was less effective running before it.[26] The Baltimore schooner was already famous, combining just the qualities of speed and handiness so useful to such endeavours. Ultimately schooners provided two-thirds of the vessels engaged in privateering if less than half the tonnage. Armament had to be sufficient only to outfight British merchantmen, but a numerous crew was also essential for boarding and providing the prize crews.[27] Beyond that hard fighting was not envisaged, although some owners were bold enough to consider taking on British sloops or Post Office packets—official vessels but not part of the Royal Navy establishment that carried mail and specie to British overseas possessions—and set to strengthening their sides and armament accordingly.[28]

Thus, as one part of American private enterprise was supplying British troops in the Peninsula with the food needed to fight the French, another strand was proving less helpful. Wellington wrote from Madrid as early as 13 August on hearing of the declaration of war that "the mouth of the Channel and the coasts of Portugal will swarm with privateers." He would later repeat his concerns on numerous occasions and was particularly exercised by "the capture and ransom of the *Canada,* horse transport, by an American privateer, with a detachment of the 18th Light Dragoons and other troops on board," and later by the prospect that "if they only take the ship with our shoes we must wait six weeks."[29] Among the most successful privateers were the *Saratoga* (18) from New York under Captain Charles Wooster and the *Rossie* (12) of Baltimore, commanded by Joshua Barney—a famous Revolutionary War privateersman—who took 18 British vessels valued at $1.5 million, including the packet *Princess Amelia* (14) after a hard fight—followed by the *Yankee* (10) from Bristol, Rhode Island, which took 8 vessels valued at

$300,000.[30] Privateers entering the Bay of Fundy, the Gulf of St. Lawrence, and the Grand Banks soon took 150 vessels in those areas, and a correspondent to the *Morning Chronicle* complained that "Jonathan's privateers" were operating with impunity.[31] They also did extensive damage to British trade in the West Indies, temporarily forcing insurance rates up as high as 30 percent, usually with a third or more rebate for convoy. But these were strictly local effects; British marine insurance rates between 1812 and 1814 were no higher than they had been in 1810 and 1811.[32]

However, as with any speculative venture, many people risked their money unwisely and lost it for good. Inadequate preparation was a recipe for disaster, and the Royal Navy was hardly an easy opponent. From the outset of war British captains were reporting captures: Lieutenant Robert Hockings RN (he would be referred to as "captain" insofar as he was senior officer on the vessel, but he was not "post captain"—that is, of the rank "captain" in the Navy List) of HM Schooner *Dominica* (14) had the pleasure of "the capture of the American schooner *Providence* [12], privateer of Providence"; Lieutenant Francis Erskine Loch RN, in acting command of HM Brig *Rover* (10), took "the American schooner, letter of marque, *Experiment*" (6); so the square rig had overtaken the fore-and-aft in two cases.[33] In the first three months the Halifax, Leeward Islands, and Jamaica Stations took 78 American privateers, and Newfoundland took 33 and recaptured two Britons by the end of September.[34] In fact, many merchant ships soon carried letters of marque, since they were easy to obtain, and if the ship were captured both she and her cargo would be forfeit in any case. Thus she might as well capture any unescorted British merchantmen she might encounter, and many British captures were primarily blockade runners and privateers only as a secondary consideration. There were large profits to be made in Nantes and Bordeaux, so the figure of 526 letters of marque issued during the war is misleading; only around half that number actually went to sea as privateers.[35] Equally, some naval historians have exaggerated their achievements, and others have minimized British efforts against them. Even in 1812 there were numerous French privateers operating; but if by that time Britain had very nearly driven them from the ocean and expelled them from home waters, it had taken nineteen years of war to do so, and in the case of American operations similar success was achieved in just three.[36]

The success or otherwise of the venture depended largely on the captains involved; some showed tremendous flair and natural aptitude for the task, but others lacked all natural ability. Flair was best supplemented with intimate knowledge of the trade routes and seasonal variations of commerce, and such experience led privateers to excel naval officers in captures. Good captains soon had reputations while poor ones ended in gaol, or dead. But it was extremely difficult business to make profitable, even if after 1813 privately armed vessels were the only successful American offensive weapon.[37]

ON LEAVING New York, Rodgers knew he had to defeat Sawyer's force piecemeal before it had a chance to concentrate; alternatively he could hope to catch a large convoy such as the Jamaica convoy—100 fully-laden merchantmen—escorted by as little as one frigate and one brig, blissfully unaware of hostilities and making leisurely course for Britain.[38] He was acting contrary to the opinion of other naval officers, who suggested a measure of dispersal, but these voices failed to recognize that privateers would snap up isolated merchantmen and, furthermore, that concentration of force increased the squadron's efficiency by greatly extending its field of vision. It also provided cover for American merchantmen now swarming homewards on the rumour of war.[39]

However, while still some hundreds of miles short of their target they encountered a solitary British frigate, HMS *Belvidera* (38), under Captain Richard Byron RN, and, led by *President,* the entire squadron altered course to intercept her. Alerted by this unnecessary and excessive interest, Byron stood away as close-hauled to the wind as he could get and heading away from the convoy. As the squadron gained on him he cleared for action, shifting two long 18-pounders to fire through the sternposts of his cabin and bringing two 32-pounder carronades to the stern of the quarter-deck; to avoid accidental discharge, the guns were loaded but not primed. The wind veered westerly and decreased, so that all the ships crept along in the heat until the wind freshened, enabling *President* to close by 4:20 P.M., when she opened fire with her bow guns, causing three hits and casualties. *Belvidera* was all set to return fire, when suddenly the second of *President*'s forward 24-pounders burst, killing or wounding sixteen men, including Rodgers, whose leg was broken, and *Belvidera* quickly added to his discomfort. Damage to decks and sides was severe, and with her chase-guns out of action *President* began yawing from side to side in order to bring her broadsides to bear. Since this manoeuvre would allow *Belvidera* to make good her escape, she aimed for the rigging, which was badly damaged. But having only the stern-chasers in action, *Belvidera*'s remaining crew set about hasty repairs, replacing and splicing the rigging

The WAR at SEA
U.S. Ships named first
LONDON
MILFORD HAVEN
Argus vs. Pelican 1813
Wasp vs. Reindeer 1814
Wasp vs. Avon 1814
HALIFAX
BOSTON
NEW YORK
Enterprise vs. Boxer 1813
Chesapeake vs. Shannon 1813
President vs. Endymion Pomone & Tenedos 1815
Nautilus captured by RN Squadron 1812
Prince-de-Neufchâtel vs. Endymion 1814
Constitution vs. Guerrière 1812
Hornet vs. Penguin 1815
Essex vs. Alert 1812
AZORES
General Armstrong vs. British Squadron 1814
Constitution vs. Cyane & Levant 1815
NORTH AMERICA
Vixen II captured by Belvidera 1813
Wasp vs. Frolic 1812
Wasp & Frolic captured by Poictiers 1812
Vixen captured by Southampton 1812
Frolic captured by Orpheus 1814
United States vs. Macedonian 1812
CUBA
AFRICA
Viper captured by Narcissus 1813
Peacock vs. Epervier 1814
Caribbean
CAPE VERDE Is.
Constitution captured Pictou 1814
Hornet vs. Peacock 1813
Atlantic
EQUATOR
Ocean
Constitution vs. Java 1812
SOUTH AMERICA
Pacific Ocean
Syren captured by Medway 1814
Essex vs. Phoebe & Cherub 1814
VALPARAISO

and "fishing" (repairing) damaged spars, tasks requiring great steadiness and discipline with heavy shot whistling all around. *Congress* took up the chase at about 6:30 P.M.; Byron threw overboard four boats and 14 tons of water, and by 8 P.M. was 2 miles clear of any pursuer. His crew was still trying to fish the damaged topmast, a difficult task with the spar in position and the ship under way. But the job was done, and by 11 P.M., with *Belvidera* 3 miles ahead, Byron altered course eastwards under studding sails, going ahead at such a rate that the Americans gave up the chase.[40]

This neat little engagement reflected very well on Byron and his crew, who reached Halifax three days later having taken some American prizes; an officer noting laconically that they had "tickled him [*President*] with four, and only four, stern chasers, which were well applied to his bows."[41] The action probably saved the convoy of which Rodgers had been informed only an hour or two before sighting the British frigate, but since *Belvidera* was running away she received no congratulatory acknowledgement from the Admiralty or the government. However, Sawyer released the prizes taken by *Belvidera* and sent a precious sloop under flag of truce for explanations from the Americans. The Americans had been perfectly entitled to engage as they had done, but in an age when chivalry was still taken seriously there was bitterness concerning the "treacherous" nature of the attack when a gentlemanly warning might have been given.[42]

Rodgers now continued on his way with the hope of intercepting the convoy, but he ran into thick weather off the Grand Banks that followed him all the way to within 150 miles of the Scillies, where he turned back on 13 July. Sawyer had planned to post single British cruisers in front of each American port, but though the West Indies convoy Rodgers sought had escaped, by creating a "fleet-in-being" he forced Sawyer to concentrate and operate away from the ports to which American merchant shipping was now flocking.[43] Had Rodgers remained in New York and obeyed the orders sent to him, he would likely have found himself bottled up by *Africa* and several frigates that appeared three weeks later, only to find Rodgers gone. His bold decision thus had a profound effect on the rest of the war. Most American merchantmen were able to get home, bringing a vital bounty of goods and experienced seamen to help man privateers. Indeed, Captain Philip Bowes Vere Broke RN of HMS *Shannon* (38) felt it necessary to make a 2,000-mile round trip taking six weeks to safeguard another West Indian convoy, a period during which American merchant ships entered home ports unmolested and even unobserved.[44] "We have been so completely occupied looking for Commodore Rodgers," noted another British officer, "that we have taken very few prizes."[45]

While Rodgers was leading his squadron out of New York, Captain Isaac Hull USN of USS *Constitution* was not even in a position to sail from Annapolis on Chesapeake Bay until three weeks after the declaration of war, being equally fearful of a blockade force penning him in.[46] But on 17 July, five days out from Chesapeake, he saw the sails of warships, four to landward and one out to sea, exactly what he would expect if it were Rodgers. But Hull was cautious, and at nightfall he beat to quarters and headed for the isolated ship. This was HMS *Guerrière* (38) under Captain James Dacres RN, rejoining his squadron after being separated off a hostile coast. But with an enemy squadron known to be at large, Dacres was as cautious as Hull. When the unknown ship made strange lantern signals his suspicions were confirmed; he kept his distance until dawn, then edged closer to what could only be an American frigate. He also sighted the British squadron under Broke's command to leeward, to which he identified himself but received no answer. It might be that the nearest ship, *Belvidera,* saw the signal and, assuming that *Shannon* had also done so, left it to her to reply. Dacres found himself between an American frigate and four unknown ships and, knowing that Rodgers had five ships under command, chose to retire; the chance to engage immediately and possibly capture *Constitution* slipped away. Hull, however, was in no doubt about the nationality of the squadron and turned away to try to escape.[47]

The wind was light and variable, and Hull mounted two 24-pounders through his cabin windows with another 24-pounder and an 18-pounder by cutting away part of the taffrail around the ship's stern. Then, with the breeze dying away completely, he set his boats to tow the ship as the British pursued in similar fashion. When a light breeze picked up at around 7 A.M., the boats were skillfully picked up while under way, whereas the pursuer could afford to leave a boat behind to be picked up by another friendly ship. But after half an hour the breeze died away again, and back out went the boats, pulling on the glassy sea in the July heat.[48] Hull's first lieutenant, Charles Morris, then made a suggestion. Soundings showed the water depth as only 25 fathoms—150 feet—so that the hands not manning oars could be put to kedging: the kedge anchor was taken out in the cutter with cables and ropes tied to make a single long cable, and when fully out the kedge was dropped to the bottom. The capstan bars were manned and the ship hauled up to the anchor while a second cable was prepared and a second kedge sent forward to repeat the action. The pursuers were prevented from following suit by the four long guns at *Constitution*'s stern, which could make matchwood of any cutter with the temerity to try. Had *Guerrière* remained within long gunshot of *Constitution* she might have prevented the American from launching her boats and enabled Broke's other ships to work up to her.[49]

At noon Hull pumped out 10 tons of fresh water and made another gain, soon lost when Broke signalled the other boats from the squadron to tow *Shannon* forward, a move that produced gloom on *Constitution.* Hull turned to Morris and said: "Let's lay a broadside on them, Mr. Morris, and fight the whole. If they sink us, at least we'll die like men."[50] But it was unnecessary; once more a light breeze sprang up, and Hull took in his boats on the run while the British had to abandon many as they jockeyed down the narrow corridors of wind, only for it to peter out once more. During the afternoon the wind held for four hours, and the sails were kept wet to catch the maximum air, just as labourious a task as kedging, to which the crew returned at nightfall when the breeze died away again. It returned around midnight, and *Belvidera* began to close a little, as did HMS *Aeolus* (38), which managed to get the weather quarter. Hull waited half an hour, then went about, all three barely making steerage way as slowly, painfully slowly, *Constitution* pulled ahead. The British had pounced and missed.[51] Next day, *Constitution* drew farther ahead when a squall came up in the evening from the east, reaching *Constitution* first, and by the time the British saw *Constitution* again she was 2 miles off with the wind blowing from *Constitution* to *Belvidera,* a barrier as impenetrable as it was invisible. The chase continued during the night as the wind slackened once more and the business of wetting the sails resumed, but by dawn *Constitution* was clear, now hull-down below the horizon, with the British squadron a straggling line and *Africa* far behind. The British conceded that her escape was "elegant."[52]

The knowledge that Rodgers was at sea with his squadron left Broke no choice but to remain concentrated: he would have liked to cover each of the principal ports along the eastern seaboard, knowing it was far easier to catch the privateers as they emerged from their home ports rather than try to hunt them down on the open seas. He also knew there was another West Indian convoy needing protection, its current escort consisting of a solitary frigate. He therefore made its safety his first priority, though this meant there was no British cruiser off Boston, thus allowing *Constitution* to gain sanctuary.[53] It also meant he would have to consider how best to refit and restock his ships: they could not stay at sea indefinitely, and three weeks later, when he left the West Indian convoy to return across the Atlantic, he detailed *Guerrière* to retire to Halifax to prepare for another prolonged period of sea service. This she did, making slow progress into head winds, while Broke continued towards New York with the remainder of the squadron.[54] Hull had awkward decisions to make as well. Being a New Englander and his ship being Boston's own, they were assured a warm welcome; but despite universal admiration for his brilliant feat of seamanship, the war remained far from popular in this Federalist stronghold. The navy agent did not even have the funds to provision and equip the frigate for another cruise; this fell to a private citizen, William Gray, who was read out of the Federalist party for making the loan. Hull knew it was important to get back out to sea before the inevitable British blockade, and he set out again at the earliest opportunity—2 August—despite the absence of orders, emerging unobserved.[55]

He took up position off Cape Race on the main transatlantic traffic lane, meeting up with a privateer on 18 August that reported a British frigate had recently chased her to the south—*Guerrière.* They met the following day, and when Dacres spotted *Constitution* he shortened sail to meet her. By now *Guerrière* was in a poor condition; although she had recently managed to take the privateer *Betsy,* she had been struck by lightning that had damaged her mainmast and bowsprit, and she was leaky.[56] But even had she been freshly refitted she was no match for the big American at 1,092 tons, carrying a much lighter broadside and undermanned, with 272 men—including 10 Americans, who were allowed to remain out of the fight—against 456.[57] Nevertheless, at 5 P.M. she opened fire, her shot falling short. Ten minutes later, Hull screamed: "Now, boys, pour it into them!" And he leapt into the air with such energy that he split his tight breeches from waist to knee. *Constitution* fired a broadside so effective that on *Guerrière,* a man below "heard a terrible crash, the *Guerrière* reeled and trembled as though she had received the shock of an earthquake. The next minute the cockpit was full of wounded."[58] *Guerrière* began dodging about in an effort to put the American gunners off their aim, but this ploy hindered the British far more. After half an hour of this, Hull decided to close for a decisive engagement.

At about 6 P.M. *Guerrière* had her mizzen-mast shot away, falling starboard aft and knocking a large hole in the ship's counter, in which some rigging stuck, acting as a sea anchor. *Constitution* now raked her from forward until the two ships fouled, with *Guerrière*'s bowsprit tangling in the starboard mizzen rigging of *Constitution.* Hull decided on boarding while Dacres went to the forecastle determined to repel the Americans; all the while the marines of both sides kept up a sharp and heavy fire. "Amidst the dying and the dead," recalled Chaplain Charles Denison on *Constitution,* "the crash of timbers, the flying of splinters, and falling of spars, the American heart poured out its pa-

4.1. *USS Constitution vs. HMS Guerrière*, painting by Anton Otto Fischer. U.S. Naval Historical Center. Courtesy of Miss Katrina S. Fischer.

triotism with loud cheers."[59] Officers of both sides were conspicuous targets, and the American first lieutenant and lieutenant of marines were hit—events which caused some delay in the boarding preparations—as were the sailing masters of both sides; Dacres himself was shot through the shoulder.

Before the boarding could take place, *Guerrière* managed to get free and across the stern of *Constitution,* where she fired a broadside at such short range that the burning wads from the guns set fire to Hull's cabin. But the foremast came down and took the mainmast with it so that she lay quite immobilized, while *Constitution* ranged ahead to make repairs to her rigging. Without her masts, *Guerrière* was rolling so badly that her main deck guns were being dipped in the sea, and Dacres set a division to secure them, another to clear the wreckage, and another to set a sail on the sprit-sail yard that warships carried but seldom used. However, it was almost immediately carried away, and when *Constitution* came up again she struck her colours from the stump of the mizzen. Casualties had been severe, with seventy-eight killed and wounded on *Guerrière* against fourteen on *Constitution;*[60] Seaman Henry Gilliam was horrified by the way "pieces of skull, brains, legs, arms & blood lay in every direction," and "the groans of the wounded were enough almost to make me curse the war."[61] Indeed, *Guerrière* was so shattered that the prize master announced she was sinking. All the prisoners and prize crew were taken aboard *Constitution,* and the hulk was set alight, blowing up shortly afterwards, presenting Surgeon Amos A. Evans with "a sight the most incomparably grand and magnificent I have ever experienced."[62]

Hull decided not to stay put; he had some 200 prisoners aboard as well as many wounded, and in twenty-five minutes of firing had consumed one-third of his ammunition, although his ship had not sustained serious damage. But he also wanted America to have news of this great victory, the most important single-ship engagement in her history to date; so he turned and battled unfavourable winds for ten days to reach Boston on 30 August.[63] The effect of the news was explosive, far more important than its physical basis: the Royal Navy humbled in bold and vigorous one-to-one combat, and a captain of the navy that Americans regarded as so arrogant brought in a humbled prisoner soon produced songs of joy.[64] When a seaman saw a shot bounce off *Constitution*'s sides, he cried: "Huzza, her sides are made of iron," and she was known thereafter as "Old Ironsides."[65] With the failure of Hull's uncle in Upper Canada, this was essential food to a people starved of good news. New York raised a subscription to buy swords for Hull and his officers, who also received $50,000 from Congress; Philadelphia sent them services of plate, and at Baltimore church bells were rung and guns fired all day long. More significantly, Congress, which at the war's start had voted barely $300,000 to repair naval vessels, rushed through a bill to construct four ships-of-the-line and six more frigates.[66]

Hull, meanwhile, having learned of the death of his brother, requested leave to arrange his brother's affairs. He was somewhat embarrassed by the attention and went to Washington to make a report before taking command of New York's harbour defences.[67] On the way he paused long enough at Philadelphia to call on Ann Hart, a celebrated beauty. She had visited *Constitution* eleven years previously when Hull was a lieutenant superintending repairs, and had expressed a desire for a piece of the curiously hard tarred rope from her cordage as a souvenir. After Ann left, Hull sent a piece made into a necklace, and now that he had returned a hero she wore it. They were married in February 1813, and Hull never held another fighting command.[68]

A week later more good news arrived from New York to bolster American spirits: the frigate USS *Essex* (32) under Captain David Porter USN had put to sea on 3 July, just as *Belvidera* reached Halifax but two days before Broke started from there with his squadron.[69] *Essex* thus got clear away and made for Bermuda, where she sighted a British convoy of seven troop-ships escorted only by the frigate HMS *Minerva* (32). During a confused night encounter, *Minerva* and most of the convoy made off largely unscathed, but Porter managed to capture the transport *Samuel and Sarah,* with 3 officers and 156 Royal Scots on board, whom he then released on parole.[70] Porter bore away and subsequently took a number of prizes, including HM Sloop *Alert* (20). He sent her to Halifax as a cartel (a vessel licensed to carry prisoners of war, civilians, or government officials to an enemy port) with some of his numerous prisoners aboard, and by the time he reached New York on 7 September had taken another nine prizes.[71] But Porter's involvement in the case of John Ervin (variously, Irvin, Irvine, and Irving), a British seaman who refused to swear allegiance to the United States and was consequently tarred and feathered, would make his name notorious in Britain.[72]

THE NEWS of the loss of the *Alert* was the first to reach Britain, and it occasioned a deep sense of shock among a nation used to unbroken success on the high seas: the first loss by the Royal Navy in a single-ship action since 1803. That the British underestimated the Americans is perhaps unsurprising, but it was also dangerous: to feel one will win is good for morale; to assume one *must* win and then to fail was profoundly disturbing.[73] On 12 August the *London Gazette* announced Vice-Admiral Sir John Borlase Warren's appointment as commander-in-chief on the Halifax and West Indies Stations to replace Sawyer. Sawyer might rightly have felt aggrieved, having deployed the force that made contact with *Constitution* before she had done anything, and having made a success of the licensing system; but this move was an important unification of command, acknowledging that considerable forces might eventually be required, since Warren was a very senior officer. But he was also past his prime, "a superannuated Admiral, whose services, such as they were, bore a very old date."[74] Warren's role would be to coordinate the considerable administrative details along the entire coast of America, but he was also empowered to make peace overtures to the U.S. government on the basis of the *status quo ante bellum.*[75] In Britain the American War was assumed to be a mistake that would be rectified once news of the repeal of the Orders in

Council was received in America. But when Jonathan Russell received a note in August that authorized him to offer peace if Britain renounced impressment, Castlereagh explained that no administration "could expect to remain in power" if it did so, and if America was so desirous of peace it should accept the revocation of the Orders in Council.[76]

Warren reached Halifax on 26 September bringing news of Wellington's success at Salamanca, and two days later every ship in port fired a twenty-one-gun salute in honour of this great victory.[77] But Warren found his command dispersed and disheartened, and with a chronic shortage of seamen he issued a proclamation summoning all British seamen in the United States to return to their true allegiance in return for pardon and the opportunity to resist "the Tyranny and Despotism of France."[78] On 30 September he sent a peace proposal to the Americans, but Madison rejected it: impressment would continue while war with France continued, as would the blockading of enemy ports to neutral shipping. At the same time, Tsar Alexander offered to mediate, although this proposal was somewhat embarrassing to Britain; given its naval strength, it was not prepared to accept third-party interference in a conflict over the question of maritime rights. Not wishing to offend a new ally now in the throes of war with Bonaparte, Castlereagh delayed making a formal reply; in the event this took until the following March to reach Washington.[79] However, Warren was empowered to negotiate with any portion of the United States prepared to make peace, and since the feverish trade with Quebec showed that New England merchants remained interested in profit, he prohibited offensives along the north-eastern seaboard.[80]

Wellington's Peninsula army continued to rely on American grain, and, given the complicated situation between the United States, Spain, and Portugal in relation to France, American merchants could still trade legally with the Peninsula. Their cargoes could be sold to either the Portuguese government or Portuguese merchants; but either would ease the burden on the British government, and if the flour found its way to British troops then so much the better. As early as September 1812 Wellington wrote: "I am very glad that Mr. Forster has given licenses to American ships to import corn to Lisbon," and he urged that Portuguese ships be similarly licensed to trade with American ports to reduce his reliance on American shipping and help reduce the temptation to American captains to try to run the continental blockade and trade with France once near the coast of Europe.[81] The effect of Warren's licences was to retain New England commercial goodwill, and American ships also carried American newspapers, a valuable source of information. But the cost was high: all such transactions had to be paid for in specie which the British government could ill afford. Consequently, while the troops fell up to six months in arrears of pay and Portuguese muleteers and middlemen into as much as a year, American merchants returned loaded with British gold and silver that would gorge New England's banks by the war's end and help pay for subsequent industrial development.[82] Furthermore, a circular of 9 November authorized governors in the West Indies to import essential commodities from New England, and as Sherbrooke continued to issue licences to New England merchants wanting to trade provisions for British manufactures, they were also authorized to issue letters of marque to shipowners interested in fitting out as privateers.[83]

When Warren arrived it seemed that American privateers were already ubiquitous; in the first four months of war they took 219 vessels carrying 574 guns and 3,108 men, mostly from the Bay of Fundy and off Newfoundland.[84] That month, Sir George Beckwith, governor of Barbados, complained that his area was "infested" with privateers, fully manned and with sailing qualities superior to those of British naval vessels.[85] He commanded 15,000 troops in eighteen stations scattered across the Caribbean, but the navy was unable to guarantee communications between them against fast American privateers, which could outsail British frigates, although the Admiralty strongly denied these charges.[86] Their privations began to affect trade in Britain, where the influential West Indian Merchants Association in Liverpool complained to the Admiralty about a lack of protection in January 1813, and it was little wonder that Warren hurriedly requested reinforcements of both ships and men.[87] Their lordships of the Admiralty pointed out that his force was twenty times that of the U.S. Navy and had apparently achieved nothing while other commanders-in-chief were complaining about American intruders disturbing their convoys and supplies.[88] "It is of the highest importance to the *character* and interests of the country," he was curtly informed.

> Their Lordships have therefore thought themselves justified at this moment in withdrawing from other important services, for the purpose of placing under your command a force with which you cannot fail to bring the naval war to a termination, either by the capture of the American national vessels, or by strictly blockading them in their own waters.[89]

And in November the Admiralty significantly increased his responsibilities by directing him to supply escorts for merchant convoys and to establish a blockade on the Chesapeake and Delaware Bays, adding six weeks later that it intended to build up his squadron to thirty frigates and fifty sloops-of-war, but that it expected a return for this investment against the tiny U.S. Navy.[90]

Warren's difficulties were exacerbated by the size of his command, covering Newfoundland, Halifax, Bermuda, the Leeward Islands, and Jamaica Stations. Bermuda's dockyard possessed only 70 artificers and labourers (compared to over 4,000 at Portsmouth), and to be effective his shore bases required constant replenishment to feed his ships, a circumstance which put further strain upon the latter: convoys had to ply regularly from Britain to Halifax and Jamaica, most gathering and dividing at Bermuda, from which place reports took an average of six weeks to reach the Admiralty; return dispatches took up to ten weeks to reach Warren, with bad weather adding another three or four weeks to the gap.[91] Not that the U.S. Navy had things completely its own way: the U.S. Brig *Nautilus* (14) under Lieutenant William M. Crane USN sailed into British hands off New York, and HMS *Barbadoes* (32) captured the revenue schooner *James Madison* near Savannah, while the U.S. Brig *Viper* (12) fell victim to HMS *Narcissus* (32) after seven weeks without taking anything herself.[92] Two weeks earlier her sister ship, *Vixen* (14), was captured by HMS *Southampton* (32) under Captain Sir James Lucas Yeo RN after five unproductive weeks in West Indian waters.[93] From this otherwise totally insignificant encounter arose, however, a series of events that would profoundly affect the war. Yeo took his prize to Jamaica via the Crooked Island Passage, where a strong current sent both aground on a long-uncharted reef. Both ships sank soon afterwards, but Yeo was exonerated by the subsequent court-martial in February 1813.[94]

Certainly the news of these minor successes did nothing to mitigate the sense of horror felt throughout Britain once news of the loss of *Guerrière,* "one of our stoutest frigates," reached London.[95] It caused as much consternation as it had joy in America; the news soured that of Salamanca, the burning of Moscow, and Brock's triumph at Detroit. This was the Royal Navy, after all. Although *The Examiner* expressed the hope that the twin blows of Detroit in America and the *Guerrière* in Britain "will rather show both parties the folly of injuring one another to no purpose," most of the press was dismayed and even condemnatory in tone; at least professional opinion supported Dacres for not prolonging an obviously hopeless cause with unnecessary bloodshed.[96] *The Times,* however, noted that "the loss of the *Guerrière* spread a degree of gloom throughout the town, which it was painful to observe," and it provided little comfort that *Constitution* was of "very superior force."[97] Dacres pointed out to Broke, following his parole, that it was not superior American gunnery that led to his defeat but the early loss of the mizzen, and Broke informed his wife that Dacres was "wishing only another frigate to go to *take his revenge.* The citizens of America (Boston) were very kind and polite to him and his officers. The American officers too rude a lot of animals for gentlemen to associate with."[98]

Writing in November 1812 following the receipt of Dacres' report, but before the arrival of other news, an anonymous correspondent in the *Naval Chronicle* urged caution. He alluded to suggestions that *Guerrière* had been unlucky and hoped British frigates would be successful in future. But, he continued, "it will be no bloodless conquest, for the Americans have manifestly great advantages, and are manned with *able* seamen." He noted that Warren had not strength enough both to watch American warships and to provide convoy escorts, and proposed swamping the American menace with heavy reinforcements of ships-of-the-line. Clearly, the U.S. Navy was not to be trifled with. But his was a lone voice: the editorial comment in the same paper expressed the hopeful opinion that a British 38 was a match for "a 44-gun ship of any nation."[99] But not only had the U.S. Navy punctured British pride; it was not finished yet.

Master Commandant Jacob Jones of the U.S. Brig *Wasp* (18) was no youngster at age forty-five, but his career was undistinguished until he sailed out of Delaware Bay after an unprofitable cruise from New York in the exultation following the news of *Guerrière.*[100] Three days out, a gale inflicted some damage and left the sea running high, but before he could repair his jib-boom he sighted a convoy at midnight which dawn on 18 October revealed as merchantmen; lying between *Wasp* and the convoy was the latter's escort, HM Brig *Frolic* (18) under Captain Thomas Whinyates RN. Both sides shortened sail for action as they closed on a tossing sea. *Wasp* was a fine vessel, if difficult to handle, while *Frolic* was a typical British gun-brig; one of scores built at yards whose resources were strained to the limit, from a design compromising seaworthiness and fighting ability with long endurance, that rolled terribly and were overcrowded but had to be employed. The fight involved no manoeuvring, as both vessels were armed with carronades and closed the range to use them. Accurate fire was extremely difficult, but the Briton, firing on the up-roll, sent her shot high while the American, firing on the down-roll, struck lower and, with the advantage of the weather gauge, was not facing the incoming sea.[101] Within fifteen minutes *Wasp* was badly cut up aloft, but her stronger scantlings gave some protection to her hull; *Frolic,* however, was badly battered all round, with heavy losses. They came close alongside, rolling so that the gun muzzles were sometimes submerged, and spray added to the confusion of the smoke. As *Frolic*'s bowsprit came across *Wasp*'s deck she got the full force of a broadside, and American boarders swept onto her deck to find the badly wounded Whinyates barely supporting himself. British losses were seventeen killed and twenty-three wounded; *Wasp* lost five dead and five wounded.[102]

Whinyates attributed defeat to the loss of his main yard during the previous night's gale, but the Royal Navy had fought French ships under greater handicaps and won. Jones put a prize crew aboard, but the sight of HMS *Poictiers* (74) en route from Halifax to Bermuda soon ended his triumph, despite a daring but unsuccessful plot by his crew to take the British ship.[103] In any case, following a prisoner exchange Jones was back in New York within a month, where he was entertained and rewarded with a gold medal on the basis of his initial success, and his crew with $35,000.[104] But the loss of *Frolic* excited far less passion in the British press than another, far more significant action that occurred almost concurrently. On 12 October the *United States* under Captain Stephen Decatur was cruising south of the Azores hoping to intercept convoys from India. *United States* was the slowest of the big 44s and known as "Old Waggoner" as a result, but she was seaworthy and provided a steady gun platform. At dawn she observed a sail on a parallel track which proved to be HMS *Macedonian,* a fine new frigate rated 38 but carrying 49 guns under Captain John Surman Carden RN, though he called it "the worst Man'd Ship in the British Navy," with 262 men and the unusually high number of 35 boys.[105] It was certainly not a happy ship, probably as a result of the first lieutenant John Hope's cat-happy love of smartness over efficiency, which the Royal Navy's invincibility at this stage sometimes engendered.[106] Carden believed he had spotted *Essex,* whose carronades would not provide long-range firepower, and *Macedonian* immediately boomed out studding sails and bore away in pursuit. Perhaps deceived by the vast spread of sail, Decatur at first took her for a 74 and wore away also, but as *Macedonian* closed and her single deck of guns became visible, *United States* put about and hoisted her colours together with the commodore's pendant that marked her as a 44 (though she carried 56) manned by 478 well-trained men. *Macedonian* was not put off; she had been abroad for some time and had no knowledge of the fate of *Guerrière,* remaining convinced that a British 38 could take any frigate afloat.

Carden chose to retain the weather gauge and hauled close to the wind. The ships passed in opposite directions, and *United States* fired a broadside although the range was too great. Carden put about, and at about 9:20 A.M. the battle began, taking the mizzen topmast off *Macedonian* and giving *United States* the advantage in sailing, continuing with *Macedonian* on her quarter at fairly long range, where her 24-pounders had the advantage over *Macedonian*'s 18s. The carronades on *Macedonian*'s foredeck were soon dismounted and the bulwark shattered before Decatur closed for the decisive action, described by British seaman Samuel Leech:

> Two of the boys stationed on the quarter-deck were killed. They were both Portuguese. A man, who saw one of them killed, afterwards told me his powder caught fire and burnt the flesh almost off his face. In this pitiable situation, the agonized boy lifted up both hands, as if imploring a relief, when a passing shot cut him instantly in two. I was an eye-witness to a sight equally revolting. A man named Aldrich had one of his hands cut off by a shot, and almost at the same moment he received another shot, which tore open his bowels in a terrible manner. As he fell, two or three men caught him in their arms, and, as he could not live, threw him overboard.[107]

Although the men "fought like tigers," by 11 A.M. *Macedonian* was a wreck, with the mizzen-mast, main, and fore-tops gone; but she set the only remaining sail on the foremast to try to make enough way to board *United States,* when "at the moment our object was to be accomplished," recalled Carden, "the fore sheet was shot away. The ship came too against the helm, our object was thus frustrated & as no other effect could be made my ship lay an unmanageable log on the ocean."[108] When *United States* now passed the bows of *Macedonian* without firing a shot, the crew of the latter began cheering their surprise deliverance; but *United States* had only stood off to refill her cartridges, which had been used up in the seventy broadsides she had fired. When she was ready and came astern the stricken British vessel at noon, the colours came down.[109]

"On taking possession," recalled American seaman Elijah Shaw, "the enemy was found fearfully cut to pieces, having received no less than a hundred round shot in his Hull alone."[110] Decatur greeted Carden heartily, the two men having met before the war at Norfolk, Virginia, and quipped about the relative merits of their ships and fighting methods. The American refused to accept the Briton's sword, "a man who has so bravely defended his ship. But I will receive your hand." Carden was utterly despondent, believing himself wholly undone, "the first British naval officer that has struck his flag to an American. What will they do to me?" Decatur tried to console him with the news of *Guerrière,* and remarked to one of his lieutenants that half the pleasure of victory was spoiled by his opponent's unhappiness.[111] Once more British casualties were much heavier than the Americans': 104 killed and wounded against 14. And *United States* was also little damaged, but the two ships had to lie together for a fortnight before *Macedonian* was fit to sail, and it was 4 December before they sighted Long Island. *Macedonian* was then purchased into the U.S. Navy, earning the victorious crew $200,000 of prize money.[112]

"The Public will learn," lamented *The Times,* "with sentiments which we shall not presume to anticipate, that a third British frigate has struck her flag to an American . . . three frigates! Anyone who predicted such a result of an American war this time last year would have been treated as a madman or a traitor."[113] Essays in *The Times* and *Naval Chronicle* pondered whether the Americans possessed a secret way of managing their guns or of making improved powder and shot, or whether the super-frigates were really ships-of-the-line in disguise.[114] Only later in the war would *The Times* pontificate on why the Americans had done so well, noting "the superior strength of his vessels, their picked crews, their practiced and murderous mode of firing, and the almost uniform advantage they possess in sailing."[115] The blow to naval prestige inflamed the debate as to whether the Royal Navy was being ruined by aristocrats, brutal discipline, slack discipline, or the wrong sort of discipline, and each party rushed to apportion blame according to its prejudices.[116] The Admiralty had to issue secret orders that British frigates were not to risk engaging the big American frigates in single-ship actions but to keep them under observation until a ship-of-the-line could be summoned.[117] The Admiralty also issued an implicitly critical circular to captains reminding them of the importance of gunnery drill, although one aspect it did not address was gunnery tactics, rather than drill. The rational tactic for a weaker ship facing one of the super-frigates would be to fire at the masts and rigging and escape. But this sort of long-range gunnery was not in the British tradition, and the Ordnance Board had recently ceased issuing dismantling shot, which the U.S. Navy used to excellent effect.[118]

Historians have tended to adopt one or two monocausal explanations for American victories, but the disparity of force between 18-pounder and 24-pounder frigates is sufficient explanation. A warship is a very complex system, and the failure of one component can lead to the failure of all. Yet contemporaries, and to a surprising degree historians, tended to interpret these actions in national and moral terms, not technical ones, giving them far greater significance than they can reasonably bear. And in strictly military terms these actions were of very limited significance: for Madison the conquest of Canada remained the only strategic policy option.[119]

5

Winter on the Lakes

Hail to the Chief, the pure son of the Ocean,
Who raises his flag on Ontario's wave;
Long may Canadians behold with emotion,
The Hero who's destined their Country to save.
Let not a laurel fade,
Gracious Heav'n lend him aid,
Every device of the foe to withstand;
Waft him to Victory
Let the full Chorus be
"Yeo" the preserver the stay of our Lands.

—Anon., *Kingston Gazette,* 1 October 1814

For Roger Hale Sheaffe victory presented the opportunity to deal with the problem of American-born residents in Upper Canada who refused to swear allegiance to the Crown and claimed exemption from militia service. On 9 November he issued a proclamation that by 1 January 1813, "every citizen of the United States" who did not report to one of the examination boards being convened at Niagara, York, and Kingston "should be considered an alien enemy and become liable to be treated as a prisoner of war or a spy as circumstances dictate."[1] Those who satisfied the boards were given passports to cross into the United States, but Sheaffe provoked disquiet in various circles, both military and civilian, and he never inspired the levels of confidence among either group that Brock had enjoyed.[2] Furthermore, over the winter he suffered from serious illness which, his aide noted, left "an irresistible melancholy on his mind, which is very distressing. I have reason for knowing that his expectations from below are by no means flattering."[3]

In America Stephen Van Rensselaer handed over command to Alexander Smyth on 16 October. The latter quickly reorganized the army on the Niagara amid plans to achieve what Van Rensselaer had failed to do: "pass into Canada and secure winter quarters."[4] Like Hull he began by issuing bombastic proclamations: "Where I command, the vanquished and the peaceful man, the child, the maid, and the matron shall be secure from wrong. If we conquer, we will 'conquer but to save.' "[5] In the same tract he managed to insult his predecessors and alarm his superiors. Madison himself took a rather dim view of it, and William Eustis asked if he had Henry Dearborn's agreement to his declared aim to "plant the American standard in Canada."[6] Military defeat nearly proved politically disastrous for Madison; he faced a strong bid in the presidential election campaign during October and November from De Witt Clinton, who offered a tempting alternative backed by Federalists and a Republican faction.[7] Although Madison won by 128 electoral college votes to 89, it was the closest election since 1800, and only Pennsylvania and Vermont of the nine states north of Maryland and Kentucky voted for him, a regional division not repeated until 1860.[8]

However, on Lake Ontario Isaac Chauncey was about to seize the initiative and change the situation dramatically, while Lieutenant Thomas Macdonough USN took command on Lake Champlain on 8 October.[9] On assuming his new command Chauncey immediately saw to the manufacture of guns, carriages, and ammunition at forced rates; he created a courier system linking New York with Sackets Harbor which could complete the round trip in six days, and dispatched 140 shipwrights and 700 seamen and marines from New York.[10] Besides the *Oneida* and various schooners already under conversion, Chauncey purchased four schooners at Oswego, including the *Scourge* and a former British trader, *Lord Nelson,* taken on 5 June 1812 on suspicion of smuggling, and strengthened their hulls and armed them with one or two long 32-pounders, which had an effective range of 3,000 yards.[11] But his tactics would be dictated by the carronades on *Oneida,* which were accurate to only around 500 yards. Otherwise they offered considerable advantages, as they gave far greater firepower but took up less space and weighed less than the long 12-pounders they replaced. They were also never known to burst even when double-shotted and required detachments of only four to seven men rather than the six to fourteen men necessary for long guns of various sizes. The Provincial Marine was aware of these factors as well, and *Royal George*—laid down in 1809 in response to the threat posed by *Oneida* but not finally commissioned until 1811—was armed with twenty 32-pounder carronades while

Earl of Moira carried ten 18-pounder carronades and four long 6-pounders. After his purchases Chauncey had ten vessels carrying 63 guns against six British vessels expected to carry 106 guns, but he was undaunted.[12]

In late October Sir George Prevost sent the first of numerous warnings to London about American naval preparations, along with requests for experienced naval personnel, especially officers, and he ordered the construction of new vessels at Kingston, York, and Amherstburg.[13] Early in November Chauncey had his first encounter with the Provincial Marine in which the latter displayed a singular lack of aggression or efficiency: despite outnumbering *Oneida,* three vessels—*Royal George* and the schooners *Prince Regent* and *Duke of Gloucester* on watch outside Sackets Harbor—allowed her to sneak back into port without challenge. On 8 November Chauncey sailed with his full squadron, including the schooners *Hamilton, Governor Tompkins, Conquest, Growler, Julia,* and *Pert,* to search for the British. The following morning they spotted *Royal George* making for Kingston and gave chase in a light wind into the Bay of Quinte, where they lost contact at nightfall. The Americans continued next morning past the village of Amherstview, where the schooner *Two Brothers* was destroyed, before sighting *Royal George* once more and proceeding to chase her into Kingston harbour, where Chauncey was forced to break off by the shore batteries after losing two dead and eight wounded to one Briton killed.[14] The balance of power had tilted suddenly: *Earl of Moira* managed to get into Kingston a few days later, but the Americans blockaded the harbour for the rest of the season, while *Prince Regent* and *Duke of Gloucester* were forced to winter at York; and soon Chauncey had additional converted schooners and a powerful new corvette—built in just forty-five days—to add to his squadron. The *Madison* was one-third larger than the ocean-going sloops-of-war *Wasp* and *Hornet* and carried twenty-four 32-pounder carronades.[15]

The officers of the Provincial Marine appeared "to be destitute of all energy and spirit, and are sunk into contempt in the eyes of all who know them," reported acting Deputy Quartermaster-General Captain Andrew Gray to Prevost; "I do not Conceive there is one Man of this Division *Fit* to Command a Ship of War."[16] "The want of seamen is so great," reported Prevost to Bathurst in turn, "that the *Royal George* has only 17 men on board who are capable of doing their Duty, and the *Moira* only 10 able seamen." He urged that the Royal Navy take over the Provincial Marine, in which he was supported by Warren, who also advocated shipbuilding on the lakes and active operations against the southern United States, including the capture of New

5.1. Sackets Harbor. *Sacketts Harbour on Lake Ontario,* engraving by Baily after Juvenal, from the *Naval Chronicle* (London), 1818, U.S. Naval Historical Center.

Orleans to isolate the belligerent states of Ohio, Kentucky, and Tennessee.[17] In due course Bathurst accepted Prevost's suggestion, although no command appointment was made initially. James Richardson, who sailed as second lieutenant on *Earl of Moira,* defended the Provincial Marine's efforts, pointing out that the squadron kept open the essential communications between the Centre and Right Divisions of the army, and it is true this was an important task. But it had wasted the availability of superior firepower to seize decisive control of the lake, and the navy would pay the penalty of this failure during the following two years.[18]

Soon after Chauncey's exploit on Lake Ontario, Dearborn's long-awaited invasion of Lower Canada began. Here the key defensive line lay between La Prairie on the St. Lawrence to Chambly on the Richelieu River, and de Rottenburg—whose "fair, beautiful, lively, discreet, witty, affable" young wife, thirty years his junior, was the talk of his officers—had used the summer to construct a strong fortified defensive position at Isle-aux-Noix effectively commanding the river, before which a force of 150 Indians was deployed as a screen.[19] De Rottenburg commanded some 2,500 regulars and 3,000 militia, and when the weather deteriorated in October he moved them into winter quarters, but still within easy reach of the defence line south of Montreal.[20] Dearborn's men were ill equipped and unprepared, lacking tents and blankets and forced to sleep in the wet and the mud. As they advanced to Champlain village, the Canadian militia flocked to arms and the British deployed. Dearborn sent 3,000 regulars across the frontier on 20 November, but the 3,000 Vermont and New York militia flatly refused to accompany them: the regulars fell into confusion in the dark, fired at each other, and retired; an army surgeon noted that they were now seized with dysentery, fevers, pleurisy, pneumonia, and other sickness "which made the very woods ring with coughing and groaning."[21] After three days Dearborn retired into winter quarters at Plattsburgh, and the invasion was over, a failure described by Charles J. Ingersoll as a "miscarriage, without even [the] heroism of disaster."[22] The British retaliated on 23 November with a raid on the American fort at French Mills, capturing forty-four men, four boats, and fifty-seven stands of arms.[23]

On 21 November there was an artillery duel between the forts across the Niagara, ordered by Sheaffe as a diversion when he thought the Americans were planning something farther upstream.[24] Dearborn having insisted that Smyth attack with a force of at least 3,000 men, Smyth was not ready to mount his first attempt to conquer Canada until a week later. On 28 November he launched simultaneous attacks with 130 men of the 15th U.S. Infantry and 70 sailors on Fort Erie at the southern end of the river—defended by 50 British regulars with two light guns—and Chippawa, where Lieutenant-Colonel Charles Boerstler led 200 men of the 14th U.S. Infantry. The latter force failed to destroy a bridge over Frenchman's Creek, and as Smyth tried to embark his main force the advance parties were driven off by British counter-attacks under Lieutenant-Colonel Cecil Bisshopp of the 49th Regiment, though at the high cost of 21 dead, 43 wounded, and 35 missing.[25] But this stiff resistance persuaded Smyth to cancel the operation, leaving the main force standing bewildered in the cold and rain. In fact, Smyth never admitted that he could not assemble the 3,000 men required; for example, only 413 of the 1,500 men of the Pennsylvania brigade were prepared to cross into Canada.[26] A repeat attempt two days later was also cancelled, after which the campaign dissolved in shambles. Winfield Scott wrote that Smyth, "though well read, brave and honorable . . . showed no talent for command, and made himself ridiculous on the Niagara front."[27] Smyth sought leave, which was granted, and he, like the cousins Van Rensselaer, never saw active service again.

In the West, success at Detroit had raised with the government in London the prospect of establishing an Indian state in the Old Northwest, and Bathurst was keen to sustain the cause and the alliance.[28] But Colonel Henry Proctor did not have to wait long for the next American thrust. Tecumseh's people were heavily outnumbered—they faced not only locally raised militia but also six mounted volunteer ranger companies—and Tecumseh fell ill and remained so throughout the autumn. At the same time, Kentucky—a state forged by Indian warfare—was raising large forces of regulars and militia under Brigadier-General James Winchester and volunteers under Major-General Samuel Hopkins.[29] William Henry Harrison had set aside the governorship of Indiana to accept a commission as a major-general of Kentucky militia, though not a resident of the state, and Eustis had also mailed him a regular commission as brigadier-general on 12 August. On 17 September Eustis appointed him to command a new North Western Army, following a subtle and gentlemanly rivalry with Winchester, a man who, despite a reputation as an Indian fighter, was held in considerable contempt by the men he commanded.[30]

Although American counter-attacks against the Indians were largely ineffective, usually destroying already abandoned villages, in October Governor Ninian Edwards of Kentucky and Colonel William Russell broke up a hostile concentration at Lake Peoria, and in December 50 men, women, and children were killed or captured at the Mississinewa River in an expedition under Colonel John B. Campbell.[31] Comprising a regiment of Kentucky dragoons and a squadron of 2nd U.S. Light Dragoons, a company of 19th U.S. Infantry, the Pittsburgh Blues, and Alexander's Pennsylvania Riflemen, the expedition set out on the 14th and marched hard for 80 miles in three days and a night, then launched the attack without pausing. Campbell ordered all the Indian cattle shot, burned three villages, then returned to the first one to camp. But that night the Americans were counter-attacked by Miamis and suffered 10 killed and 48 wounded, with a further 303 casualties badly frost-bitten as they retreated through the snow.[32] The main effect of these attacks was to force the Indians to seek British supplies, thus reinforcing their alliance, and the year ended with no American soldiers on Canadian soil apart from the prisoners languishing in Quebec, while the British Union flag fluttered over Fort Mackinac and Detroit. America's war had begun inauspiciously, but winter could bring only a temporary respite to Canada's defenders.

IN AMERICA in early December there was speculation that "the French emperor may be dictating peace in Moscow."[33] On the 5th the Baltimore *Weekly Register* boldly declared: "Peace before this time has been dictated by Bonaparte."[34] In fact, Bonaparte was already in retreat and that same day abandoned the Grand Armée on the banks of the Beresina to hurry back to Paris. The disastrous result of Bonaparte's Russian campaign was a godsend for the British, a bitter blow to the Americans, and equally unforeseen by either. But the British had been weakened in Canada, not least by the loss of the energetic and charismatic Brock, and the U.S. government remained determined to seize the country. In January 1813 Matthew Clay, a veteran representative from Virginia, made the clearest statement of reasons when he told Congress:

> We have the Canadas as much under our command as she [Britain] has the ocean; and the way to conquer her on the ocean is to drive her from the land . . . I would take the whole continent from them, and ask them no favors. Her fleets cannot then rendezvous at Halifax as now, and having no place of resort in the North, cannot infest our coast as they lately have done . . . if we get the continent, she must allow us the freedom of the sea.[35]

The Americans were also likely to be better prepared. Stephen Van Rensselaer's defeat was born of factors beyond his control, but the myopia and lethargy of Dearborn had surely earned that individual his dismissal. Yet Dearborn lingered in command as visible proof that the administration was slow to learn the harsh lessons of war. At least Madison accepted Eustis' resignation on 3 December, replaced by John Armstrong on 5 February.[36] Armstrong was now fifty-four years old and at the outbreak of war had used his connections to obtain a regular commission as brigadier-general in charge of New York's harbour defences. Despite holding the post for only six months he thereafter expected to be addressed as "general" and rather fancied himself as a strategist, having penned a pamphlet titled *Hints to Young Generals from an Old Soldier,* although this amounted to little more than four days' worth of cribbing from the work of the Swiss theorist Antoine-Henri Jomini.[37] Armstrong's appointment would bring political advantages in New York State, which faced a crucial gubernatorial election in April 1813; but there was something about his character that always created distrust in those associated with him, as his narrow eighteen-to-fifteen Senate confirmation vote demonstrated. Less contentious was the replacement of the drunkard Paul Hamilton as secretary of the Navy after his resignation on 29 December. William Jones, an experienced fifty-two-year-old ship-owner from Philadelphia, took over, and emphasized that "the success of the ensuing campaign will depend absolutely upon our superiority on all the lakes & every effort & every resource must be directed to that object."[38]

Control of the lakes, and of Lake Ontario in particular, was the key to the control and defence of Upper Canada. As Assistant Surgeon William "Tiger" Dunlop noted, the St. Lawrence was the key to the lake:

> Every kind of Military and Naval Stores, every bolt of canvas, every rope yarn, as well as the heavier articles of guns, shot, cables, anchors, and all the numerous etceteras for furnishing a large squadron, arming forts, supplying arms to the militia and the line had to be brought from Montreal to Kingston . . . exposed to the shot of the Enemy.

He estimated that four field guns and a corps of riflemen along the American shore of the river could have cut communications with Upper Canada. "If they had done so with any spirit," he concluded, "we must have abandoned Upper Canada . . . and leaving it to its fate, confined ourselves to such parts of the Lower Province as came within range of our own empire, the sea."[39] But political difficulties in New England, combined with lack of strategic vision in Washington, ensured that the Americans would keep hacking at Canada's branches, rather than launching a concentrated assault on her trunk.

Armstrong faced three serious problems: a wholly inadequate logistical apparatus, a chronic shortage of trained regular troops, and a near catastrophic shortage of funds. By February barely one-third of the regular army establishment was under arms.[40] But more than anything else the U.S. Army needed well-trained and experienced commanders, particularly to control the militia; something the British government understood very well, as Bathurst pointed out to Prevost. In comparing forces, they could not ignore "the vast superiority which the general composition & discipline of the British Army supported as it is by the good disposition of all classes of the inhabitants must give to any Military operation against an American Force acting beyond their frontiers."[41] Gallatin recommended reducing expenditure on western operations, and Armstrong was happy to agree; he had no confidence in Harrison and wanted to concentrate on the east. Nevertheless, Harrison spent the autumn and winter building a large army that soaked up federal funds at an alarming rate, but as the local economy boomed it kept the war popular there.[42] On 19 December *The Supporter* of Ohio reported the "March of the Four-Footed Troops" as 4,648 pigs headed from Chillicothe to the North Western Army.[43] Harrison had, with his chief engineer, Captain Eleazer D. Wood, selected a point on the east of Maumee River at the foot of the rapids for a forward fortified post, which was named Fort Meigs after Governor Return Johnathan Meigs of Ohio.[44] During February Wood divided the work so as to create a constructive competition among the units, noting: "In the use of axe, Mattock and spade, consists the chief military knowledge of our army."[45] Although it was the finest natural position for a fort along the Maumee and recognized as a key to all subsequent operations in the north-west, a Virginia militiaman engaged in its construction noted: "It will never answer to invade a country with militia; some will not cross the line—others will not submit to any kind of subordination and, in fact, would rather be at home than courting fame on the embattled field."[46]

As Harrison's three columns struggled to get into position at Fort Wayne, Winchester's vanguard had serious difficulties getting supplies, particularly across the "Black Swamp" region. Caravans often made no more than 5 miles a day as horses and waggons floundered in the mud, leaving no choice but to sit and wait, a situation guaranteed to bring out the worst in the men, especially those from Ohio, who had not been paid in three months and were chronically short of clothes, food, and medicine, the last exacerbated by the inexperience of officers and men in the matters of camp hygiene.[47] Camps soon stank, and serious illness—pneumonia, measles, typhus, intermittent fever, and dysentery—took an increasing toll as the men lived on stringy beef and hickory roots.[48] Harrison wanted to sweep the area of Indians and retake Detroit, but, remembering that Wayne's legion had nearly starved in the same region in the 1790s, he insisted that one million rations be within reach of his columns before he began towards Canada. However, the contractors fouled things up: one who stood to make $100,000 from army contracts would rather see the men starve, said Harrison, than give up $5 of profit. Eventually he failed to lay down the necessary provisions, and Harrison resorted to Augustus Porter, the man who had supplied Hull's army.

In mid-October Harrison bought 100 ox-drawn waggons, since oxen could forage in the woods where horses could not; but ox-drivers were scarce and expensive.[49] Besides, it was impossible to move a waggon through the November mud, and pack-horses, already in short supply, were rendered useless by hunger and the wet weather. What few supplies did get through were frequently spoiled, including two-thirds of those deposited at Fort Meigs. Flour was reputedly bought at $100 a barrel, but pack-horses could carry only half a barrel and in turn required others carrying forage for that animal and themselves. A pack-horse could carry 3 bushels 60 miles but would consume one-ninth of the load in the process, a circumstance which, at $1 per bushel, made the whole arrangement extremely expensive. Few horses survived more than one trip, and of 4,000 scarcely 800 remained by spring. In early December an attempt was made to bring up 200 barrels of flour by boat, but ice prevented its arrival.[50] Thus Winchester led his men on the march on 29 December. Elias Darnell, who participated, recalled it as

> one of the most serious marches ever performed by the Americans. Destitute, in a measure of clothes, shoes and provisions, the most essential articles . . . and more particularly in this cold climate. Three sleds are prepared for each company, each to be pulled by a packhorse which has been without food for two weeks, except brush.[51]

The plan was to concentrate Harrison's scattered forces at Maumee Rapids (near modern Toledo, Ohio). Winchester built Fort Winchester in the ruins of the old French Fort Defiance but could proceed no farther without supplies as his men sat hungrily shivering in summer clothing. Another volunteer, Private Nathan Newsom, thought the army an "object of charity"; far from constituting an imposing force poised for invasion, nearly half the men were sick and the other half "almost naked . . . it is ardently wished by every naked man in camp that something would arrive where with he might cover his nakedness, keep his body warm and his feet dry so that he would be able to do his duty as a soldier."[52] Not until December did they receive any clothing, and this was not army issue but blankets, knitted socks, and hunting shirts forwarded by the women of Kentucky.

"Tecumseh, I fear," reported Proctor on 13 January, "has scarcely recovered his health" to lead his warriors when five days later, without waiting for Harrison, Winchester led 900 regulars and militia to attack Frenchtown (near modern Monroe, Michigan), held as a British outpost on the west side of the now frozen Detroit River, 26 miles from Detroit.[53] The Americans, led by Lieutenant-Colonel William Lewis, quickly drove off the few militia under Major Ebenezer Reynolds and the allied Indians defending it, losing 14 killed and 53 wounded in the process—a very rare example of Canadian militia fighting without regular support—and settled down without taking defensive precautions. Winchester camped some way off from his disaffected men, little expecting the British to react.[54] But on 18 January the garrison officers were in Mrs. Draper's Tavern in Amherstburg, where a military ball was being held in celebration of Queen Charlotte's birthday, when, recalled a participant, in walked Colonel Thomas Bligh St. George dressed for the field.

> "My boys," said he, in a loud voice, "you must prepare to dance to a different tune; the enemy is upon us, and we are going to surprise them. We shall take the route about four in the morning, so get ready at once."
>
> Of course there was some confusion and surprise, but I believe the fellows liked the fighting as much as the dancing. The ball broke up at once, and every man was at his appointed post at the proper time.[55]

The British force marched for two days, halting to make camp on 21 January about 5 miles from the Americans. In command the fifty-year-old Proctor lacked the dash and fire of Isaac Brock. The Anglo-Irishman was a steady and professional career soldier, but had little battlefield experience and lacked obvious leadership skills or the ability to promote teamwork. He was not on good terms with the Indian Department, regarding it as incompetent; he found the militia unreliable and regarded the civilian authorities in Detroit as treasonable.[56] But neither was he helped by his superiors, Sheaffe and Prevost, who were more concerned with matters farther east. He was starved of resources, especially manpower, and appealed in vain for another regiment to help garrison the frontier and stiffen Indian resolve. Prevost regarded the Indians and not regular troops as the guardians of the west, and failed to understand the need to demonstrate British resolve, which required both men and aggressive action.[57] But Proctor knew he could not afford to sit around while the Americans gained strength, that he must act quickly before they consolidated themselves.

On 22 January he led 334 regulars and fencibles, 212 militia, and 28 Provincial Marine sailors, supported by around 600 Indians under a chief called Roundhead, in an immediate counter-attack that found Winchester's men on the north bank of the Raisin, unprepared and vulnerable, having failed to post piquets on the sole approach road and the river behind them.[58] But the British failed to take the Americans completely by surprise, and as they advanced a Kentucky sentry opened fire "and hit Gates, the leading grenadier of the 41st, right through the head," recalled Major Reynolds. "The ball went in at one ear and out of the other."[59] Proctor ordered his sled-mounted 3-pounders to engage the enemy, which they did with little effect in the murky half-light; as the regulars formed up they mistook a five-foot split-rail oak fence for the American lines, which in fact lay farther back.[60] Winchester himself and the reserve ammunition were on the far side of the river, but the American fire took a heavy toll on the centre of the British, whom Proctor kept within range of the fence and under fire. Proctor's conduct here was later much criticized by John Richardson, whose younger brother was badly wounded after taking part in the advance in defiance of his father, Robert, a hospital assistant.[61] Afterwards these criticisms were widely repeated: the British line was exposed for over two hours, with no fewer than 111 cut down by the Kentuckians, who were able to rest their rifles on the palings to aim. But the British guns blasted the Americans, and Roundhead threw his warriors against their right flank, forcing them back across the frozen river with mounted Wyandots hunting down stragglers. Proctor then halted the frontal assault and tried to secure some farm buildings on his left, a tactic which saw Colonel St. George wounded four times, and American Ensign William O. Butler twice running into a barn under heavy fire in order to set it alight, leaving unharmed but with his clothes riddled by shot.[62]

Winchester had now arrived with his uniform pulled over his nightshirt and tried in vain to rally his men, but many threw away their arms as they floundered in the deep snow, and the Indians closed in; "with infernal yells [they] followed close on the heels of the fugitives very few of whom received quarter," shooting them down or dispatching them by tomahawk.[63] Barely thirty escaped to reach the Maumee Rapids, and Winchester was among those captured. Some weeks later the *Morning Chronicle* in London reported the event:

> The Indian according to the laws of nations and courtesy due to the prisoners of war, stripped the American commander of his fine waistcoat and shirt and then daubed his skin with paint. In this ludicrous state, having dressed himself in his regimentals, he [Roundhead] presented him to Colonel Proctor who with difficulty succeeded in getting the discomfited general his coat, sword and hat.[64]

Proctor persuaded Winchester to surrender the remainder of his force, and a message was sent to Major George Madison, commanding them, and following a protracted parley a surrender was agreed at 11 A.M.[65] Among the wounded was Private Shadrach Byfield of the 41st Regiment, who was "much affected by seeing and hearing a lad, about 11 or 12 years of age, who was wounded in one of his knees. The little fellow's cries from the pain of his wound, his crying after his dear mother; and saying he should die, were so affecting that it was not soon forgotten."[66] Alarmed by a false report that Harrison was only 8 miles away, and with so many prisoners on his hands, Proctor decided to get away to Detroit as quickly as possible, although Reynolds insisted that he "need not have retired so precipitately."[67]

Proctor left around 80 American wounded behind in houses at Frenchtown to await sleds that were to be sent the following day, or the widely expected arrival of Harrison.[68] But they were poorly guarded, and next morning they were found by drunken Indians who went from house to house beating and killing the Americans, and setting fire to the buildings, and some bodies were thrown in the streets to be scavenged by pigs. Gustavus M. Bowers was a surgeon's mate of the Kentucky militia who saw what happened, and "my blood runs cold in my veins when I think of it." He was roughed up and threatened with scalping by the Indians but spared, although he was close enough to another unfortunate when he was tomahawked "to receive the brains and blood after the fatal blow, on my blanket."[69] Now seventy-four years old, Matthew Elliot was inured to cruelty and had neither the will nor the desire to control the Indians. And although whiskey was involved it was not the cause of the massacre; retaliation for previous American behaviour also played some if not a large part in it.[70] In total between 30 and

60 were killed (depending on the source); those who escaped death were taken to Detroit whence they were eventually ransomed for a small fortune by a young merchant, John McDonnell.[71] The British had lost 24 killed and 158 wounded, and there "was much ammunition and many muskets, Rifles, Swords and Pistols which it was politic to allow the Indians to take away with them," while the Americans lost 292 dead and 592 prisoners, although the disaster was made more unbearable by the atrocities.[72]

The horrific events at Frenchtown were amplified and distorted by wartime propaganda, but they also inspired genuine anger. Proctor was universally vilified in the American press as being personally responsible, the bloodthirsty agent of "fiend-like depravity."[73] He or a subordinate did post guards, but even Indian leaders, quite apart from British officers, had little power to restrain the wilder elements among their followers. Not all captives were treated harshly as some Americans supposed, but Indians saw little point in releasing enemies captured in war whom they would only have to fight again. Besides, they felt they had a right to avenge their own fallen brethren. As Proctor informed Sheaffe, "it is almost impossible to save any prisoner . . . where the Indians have lost lives."[74] This was an important part of tribal societies with no formal criminal justice system, as it deterred offenders from injuring others; but it cut no ice with white people. Some British observers were equally disturbed, as Dr. Richardson noted: "Be assured we have not heard the last of this shameful transaction. I wish to God it could be contradicted."[75] As a result, the north-west had a new rallying cry: "Remember the Raisin!" And the unwounded prisoners also faced the ordeal of a 280-mile march, scavenging for apple peels and frozen potatoes and running to keep from freezing.[76] Prevost, however, accepted Proctor's version of the battle and did not inquire why casualties exceeded 40 percent among his precious regulars. Relieved that the threat to Detroit had been lifted, he granted Proctor the local rank of brigadier-general; both in Canada and at home his great victory was acknowledged and he was declared a hero.[77]

The course of the war had taken both sides by surprise. The conquest of Canada, supposedly naught but a matter of marching, clearly involved much, much more, and the U.S. government was under increasing pressure to gain control as winter approached. The new Congress tried to implement improvements in the U.S. Army and to increase recruiting for both regulars and militia. Money, as ever, would be a major problem, and although upon declaring war Congress had doubled import tariffs, both to raise revenue and to encourage American manufacturing, most merchants preferred to trade even if doing so meant smuggling or trading with the enemy.[78] In London two parliamentary debates on the American War were held on 3 and 18 February 1813, in which virtually every member expressed reluctance to fight the United States but agreed that once involved the only possible reaction was to strike aggressively and quickly. A common belief was that one of America's motives was a desire to help Bonaparte, and that Madison had carefully timed his "stab-in-the-back" to exploit British economic depression.[79] That same month Prevost learned from American newspapers that Congress had approved a $16 million war loan with the assistance of three wealthy merchants, Stephen Girard, John Jacob Astor, and the German-born financier and land speculator David Parish—all at a healthy discount that highlighted the need for taxes, which Republicans still strongly resisted.[80]

Once Gallatin had arranged these loans, $13,320,000 was allotted to the War Department, but Armstrong was told that monthly expenditures were not to exceed $1,480,000 per month, and he in turn warned Dearborn that "economy must be your alpha & omega as well as mine."[81] Four regular major-generals were appointed, including Harrison, plus seven brigadier-generals, and Madison was authorized to raise another twenty regiments for one year's service.[82] Armstrong also reorganized the former Northern and Southern Departments into nine military districts, the most important being No. 9, embracing Pennsylvania, New York, and Vermont under Dearborn, followed by No. 8 under Harrison, comprising Kentucky, Ohio, Michigan, Illinois, Indiana, and Missouri.[83] But the disaster at Frenchtown caused Armstrong to lose confidence in Harrison, who had to suspend plans for an attack on Fort Malden until control of Lake Erie had been won. Armstrong also ordered that Harrison dispose of his heavy train of draught horses and oxen, forbade him to draw more than $20,000 per month upon the department, and imposed restrictions on militia service, while Harrison began to suspect almost everyone of embezzlement.[84]

In Canada the army bills proved very successful, with most of the burden of the war falling on the already groaning shoulders of the British taxpayer, who now had to forgo the benefit of £12 million worth of trade with the United States just when another poor harvest drove up food prices. Labourers without work broke up machinery and rioted, leading some American commentators to predict imminent crisis in Britain; but few in Britain shared this view, regarding America as having "an aspiring, grasping commercial character," and a military capability, if recent performance was anything to go by, "almost beneath contempt."[85] And lack of money only exacerbated an already serious supply problem. Despite their small numbers the British faced increasing difficulties in supplying their troops at Kingston and Prescott; commissariat officers and agents found Canadian farmers reluctant to sell provisions or forage except for specie, which was sorely lacking. The Commissariat Department had struggled since the beginning of the war to make up the shortages of clothing, shoes, blankets, and the material to make them, as well as food, forage, and firewood. The department had been severely undermanned before the war, and most of the ire fell on the unfortunate Deputy Commissary-General, Edward Couche, who was forced to improvise a system as best he could, which was not very well, and this state of affairs drove Lieutenant-Colonel Robert Nichol of the Upper Canada militia "crazy," impelling him to declare that Couche "should be hanged."[86] If British resistance was to continue into 1813 it was clear that assistance must come from home, and in successive letters Bathurst assured Prevost that this would be forthcoming: a Royal Artillery company and detachments of the Corps of Royal Artillery Drivers and the Corps of Royal Sappers and Miners (formerly the Royal Military Artificers), with the 13th (1st Somersetshire), 2nd/41st, 70th (Glasgow Lowland), and 98th Regiments, plus drafts for existing units in theatre, and, with the French threat in the Mediterranean decreasing, the Swiss mercenary Régiments De Meuron and De Watteville.[87]

However, these reinforcements depended on the availability of shipping; the 445 men of the 2nd/41st Regiment were now in Bermuda, while the 1,300 of the Régiment De Watteville were in far-away Spain. The vast and often densely wooded Canadian terrain, where the chief means of transport was by boat and forage was sparse, meant that cavalry was not regarded as useful. Nevertheless, on 6 March the 19th Regiment of (Light) Dragoons was ordered to prepare three squadrons of 80 men each for service in North America.[88] Prevost decided to move reinforcements overland from New Brunswick before the St. Lawrence was open for shipping. The 104th Regiment was deemed the best suited to such a move, including as it did some 200 French Canadians, many of whom were experienced woodsmen.[89] After Prevost wrote of his plan on 16 January 1813, training was stepped up, including marching in snowshoes. Meanwhile Warren received orders to attempt a diversion to assist Prevost by making a landing on the American coast. The landing force was to be commanded by Colonel Sir Thomas Sidney Beckwith, a Peninsula veteran sent to become quartermaster-general in North America, and would likely take place in the vicinity of Chesapeake Bay and the Delaware River, whose ports Warren blockaded on 6 February.[90]

Early that month the 104th Regiment concentrated six companies about 550 men strong at Fredericton with its detachment at Saint John relieved by the 2nd/8th Regiment, leaving behind the boys and older men.[91] Lieutenant John Le Couteur was quite nostalgic: "I shall never forget the morning parade of that Sunday for although we marched with the best intentions it was impossible not to feel, in a certain degree, low-spirited, as our bugles struck up the merry air *The Girls We Leave Behind Us*."[92] On 16 February Lieutenant-Colonel Alexander Halkett and the Grenadier Company set out led by four Indian guides. Two horse-sleds took each company on the first day's march, whereafter they continued on foot, another company stepping out each day with the Light Company as rearguard on the 21st. They followed an old postal route through wilderness where deep snow precluded horse transport and shortage of dogs meant the men had to drag their own baggage, two to a toboggan carrying muskets, knapsacks, one blanket each, snowshoes if not wearing them, and fourteen days' rations. Lieutenant Charles Rainsford was extremely critical of their poor and scanty clothing, "their snowshoes and moccasins miserably made, and even their mittens were made of poor thin yarn, and yet in spite of all this they endured cheerfully all the discomforts and privations of their long and dreary tramp through the storms and cold of a most rigorous winter."[93] The winter was an intense one. At Fredericton on 1 February there was more snow on the ground than there had been for nine years, and the cold persisted once the march began. Le Couteur's company, being a later starter, might have expected a well-packed trail, but he reported incessant snow with another 8–12 inches covering the track made twenty-four hours previously, and the way was difficult, with much floundering.

For the first six or seven nights they found lodgings in houses and barns, but as the country became less settled, they had to build shelters. Reveille was sounded two hours before dawn to enable the men to prepare a meagre breakfast and be ready to leave as soon as it was light enough to ensure no equipment was left behind. They marched until the early afternoon, then hung their kit in the trees to prevent losing it in the snow before building wooden shelters, digging out the snow to reach the frozen ground beneath while the company axemen cut poles to form frames over which evergreen boughs were laid. Each shelter was completely enclosed apart from a small opening covered with a blanket with a hole in the roof to allow smoke to escape. The ration of one pound of salt pork (including bones) and 10 ounces of biscuit providing two meals per day was used up more quickly than expected: the allowance of only fourteen days to reach the St. Lawrence, where they were to be resupplied, was too optimistic, and by the time Le Couteur's company reached Grand Falls on 1 March, many men were frost-bitten. Lieutenant A. W. Playfair later recalled that the men could think and talk of nothing but food,

> yet, in the midst of our privations, we had some hearty laughs. Some of the men would run toboggans down the hill sitting on them, and would frequently capsize. Our big black drummer straddled the big drum, which was lashed to a toboggan, to try the experiment, but it got off the track, shooting him off at high velocity, and the sable African came up some distance from where he disappeared, a white man exciting roars of laughter.[94]

The African was Harry Grant; another was George Lawrence, a giant nearly seven feet tall.

At Lake Temisconata a blizzard forced Captain George Armstrong's company to abandon the 18-mile crossing and huddle in shelters for three days with Captain George Shore's Light Company. With starvation threatening, Rainsford and two privates with local knowledge offered to fetch help and set off to cover the 54 miles to the nearest settlement, at St. André. On the way they met William Long, a Canadian guide out looking for them, who set them on the right road, and they reached the regimental quarters on the St. Lawrence at Rivière du Loup whence a rescue party was dispatched. Once the two companies reached St. André and thawed out, the remaining march was along packed roads and without incident, and they assumed garrison duties at Quebec soon afterwards, and were sent on to Montreal and then Kingston some three weeks later. One man was left sick at Woodstock and died some weeks later, though not from the cold but from fever. Le Couteur noted that many men fell sick soon after the march, and within six weeks a corporal and nineteen privates died, although he hastened to note they were all heavy drinkers.[95] Prevost appeared singularly unimpressed by their achievement, but while couriers and small parties made the same trip repeatedly they did not face the same difficulties of food and shelter posed by large parties.[96]

Fortunately for the British, news from the busy smugglers along the frontier that Dearborn was collecting sleds for a winter campaign proved false: once snow fell and the St. Lawrence froze, American farmers were only too happy to take advantage of the higher prices paid by the British.[97] Everywhere business flourished on contracts for food, clothing, and other supplies while tavern keepers did an excellent trade with the troops. Prevost made adjustments to the militia and raised three troops of Canadian Light Dragoons and a small Corps of Provincial Royal Artillery Drivers, and the Corps of Canadian Voyageurs was replaced by the Provincial Commissariat Voyageurs, some 425 strong.[98] When intelligence reports of a large American build-up at Sackets Harbor and Buffalo made another invasion of Canada seem imminent once the snows melted, Prevost decided to move reinforcements to Kingston; a company of Glengarry Light Infantry and some gunners arrived at the end of January, releasing a 49th company there to move to York; four companies of the 1st/8th Regiment were dispatched to Kingston and two more on 21 February to Prescott, where Prevost himself arrived a few hours later, having prorogued the Lower Canada Assembly.

He was immediately pressed by Lieutenant-Colonel Thomas Pearson and Major "Red George" Macdonell to lance the boil of Ogdensburg across the river whence Benjamin Forsyth's riflemen had made a daring raid on Elizabethstown (now Brockville) two weeks earlier and seized fifty-two prisoners, earning Forsyth promotion to major.[99] Another patrol had also taken three farmers and a team of horses and insulted Macdonell when he went to remonstrate under a flag of truce. The New York militia were known to be deserting in numbers, a development which would assist a surprise attack, although two of the Prescott garrison also deserted that evening, and Prevost's presence would also be known of in Ogdensburg. A demonstration was made to cover Prevost's departure for Kingston when he left early the next morning, but he warned against an attack.[100] Nevertheless, Macdonell chose to implement an existing plan using two columns: one under his own command, comprising 150 regulars and 230 militia; and one under Captain John Jenkins, with his own company of Glengarry Light Infantry and 70 militia.[101] Behind the Glengarrys came their warrior priest, Father Alexander Macdonell, who encouraged the more reluctant to do their duty and, when one man refused to move forward despite two warnings, excommunicated him on the spot.[102]

As they crossed the iced-up St. Lawrence, more than a mile wide, on which the Americans were used to watch them parade, Sergeant James Comins of the 8th Regiment recalled the American gunners did not open fire until they were over halfway across.

> Their firing had not much effect as their gunners were undisciplined, most of their shots going over our heads. On our nearer approach their soldiers abandoned their posts, leaving the Inhabitants to Protect their own Property; some of them fired upon our men from their windows

> . . . all this time the soldiers were retreating and ours were ordered to pursue them while others took possession of the town.[103]

The second column ran into difficulties because the sleigh-mounted artillery could not keep up with them, and Jenkins was severely wounded in both arms, losing one.[104] But Forsyth realized he would be cut off and abandoned the fort, retreating towards Sackets Harbor. The Americans lost 20 dead and 70 captured, mostly wounded, while British losses were 7 killed and 48 wounded, including "Red George" Macdonell.[105]

At this point Macdonell received a note from Prevost written en route ordering him not to take offensive action without permission of de Rottenburg at Montreal, "unless the imbecile conduct of your enemy should offer you an opportunity for his destruction."[106] He later tried to spin his dispatches to gain some credit for the success and belie his caution. The British burned the schooners and gunboats frozen in the ice and carried off the military stores, and subsequently Ogdensburg remained garrisonless for the rest of the war. Apart from a brief period in early November, the St. Lawrence line of communications remained firmly in British hands, while Captain Reuben Sherwood and others roamed freely on the American side to provide a steady stream of intelligence to Kingston, Cornwall, and Prescott, and soon both sides were crossing to fraternize with the other.[107]

When Dearborn learned of the defeat at Ogdensburg on 25 February, he moved to reinforce Sackets Harbor, fearing that Prevost had concentrated 6,000–8,000 men for a move across Lake Ontario.[108] More significantly, however, the British lacked the manpower and resources to compete on Lake Erie and would lose control of it as a result, changing the nature of the war in the west. Over the winter 200 naval personnel were given a warning order to prepare for service in North America. Most of these men had been operating gunboats in defence of Riga in the Baltic and would be familiar with the conditions of a Canadian winter; by early March their numbers were increased to 465 due to sail on the transport HMS *Woolwich* (22).[109] On 19 March the appointment of Sir James Yeo as commodore and commander-in-chief was announced; his Admiralty instructions specified that his "first and paramount" objective was defence of the North American provinces under Prevost's command, but he was also to take orders from the Admiralty, and he could also request assistance from Warren, who had already provided Prevost with nine Royal Navy lieutenants and some gunners to serve with the Provincial Marine, including three senior lieutenants to act as "captains of corvettes" on

Lake Ontario.[110] As events unfolded, Yeo would find himself answering to too many masters, although Prevost was the principal amongst them, and Warren and the remote Admiralty could exercise little effective influence. And despite the launch of *Wolfe* and two gunboats at Kingston on 20 April, raising British forces to six vessels carrying 96 guns, the U.S. Navy now had three ships and fourteen schooners carrying 111 guns, although their total broadside weight was no greater.[111]

In the meantime Chauncey was to be joined by twenty-seven-year-old Master-Commandant Oliver Hazard Perry, who would prepare a squadron for service on Lake Erie to support Harrison's summer campaign.[112] Chauncey had transferred his command to Erie village on Presque Isle (now Erie, Pennsylvania), where the stores and guns for two 20-gun brigs and four schooner gunboats were being assembled by the energetic shipbuilder Noah Brown, and where Perry arrived in March.[113] "You are the very person," said Chauncey, "that I want for a particular service, in which you may gain reputation for Yourself and honor for your country."[114] Brown's designs were totally functional and employed green timber, since his new ships would be required for one battle only; with competent shipwrights, ample finances, and naval stores available via secure routes from the New York and Philadelphia yards, and ironware from Pittsburgh, it was obvious that the Americans enjoyed an immense logistical advantage.[115] But it was equally obvious that it would be well into the summer before the U.S. Navy would be in a position to bid effectively for control of Lake Erie. Therefore Chauncey concentrated on Lake Ontario and Perry on Lake Erie, where, with Daniel Dobbins, he worked frantically to complete four ships under construction.[116] And although Congress had sanctioned the building of four ships-of-the-line and more super-frigates and sloops, the Royal Navy's blockade ensured that American blue-water vessels were confined to port, releasing considerable drafts of officers and men for service on the lakes.[117]

6

Spring on the Frontier

Hark, now the drums beat up again,
For all true soldier gentlemen,
Then let us 'list and march, I say,
Over the hills and far away.
Over the hills and o'er the main
To Flanders, Portugal and Spain
King George Commands and we'll obey,
Over the hills and far away.
Over river, bogs and springs,
We all shall live as great as kings,
And plunder get both night and day
When over the hills and far away.

—Anon., "Over the Hills and Far Away"

In early February Congress secretly approved the occupation of West Florida, and Armstrong sent orders to New Orleans to occupy the territory as far as the Perdido River. An expeditionary force was hastily arranged and dispatched to seize Mobile and Fort Charlotte nearby, a task achieved bloodlessly on 15 April. This modest undertaking would prove one of America's few successes of 1813, and would represent its only permanent territorial gain of the war.[1] Armstrong's main plan for the year called first for the seizure of Kingston—the principal British naval base on Lake Ontario—followed by the seat of government at York and the reduction of Forts George and Erie, leaving the rest of the Niagara front as mopping-up operations.[2] The plan would secure Lake Ontario and all points westward and was readily accepted by Chauncey and Dearborn in early February; but it made significant errors in estimating the difficulties of the ground and British opposition.

The difficulties of manoeuvring armies across largely unmapped trackless wastes of forest and bog were difficult to imagine in London or Washington, and large-scale maps portraying lakes as overgrown duckponds belied their treacherous natures.[3] The cabinet approved Armstrong's initial plan on 10 February, but almost immediately he began fiddling with it and suggesting to Dearborn little diversions here and there; these "hints," as he called them, hardly served to convince Dearborn of Armstrong's commitment to the plan.[4] Armstrong also managed to antagonize the other cabinet members with his penchant for intrigue, riling Monroe and Gallatin and losing the trust of his navy counterpart by the summer, leading Jones to declare: "the 'Old Soldier' [Armstrong's nom de plume] is not a legitimate son of Mars."[5] Worse, the American economy was crumbling. Financial crisis was prompted by the failure to provide an adequate taxation system for war, and the final collapse by New England antipathy to it. Congress had been forced to approve the $16 million loan in February made possible only by a 12 percent discount, and even then prosperous New England gave precious little support; Boston, for example, providing only $75,000. Although the suspension of imports provided a stimulus to manufacturing and generated specie as the south and west languished, New England Federalists refused to subscribe to government loans.[6] Congress also approved $5 million worth of Treasury notes to replace those issued the previous year, but after twelve years at the Treasury Gallatin resigned, weary of congressional opposition. He handed over temporarily to Navy Secretary Jones, who could do little to ease the crisis and was eventually replaced by George Washington Campbell of Tennessee, a man who inspired no confidence in the financial community.[7]

In March Congress authorized $10 million in Treasury notes and $25 million in loans, but little more than $10 million was realized. On 24 May Madison called a special session of Congress that finally agreed to impose internal taxes, including some $3 million apportioned among the states and further excise duties, plus a further loan of $7.5 million, once more at a considerable discount to try to attract investors.[8] Thus the two parties traded their traditional places: it was now the Republicans who imposed taxes, turning loose upon the land the tax demon they had once denounced as representing tyranny and opposed by the Federalists.[9] Before this, however, the Russian offer to mediate in peace negotiations finally reached America and was promptly accepted by the administration on 11 March, as military failure and news of Bonaparte's disaster in Russia compounded the sense of financial and administrative chaos the war had created. Republicans realized they must temper "idealism" with "realism" while British commercial and diplomatic interests appeared, by contrast, relatively secure.[10] Yet even now Madison, Armstrong, and others were seeking to expand the war with more grandiose schemes of conquest; and as Madison would spend most of 1813 seriously ill, it would fall to Armstrong to do most of the directing.[11]

On 14 March Prevost returned to Montreal having completed his tour of inspection, although this was not known in Sackets Harbor for another week. Dearborn remained fearful as reports indicated major troop movements and as companies of the 1st Royal Scots, the 8th Regiment, and Voltigeurs Canadiens moved westwards by stages, now that Bathurst's dispatches had assured Prevost of reinforcements to come. But Prevost remained cautious and informed Sheaffe that these extra troops were for defensive purposes only.[12] Dearborn had managed to convince himself that Prevost had assembled 6,000–7,000 men at Kingston and was within forty-eight hours of an attack on Sackets Harbor, and Chauncey appears to have contracted his pessimism. On 20 March Dearborn used these fears and that of ice at the eastern end of the lake to request that Armstrong change the plan, supported by Chauncey: York, not Kingston, would now be the first objective, and Armstrong agreed.[13] York's isolation made it an unsatisfactory naval base where over the winter the construction of a new ship, *Sir Isaac Brock,* partly from the dismantled *Duke of Gloucester,* was being steadily bungled.[14] Its defences were equally woeful: a fort had been outlined but only partially dug, and an earthwork battery with two 12-pounders mounted; but a good beach to the west of town made a landing difficult to defend against, and a western battery was constructed with two condemned 18-pounders that lacked trunnions, clamped into a log base which could fire at long range. The mixed garrison of 700 included two companies of the 1st/8th Regiment, one of Glengarry Light Infantry, and a company-sized detachment of the Royal Newfoundland Regiment, 300 dockyard workers, the 3rd York Regiment of Militia, and about 50 Mississauga and Chippewa Indians.[15]

During March and April the Americans collected around 4,000 men at Sackets Harbor from the 2nd U.S. Light Dragoons, the Light Artillery, and the Rifle, 6th, 9th, 15th, 16th, and 21st U.S. Infantry Regiments, organized in two brigades under Brigadier-Generals Zebulon Pike and John Chandler.[16] Pike had spent the winter with his brigade based at Plattsburgh, struggling against the winter weather in summer uniforms that brought on a virulent strain of pneumonia, and trying to stem smuggling along the New York and Vermont borders. On 2 April Lieutenant Lorinn Austin and 50 dragoons surrounded the New York village of Americus and arrested thirteen men on suspicion of smuggling and marched eight of them to Sackets Harbor. But the smugglers were soon out of goal and Austin inside instead, for whom Pike had to send bail money, such was the hostility of the border regions to interference with free trade.[17]

On the evening of 26 April fifteen American vessels carrying 1,700 regulars were sighted by sentries on Scarborough Bluffs, and the alarm was sent by semaphore, but adverse conditions prevented the Americans from getting ashore before the next morning. Given the paucity of forces, Sheaffe's only hope was to keep his small force concentrated and to counter-attack quickly before the Americans got established ashore, and only the Glengarrys and Indians were sent to oppose a landing near the old French fort, built in 1749, of Rouille, or *Tarontah,* meaning "Trees on the Water," that later gave its name to Toronto.[18] Seaman Ned Myers helped row the soldiers ashore: "They were mostly tall, pale-looking Yankees, half-dead with sickness and the bad weather—so mealy, indeed, that half of them could not take their grog which by this time I had got to think was a bad omen." But in the event the assault boats were carried west of the proposed landing site by the wind, and the two sides did not clash until about 8 A.M. Then, as they came under fire, Myers' opinion of his passengers changed as "they became wide awake, pointed out to each other where to aim, and many of them actually jumped into the water, in order to get ashore sooner."[19] Led by Forsyth's riflemen to cover the landing, Pike took three companies forward and soon forced the 8th's Grenadier Company back towards the town, killing or wounding almost half of them.[20] Sheaffe failed to keep his force together, and they were defeated piecemeal despite the narrow paths through the forest slowing the eastward movement of the Americans, as Chauncey's schooners kept up a steady 12-pounder fire that effectively covered the American right flank.[21] After some three hours the British were forced back to the western battery, where the open magazine was suddenly detonated by a careless gunner, an incident witnessed by a young boy, Patrick Finan, who saw the men blown into the air, "and the *dissection* of the greater part of their bodies was inconceivably shocking!" He watched as the survivors were brought into the hospital, and

> a more afflicting sight could scarcely be witnessed . . . One man in particular presented an awful spectacle: he was brought in in a wheelbarrow, and from his appearance I should be inclined to suppose that almost every bone in his body was broken; he was lying in a powerless heap, shaking

> with every motion of the barrow, from which his legs hung dangling down, as if only connected with his body by the skin, while his cries and groans were of the most heart rending description.[22]

The battery quickly fell, and the Americans pressed on to attack the unfinished fort. Sheaffe remained cool and decided to retire. It was a sound decision, but York was the provincial capital and home to influential men already critical of him; he was later accused by civilian witnesses of doing nothing to animate the soldiers.[23] Although it was only early afternoon, having lost sixty-two dead and ninety-four wounded, Sheaffe decided to retreat to Kingston, though he left the Union flag flying above the fort to deceive the Americans into thinking it was still strongly held and instructions to the militia officers who would remain behind to seek the best possible terms. He then ordered the unfinished *Brock* destroyed and the "Grand Magazine" blown up.[24]

Pike was interviewing a prisoner when huge rocks from the explosion landed amongst townsfolk and Americans alike that seemed as if "the heavens and earth were coming together," killing 38 of the latter and wounding 222.[25] George Howard later reported to his wife that Pike was struck by a large stone "on the forehead [that] Stamped him for the Grave"—he died later on USS *Madison,* resting his head on a British flag brought as proof of victory.[26] Total American losses were 320, and the overstretched American surgeons "waded in blood cutting off arms, legs and trepanning [boring holes in the skull to relieve pressure]," recalled Dr. William Beaumont, who cut and slashed for forty-eight hours, without food or sleep. "My God! Who can think of the shocking scene where his fellow creatures lye [*sic*] mashed & mangled in every part, with a leg—an arm—a head, or a body ground to pieces without having his heart pierced with the acutest sensibility & his blood chilled in his veins."[27]

Dearborn was appalled and came ashore to assume command, in no mood to discuss terms with anyone. The militia officers were paroled to their homes and the men cooped up, the wounded receiving no treatment. But the following day Dearborn had cooled down enough to sign a capitulation guaranteeing private property, and did his best to ensure the terms were kept.[28]

Following victory American discipline broke down, however, and although there was no murder or rape, nor theft from occupied homes, many empty houses were robbed. Forsyth's riflemen were accused of being among the worst culprits in retaliation for Ogdensburg, but Ned Myers admitted stealing sugar, tea, liquor, and enough other items to fill a purloined canoe twice over. "Every house they found deserted was completely sacked," recalled resident Penelope Beikie.[29] Then on 30 April Parliament House was set on fire—probably the unauthorized work of American sailors—as the "Town thronged with the Yankees," wrote Ely Playter, "many busy getting off the public stores. The Council office with every window broke & pillaged of every thing that it contained. The Government building, the Block House and the building adjacent all burned to ashes," although another resident, Isaac Wilson, praised the Americans and blamed the looting on other locals, "who made shameful work."[30] On 1 May the remaining public buildings were deliberately torched as the Americans departed, taking with them provisions and military stores and £2,500 from the public treasury. This had been hidden but was given up under the threat that the whole town would be burned; the Americans also took books from the subscription library—most of which were personally returned by Chauncey in November and after the war; but the government mace was not returned until 1934.[31] Sheaffe was especially displeased, as among the "public" property was his "most superb Scarlet coat," which was sold at auction at Niagara a few weeks later. The Americans also destroyed the possessions of Major James Givins and his family, being particularly bitter against those who led the Indians.[32]

Although the British had destroyed *Brock,* the Americans seized *Duke of Gloucester* as well as a large quantity of naval stores; losses which would help the Americans maintain parity on Lake Ontario and which severely hampered other British plans, as Prevost reported to London: "The ordnance, ammunition and other stores for the service on Lake Erie were either destroyed or fell into enemy hands when York was taken."[33] But the Americans had been in York longer than they intended, since a gale prevented their departure, and when they finally sailed Chauncey's schooners were so crowded that only half the troops could get below to shelter from the rain and lashing waves. By the time they reached Fort Niagara on 8 May, they were in no state to make an attempt against Fort George and had, in any case, lost the element of surprise. So Chauncey took the squadron back to Sackets Harbor, where the men stumbled ashore in appalling condition, a great many suffering from sickness.[34]

Prevost refrained from criticizing Sheaffe in his reports to Bathurst, blaming defeat on inferior forces; but neither did he praise him for saving half his army. Having already criticized him for failing to follow up victory at Queenston by taking Fort Niagara, he transferred Sheaffe to Montreal at the end of May, replacing him as commander-in-chief and administrator of Upper Canada with de Rottenburg, who assumed command on 19 June. In this decision he was strongly influenced by the indignant reaction to the attack on York written by Reverend John Strachan and signed by six other prominent citizens.[35] Sheaffe remained at Montreal until November, when he was recalled to Britain at Prevost's request. The reasons behind his dismissal appear flimsy, especially given that there was no court-martial or inquiry.[36] No mention was ever made of the fact that the two companies of the 8th Regiment were in York only by chance, and Prevost failed to mention that guns and other stores promised for its defence had not arrived, and Prevost was soon facing criticism himself from local dignitaries who disliked his defensive strategy.[37]

IN THE WEST, Shawnee and Delaware Indians fought a skirmish against militia in southern Indiana on 23 March that became known as the battle of Tipton's Island.[38] On 2 April the command of Fort Meigs fell to Major Amos Stoddart following the departure of militia under Brigadier-General Joel Leftwich when the terms of his men had expired and they went home; not that Captain Eleazer D. Wood thought him any loss, calling Leftwich "a phlegmatic, stupid old granny."[39] At the same time, Proctor had assembled 423 men from the 41st and 63 of the Royal Newfoundland Regiments, with 30 Royal Artillery men, a captain of Royal Engineers with a field train, 462 militia, and a small commissariat.[40] He would be supported by 600 warriors serviced by the Indian Department gathered under Roundhead, who had been purifying themselves for weeks with sweat-baths and dances to gain spiritual favour for an attack on Fort Meigs. With an early thaw having freed Proctor's flotilla of six ships, two gunboats, and *bateaux* transports on Lake Erie, all they awaited now, Proctor informed Sheaffe, was "the cooperation of Tecumthe [*sic*]." Once again Proctor knew he must strike before the Americans could overwhelm him with numbers. "If I tamely permit the enemy to await his reinforcements and mature his plans, he will become too formidable."[41]

Tecumseh reappeared after an absence of seven months, bringing warriors and their dependants, for whom he asked for five days' grace to settle in the protective custody of the Great Father. On 23 April Proctor was ready to embark as Tecumseh led the Indians, reinforced to a total of 1,200 warriors, around the lake to the mouth of the Maumee River towards Fort Meigs. When he arrived in front of the fort on 26 April, Tecumseh found the British busy unloading, and next morning Proctor outlined his plans. Fort Meigs was sited on a plateau south-east of the river and some 60 feet above it. It was a truly formidable position now garrisoned by 1,200 men—half regulars and volunteers, and half Ohio and Kentucky militia—and encompassing nine acres with stout 15-foot pickets embedded 3 feet deep, including seven blockhouses and five raised batteries, with five 18-pounders, five 12-pounders, four 6-pounders, and five howitzers, and the ammunition lodged in two underground magazines.[42] Proctor sited his guns on the far bank, which was slightly higher, while the Indians and militia sealed off the fort from the other directions, but the weather remained bitterly cold as preparations were put in hand. On the 29th a column of 200 men with several oxen slipped and struggled along the dirt road that heavy rain had turned into deep mud, to bring forward their heavy guns into four batteries designated "King's," "Queen's," "Sailors," and "Mortar," supported by the 9-pounders aboard the *Myers* and *Eliza.* A bombardment began on 1 May, as a result of which inside the fort "the spades and dirt flew faster than any of us had before witnessed," recalled Private Alfred M. Lorraine of the Virginia militia.[43] But most of the rounds fired buried themselves harmlessly in skillfully built traverse earthworks 20 feet wide and 12 feet high that Eleazer Wood had created behind a line of tents.[44] "When the tents were struck," wrote Wood, "that beautiful prospect of beating up our quarters, which but an instant before presented itself to the view of the eager and skilful [British] artillerists, had now entirely fled, and in its place suddenly appeared an immense shield of earth, obscuring from his sight every tent, every horse . . . Those canvas houses, which in a great measure covered the growth of the traverse, by keeping from the view of the enemy the operations about it, were now with their inhabitants in them entirely protected in their turn."[45]

The Americans dug recesses in the far side of the traverse to provide shelter bays during bombardments; they were damp, muddy, and uncomfortable, but proof against the roundshot and shrapnel from the British guns—two 24-pounders taken at Detroit, a mortar, a howitzer, and three 12-pounders. "The Enemy," Proctor reported miserably, "had during our Approach so completely entrenched, and covered himself as to render unavailing every Effort of our Artillery."[46] Tecumseh taunted Harrison to come out and give battle, and not to hide "behind logs and in the earth like a ground hog," and Proctor demanded a surrender, but Harrison wisely refused.[47]

For several days a brisk if ineffectual fire was maintained, the Americans mostly conserving their scarce ammunition, and patiently recovering British shot for which Harrison offered a bounty. Heated shot fizzled in the wet earth, and roundshot and shells damaged the roofs of blockhouses and the main magazine; but it was Indian sniping that accounted for most American casualties, especially on parties trying to fetch water from the river.[48] A second British battery was placed to the south just 300 yards from the fort, but Wood quickly threw up new traverses, and few casualties were suffered by the defenders. It was plain that the bombardment was failing—to the intense annoyance of the Indians; then at 11 A.M. on 4 May Harrison received word that a 1,200-man relief force from Kentucky under Brigadier-General Green Clay had arrived in boats along the Maumee Rapids, deepened by snow-melt and the heavy rain, and was two hours upriver. Harrison planned a counter-attack the next morning against the northern battery by means of intrepid couriers slipping through the Indian cordon.[49] But it was a risky enterprise, since one of Clay's two Kentucky regiments, under Lieutenant-Colonel William Dudley, would be isolated as they landed to spike the British guns before retiring to the fort. "Hearing that we were certainly to fight," recalled one of Dudley's officers, Lieutenant Joseph R. Underwood, "I began to look upon all the surrounding objects as things which to me might soon disappear forever and my mind reverted to my friends at home, to bid them a final farewell."[50]

After a struggle with wind and currents Clay's men landed in two parties at about 9 A.M., and Dudley's men, after marching some 2 miles in three columns across an open plain, reached the northern battery. They raised an almighty whoop, charging forward with their new battle cry, "Remember the Raisin!" they rushed the position and spiked the guns, improperly as it later turned out, for they had not brought the right tools.[51] And, recalled Lieutenant Joseph H. Larwill of the 2nd U.S. Artillery, having "accomplished this objective, [Dudley's] orders were peremptory to return immediately to his boats and cross over to the fort; but blind confidence which generally attends militia when successful proved their ruin."[52] Disregarding their orders they continued in disorganized pursuit after some Indians who fired on them from the woods to the left. The Indians led them on, and the Kentuckians soon found themselves deep amongst the trees. Now isolated, they were in turn attacked by three companies of the 41st Regiment supported by the militia under Captain Adam Muir along the river and, more ominously, by Indian reinforcements. A sixteen-year-old volunteer, Thomas Christian, recalled, "that portion of the enemy upon the opposite side of the river [had] ample time to cross over in our rear, completely hemming us in upon every side. Our case was then hopeless."[53] Deeply alarmed, Harrison launched a sally from the fort to cover them and offered a $1,000 reward for any man who would cross the river and bring Dudley's men back.[54] At the same time, Colonel John Miller led another sortie from the fort to attack the British battery to the south, which they spiked, taking forty-one prisoners before being vigorously counter-attacked by Indians under Tecumseh, who retook the guns and attempted to outflank Miller's force. Miller's regulars made a spirited charge to extricate the endangered wing and regained the fort having lost about thirty dead and ninety wounded.[55]

Soon Dudley's men were fleeing for their lives as the Indians chased them with tomahawks and scalping knives, "painted with most every color, their heads tipped off with bird wings, huge bunches of feathers, and skins of animals."[56] In complete disorder Dudley's men rushed back past the battery with almost half their number killed or captured. Joseph R. Underwood "received a ball in my back which remains in my body. It struck me with a stunning, deadening force and I fell on my hands and knees."[57] He was lucky to survive: British troops also moved to cross the river but arrived as the action ended, where Private Shadrach Byfield saw a Kentuckian, disabled and scalped, lying "in a miserable plight . . . begging for water," until other warriors came and finished him off.[58] Another British force assembled at their headquarters advanced to retake the guns, and those Kentuckians who had not escaped upriver or made it back to the boats, and thence to the sanctuary of the fort, tried to surrender to British troops wherever possible. But Dudley and many of his men were already dead, and the battle was over around noon.[59]

Collecting their prisoners, the British sent them with an escort of fifty men to Fort Miami, an old ruined British fort from the days before American independence which they used as an enclosure. But the column was soon surrounded by Indians who pestered and cajoled the prisoners, stealing watches and money, and not only valuables but items of clothing. At the entrance to the fort where it passed over a ditch the Indians formed a "gauntlet" of two lines. Leslie Combs, who was among the prisoners, later claimed that ten or twelve bodies already lay nearby, and as they approached the gauntlet, "a man who was walking behind stepped before me. Just as he entered the defile an Indian put a pistol to his back and fired. He fell. I ran through without being touched."[60] Many others received blows, and there was much jeering, but once inside they were still not safe. Indians began to push the sentries aside and clamber over the walls. When Private Russell of the 41st, "an old and excellent soldier" according to John Richardson, tried to protect the Americans, an Indian shot him down.[61] One fearsome-looking warrior shot three prisoners from the wall in succession, calmly reloading his musket each time, before leaping down with an axe and setting about a fourth, then proceeding to scalp his victims as the horrified onlookers struggled to escape. "Without any means of defense or possibility of escape," recalled Combs, "death in all the horror of savage cruelty seemed to stare us in the face."[62]

At this point Tecumseh and Matthew Elliott arrived. A worthless Ojibwa identified as Split Nose or Normee was said to have been behind the assault as an easy way of obtaining scalps, having missed the battle, and certainly many of those present were Ojibwas and Potawatomis, who could not understand Tecumseh's speech. But he gained control of the mob and, in saving the lives of the remaining prisoners, passed into legend. However, as Ensign James Cochran noted:

> Had they been amenable to British laws the perpetrators of this massacre would have been severely punished—as it was most of the principal chiefs, who with the brave Tecumseh had endeavored to check it, but whose exhortations were lost on such maniacs, convened a meeting in conjunction with the Chippewas, before which Spilt Nose was summoned, but he had wisely taken himself out of the way and his crime was soon nearly forgotten.[63]

One story often repeated was that Tecumseh turned to Proctor when the latter complained the Indians were uncontrollable and told him: "Begone! You are unfit to command. Go and put on petticoats!" The truth of this and other stories is unverifiable, but Proctor was already severely embarrassed after the Raisin murders, even if the number of dead in this second incident was far fewer than the forty Harrison believed. But a terrible tragedy had undoubtedly occurred, and Proctor completely ignored it in his dispatch. Tecumseh's defence of the American prisoners would become an important foundation block in his legend, but equally significant was his defence of four Shawnee captives who had served with the Americans.[64]

During the afternoon a white flag appeared above the fort, but it was not to offer surrender, only to arrange a prisoner exchange.[65] Many Indians, including most of Dickson's Sac, Fox, Menominee, and Chippewa warriors, now deserted in search of plunder, and the Canadian militia informed Proctor that they really had to get back to their farms to plant crops, a plausible and convenient excuse to avoid unpopular and potentially dangerous service.[66] With the siege plainly unsuccessful and his force massively diminished, Proctor marched away on 9 May reporting that "under present circumstances at least, our Indian Force is not a disposable [useful] one . . . Daily experience more strongly proves that a regular force is absolutely requisite to ensure the Safety of this District."[67] The Americans had lost 135 killed, 188 wounded, and over 630 prisoners to British losses of 14 dead, 47 wounded, and 41 prisoners.[68] But the fort, albeit overcrowded, disease ridden, and ill provisioned, had withstood the test largely thanks to its excellent construction, and its successful defence inspired Harrison and his army for the later campaign in Canada.[69]

SIR JAMES YEO arrived at Quebec on 5 May accompanied by three commanders, including William Howe Mulcaster, eight lieutenants, and 440 men.[70] He learned of the fall of York and set out next day for Kingston with 150 men, catching up with Prevost en route; arriving in Kingston together on the 15th, they met Lieutenant Robert Barclay RN, who had already achieved considerable feats in the two weeks he had been there.[71] Barclay was the son of a Church of Scotland minister at Kingskettle, Fife, where John Strachan gave lessons. He had served on *Swiftsure* at Trafalgar, and in 1808 on the frigate *Diana* he had lost his left arm to a ball from a swivel gun while fighting a French convoy.[72] In the meantime other naval officers had also arrived, and the Lake Ontario squadron now consisted of *Wolfe* (23)—launched on 20 April and awaiting her guns—*Royal George* (21), *Earl of Moira* (14)—now re-rigged as a brig—*Prince Regent* (14)—shortly to be renamed *General Beresford*—and the converted merchant schooner *Sir Sidney Smith* (12). Plans had been made to lay down a ship to replace the one lost at York, together with six gunboats. As Yeo was keen to promote his own officers, he sent Barclay to command on Lake Erie with three lieutenants, a surgeon, a purser, an ailing master's mate, and nineteen seamen who were, said Barclay, "the most worthless Characters that came from England with" Yeo. This move marked the beginning of a long struggle to obtain adequate reinforcement for the painfully weak Lake Erie squadron.[73]

Lack of provisions was another serious problem: as early as 7 June John MacGillivray warned Simon McTavish of the North West Company that the entire British position in Michigan was "doomed to be forced to surrender for want of provisions and ammunition," a problem exacerbated by poor harvests and lack of rainwater in the streams to drive the mills.[74] At Long Point Barclay found the schooners *Lady Prevost* and *Chippewa,* plus the transport *Mary,* but he would have to strip the shore batteries to provide guns for new ships, including the powerful *Detroit* under construction at Amherstburg;

and it was clear that while Yeo had barely enough seamen for Lake Ontario, there was little he could do for Barclay.[75] Yeo knew that Chauncey's vessels packed heavier armaments than his own and that once Chauncey's new corvette was complete, with its twenty-six long 24-pounders, the American squadron would be too powerful to attack. He therefore wrote to the Admiralty on 26 May that he would "put to sea" while there was still rough parity between them, "as the possession of Upper Canada must depend on whoever can maintain Naval Superiority on Lake Ontario."[76]

Prevost was also alarmed by the growing disparity of strength in Upper Canada and complained to Bathurst that the demands of the militia laws combined with the demands of agriculture were undermining the province's defences.[77] With the threat to Kingston and the British position on Lake Ontario, on 19 May Prevost sent the 2nd/89th Regiment by ship from Halifax to Quebec, where it arrived on 5 June, thereafter marching the 400 miles to Kingston in nineteen days.[78] Fortunately reinforcements were beginning to arrive; the 400-strong 2nd/41st and the 98th Regiments reached Quebec a few days earlier and these units were sent westwards, together with the balance of 1st Royal Scots, a car brigade (battery) of light artillery, a troop of Canadian Light Dragoons, four assorted grenadier companies, and the 1st Light Battalion—a unit organized six weeks before from the flank companies of the Select Embodied Militia of Lower Canada and the light companies of the regular units in Lower Canada. A 2nd Light Battalion had also been organized, and other troops were arriving in Montreal. Soon after Prevost sent these orders, however, came news that the Americans had started bombarding Fort George and had set all the log buildings within it alight.[79]

Fort George was garrisoned by around 1,000 troops from the 1st/8th and 49th Regiments, Royal Newfoundland Regiment, and Glengarry Light Infantry, and 300 continuing militia flank companies under Brigadier-General John Vincent, commanding the Centre Division, with another 750 troops posted along the Niagara front and several hundred militia available for duty.[80] During May American forces at Sackets Harbor increased, and when Lieutenant-Colonel Electus Backus arrived with almost 400 unmounted 1st U.S. Light Dragoons and another 250 men of the 1st and 9th U.S. Infantry, bringing the total assembled to around 4,500 men, Chauncey could delay no longer. He weighed anchor on 23 May, but adverse winds prevented his arrival at Four Mile Creek for two days. Meanwhile American gunners across the river from Fort George opened fire on Newark on the 24th. John D. Carroll was a young boy and years later remembered

> a crashing sound went through the house; it was a cannonball which passed through both walls of the room we were in, over our heads. Mother, who had been several years in a state of religious melancholy, so that she largely omitted her old-time care for her family; now, to use her own words, "ceased caring for her soul and commenced caring for her children." The war cured my mother.[81]

They fled. The following day Chauncey came up to add his ships' broadsides to the barrage and provide cover for a landing.[82] The first wave was led by Colonel Winfield Scott to take the fort in the rear, followed by a second and third under Brigadier-Generals John Boyd and William H. Winder. Winder was a prominent Baltimore lawyer and had commanded a regular regiment raised in that city, while Boyd had served as a lieutenant in the regular army from the end of the Revolution to 1789, and then as a mercenary in India for nineteen years, returning to the U.S. Army in 1808 as a colonel and leading the 4th U.S. Infantry at Tippecanoe. But he was not highly regarded by his peers or subordinates; Major-General Morgan Lewis, now commanding the Niagara front, said he was "better adapted to the bully of a brothel than to a soldier."[83]

"It was a grand and imposing sight," recalled Captain Ephraim Shaler of the 25th U.S. Infantry, "to see 180 boats carrying in all about 3,000 men, gliding swiftly over the blue waters to meet in a few minutes in deadly combat the proud sons of Britain." Once they landed, the Americans encountered a steep embankment.[84] Heavily outnumbered, Vincent had deployed Lieutenant-Colonel Christopher Myers with some 600 men to meet this threat, but they came under intense fire from up to twenty-four guns mounted on the American ships, which "kept up a steady fire with grape and cannister, until the boats had got in-shore and were engaged with the enemy," recalled Ned Myers.[85] Another American officer described the scene as they splashed ashore: "Some of the regiments, when they had reached the crest near enough to aim over it, halted as it were behind a breastwork, poured in a volley among the trees, which were as red with the enemy as if a fire were spreading through the underbrush."[86] Vincent was forced to order a retreat to the south after suffering heavy casualties: 52 dead and 306 wounded or missing, against 40 dead and 113 wounded Americans.[87] Also taken were Burgoyne's four brass pieces lost at Detroit the previous year, and Scott was keen to begin a pursuit when he was ordered by Lewis to return to the fort.[88] The loss of Fort George exposed the entire British line on the Niagara, and Vincent ordered its abandonment from Queenston to Fort Erie, positions eventually occupied by the Americans. But although the United States now controlled the entire frontier, they failed to follow up their victory, and Vincent regrouped at Burlington Heights (now modern Hamilton) at the western end of Lake Ontario.[89]

Having confirmed Chauncey's absence, on the morning of 29 May the British counter-attacked at Sackets Harbor. Prevost later claimed that "light and adverse winds" prevented the squadron from approaching the fort earlier to attack before dawn.[90] Yeo, however, with prior experience of combined operations, disagreed. He knew that conditions were never perfect and that keeping troops cooped up onboard would do them no good: but he was only the naval commander.[91] At least the Mohawks and Mississaugas accompanying the British were able to attack a flotilla of *bateaux* carrying elements of the 9th and 21st U.S. Infantry, 115 of whom chose to surrender to the British squadron rather than risk massacre. Next morning Yeo's fleet landed 750 men under Colonel Edward Baynes—a 27-man detachment of 1st Royal Scots, two companies from the 1st/8th, the Grenadier Company of the 100th, and four companies of the 104th Regiment, one company of Glengarry Light Infantry, two companies of Voltigeurs Canadiens, and a section of two 6-pounders—at dawn on Horse Island, a wooded area joined to the mainland by a neck of sand and gravel. The defenders immediately to hand under Backus numbered over 700 regulars, some 200 sundry shipyard workers and marines, and 700 New York militia, with the militia drawn up to repel a landing until the bayonets of the British struck fear into them.[92] As they approached Horse Island the British came under heavy fire; Lieutenant John Le Couteur saw a *bateau* split by roundshot and quickly sink, but the grenadiers in it "behaved admirably, raised their firelocks high, and could just touch the bottom. We little fellows would half of us [have] drowned."[93]

When the British landed, the American militia took to the woods in confusion and remained there until the action was over, but the regulars made good use of the cover provided by their well-prepared defensive works to maintain a sharp fire on the attackers throughout, and as Midshipman John Johnston RN recalled, "the country being woody, their riflemen picked us off without being perceived."[94] Meanwhile a continuing onshore breeze prevented Yeo's ships from getting close enough to batter the defenders' posts. "I do not exaggerate," wrote Edward Brenton afterwards, "when I tell you that shot, both grape and musket, flew like hail."[95] The British continued towards Fort Tompkins, and in the confusion Midshipman John Drury USN ordered fires to be set on the dockyard, where a powerful ship, *General Pike,* was under construction; but the British could not penetrate the blockhouses or the fort before Prevost ordered a withdrawal.[96] Prevost has been widely criticized for this move, but he claimed that several American vessels had been sighted and the withdrawal was unhurried, enabling the British force to take away guns and prisoners.[97] Sergeant Comins was not impressed, however:

> We brought all our wounded away it was possible to remove and embarked on board ship tired, hungry, wet and thirsty and looking very sheepish at one another; you would hardly have heard a whisper until that powerful stimulant grog was served out when the Tower of Babel was nothing like it, everyone blaming another, nay some of them were rash and imprudent to lay the blame on anyone but themselves.[98]

American losses were 22 killed, 85 wounded, three 6-pounders, and 154 prisoners, with British losses 47 dead, 154 wounded, and 16 missing.[99]

Sackets Harbor was one of the more confused actions of a confusing war, and Midshipman David Wingfield RN was far from alone in being disgusted by it: "We lost nearly 400 [*sic*] men killed and wounded in this disgraceful affair when, in every probability, the place might have been taken without the loss of a single man had things been conducted as they ought"; and Le Couteur called it "a scandalously managed affair."[100] Later Jacob Brown wrote in his report that Prevost had been on the verge of defeat, and claimed credit that really belonged to Backus, who was mortally wounded during the fighting; Brown was appointed a regular brigadier-general as a result.[101] Chauncey hurried back on 31 May, but despite promising Jones that he would confront Yeo on the lake if Yeo came to meet him, he remained the entire month at Sackets Harbor waiting on a new ship and writing to Jones, "I trust you will approve of my determination to put nothing at hazard until the new ship is fitted."[102] He was convinced that the attack was the result of information given to the British by Samuel Stacey and recommended that Stacey be hanged. But Jones disagreed because Stacey was a civilian and therefore could not be treated as a spy. And by choosing to remain at anchor, Chauncey handed control of Lake Ontario to the British, who were already benefiting from his absence.[103]

ON LAKE CHAMPLAIN the Americans held the balance of power until the middle of the year, when on 3 June Lieutenant Thomas Macdonough, commanding the American flotilla, ordered Lieutenant Sidney Smith USN to patrol the northern reaches with *Eagle* and *Growler* (both 11).[104] Unfortunately, the over-eager Smith sailed into the shallow waters of Isle-aux-Noix, a garrison commanded by Major George Taylor with six companies of the 100th Regiment and a Royal Artillery detachment, where he found he could not manoeuvre to withdraw. The British mounted 6-pounders in gunboats rowed by infantry that were too low in the water for the Americans to engage effectively, while more infantry engaged the ships from the shore for three hours wherever they came in range, and "they kept up a continual fire upon us," recalled Private Joseph Penley of the Maine Volunteers, "their bullets whistling through the sloop's rigging and against her sides like hailstones."[105] Eventually, recalled his comrade, Captain Daniel Holden, "The only alternative was to surrender at discretion or cause the enemy to purchase what they must eventually get at the price of blood."[106] The Americans lost one dead and eight wounded and the British three wounded; once refitted, the vessels were renamed *Broke* and *Shannon,* and control of the lake passed to the British, depriving the Americans of an important supply route and securing essential British trade with the farmers of Vermont. The Champlain Valley in particular was orientated to Canadian markets, and throughout the summer smuggling was rife.[107]

The British loss of Fort Erie had also uncovered Perry's vessels at Black Rock, the brig *Caledonia,* three schooners—*Somers, Trippe,* and *Ohio*—and a sloop, *Amelia.* What followed was the first instance of "Perry's luck," as they were greatly outnumbered and outgunned by the British Lake Erie squadron. But departing on 14 June and hugging the southern shore, Perry managed to bring them safely to his base at Presque Isle Bay four days later, a difficult task made possible only by 200 soldiers supplied by Dearborn.[108] Meanwhile Yeo sailed on 4 June to harass Lewis at the other end of Lake Ontario and to take stores and 200 reinforcements to Vincent.[109] Lewis had finally recognized his error in failing to pursue Vincent towards Burlington, but not until 1 June did he order two brigades—some 2,600 men—to pursue under Winder and Chandler. Neither had much military experience, and when about half the American force camped at Stoney Creek 7 miles from the British position on the night of 4 June, Ensign Joseph H. Dwight of the 13th U.S. Infantry noted: "we saw the blessed effects of having plow-joggers for generals whose greatest merits consist of being warm partisans and supporting the administration right or wrong."[110] According to Sergeant Comins, Captain H. B. O. Milnes (Prevost's aide-de-camp) dressed in mufti and took a waggon-load of potatoes to sell to the Americans, thus gaining an idea of their dispositions.[111] The Americans were taken by surprise the morning of the 6th after Lieutenant-Colonel John Harvey had made a reconnaissance and found them badly deployed with few sentries, although the Americans were not wholly unprepared.[112] Harvey told Vincent that a night attack would be easy to mount from the surrounding forest, and Vincent agreed to send Harvey the following night with 700 men—about half his total from the 8th and 49th Regiments. Led by a militia scout, Private Billy Green, and having learned the American password from a paroled prisoner, they were able to bayonet or capture the American piquets and achieved complete surprise as they burst into the centre of the camp.[113]

However, illuminated by the camp fires the British were soon under a heavy fire, and the fight quickly degenerated. At one point Harvey rode up to an American battery and then galloped away towards the British side. But when the American artillery commander, Captain Nathan Towson, gave the order to fire, nothing happened. At first he suspected that his guns had been spiked through treachery, but the problem proved to be no more than damp powder, and they were soon in action.[114] Lieutenant William H. Merritt heard "our men set up a tremendous shout, which continued along the whole line, and was the cause of throwing the enemy into the greatest disorder and confusion imaginable."[115] Private Elihu H. Shepard of the New York militia also heard the British shouting,

> Indians yelling, arms clashing, men screaming, begging, groaning, dying, swearing and fighting . . . our men and the British commingled; some holding each other fighting, stabbing and cutting; others with clubbed muskets thrashing the enemy down with buts [*sic*]; others running or trying to run across a stream and all making the most hideous and indescribable noise possible.[116]

Eventually the Americans retreated in disorder, during which Chandler was taken prisoner after being dumped by his horse in the middle of a party of British. Winder was about to offer his pistol in surrender when Sergeant Alexander Fraser of the 49th charged his bayonet at him and cautioned: "If you stir, Sir, you die." Winder dropped the pistol and his sword and replied, "I am your prisoner." This was very wise: Fraser had already bayonetted seven of the enemy and his younger brother beside him four.[117]

Colonel James Burn of the 2nd U.S. Light Dragoons took command of the remnants and decided to withdraw to Forty Mile Creek (modern Grimsby), but the British had suffered serious losses—23 dead, 136 wounded, and

55 missing, to 55 Americans dead and 100 missing.[118] They had, however, secured the position together with 500 tents, 200 camp kettles, 140 barrels of flour, plus muskets, horses, boats, and assorted public and private baggage.[119] The army daily expected a clash between Yeo and Chauncey, but Yeo failed to locate his rival and had to be satisfied with taking merchantmen—three schooners, two sloops, and a raft—and plundering American storehouses ashore, before returning to Kingston laden with booty.[120] Vincent was also thrown from his horse and got lost during the action at Stoney Creek, not appearing until noon the following day; his failure to pursue the Americans beyond Forty Mile Creek left Lieutenant James FitzGibbon of the 49th Regiment with the impression he was "a feeble man, both in mind and body."[121] But those Six Nations Indians who had been wavering in their support for the British took great heart from the victory and now began to harass the Americans severely.[122]

Dearborn claimed that the local Canadians were supportive of his men, and indeed, Joseph Willcocks, a former member of the Upper Canada legislature, offered to raise a small mounted unit of Canadian Volunteers who acted as scouts that rendered useful service to the Americans in 1813 and 1814.[123] But these traitors gained notoriety by their conduct north of the border, helping identify militia leaders and other prominent citizens who were then seized as prisoners of war. And Vincent also found local support as he advanced to re-occupy the depot at Beaver Dams with the flank companies of the 104th Regiment, a company of Glengarry Light Infantry, and drafts for the 8th and 49th Regiments—a 2nd Battalion of the latter being raised in England on 2 June as a depot unit—and recommending that the balance of the 1st/41st Regiment, its headquarters and around 100 men, join Proctor at Amherstburg. On 7 June Yeo arrived with reinforcements and slipped a schooner into the creek to bombard the American camp. Three days later a raiding party took eighty prisoners and destroyed valuable supplies, and Lewis, already under orders to break the camp, retreated the following morning to Fort George—a position more resembling a prison than a bastion—in such haste that further vast quantities of stores were abandoned.[124]

The Americans also abandoned Fort Erie and Chippawa, and Dearborn sank into gloom, complaining of ill-health and effectively giving up direct command of his army.[125] On the defensive and keen to restore American prestige, Lewis ordered Lieutenant-Colonel Charles Boerstler to lead some 550 men from the 6th, 14th, and 23rd U.S. Infantry with a company of the Light Artillery Regiment equipped with a 6- and a 12-pounder, a troop of

2nd U.S. Light Dragoons, and some 40 volunteers to march 16 miles from Fort George to destroy the forward British position at a fortified farmhouse called DeCou's near Beaver Dams, an area of marsh and ponds near Twelve Mile Creek. It was now that a Queenston farmer's wife and mother of five, thirty-eight-year-old Laura Secord, earned undying fame as a Canadian heroine. After overhearing the plan either from her husband or from Major Cyrenius Chapin, who came to her house with some other officers demanding a meal and talking loudly, this "person of slight and delicate frame" slipped past the American sentries and walked for 20 miles through unfamiliar territory on 22 June to warn Lieutenant James FitzGibbon's company of the 49th Regiment.[126] FitzGibbon listened intently to her information, but he could not know it was true: the frontier crawled with spies, including many who burned the candle at both ends, and he was already appraised of American moves from his own sources. But to make the gruelling trek was testimony to Laura's courage, stamina, and loyalty.[127]

As the Americans approached Beaver Dams at about 8:30 A.M. on 24 June, they saw redcoats in the distance and heard bugles and muskets sound the alarm. Despite losing the element of surprise, Boerstler proceeded anyway until suddenly ambushed by 300 Grand River Mohawks led by a Frenchman, Captain Dominique Ducharme, joined by 100 more led by Captain William Kerr.[128] Major Isaac Roach, whose company of 23rd U.S. Infantry was near the rear of the column, watched the dragoons charge, but the Mohawks fired a "smart volley," and the dragoons retreated, plunging through Roach's line and "knocking down and breaking about one third in each platoon."[129] The Indians promptly scalped the dead. A firefight then developed, with Boerstler resorting to bayonet charges to drive the Indians off. During a lull the Americans loaded their waggons with wounded and prepared to issue a whiskey ration, but could not do so before the Indians renewed their attack. The Americans became increasingly anxious as their ammunition dwindled, and Boerstler sent forward a flag of truce to negotiate a surrender, but the Indians kept firing: the only reason Ducharme did not accept their surrender was his inability to speak English.[130]

The Indians themselves were beginning to drift away some three hours after the fight had begun when they were reinforced by FitzGibbon's company across the American line of retreat. Although the British and Indians were now heavily outnumbered, FitzGibbon rode forward under a flag of truce and, exaggerating the size of his force, persuaded the Americans to surrender. When a subordinate made a suggestion that would enable the Americans to see the small size of his company, FitzGibbon said loudly: "Do you think it prudent to march them through with arms in their hands in the presence of the Indians?" Fearing a massacre, Boerstler demanded that the Americans be allowed to lay down their arms immediately and duly surrendered 462 men to 47.[131] "Not a shot was fired on our side by any but the Indians," wrote FitzGibbon, giving credit where it was due. "They beat the American detachment into a state of terror, and the only share I claim is taking advantage of a favourable moment to offer them protection from the Tomahawk and the scalping knife."[132] Casualties among the Indians are unclear; up to 20 dead and 30 wounded. Besides prisoners the Americans lost 30 dead, 70 wounded, their guns, and the colours of the 14th U.S. Infantry, but later the Indians complained about not receiving the praise or presents due to them for this victory, and many went home before the British made belated efforts to pay them prize money.[133]

Towards the end of the month Yeo tried a sneak raid to attack Chauncey's squadron at anchor and get at *General Pike,* which had survived the fire in Sackets Harbor dockyard, and which he knew would give Chauncey the upper hand on Lake Ontario. Unfortunately, having landed and camped in a nearby forest on 30 June, when roll-call was made the next morning it was discovered that two men of the 100th Regiment had deserted, and with security compromised the raid was cancelled.[134] Nevertheless, the British now held the initiative and took the war to the Americans all along the Niagara. On 5 July a party of militia attacked Fort Schlosser and made off with the supplies there, and three days later Indians attacked and killed all but 5 of 39 Americans under Lieutenant Joseph C. Eldridge sent out from Fort George to relieve the guard.[135] De Rottenburg's arrival also took effect as he countermanded Vincent's recommendation and Prevost's directive; he scuppered any hopes of Proctor and Barclay for additional support to the Right Division and detained the balance of the 41st Regiment on the Niagara frontier, causing Proctor to complain directly to Prevost.[136] He also continued to send raids against the Americans; when they abandoned Fort George the British had buried a large cache of medicines nearby, which were now in such short supply that they sent a detachment to dig them up. This involved approaching perilously close to the fort, and a skirmish ensued, but they came away with the precious cache.[137] De Rottenburg's justification was an operation a week later, when another British force of 300 regulars and 40 militia burned the military post at Black Rock, set fire to the barracks, and ate breakfast at Peter B. Porter's house before carrying off more supplies. Porter rallied the militia and Tuscarora Indian allies of the Americans, attacking the British as they were re-embarking and subjecting them to a withering fire as they floated downriver. During the retreat, which was delayed in order to bring away 123 precious barrels of salt, then extremely scarce in Upper Canada, the British lost 13 killed and about the same number missing, with 27 wounded, including Lieutenant-Colonel Cecil Bisshopp, who died five days later, not yet thirty years old.[138] Both raids were designed to force the Americans to abandon Fort George or to overextend themselves, and Armstrong could not disguise his "*surprise* occasioned by the *two escapes of a beaten enemy;* first on the 27th ultimo [Fort George] and again on the 6th instant [Stoney Creek]." On 6 July he finally relieved Dearborn of his command.[139]

7

Raids and Blockades

The bold Chesapeake
Came out on a freak,
And swore she'd soon silence our cannon;
While the Yankees in port
Stood to laugh at the sport,
And see her tow in the brave Shannon.

Quite sure of the game,
As from harbour they came,
A dinner and wine they bespoke:
But for meat they got balls
From our staunch wooden walls,
And the dinner engagement was—Broke.

—Anon., "Impromptu"

BETWEEN 1689 and 1815 Britain fought eight wars with France, and in every one the primary strategic aim was the protection of the British Isles from invasion.[1] Until Wellington's army crossed the Pyrenees in early 1814, the British never seriously contemplated invading France, and even then they could do so only as the vast armies of Britain's continental allies pressed Bonaparte's shrinking army back onto France's eastern borders. Not surprisingly, just as blockade was the cornerstone of British naval strategy against France, so it became the cornerstone of British strategy against the United States. But no sea power can ever guarantee the absolute success of a blockade, and with most of the Royal Navy's ships operating around Europe, the maintenance of a close blockade was practically impossible; it would always require far more ships than were available, especially since some vessels would always need to return to port for repairs and replenishment, so that even British strength could not hope to close every nook and mouse-hole along a coast as long and complicated as America's.[2]

The Royal Navy had learned during the Revolution that it was impossible to maintain the north-east coast of the United States under continuous blockade during the winter because the strong prevailing westerly winds kept blowing them off station; they therefore expected the U.S. Navy to try to break out of these ports during foul weather. In December 1812 the US Brig *Argus* (20) returned to New York after nearly running foul of the frigate HMS *Dragon* (38) in a moonlit chase, when "no smuggler or wrecker ever more devoutly wished the moon extinguished than did the crew," who were saved by a sudden squall the following morning.[3]

Neither Boston nor Narragansett Bay could be closely and continually blockaded on "dark blowing nights," and in blizzards there was always the chance that sloops or frigates would slip out to sea; in the spring of 1813, according to Captain Thomas Capel RN, *Shannon* and *Tenedos* (38) were "invariably as close off the port of Boston as the circumstances of the weather would permit, but the long continued fogs on this part of the coast at this season of the year give the enemy great advantage."[4] But the Royal Navy also knew that the southern portion of the coast was not subject to these westerlies, and could be successfully contained.[5] This Warren had proceeded to do from Charleston south to Spanish Florida from the autumn of 1812, and in March 1813 the blockade was extended to the Chesapeake and Delaware Bays and to other ports and harbours in the southern and middle states, becoming practically complete. Lieutenant Charles Loftus RN was aboard *Poictiers* blockading the Delaware; after three weeks of inactivity an expedition was sent by boat to capture a schooner that was believed to be fitting out as a privateer, but finding "she was nothing more than a coasting vessel, loaded with cheeses, hams and all sorts of marketable produce . . . [we] quickly cleared her of all her cargo."[6] But it was never possible to close every single cove and river mouth, and Warren did not formally proclaim the extension until 16 November 1813, eight months after receiving the directive from London.[7]

In the autumn of 1812 the U.S. government decided to put strong squadrons to sea, including the Pacific, in order to disrupt the British whaling fleet and other commerce. Command was given to Commodore William Bainbridge USN, who had succeeded Hull on *Constitution,* to be accompanied by *Essex* and *Hornet* under Master-Commandant James Lawrence USN. They would rendezvous off the coast of Brazil, whither Porter's *Essex* departed on 27 October 1812 from the Delaware River, the other two leaving Boston on the 30th.[8] But when the latter pair arrived they found no sign of *Essex,* and Bainbridge ordered *Hornet* into San Salvador on 13 December to make inquiries as Bainbridge absurdly challenged HMS *Bonne Citoyen* (20) to fight *Hornet.* Captain Pitt Barnaby Greene RN wisely refused; she was carrying £500,000 worth of gold and silver, and *Constitution* stood some 30 miles off the coast. At 2 A.M. on 29 December she was spotted lying hove-to by HMS *Java* (38), which was convoying Lieutenant-General Thomas Hislop, the new governor of Bombay, with his entourage to his posting. *Java* was formerly the *Renommée* out of Toulon, captured in February 1811; her crew was raw in the extreme, with 23 boys, 60 Irish landmen, and 50 seamen suspected of mutinous intentions. Indeed, fewer than 50 of the 300 had ever been in action, and Captain Henry Lambert RN had only 8 volunteers from HMS *Rodney* who were real sailors; having taken the American merchantman *William,* he had lost his master's mate and 19 men to form a prize crew, although by now the East Indiamen he was convoying felt safe enough to proceed alone.[9]

The two ships made recognition signals which neither could recognize, and *Constitution* wore away with *Java* in pursuit under a press of sail. With the wind and sea coming up at 1:40 P.M., *Constitution* shortened sail and hoisted her colours. The action began at 2:10 P.M. with *Java* closing and firing an effective broadside that took away the wheel and killed four Americans while *Constitution* tried to wear away and increase the range. More broadsides were exchanged, and *Java* passed close under *Constitution*'s stern, although instead of a devastating broadside she managed only one shot, probably because her inexperienced gunners had not reloaded in time. But she gained another chance when *Constitution* wore away again and this time was more successful. By 3 P.M. *Java* had given a good account of herself, but Bainbridge decided to close and gave her a serious pasting from his well-served guns, seriously damaging *Java*'s rigging and taking out the foremast, which smashed the forecastle and blocked the deck. Now *Java* was subject to a tremendous fire of all arms, and at 3:30 P.M. Lambert was mortally wounded by a musket-ball, with command devolving on Lieutenant Henry Ducie Chads RN, who was also wounded but kept the deck. At 4 P.M. the mizzen-mast went, but the two ships fell away, and *Java* gave one of her best broadsides yet, although her gunblasts set fire to the wreckage hanging down her side. When *Constitution* pulled away to deal with her own wreckage, the crew of *Java* cheered, thinking she was retreating. They managed to rig some sails to the stumps of her spars and got under way as *Constitution* came in once more, both sides trading shot for shot; but by 6 P.M. *Java* was little more than a hulk and, feeling "that on having the great part of our crew killed, our bowsprit and three masts gone, several guns useless, we should not be justified in wasting the lives of more of those remaining," Chads ordered the colours to be struck. They had suffered 124 casualties against 34 in the *Constitution,* according to Bainbridge's account, although the British officer prisoners estimated American deaths at 52.[10]

With *Java* sinking, Bainbridge ordered all the prisoners and their baggage to be transferred in the only one of his eight boats capable of taking the water, a process that took a whole day. On 31 December *Java* was set on fire and blew up at about 3 P.M. The officers of *Constitution* were criticized for trying to induce the seamen prisoners to join the U.S. Navy, but in the event only three of the Irishmen were persuaded to do so. Just as *Java* was on the point of blowing up, one of them told Bainbridge that a large part of the cargo was gold bars which he had helped to stow, but after enjoying Bainbridge's discomfort at this news for a while the British officers assured him that the metal was, in fact, copper. Part of the prize was a handsome silver service that Bainbridge graciously returned to Hislop, who returned the compliment with the present of a handsome sword. Captain Lambert died on 4 January 1813, the fatal bullet having lodged in his spine.[11] He was buried at Fort St. Pedor at a ceremony attended by the governor of the fort, but not by the American officers, although Bainbridge wrote to Hislop that although Lambert had been an enemy, he could not

> but greatly respect him for the brave defense he made with his ship; and Commodore Bainbridge takes this occasion to observe, in justice to Lieutenant Chads, who fought the *Java* after Captain Lambert was wounded, that he did everything for the defense of that ship that a brave and skilful officer could do, and further resistance would have been a wanton effusion of human blood.[12]

But although it was another tactical victory, the damage sustained by *Constitution* was so great that it might have been termed pyrrhic. Just as *United States* had been forced to return home rather than track the East Indies convoy, *Constitution* was too badly damaged to continue round to the Pacific, and had to return to Boston for repairs. But *Hornet* continued to blockade *Bonne Citoyenne* until 24 January 1813, when she was chased away by HMS *Montagu* (74).[13]

On 14 February Lawrence took a British packet, the brig *Resolution* (10), and burned her after relieving her of £5,000 worth of specie; he then chased another sail to the mouth of the Demerara River off the coast of British Guiana. This was HM Brig *L'Espiegle* (18) under Captain John Taylor RN, a "fat pursy fellow with shifting eyes," according to Frederick Marryat, who brutalized his crew and stayed ashore rather than accept action.[14] But Lawrence then spied HM Brig *Peacock* (16) under Lieutenant William Peake RN. Known as "the Yacht" from her brilliant appearance, she was, in fact, rotten, and unprepared for a fight. After manoeuvring for position, the two vessels traded broadsides at 50 yards' range, and *Hornet*'s 32-pounders immediately did severe damage while *Peacock*'s 24-pounders cut about *Hornet*'s rigging but largely missed her hull. *Hornet* then got onto *Peacock*'s starboard quarter, where she could fire her full broadside while *Peacock* could reply with only two after guns, whose detachments were soon all killed or wounded. *Peacock*'s topsails and gaff halyards were shot away and the mainsail rendered useless when Peake, already wounded, was cut down by a roundshot. Less than half an hour after the action started and with 6 feet of water in her hold, the senior lieutenant had to wave his hat to signal surrender, as her colours had been shot away with the gaff.[15] Although *Hornet*'s crew worked fast to remove their prisoners and plug her holes, *Peacock* was so badly damaged that she went down with men from both crews still aboard and 9 Britons and 3 Americans drowned. As one officer noted: "If the *Peacock* had been moored for the purpose of experiment she could not have sunk sooner."[16] The British lost a further 9 killed and 28 wounded from 122; the Americans one dead and 2 wounded from 135. Off the West Indies there had been little action for some years, and the loss of *Peacock* was attributed at the court-martial to "want of skill in directing the fire, owing to an omission of the practice of exercising the crew in the use of the guns for the last three years."[17] But equally galling was the news that *Constitution* had managed to slip back into Boston nearly two months after her defeat of *Java,* a failure of the blockade caused by very heavy weather and snowstorms.[18]

Having failed to make his rendezvous four times, David Porter decided to cruise the Pacific alone, a decision made chiefly for reasons of profit and glory, an attempt to emulate Lord George Anson's exploits against the Spanish in 1741–1744. After undergoing initiation into the Noble Order of Neptune upon crossing the Equator, eleven-year-old Midshipman David Farragut, caught chewing tobacco, had a first taste of Porter's discipline; Porter simply put his hand over the boy's mouth and ordered him to swallow. Farragut was never interested in any form of tobacco ever again, but went on to become Porter's favourite middie.[19] On 26 January 1813 *Essex* set off from St. Catherine's, 500 miles south of Rio de Janeiro, making for Cape Horn, a "boisterous and unpleasant" voyage, if not quite so bad as Porter made out in his *Journal,* which Samuel Eliot Morison describes as "a salty narrative . . . the best of the sea literature of the period."[20] In the Pacific Porter and the *Essex* waged almost a separate war for a year and a half. Even though formally unopposed by the Royal Navy, the ship achieved remarkable feats: she went first to the Galápagos Islands and then to the Marquesas, surviving entirely on what she could capture from British prizes in the Pacific, preying notably on the whaling fleet, which was not entirely defenceless, as many were armed and carried letters of marque. Over the next few months Porter took twelve of them—60 percent of the fleet—and recaptured an American whaler taken by a British privateer. They were either overawed by *Essex* herself, by her boats, or by *Georgiana* or *Atlantic* (renamed *Essex Junior*), two prizes armed by Porter. However, none of his prizes reached America, nor did he wreak anything like the $5 million worth of damage he somewhat wildly claimed.[21]

The first moves to combat *Essex* were taken by the Admiralty in March 1813, when it dispatched HMS *Phoebe* (36) under Captain James Hillyar RN to proceed to Rio, with "most secret" instructions for the commander-in-chief of the South Atlantic Station to deal with *Essex.* Among these instructions were some for Hillyar himself that were not to be opened until he was 30 miles south of Rio, which *Phoebe* reached on 11 June; he was to round the Horn and to "totally annihilate" any American fur-trading establishment on the Columbia River so that its place could be taken by the North West Company. But on arrival these orders were superseded by the task of finding the *Essex.*[22] Hillyar left Rio a month after his arrival accompanied by HM Sloop *Cherub* (18) and made the arduous passage round the Horn to begin the long search for the American.

ON 8 FEBRUARY in Chesapeake Bay the frigates HMS *Belvidera, Maidstone* (36), *Junon* (38), and *Statira* (38) put down nine boats with 200 men under Lieutenant Kelly Nazer RN to confront a strange schooner which turned around and tried to flee. Under heavy fire the Royal Navy boats caught up and boarded the schooner, but her crew put up a game fight on deck as well, until finally forced to surrender. The British suffered thirteen casualties, but nineteen of the twenty-eight Americans were killed or wounded.[23] Thus the privateer *Lottery* (6) became the first prize taken by the Royal Navy in the bay, and six days later they took *Cora* (8) and her forty-man crew, said to be the fastest schooner out of Baltimore.[24] But when on 20 February Warren told the Admiralty he needed three frigates and five sloops or schooners plus smaller vessels simply to protect Nova Scotia properly, he was again rebuked for "the facility and safety with which the American Navy has hitherto found it possible to put to sea," although even the Admiralty had to acknowledge the length and complicated nature of the American coast, together with the severe winter weather that made an effective blockade very difficult.[25]

At least the unsuccessful frigate actions aided Warren's appeals for reinforcements, and the Admiralty strengthened its forces in American waters by early 1813 to 10 ships-of-the-line, 38 frigates, and 52 smaller vessels and proposed to send him two battalions of Royal Marines.[26] Among these reinforcements was HMS *Marlborough* (74) under Rear-Admiral George Cockburn—newly appointed at age forty to inject some dynamism into the arena. Cockburn, a Lowland Scot with a high voice, had little regard for the Americans, particularly for the American militia, but in turn he would come to be reviled by them.[27] Yet to fifteen-year-old Midshipman Robert Barrett, Cockburn with his "sun-burnt visage and . . . rusty gold-laced hat" was "an officer who never spared himself, either day or night, but shared on every occasion, the same toil, danger, and privation of the [lowliest sailor] under his command."[28] Cockburn was ordered to Bermuda, where he would be assigned a squadron to take the war into the mid-Atlantic states, the aim of which was to draw off American forces attacking Canada.[29] He arrived in the middle of January 1813 but was unable to meet Warren as previously agreed because *Marlborough* badly needed caulking in the Bermuda dockyard, and awaiting him were orders to proceed to Chesapeake Bay and take command of four other third-rates, *Poictiers, Victorious* (74), and *Dragon* (74), along with seven smaller vessels and an additional four frigates in the bay itself. He was directed to blockade the ports and rivers of the Chesapeake and Delaware areas up to Long Island Sound, capture and destroy shipping, and investigate USS *Constellation* and determine the best means of destroying her.[30]

Cockburn arrived on station on 3 March and was joined ten days later by Warren, who took direct control of operations in the Chesapeake. He approached within 25 miles of Washington but decided he lacked the strength to attack it, and ordered Cockburn to intercept the trade between Philadelphia and Baltimore.[31] Much of the area was uncharted and unsurveyed, but within ten days of Warren's arrival Cockburn produced a comprehensive appreciation of the situation. As the admirals saw things, the Chesapeake and Delaware Bays laid three states open to attack. Cockburn knew that *Constellation* had moved closer to Norfolk, which was garrisoned by at least 3,000 men, and to approach her would be difficult in daylight.[32] One night approach had been made, unsuccessfully but yielding two schooners, and it was clear that vessels of shallow draught were necessary to make a fresh attempt, as were additional troops: he was unaware that the 102nd Regiment and two Royal Marine battalions were currently Bermuda-bound from Britain for this purpose, although it says much for American intelligence that their newspapers already had wind of this development.[33] But already his presence was being felt, he noted, since "the capture of ships so high up one of their rivers and the possibility of similar excursions elsewhere has set the whole country in a state of alarm causing the continuation of hostilities with us to be now as unpopular in this area as it has been in other parts of the United States."[34]

On 3 April five boats under Lieutenant James Polkinghorne RN pursued four American schooners up the Rappahannock, and although the captain of the schooner *Arab* ran his vessel ashore and set her on fire, she was saved and refloated and taken along with *Dolphin, Racer,* and *Lynx,* with 219 men and thirty-one guns, for the loss of one man killed and eleven wounded.[35] Then on 5 April seven more schooners and two brigs were sighted and chased by three of the prizes to a position between the Potomac and Patuxent Rivers. The following morning, in sight of thirty-six enemy vessels ahead of them, but flying American colours, the prizes were offered a pilot, whom they refused, saying they were being chased by the British. Quickly coming up alongside their targets, they exchanged their false colours for British ones and, recalled Lieutenant James Scott RN:

> the broadsides of the schooners opened out upon all around. The scene of dismay, confusion and indecision exhibited onboard the unlucky craft might be compared to the fright of a flock of sheep surprised by wolves leaping suddenly into the midst of them; one endeavored to escape here, another there, but they were speedily stopped by the fire of their unmasked foes . . . The *ruse de guerre* completely succeeded; not one it appeared, entertained the slightest suspicion.[36]

In the Patapsco River more prizes were taken, and throughout these operations the business of surveying was assiduously carried out, so that in time the British would be as familiar with the waters of the Chesapeake as were the Americans themselves.

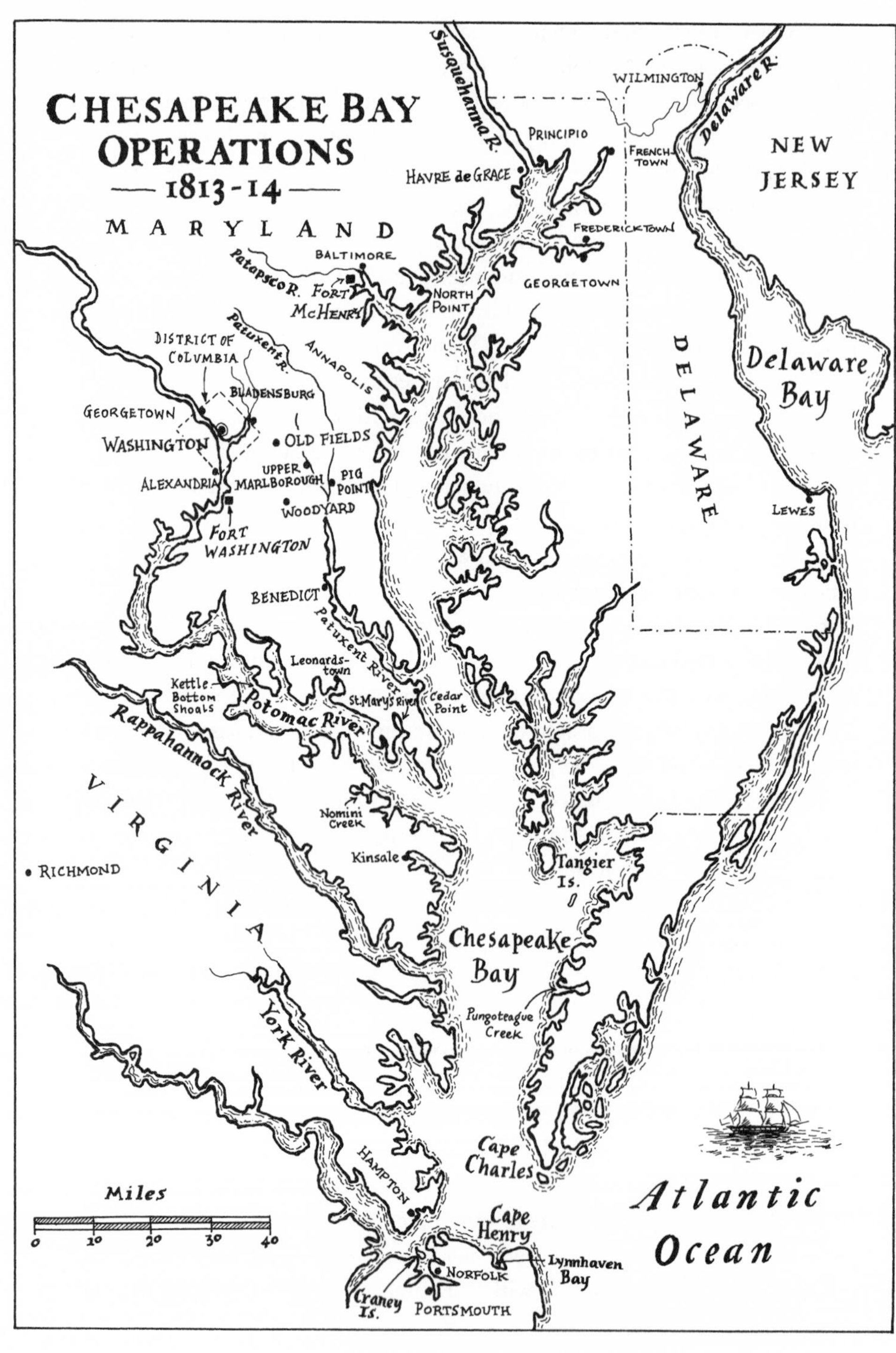

CHESAPEAKE BAY OPERATIONS
1813-14
MARYLAND
VIRGINIA
DELAWARE
NEW JERSEY
Susquehanna R.
Delaware R.
WILMINGTON
PRINCIPIO
FRENCH-TOWN
HAVRE de GRACE
FREDERICKTOWN
GEORGETOWN
BALTIMORE
Patapsco R.
FORT McHENRY
NORTH POINT
Patuxent R.
ANNAPOLIS
DISTRICT OF COLUMBIA
BLADENSBURG
GEORGETOWN
WASHINGTON
OLD FIELDS
ALEXANDRIA
UPPER MARLBOROUGH
PIG POINT
WOODYARD
FORT WASHINGTON
BENEDICT
Patuxent River
Leonards-town
Kettle Bottom Shoals
Potomac River
St. Mary's River
Cedar Point
Rappahannock River
Nomini Creek
Kinsale
Tangier Is.
RICHMOND
Chesapeake Bay
Pungoteague Creek
York River
Delaware Bay
LEWES
Cape Charles
HAMPTON
Cape Henry
Lynnhaven Bay
NORFOLK
Craney Is.
PORTSMOUTH
Atlantic Ocean
Miles
0
10
20
30
40

In April Warren received an important letter from André de Daschkoff, the Russian minister in Washington, offering to act on behalf of the tsar to mediate in peace negotiations.[37] Dispatches to this effect were duly sent via Gothenburg, and, without waiting for a reply from the British, Madison named Gallatin and Federalist James A. Bayard, together with John Quincy Adams—son of the second president, John Adams, and currently minister in St. Petersburg—as peace commissioners, and sent them to Europe.[38] But in the meantime the war continued, and on 6–7 April Lewes, Delaware, suffered a two-day bombardment by a British squadron under Captain Peter Beresford RN, sent by Cockburn to blockade Delaware Bay and River. *Poictiers, Belvidera,* and a schooner demanded fresh provisions from the town and were refused, Governor Joseph Haslet of Delaware being determined to resist. But because so many trees obstructed the view of the ships, very few shots actually struck property, and the final damage was small, some $2,000 worth; the only casualties were a chicken that was killed and a pig whose leg was broken.[39] On 23 April Cockburn's forces seized Spesutie Island, at the head of Chesapeake Bay, carrying off pigs and cattle; the residents fled their homes but returned on receiving assurances they would not be molested.[40]

On 28 April Cockburn attacked Frenchtown, on the Elk River, where a large depot of military and other stores was reputedly kept. Following a brief bombardment from carronades in his boats which silenced the defending battery of six guns, the naval brigade landed aided by escaped slaves who enabled him to move quickly across country, and the militia promptly fled.[41] The valuable stores were destroyed and its guns disabled, while Cockburn paid for the cattle he took, making clear that "I shall give the owner bills on the Victualling Office for the fair value of whatsoever is taken but should resistance be made, I shall consider them as prize of war."[42] The admiral did not mention that such bills would not be redeemable until after the war was over, and Midshipman Frederick Chamier, who watched Cockburn at work in southern Maryland in the summer of 1814, was unimpressed:

> A bullock was estimated at five dollars, although it was worth twenty; and sheep had the high price of a dollar attached to them, they being in reality worth six at least . . . But supposing, and I have seen it one hundred times, that the farmer refused the money for his stock; why then we drove sheep, bullocks, and geese away, and left the money for the good man to take afterwards.[43]

Lieutenant-Colonel Charles Napier of the 102nd Regiment felt similar qualms about this type of warfare:

> Strong is my dislike to what is perhaps a necessary part of our job, viz. plundering and ruining the peasantry. We drive all their cattle and of course ruin them; my hands are clean, but it is hateful to see the poor Yankees robbed, and to be the robber. If we should take fairly it would not be so bad, but the rich escape; for the loss of a few cows and oxen is nothing to a rich man, while you ruin a poor peasant if you take his only cow.[44]

Cockburn announced that resistance would generate destruction but that communities which submitted would be spared. The inhabitants of Havre de Grace, at the entrance of the Susquehanna, chose the latter course. As Cockburn's squadron set off to nearby Spesutie Island to re-form, the overconfident townsfolk hoisted colours and opened fire from the "Potato Battery," so called because of its shape. Reasoning that if a place was worth defending it was worth attacking, Cockburn assembled his boats by night, and on the morning of 3 May the British approached with Congreve rocket-boats in the lead under Lieutenant George Augustus Westphal RN, first lieutenant of *Marlborough*.[45] Although the defending force amounted to about 2,000, recalled Captain Marmaduke Wybourn of the Royal Marines (RM), the Americans were quickly driven from their guns, having

> not the courage to await our attack though perhaps the circumstances of a Congreve rocket having been well directed at the outset put them in confusion. It passed through the Battery and struck a man in the back, when not a single vestige of him was to be found. This tremendous engine of death afterwards struck the ground & forced itself full a mile into the country, tearing up everything in its way.[46]

In fact, this poor man—a citizen named Webster—appears to be the only recorded fatality of this notoriously unreliable weapon during the war, but John O'Neill continued to serve his gun when all the others fled, despite being wounded.[47] He was captured and supposedly threatened with death, having been born in the west of Ireland; but he was later freed, and, as John Scott repeatedly pointed out, American newspaper reports of all these actions were prone to whining self-pity amid massive distortions of reality.[48] Indeed,

Hezekiah Niles went as far as to explain on 4 May 1813 that in war it was "a sound maxim that the truth should not be told at all times."[49]

Soon the roads all around were filled with "flying distressed women and children, half-dressed in every direction, not knowing where to go or what to do, having been stripped of their all."[50] At about noon the Philadelphia-to-Baltimore stage-coach arrived and stopped at the inn before driver and passengers realized they were surrounded by Britons. "Milliners with the latest fashions from Paris, merchants and tradesmen, were alike pretty considerably confounded," recalled Scott, "wondering how we had reached the high road between their two most flourishing and principal towns."[51] Cockburn forbade a pursuit but then learned of the nearby Principia Foundry, one of the largest armament factories in the country. He led a small party against it and destroyed fifty-one large-calibre guns and 130 stands of small arms, adding to the tally five vessels in the Susquehanna and a flour depot.[52] Cockburn noted that the Americans

> took every opportunity of firing their rifles from behind trees or haystacks, or from the windows of their houses upon our boats whenever rowing along the shore within their reach, or upon our people when watering . . . in short, whenever they thought they could get a mischievous shot at any of our people without being seen or exposed to personal risk in return.

He therefore felt justified in following and publicizing a policy of retribution on inhabitants who treated their dwellings as "a place of arms," and set fire to those houses abandoned by their owners, so that his sailors "soon became experts at the art of burning Yankee property" in order to teach them "what they were liable to bring upon themselves by building batteries and acting towards us with so much useless rancour."[53]

On 6 May it was the turn of Georgetown and Fredericktown, on the Sassafras River, which were first warned by Cockburn's sending forward by boat two Americans to inform them of their fate should they resist. When he then approached and came under heavy musketry fire, his guns and rocket-boats returned fire with rapid effect, and the towns were soon taken, the militia fleeing at the sight of bayonet-armed Royal Marines. "I kept my word respecting the towns," said Cockburn, "which (excepting the houses of those who had continued peaceably in them and taken no part in the attack), were forthwith destroyed, as were four vessels lying in the river, and some stores of sugar, lumber, leather and other merchandise." These raids may have caused indignation, but they worked; Charlestown and others sent deputations to assure Cockburn that no guns or militia "would be suffered there."[54] "On my way from Philadelphia to Washington," moaned Charles J. Ingersoll, "I found the whole country excited by these depredations" as the British moved freely about the countryside for twelve days without meeting effective resistance.[55] Yet despite the opprobrium heaped upon him by the American press, Cockburn operated within the accepted rules of war as they stood at the time.[56]

All along the coast the blockade was now beginning to bite as foreign trade was sharply reduced and customs revenues dried up. "Commerce is becoming very slack," reported John Hollins of Baltimore on 8 April; "no arrivals from abroad, & nothing going to sea but sharp [fast] vessels."[57] And as the lists of American vessels taken grew steadily longer, it was not merely the foreign carrying trade that suffered; en route to Boston alone the following vessels were taken: *Lively* from St. Bartholomew's, carrying molasses and sugar; *New Foye* from New York, with sugar, earthenware, and other items; *Polly* from Charleston, with rice, cotton, shoes, and tanned leather; *Eliza* from Philadelphia, with pig-iron, sixteen 9-pounders, gin, flour, dry goods, and sundry other items. In the first lists published there were 200 other names, and supplementary lists were published every month.[58]

Not all American trade suffered, however. In early January *The Times* had reported that in the first twenty-five days of December 1812 no fewer than 116 American ships had entered the Tagus, bringing an estimated 148,000 barrels of flour, 100,000 bushels of wheat, and 24,000 barrels of Indian corn, leaving Portuguese markets "literally glutted with grain."[59] And although *Chesapeake* had seized *Julia,* an American ship trading with Lisbon under British licence that was ruled illegal intercourse with the enemy by Judge Joseph Story at end of 1812, it was not until July 1813 that Congress finally agreed to outlaw the use of British licences and to treat vessels doing so as enemies with severe penalties, including confiscation of ship and cargo; but in fact by this point the Peninsula army no longer needed American grain.[60] This drawdown in the grain trade pleased the administration, but it failed to stop the supply of provisions to British cruisers off the American coast, a profitable business made easier as British ships disguised themselves as non-American neutrals. Ineffectual general orders were issued to the U.S. Navy to prevent intercourse with blockaders and to be on the lookout for violations under the "specious garb of friendly foreign flags."[61] Madison was especially annoyed by the Royal

Navy's policy of blockading the mid-Atlantic and southern states but leaving New England's ports open to maintain the flow of supplies to Canada and the West Indies.[62] He once more proposed an embargo but got nowhere as an obstreperous and uncooperative Congress showed no enthusiasm for restricting trade, although it was prepared to boost privateering.[63]

While privateering proved troublesome for the British, it was not without cost to the Americans themselves. It skimmed the cream of her seamen away from the U.S. Navy, and because privateers sought profit above national welfare—they were commercial rivals before they were brothers-in-arms—prizes were sought for their monetary rather than for their military value, so that a fat East Indiaman loaded with spices was more appealing than a coasting brig with 20 tons of Wellington's vital shoes, although there can be little doubt which would have had most effect on the British government. But privateers were hardly alone in this focus; even the Royal Navy had to drop continuous hints to its captains and flag officers to concentrate on military duties and not be distracted by the search for prizes. Another problem for the privateers was discipline, especially in the face of a determined enemy. A privateersman being entered on the ship's rolls in return for a share of the proceeds of the voyage would all too likely claim the rights of a shareholder, and some of them might say even in the running of the enterprise. And while occasionally they would fight desperately, all too often they would give up with little or no fight at all. Only radical measures by the government would have reduced the disadvantages in the system, but the organization necessary was never going to be forthcoming under Madison's political direction. Eventually he persuaded Congress to allow a small incursion by federal forces into the commerce-destroying business, and into the purchase or construction of schooners to be employed as naval vessels for that purpose; but by then it was American commerce that had been effectively driven from the seas, and the scheme came to nothing before the war ended.[64]

Although the opening months of the war brought rich pickings for the U.S. Navy, 1813 proved far leaner, as its ships were mostly bottled up in port. Even those that managed to get out often returned empty-handed as British warships sailed in squadrons and merchantmen in convoys, which by the war's end had reached an unprecedented level of complexity and efficiency.[65] On 23 April Commodore John Rodgers sailed from Boston in USS *President* (44) accompanied by USS *Congress* (36), and in foul weather a week later succeeded in evading the British squadron of *Shannon, Tenedos, Nymph* (38), and *Curlew* (18).[66] American warships were under orders to cruise separately and to avoid contact except in favourable circumstances, their mission being "to destroy the commerce of the enemy from the Cape of Good Hope to Cape Clear."[67] *Congress* had an uninspiring cruise, taking just four small prizes, and returned eight months later to Portsmouth, New Hampshire, where she spent the rest of the war bottled up; but *President* enjoyed a far more dramatic voyage that would cause great embarrassment to Warren. She sailed to the Azores, Shetlands, and Orkneys, around Ireland, and across the Grand Banks and returned on 27 September with a dozen prizes, the last being a former privateer schooner now in British service, *High Flyer* (5), taken off Nantucket on the 23rd.[68] But although *United States* and *Macedonian* managed to escape from New York on 24 May, when they tried to reach the open sea out of Long Island Sound on 1 June with *Hornet*, they were chased into the well-defended port of New London, Connecticut, by a British squadron commanded by Captain Sir Thomas Masterman Hardy RN—Nelson's former flag captain on the *Victory*, who was, according to Lieutenant Henry Edward Napier RN, "an honest, plain, sensible man and good officer."[69] The Americans subsequently had to scurry 8 miles up the Thames to be defended by earthworks dubbed "Fort Decatur" with a huge chain protecting them downriver, where except for *Hornet* they would languish for the rest of the war.[70] Also effectively neutralized were *Constellation* at Norfolk, *Adams* at Alexandria, and *Constitution* and *Chesapeake* at Boston.[71]

Chesapeake was originally laid down as a super-frigate but later finished according to new plans by Josiah Fox equivalent to "the largest size frigates in the British Navy," and, in order to be completed in half the time and at half the cost, built largely with slave labour.[72] James Lawrence was appointed to command her but had trouble finding an experienced crew, as many of her veteran sailors were in dispute over prize money and refused to sign on again, and he had to accept raw recruits.[73] Cruising off Boston were *Shannon* and *Tenedos*, the former having been under Broke's command since 1806 with the benefit of a settled and experienced crew. Broke was so devoted to the concept of single-ship action that he eschewed merchant prizes to avoid having to reduce his efficiency by providing prize crews. Furthermore, he trained his men intensively in gunnery for an hour a day, to operate in perfect silence so that orders could be clearly heard, and mounted a 9-pounder on the quarterdeck specifically to shoot away the enemy's wheel.[74] The men also spent an hour and a half each day on boarding drill, and he had personally directed the mounting of his guns to fire in a single horizontal line, with target practice twice a week—the extra cost of powder and shot coming from his own purse.[75] As *Chesapeake* was preparing to sail, he sent *Tenedos* away and issued a challenge to Lawrence for a meeting "Ship to Ship, to try the fortunes of our respective Flags."[76]

Soon afterwards *Shannon* intercepted a fishing boat whose captain, Eben Slocum, hurled imprecations and shook his fist at Broke, "and he abused our captain very much."[77] Instead of sending the boat on its way, as he normally would have done with such worthless vessels, Broke had Slocum's boat burned. Lawrence emerged soon afterwards—before the challenge arrived—flying a banner that read "Free trade and Sailors' Rights," and made straight for *Shannon.* "The notice of the fight deeply interested our inhabitants," recalled local pastor William Bentley, "who went in throngs to Legge's Hill & the heights . . . Legge's Hill in sight was black like a swarm of bees and we left them eager to follow with their eyes & hearts the Am[erican] frigate."[78] Perhaps it was a case of overconfidence; it was certainly a rash move, given that Lawrence's inexperienced crew had drilled at their guns only ten times since the beginning of May and that his orders were the destruction of British merchant shipping; so engaging a frigate could only hamper this mission, as it would, at the very least, entail returning to port for repairs.[79]

Shannon was running with the wind on the starboard tack, but *Chesapeake* had more way and a slight advantage of position. She tried to cut across *Shannon*'s stern and rake her, but *Shannon* put her helm to starboard, bringing them parallel. William Mindham, captain of No. 14 gun, had orders to open fire when his gun would bear on *Chesapeake*'s second main-deck gun port.[80] *Chesapeake* having more way on her, he did so at 5:50 P.M., and, recalled G. Raymond, then a mate awaiting a lieutenant's commission, "as she came up we delivered all our starboard guns into her bows as they bore."[81] *Chesapeake* fired similarly as her guns bore; then all the carronades that could be brought to bear were fired. Charles Reece Pemberton eloquently described a naval gunfight as a

> leaping, tugging, clattering of ropes and grumbling of blocks as if the tenants of the lower regions, black from the smoke, had broken loose and gone mad . . . smoke bursting forth from the many black iron mouths and whirling rapidly in thick rings, till it swells into hills and mountains, through which the sharp red tongue of death darts flash after flash, and mingling fire and smoke slowly rolls upward like a curtain, in awful beauty, and exhibits the glistening water and the hulls of the combatants beneath; while the lofty mastheads and points of yardarms seem as if cut

> away from the bodies to which they belong, and sustained or resting on the ridges of the dense massy vapors alone.[82]

Shannon had the better of this exchange. Lawrence was careless: neither he nor his first lieutenant noticed that the boatswain had failed to sling the topsail yards when clearing for action. One of *Shannon*'s first shots cut the foretopsail tie, and the yard came down with a run; *Chesapeake* luffed into the wind and was repeatedly raked, with her officers cut down.[83] Lawrence was hit in the leg by a musket ball early on, and the first and fourth lieutenants and marine officer were all struck down. As Lawrence ordered his men to prepare to board, he was hit again in the groin and had to be carried below. Broke's 9-pounder destroyed *Chesapeake*'s wheel, causing her to luff further, and though Broke wanted to manoeuvre away to continue the damage at range, a round cut his jib-sheet, and *Chesapeake* crashed into *Shannon* about 50 feet below the bow. Broke immediately led his men to board the American as a British grenade exploded an arms chest on the American quarterdeck. As Raymond noted,

> we boarded from the fore-top, fore-chains, and starboard gangway; and the Americans did not, in my opinion, attempt to come up. We met only a few. One thing we certainly had the advantage. She [*Chesapeake*] being a flush vessel, they could only get up the fore and after hatchways. The after was on boarding immediately secured, and therefore they were compelled to go forward; but could not muster enough to face our brave fellows who followed, sword in hand.[84]

Lawrence earned enduring fame by uttering the cry "Don't give up the ship!" as he died, but the casualties suffered by his men forced them to surrender.[85] The entire action lasted no more than fifteen minutes, probably less; George Dodd, who was among the crowds that watched the entire fight from the shore, was "of the opinion from every circumstance that I saw, that the Chesapeake was boarded and carried in ten minutes from the time the first gun was fired."[86] With British victory confirmed, all Boston "became one scene of silence and mourning," and the planned victory dinner had to be cancelled.[87]

Losses were heavy: the British had twenty-four killed and fifty-eight wounded, including Broke twice, one of these injuries being a severe cutlass wound to the head. Seaman Charles Roche recalled that night: "The moon shone bright and revealed a horrible sight to the decks, the bulwarks, torn

7.1. *Shannon* returning with *Chesapeake* to Halifax. *Chesapeake vs. Shannon,* painting by J. C. Schetky. U.S. Naval Historical Center.

hammocks and pieces of rope all stained with blood, while there could be heard the groans and cries of the wounded below in the cockpit."[88] American losses were even greater; sixty-one dead and eighty-five wounded. Lieutenant Provo Wallis RN was the only unwounded officer left on *Shannon* and now had the difficult task of taking in the two ships, crowded with dead and wounded on an enemy coast, although both remained seaworthy, and *Chesapeake* was sailed to Halifax in triumph amid wild celebrations from the inhabitants, a town whose economy was booming thanks to the war.[89] Thomas Akins, then a small boy, later recalled: "The upper streets were full of brothels; grog-shops and dancing houses were to be seen in almost every part of town." In the area around Brunswick Street, "nearly all the buildings were occupied as brothels for the soldiers and sailors. The streets of this part of town presented continually the disgusting sight of abandoned females of the lowest class in a state of drunkenness, bare-headed, without shoes, and in the most filthy and abominable condition."[90]

In Britain the public greeted the news with delight and relief; Broke's exploit restored the navy's pride, and some towns celebrated his victory like another Trafalgar: "Captain Broke and his crew," noted the *Morning Chronicle,* "have vindicated the character of the British Navy."[91] Cobbett's *Political Register* declared:

> This is of far greater importance than the victories of Lord Wellington, and as such the public appear to feel it; for every one runs cackling about it to his neighbour with as much glee as a long-married husband carries the news of the birth of his first child. Why there is more boasting about the defeat of one American frigate than there used to be about the defeat of whole fleets. This is no small compliment to the Americans.[92]

Warren offered his congratulation in terms expressing the great sense of relief felt in Royal Navy circles: "At this critical moment you could not have better restored to H.M. Naval Service the pre-eminence it has always deserved, or contradicted in a more forcible manner the foul aspersions and calumnies of a conceited and hostile enemy than by the brilliant action you have just performed."[93] Broke received a baronetcy and the key to London and was showered with gifts from a grateful nation, but he never served again at sea, instead retiring to a peaceful life in Suffolk, where his influence helped establish HMS *Excellent,* the naval gunnery school at Portsmouth in 1830.[94] Lawrence and Lieutenant Augustus Ludlow USN were initially buried at Halifax, escorted by six companies of the 64th (2nd Staffordshire) Regiment; but after the intervention of Captain George Crowninshield of Salem, Massachusetts, Lawrence's body was repatriated and re-interred at a hero's funeral in New York on 23 August, reputedly attended by 50,000 people.[95] "Don't give up the ship!" became a rallying cry for the U.S. Navy, and Perry named his flagship on Lake Erie after him.[96] Ludlow was later vilified, as was acting Lieutenant William S. Cox USN, a young officer who helped carry his wounded captain below; Cox became a scapegoat for the defeat and was branded a coward until a joint resolution of Congress exonerated him in 1952.[97]

ON 5 JUNE the boats of *Victorious* discovered a "powder machine" (a "torpedo," or floating mine) designed by the famous engineer Robert Fulton, "no doubt destined for the *Victorious* or one of the other ships here," Cockburn noted indignantly, "the American government intending thus to dispose of us by a wholesale six hundred at a time," although, he noted, "they will be as likely to come in contact with neutrals or indeed some of their own countrymen."[98] In March Congress had passed what became known as the Torpedo Act, which promised to pay any citizen who burned, sank, or destroyed a British vessel half her value plus half "the value of her guns, tackle, and apparel," a measure that prompted a number of entrepreneurs to try their hands with floating bombs.

On 15 June a New York businessman called John Scudder Jr. tried to sink HMS *Ramillies* (74) by turning the schooner *Eagle* into a floating bomb which was allowed to be taken by the British as though she were a hastily abandoned merchantman carrying flour.[99] For some reason Hardy ordered her away with another prize; when she went up a "body of fire appeared to rise upward of 900 feet into the air, with a black streak on the spout side, and then burst like a rocket."[100] The explosion killed ten and showered *Ramillies* almost a mile away with tar and pitch. The ship had been loaded with explosives and rigged to blow when the cargo was moved, and the incident produced a chorus of condemnation in the British press. Unable to protect its citizens around Chesapeake Bay, the American government decided to fit out some lateen-rigged and oared gunboats under Commodore Joshua Barney. The effectiveness of shallow-draught oared vessels was demonstrated in a dawn raid on 20 June, when fifteen boats from *Constellation* attacked HMS *Junon* in Hampton Roads and were driven off only with the assistance of HMS *Barrosa* (36) and HMS *Narcissus* (32).[101] Throughout the summer the American coast was alive with petty warfare, such as the torpedo supplied by Fulton to the "intrepid, Zealous" Elijah Mix, who tried to attack HMS *Plantagenet* (74) near Cape Henry on 25 July, although he succeeded only in drenching the vessel when the device detonated prematurely.[102]

As the blockade intensified through the summer, British naval power was not only an application of economic pressure, but a means to bring the war home to the people of the United States. Cockburn's success also had other consequences; slaves from surrounding plantations began deserting their owners to join the squadron. Ultimately some 4,000 would gain their freedom this way, giving the British a valuable propaganda tool.[103] Able to provide invaluable local information, they were at first well received, while, unsurprisingly, the locals did all in their power to prevent the exodus of a valuable commodity. When Lieutenant William Stanhope Lovell RN encountered freed slaves the following year he expressed a sentiment common among the British:

> Republicans are certainly the most cruel masters, and the greatest tyrants in the world towards their fellow men. They are [actuated] by the most selfish motives to reduce every one to a level with, or even below themselves, and to grind and degrade those under them to the lowest stage of human wretchedness. But American liberty consists in oppressing the blacks beyond what other nations do, enacting laws to prevent their receiving instruction and working them worse than donkeys. "But you call this a free country, when I can't shoot my nigger when I like—eh?"[104]

On 7 June Cockburn received a letter from an American officer requesting permission to interview runaways and to allow those wishing to return to do so, explaining that if he refused, the Americans would lose their "property." Cockburn agreed, but, unsurprisingly, none of the former slaves chose to return. When a second request was made two days later, he again agreed, although he could not see why the second attempt should succeed any more than the first, and his reply contained a sting: he was happy, he said, to alleviate the sufferings of war, especially for those who had no part in or responsibility for starting it.[105]

In mid-June Cockburn received word that Warren would shortly return from Bermuda with Colonel Beckwith commanding a land force of two battalions of Royal Marines, two Independent Companies of Foreigners—formed from French prisoners of war who had enlisted to avoid the horrors of Dartmoor prison—and the 102nd Regiment.[106] His instructions were to raid with the aim of diverting American forces away from Canada, and not to try to hold ground. In the process all government stores, shipping, and other facilities were to be destroyed. He had specific instructions not to encourage slaves to rise against their owners, but he was permitted to allow individuals to accompany him, and any who assisted him were to be offered the chance to enlist in the West India regiments.[107] With instructions from the Admiralty to find an objective that would help cripple the U.S. Navy, Warren was determined to attack Norfolk, Virginia, where *Constellation* was lurking.[108] A reconnaissance had been made of Craney Island, which dominated the Elizabeth River, defending the approaches to Norfolk, and Cockburn submitted this to Warren and offered to coordinate the attack, but was turned down on the grounds that plans had already been completed and the assault would be led by Captain S. J. Pechell RN of HMS *San Domingo* (74). Beckwith would command an assault force of 2,400 men, including the two Royal Marine battalions with a company of Royal Marine artillery equipped with rockets.[109]

On 12 June the crew of *Narcissus* boarded the U.S. revenue cutter *Surveyor* (6), which resisted so gallantly that when the American captain tendered his sword in surrender, it was returned to him. The British lost 4 killed and 6 wounded; the Americans, 5 wounded.[110] Meanwhile Brigadier-General Robert B. Taylor, in charge of local defences, assembled 737 militia and constructed two batteries on and near the fortified Craney Island, protected in front by a line of gunboats.[111] Private James Jarvis of the Virginia militia recalled that with every "arrangement thus made to defend the post, we waited the approach of the enemy and felt we were prepared to give them a decent reception for the troops were full of ardor."[112] The British plan was to land on the mainland west of Craney Island while 1,500 men approached it in barges. On 22 June the assault went in but ran into so many natural obstacles—sandbanks among the waters and deep creeks on land—and such heavy fire from the defenders that it quickly degenerated into complete chaos, and the British retreated in total confusion, after losing some 16 men killed and 62 missing.[113] Colonel Thomas Armistead of the Virginia militia noted that the British fired several rockets "without the least effect and these instruments of war have ceased to excite the apprehensions of danger which the newspaper accounts of them were calculated to inspire."[114] Afterwards the barge *Centipede,* which had run aground, was given to the militia, although Private Jarvis complained "that she should have been retained as a trophy of the artillery."[115]

On 25 June the British once more embarked to attack Hampton, but this time under Cockburn's direction. The 450 Americans defending could not deflect the 2,000 attackers, who lost 5 killed, 33 wounded, and 10 missing to a total of some 300 Americans, a third of whom were posted as missing but had simply returned home.[116] The British stayed for ten days while the Independent Companies ran amok and subjected the inhabitants to fearsome abuse.[117] "Well!" declared Charles Napier: "Whatever horrible acts were done at Hampton, they were not done by the 102nd, for they were never let to quit the ranks, and they almost mutinied at my preventing them joining the sack of that unfortunate town."[118] The Independent Companies, complained Napier, committed every horror "with impunity, rape, murder and pillage: and not a man was punished!"[119] However, James Scott noted that the American press did not feel restricted to reporting what had actually happened, and while acknowledging the excesses of the Independent Companies he noted: "Never was there, I believe, a concatenation of more monstrous absurdities or glaring falsehoods hazarded on any occasion than that vomited forth by the press of the United States in the affair of the capture of Hampton."[120] What exactly their crimes were is difficult to determine, given the vague generality of British reports and outraged American propaganda.[121] But American protests did result in a British investigation: "The murder of the old *bedridden* Man, and his Aged Wife were but too true, and repeated Circumstances have transpired since . . . to prove it was their [the Independent Companies] Intention to desert as a Body to the Enemy, most probably at the same time murdering Capt. Smith and such of his Officers as had interfer'd, or endeavoured to check their horrid proceedings."[122] Despite being swiftly withdrawn from frontline service to garrison Halifax, their behaviour did not improve. "The Inhabitants of Halifax are in the greatest alarm about these fellows," reported a worried Sherbrooke.[123]

Cockburn transferred his flag to HMS *Sceptre* (74), and a few days later, on 2 July, led another landing force to attack Ocracoke Inlet, North Carolina, a valuable entry point for ships trying to reach Norfolk by inland navigation, where they took a brig, *Anaconda* (18), and a Philadelphia privateer schooner, *Atlas* (10).[124] In addition, some 600 slaves were liberated, although few were willing to enlist in British service and were sent to Bermuda; still, it was a development deeply troubling to southerners. A northern congressman reported: "All accounts agree that [the British] are recruiting rapidly from the Plantations [and] there begins to be loud howling on this subject."[125] But the British were not finished yet: on 12 July the 102nd Regiment made another raid on Ocracoke Island and Portsmouth, North Carolina, where two vessels were captured and cattle and provisions were purchased. Two days later this force entered the Potomac, but with orders not to go above Cedar Point.[126]

At the beginning of August Cockburn established a base on Kent Island, the largest in Chesapeake Bay, where he stayed for three weeks sending out ineffective expeditions; to St. Michael's on 10 August, where they suffered twenty-nine casualties for no return, and to Queenston on the 13th.[127] At about this same time Hardy learned of another plot to blow up British ships off New London, and on 21 August a British naval party raided East Hampton on Long Island and seized Joshua Penny, an alleged plotter, who had previously been pressed into the Royal Navy. "My wife followed us to the door and shrieked; upon which a sergeant of marines struck her with the breech of a gun, the point of which he thrust at her left breast with such force that she is unwell from that cause to the present time." Penny was taken aboard *Ramillies* to be questioned about torpedoes and sent to Melville Island prison at Halifax before being paroled and released nine months later at Salem, Massachusetts.[128]

Cockburn finally returned to Lynnhaven Bay on 2 September, when what was known as the "sickly season" arrived. The unceasing activity of Cockburn's squadron had extracted a price in the health and well-being of his men; rations were always precarious, and the supply of fresh vegetables in particular was very erratic, so that scurvy made an occasional appearance. Now fever took an increasing hold of his force, and it was imperative that it be dealt with. Warren took the prizes to Halifax, leaving Cockburn and his men to retire to Bermuda for a well-earned rest, where they remained for the rest of the year. He was dismayed by the hospital facilities provided in an unsanitary hulk, the *Goree,* surrounded by liquor shops, and he spent much of his time supervising the building of a new hospital on Tatham's Island.[129]

8

Tecumseh's Tragedy

> Where today are the Pequot? Where are the Narragansett, the Mohican, the Pokanoket, and many other once powerful tribes of our people? They have vanished before the avarice and the oppression of the White Man, as snow before a summer sun. Will we let ourselves be destroyed in our turn without a struggle, give up our homes, our country bequeathed to us by the Great Spirit, the graves of our dead and everything that is dear and sacred to us? I know you will cry with me, "Never! Never!"
>
> —Tecumseh of the Shawnees

THROUGHOUT the summer following their victory at Beaver Dams the "Nitchies,"[1] as the British called their native allies, mounted a campaign of sniping and skirmishing against the American posts around Fort George, where the Americans were "panic struck—shut up, and whipped by a few hundred miserable Savages."[2] It was just as well, because the British hated service in the humid Niagara summer, a place, according to John Le Couteur, where "only misery, wretchedness, Broken heads and no honour or credit can be met with."[3] Captain Jacques Viger, in camp at Point Henry near Kingston with the Voltigeurs Canadiens, was disturbed only by false alarms and myriad biting wildlife.

> Sharing our blanket with reptiles of varied species; carrying out the precepts of the most self-sacrificing charity towards ten million insects and crawling abominations, the ones more voracious and disgusting than the others. Phlebotomized by the muskitoes [*sic*], cut and dissected by gnats, blistered by the sand flies, on the point of being eaten alive by the hungry wood rats as soon as they shall have disposed of our provisions. Pray for us! Pray for us! ye pious souls . . . Oh ye gods, what a place this is![4]

Reinforcements trickled in, but few units were experienced. On 5 May 1813 the Régiment De Meuron, 1,100 strong under Lieutenant-Colonel François-Henri de Meuron-Bayard, embarked at Malta and proceeded via Gibraltar to Halifax, arriving on 5 and 6 July, by which time its sister Régiment De Watteville was already at Kingston.[5] The Meurons moved south of Montreal to garrison the fort at Chambly, where they were inspected by Sheaffe, who wrote to Prevost that he was "satisfied with their military appearance; it is weak in officers, but in other respects seems *tout à fait à la hauteur de sa tâche* [well suited to the task]!"[6] It was just as well he was satisfied, as other regiments suffered from desertion: between June and September the 104th Regiment had 40 desertions, including 10 in the face of the enemy.[7] On 7 July de Rottenburg proposed to execute a member of the 41st Regiment for desertion and by September complained bitterly that 5 or 6 men a day were running as the weather continued oppressively hot.[8]

In the early hours of 19 July the American privateers *Neptune* and *Fox* from Sackets Harbor captured the gunboat *Spitfire* and a convoy of 15 *bateaux* carrying 250 barrels of pork, 300 bags of bread, plus ammunition and stores, and defeated the expedition sent from Kingston to recover them two days later in Cranberry Creek, taking over 60 prisoners in the process.[9] But this episode had little significance in the overall conduct of the war along the frontier, and Kingston and the upper St. Lawrence Valley experienced a quiet summer. After success on Lake Champlain in June Prevost was emboldened to minor offensive action and sent the 50-man crew of HM Sloop *Wasp* to man the lake's gunboats. Lieutenant-Colonel John Murray had 39 officers and 907 men of the 13th, 100th, and 103rd Regiments, the Canadian Fencibles and 1st Battalion, Select Embodied Militia, along with 24 Royal Artillerymen and two 3-pounders in two sloops, three gunboats, and a number of *bateaux,* and set out on 29 July to raid Plattsburgh the following day. Major-General Benjamin Mooers of the New York militia was frantically trying to collect men to defend the town but could assemble only one 6-pounder and 300 men, who ran away without firing a shot. The British destroyed the arsenal, a blockhouse, and commissary stores after taking away whatever they could from them.[10] Private George Ferguson of the 100th Regiment and a lay Methodist preacher was among them, and recalled

> a grand wealthy village. The few [people] that remained in it were filled with fear and consternation. Most of the inhabitants had fled, and carried with them as much property as they could. No females in the town

> and everything wore a gloomy aspect. Our men began to plunder all they could get; but I was determined to take nothing. Every eye was upon me, and I resolved that no plunder should be found with me, as so much depended upon our circumspection and watchful piety.[11]

On 31 July Burlington was bombarded by vessels under the temporary command of Commander Thomas Everard RN, who had been seconded from *Wasp* for a fortnight, and who cruised at will, taking a number of lakers.[12] Resident Daniel Coit recalled that the British "shot a number of 24 pdr balls into the village—one struck the roof of a house and lodged in a lower room, which was about all the damage that was done."[13] In August another 800-man force raided Plattsburgh and other settlements around the lake, destroying stores, blockhouses, barracks, and all possible supplies without resistance from the inept local forces.[14]

More significant was the continued rivalry between Chauncey and Yeo on Lake Ontario. Despite having been damaged in the raid on Sackets Harbor, *General Pike* was ready to sail on 20 July, and Chauncey set out with three ships and ten schooners to look for Yeo.[15] On 22 July the brig *Lord Melville* was launched to strengthen Yeo's battle line on Lake Ontario, to which were added several gunboats, and three days later Midshipman John Johnston wrote home to his mother: "You must not expect me back so soon as we expected for we have now a Regular fleet on the lake . . . We are not so numerous but have more heavy Ships . . . We expect to sail in 4 or 5 days to meet the Yankees, as long as the American war lasts we shall keep a Naval Force, as the fate of Cannada [*sic*] depends upon us!"[16] On 31 July Chauncey again raided York, burning storehouses and seizing eleven boats and property including five guns, although there was little public property left. John Strachan's complaint that the Americans were plundering private warehouses of flour was answered with an abrupt declaration that provisions constituted a "lawful prise [*sic*], because they were the subsistence of armies."[17] When Chauncey left once more it seemed likely that the decisive naval engagement to control the lake would finally take place. Yeo sailed from Kingston with his squadron and on 7 August came up to the Americans anchored off Fort Niagara.[18] The American squadron was slightly superior in force but less well handled as a unit than the British. In the long run, neither Chauncey nor Yeo was prepared to take risks to ensure a decisive victory, though both claimed they were seeking action. But whenever they came close, one or the other would avoid it, since both were seeking to fight on their own terms, and these were fundamentally different. The Americans had a significant advantage in long guns while the British had more weapons, but mostly short-range carronades, so that both sides wanted to engage at their optimum range. While not entirely satisfactory, this stand-off at least suited the defensive British strategy, always less concerned with winning than with not losing; and that night the Americans lost two schooners, *Scourge* and *Hamilton,* which foundered in a squall with most of their crews, only sixteen men surviving.[19] Then on 10 August the Americans lost two more schooners, this time to the British squadron in pursuit off Twelve-Mile Creek, when *Growler* and *Julia* managed to become separated from their sisters.[20] However, eight days later the Americans launched another powerful schooner, *Sylph* (16), just twenty-one days after laying down her keel, and the balance on the lake tilted once more.[21]

AMERICAN ascendancy on Lake Ontario increased pressure severely on the British position further west, but it was not until the summer that relations between Tecumseh and Proctor seriously broke down, when they began to disagree about strategic priorities. The British suggested that the Indians quarter themselves in Michigan Territory, where they could live off the land to a certain extent, and that their presence might provide a basis for permanent settlement in the event of peace. Proctor understood the need to keep the Indians onside by taking the offensive, as the Indians contented themselves with raids around Fort Meigs, such as the killing or capture of all but two men in a sixteen- or eighteen-man detail a few miles away on 2 July.[22] As early as 1 June Barclay—whom Tecumseh called "Our Father with One Arm"—had pleaded with Yeo to "see the necessity of sending me a reinforcement of *good Seamen* that by mixing with these [I have] I may be able to perform any service with honour to ourselves and advantage to the Country," and Prevost tried to press Warren on Barclay's behalf.[23] But although he repeated his requests throughout the summer and was supported in them by Proctor, they were in vain, as Yeo had not enough men for Lake Ontario and had also to consider the needs of the Richelieu River and Lake Champlain flotilla, now under Commander Daniel Pring RN.[24]

With provisions in desperately short supply and American attacks in Niagara and on Lake Ontario interdicting his tenuous supply line, and, most ominously of all, with Perry's fleet at Presque Isle threatening to take control of Lake Erie, Proctor bombarded Prevost with requests for support. But within his command he was a poor communicator, and he failed to reconcile his difficulties with the Indians and British subordinates: those officers who were in his confidence knew more than their superiors, and bad relations with the Indian Department hampered communications with the Indians themselves. And Tecumseh, who had a poor grasp of naval and logistical matters, was clamouring for action against Fort Meigs.[25] With the arrival of thousands more Indians—Ojibwas, Sioux, Menominees, and Potawatomis—rallied by Robert Dickson, the pressure on the commissariat became unbearable, and Proctor agreed to invade Ohio once more.[26] On 20 July, with barely 450 regulars and a disappointing number of Indians, he crossed the lake and occupied the old camping ground near Fort Meigs, itself strongly reinforced under Brigadier-General Green Clay.[27]

Although they collected oxen and horses and surprised and killed a small patrol, the siege was pursued half-heartedly; Proctor did not even bother to erect batteries. Reports that Harrison was marching to relieve the post proved false, and a plan devised by Tecumseh to lure the Americans out by staging a fake battle on 26 July failed.[28] The Indians began returning to their villages, and Proctor decided to go down the Maumee and up the Sandusky Rivers to Fort Stephenson (modern Fremont, Ohio) with some 400 troops and 200–300 Indians.[29] Harrison was convinced that this small post on the Sandusky—held by 7 officers and 160 men under twenty-one-year-old Major George Croghan—was indefensible, and sent orders for Croghan to abandon it.[30] But Croghan refused: "We have determined to maintain this place," he wrote to Harrison, "and by heavens we can"; to which Harrison replied that Croghan would be immediately relieved.[31] But Proctor came up on 1 August and made the customary call to surrender, which was refused, and the gunboats *Eliza* and *Myers* began to bombard the fort.

On 2 August Proctor ordered an assault. At 4 P.M. 350 men under Lieutenant-Colonel William Shortt advanced in three divisions towards the fort. The first division, with Shortt in the lead, was so obscured by smoke that it got within 20 yards of the fort before it was detected by the defenders. But here the British reached a ditch, where they were cut down by a concealed gun called "Old Betsy" and Kentucky sharpshooters who, recalled Private William Gaines, "shot through loop holes in the pickets and port holes in the blockhouses."[32] Among the attackers, John Richardson recalled:

> Not a fascine, however, had been provided; and although axes had been distributed among a body of men selected for the purpose, they were so

> blunted by constant use, that it would have been the work of hours to cut through the double line of pickets, even if an enemy had not been there to interrupt its progress. In defiance of this difficulty, the axe-men leaped without hesitation into the ditch, and attempted to acquit themselves of their duty; but they were speedily swept away.[33]

The 160 men of Lieutenant-Colonel Augustus Warburton's division arrived in its position late, after Shortt's column had been repulsed, and advanced along a ravine until it encountered heavy musketry. Private Nathaniel Vernon of the Pennsylvania militia recalled that "our men kept up such a destructive fire that the enemy, unable to breast the storm, broke and fled in the wildest confusion."[34] Most broke for the cover of some woods 300 yards away, leaving Warburton and 3 officers and a dozen grenadiers pinned down 20 yards from the fort, where they remained until nightfall before escaping.[35] The Americans lost one dead and 7 wounded, while after losing 29 killed, 28 missing (mostly killed), and 44 wounded, Proctor was forced to give up the assault and march back to Canada.[36] Croghan then embarrassed Harrison by explaining his insubordination, saying that it would have been more dangerous to follow orders than to stand and fight; Harrison was obliged to reinstate him, and Croghan won the thanks of Congress, numerous swords and medals, and was brevetted lieutenant-colonel, while Proctor was chided by Prevost for "having allowed the clamour of the Indian Warriors to induce you to commit a part of your valuable force in an unequal and hopeless conflict."[37]

In a dispatch that failed to praise a single officer, Proctor blamed the Indians, who had demanded action and then promptly quit the field when the fighting began, concluding: "A more than adequate Sacrifice having been made to Indian Opinion, I drew off the brave Assailants."[38] The Indians were equally scathing in return. Black Hawk, a Sac chief, later recalled his impression of the white man's fighting methods:

> Instead of stealing upon each other, and taking advantage to *kill the enemy and save their own people,* as we do, (which with us is regarded as good policy in a war chief) they march out, in open daylight, and *fight,* regardless of the number of warriors they may lose! . . . They all fought like braves but would not do to *lead a war party with us.* Our maxim is, "*to kill the enemy and save our own men.*" Those chiefs would do to *paddle* a canoe, but not to *steer* it. The Americans shoot better than the British, but their *soldiers* are not so well clothed, or provided for.[39]

Prevost was dismayed but had no better officer to replace Proctor, and could send no more reinforcements than the understrength 2nd/41st Regiment and a Royal Artillery detachment.[40] But the consequences of failure to support the native alliance adequately were now increasingly clear. Harrison's careful "seize and hold" strategy negated the Indians' strengths as guerrilla fighters and, as they proved unable to defeat his fortifications, removed the opportunities of plunder and personal glory that sustained them; they lacked the stamina and organization to maintain the campaign and were increasingly worried about the plight of their families, now reliant on British provisions.[41]

At Presque Isle over the winter of 1812–13 and into the spring, Perry had pursued a ship-building programme that had produced two new brigs to add to those vessels brought from Black Rock. But he complained bitterly about the quality of his men, claiming that Chauncey was keeping the best for his own squadron.[42] Fortunately Harrison supplied him 130 volunteer seamen from his army, and with these he manned the new brigs, his new flagship *Lawrence* (20) and *Niagara* (20), commanded by Jesse Elliott. Concentrating his nine vessels at Put-in-Bay in the Bass Islands, at the western end of the lake, he could observe the British squadron now anchored near Fort Malden.[43] Surgeon Usher Parsons recalled: "No one who hears me can form any idea of the difficulties encountered in obtaining cordage, canvas, cannon, powder, balls and all other outfits, which were to be brought to Erie, mostly from a distance of four or five hundred miles, over bad roads."[44] "The government was to send iron, pitch and oakum," recalled Perry's shipwright, Noah Brown, "but the roads were so bad that I had almost finished the fleet before any arrived."[45]

Barclay's difficulties made Perry's look trifling, however. Desperately short of personnel (he had 7 Royal Navy and 108 Provincial Marine seamen, 106 soldiers of the 41st, and 54 of the Royal Newfoundland Regiments), Barclay was also a third weaker in vessels that carried far fewer carronades, and was forced to mount guns from Fort Malden on his best ship, *Detroit,* named after the one taken by Elliott the previous October. These guns lacked proper firing mechanisms and could be fired only by discharging a pistol over the touch hole.[46] He also had *Queen Charlotte* (18), *Lady Prevost* (12), *General Hunter* (10), *Little Belt* (2), and *Chippewa* (1). Proctor pressed Barclay to reopen communications with Long Point, where desperately needed supplies of every description had accumulated, waiting for transport along Lake Erie to Amherstburg and Detroit; but the loss of stores from the American raid on York was critical. In April Chauncey had reported finding twenty guns at

York ranging from 6- to 32-pounders and having destroyed $50,000 worth of stores irreplaceable to the British, "for independent of the difficulty of transportation, the articles cannot be replaced in this country."[47]

On 16 July Barclay informed Prevost that he had no seamen, supplies, or ordnance for *Detroit,* and Prevost sent an urgent request to Warren at Halifax for these.[48] Warren, however, was not at Halifax; he was on the Chesapeake, and it was not until late August that emergency measures to send seamen from Halifax were taken. But the British rather more than the Americans understood the fundamental importance of retaining, or at the very least contesting, control of Lake Ontario: defeat on Lake Erie would not result in losing Canada, while Upper Canada would surely fall if Lake Ontario was lost, and they allocated resources accordingly.[49] On 1 August Prevost dispatched to forty seamen who had formed the crew of a troop-ship, but he did not stipulate their use on Lake Erie, so Yeo retained them on Lake Ontario. Bathurst indicated that demands in the Iberian Peninsula meant that few reinforcements could be spared, and Barclay received a final rebuff: "obtain your Ordnance and naval Stores from the Enemy."[50] Barclay also struggled with food shortages as British officials at Amherstburg tried to feed a large body of Indians, including many women and children.[51]

Michilimackinac was even more desperate for food, and on 31 August Proctor sent the schooner *Nancy* loaded with flour—the last support it would receive from its base—with a crew themselves on short rations, and with Captain Richard Bullock of the 41st Regiment to relieve the ailing Roberts of command.[52] By early September the local commissary officer wrote that the Indians were so desperate for food they had "killed working oxen, milk cows, hogs, sheep and even dogs belonging to the inhabitants. They had waited upon me threatening to take me to their camp and there keep me without provisions."[53] Barclay reported "not a days flour in Store, and the Crews of the Squadron under my Command were on Half Allowance of many things." Desperately short of everything and goaded by the army, he decided to "risk everything" to open his lines of communication by challenging Perry's squadron.[54]

During June and July Perry had prepared at Presque Isle while Barclay was prevented by a sand-bar across the mouth of the harbour from sailing in and raking the American ships. Had Barclay maintained a tight, continuous blockade, the Americans could not have risked dragging their vessels across the bar, but he apparently believed the Americans were not yet ready and inexplicably and disastrously left it unguarded between 29 July and 4 August.

Perry took advantage of the gap to drag his vessels across the bar in a remarkable feat using "camels"—watertight boxes submerged beside a ship, then pumped out to help float them in shallow water—to fit them out and sail to take control of Lake Erie.[55] Barclay was effectively doomed to defeat from that moment. His small squadron lacked power, carrying no 32-pounders and fewer than twenty 24-pounders, and though he received 36 seamen on 5 September, including 2 lieutenants, a master's mate, and 2 gunners, his total manpower of 364 included 214 soldiers.[56] He met with Proctor, who pointed out that an attempt must be made to re-open communications, and on 8 September they agreed that all must be risked on a decisive engagement.[57] Perry had nine vessels that carried fewer guns in total, but these included over forty 32-pounders. But Perry also had manpower difficulties: of his original total of over 500 men—some quarter of whom were African-Americans—a fifth were now sick or otherwise unfit for duty; he begged for more and threatened to resign if he did not receive them.[58]

Barclay sailed from Amherstburg at 11:00 A.M. on 9 September, and as dawn broke on 10 September the two forces spotted each other, with Barclay initially holding the weather gauge. Barclay reduced sail to await the American force. Then in mid-morning Perry's luck changed, and the wind backed 90 degrees into the perfect direction for the Americans, who approached in a 2-mile line, *Lawrence* shooting ahead.[59] Although the British opened fire at long range—their only real chance—Perry quickly closed in to make the most of his superior firepower. Perry's ships carried 248 pounds of long-gun power and 1,248 pounds of carronades to Barclay's 196 and 460 pounds respectively. Elliott, however, for reasons that have never been satisfactorily explained, stood off and relied on his long guns.[60] Thus Perry was shorn of close support from his second-largest ship, and the *Lawrence* found herself trading broadsides for two hours with *Detroit* and *Queen Charlotte* in a fight so intense that a Royal Marine who had been at Trafalgar claimed that it had been "a mere fleabite in comparison to this."[61] On *Lawrence* "a shot struck a man in the head who was standing close by" to Seaman David Bunnell, and "his brains flew so thick in my face that I was for some time blinded and for a few minutes was at loss to ascertain whether it was him or me that was killed."[62] After two hours all three ships were seriously damaged, and *Lawrence,* having suffered severe casualties, "presented a picture too horrid for description," recalled Sailing Master William V. Taylor, with "nearly the whole crew and officers all prostrated on the deck, interlined with broken spars, rigging, sail, and in fact one confused heap of horrid ruins."[63]

Yet though his ship was a floating hulk Perry steadfastly refused to surrender and called the walking wounded on deck to help continue the fight; and with the day clearly going against him, he took a decision that Barclay conceded "made a noble, and alas, too successful an effort to regain it."[64] He took a boat and rowed to take command of *Niagara,* which he led back into the heart of the British squadron, taking fire from three ships this time; and when *Detroit* and *Queen Charlotte* fouled each other's rigging, he was able to shoot them to pieces at leisure, and after another three hours the commanders and their successors of all six British vessels had been killed or wounded.[65] Barclay's good arm had been mangled; he had a deep wound to his thigh and several other wounds. Before that, Barclay noted, the "few British seamen I had behaved with their usual intrepidity and as long as I was on deck, the troops behaved with a calmness and courage worthy of a more fortunate issue to their exertions."[66]

Lieutenant George Inglis RN, who took over *Detroit* after Barclay was wounded the second time, noted that once *Detroit* and *Queen Charlotte* were disentangled the former was

> completely unmanageable, every brace cut away, the Mizzen Topmast and gaff down, all the masts badly wounded, not a Stay left forward, Hull shattered very much, a number of Guns disabled, and the Enemy's Squadron raking both Ships ahead and astern, none of our own in a situation to support us, I was under the painful necessity of answering the Enemy to say we had struck, the *Queen Charlotte* having previously done so.[67]

Four of the British vessels struck, and the other two were chased down when they tried to get away. When the victors boarded *Detroit* they found a pet bear lapping up the blood, and Indians who were supposed to be serving as musketeers in the tops hiding in the hold.[68] Sergeant Alfred Brunson later inspected *Detroit* and declared: "Her side next to our guns was so full of balls, shot and holes made by heavy shot that, it seemed to me, a man's hat, laid on her at any place, would touch more or less of them."[69] Losses on both sides were heavy, with 41 British killed and 94 wounded, to 27 Americans killed and 96 wounded. The highest losses were suffered among the crews of *Lawrence* (22 killed) and *Detroit* (13 killed and 38 wounded).[70]

Victory was a tribute to Perry's personal resolution and determination, to the employment of superior resources, but especially to the remarkable work of Noah Brown, whose achievement, wrote Howard Chapelle, "makes some of the modern wartime production feats something less than impressive. The man was tireless and ingenious."[71] On the back of an old letter Perry wrote a note to Harrison: "We have met with the enemy and they are ours: Two Ships, two brigs one schooner and one sloop."[72] In fact, he had taken two ships, two schooners, a brig, and a sloop. As the schooner *Nancy* evaded American militia at the mouth of the St. Clair River on 3 September to escape and begin a furtive new life on Lake Huron, so Lake Erie had been swept clean of British naval forces, and the return mail informed Perry that Madison had been pleased to promote him captain.[73] Yeo concluded that Barclay had not been justified "in seeking a contest the result of which he almost foresaw would prove disastrous," and that Proctor had no need to urge him to "so hazardous and unequal a contest."[74] Yeo tried to blame Barclay for not supporting Proctor effectively and for evading the enemy, and Warren passed this disquiet up to Melville at the Admiralty.[75] But Prevost defended him, and when he was released by Perry to seek treatment for his wounds, Barclay was well received by the inhabitants of Quebec City, who presented him with a gift of plate, largely at the behest of John Strachan.[76] He wrote to his fiancée in London, Agness Cossar, to describe his battered condition, and discreetly offered to release her from the engagement. She replied that if there was enough of him left to contain his soul, she would marry him, which she did following Barclay's repatriation in the summer of 1814.[77] He faced a mandatory court-martial in September that "most fully and most honourably acquitted" him and his surviving officers and men. He considered that the only honourable course of action had been to risk everything; he had Proctor's support and anticipated that of Prevost.[78] "Had I not risked an action," he argued, "the whole disgrace of the retreat of the Army would have been attached to me, and I should have been justly involved in the shocking imputation of Cowardice."[79]

THE BATTLE of Lake Erie was a defining engagement of the war; it made Perry an American national hero and earned him and his men considerable prize money. More importantly, it isolated Proctor's Right Division from the Centre, and Perry could now starve it of supplies: retreat was inevitable.[80] "The Loss of the Fleet is a most calamitous Circumstance," wrote Proctor; "I do not see the least Chance of occupying to advantage my present extensive Position."[81] There was practically no food left in the stores, nor was there cash to pay the troops, who were already in arrears, and having stripped Fort

Malden of guns to arm the fleet and lost over 200 soldiers with it, he was in a "truly alarming" situation.[82] While the total troops under Proctor's command numbered no more than 900, including sick, Harrison had raised more troops and persuaded the governor of Kentucky, Isaac Shelby, to take the field. Known as "old King's Mountain" after a battle he had fought in during the Revolution, the sixty-three-year-old Shelby brought 3,000 Kentuckians with him following a stirring plea to lead them in person, and many brought their horses with them.[83] Of these only 1,200 selected men were permitted to take their mounts into battle under the command of former congressman Colonel Richard M. Johnson, but this resource gave Harrison an added dimension of mobility.[84] Harrison's total force now amounted to around 5,500, and would have been greater except that he had to turn away large numbers of Ohio volunteers for lack of supplies to support them.[85]

Even victory over these forces would not free the lake, and by 11 September, when Proctor knew of the loss of the fleet, with his forces consuming fourteen head of cattle and 7,000 pounds of flour per day, and with the Americans now capable of turning his flank at will, he had no choice but to retreat.[86] But he was gripped by a state of funk. On 13 September he ordered the dismantling of Fort Malden, a move that threw Tecumseh into a "violent passion."[87] Tecumseh was disgusted that with no American troops even in sight and not having lost a pitched battle, Proctor should choose to retreat. It was perhaps unfair to expect him to understand the nature of Proctor's position now that the Americans were supreme on Lake Erie. Tecumseh was certain of only one thing: the British were deserting the Indians just as they had in 1783 and 1794. "Our Great Father, the King, is the head, and you represent him," he reminded Proctor. "You always told us that you would never draw your foot off British ground; but now, Father, we see you are drawing back, and we are sorry to see our Father doing so, without seeing the enemy. We must compare our Father's conduct to a fat animal that carries its tail upon its back; but when affrighted it drops it between its legs and runs off."[88] But the vociferous and humiliating protests of the Indians and the Indian Department were to no avail. Proctor insisted that retreat was the only option, although he did apparently promise to make a stand at the forks of the Thames River as he withdrew along it. He probably had no intention of fighting a major engagement at that point, but he would rather secure his retreat first against a possible flanking move across the lake.

Nevertheless, preparations for the march took more than a week after news of Perry's victory arrived; and as the Americans were reported among the islands in Lake Erie and could be expected any time at Fort Malden, Proctor sent women, children, and stores by boat up the Thames.[89] Even when Tecumseh agreed to accompany Proctor as far as Moravian Town (Fairfield) there was no hurry; ordnance stores were sent ahead, and on 22 September Proctor burned the dockyard at Amherstburg, and the public buildings went up in smoke the following morning. He then marched the 15 miles to Sandwich in the teeth of fierce Indian protests: the Indians also objected to the destruction of bridges in his wake, and such was his indecision that the Americans duly found them intact on their advance. The remaining bulk stores at Detroit were burned on the 24th, and the garrison crossed over the river. Although Fort Malden—symbol of the British-Indian alliance—was fired on 26 September, Proctor was still at Sandwich next day when he heard that the Americans had landed at Amherstburg.[90]

Harrison had reached the Sandusky River on 12 September, when he received Perry's terse message of victory on the lake. He quickly arranged transport for his men to take Fort Malden and sent Johnson with 1,000 mounted Kentucky riflemen to take Detroit. As Harrison's force disembarked at Amherstburg, Proctor made a hasty retreat towards the Thames, taking with him around 1,200 bitter and disillusioned Indians—many were already deserting the cause to try to make a separate peace with the Americans.[91] Apart from 150 Pennsylvania militia who refused to do so, all of Harrison's army crossed into Canada, but he was slow to pursue. He did not expect to catch up with Proctor—erroneously believing that Proctor had 1,000 horses—but Proctor moved in a dilatory fashion, having now lost the confidence of his British troops, as well as the Indians, by showing greater concern for his family and baggage than for issuing the necessary instructions: over the course of three weeks the retreat turned into a rout.[92]

Only on 2 October did Harrison commence the pursuit. Proctor had ignored his promise to fortify the fork of the Thames, again driving Tecumseh into a rage and reducing Elliott to tears; instead he went ahead of the army to reconnoitre the area around Moravian Town while the Indians skirmished with the advancing Americans. Lieutenant-Colonel Augustus Warburton's urgent request for instructions was ignored, and on 4 October the retreat continued, although the column was frequently forced to stop by the numbers of Indian women and children trudging along with it; on the morning of the 5th came news that the Americans had captured abandoned British baggage as well as two gunboats on the Thames River carrying Proctor's reserve ammunition. Proctor's men, who expected to fight at Moravian Town, where the heights were suitable for defence, were met by Proctor 2 1/2 miles short of the village and told that he had decided to face the Americans there, before they were overtaken and apparently because the woods would offer some protection against the American mounted force. Besides, the women, children, and sick accompanying the army were still at Moravian Town. The swampy ground did offer some advantages, and he deployed in two thin lines from the river to a large swamp with his only gun—a 6-pounder loaded with spherical and common case, for there was no other ammunition—on the road alongside the river; eventually his first line comprised some 280 men remaining to him of the 41st and Royal Newfoundland Regiments and 10th Royal Veterans, with some 80 more and a small party of Canadian Light Dragoons in a second line 100 yards behind them across the road and amidst trees.[93]

By this time the 41st Regiment was in a very poor state. All were at least six months in arrears of pay and lacked greatcoats or blankets against the approaching autumn weather; with a growing sick list they had not eaten properly for two days and now stood waiting for three hours, shuffled and reshuffled by Proctor, so that, as Ensign James Cochran noted, "the order of the lines was neither *extended* nor *close* but somewhat irregularly between both, and the trees were rather of a late growth but not sufficiently large to afford protection to the numbers that crowded behind them."[94] Lieutenant Richard Bullock heard the men grumble that "they were willing to fight for their knapsacks, wished to meet the enemy, but did not like to be knocked about in that manner, doing neither one thing nor the other."[95] Proctor also had about 500 Indians—all that was left of their once great force—and these deployed in the woods.[96] Harrison had some 3,500 men, and it took some three hours for them to come up to the thin British line. Harrison did not follow the frontier custom that suggested he use his mounted riflemen against the Indians, who had never developed an effective defence against horsemen; instead he put them in the centre of the line and strengthened his left flank nearest the swamp, with infantry under Joseph Desha, to prevent the Indians from outflanking him.[97] But when the Americans saw the British line, Johnson asked permission to make a frontal assault with his mounted men, and although they were not cavalry, Harrison agreed because "American backwoodsmen ride better in the woods than any other people," he said later. "I was persuaded too that the enemy would be quite unprepared for the shock and that they could not resist it."[98]

The Kentuckians charged, shouting "Remember the Raisin!" Private Nat Crain thought the British line "apparently as cool and collected as if on

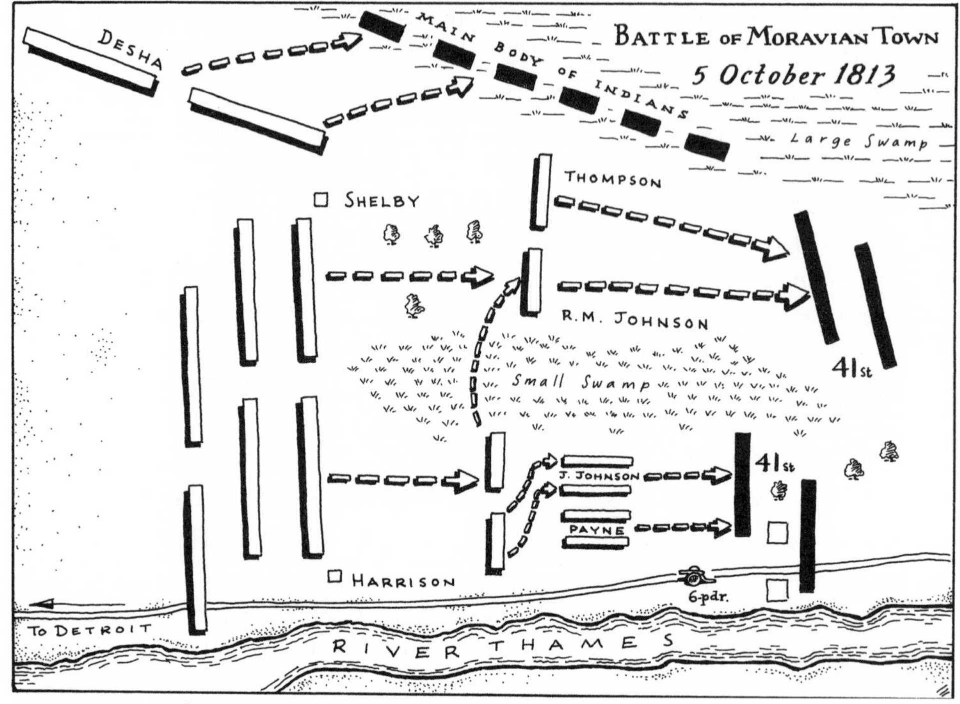

parade, it was a sight well-calculated to cool the ardor of a youngster."[99] But facing them Private Shadrach Byfield recalled:

> The Attack commenced on the right, with the Indians, and very soon became general along the line. After exchanging a few shots, our men gave way. I was in the act of retreating, when one of our sergeants exclaimed, "For God's sake, men, stand and fight." I stood by him and fired one shot, but the line was broken, and the men were retreating.[100]

The Kentuckians easily burst through on the right, suffering only three men wounded. They then dismounted and took the line in enfilade, forcing it to surrender, many like Byfield after firing only once, and the 6-pounder not at all. The second line was quickly overwhelmed, and the battle was effectively over, the British raising their arms in surrender as "passive as sheep."[101] But the Indians bravely fought on as Johnson's men got amongst them, led by Jacob Stucker's company formed as skirmishers on foot. Johnson himself was hit four times but kept his grey mount, while Colonel James Davidson, who led his left-hand column, was hit in chest, stomach, and thigh. As their horses floundered in the swamp many Kentuckians were forced to dismount, but the militia were now coming up to support them. Tecumseh fought and rallied his men until "one of the Big Knives raised a gun loaded with ball and several buckshot and aimed at the left side of the chief's chest and fired."[102]

When the Indians got word of Tecumseh's death, recalled Private William Greathouse of the Kentucky militia, they "gave the loudest yells I ever heard from human beings and that ended the fight."[103] Johnson was later credited with killing Tecumseh, and although this was later disputed he would ride this reputation to the vice-presidency in 1836. But many men claimed to have been in on the kill; how Tecumseh really died and the truth about what happened to his remains have been subject to conjecture ever since.[104] Certainly the Americans took clothing, hair, and patches of skin from what they believed to be his body; one veteran later recalled that "I [helped] kill Tecumseh and [helped] *skin him,* and brot [*sic*] two pieces of his yellow hide home with me to my Mother & Sweet Harts."[105] In total the Americans lost just 7 dead and 22 wounded, although 5 of these later died of wounds; the British suffered 18 dead, 25 wounded, and 591 taken prisoner. The Americans counted 33 Indian dead on the field, but others may have been carried away, possibly including Tecumseh.[106] "Having in vain, endeavoured to call the men to a sense of duty," complained Proctor afterwards, "and having no chance by remaining but of being captured, I reluctantly quitted the ground and narrowly escaped being taken by the enemy's cavalry."[107] He made off with 246 men to the head of Lake Ontario, where he was eventually joined by around 2,000 Indians, mainly women and children, leaving the Detroit frontier in American hands.

Among those pursuing him was Captain Stanton Sholes of the 2nd U.S. Artillery, who enjoyed "a very pleasing ride to Detroit in Proctor's carriage. I found a hat, a sword, and a trunk partly filled with letters mostly by Proctor's wife to her darling Henry."[108] Given his reputation among the Americans, Proctor may have been glad to have got away: for several months following the victory, twenty-three British officers were held at Frankfort penitentiary in close confinement with thieves, rapists, and murderers, victims of a change in policy from earlier in the war in retaliation for British treatment of the twenty-three disputed "British" prisoners taken at Queenston the previous year.[109] In response Madison had ordered confinement of the same number of British prisoners, and Prevost responded by ordering the confinement of another forty-six Americans, in turn equalled by Madison, a situation that

8.1. The death of Tecumseh. *Battle of the Thames,* lithograph by William Emmons. *Source:* Library of Congress, Prints and Photographs Division.

inflicted great suffering on prisoners of both sides. At the outset of war the United States had no policy for prisoners, and although many were exchanged or paroled through the British agent, Thomas Barclay, who negotiated a cartel on 12 May 1813 with the American commissary-general of prisoners, John Mason, which the United States ratified immediately, the British government rejected it. Unfortunately news of this move did not arrive until January 1814, and the matter was not fully resolved until the peace, by which time the affair had petered out.[110]

The Americans spent the night on the battlefield near Moravian Town—a prosperous village of some sixty homes—and were fed by the inhabitants. Relations were cordial until several boxes of papers belonging to Proctor were discovered, whereafter the village was ransacked and plundered. Harrison declared it "an English garrison town" and put Captain Robert McAfee in charge of a fatigue party charged with transporting the village booty down the Thames on seventeen rafts. After stripping it, McAfee put it to the torch on 7 October.[111] Harrison and his army returned to Detroit, eschewing the opportunity of attacking Vincent's exposed left flank, probably because Shelby's sixty-day volunteers were clamouring to return home, and he had few regulars and limited provisions as winter approached. By 10 October Harrison was at Sandwich, where a violent storm capsized a schooner and several boats containing much of the campaign booty. The Kentucky volunteers—keen to get home to proceed with wheat flailing, corn-husking and "*hawg-butcherin'*"—were heading for home by 13 October and were discharged on 4 November.[112] On the 16th Harrison signed a treaty with the Indians gathered there and accepted a number of their women and children as hostages to good behaviour. Perry agreed that it was too late in the season to attempt to recover Mackinac and instead sailed for Buffalo with nearly 1,200 regulars, leaving just another 400 with 1,300 Ohio militia to garrison the area.[113]

The battle of the Thames was a great victory for the United States, and the death of Tecumseh shattered the Indian Confederacy; but the Americans had only recovered what was previously lost.[114] Prevost publicly blasted Proctor for the disaster in general orders but refused his request for a court-martial. Proctor appealed to the Duke of York, but by the time of his court-martial, which concluded in January 1815, opinion had been thoroughly primed against him; he was convicted of misconduct, suffered a loss of rank, and was suspended from duty for six months. The Prince Regent directed that his own "high disapprobation" be conveyed to him and included in the general orders read to every regiment in the British Army; he spent the rest of his career on the unattached list.[115]

ON LAKE ONTARIO, having carried Prevost to York on 27 August, Yeo took his squadron on a cruise to the south in early September and spotted Chauncey on the 3rd and tried to maintain station as bad weather set in. Chauncey kept to the Niagara River, exercising his crews, and emerged at dawn on 7 September; over the next four days the two squadrons circled warily trying to gain an advantage via Scarborough Bluffs near York, west into Burlington Bay, and eastwards along the southern shore throughout the 10th. Early in the morning of 11 September Yeo found himself becalmed off Braddock Bay, and Chauncey was able to engage with his long guns as the two forces drifted slowly down towards the mouth of the Genesee River. For ninety minutes the Americans were able to work on the British squadron, which put down boats to tow the *Royal George* and *Melville* clear. The British suffered four killed, five wounded, and damaged rigging before a breeze enabled them to pull clear to the north-east, where Chauncey held back as Yeo went among islands south-east of Prince Edward peninsula.[116]

Prevost was becoming frustrated with Yeo's failure to bring Chauncey to a decisive engagement and sent instructions that he wanted Yeo to escort a supply convoy to de Rottenburg's army, and then plan offensive operations against the mouth of the Niagara River. Yeo came into Kingston, where he made modifications to his ships' armament and sailing configurations and received the written instructions from Prevost he had requested, detailing his tasks with regard to de Rottenburg, when news arrived on 19 September of Barclay's defeat at Put-in-Bay. Chauncey had sailed with his squadron the day before, having been instructed by Armstrong, who was visiting Sackets Harbor, that his first priority would now be supporting the autumn ground offensive rather than pursuing Yeo. On 20 September Yeo sailed, although neither commander was aware that each had similar instructions likely to preclude a decisive engagement, and the convoy put into Burlington Bay on the 26th. Leaving the transports, Yeo then moved north towards York, and Chauncey came up on the 28th, the two spotting each other at around midday.[117]

Both squadrons formed line for battle and began to move south, 12 or 15 miles south of York on the back of a strong and strengthening westerly; but Chauncey had the weather gauge and began to manoeuvre closer to the

British, assuming they would try to steer clear. Instead Yeo, leading the line in his flagship, *Wolfe,* tacked abruptly to head north towards him and engage Chauncey's flagship, *General Pike,* at the head of the American line. Chauncey also tacked, and as the two lines converged *General Pike* gave *Wolfe* a powerful broadside with fourteen long 24-pounders that sent a hail of round and chain shot, knocking her a couple of points off course; but her reply damaged the American's upper topmast. Broadsides were once more exchanged, this time with disastrous result for the British: *Wolfe*'s mizzen topmast was brought down and took the main topmast with it, crashing onto the deck and over the side. Amid the confusion on her decks the Americans immediately sought to bear down and finish off their wounded adversary, but in an elegant and effective counter, Commander William Mulcaster RN on the *Royal George* got between *Wolfe* and *Pike* and poured repeated broadsides into the American, enabling Yeo's crew to regain control of *Wolfe* and get clear; and so began a chase that became known as the "Burlington races."[118]

The Americans snapped at the heels of the British as they sped away to the south-west, firing on any target that offered itself as the wind rose to become a gale. They covered some 15 miles in ninety minutes, but in the process one of *Pike*'s 24-pounders burst, killing and wounding twenty-two men and tearing up the deck, and four other guns showed ominous cracks. Chauncey decided to break off, as *Pike* was shipping too much water and the rising gale, now easterly, was pushing his ships against a shore where de Rottenburg's guns might soon add to his discomfort, thus leaving Yeo to anchor and set about urgent repairs. Captain Arthur Sinclair USN of the *Pike* was not best pleased: "My opinion is that had the schooners been properly managed with their long guns, and in such light, smooth weather, the enemy's fleet might have been stopped and a decisive battle fought."[119] The British lost five killed and thirteen wounded; the Americans suffered twenty-seven casualties and were faced with a fierce struggle against the elements that now built against them across the lake.[120]

Yeo complained to Warren that "the great advantage the Enemy has over us from their long 24 Pounders almost precludes the possibility of success, unless we can force them to close Action, which they have ever avoided with the most studied circumspection."[121] But Chauncey was to have better luck a week later; on 5 October he intercepted six of seven schooners transporting the two flank companies of Régiment De Watteville, together with a large number of sick and wounded en route from York to Kingston, taking 252 prisoners, including 18 officers. In writing to Horse Guards to request replacements, Prevost complained that Yeo had been expected to provide escorts, which he had failed to do; relations between them were becoming strained. Chauncey had established a clear ascendancy on Lake Ontario, but it was nullified to a large extent by the decision to transfer 3,000 troops from Fort George to Sackets Harbor as part of plans for an autumn offensive towards Montreal; this move would leave at Fort George a force of only 1,800, which posed little threat to the British. Although Chauncey found troop transportation extremely irksome, over four weeks Yeo had suffered a series of setbacks quite unlike anything in his career to date.[122]

9

Crysler's Farm

How happy the soldier who lives on his pay,
And spends half a crown on six pence a day;
He fears neither justices, warrants nor bums,
But pays all his debts with a roll of the drums,
With a Row de dow, Row de dow, Row de dow, dow
And he pays all his debts with a roll of his drums.

He cares not a Marnedy how the world goes;
His King finds his quarters, and money and clothes;
He laughs at all sorrow whenever it comes,
And rattles away with the roll of the drums.
With a row de dow, row de dow, row de dow, dow
And rattles away with a roll of the drums.

—Trad., "How Happy the Soldier"

FOLLOWING Dearborn's removal Armstrong replaced him with another singularly poor choice, a man whom Winfield Scott regarded as "an unprincipled imbecile."[1] In 1791 James Wilkinson's dodgy financial ventures had collapsed, but his connections secured him a commission as a lieutenant-colonel in the regular army. Six months later he was promoted brigadier-general and became the senior officer of his rank in 1796; but his tenure of this post over the next twelve years had a thoroughly debilitating effect on the peacetime army, since officers' career prospects depended on retaining his favour, yet many disliked and distrusted him.

Arrogant, unscrupulous, and overly fond of liquor, Wilkinson was the only man John Randolph knew "who was from the bark to the very core a villain."[2] He received a $2,000 retainer from Spain to support its interests in the western territories, a treasonable arrangement typical of the man, who if caught behaving improperly would seek "to the utmost of his not inconsiderable ability to shift responsibility for any misfortunes to other shoulders."[3] Nevertheless, he was appointed to command the new Louisiana Territory in 1803 and then became involved in Aaron Burr's plan to establish a separate nation west of the Mississippi. Wilkinson narrowly avoided indictment by acting as chief witness against Burr, and returned to Louisiana, where he plunged back into intrigues to enhance his personal wealth. These intrigues led to a congressional inquiry in 1810 from which he emerged yet again unscathed, while his incompetence in the notorious Terre-aux-Boeufs camp in Louisiana during the winter of 1809–10 cost the army 1,000 men to disease and desertion—about one-fifth of its entire strength at the time.[4] In 1811 Madison ordered a court-martial on charges of "treason, conspiracy with Colonel Burr, [and] corruption of the Spanish governor of Louisiana"; but although the court discovered many "queer transactions of a political and mercantile character," Wilkinson was acquitted of treason and restored to his post.[5]

By 1813 it was said that much of the Louisiana militia would absolutely refuse to serve under him, and his state's senators were demanding his removal.[6] To quiet this brewing mutiny, Armstrong, who knew Wilkinson well from Revolutionary War days, diverted him on 10 March to the Canadian frontier to serve under Dearborn; an order sweetened two days later with appeals to his patriotism and an offer of immediate promotion to major-general.[7] Thanks to slow mail and Wilkinson's absence from New Orleans, he did not read these appeals until 19 May, but in due course, despite having a new young and pregnant wife, he agreed, and set off from New Orleans with her on 10 June. He made a leisurely progress northwards, reaching Washington on 31 July, and five days later Armstrong showed him his new plan, recently approved by the cabinet. Armstrong wanted to combine the forces at Fort George and Sackets Harbor and attack either in Niagara or against Kingston, but wavered in his approach to strategy. His preference was for a move against Kingston, but in July the cabinet had to approve Montreal as an alternative objective, since a British reinforcement of Kingston might expose Montreal, which could also be attacked from the Lake Champlain area. Montreal had always been a distant goal, but with Madison's handling of the war proving unpopular, and the president having been ill for most of the year and playing little part in the war's direction, it now loomed large; Armstrong knew the administration desperately needed success to redeem itself. But all operations were dependent on

Chauncey's securing control of Lake Ontario, and the final choice of objective would rest with the commanding general, who would be Wilkinson; except Wilkinson did not like the plan.[8]

Any operation involving the division at Lake Champlain was bound to be unwelcome to Wilkinson, as it was commanded by Brigadier-General Wade Hampton. A sixty-one- or sixty-two-year-old North Carolinian, Hampton had become one of the largest land- and slave-owners in South Carolina and Mississippi. In 1808 he was appointed a regular brigadier-general and immediately complained bitterly to Eustis about Wilkinson's behaviour, and was greatly angered by Wilkinson's acquittal in 1811.[9] In accepting his command on 3 July, Hampton insisted on receiving orders direct from Armstrong, guaranteeing separation of command from both Dearborn and Wilkinson despite operating in Dearborn's Military District No. 9, although he at least consented to respect Wilkinson's seniority should the two forces ever combine.[10] Dearborn's removal upset this carefully constructed house of cards, leaving the two bitterest enemies in the U.S. Army in a direct-command relationship requiring cooperation. Armstrong decided to go north to soothe the inflammation, while Wilkinson demanded that no improper communication be permitted between his subordinate and the secretary of war. And before departing for Sackets Harbor on 11 August, Wilkinson wrote to Hampton, so infuriating him that Hampton was placated only with difficulty by Armstrong, although Hampton insisted that if he was not killed in the forthcoming operations, he would still resign.[11]

To the U.S. Army Wilkinson was the "Big Bug from the south," as all generals were "Big Bugs" to American soldiers just as they were "Big Wigs" in the British Army. On his arrival at Sackets Harbor on 20 August a council of war was held involving Morgan Lewis, Chauncey, and Brigadier-Generals Jacob Brown and Robert Swartout, the quartermaster-general. It concluded that the main strength of the American army in the north should concentrate 7,000 men at Sackets Harbor under Wilkinson, making a bold feint towards Kingston and its main effort along the St. Lawrence towards Montreal, where it would meet Hampton's 4,500 men moving up from the Champlain Valley.[12] But Wilkinson had little confidence in this plan as he set off to visit Fort George: he had ample cause to fear that Armstrong would not provide him with adequate resources, failures that stemmed from American weakness rather than British strength. And his original intention to set off in mid-September foundered when he discovered the state of his army, while lack of naval control of Lake Ontario delayed him further.[13]

Following defeat at the battle of the Thames, Prevost shifted his strategic focus eastwards, and he initially ordered all forces to withdraw to Kingston. But bad weather and the stubbornness of local commanders prevented this move: Brigadier-General John Vincent insisted on holding Burlington rather than abandon the Indians in the vicinity, and through de Rottenburg he was able to persuade Prevost of the necessity of not doing so.[14] Having already called out 3,000 sedentary militia in Lower Canada, Prevost now called up another 5,000, and William Dunlop, who was travelling to join the 2nd/89th Regiment in Upper Canada, encountered several units.

> They all had a serviceable effective appearance—had been pretty well drilled, and their arms came direct from the tower [of London], were in perfectly good order, nor had they the mobbish appearance that such a levy in any other country would have had. Their capotes [hooded cloaks] and trowsers of home-spun stuff, and their blue *tuques* (night caps) were all of the same cut and color, which gave them an air of uniformity that added much to their military look . . . They marched merrily to the music of the voyageur songs, and as they perceived our [scarlet] uniform as we came up, they set up the Indian War-whoop, followed by a shout of *Vive le Roi* along the whole line.[15]

Thus they displayed that light-hearted attitude noticeable in *Canadiens* generally, and in *Canadien* soldiers in particular, that is often the cause of bafflement among their more dour anglophone compatriots.[16]

Canadiens were more willing to fight in 1812 than they had been in 1775; they were royalists in sentiment and resented republicanism, while the depressed economy left a large pool of unemployed who sought military service for income. Although conscription to form the five battalions of select embodied militia saw some resistance, they were kept up to strength with drafts.[17] However, the majority of the sedentary militia were not armed but were intended to provide the logistic support for the 6,000 regulars, fencibles, and select embodied militia stationed along the frontier and in reserve. Command of the frontier fell to Major-General Louis de Watteville, a thirty-seven-year-old Swiss with two decades of campaigning experience in Europe who had accompanied his own regiment to Canada in the spring, and command of the reserve to Sheaffe.[18] By contrast, Colonel Robert Purdy of the 4th U.S. Infantry later wrote that Hampton's force "was composed principally of recruits who had been but a short time in the service, and had not been exercised with that rigid discipline so essentially necessary to constitute a soldier."[19] Hampton tried to train his army and instil a measure of discipline with six hours' drill per day, but it seems that the officers, especially the junior ones, failed to grasp that their prime responsibility was towards the men under their command and not their personal gratification.

Hampton imposed harsh order which was often as brutal as the flogging that had been abolished by the government at the outbreak of war. Men were sentenced to ride the wooden horse—a most painful and injurious punishment.[20] Another common punishment was running the gauntlet, in which the condemned man's comrades beat him with their bayonets; as was "Cobbing," or caning, of which Hampton was so fond he was nicknamed "Old Hickory" by his men.[21] On 8 September he began transferring his 4,000-strong division across the lake from Burlington to Cumberland Head, near Plattsburgh, and on the 19th they began to move north towards Odelltown, on the Canadian side of the border. He then chose to move west to the Châteauguay River rather than continue north along the Richelieu River.[22] This decision necessitated a difficult cross-country march of 70 miles that after four days brought them to the village of Four Roads in New York State at the head of the Châteauguay, where they paused and improved the road behind them. Armstrong approved the move to the west but emphasized that Hampton was not to proceed until Wilkinson's force was ready to do so.[23]

Wilkinson agreed that if naval superiority could be assured, a move against Kingston was best, but if not he preferred to concentrate all forces in Niagara and move towards Amherstburg. Armstrong insisted that the primary objective must be Kingston but left it to Wilkinson whether this was to be achieved by direct or indirect means, and discussed the advantages of attacking Kingston directly or going for a point down the St. Lawrence. On 15 September he left Wilkinson with typically ambiguous instructions: "Think of this, if you like it, choose your part, go first or last, sever the communication or take Kingston."[24] But Wilkinson had fallen ill with "lake fever" and taken to his bed. When he rose on 20 September he held a council of war to discuss whether to proceed in Niagara or move up to Sackets Harbor, and it was agreed that if the regular army should leave Fort George it was to be "razed and abandoned."[25] Armstrong had reminded Wilkinson again of the importance of Kingston on 18 September and that it was held only by the Régiment De Watteville, which was "completely disaffected," and that "nothing forbids and everything invites to a prompt and steady prosecution of the plan of operations already prescribed to you."[26] This was strong language for Armstrong, and Wilkinson knew he would have to obey, yet still he procrastinated until the news of Perry's victory at Put-in-Bay arrived on the 22nd. Armstrong had instructed Harrison to clear the Niagara Peninsula from the west, and if he did so Wilkinson's fear about Fort George would be groundless.[27] On 25 September he launched his first wave in a motley collection of *bateaux,* Durham boats—a Durham had a rounded bow and square stern, a rudder, and a mast, and could transport sixty to seventy-five men plus stores—and other small craft, but turned back because of adverse winds.[28] Then two days later Yeo's squadron was sighted, and all movement on the lake was halted until the ensuing battle between Yeo and Chauncey and the "Burlington races." The troops finally began to embark on 1 and 2 October, but the move was disrupted by bad weather, and Wilkinson did not return to Sackets Harbor until the 3rd, meeting there with Armstrong the following day. Armstrong still wanted an attack on Kingston, but Wilkinson now insisted that Montreal should be the objective, and the discussion marked the beginning of a rift between them. At least the confusion ensured that the British remained ignorant of American intentions.[29]

Wilkinson's health was now a major cause for concern; he had arrived in the north so enfeebled that he would have been considered unfit for most duty, and a particularly harsh bout of fever on 5 October prompted a desire to retire from the service. But Dr. E. W. Bull, the attending surgeon, managed to dissuade him, and Armstrong was seemingly desperate to retain him. "I would feed the old man with pap," he supposedly said, "sooner than leave him behind." On the same day Armstrong issued an ambiguous directive produced in a council involving himself, Wilkinson, Jacob Brown, and Morgan Lewis, stating that if the British fleet did not escape or Kingston receive reinforcement, it would be the objective; "otherwise we shall go directly to Montreal."[30] Chauncey was very keen to move against Kingston, a tactic which he hoped would lead to a general action against Yeo, but Wilkinson was unenthusiastic about his part in the plan; he wanted specific instructions in order to avoid the blame if things went wrong.[31] On 16 October Armstrong learned that the British had reinforced Kingston and immediately changed his mind about Wilkinson's objectives, but for some time both men remained unaware that Hampton had suffered a serious setback.[32]

HAMPTON was due to advance along the Châteauguay River, but most of his militia (some 1,000 men) refused to cross the border, and his regulars were little more reliable. Nevertheless, he commanded 4,000 infantry supported by 200 dragoons and ten guns, his advance supplied by slow-moving farm waggons which were delayed because the bridges on every small stream had been previously demolished. He began by making attempts to divert the British with raids and learned that he was facing only 2,100 men, one-third of whom were militia under Lieutenant-Colonel Charles de Salaberry who were preparing defences where the Châteauguay River made a fairly sharp bend.[33] On 16 October Hampton issued six days' rations in preparation for the advance, and Brigadier-General George Izard arrived to command his second brigade. But it was not until the 21st that they set out, the troops "in the best of spirits" according to Corporal Richard Bishop of the 29th U.S. Infantry.[34] Sergeant Alexander Neef of the 4th U.S. Infantry remembered "every countenance was bright, each soldier appeared to feel as men ought to feel on such occasions," and nothing "but opportunity was wanted to add fresh laurels to the splendor of American arms."[35] However, they made only slow progress over two days across appalling roads which had to be improved and the bridges rebuilt. As Private Charles Fairbanks of the New Hampshire Volunteers recalled, "often the wheels of the baggage wagons cut up the road so we had to lay logs across for miles; we often had to wade in the river up to our knees, or above them, lugging logs and timber. Such is the work of the poor soldier on half rations." He complained that they "would receive six or eight days rations at a time, and a day before our time was out, our rations would be out no matter how hard we hoarded the scanty allowance, and then we had nothing to eat."[36]

ON 20 OCTOBER Prevost was at Kingston when he received news of Hampton's move, and he asked Lieutenant-Colonel "Red" George Macdonell, now commanding the composite 1st Light Battalion, when his men could set out for Lower Canada. "When the men have finished their dinner, Sir," replied Macdonell.[37] It took three days to make an arduous 170-mile journey by boat and a 40-mile forced march, achieved without losing a man, to reach the position. At the same time the Americans concentrated at Spears Farm, near the junction of the Châteauguay and Outardes Rivers, and Hampton confidently decided to attack the Canadian position before him.[38] At Châteauguay de Salaberry's defences were approved by de Watteville, being well sited on swampy and wooded ground cut by gullies and ravines where the river was some 40–100 yards across and 5 or 6 feet deep, although there was a ford a short way downstream. The road, which ran some 300 yards to the left of

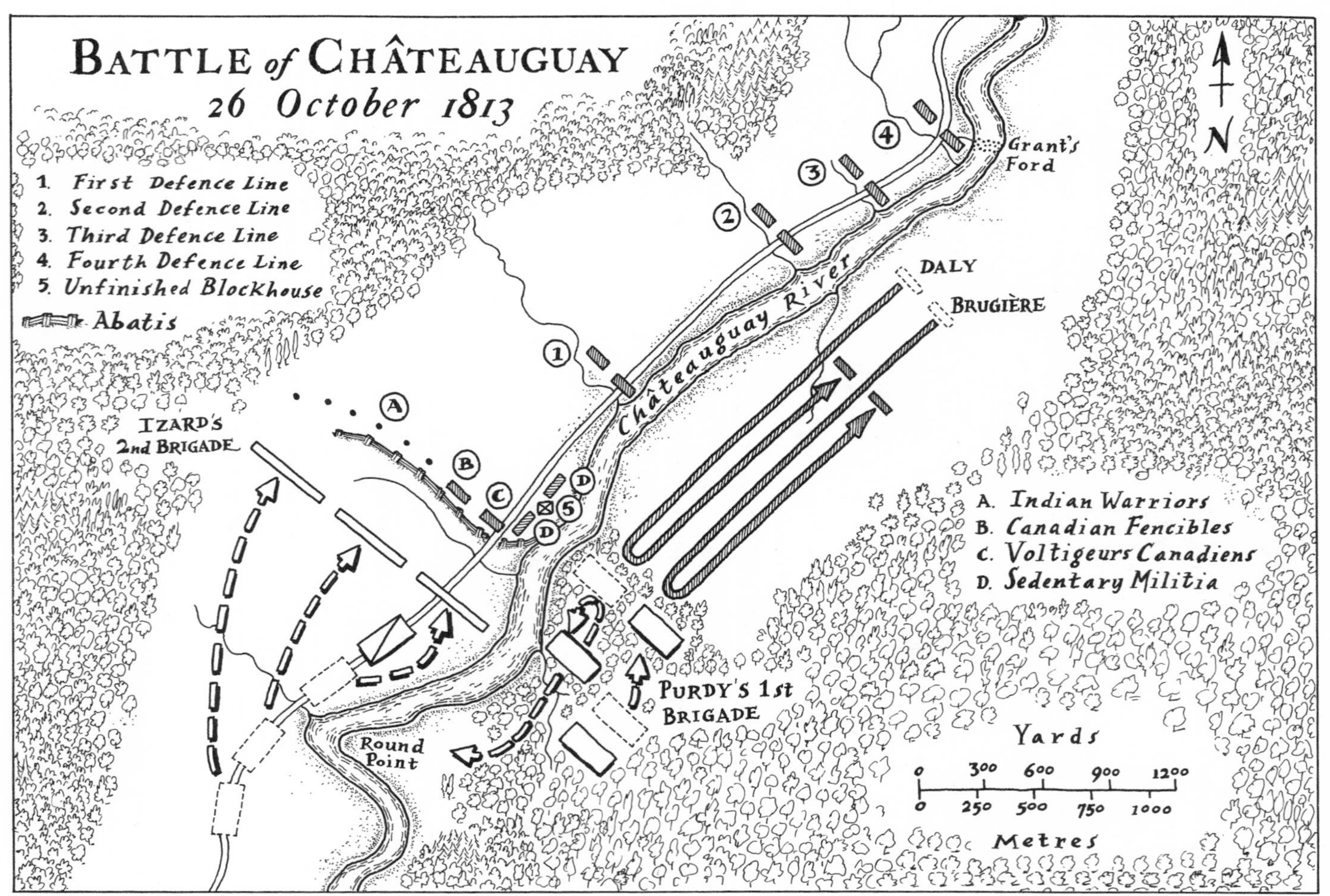

BATTLE of CHÂTEAUGUAY
26 October 1813
1. First Defence Line
2. Second Defence Line
3. Third Defence Line
4. Fourth Defence Line
5. Unfinished Blockhouse
Abatis
N
Grant's Ford
DALY
BRUGIÈRE
Châteauguay River
IZARD'S 2nd BRIGADE
PURDY'S 1st BRIGADE
Round Point
A. Indian Warriors
B. Canadian Fencibles
C. Voltigeurs Canadiens
D. Sedentary Militia
Yards
0 300 600 900 1200
0 250 500 750 1000
Metres

the river as the Americans advanced, was intersected at the bend by a deep re-entrant where a cleared area provided a limited field of fire, and the defenders erected a line of breastworks and abatis (fortifications made with felled trees) with a blockhouse next to the continuing forest. Behind this position, manned by 50 Canadian Fencibles, 150 Voltigeurs Canadiens, 100 sedentary militia, and a few Indians, four reserve lines were laid out from the river to a marshy area on the far side of the road, each manned by two companies of select embodied and one of sedentary militia, amounting to around 160 of all ranks, creating defence in depth back to Grant's Ford.[39] On the right bank Macdonell could manoeuvre a supporting force of 300 Voltigeurs Canadiens, 480 select embodied and 200 sedentary militia, and about 150 Indians.[40] Hampton was well informed about de Salaberry's position, and local guides assured him that he could outflank it. He planned to do so with Colonel Robert Purdy's first brigade moving towards the ford on the right while mounting a frontal assault with Izard's second brigade. But this was a risky plan, since it involved splitting his forces across a river.[41] Purdy's 2,300 men moved out on the night of 25 October under a light drizzle to march 10 miles across marsh and through thick brush, but it was soon apparent that the guide "knew nothing of the country having never been that way."[42]

Hampton may have had second thoughts, but it was too late, and early in the morning he ordered Izard to "attract the enemy's notice while Purdy gets in the rear."[43] They were fired on by Canadian piquets at about 10 A.M., and both de Salaberry and Macdonell moved forward at the sound of firing, de Salaberry organizing his men and placing himself in the centre of the front line just as "a strong column of infantry advanced thro' the plain in front of the abatis," and he himself "fired the first shot which was seen to bring down a mounted officer," although this was probably a dragoon.[44] Hampton ordered Izard to deploy the 250 men of the 10th U.S. Infantry in the clear area in front of the abatis; seeing them do so, de Salaberry had his bugler sound to commence firing, and a brisk twenty-minute action ensued until the 10th ran short of ammunition.[45] On the right bank Purdy tried to orientate himself to the sound of firing, and his two lead companies, moving in single file some way in advance of his main force, were roughly opposite the second left-bank defence line when they encountered Captain Jean-Baptiste Brugière's sedentary militia company posted as piquets. A sharp fight saw both sides retreat, with Brugière re-forming on Captain Charles Daly's company of select embodied militia sent across by Macdonell, who together cautiously followed up Purdy's vanguard as it withdrew into the thick brush.[46] As the rest of Izard's

9.1. *The Battle of Châteauguay,* painting by Eyving H. Dirkine Holmfeld. Château Ramezay Museum collection, Montreal.

brigade came up and Hampton realized from shouted messages across the river that Purdy had not gained the ford, he decided to attack again on the left bank. Izard's three regiments advanced at about 2 P.M.

The volleys of the Americans tended to go high and were further hampered by using "buck and ball," combining three buckshot pellets with each bullet, thus diminishing both accuracy and range. They were answered by much more effective individual shooting from the Canadians, initially from in front of their abatis, but who sensibly retired behind their cover. The Americans mistook this movement for a retreat, and a bout of cheering broke out, echoed by the Canadians, and prompting de Salaberry to have his bugler sound the "Advance" just as Macdonell, who was moving forward to support him, was joined by a party of Indians whom he deployed to his right to scream their war-yells and attack Hampton's left. At about the same time, Daly's and Brugière's companies again made contact with Purdy's brigade, and someone heard the word "retreat"; confusion spread among the Americans, whose officers could not maintain order in the dense undergrowth, and many of whom abandoned their men.[47] Perhaps a dozen officers tried to reach Izard's brigade across the river, much to his disgust. Purdy's brigade was able to hold off the two Canadian companies, being perhaps 1,500 men against 80, but Daly and Brugière decided to mount another attack, which unsurprisingly was driven off, with both men wounded.[48] But as the Americans pursued them into the open, they found themselves exposed to the fire of two companies posted by de Salaberry on the left bank to guard against just such an eventuality, and their fire checked the American advance.

It was now about 3 P.M., and Hampton, realizing his plan had failed, ordered a withdrawal. Izard's brigade accomplished this in reasonably good order, although in a night of torrential rain Private Fairbanks recalled "there was mud in abundance and, the rain kept making it softer; we could see nothing and had to almost find the way by the sense of feeling." After floundering through the night, one "can easily imagine what grotesque appearance we must have presented that morning, the mud and water dropping from our uniforms; we in fact presented an appearance unlike human beings."[49] Purdy's brigade had to find its way back without assistance for his wounded and harassed by Indian shouts, although they were not actually attacked. Canadian losses were two dead, sixteen wounded, and four taken prisoner; American losses were between forty and eighty. Prevost and de Watteville arrived in time to justify their submitting dispatches, thus preventing de Salaberry from doing so of the victory he had won.[50] But the Legislative Assembly of Lower Canada thanked him officially, and the Prince Regent was pleased to grant colours for the five battalions of select embodied militia that took part, although this award overlooked the fact that at least one company of sedentary militia was as heavily engaged as any other troops.

The most significant aspect of this victory was that it was entirely Canadian, anglophone and francophone together, although years later their relative contributions would become the subject of debate.[51] The Canadians won through superior professionalism, the quality of American leadership at all levels being woeful; the battle was "from its inception to its termination a disgrace to the United States Army," according to Major John Ellis Wool.[52] Hampton's nerve was shattered by his defeat as his army slowly returned to its base at Four Corners. When he saw an order signed by Armstrong to prepare winter quarters, he concluded on 1 November that the administration was not really interested in pressing the invasion. "This paper sank my hopes," he wrote later, "and raised serious doubts about receiving the efficacious support which had been anticipated."[53] Such hopes were further dented when Governor Martin Chittenden of Vermont issued a proclamation ordering his state's militia home, causing a great political furore and demonstrating the continuing divisions between New England and the rest of the country over the conduct of the war; he refused to deploy Vermont militia in defence of New York or to serve under regular officers, but was eventually prepared to allow them to defend Plattsburgh as volunteers.[54]

ON 16 OCTOBER the first units of Wilkinson's 7,000-man army, which included Forsyth's riflemen, fourteen infantry regiments, two regiments of dragoons, and three of artillery (some serving as infantry), began their move from Sackets Harbor, heading initially for Grenadier Island, the transport of men and stores proving a herculean task. They were carried in some 300 *bateaux* and other small craft with twelve gunboats for protection, but news of their movement reached Kingston that evening, and for thirty-six hours the wind blew so fiercely that they lost fifteen boats and nearly half the army's rations with large quantities of other stores; they were then marooned and delayed on the island and assailed by heavy snowfalls at the end of the month.[55] But life was not without compensations. One young woman living on the island whom the officers christened the "lady of the lake" became the "object of more interest and admiration than often falls to the lot of the most dominant city belle," though she spurned all advances.[56] Drummer Jarvis Hanks of the 11th U.S. Infantry was more interested in a field of potatoes, for which the farmer was offered 50¢ a bushel. Foolishly he declined, claiming he could get $1 in Kingston, and soon found he had no potatoes at all. When he then "applied to the officers to remunerate him for his loss, they gave him no encouragement, or consolation, in the premises, and he retired, lamenting his unwise decision."[57] Two days after his order to move out, Wilkinson still insisted that he planned to attack Kingston, the capture of which would yield all of Upper Canada and Lake Ontario and end the Indian war; if Armstrong now wanted the column to attack Montreal, Wilkinson would require a direct order with presidential authority to that effect.[58]

Armstrong and Wilkinson continued with a confused correspondence in which Armstrong sent strong recommendations but withheld the direct order. Yet somehow the priority was changed, and nobody bothered to inform Chauncey, who still expected to attack Kingston until as late as 29 October.[59] Throughout this time the British continued to wonder about American intentions and also expected an attack against Kingston, though Prevost also prepared the defences in front of Montreal.[60] Shepherded by Chauncey's squadron, Wilkinson's army made steady progress down the St. Lawrence, entering the Thousand Islands and reaching a rendezvous at French Creek on Wolfe Island. There they were attacked on the morning of 1 November by William Mulcaster commanding two brigs, two schooners, and four gunboats. With Chauncey still out on the lake it fell to Brigadier-General Jacob Brown to fight off the British boats with a skilfully placed battery and a furnace to heat shot, forcing Mulcaster to withdraw the next day.[61] The two squadrons on Lake Ontario continued their stand-off, but early on the 6th Yeo withdrew to Kingston, and Chauncey also chose to withdraw to Sackets Harbor, albeit in stages, and he wrote to Jones on 11 November describing an interval of pleasant weather that "I have no doubt, but that [Wilkinson] has taken advantage of and I presume by this time is in Montreal."[62]

In fact, Wilkinson faced a 150-mile journey to Montreal along the St. Lawrence that would entail running five notoriously dangerous sets of rapids.[63] With British guns at Fort Wellington dominating the river at Prescott, he landed his army above Ogdensburg and floated the empty boats downriver in the dark, then re-embarked upstream despite unrelenting fire from Fort Wellington's guns. But these were at extreme range of some 1,800 yards, and only one American boat was hit, with one man killed and three wounded.[64] Once it was clear where the Americans were heading, de Rottenburg implemented his instructions from Prevost of 12 October to pursue them.[65] On 7 November the battalion companies of the 49th Regiment (now reduced to under 400 men) and the 2nd/89th Regiment less the Light Company (some 480 men), with a score of gunners manning two 6-pounders, embarked on the schooners *Beresford* and *Sir Sidney Smith,* seven gunboats, and a number of *bateaux* commanded by Mulcaster. The "corps of observation" was commanded by Lieutenant-Colonel Joseph Morrison of the 2nd/89th Regiment, whom, despite having little combat experience, Prevost regarded as an "active and intelligent officer."[66] He was supported as second-in-command by Lieutenant-Colonel John Harvey, an officer of wide combat and staff experience with a reputation for "zeal, intelligence and gallantry."[67]

Canadian militia were acting against Wilkinson's rear and taking artillery potshots wherever the river narrowed sufficiently, so Wilkinson put down 1,200 men under Colonel Alexander Macomb at Iroquois Point to drive them off and act as advance guard.[68] In the afternoon of 8 November Wilkinson called a council of war to decide whether to proceed and received an endorsement from four of his six brigade commanders, while the other two saw no alternative.[69] In fact, most of his army was suffering from sickness, particularly dysentery, and the army's precious rations were being rapidly lost or stolen; a civilian who saw them pass through Ogdensburg thought they resembled "a moving Hospital, much more than they did an invading army." The sick were to be left in the United States, and there was "scarce a house" within 30 miles of Ogdensburg without "more or less of these miserable sick soldiers in them," left without provisions or attendants.[70] The council did not know that at the same time Hampton was deciding to move away from Montreal and no longer support the main advance. Covered by Izard's brigade, the retreat was very unpopular and took eight days to reach Plattsburgh, and when the men arrived there were no winter quarters, so they had to erect shelters in the middle of a snowstorm. Izard, like so many of his men, fell ill, noting that the "ignorance of the surgeons who attended me did me more harm than the disease itself."[71]

Early on the evening of 8 November Morrison's force landed at Prescott after making a 70-mile journey in twenty-two hours; here he would have to leave *Beresford* and *Sydney Smith,* unable to descend the rapids below. The men transferred to *bateaux,* and he received 240 reinforcements, the flank companies of the 49th Regiment, three companies of Voltigeurs Canadiens, a detachment of Canadian Fencibles, a militia artillery detachment with a 6-pounder, and half a dozen Provincial Dragoons to act as couriers, bringing his total to around 1,200. This force left Prescott early on 9 November and advanced towards John Crysler's farm.[72] Wilkinson's plan was for Brown to land 2,600 men on the Canadian shore to clear the way to Cornwall, while Boyd was to detail those troops not needed to navigate the Long Sault Rapids into a rearguard to hold off Morrison's force, which had now been reported to Wilkinson. Skirmishing began on the morning of 10 November, which a British participant described as a "smart little brush."[73] Boyd remembered spending the day "marching, counter-marching and skirmishing" over sodden fields in a constant downpour, often under fire from two 6-pounders firing shrapnel under Captain George Jackson RA. In the afternoon American discomfort was compounded when Mulcaster's seven gunboats appeared and began attacking the rear of the American flotilla, threatening to pin it in place above the Long Sault Rapids, until Wilkinson arranged support from a battery onshore and forced Mulcaster to withdraw.[74]

Brown made slow progress over appalling roads punctuated by destroyed bridges; in the early afternoon, having covered about 11 miles, Forsyth's riflemen in the vanguard reached Hoople's Creek and were fired upon.[75] Their assailants were some 300 Canadian militia from Cornwall, 12 miles away, under

Major James Dennis of the 49th Regiment. Brown estimated their strength at 400–800 and ordered up his artillery, comprising two 6-pounders. Dennis withdrew, having delayed the Americans for an hour, and they would still have to repair the bridge. More significantly, Dennis had ensured he would have enough time to evacuate the stores at Cornwall, including provisions Wilkinson would need if his army was to reach Montreal.[76] That evening Morrison advanced to establish his headquarters at Crysler's farmhouse to the west of the American camp, where he received orders to break off the pursuit and return to Kingston because of a report of another 5,000 Americans threatening Kingston. Not knowing that the report was false, Morrison called his subordinates together and, having decided he could not break off contact with Wilkinson, sent letters to explain his fateful choice to de Rottenburg and Prevost.[77]

Wilkinson was also hampered by other problems: bad weather in the form of heavy rain and sleet on the night of 10–11 November, and illness, which he treated with massive doses of laudanum, an opiate tincture unlikely to promote sharpness of thought, which he conceded gave him a "giddy head." Another officer observed he was "very merry" as he sang songs and told stories.[78] The Americans were within sight of the Long Sault Rapids, but with the British now close enough to interfere with their further movements. A cold and steel-grey dawn on 11 November found the men of both sides huddled miserably under whatever shelter they had managed to find, although at least the rain had petered out. At about 8 A.M. the alarm was sounded when desultory firing caused both sides to believe the other was about to attack. Wilkinson planned to run the rapids that day and turned over command ashore to Morgan Lewis; but now confusion reigned as to who was in command as Mulcaster renewed his attack on the American gunboat flotilla, which he broke off at around 11 A.M. By noon Morrison was becoming impatient, his men standing in the rain once more. So he sent Major Frederick Heriot, commanding three companies of Voltigeurs Canadiens and some 30 Mohawk warriors, to push forward closer to the enemy camp through the woods to the north.[79] Wilkinson does not appear to have formally resumed command but continued to issue orders nonetheless, apparently still planning to move down the rapids to join Brown, who had now occupied Cornwall. He ordered Boyd, whose men had also been standing in the drizzling rain all morning, to "beat back" any British attempt to harass his rear.

When Heriot's light troops appeared, Boyd chose to do just that, starting forward immediately with three brigades, some 2,300 regulars, in three

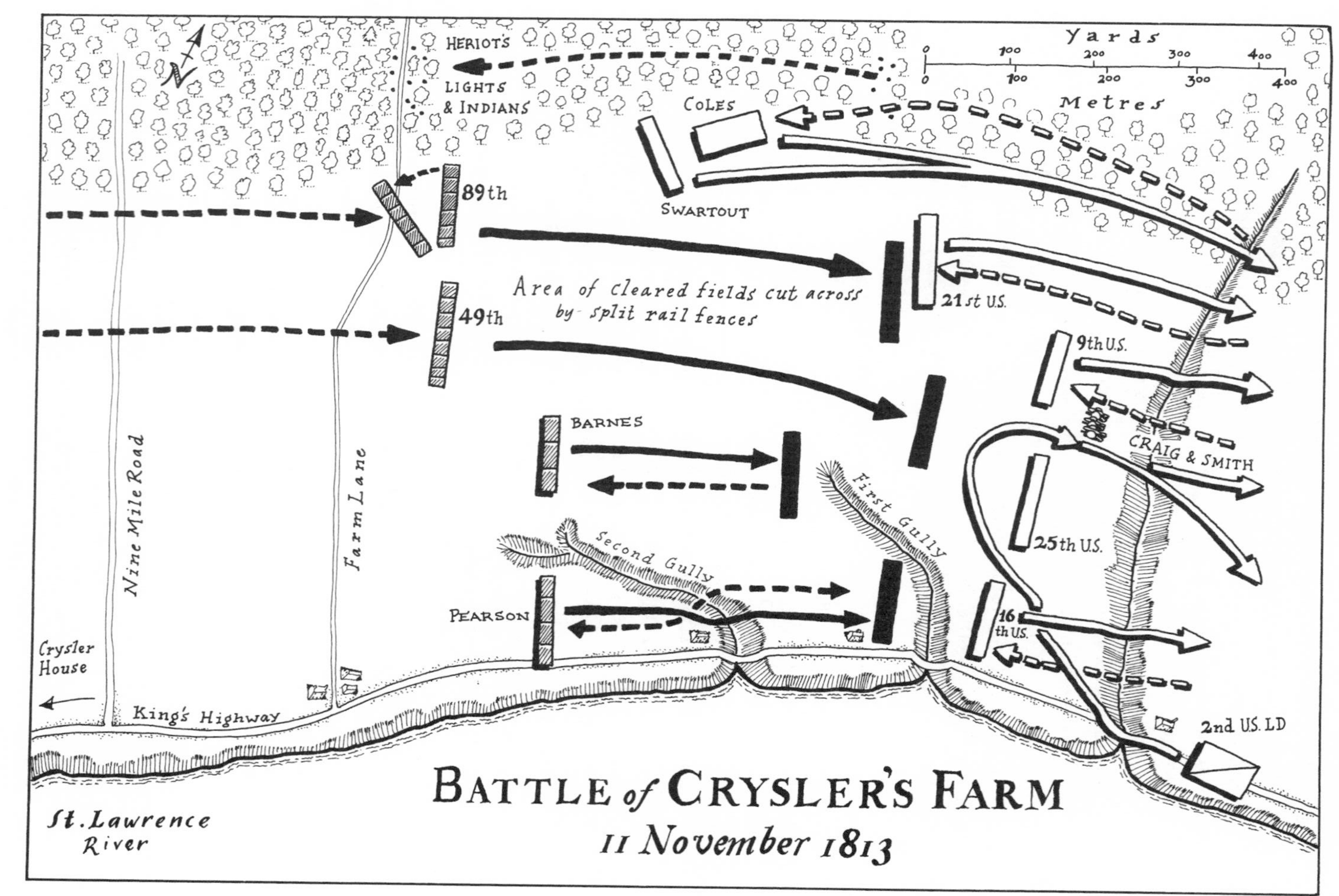

BATTLE of CRYSLER'S FARM
11 November 1813
Yards
0
100
200
300
400
Metres
HERIOT'S
LIGHTS
& INDIANS
COLES
SWARTOUT
89th
49th
Area of cleared fields cut across
by split rail fences
21st U.S.
9th U.S.
CRAIG & SMITH
BARNES
First Gully
Second Gully
25th U.S.
PEARSON
16th U.S.
2nd U.S. LD
Nine Mile Road
Farm Lane
Crysler House
King's Highway
St. Lawrence River

columns supported by around 130 dragoons and two 6-pounders. The Americans easily drove back the skirmish line of Voltigeurs Canadiens through the woods, but at about 2 P.M. they emerged to be confronted by a line of British regulars. On the right near the King's Highway in the first gully stood the flank companies of the 49th Regiment—dressed in their long grey greatcoats, which may have led the Americans to believe they were militia—and a detachment of Canadian Fencibles under Lieutenant-Colonel Thomas Pearson.[80] Supporting them and somewhat to the rear in the second gully were three companies of the 2nd/89th Regiment under Captain George Barnes, whose red tunics were not covered by greatcoats, in a position to maintain contact with the main body, consisting of the eight battalion companies of the 49th Regiment and five remaining companies of the 2nd/89th Regiment, formed in open columns on a farm lane; as the firing drew nearer to their front, the columns deployed into line. Boyd chose to attack by sending the 1,300 men of the First and Fourth Brigades under Colonel Isaac Coles and Brigadier-General Robert Swartout to make a flanking attack through the woods against the British left.[81] They stumbled through the undergrowth in columns harassed by Heriot's sharpshooters, and covered on their own left flank by the 21st U.S. Infantry of Coles's brigade advancing in line across the open fields. As the Americans emerged from the cover of the woods, they immediately came under effective fire from the British guns firing shrapnel and supported by Mulcaster's gunboats. They were soon disordered; the American army had recently been re-organized and had not been able to train in brigade manoeuvre, and different regiments had trained according to different drill manuals.[82]

As the Americans advanced clear of the woods, they shouted and cheered and began a ragged firing as their officers struggled to deploy them into line, displaying their inexperience.[83] The British stood still and quiet, their long experience, by contrast, having shown this to be the best way both to maintain discipline and to produce effective fire. Hearing the noise of the American advance and with the 21st U.S. Infantry clear of the woods marking their progress, Morrison realigned the 2nd/89th Regiment some 45 degrees to counter this move "forming en-potence [at an angle] with the 49th," and at about 2:30 P.M. the action became general, with the 2nd/89th Regiment firing by platoons "when within half musket shot the line formed under a heavy but irregular fire from the enemy."[84] The result was a rolling British volley of continuous and devastating effect, added to by Jackson's guns, with both British regiments now moving forward occasionally. Harvey recalled that the Americans "advanced quickly at the *pas de charge à la Française* which was quickly changed by a well-directed fire from our field pieces to one more comporting with the dignity of the American nation."[85] Captain Jackson noted, somewhat less smugly: "The American columns soon began to waver, and one after the other broke and ran, during which they suffered dreadfully from our firing Shrapnel shells. The enemy's columns were at one time not much more than two hundred yards from my guns, their light troops much nearer, as my men were wounded by musket balls."[86] Reeling in confusion, the Americans ran back to the cover of the woods, where Heriot's Voltigeurs and the Mohawks resumed their sniping; the 21st U.S. Infantry also withdrew to the skirt of the woods.[87]

Meanwhile the 1,100 men of Brigadier-General Leonard Covington's Third Brigade advanced in extended line towards Pearson's flank companies in the first gully, where the stream was swollen by autumn rain. Pearson was unconcerned by the overwhelming odds: in 1811 he had fought with the 23rd Regiment (Royal Welch Fusiliers) in the Fusilier Brigade at Albuera, described by Fortescue as one of the four hardest-fought battles of the British Army, when they swept away a French attack and less than half the fusiliers were left standing.[88] Now his four companies delivered a destructive volley into the 16th U.S. Infantry that caused many casualties, including Covington, who was advancing on foot with his men and was hit in the stomach.[89] Calmly, Covington told Colonel Cromwell Pearce that "he was mortally wounded; and that command of the brigade now devolved upon him," and was carried back to the shelter of the gully. Pearce showed considerable resolution and returned the British fire, supported now by the 25th U.S. Infantry, and with Pearson's horse shot from under him and the British beginning to waver, Pearce ordered an immediate bayonet charge.[90] As they began to advance, Pearson withdrew behind the second gully, leaving the 16th U.S. Infantry to crawl up and re-form on the west side of the first, paralleled on their right by the 25th and yet further to the right by the 9th U.S. Infantry. Morrison was now aware of the threat on his right and began to advance the main line, taking care not to expose them to renewed flank attack out of the woods. Despite the wet ploughed earth and split-rail fences the advance was relentless; the two lines opened a steady fire at each other lasting for some ten to fifteen minutes when the Americans, now running short of ammunition, began to fall back. Only now, some ninety minutes after the battle started, did the American artillery come into action.[91]

Lieutenant Henry Knox Craig was in command of six iron 6-pounders that had finally been brought forward, four in the centre of the American line and two on the left. These commenced firing at the British line, aiming for the colour party of the 49th Regiment and causing heavy casualties, including Lieutenant-Colonel Charles Plenderleath, who was hit in the thigh but refused to leave the field. In ten minutes the 49th lost "eleven officers out of eighteen and men in proportion," noted Lieutenant John Sewell, but re-formed their ranks and advanced directly on the guns.[92] Harvey and Morrison saw the 49th shudder at the effects of the fire, and at Harvey's suggestion Morrison ordered Plenderleath to advance and engage the guns to his front. But Plenderleath soon realized this feat was impossible as large gaps opened in his line, and he calmly withdrew his men out of canister range and commenced long-range firing at the American artillery. Barnes also brought his three companies of the 2nd/89th Regiment to engage the gunners, forcing Craig to withdraw three guns covered by the fourth. Colonel John Walbach, the American adjutant-general, who was near Major John T. Woodford's squadron of 2nd U.S. Light Dragoons, first suggested that a charge be made to save them. Woodford readily agreed, whereupon Walbach, whose real name was Jean-Baptiste de Bart Walbach and who had never lost his aristocratic German accent, ordered Woodford to "Charge mit de dragoons!"[93] Woodford had first to traverse the ravine and re-form on the far side, where he immediately came under artillery and musket fire; the dragoons quickly formed line two ranks deep and advanced on the 49th Regiment, riding across the front of the Pearson and Barnes detachments and taking fire all the way, including at least one round of canister from a 6-pounder. The dragoons lost their formation and impetus as men and horses were tumbled to the ground, but they continued to hurtle towards the 49th Regiment's right flank company commanded by Lieutenant Dixie Ellis, a thirty-five-year-old Irish veteran who had been with the regiment since 1803, having served nine years in the ranks before gaining his commission. Ellis timed his riposte nicely; he fired at short range just as Barnes's men fired another volley into the dragoons' rear, and left "many saddles emptied ere they went right about."[94] Woodford's squadron disintegrated, the survivors wheeling away to seek shelter in the woods.

At least Craig was able to get his three guns away, although the fourth, defended to the last by Lieutenant William Smith, who was badly wounded, was captured as Barnes's detachment rushed forward; whereupon a sudden lull fell over the field, which Morrison used to push his entire force forward to the west side of the ravine, within good musket range of Boyd's re-formed line whose three brigades had replenished their ammunition, and the artillery duel recommenced.[95] Watching the steel-tipped British line advancing steadily once more after two hours of hard fighting, Boyd began to have doubts:

> My orders from General Wilkinson were, should the enemy advance upon us, beat them back. They first attacked us in the woods; we drove them from thence, into a plain; from the plain to a ravine, where their main body was posted, from thence into an open space interspersed with smaller ravines, and raked by their gunboats . . . Considering my orders to have been executed, and some of our troops giving way, I ordered the main body to fall back, and re-form where the action first commenced.[96]

Having somehow thus reconciled his retirement with his orders to beat the British back, the Americans duly went back farther, and then beyond to the boats, where Boyd received an order to retire from Wilkinson (who otherwise played no part in the battle), although many in the American ranks could not understand why such an order was issued and no senior officer would subsequently accept responsibility for it. Major William Cumming of the 16th U.S. Infantry was disgusted: "We were marched now here, marched now there, without any system, or any apparent design but to learn whether the army liked cannon shot as little as certain generals."[97] Captain Jackson took the opportunity to hurry them along with shrapnel as the day, and the action, drew to a close at around 4:30 P.M.[98]

The British suffered 22 killed, 148 wounded, and 9 missing, although in reality their losses may have been slightly higher;[99] American losses were 102 killed, 237 wounded—including Covington, who died after some thirty-six hours of agony from his stomach wound—and well over 100 taken prisoner. (Woodford's dragoons had lost 18 men killed and 12 wounded plus 25–30 horses.[100]) Afterwards Jackson complained: "The whole army are much annoyed that Sir George Prevost did not reinforce us and let us immediately attack the Americans, and at the same time push on from the Chateguay [*sic*] frontier, by which we should have had them between two fires . . . Sir George has probably lost by it the most favourable opportunity of destroying that army he is ever likely to have."[101]

Although Brown had cleared the way to Cornwall, Wilkinson could not now hope to cope with the forces that Prevost would surely be concentrating before Montreal. The troops were re-embarked and had negotiated the Long Sault Rapids when Wilkinson received a letter from Hampton on 12 November in which Hampton, convinced that Armstrong was not counting on the capture of Montreal in 1813, refused to join Wilkinson at St. Regis. With the perfect excuse to blame Hampton, the subsequent council of war agreed to call the whole campaign off, a decision which Wilkinson announced the next day.[102] He then wrote to Hampton claiming that "such resolution defeats the grand objects of the campaign in this quarter, which before the receipt of your letter, were thought to be completely within our power, no suspicion being entertained that you would decline the junction directed, it will oblige us to take post at French Mills, on Salmon River, or in their vicinity for the winter."[103] In fact, had Wilkinson continued towards Montreal he would have encountered a considerable array of British forces, as Prevost had collected some 6,000 men, including five regular battalions. At the end of October two Royal Marine battalions and their accompanying two artillery companies and rocket company had arrived at the St. Lawrence after their Chesapeake operations, although when the 70th Regiment arrived from Ireland, their commander, Major Charles McGregor, reported to Prevost that "we are very young and small," and the best men had been left behind on leave or on recruiting duties, so that the regiment was in a "very infant state."[104] But they were supported by five battalions of select embodied militia, almost a full regiment of combined British and Canadian dragoons, and three companies of field artillery.[105]

These now returned to winter quarters, and Morrison's British troops returned to Prescott or Kingston, where, as William Dunlop fondly recalled, "we passed the remainder of the winter as officers are obliged to do in country quarters. We shot, we lounged, we walked and did all the flirtation that the neighborhood of a mill, a shop, a tavern, with two farm houses within a forenoon's walk could afford."[106] Morrison was selected to take the official dispatches of his victory to the Prince Regent, a journey which would not only reunite him with his young family but earn him automatic promotion. Unfortunately he arrived too late in Quebec City to embark and had to console himself with a restful staff appointment and being lionized by society. Prevost's seventeen-year-old daughter, Anne, recalled that the social scene was in full swing that winter. "On 7 January [1814] a grand Ball and Supper were given by the Officers of the Garrison to my Father. I have never thought so much of any ball in my life . . . and it had been arranged that I was to open the Ball with Colonel Morrison. Dear Colonel Morrison!—more interesting and agreeable than ever—Our victorious Hero!"[107] At Kingston the highlight of the social calendar was the marriage of Commander Alexander Dobson

RN and Miss Mary Cartwright on 17 February, after which the dancing went on until the small hours, although a false alarm about an enemy attack prevented the newly-weds from travelling to Montreal for their honeymoon. "So you see," wrote John Johnston, now a Royal Navy lieutenant, "we are quite gay in the wilds of America."[108]

The Americans in their quarters enjoyed no such pleasures: they retired to French Mills—renamed Fort Covington after the war—a desolate place 2 miles inside the United States with hardly any accommodation, where they suffered terribly from severe winter conditions and lack of supplies, being soon put on half-rations in the bitter cold. "Even the sick had no covering except tents," reported a doctor. "Under these circumstances sickness and mortality were very great."[109] Boyd, Swartout, and Morgan Lewis soon disappeared to their homes amidst much bickering, but Wilkinson, despite his ill-health, displayed considerable energy in shifting blame for the disaster and continued in command.[110] Only the arrival on 13 December of Dr. James Mann to supervise the medical services averted disaster; Mann worked in conjunction with Jacob Brown, who had succeeded Boyd. Finally Brown felt secure enough to celebrate the new year with a ball in his quarters, recorded Lieutenant Reynold M. Kirby wistfully—not being among the guests—with ladies "from the distance of 20 miles & might have amounted, I am told, to twenty."[111]

10

Drummond's Winter Offensive

Eyes right, my jolly field boys, who British bayonets bear,
To teach your foes to yield, boys, when British steel they dare!
Now fill the glass, for the toast of toasts,
Shall be drunk with the cheer of cheers,
Hurrah! Hurrah! Hurrah! Hurrah!
For the British Bayoneteers.
Great guns have shot and shell, boys, Dragoons have sabres bright.
Th'artillery's fire's like hell, boys, and the horse like devils fight.
But neither light nor heavy horse,
Nor thundering cannoneers
Can stem the tide of the foemen's pride,
Like the British Bayoneteers.

—Trad., "The British Bayoneteers"

In Tennessee the public demanded revenge for the Duck River killings and Martha Crawley's capture. Prominent among those demanding action was Andrew Jackson, who had risen from poverty on the Carolina frontier. Jackson's Scots-Irish immigrant parents left him orphaned at fourteen with little formal education, after which he was successively a saddler's apprentice and schoolteacher before studying law and moving to Tennessee. He plunged into politics and was soon a successful lawyer, planter, slaveholder, and judge, a devotee of cock-fighting and horse-racing. Though he was not so rough-hewn as opponents sometimes portrayed him, he possessed strong prejudices and a violent temper, making him a celebrated duellist. As major-general of the Second Division of Tennessee Militia, Jackson feverishly implored Governor

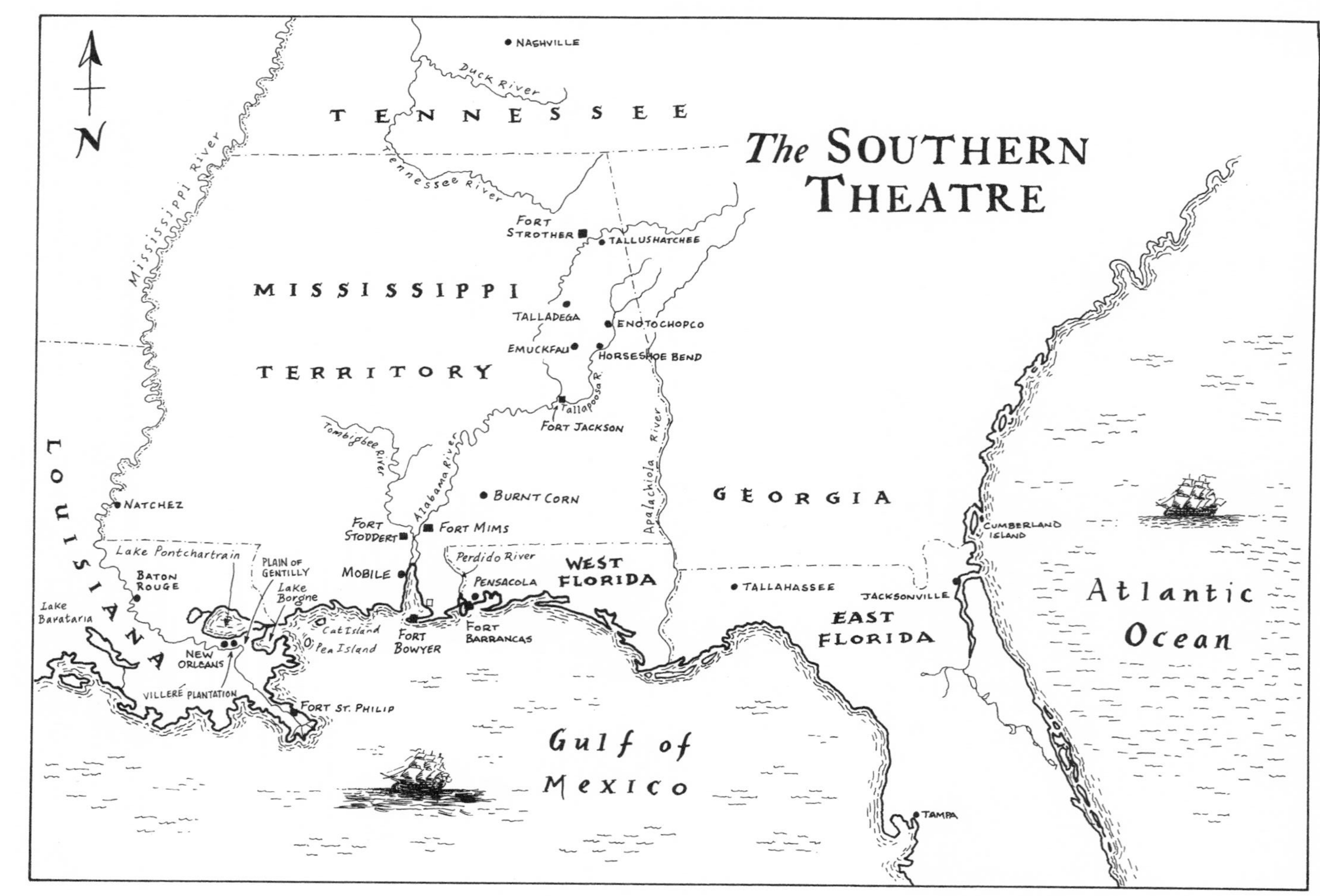
N
The SOUTHERN THEATRE
TENNESSEE
NASHVILLE
Duck River
Tennessee River
Mississippi River
FORT STROTHER
TALLUSHATCHEE
MISSISSIPPI
TERRITORY
TALLADEGA
ENOTOCHOPCO
EMUCKFAU
HORSESHOE BEND
Tallapoosa R.
FORT JACKSON
Tombigbee River
Alabama River
Apalachicola River
BURNT CORN
GEORGIA
NATCHEZ
FORT STODDERT
FORT MIMS
Perdido River
WEST FLORIDA
Lake Pontchartrain
PLAIN OF GENTILLY
Lake Borgne
MOBILE
PENSACOLA
BATON ROUGE
Lake Barataria
LOUISIANA
Cat Island
Pea Island
FORT BOWYER
FORT BARRANCAS
NEW ORLEANS
VILLERÉ PLANTATION
FORT ST. PHILIP
TALLAHASSEE
JACKSONVILLE
EAST FLORIDA
CUMBERLAND ISLAND
Atlantic Ocean
Gulf of Mexico
TAMPA

Blount of Tennessee to send the army against the Creeks. But although Blount was sympathetic, he had to consult the War Department, and the government wished to defuse the situation via their Creek agent, Benjamin Hawkins.[1]

Hawkins used his position to persuade certain Creek leaders to agree to hunt down the perpetrators and secure Mrs. Crawley's release as lurid rumours circulated about her fate, feeding Indian hatred among Tennesseans. Jackson chafed at the bit as local newspapers stirred the pot demanding retribution, the Nashville *Clarion* demanding in July 1812 that Americans must act "as your forefathers, and at the point of the bayonet subdue or extirpate the savage foe. The softer emotions of humanity are out of the question; it is folly to spare the viper that he may poison your family." In fact, she had already escaped with help from a blacksmith called Tandy Walker and was safe.[2] However, Mrs. Crawley's escape coincided with Creek leaders' compliance with Benjamin Hawkins' demand to pursue the Duck River murderers; the latter were hunted down and killed, but only at the cost of tribal civil war, which forced many pro-white leaders to flee to American agents for protection, and with the Red Sticks in the ascendancy, Indian raids increased.[3]

Following a detailed reconnaissance of the Gulf of Mexico in November 1812, Lieutenant James Stirling RN wrote to his uncle Vice-Admiral James Stirling, commander-in-chief of the Jamaica Station, recommending an alliance with the Creeks and an immediate blockade of New Orleans, but this proposal was not taken up.[4] In the autumn of 1812 Eustis asked Blount for 1,500 militia to help defend New Orleans, a force that both he and Madison hoped might be used to invade the Floridas. Tennessee was enthusiastic about war, and Jackson soon raised 2,000 men, who left Nashville on 10 January 1813 and reached Natchez a month later.[5] Although the United States had not gone to war with Spain in 1812, many in the south were willing to use the opportunity presented by war with Britain to seize the Floridas, where an American-inspired insurrection—the so-called "Patriot" War—continued in East Florida into 1813.[6] Throughout the spring and summer, tensions simmered until a group of Red Sticks led by half-breed Peter McQueen visited Pensacola to trade and collect arms promised by Spanish officials.[7] As they returned with their pack train, they were attacked on 27 July 80 miles north of Pensacola by 180 Mississippi militia in a fight known as the battle of Burnt Corn. Although the Americans managed to secure most of the supplies, they were driven from the field; this result emboldened the Red Sticks, transforming what had been a Creek civil war into one against the United States that would lead to their destruction.[8]

On 30 August the Red Sticks retaliated at Fort Mims in Mississippi Territory, a stockade 40 miles north of Mobile occupied by about 300 people, including 120 militia under a regular officer, Major Daniel Beasley. Beasley paid little attention to his duties and failed to put the fort in a state of defence, and when two slaves reported Indians nearby they were flogged for lying. With the gates left open the defenders were surprised and overwhelmed. Later an American burial party reported a horrifying spectacle: "Indians, Negroes, white men, women and children lay in one promiscuous ruin. All were scalped, and the females of every age were butchered in a manner which neither decency nor language will permit me to describe. The main building was burned to ashes, which were filled with bones. The plains and the woods around were covered with dead bodies."[9] Although at least 100 Indians were killed and many more wounded, they in turn killed nearly 250 white occupants, including many women and children, and perhaps another 150 blacks and friendly Indians (although newspapers reported much higher figures still wildly bandied about today). Only a few whites escaped, and some slaves also survived to be taken away by the Indians.[10] The massacre stirred people in the south-west much as the Raisin had those in the north-west, and so Andrew Jackson finally had his war with the Creeks. But despite appeals to the Spanish for a joint attack on Mobile, and to the British in the Bahamas to send assistance via the Apalachicola River, the Creeks would fight alone, divided amongst themselves and surrounded by their enemies.[11]

Initially expeditions were mounted from Georgia and Mississippi Territory which took a heavy toll on the Indians but were inconclusive. Georgia operations under Brigadier-General John Floyd saw 11 Georgians killed and 54 wounded at Auttose (in modern Montgomery County, Alabama), for which price Floyd estimated 200 Indian dead.[12] Tennesseans rushed to the colours as well, and by autumn 2,500—including a young Sam Houston and Davy Crockett, who would later find fame defending the Alamo—assembled for a punitive expedition under Jackson, who planned to wipe out the Indians and then seize Spanish Florida.[13] Jackson moved rapidly south to the Coosa River, where he built Fort Strother as a forward base. On 3 November his most able subordinate, Brigadier-General John Coffee, attacked the Indian village of Tallushatchee, less than 15 miles from Fort Strother, killing around 200 and capturing 84 women and children.[14] Several days later, Jackson learned that 1,100 hostile Creeks were besieging a friendly village at Talladega, and he marched with 2,000 men to relieve it. On 9 November he attacked the Indians, killing some 300 for the loss of 100 men, although most of the hostile Indians escaped. But with provisions low, Jackson was forced to suspend campaigning and return to Fort Strother.[15] Jackson, like all other American generals, had to contend with the vagaries of a supply system that relied on private contractors, who he claimed were responsible for the delays and difficulties suffered during his campaign.[16] He also found people around him losing heart, including Blount, and had to use sheer force of will to keep his army together. Twice he levelled his own gun to stop militiamen leaving; but as the year drew to a close he was eventually forced to allow men to return home.[17]

Some 750 Creek warriors had been killed from a total of 3,500–4,000, but their main force remained unbroken. A force of Mississippi militia and regulars under Brigadier-General Ferdinand L. Claiborne left Fort Stoddert on the Alabama River on 13 December, and attacked the village of Econochaca (in modern Lowndes County, Alabama) at the battle of the Holy Ground ten days later. Some 30 Indians were killed for the loss of one American killed and 6 wounded.[18] But the campaign was not being clearly directed. In January 1814 Jackson once more assembled 1,000 men in order to resume operations and marched deep into Creek territory. On 22 January, and again two days later, he fought inconclusive actions at Emuckfau (in Tallapoosa County, Alabama) and Enotochopco Creek. Meanwhile Floyd fought a bitter and bloody engagement at Tuchaubatchee on the Tallapoosa.[19] Returning once more to Fort Strother, Jackson built up his force to 4,000, stiffened by 600 regulars of the 39th U.S. Infantry, but he continued to have disciplinary problems with his militia.[20] John Woods, a young soldier who refused to obey an order, was court-martialled and shot—the first such instance since the Revolution. "An army cannot exist where order & Subordination are wholly disregarded," said Jackson, and "a strict obedience afterwards characterized the army."[21]

Thus ensuring that his army feared him more than it did the enemy, Jackson led his force once more against a Creek concentration at Tohopeka (Horseshoe Bend) on the Tallapoosa River. On 27 March he launched a combined assault using canoes stolen earlier from the Creek positions by friendly Indians and slaughtered around 800 Indians for the loss of just 45 Americans.[22] The power of the Upper Creek was broken, and the brief Creek War drew to a close. Among those who surrendered was the half-breed chief Red Eagle, or William Weatherford, who reportedly cried: "My people are no more!! Their bones are bleaching on the plains of the Tallushatches, Talladega, Emuckfau."[23] For his part, Jackson succeeded Brigadier-General Thomas Flournoy on 22 May to command the Military District No. 7 based at Mobile, and was promoted as a regular major-general six days later.[24]

THE TSAR'S willingness to broker a peace settlement may have been acceptable to the Americans, but it was wholly unacceptable to the British, although Castlereagh was far too astute a diplomatist to risk offending Britain's most powerful ally in the European war by saying so. Lord Liverpool was deeply interested in foreign policy but left its execution to Castlereagh, who was granted wider powers than any previous British statesman in similar circumstances. Castlereagh therefore evaded the issue for most of the year, eventually informing the tsar in November 1813 that Britain would prefer to offer formal direct negotiations with the United States.[25]

Most of the European continent was now free to British trade, and Madison, needing to raise $45 million just to keep the nation afloat in 1814 while Jones estimated government income at $16 million, saw the nation facing bankruptcy and dissolution unless new taxes were raised, a prospect which Republicans bitterly opposed.[26] As 1813 ended, Britain and her continental allies were approaching the borders of France for the first time since 1793. The tide of war had swung decisively in their favour, but the tsar's intervention had done nothing to resolve the conflict in North America, largely because Britain was determined to yield nothing on maritime rights. On 30 December HM Schooner *Bramble* (10) duly arrived at Annapolis carrying a letter from Castlereagh dated 4 November suggesting that British and American peace commissioners meet to discuss terms; the letter contained a thinly disguised promise that Britain would insist on maintaining the right of impressment. On 26 December Castlereagh issued explicit instructions that peace was to be negotiated on the basis of "the *status quo ante bellum* without involving in such Treaty any decision on the points of dispute at the commencement of hostilities."[27] The timing was, however, left open, and at various stages the British government flirted with proposals from lobbyists representing Canadian merchants, Indian traders and agents, and old Tories.

With Castlereagh's letter came London newspapers telling the Americans of Bonaparte's comprehensive defeat at the battle of Leipzig, indicating that he would probably have to abandon Germany completely.[28] Congress quickly appointed Henry Clay and Jonathan Russell as additional peace commissioners, although it was not until late February 1814 that they sailed in the *John Adams* to join their colleagues at Gothenburg carrying a list of demands that included an end to impressment.[29] The Americans initially intended that the negotiations would be held in Sweden, which had a strong material interest in peace, and as late as March they believed that Sweden would mediate in America's favour; but by the time Russell and Clay reached

Gothenburg the war in Europe was over, and Britain insisted that the commission meet in Ghent.[30] And before 1813 drew to a close there was another outbreak of fighting along the Canadian border.

The departure of most of the regulars from Fort George with Wilkinson in early October was not disastrous, as Colonel Winfield Scott remained with 800 men to supplement the garrison under the command of Brigadier-General George McClure of the New York militia. But Scott believed the frontier to be secure and crossed the Niagara River on 13 October, leaving McClure in charge with just a handful of regulars, some 250 pro-American Indians, and about 1,000 militia, who were badly affected by the perennial problem besetting United States forces: arrears of pay.[31] This decision would have dire consequences for which Scott has been criticized, and probably contributed to the plundering and pillaging of the Canadian inhabitants, to whom McClure offered feeble apologies, lamely admitting that he could not "promise complete security."[32] In November American patrols led by renegade Canadian scouts proved to be as interested in looting and the kidnapping of militia officers as they were in gathering military information on British dispositions, and a number of prominent citizens gathered in Port Dover to discuss the matter. Led by militia Captain John Bostwick, they sprang into action on 11 November, killing 5 raiders and capturing 16 at Nanticoke Creek; two weeks later they attacked a marauder outpost near Chatham, killing several and capturing others.[33]

There came a temporary improvement for McClure when Harrison reached Buffalo with some 1,200 westerners; but late in November Harrison departed for Sackets Harbor, and McClure's position rapidly deteriorated. Despite the offer of illegal bounties his militiamen drifted away, and when their terms of enlistment expired they were discharged without pay. Left with just 60 regulars, he made plans to evacuate Fort George and burn it down. Prevost had been seriously displeased with de Rottenburg for having ordered Morrison and Mulcaster to withdraw to Kingston when they were pursuing Wilkinson along the St. Lawrence, even though de Rottenburg had cancelled the order once it became clear that the American objective was Montreal. On 10 December McClure heard a rumour that the British were "advancing in force" and hurriedly abandoned the post, though not before burning the 150 private homes of Newark, allowing the inhabitants only twelve hours' notice in zero-degree weather.[34]

McClure appears to have misunderstood his instructions from Armstrong: he had authority to do this only in the event of defending Fort George and needing to improve his fields of fire; but he may have been encouraged by Joseph Willcocks, whose 70 renegade "Canadian Volunteers" played a major part in the act.[35] An American eyewitness described Willcocks leading "a banditti through the town on that fatal night . . . applying the epithet of Tory to all who disapproved of this flagrant act of barbarity."[36] "Every building in Newark is reduced to ashes," reported McClure, and as the American side was thrown into turmoil expecting retaliation, he reported that "the enemy is much exasperated and will make a descent on the frontier if possible."[37] Although the U.S. government subsequently dissociated itself from his action, McClure was not wrong. The British found the once beautiful town turned to "ruin, nothing to be seen but brick chimneys standing."[38] Lieutenant-Colonel Elliot of the 100th Regiment said of McClure: "The cowardly wretch with the whole of his minions abandoned Fort George and fled across the river. Not the slightest opposition did he make. He was in too much haste to destroy the whole of his magazines or even remove the tents."[39] Houses worth £37,625 were destroyed, supposedly to deny the British shelter, yet tents for 1,500 men were left pitched close by, and Fort George itself—the one structure of military value—was not only untouched but left stronger than when the British had been forced to relinquish it: all that was accomplished was the spiking of its guns, which had been thrown into a ditch.[40]

On 16 December a new British commander, Lieutenant-General Sir Gordon Drummond, arrived in the Niagara Peninsula to replace de Rottenburg as administrator of Upper Canada, while de Rottenburg went to command the Left Division in Lower Canada and Sheaffe was quietly returned to Britain.[41] Drummond was forty-one years old and had seen active service in the Netherlands, the West Indies, and Egypt, and had served in Canada as major-general from 1808 to 1811.[42] He was accompanied by thirty-eight-year-old Irishman Major-General Phineas Riall, who would take command of all troops west of Kingston, a command that now became the Right Division, replacing the ailing Vincent, who temporarily took command of the troops at Kingston and along the St. Lawrence, which became the Centre Division.[43] Drummond had orders to exploit any American weakness; he was furious and determined to avenge the destruction of Newark and the eviction of its residents. Preparations for attacking Fort Niagara began immediately after taking Fort George, but billeting difficulty and extremely cold weather caused a delay. The Americans had taken the precaution of destroying river craft, and only two boats could be located. Nevertheless, the Canadian militia eagerly volunteered to fetch sufficient *bateaux* from Burlington, 50 miles away, and these were brought down by night and across the snow to Longhurst Ravine and carefully concealed.[44]

On 18 December a force of 562 men (12 Royal Artillerymen, the Grenadier Company of 1st Royal Scots, the flank companies of the 41st—whose two battalions had been consolidated following the disaster of the Thames—and 350 men of the 100th Regiments) under Lieutenant-Colonel John Murray assembled at St. Davids, where the ground hid them from prying American eyes. At 10 P.M. on a bitterly cold night they set off to cross the Niagara. All knew it was an extremely risky operation, to be carried out by the bayonet with unloaded muskets, and Lieutenant Maurice Nowlan of the 100th Regiment's Grenadier Company wrote to Agathe, his wife of eighteen months, that it broke his "heart to write you now until this business is over, for I have great hopes to survive, tho' it will be wicked business."[45] But the snow enabled the forlorn hope, led by Lieutenant Irwin Dawson and Sergeant Andrew Spearman of the 100th Regiment with 20 Canadian volunteers, to get close to a tavern where Americans were spied playing cards. Spearman surprised the sentry, extracted the password, and left the man dead, and the rest of the small party rushed the tavern and bayoneted the occupants. A second public house on the way to Youngstown was similarly dealt with, and the force approached the fort, their nerves stretched when an accompanying horse let out shrill neigh that was answered by an equally shrill reply from within.[46]

Reaching the fort, they found the drawbridge down, and when the guard marched out to relieve those on duty they rushed the gate and secured entry. The defenders had taken no precautions, but as the British split into three groups they made the mistake of cheering, and the noise roused the defenders, who began firing from the interiors of the buildings while their women, "supposing we had Indians with us, were greatly frightened," recalled Private George Ferguson, "and ran around shrieking most piteously."[47] McClure reported with horror: "Our men were nearly all asleep in their tents, the Enemy rushed in and commenced a most horrid slaughter," which Lieutenant Henry Driscoll admitted included many "crying out for quarter."[48] The British inflicted 65 dead and 14 wounded, mostly with the bayonet, and took 350 prisoners, including the commander, Captain Nathaniel Leonard, who had been at home 3 miles away and rode up to the gate and into the bag; they suffered only 5 wounded and 6 killed in return.[49] Unfortunately this toll included Lieutenant Nowlan, who was found surrounded by three dead Americans, killed by his sword or pistol, but with his own "breast pierced by a deep bayonet wound at the bottom of which were a musket ball and three buckshot."[50]

The British also secured a huge quantity of war material: "The amount of cannon, muskets, shot, shells, powder, fixed ammunition, clothing & other supplies in Fort Niagara was immense," according to Governor Daniel D. Tompkins. "The acquisition of them will be of the greatest importance to the British, & an irreparable loss to us."[51]

Drummond had not expected quite so easy a time at Fort Niagara and had provided another force as a reserve under Riall, comprising battalion companies of the Royal Scots, 8th, 41st, and 100th Regiments and several hundred Indians under Matthew Elliott, which also crossed into American territory on 18 December. The following morning this force advanced on Black Rock led by the Light Company of the 2nd/89th Regiment, once more surprised the enemy piquets and took them prisoner, then seized a battery of five 6-pounders.[52] "The troops engaged were principally raw militia," recalled one defender, Private David Brayman, "and seeing for the first time the bursting of shells and rockets, and hearing the whizzing of bullets and hearing the horrid yells of savages, it is no wonder they did not fight better."[53] Nor could American officials persuade the militia to intervene; most of the men in the region had already served in several drafts and would not serve again. McClure reported that even those who were prepared to do so were unsurprisingly more interested "in taking care of their families and property by carrying them into the interior, than in helping us to fight."[54]

In fact, few were willing to serve under McClure, who was universally detested for his withdrawal and who shouldered the blame for the collapse of the front. McClure was replaced on Christmas Day at Batavia by Major-General Amos Hall; the following morning Hall set up his headquarters between Black Rock and Buffalo, which the British now threatened, and managed to raise 2,000 militia to face the British near Black Rock at the end of December.[55] Drummond approached Black Rock on the 29th and routed the militia guarding the bridge across the Shogeoquady Creek, and another 800 men sent forward by Hall to block them melted away, leaving him with just 1,200 men. Undaunted, he advanced on 30 December and briefly put up a show, but when the British rapidly threatened to envelop his force he ordered a retreat resulting in some disorder, and militia ran helter-skelter through Buffalo, panicking the civilian population.[56] Although Hall managed to cover the retreat, the British proceeded to destroy Lewiston and Buffalo, four armed schooners that had formed part of Perry's Lake Erie squadron wintering there, and large quantities of stores; their total losses came to 31 killed and 72 wounded.[57] Prevost deprecated the need for the destruction of towns, an action which in an indignant proclamation of 12 January 1814 he said was taken in direct response to the destruction of Newark. Future generations would scarcely believe "that in the enlightened era of the 19th century, and in the inclemency of a Canadian Winter, the troops of a nation calling itself Civilised and Christian . . . forced 400 helpless women and children . . . to be mournful spectators at the conflagration and total destruction of all that belonged to them."[58] The British government later approved the action, although Bathurst expressed hope that a repetition would not prove necessary.[59]

Lewis Cass arrived in Buffalo a week later to find the whole region depopulated as people fled their homes, and described "a scene of distress and destruction such as I have never before witnessed."[60] Thus the year ended with the Niagara Valley in flames, with 334 buildings worth £350,000 "enlightened" by British torches. "The whole frontier," lamented Tompkins, "from Lake Ontario to Lake Erie is depopulated & the buildings & improvements, with a few exceptions, destroyed."[61] Another witness later recorded the depredations wrought by the Indians, who had found liquor: "The sight we here witnessed was shocking beyond description. Our neighbors were seen lying dead in the fields and roads, some horribly cut and mangled with tomahawks, other eaten by the hogs."[62] However, there was no widespread assault or murder of civilians; four men were killed by drunken warriors at Lewiston in a brawl that also left two Indians dead and two British soldiers wounded, and much of the looting at Buffalo was carried out by American militia.[63]

Prevost could not afford to relax, although his efforts were appreciated in London, as he would discover in a dispatch from Bathurst, sent before news of victory at Châteauguay and Crysler's Farm had reached Britain, that absolved him of blame for the summer's misfortunes. Bathurst stressed the importance of maintaining the Lake Ontario fleet in being, and later, having learned of the victories before Montreal, he encouraged Prevost to continue to trust his own judgment, as "Justice will always be done to you. The Result of the Campaign is that to which the public will always look. Against occasional failures no man can guard. An extended line of frontier cannot everywhere be defended, against the Troops which the Enemy may be able, with their resources on the spot, to collect; with a force double what you have."[64] The British would hold Fort Niagara until the end of hostilities; in one month Drummond had more than cancelled American successes of the summer and brought "hard war" to American soil.[65] And except at Amherstburg, the Union flag still flew along the entire length of the "wide extended frontier."[66]

10.1. *The Refugees from the Niagara Frontier,* painting by Stanley Massey Arthurs, from *Scribner's Magazine,* 1905. *Source:* Picture Collection, Branch Libraries, New York Public Library, Astor, Lenox and Tilden Foundations.

As early as January 1814 Bathurst wrote to the Duke of Wellington that the time had come to start sending parts of his army in Spain to America. A month passed before Wellington replied, when he noted that the Royal Navy must dominate the lakes before ground operations could commence; and he cautioned that even then, it was doubtful that operations could so injure the United States as to cause it to sue for peace on any punitive terms.[67] Prevost was against any offensive measures at this stage, as James Monroe was now suggesting an armistice. Prevost did not have authority to accept such a proposal, but a prisoner exchange was agreed, releasing all prisoners in Canada and the United States except the twenty-three British hostages held in close confinement against the twenty-three Americans now held for treason in Britain as native-born subjects. After informing London of these developments, Prevost was curtly instructed to get on with fighting the war immediately.[68] The exchange of prisoners was a complicated matter which became increasingly difficult to manage on an equitable basis, as the British were taking so many along the eastern seaboard. Thomas Barclay in New York faced frequent angry mobs outside his house in Harlem reacting to "illegal" seizures of American ships and crews, while at the same time being widely criticized among Royal Navy officers for being weak and vacillating. In March he wrote to Cockburn to inform the latter of his move to Bladensburg, a village outside Washington, D.C., to facilitate communications, and stressing that in the one-sided exchange of prisoners Cockburn should ensure that American prisoners not be landed from His Majesty's ships without first receiving a similar number of Britons. Far too many captains were taking the easy way out by assessing enemy crews as "non-combatants" and landing them to avoid the difficulty of having to guard, feed, and transport them.[69]

Prevost was, however, still very short of men, having a total of around 15,000 regulars and fencibles—including sick and wounded—and very little by way of artillery, and he continued to press London for reinforcements. In January he therefore ordered six companies of the 2nd/8th Regiment to march overland from New Brunswick to Quebec City as the 104th had done the previous year. Lieutenant Marshall MacDermott described the march, which took forty-two days, but since two provision depots had now been formed along the line of march, this was broken into three stages of fourteen days each. When they reached the St. Lawrence still 90 miles short of Quebec, "the spontaneous kindness of the French Canadians could not have been exceeded," he recalled. "The Carrioles, sleighs and sledges of the whole district were assembled, and no man was suffered to march. They also fed the

Regiment during the whole route."[70] Prevost also received the 103rd Regiment and 2nd Battalion, Royal Marines, as reinforcements, although these were not enough to cover his losses, and he would be forced to rely heavily on the militia and Indians. He was also desperately short of money to pay the troops and feed dependants.[71]

In order to fight treasonous elements, Drummond urged the parliament of Upper Canada to suspend habeas corpus and to establish martial law for the procurement of supplies and setting of prices; the legislature agreed but took the opportunity to point out to the Prince Regent that the war had withdrawn 15,000 men from agriculture and that as a result of several harvest failures the province was suffering from genuine hunger.[72] Keen to improve his position, Prevost cautiously agreed when Drummond and Yeo planned a joint attack to finish off the Lake Erie squadron and even to recapture Detroit, which was defended by only 600 Americans. Drummond would leave 1,200 men to guard the Niagara frontier and take 1,760 picked men, equipped with bill-hooks, hatchets, and axes, over land and ice by sled at an estimated 30 miles per day.[73] But unusually mild conditions that made the 2nd/8th Regiment's march less arduous than the 104th's a year earlier—one man was killed by a falling tree, and fourteen were later discharged on account of severe frostbite—also melted the ice on the rivers necessary for a quick strike and forced Drummond to cancel his operation.[74]

Over the winter of 1813–14 and into the spring the Americans used Detroit as a base to send expeditions as far as the Long Point region, but neither side attempted a decisive manoeuvre.[75] Following Proctor's defeat at the Thames, the western portion of Upper Canada lay open to American invasion, but the Americans did not occupy it in force, and the war degenerated into a series of destructive marauding expeditions by American troops and Canadian renegades who took the opportunity to settle old scores by capturing militia officers and sending them to Detroit.[76] As the final report of the Loyal and Patriotic Society—founded by John Strachan—noted, Captain Daniel Springer "exerted himself in defending the province, by actively performing his duty on all occasions; he as usual therefore became obnoxious to the enemy and the disaffected, a party of whom seized him on the 1st February, 1814; and after binding him, took his own horses and sleigh, and placing him in it carried him to Kentucky."[77]

With the British and the militia too weak to hold a front, pitched battles of any sort were rare. The most notable was known as the battle of Long Woods, west of Burlington Heights, on 4 March, which saw some 240 British and

Canadians under Captain J. L. Barden sharply engaged by some 160 Americans under Captain Andrew H. Holmes, who had the better of it, leaving 14 British dead and 52 wounded against 4 Americans killed and 3 wounded.[78] But it was increasingly obvious that with the tide of war turned in Europe, it was no longer America that would be doing the invading, even if the Admiralty faced unusual problems on the lakes by having to build ships to gain ascendancy.

THE BALANCE on the lakes was always finely poised: at the end of July 1813 Bathurst had ordered that 300 seamen be sent there from Britain, and that Warren furnish another 300 from the North American Station at Halifax. But those from Britain did not arrive until November, by which time the disaster on Lake Erie had already placed fresh demands on Warren. Bathurst learned of the disaster on Lake Erie in November from an American newspaper and immediately wrote to Prevost to make every possible exertion to regain it.[79] In London discussion of the importance of control of the Great Lakes led the government to give the Royal Navy complete control. In January Yeo was promoted to commander-in-chief of His Majesty's ships and vessels employed on the lakes, removing them from Prevost's direction and from subordination to the admiral commanding the North Atlantic Station; but this step gave Yeo—a junior captain in a rear-admiral's command—massively more responsibility than he had experience to manage.[80] It was also a move likely to exacerbate inter-service rivalry by breaking the principle of unity of command, although at least reinforcements would be forthcoming. In December Yeo had requested that another 200 or more seamen for Lake Ontario be sent overland from Halifax to Quebec to be available for the spring of 1814. This transfer necessitated laying up four ships in Halifax and marching the men west through the snow, arriving at Kingston in March. Commander Edward Collier RN was also able to make the overland journey by snow-shoe and sleigh with 216 men, of whom 191 essential Royal Marines and Royal Navy personnel arrived fit for duty.[81] Captain George Downie RN led three other newly promoted captains and 900 junior officers and men from Britain for lake service, for which two sea-going ships had to be deactivated; and in March another 600 sailors and dockyard workers arrived in Canada, although Prevost had difficulty finding transport for them.[82] These reinforcements were essential, as in early March the Royal Navy would be behind, at least temporarily, in the crucial shipbuilding race on Lake Ontario: the British had eight ships carrying 76 long guns and 108 carronades, with two under construction, and although the launch of *Prince Regent* (56) and *Princess Charlotte* (42) on 14 April gave the British an advantage of about 25 guns overall, this was still not enough to change Yeo's stance to an aggressive one.[83] Meanwhile the rumours arriving from the American shore prompted the laying down of a third frigate that would eventually grow into a behemoth of oceanic proportions more powerful than Nelson's flagship at Trafalgar—HMS *St. Lawrence* (102).[84]

Warren continued to believe that Canada's defence would be best served by diversionary raids against the coast of the United States, and suggested New Orleans and Chesapeake Bay as rewarding targets; he also urged using disaffected minorities—Indians, Spanish, African-Americans—and referred with revulsion to the "British money . . . now used in the vindictive war carried on against us": a U.S. government loan of $7 million had been arranged in part by Baring Brothers of London.[85] But in 1813 British raiding operations along the Atlantic coast had failed to draw American regular troops from the critical Canadian frontier, where the U.S. Army now concentrated its best men. And with her ships bottled up in blockaded ports, the U.S. Navy was able to divert its best to the lakes. Plans to lay down two frigates and two brigs at Chatham dockyard and transport them across the Atlantic to the St. Lawrence overlooked the difficulties of getting them to the lakes, and more important was the critical shortage in Canada of ordnance, ammunition, anchors, sails, cordage, and other naval stores.[86] The costs involved in rectifying these shortages were extremely high; guns had to be hauled overland to avoid the threat of capture, and 200 ox-teams were secretly hired in New Hampshire and Vermont to sled them, so that it cost £6,000 to haul forty-six guns to Kingston.[87]

ON THE AMERICAN side Congress increased the regular army enlistment bounty on 27 January; this move was designed to bring in 14,000 recruits by September, as it was now clear that only regular troops were useful in a war against a professional army like the British. On 10 February three new rifle regiments were authorized, the original becoming the 1st, although the new units could raise only 1,006 men between them—only one-third of their theoretical strength.[88] And the general quality of regular recruits was never very high: few men enlisted out of patriotism; most did so from sheer economic necessity.[89] The most significant developments were an almost total changeover in command arrangements. Hampton was quietly invalided out to avoid embarrassing Armstrong, who in December 1813 recommended promoting

George Izard and Thomas Flournoy to major-general, passing over Andrew Jackson and Jacob Brown. Despite mounting pressure, Madison continued to support Armstrong, and he nominated Izard and Brown to Congress.[90] Soon enterprising young colonels, including Alexander Macomb, Edmund P. Gaines, Winfield Scott, and Eleazer W. Ripley, with an average age of thirty-three, were promoted to brigadier-general.[91] William Henry Harrison, however, resigned in May when it became apparent that he was being sidelined.

For the forthcoming campaign practically everyone agreed that Kingston had to be the primary objective, but Armstrong would end up directing operations against Niagara because of continuing communications problems with his commanders in the field.[92] Wilkinson bombarded him with embarrassingly half-baked schemes, then decided to break up the camp at French Mills. At the end of January Brown was ordered to march 2,000 men to Sackets Harbor while Wilkinson took the rest to Plattsburgh. They prepared to move on 3 February, burning the flotilla, including twelve gunboats and dozens of river craft stuck in the St. Lawrence ice, their blockhouses and accommodation, and any stores they could not carry away. The sick, who still numbered over 400, were sent by sleigh to Burlington, and the army marched out on the 9th.[93] Spies reported this activity to the British at Cornwall, and Lieutenant-Colonel Morrison—now returned from his sojourn in Quebec—decided to take pre-emptive action and sent a raid on Madrid, New York, where a sale of goods taken during the invasion was being organized.[94] The Americans were then pursued by a small detachment of the 89th and 103rd Regiments close to Plattsburgh that took 100 sleigh-loads of stores, including one carrying a hogshead of whiskey. But the contents never reached Canada: "soldiers ran up behind the sleigh, bored a hole with a bayonet, and secured in jugs the coveted fluid."[95]

The British were now free to roam the south bank of the St. Lawrence at will, creating a great feeling of insecurity among the inhabitants, although around ninety troops took the opportunity to desert. Prevost complained of the standard of soldier sent out to him: too many were convicts from the hulks, and no manner of discipline would turn them into soldiers.[96] In a theatre rife with disaffection on both sides, and where English-speakers could pass easily for either nationality, espionage was widespread, although the matter has been largely untouched by scholars owing to the absence of documentation; commanders were naturally reluctant to keep records in copybooks and journals. Prevost placed Edward Doyle at Prescott and Leon Lahanne at Montreal in charge of issuing licences to trade in Canada to

American merchants, in exchange for information, and they were also given information to pass on to the American authorities so that illegal trading would be overlooked.[97] But Major-General Sir Frederick Robinson was later highly critical of Prevost's refusal to allocate funds for intelligence-gathering. "Such doctrine is in direct opposition to the long established opinion that the lower class of Americans will do anything for money."[98] Equally the Americans tried to exploit disaffection in Upper Canada, and the letterbooks of Dearborn and Wilkinson are littered with references to unnamed spies, while renegade Canadians were regularly landed on the north shore of Lake Erie by Captain Arthur Sinclair to provide "considerable information as to the numbers, situation and movements of the enemy."[99] The tale of David Kilbourn might be typical: an American who moved to Upper Canada following the Revolution, he remained loyal to the United States and reported British military movements to Wilkinson via one of his agents. When confronted with his treachery he made his way to Wilkinson's camp at French Mills and later received some compensation from the American government, though not enough to cover the confiscation and sale of his property in Canada.[100]

Throughout January and February Armstrong was preparing to relieve Wilkinson of command, but he was not ready to make a decision until 24 March. He was too late; with his keen nose for impending trouble Wilkinson had roused himself for another foray into British territory, leading 4,000 men towards Montreal while requesting a court-martial to clear him of the "slanders and misrepresentations" he was suffering from the press.[101] On the 30th the American light troops entered Odelltown followed by three infantry brigades accompanied by a light dragoon squadron and eleven guns, and drove off the British piquets. They then attacked the post at Burton Ville held by two Canadian companies, which gave them such a warm reception that they were turned aside to attack the post at Lacolle Mill (modern Cantic, Quebec), a stone fortification on the river of the same name, defended by 180 men, including 70 Royal Marines under Major Richard Butler Handcock of the 13th Regiment.[102] Having gained possession of a wood before the post and detached a force to cut off Handcock's line of retreat, Wilkinson labouriously brought up two 12-pounder guns to assault the position, but they made little impression on the structure, as a disgusted civilian witness, James Wood, related to Armstrong; "what appears very extraordinary is that there was not energy enough to have got there an eighteen pounder, which was within three or four miles, and which was amply sufficient to have thrown the walls about their ears in a few moments."[103] Soon afterwards the flank companies of the

13th arrived from the blockhouse at Isle-aux-Noix. Handcock ordered them to cross the river and charge the guns, which they did but were driven off. Further reinforcements then arrived in the form of the Grenadier Company of the Canadian Fencibles, who because of snow-melt "were obliged to wade through mud and water up to their waists for many miles," and a company of Voltigeurs Canadiens. These four companies renewed the assault and drove the American gunners from their pieces, although they were unable to hold the position.[104]

Despite vastly outnumbering the British, Sergeant Jesse P. Harmon of the 11th U.S. Infantry recalled sadly: "We were exposed to a galling fire from the enemy and my brother received a mortal wound in his breast while fighting at my side."[105] The British were then further reinforced by two gunboats coming up the Richelieu River, forcing the Americans to retire. British losses were 13 killed and 50 wounded to 144 Americans killed, wounded, and missing; Wilkinson gave up his offensive and retired to the United States claiming that his ill-fated and ill-run expedition had produced a tonic effect on the U.S. Army.[106] Wilkinson had finally had enough, but to avoid an actual resignation his request of a court of inquiry on his conduct of the 1813–14 campaign was granted, although it did not sit until January 1815, and on 21 March he was acquitted of all charges when it became apparent that much of the blame lay with Armstrong. But the verdict came three weeks after Congress had reduced the size of the army, and he was dropped from the rolls, his long and far from illustrious career finally ended.[107]

American strategy for 1814 ignited from the embers of Buffalo, but Armstrong still managed to spread confusion among his subordinates. On 28 February he sent two letters to Major-General Jacob Brown, now commanding the Left Division of Military District No. 9 at Sackets Harbor, to try to revive the scheme for an attack against Kingston if certain conditions were met: good roads, good weather, and Chauncey's cooperation.[108] If this was the case, instructions contained in the second letter formed the basis of a deception cover plan, ordering Brown to join Winfield Scott at Batavia and await orders to attack Niagara.[109] Brown and Chauncey decided that the first plan put forward was too difficult, and Brown, taking the second as an alternative, set off as ordered. At Geneva he met Brigadier-General Edmund P. Gaines, who persuaded him that he was mistaken, and on 21 March Brown wrote to Armstrong to say he would return to Sackets Harbor. There he conferred once more with Chauncey, who convinced him that their original interpretation had been correct, and he now wrote to Armstrong for clarification, as he was "the most unhappy man alive."[110] He set out on 31 March to return to Batavia, where he received a letter from Armstrong dated 8 April saying he had been mistaken; Armstrong's original intent and the westward move had been intended as a feint.[111] This confusion was all the more annoying because conditions really did inhibit a move against Kingston, but Brown was a junior major-general and keen to make his mark while Armstrong's instructions were unnecessarily vague; he was trying to be too clever. Finally Armstrong submitted a plan to Madison on 30 April for an advance in Niagara, once more failing to aim at the crucial points of Kingston or Montreal, because although the U.S. Navy held control of Lake Erie it remained disputed on Lake Ontario.[112] Thus Armstrong ended up failing, as he had in 1813, to provide a clear and consistent policy, generating the fog of war rather than clearing it.[113]

On Lake Ontario the Americans were dilatory and did not begin enough ship construction to hope to ensure even a balance of power by early summer. In February two 22-gun brigs were laid down together with a frigate, *Superior,* intended for 60 guns but eventually built for less. A second frigate, *Mohawk* (42), was started in May and when completed in mid-summer gave the eight ships of the American squadron a slight advantage, but in no way a decisive one. A similar story obtained on Lake Champlain, where Macdonough launched *Saratoga* (26) on 11 April, just forty days after the trees in her were cut from the forest, to be followed by *Ticonderoga* (17) and *Preble* (7).[114] On 14 May Captain Daniel Pring RN sailed from Isle-aux-Noix with the intention of destroying American vessels being prepared at Vergennes, on Otter Creek in Vermont; but he found them too well defended, and, lacking a landing party, he retired without inflicting any serious damage.[115] There was then little action in the Lake Champlain region until the autumn; in the interim both sides concentrated on building their fleets.

With spring came news that the war in Europe was finally over. Bonaparte abdicated on 11 April, and four days later *The Times* thundered that with the tyrant now

> consigned to infamy, there is no public feeling in this country stronger than that of indignation against the Americans. That a republic boasting of its freedom should have stooped to become the tool of the Monster's ambition; that it should have attempted to plunge the parricidal weapon into the heart of the country whence it is derived; that it should have chosen the precise moment when it fancied that Russia was overwhelmed, to attempt to consummate the ruin of Britain—all this is

> conduct so black, so loathsome, so hateful, that it naturally stirs up the indignation that we have described.[116]

In America Federalists rejoiced, assuming the news would herald peace, but Republicans were sceptical.[117] According to reports reaching America, wilder voices in Britain were already calling for a new Indian boundary, exclusion from the Canadian fisheries and British West Indies, even the cession of New Orleans or a boundary 100 miles below the Great Lakes; "chastisement" was a word commonly bandied about.[118] America would now have to fight, said the Maryland lawyer and politician Joseph Nicholson, "not for free Trade and sailors rights not for the Conquest of the Canadas, but for our national Existence."[119]

11

Atlantic and Pacific

Roll on, thou deep and dark blue Ocean—roll!
Ten thousand fleets sweep over thee in vain;
Man marks the earth with ruin—his control
Stops with the shore;—upon the watery plain
The wrecks are all thy deed, not does remain
A shadow of man's ravage, save his own,
When for a moment, like a drop of rain,
He sinks into thy depths with bubbling groan,
Without a grave, unknell'd, uncoffin'd, and unknown.

—George Gordon, Lord Byron, *Childe Harold's Pilgrimage*

In July 1813 the US Brig *Argus* sailed for France under Captain William Henry Allen USN with the new American minister to that country.[1] On 20 July she left L'Orient and cruised into the English Channel, around Cornwall, and up the west coast of Ireland. On 1 August she sailed into the River Shannon, fooling the signal station on Kerry Head by showing British colours; she then took twenty prizes, arousing great excitement and amazement in Britain that such a thing could happen barely 60 miles from Cork, the headquarters of Vice-Admiral Edward Thornbrough, commander-in-chief of the Ireland Station. But this time the U.S. Navy had overreached itself, and a strong reaction was inevitable. Early on 14 August 1813 *Argus* was spotted off the south-west coast of Ireland by HM Brig *Pelican* (18), commanded by Captain John Maples RN.[2] The crew of the *Argus* may have been hung-over after capturing the *Bedford,* loaded with wine, the night before, and might have escaped had she chosen; she was a better sailor and faster than *Pelican.*[3] But though Allen's orders emphasized the importance of commerce-raiding and the defeat of a Royal Navy warship would contribute little to what Navy

Secretary Jones wanted *Argus* to accomplish, Allen felt his personal honour to be at stake and that his orders permitted engaging light cruisers.

The action began at 6 A.M.; within minutes Allen had his leg shot off and soon lost consciousness, and in rapid succession the rigging was smashed and officers either killed or wounded, leaving Lieutenant Howard Allen USN in command. But the key to her defeat was her failure to rake *Pelican* when she got into a position to do so, and *Pelican*'s subsequent broadsides were so devastating that within half an hour *Argus* was unmanageable. Although the wounded first lieutenant, William Watson, regained the deck after having had his scalp stitched, before the British could board the American struck her colours, having lost ten dead and eight wounded; the British suffered two dead and five wounded.[4] The noise of battle was heard 20 miles away at Milford Haven, where the inhabitants were "alarmed by a tremendous firing."[5] The prisoners were brought ashore and sent to Dartmoor prison, officially styled "The Depot for Prisoners of War at Dartmoor," a facility scheduled to hold 10,000 men, although it rarely held more than 8,000. At the time it contained some 600 Americans, including some of the 2,500 former American Royal Navy personnel who refused to continue to serve during the war with America. There on 18 August the mood changed abruptly when one of their number, John Robinson, announced that he was, in fact, James Hunter of Dundee, and that seven men among the prisoners were really British. That same night Captain Allen died; he was buried three days later with full military honours.[6] Meanwhile, a thorough investigation found that none of those accused by Robinson/Hunter was in fact British, and Robinson himself escaped.[7]

Following her capture *Argus* was operated as a British privateer, *Vittoria,* and later took the Baltimore schooner *Eliza* while operating out of Guernsey.[8] But on 5 September the Americans gained a measure of revenge when US Brig *Enterprise* (16) defeated HM Brig *Boxer* (14) off the coast of Maine in an hour-long action in which both captains—Captain Samuel Blyth RN and Lieutenant William Burrows USN—were killed.[9] The American enjoyed a manpower advantage (120 to 66), and in considering this engagement, William James noted that not only was the American vessel bigger and altogether a better sailor, but also American carronades were superior, being both heavier and therefore more stable, and longer, giving greater range. But he also acknowledged superior American gunnery.[10]

On the Pacific coast Fort Astoria was the first permanent U.S. settlement, a fur-trading post established in 1811 by John Jacob Astor's Pacific Fur Company;

but on eventually hearing of the declaration of war in July 1813, the company partners held a meeting and agreed that they could not defend Astoria against the British.[11] A resolution was signed dissolving the company and agreeing to abandon the area to the North West Company the following year, but on 7 October John McTavish arrived with a party of seventy-one North West trappers. He produced a letter to the effect that an expedition had sailed from London with orders to seize Fort Astoria. When the ship did not arrive as expected, and since McTavish and his men were being supplied by the Astorians, negotiations began for Astoria's sale, which was finally signed on 12 November. On 30 November 1813 HMS *Racoon* arrived, and Captain William Black RN took formal possession, declaring Fort Astoria a conquest of war and promptly renaming it Fort George.[12]

On the Atlantic coast on 7 November Fort Sullivan at Eastport, Maine, fired its guns in anger for the first and only time during the war to force a large sloop, the *Venture* of Saint John, to heave to. It appeared that the previously peaceful accommodation along the north-east border was at an end until a worried correspondence confirmed that Captain Sherman Leland of the 34th U.S. Infantry had not, in fact, zealously chosen to open hostilities in the region, but was merely acting as "an auxiliary to the Revenue department" and intercepting a suspected smuggling vessel. Leland was awarded thousands of dollars for the prize, despite having used federal arms and soldiers to accomplish his feat, and promptly resigned his commission, thus avoiding service on the active northern frontier. He later appeared at Dorchester, Massachusetts, where he made a patriotic Independence Day speech in which he insisted that only "a servile wretch would sell his country for gold."[13]

Yet if trade is considered as another front in the war, its continuance through smuggling might be considered as serious a defeat for America as was the loss of Detroit or the *Chesapeake*. For smuggling in the Passamaquoddy region, through deception, twisting the law, and where deemed necessary outright violence, resulted in no less than the effective loss of an entire regiment sent to stamp it out.[14] As the war raged in the Canadas, neighbouring New Brunswick, founded in 1784 as a refuge for Loyalists fleeing the American Revolution, remained not only unscathed but unthreatened; only the distant deployment of the 104th Regiment and privateering by its seamen served as reminders of the war. Hostilities stimulated economic development to such an extent that Fredericton became "shockingly dull."[15] Officials in New Brunswick and Nova Scotia remained quite unconcerned by the origin of New England lumber and provisions. Conversely, as the British blockade bit deeper, it distorted the American economy by forcing traders to rely on the hopelessly inadequate road system, creating gluts and shortages in equal measure. By the end of 1813 the shortage of imported manufactures was also leading to panic buying, and coffee, sugar, salt, molasses, cotton, and spices trebled or even quadrupled in price.[16]

As Bonaparte slid to defeat in Europe, the situation of his friends across the Atlantic grew increasingly uncomfortable. Until 1813 American grain was still important to feeding Wellington's army; only as 1813 drew to a close, with the markets of Europe once again open to Britain, did Madison choose to extend the embargo on American trade in a way that could do no harm to anybody save Americans. On 17 December he persuaded Congress to prohibit food and contraband from being taken to sea—a measure aimed primarily at New England and which only intensified the bitterness felt there towards the administration, further heightened when Armstrong began talking of conscription.[17] Licensed flour exports, which had been close to a million barrels in 1812 and 1813, rapidly fell to 5,000 in 1814, by which time the insurance rates on Boston shipping had reached 75 percent, coastal shipping was at a complete standstill, and New England was considering secession.[18] Although the British did not extend the blockade to New England until April 1814, by the previous autumn there were already 250 ships idle in Boston, and people were leaving the city to look for work.[19] And although there remained rich pickings to be made from the war for those with an eye for the main chance—especially through smuggling and privateers, always as much a search for profit as a pursuit of war—by 1813 American privateers found chances of success far smaller, since most British merchantmen now sailed in convoy. One captain reported "vexing the whole Atlantic" without sighting a single British vessel.[20] Only by sailing close to the West Indies and the British Isles, where merchant ships travelled unescorted, could Americans find prizes; in 1813 there were so many American privateers in the Caribbean that they almost succeeded in blockading Jamaica.[21] On 21 November 1813 the *Lapwing,* a packet on which Ensign Henry Senior of the 60th Regiment was travelling to join his fellows at Bermuda, was taken by the American privateer *Fox* after a stiff fight.[22]

The most spectacular of these cruises was by the brig *True-Blooded Yankee* (16), a small vessel fitted out by a Rhode Islander called Preble living in Paris and captained by James DeWolf. The crew was drawn from Americans willing to exchange their cells in French prisons for the chance of prize money, and included an Englishman called John Wiltshire masquerading as American John Riley. *True-Blooded Yankee* took twenty-seven prizes on a thirty-seven-day cruise around the coasts of Britain, including the *Margaret,* on which John Wiltshire went as a member of the prize crew. When *Margaret* was recaptured shortly afterwards, Wiltshire was hanged.[23] The crew also occupied an Irish island for six days and brazenly sailed into Bowmore on Islay, where they burned seven vessels. "She outsailed everything," noted another British officer; "not one of our cruisers could touch her."[24] Nevertheless, she was later taken by HM Brig *Hope,* whose master, James Weddell, would later find fame as an Antarctic explorer. In the North Sea and off North Cape the *Scourge* (15) under Captain Samuel C. Nicholls and the *Rattlesnake* (16) under Captain David Maffet—two of the outstanding privateer captains of the war—made equally good hunting, taking twenty-three prizes between them, which they sent to Norwegian ports for condemnation. *Scourge* then made another successful cruise and took more prizes on her way home. This form of commercial warfare bedevilled Britain throughout 1813 and into 1814.[25]

A weakness in historical writing about the war, however, is the failure to evaluate the effect of privateering; for example, knowing the British were short of seamen, the U.S. government offered a bounty for each prisoner brought in, starting at $20 in 1812 and rising to $100 in 1814.[26] For individuals it was a means of ekeing out a living in hard times, and a risky means too, since they were not always successful. One famous privateer was the *Grand Turk* (14) out of Salem, Massachusetts, a purpose-built 310-ton vessel whose wide-ranging cruises took her to Brazil, the West Indies, and the English Channel and netted some thirty prizes. Her various brushes with the Royal Navy included an epic chase by two frigates. But she failed against the packet *Hinchinbrook* in May 1814, which, though heavily outgunned, prevented the American crew from boarding and fought her off.[27] Eventually Lloyd's counted 1,175 British ships as taken by the Americans during the war (less 373 recaptured, for a total loss of 802)—considerably fewer than the numbers sometimes bandied around—and this figure was less impressive than it might appear because the British merchant fleet comprised over 25,000 ships, and overseas trade grew rapidly throughout the period, seemingly little affected.[28]

There were also 41 Canadian privateers. As soon as war erupted, Nova Scotia ship-owners, mainly from Liverpool and Lunenburg, became particularly interested in obtaining letters of marque, and they captured at least 207 American ships during the war, outstripping the number taken by the Americans.[29] The most redoubtable of the Canadian privateers was the *Liverpool Packet* (5) under Joseph Barss and Lewis Knaut, which alone took some

50 prizes worth an estimated £52,800. In June 1813 she was herself taken by the *Thomas* of Portsmouth, New Hampshire.[30] (Three weeks later *Thomas* was itself taken by HMS *Nymphe.*) She operated briefly as the *Portsmouth Packet* until taken by HMS *Fantôme* in October, whereafter she was commanded by Caleb Seely for another successful eleven months from December 1813—exploits worthy of the best adventure films.[31] But the most significant difference with the Americans was one of scale: most American vessels hunted larger, more valuable quarry in the West Indies or in European waters, while Nova Scotia and New Brunswick crews focused on smaller coastal traders close to home.[32] And Canadians were not the only privateers operating in American waters: the British privateer *Dart* preyed upon shipping in Long Island Sound for some time, taking over 20 vessels. On 4 October 1813 Captain John Cahoone of the U.S. Customs Service spotted her off Newport with two freshly caught prizes; taking twenty Navy volunteers on board to augment his regular crew, he boldly sailed the revenue cutter *Vigilant* well within gun range of the more heavily armed sloop and loosed a broadside, which stunned the privateer; a boarding party from the revenue cutter quickly scrambled aboard as she brushed alongside her quarry and quickly took her, losing two men who fell into the water and drowned.[33]

Once the British blockade closed in along the New England seaboard, however, Canadian privateering in the area became commercially unviable, and by 1814 it had ceased entirely, since the booming wartime economy offered better alternatives.[34] Privateering also declined sharply in the United States, as those ships that did manage to sneak out through the blockade could not sneak their prizes back in for condemnation. Later they would often simply take what was valuable off a victim and scuttle her. Privateering also held another kind of risk: privateers may have been fast sailors, but their victims seldom were; some two-thirds of prize crews were captured before they could reach port, so that many privateersmen ended up spending the war languishing at Melville or Dartmoor prisons. Investors persisted only as long as there were profits to be made, but they began to agitate for peace when these prospects diminished.[35]

BY 1813 Sir John Borlase Warren was not well regarded at the Admiralty, where his frequent requests for reinforcements elicited sarcastic replies. His suggestion that he be relieved of the Jamaica and Leeward Island commands also raised eyebrows, as the Admiralty did not favour senior officers who sought to reduce their responsibilities. The North American and West Indies Stations had been united early in the war to promote coordinated action against the United States, but the West Indies had continually complained of being neglected and were seemingly at the mercy of privateers. On 4 November 1813 Croker informed Warren that the commands would, indeed, be separated, but that Warren was to return to Britain.[36] Warren wrote of his hurt at being relieved "after having zealously and faithfully served my sovereign and country under so many disadvantages."[37]

In the meantime he implemented Admiralty instructions, which ordered that 10 "razees" (cut-down 74s large enough to cope with super-frigates), 20 frigates, 25 ships or sloops rated at 20 guns, and various smaller craft be stationed at Halifax. Jamaica and the Leewards would each have a flagship, 2 and 3 frigates, and 15 and 12 smaller frigates and sloops respectively. Nevertheless, these strengths were not maintained, and Warren continued to press for reinforcements, pointing out that the British suffered from lack of convoy escorts and from craft capable of challenging the superior sailing qualities of American privateers.[38] Even so, in November he extended the reach of the blockade to cover Long Island Sound, though still leaving New England clear. It now stretched all the way south to the Mississippi and severely affected American trade.[39]

The U.S. Navy was rightly wary: in late December the schooner *Vixen* (18) was taken off Wilmington, North Carolina, by *Belvidera.* In early January Cockburn nearly came to grief when the ageing *Sceptre* almost foundered in a heavy gale and had to be nursed back to Bermuda. On the 31st he hoisted his flag on HMS *Albion* (74); it was, noted Captain John Robyns RM, "the coldest day I ever remember . . . Blocks of ice were formed on the yards, and the Ropes were all frozen, the Deck was also a sheet of ice."[40] Early in December Commodore John Rodgers managed to slip out of Providence with *President* and cruised the West Indies, evading the blockade and returning to Sandy Hook on 18 February 1814, having taken no prizes.[41] Although HMS *Loire* (38) might have intercepted her, she adhered to Admiralty policy that 18-pounder frigates were not to take on American 24-pounder vessels in single-ship engagements. On 1 January *Constitution* slipped out of Boston under Captain Charles Stewart USN and also cruised the West Indies and off Guinea; she also took few prizes, although these included HM Schooner *Pictou* (14). On 3 April she slipped skilfully back into Marblehead despite the presence of *Junon* and *Tenedos* standing off that port, and subsequently made Boston.[42] Off New London, Connecticut, Captain Sir Thomas Masterman

Hardy was conducting the blockade of Decatur's squadron, and the British were supplied with everything they needed from local sources: "Fortunately for us," Hardy wrote to his father, "Block Island has no guns on it, therefore we get plenty of water and stock from it and we also get our linen washed there. The inhabitants are very much alarmed and of course they are most completely in our power, but as long as they supply us we shall be very civil to them."[43] Decatur was well aware of the climatic vagaries of this stretch of coast and that heavy rainfall was often followed by severe frosts, so he planned to time his escape for a period when the sails of the British ships might be frozen hard and unspreadable. But although his reasoning appeared sound, he did not know that the British had taken the precaution of covering their sails with white painted cloths to protect them from just such problems. And the local population was far from sympathetic to their countryman; they kept the British fully informed of Decatur's position. When he made an attempt to slip out, somebody ashore signalled to the British by flashing blue lights, and he found himself forced to turn back and abandon the attempt, taking his frigates as far upriver as possible, where they remained for the rest of the war.[44]

In due course Warren's replacement at Halifax would be a fifty-six-year-old Scot, Vice-Admiral Sir Alexander Forrester Inglis Cochrane, youngest son of the impecunious eighth earl of Dundonald; a consummate professional with considerable experience of the West Indies since 1800, he had previously served as governor of Guadeloupe.[45] Cochrane arrived in March, although much to his annoyance Warren delayed formally handing over until 1 April, but this was an especially favourable time: French resistance was finally collapsing, and Cochrane could look forward to far more support than Sawyer or Warren had enjoyed; he also brought much-needed energy.[46] He had already asked the Admiralty for an additional thirty frigates, forty sloops, and twenty armed vessels together with an additional 1,000 men to bring ships already on station up to complement.[47] Furthermore, he was relieved of responsibility for the Jamaica and Leeward Islands Stations, while Rear-Admiral Anselm John Griffith had been directed to conduct the blockade of Boston, reporting directly to the Admiralty, so that Cochrane did not have to divert energy to logistical matters north and south of his main area of operations centred on the Chesapeake.[48]

Gentlemen officers detested blockade duty as both boring and cruel. HMS *Nymphe* (38) was engaged in blockade off Boston in 1814, and Lieutenant Edward Napier RN recalled the tedious nature of such duties:

> Found the month of April, on and about St. George's Bank, extremely unpleasant and changeable from *bad* to *worse;* very cold, with damp, penetrating fogs, constantly and alternately changing to rain with the wind from west round by south to east, when it hardens into snow and sleet, which continues till it veers to the westward of north, a sure indication of a hard frost; thus the comforts of a winter cruise on the coast of North America are inexhaustible.[49]

He recorded that his flotilla burned two vessels but allowed a third to pass simply because it belonged to an old man with eight children who had lost $20,000 worth of shipping in the previous two years. They burned a sloop with shingles aboard that belonged to three "females" who had been given the shingles in lieu of payment for teaching, and the officers made personal donations as recompense for their loss. A small ship-owner with a wife and seven children was obliged to pay $200 ransom; he "with great difficulty scraped up by sixpences and shillings the amount . . . and came on board with tears in his eyes." Napier decided it was "an ungenerous war against the poor, and unworthy of Englishmen."[50] But however distasteful it may have been to young men like Lieutenant Napier, blockade was an effective weapon, as Bonaparte had learned to his cost.

Although Madison responded to the British blockade by denouncing it as illegal, hoping that European neutrals would oppose it, with Bonaparte defeated nobody dared challenge British naval mastery.[51] Exports and imports were severely curtailed as the American shipping tonnage engaged in foreign trade dropped from 948,000 tons in 1811 to just 60,000 tons in 1814, the rest rotting—a considerable capital loss—while the economic bottlenecks that had appeared in 1813 got progressively worse: merchants and fishermen could not put to sea, and farmers could not move their produce to foreign markets. Although the effects were partly offset by new economic activity, including privateering, and western cities such as Pittsburgh, Cincinnati, Louisville, and St. Louis saw a wartime boom, the total effect of war on the American economy was starkly negative, driving the government toward financial crisis.[52] By September 1814 American exports had dropped to just $7 million from a pre-war level of $45 million; yet supplies still reached Canada. Indeed, the south was more badly affected than New England, with Virginia exporting goods worth just $17,851 for the whole of 1814, although New York managed only $209,000, while the restrictions on trade between sections drove prices still higher. Government receipts fell, and the financial situation of the country became critical, forcing the repeal of the embargo in April, having achieved nothing except, as in 1808, to stir resentment in New England.[53]

On taking command on 2 April, Cochrane immediately announced the extension of the blockade to the entire coast of the United States and declared his determination to pursue his campaign with particular ruthlessness.[54] Cochrane's proclamation also informed those who desired "to emigrate" from the United States that they would be received aboard His Majesty's ships and could either join British forces or be sent as free settlers to British possessions in North America or the West Indies. Although slaves were not specifically mentioned, it was plain to whom this appeal was addressed, and it later caused him some difficulties when reports, though baseless, reached Britain that some escaped slaves had been sold in the West Indies or sent to Cochrane's own plantation in Trinidad.[55] He also extended raiding operations to include New England. Captain Richard Coote RN, part of the blockading force off New London, was ordered on 7 April to lead a force 6 miles up the Connecticut River to destroy privateers and other vessels equipping there or under construction. The raid was facilitated by an American traitor who volunteered to guide the British on the promise of a handsome cash reward in the event of success. The next morning at 3:30 A.M. Coote led a party of 136 men to Pautopaug Point, where they destroyed twenty-seven vessels, including three large privateers, fully equipped and provisioned and ready to put to sea, and pierced for 134 guns, totalling 5,110 tons worth $150,000, then slipped past the militia in the dark to reach safety, losing two men killed and two wounded.[56] The traitor received $1,000 subscribed for him by the blockading squadron, and Cochrane directed that he should receive another $1,000 to encourage others to follow suit, although this proved an isolated incident.[57]

Throughout the war British sailors spent many long and boring weeks on "far distant, storm-beaten ships," as Admiral Mahan described them, on tedious and unglamourous blockade duty through watch upon watch upon watch.[58] Watches were the means by which the crew was organized to run the ships, there usually being two—larboard and starboard. Each would work four hours on and four hours off, while in the early evening there would be two "dog watches" of two hours each, so that the men would not work the same hours every day. A small portion of the crew—cooks, carpenters, and specialists of one sort or another—would not be part of the watches but were known as "idlers," and would work a more regular day, beginning when the crew—at least that part not already on watch—would be roused and hammocks stowed, usually at around 7 A.M., depending on latitude and time of year. All hands would then be piped to breakfast, regarded, as were all meals, as one of the high points of the seaman's day.

Theoretically each man was entitled to a pound of bread, or more usually biscuit, per day, together with 4 pounds of beef, 2 of pork (fresh if possible but usually salted), 2 of peas, one of oatmeal, 6 ounces of sugar, 6 of butter, and 12 of cheese spread over the week, although any part of this might be replaced by other items, such as rice for bread or biscuit, according to availability. Cooking simply involved boiling in large kettles, and although nobody ever praised monotonous naval food, neither did they condemn it. Water was available, but most men preferred beer, to which they were entitled to a gallon per man per day, or a pint of wine or half-pint of rum—watered into "grog"—brandy, or other spirits in lieu. Strong liquor was intended to keep the men contented but was often the cause of mistakes and indiscipline.[59] On station off America, just like the army along the Canadian border, the Royal Navy always found it possible to receive fresh vegetables and cattle for good, hard cash. "The fact is notorious," complained the Lexington *Reporter*, that the Royal Navy "derive their supplies from the very country which is the theatre of their atrocities."[60] Not that they often had to resort to threats, finding no shortage of takers for their gold and silver; British ships were freely supplied by the locals. Chesapeake Bay, Vineyard Sound, and Long Island Sound fairly teemed with little coastal vessels offering supplies, with some sixty operating in the last alone.[61]

On 25 April 1814 Cochrane re-ordered the blockade to include New England by assigning two 74s and supporting vessels to the area between Long Island Sound and Nantucket, and a similar force to continue the line to New Brunswick. At the end of May he denied a request from Halifax merchants to allow trade under licence with American ports, noting that the latest embargo had just been lifted because of the parlous state of America's finances, and that any trade now would help the United States to raise money.[62] When the Assembly of New Brunswick recommended the seizure of eastern Maine in order to shorten the line of communication with Canada, the plan was approved in London by Bathurst, who was also eyeing New England with a view to potential future boundaries.[63] Little opposition was expected from the New Englanders, and he sent directions for the occupation of the islands in Passamaquoddy Bay, on the New Brunswick–Maine border; this operation would come under the command of Captain Hardy, and troops would be provided by transferring the 102nd Regiment under the command of Lieutenant-Colonel Thomas Pilkington from Bermuda in early 1814 to gather at Halifax and Shelburne under Sherbrooke, avoiding Saint John, as this would cause alarm.[64]

Meanwhile Cockburn had been back on station at Lynnhaven Bay since 23 February, while *Constellation* remained in her berth at Norfolk protected by twenty-two gunboats.[65] Although Cockburn remained keen to get at her, throughout March severe weather conditions permitted only the maintenance of the blockade, and during April he began preparing Fort Albion, a small base on Tangier Island in Chesapeake Bay. In early May he received instructions from Cochrane:

> You are at perfect liberty as soon as you can muster a sufficient force, to act with utmost hostility against the shores of the United States. Their government authorise and direct the most destructive war to be carried on against our commerce and we have no means of retaliating but on shore where they must be made to feel in their property what our merchants do in having their ships destroyed.[66]

He went on to explain the need to draw off American forces now gathering for another tilt at Canada, noting the destruction wrought against civilians at Newark and elsewhere during the most inclement season of the year. Cochrane also agreed with Cockburn's proposals for Tangier Island, including the raising of a Colonial Corps from among escaped slaves to help garrison it, clothed from Royal Marine uniforms and paid a $20 bounty, following a suggestion by Charles Napier.[67]

In May the command of the Colonial Marines at Fort Albion on Tangier Island was given to a senior Royal Marine sergeant with acting rank of ensign and adjutant, and the small corps proved remarkably successful in sorties from the island, which yielded over $1 million worth of booty and helped in a successful boat attack at Pungoteague, Virginia.[68] Supported by a rocket-boat and carronades mounted on launches, a force of Royal Marines, bluejackets (sailors), and Colonial Marines captured a battery and destroyed a barracks on 30 May. In this action the former slaves gave "a most excellent specimen of what they are likely to be. Their conduct was marked by great spirit and vivacity, and perfect obedience."[69] Already many slave families had arrived only to meet disappointment, since Cockburn was in no position to grant them the utopia they expected; some even asked to be returned to their former owners. He allowed some visits by American militia to make these transfers, but this process had to cease when it became too difficult to control, and feeding the extra mouths while his own seamen were already on short rations, and finding transport to take the refugees to Bermuda, both proved massive problems and posed continuing difficulties.[70]

By now Joshua Barney had assembled a flotilla of some thirty craft at Baltimore, including his flagship, *Scorpion,* mounting eight carronades and a long gun, and another nineteen gunboats with a long gun in the bow and another in the stern on a traversing carriage, each manned by a crew of forty to sixty.[71] Barney sailed on 24 May to join other flotillas at Norfolk and in the Potomac, hoping to be able to release *Constellation* and to confront Cockburn once and for all; but this depended on Barney's ability to evade the British watch between Tangier Island and Smith's Point, on the southern stretch of the Potomac. His luck did not match his daring: on 1 June his twenty-five-strong flotilla of gunboats with a few sloops and schooners met HM Schooner *St. Lawrence* (14) and a number of ships' boats under the command of Captain Robert Barrie RN of HMS *Dragon* (74) out on a reconnaissance near Cedar Point.[72] Skilfully using his boats as decoys, Barrie lured the Americans forward while he rejoined *Dragon,* which was now under sail. Barney had no option but to shelter in the Patuxent River, where he was blockaded and never subsequently escaped. Although Barrie could not risk *Dragon* in the river, with the aid of smaller vessels he was able to press Barney farther upriver into St. Leonard's Creek.[73] Cockburn was delighted, writing to Barrie: "I am sorry the *Dragon* was not able to get up with the Baltimore flotilla before they housed themselves in the Patuxent. It is, however, of all the rivers in the Chesapeake, the best to have them in."[74] On 6 June Barney attacked his oppressors, and *St. Lawrence* was grounded on her way downstream; only by stationing officers in the tops of other vessels was Barrie able to prevent her loss. Four days later he counter-attacked, and thereafter many attempts were made to lure Barney out of his anchorage, but without success; various landings were made in which vast quantities of tobacco were taken, but Barney ignored the bait, although Cockburn admitted that he "has occasioned me much anxiety and difficulty."[75]

In June, on learning that two ships were ready for launching in Buzzard's Bay, Massachusetts, one being a 444-ton ship and the other a 300-ton privateer, the New London squadron prepared for a second raid in which both vessels were burned, along with fifteen other vessels amounting to 2,552 tons and a large cotton mill.[76] In the middle of the month Barrie managed to get as far up the Patuxent River as Benedict, Maryland, which he found hastily deserted, but there a skirmish was fought with local dragoons.[77] He then went upstream to Marlborough, whence he reported:

> Marlborough is near the seat of government. I thought an attack on this town would be a sad annoyance to the enemy and oblige the regulars and militia to try their strength with us, but I was deceived as both the militia and the inhabitants made off to the woods and we were allowed to take possession of a town admirably suited for defence. Here we passed the night without molestations *though only 18 miles from Washington.*[78]

But Washington was alarmed, and Barney was ordered to destroy his flotilla, the Americans hoping that this move would persuade the British to withdraw. The order was rescinded only when a colonel offered to drive the British off with artillery established to command St. Leonard's Creek. On 26 June a simultaneous attack by the American gunboats and this battery forced *Loire* and *Narcissus* to withdraw to Point Patience while the American flotilla moved farther upstream having lost two gunboats.[79]

Cochrane utterly detested the Americans, whom he regarded as a "whining, canting race," an opinion shared by Captain David Milne RN, who thought them a "sad despicable set" totally ruled by self-interest.[80] Rear-Admiral Henry Hotham, commanding at Bermuda, had previously suggested that "the place where Americans [were] most vulnerable is New Orleans and . . . [its capture] will be the severest blow America can meet with," implying that such a blow would halt American "operations against Canada."[81] Cochrane agreed, and wrote to the Admiralty urging approval for an expedition against New Orleans, believing that action in the region could exploit discontent within the Indian, French, and Spanish populations. But Bermuda was as yet undeveloped to support any large expedition: Cochrane had first to institute dredging operations and improve hospital facilities and the defences of St. George's Bay; the dockyard lacked sufficient stores and skilled craftsmen; and the war had exacerbated the costs of feeding and otherwise supplying increased military and naval personnel—a problem that also affected Jamaica.[82] When Milne arrived at Bermuda later that year in HMS *Bulwark* (74), he reported that although they managed to get a good supply of everything, "lucky it was for us, this is the most miserable place to get any supplies that I ever was at. Beef (perfect carrion) 4s a pound, eggs 6s a dozen, poultry 10s a couple and fish 10d a pound."[83]

Since the outbreak of war, the British had wanted to use Florida and local Indians as a base to attack the United States, but they were not in a position to do so until 1814.[84] Now Cochrane ordered Captain Hugh Pigot RN of HMS *Orpheus* (22) accompanied by HM Schooner *Shelburne* (12) to establish contact with the Creek Indians and supply them with arms.[85] Pigot anchored near the Apalachicola River on 10 May and following meetings with tribal chiefs reported to Cochrane that some 2,800 Creeks were ready to cooperate with the British, that another 1,000 might be recruited from the swamps near Pensacola, and that Georgia African-Americans might also be willing to join them if arms were available. He thought Baton Rouge might then fall to "a handful" of British troops, and from there New Orleans would be an easy conquest; some 800 pirates at Barataria would also assist if promised protection.[86] Pigot's report was hopelessly optimistic: it not only underestimated American efforts to defend Mobile and New Orleans but also completely ignored the crushing effect of Jackson's victories over the Creeks. Cochrane sent Captain William Percy RN of HMS *Hermes* (22) with three other vessels to blockade the mouth of the Mississippi and convey Major Edward Nicolls RM with 115 men to organize and train the Indians.[87] Nicolls took two howitzers, a gun, 1,000 stands of arms, and instructions to enlist any African-Americans he could muster; he was also to conduct reconnaissance west of the Apalachicola River.[88] On the basis of Pigot's report, on 20 June Cochrane urged the government to mount an expedition, claiming that if 3,000 British troops were landed at Mobile, "they would be joined by all the Indians, with the disaffected French and Spaniards, [and] would drive the Americans entirely out of Louisiana and the Floridas."[89] Stating that he would lead the expedition himself, he proposed October and November as the best season, and requested shallow-draught boats to enable him to operate along the coast from Mobile to Lake Pontchartrain, whence he would attack New Orleans.[90] Cochrane was confident of success in the mild autumn weather; for over two years the warehouses of New Orleans had accumulated sugar, tobacco, cotton, and hemp that he estimated to be worth £4 million, and as commander-in-chief he stood to gain around £125,000 should the city fall, though whether this was Cochrane's prime motivation for the New Orleans expedition remains a contentious point.[91]

Bathurst cast about for a military commander for operations south of Canada, considering two of Wellington's most able subordinates, Sir Thomas Picton and Sir Rowland Hill, and eventually settling on the latter. But although the government decided in July to adopt Cochrane's plan, the slowness of communications meant that the reply from London did not reach Cochrane until 10 August. The Admiralty informed him that a force of such size would not require a general of Hill's seniority to command it.[92] Instead he would have Major-General Robert Ross's force—then engaged at Washington—available for his enterprise, to be reinforced in mid-November by another 2,130 men due at Jamaica, where he would be supplied with twenty shallow-draught vessels, and would be further reinforced by the 5th West India Regiment and 200 pioneers (construction troops); their lordships also judged the climate unfavourable for operations before December.[93]

CAPTAIN David Porter USN spent the autumn of 1813 refitting in the Marquesas, where Lieutenant John M. Gamble of the U.S. Marine Corps was given an independent command. Little occurred for several months until there was a mutiny during which Gamble was wounded in the foot. He escaped, beat off an Indian attack, and sailed for Hawaii, where he eventually surrendered to HM Sloop *Cherub*.[94]

Porter and *Essex* arrived off the coast of Chile at Valparaiso, where Captain James Hillyar RN finally caught up with him on 8 February 1814 and found Porter anchored with two of his prizes. The crews were in good spirits as at the top of the fore top-gallant mast the Americans hoisted a white flag bearing the motto: "Free Trade and Sailors' Rights." Hillyar's *Phoebe* responded with one reading "God and Country; British sailor's best rights; traitors offend both."[95] Hillyar put to sea on 15 February and cruised offshore for six weeks, waiting for chance to nail the American. On 25 March Porter burned the prize *Hector* in Valparaiso harbour, an act that Hillyar regarded as violating the neutrality of the Chilean port. Two days later *Essex* put to sea, with Porter hoping to persuade Hillyar to engage him singly; but when Hillyar refused despite abusive songs from the American crew, Porter returned to the bay.[96] The British had too much experience of war to indulge in pointless bravado, and the fifty-year-old Hillyar was a cool and calculating professional intent on victory; besides, engaging Porter in single-ship action would contravene specific Admiralty orders. Farragut in later life would sympathize with Hillyar's decision, and even come to question the judgement of his captain and foster-father.[97] *Essex* was probably a better sailor than *Phoebe* and had the edge at short range, with forty 32-pounder carronades and six long 12-pounders; but combined the two British ships were superior, with *Phoebe* carrying twenty-six long 18-pounders, four long

9-pounders, and fourteen 32-pounder carronades; *Cherub* carried eighteen 32-pounder and six 18-pounder carronades with two long 6-pounders.

On 28 March a strong wind broke Porter's larboard cable and dragged his starboard anchor to sea, forcing him to make sail quickly. At 4 P.M. "the Enemy came out and the action immediately commenced," wrote Lieutenant Charles Sampson RM to his brother.[98] *Phoebe* and *Cherub* beat to quarters, but before battle was joined a sudden squall destroyed Porter's main topmast, which plunged into the sea, drowning the men who had been on it. Porter tried to put into the shelter of his anchorage but could not reach it and instead put into a small bay, hoping to repair the damage, and the British pursued. At about 4:40 P.M. the British opened fire but could not make it effective and struggled to manoeuvre in the strong wind. After an hour and a half they were able to make their guns bear, and Hillyar intended to anchor and make the most of his range advantage. The Americans took a fearful pounding. Farragut would never forget "the horrid impression made upon me at the sight of the first man I had ever seen killed. He was a boatswain's mate, and was fearfully mutilated. It staggered and sickened me at first; but they soon began to fall around me so fast that it all appeared like a dream and produced no effect on my nerves."[99] Porter cut his cable and tried to close, but when this effort failed and with *Essex* on fire, he made a desperate attempt to run ashore and destroy her; but a wind shift made this impossible, and the thousands of spectators lining the hills watched as American sailors dived overboard and attempted to swim to shore. After a hard-fought contest *Essex* was forced to strike her colours, although the British did not cease firing immediately, and Porter considered hoisting them again before they did. The Americans complained about that and about being attacked in neutral waters, but they were well treated and later paroled.[100] Of a crew of 255 Porter had lost 58 killed, 66 wounded, and 31 missing (probably drowned). *Phoebe* lost 4 killed and 7 wounded, and *Cherub* lost one killed and 3 wounded. Not until November 1814 did *Phoebe* anchor in Plymouth Sound, having been away for twenty months.[101] Meanwhile, on 5 July 1814 parolee David Porter escaped from the *Essex Junior* and rowed ashore to Babylon, Long Island, where he was held as a British spy until official papers he was carrying established his true identity. But he held no further active commands during the war.[102]

Early in 1814 American shipbuilders completed three new sloops, *Frolic, Peacock,* and *Wasp,* each mounting twenty 32-pounder carronades and two long 18-pounders. In February *Frolic* sailed from Boston under Captain Joseph Bainbridge USN. Unfortunately for her, on 20 April she encountered

HMS *Orpheus* (22) and HM Schooner *Shelburne* (12) off Cuba, and following a chase of 60 miles in which she made desperate efforts to elude her pursuers, including jettisoning half her guns, this "remarkably fine ship" was taken because, as American seaman Benjamin Waine explained, "Being under the frigate's guns, one broadside would have sent us to eternity."[103] Next to sail was *Peacock* under Captain Lewis Warrington USN, which managed to escape from New York in March and sailed south to enjoy far greater success than her sister. At about 8 A.M. on 29 April off Cape Canaveral (now Cape Kennedy) she intercepted a Bermuda–Havana convoy escorted by HM Brig *Epervier* (18) under Captain Richard Wales RN, who besides being outgunned was outmanned, with a crew of 121 to *Peacock*'s 166. *Epervier* immediately put herself between the American and the convoy, and at 9:50 A.M. the action opened with damage to both ships, *Peacock* having her fore-yard disabled. Thereafter, however, she pressed home her advantages, and by 11 A.M. most of *Epervier*'s larboard guns were out of action, and Wales was unable to manoeuvre in order to make his starboard guns bear, as his rigging had been cut to pieces, the main boom shot away, and the foremast severely damaged. He struck his colours although casualties on both sides were light: the British had suffered 7 killed and 10 wounded, the Americans just 2 slightly wounded.[104]

The completeness of the victory was later found to be due as much to the inefficiency of the crew as to its weakness in numbers, the product of the shortage of trained seamen and harsh discipline, itself the product of deficient leadership; something that had not previously been a major factor when fighting the French but which was a decided disadvantage against the enthusiastic and efficient Americans. The first lieutenant thought that not more than twenty of *Epervier*'s crew had seen action before; "they were a weak crew and not bred as seamen." The master went further, claiming he had never seen a worse crew in his life.[105] Noting that the British sloop had been cut to pieces and the American barely scratched, Captain Edward Codrington RN, who was Cochrane's flag captain on HMS *Tonnant* (80), blamed the loss of *Epervier* on excessively harsh discipline. "This is the case with many former crack ships," he said. There was too much favouritism in the Royal Navy, whereas American officers were chosen on merit. Furthermore, "the people, from being tyrannically treated, would rejoice in being captured by the Americans, from whom they receive every encouragement."[106]

Wasp left Portsmouth, New Hampshire, on 2 May 1814 under the Irish-born Captain Johnston Blakeley (sometimes "Blakely") USN and crossed the Atlantic to take up a position in the Western Approaches, where she spent

June blithely burning and sinking merchantmen until sighted on 28 June by HM Brig *Reindeer* (18) under Captain William Manners RN.[107] It was another uneven contest, as the British ship carried only sixteen 24-pounder carronades, a 12-pounder in the bow, and two long 9-pounders, and she was manned by 118 men against 170 Americans. But she was no *Epervier.* There was very little wind, and the action took some time to begin, but having got into a position forward of the *Wasp* at about 3:30 P.M., the British were able to unleash their nine portside guns at point-blank range, tearing two of Blakeley's pieces violently from their carriages. However, by triple-shooting their weapons, the British had greatly reduced their penetrative power against *Wasp*'s stout new timbers. "The *Wasp*'s bow is composed of solid oak," lamented a survivor, "which proved impenetrable to *Reindeer*'s shot."[108] Manners did his utmost to close for boarding, but by the time he had done so, *Reindeer* was badly damaged and himself badly wounded in the legs. One attempt to board was repulsed, and as Manners led another he was shot through the head and killed, enabling the Americans to take possession quickly. *Wasp* lost 5 killed and 21 wounded; *Reindeer* had lost 33 killed and 34 wounded and was so badly damaged she had to be destroyed the following day.[109] *Wasp* then put into L'Orient to refit.

Some other American ships managed to get to sea during the summer. On 12 July the small brig *Syren* was en route to the African coast when she was taken by HMS *Medway* (74). Samuel Leech, who had joined the U.S. Navy after being captured on *Macedonian,* watched in dismay as the out-gunned Americans came to, and "our foe came rolling down upon us, looking like an avalanche rushing down the mountainside to crush some poor peasant's dwelling."[110] Soon after emerging from her French sanctuary in late August, *Wasp* captured two more merchantmen and managed to cut out and seize a ship under convoy escorted by a 74. At 6:30 P.M. on 1 September Blakeley sighted four more sails and set off to chase the most westerly, which turned out to be HM Brig *Avon* (18) under Captain the Honourable James Arbuthnot RN. She carried sixteen 32-pounder carronades and two long 9-pounders with a crew of 117. The action began at about 9:30 P.M., and, anxious to conclude matters swiftly, Blakeley came in close and poured a heavy fire into the British ship, which struck her colours within the hour with 7 feet of water in her hold, the magazine flooded, and the tiller, fore-yard, and main boom shot away. *Wasp* had to flee before the other ships came up, which proved to be a good decision, as her victim sank. *Avon* lost 10 killed and 32 wounded to *Wasp*'s 2 killed and one wounded, and once more she had received only slight damage thanks to her stout frame and her superior gunnery.[111] *Wasp* set off once more to continue her remarkable cruise and was sighted by a Swedish vessel on 9 October some 300 miles north-west of the Cape Verde Islands, and never seen again: no trace of her or her crew was ever found.[112]

Despite the exploits of *Wasp* and *Peacock,* the U.S. Navy made little impact during 1814. In June Isaac Hull, now commanding Portsmouth Navy Yard, was told by the Navy secretary that it was not worth defending, as the ships were now useless.[113] In a reversal HM Brig *Borer* (18) passed between the shoals of Martha's Vineyard and the mainland flying a Swedish flag and then began wreaking havoc with the merchant shipping, capturing five and destroying many more.[114] The privateer *Rattlesnake* was taken by the heavy frigate HMS *Leander* (58) under Captain Sir George Ralph Collier RN, and by year's end the U.S. Navy was wholly blockaded in port. Although the Americans had three 74s belatedly under construction, which the Admiralty noted were actually as powerful as three-deckers and were therefore not to be engaged on single-ship terms by British 74s, this theoretical superiority would remain theoretical if they remained bottled up.[115] In the autumn the collector of customs at Boston, on instructions from Washington, ordered all lighthouse keepers to "cause the light [under] their care to be extinguished until further orders," as the only ships to which they were of any service were British.[116] America's naval presence was felt on the high seas only through the continued success of her privateers. Throughout the summer light and fast schooners came into the English Channel and Irish Sea, and the Royal Navy could not catch them in the light breezes. Once autumn's stronger winds arrived, however, the situation improved.[117]

12

The Far Northwest

Fifty I got for selling me coat,
Fifty for selling me blanket.
If ever I 'lists for a sodger again,
The Divil shall be me sergeant.
Poor old sodger, poor old sodger.
Twice tried for selling me coat,
Three times tried for desertion.
If ever I be a sodger again,
May the Divil promote me sergeant.
Poor old sodger, poor old sodger.

—Trad., "The Rogue's March"

WOMEN FORMED an essential part of the logistical support of armies of the period, although they are often dismissed as mere "camp-followers." The British policy was for one soldier's wife to accompany a regiment for every ten men; their task was to provide essential help in cooking, cleaning, and tending the sick, although the dispersed nature of regimental service in North America meant that detachments often served without them.[1] As many as five women supposedly took part in the war as combatants. In 1814 Sophia Johnson went in disguise in search of her brother and travelled across New York State. When she found him he had another eleven months of his enlistment to serve, so she too joined up. She was soon in action and wounded, losing an arm, and later became a schoolteacher. Almira Paul shipped out of Halifax as "Jack Brown" and served on British warships and American vessels. Lucy Brewer, also known as Louisa Baker and by her married name, Eliza Bowen Webb, supposedly served as a Marine aboard the *Constitution* for three years.[2]

If true, these stories represent greater enthusiasm for the war than many men showed. During its course some 1,570 enlisted men deserted from British regular units stationed in Upper and Lower Canada, compared with 2,733 lost through combat and sickness.[3] The Americans took every opportunity to encourage desertion, especially if operating on the American side of the frontier, and it is little wonder that British troops were prone to it, with poor conditions and harsh discipline.[4] Between 22 April and 1 October 1813 37 soldiers of the 103rd Regiment were tried by courts-martial, of whom 31 were found guilty: of these, one received 300 lashes, one received 200 lashes, 6 received 100 lashes, and the rest fewer than 100.[5] But the problem was even worse in the U.S. Army, which lost an estimated 5,000–5,700 men, or around 10 percent of its authorized strength of 58,254 enlisted men fit for service, though it never reached more than half this establishment. To quell this exodus the Americans had to resort increasingly to the death penalty; only 3 men were condemned in 1812, but 146 were shot or hanged in 1814.[6]

That desertion was such a problem should be no surprise given that living conditions for the troops, especially in camps, were abominable.[7] Captain Benson Hill RA described his breakfast one morning before New Orleans:

> A black jack filled with coffee, served in tin tots; brown sugar in a paper bag; slices of bullock liver, grilled upon wood-ashes; and biscuits, which had been toasted to destroy the wevils, constituted our repast. Little did I dream, when, as a youngster, I used literally to "quarrel with my bread and butter," that the day would arrive when such fare would be acceptable.[8]

But as he and so many other soldiers have learned over the years, all food is precious, and they are naturally adept at acquiring it. Each American invasion attempt on Canada trailed ruination in its path; as Wilkinson's army moved along the St. Lawrence in the autumn of 1813, it hoovered up local produce. Michael Cook, a forty-eight-year-old loyalist born in Philadelphia, was running a tavern at Williamsburgh Township on the Canadian shore of the St. Lawrence when Wilkinson's hordes arrived. Some of what was taken was paid for in very welcome silver, but much was not: fence rails were removed for firewood, and his wheat, oats, peas, corn hay, sheep, potatoes, a yearling calf, half a bushel of salted sausages, beehives and honey, and all the farm's poultry were swept into the maw of the American army.[9] And not only food was taken. The most notorious on the American side were Forsyth's Riflemen, who would strip British officers and Canadian civilians of valuables and could make "several hundred dollars in one battle," it was reported, being quite prepared to beat "silver embossed urns, tureens and plate of every description to get them in their knapsacks. The officers, generally attempt to prevent it, but Forsyth is a perfect savage himself."[10] But the British were no better; as John D. Carroll recalled, "when they came, they stole everything."[11]

John Crysler's farm suffered as the British force that would shortly fight on his land consumed everything it could find, including 50 bushels of potatoes, 20 bushels of apples, pigs, sheep, honey from his hives, and, inevitably, his fence rails on which to cook it all.[12] A settler near York asked to billet a group of soldiers en route to Kingston discovered the following morning that his prize pig had mysteriously disappeared. A thorough search of boats and farm yielded no trace of the porker, and when the party embarked next day the officer commanding, his curiosity thoroughly roused, promised pardon to the offenders if they would reveal the animal's fate. Turning over one of the boats, the men revealed it split lengthwise and nailed like a sheath to the keel, and the officer's curiosity was sated, as no doubt was his appetite that evening with fresh roast pork.[13] British troops referred to acquiring material in this fashion as "hooking," from the practice of using a hooked stick to filch goods from a merchant's counter when he was not looking.[14] It was hardly surprising, therefore, that on 4 September 1813 Lieutenant Thomas Gibbs Ridout of the Commissary Department wrote to his father of the "ungracious reception" he had received from a Niagara district farmer. While senior officers were dined and accommodated in the main house, he and two junior officers were relegated to an abandoned shack at the rear and were refused anything to supplement their meagre army rations beyond some carefully measured milk. Not that this prevented them from eating extremely well over the next few weeks as they indulged in "an extensive robbing of peas, apples, onions, corn, carrots" and other items, including that staple fuel, the farmer's rail fences. On 21 September Ridout reported a plan "to make a grand attack on the onions. The nests are kept very clean from eggs . . . We feed a turkey close to the door, which is doomed for Sunday dinner," while "somehow a cow happens to get milked over night."[15]

Given the dreadful quality and frequent scarcity of army rations, such larceny was inevitable. Noting that British soldiers had their every requirement looked after for them in barracks, William Dunlop deplored their lack of self-reliance in the field, where they were expected to be able to fend for themselves. The militia, in contrast, "erected shanties, far superior, in warmth, tightness and comfort, to any canvas tent."[16] As Surgeon John Douglas of the 8th Regiment noted, British soldiers "slept cold and comfortless in the barns and out-houses of the settlers [or] sometimes, when overtaken by night, a fire was kindled in the woods, around which they stretched themselves till morning."[17] Earlier that summer Lieutenant William MacEwen of 1st Royal Scots described his situation in a letter to his wife: he was huddled under a lean-to built of sticks and leaves called an "Indian Shelter," and forced to rely on issue rations because the locals absolutely refused to part with any produce. Rations could be described only as "bad," and "too little for any man in good health." The inhabitants were "indifferent who gains the day," complained MacEwen. "They are determined to do nothing themselves. Where I am obliged to live, the people would not sell me a fowl nor a potato, and even grumble when my men use their dishes." He asked his wife to send "tea, sugar, pepper, mustard and any other thing you can think of."[18] On the march towards Crysler's Farm, Dunlop enviously noted the two volunteer corps formed by the gentlemen of Montreal, one of artillery and one of sharpshooters, who were in

> a perfect state of drill, and in their handsome uniforms had a most imposing appearance. But if their discipline was commendable, their commissariat was beyond all praise. Long lines of carts were to be seen bearing in casks and hampers of the choicest wines, to say nothing of the venison, turkeys, hams, and all other esculents necessary to recruit their strength under the fatigues of war . . . There can be little doubt that a gourmand would greatly prefer the comforts of dining in a mess of privates of these distinguished corps to the honour and glory of being half-starved (of which he ran no small risk) at the table of the Governor-General himself.[19]

For British regulars such luxuries were the stuff of dreams as they remained on very basic army rations.

Each man in the field was supposed to receive daily 1 1/2 pounds of bread or hardtack biscuit and one pound of fresh or salt beef or 10 1/2 ounces of pork—but this included fat, gristle, and bones—and half a gill of rum (2 ounces, or 70 millilitres). In addition to the monotony of this diet, the caloric intake for men doing heavy work was inadequate, being estimated at 2,700 calories, while the current recommendation for modern, sedentary adult males is 3,000 calories, and the energy expended in the field would have far exceeded these levels.[20] Fresh bread was rare at the best of times, and regulations stipulated that it be issued as a 6-pound loaf once every four days. However, transport was so primitive that John Kilborn of the Incorporated Militia of Upper Canada noted that the waggon that brought it one summer's day "was pretty well filled with dust and gravel," although that did not stop the men from "gladly eating and drinking such as could be got."[21] Yet as Dunlop observed, the mercenary Régiment De Watteville, consisting of all the nationalities of Europe, had learned to make the most of a bad bargain:

> . . . they greatly excelled themselves in gastronomic lore; and thus while our fellows had no better shift than to frizzle their rations of salt provisions on the ends of their ramrods, these being practical botanists, sent out one soldier from each mess, who gathered a haversack full of pot herbs, with which a little flour their ration was converted into a capital kettle of soup.[22]

But even when it was functioning properly the commissariat often deprived men of their entitlement. It seems that rum was seldom available in Upper Canada, although this was no bad thing: British soldiers were notorious drinkers, and both their behaviour and health suffered accordingly. Senior officers in Quebec were perfectly aware of deficiencies and expected soldiers to supplement their rations by local purchase, but in sparsely populated Canada this was never simple.

Food production in Upper Canada was barely above subsistence levels in the best of years, and mobilizing the militia distorted and reduced production. For example, in the summer of 1814 commissariat officers in central Upper Canada had to feed 3,939 regulars and 527 militia in eight widely scattered posts. Doing this required 75 tons of flour to provide bread for thirty days, while the Indians assembled at Burlington Heights would require about the same—Drummond's need to feed these extra mouths was debilitating.[23] All these people would consume almost 1,000 head of cattle, but the farmers of the Burlington Heights region were estimated to have only 300 between them in September 1813. Draught animals required even greater quantities of forage and consumed 168 tons of grain in a month, more than the Indians' ponies.[24] As the peacetime garrison of Canada expanded to almost 30,000 by the summer of 1814, the provision of food took on greater and greater importance, but Canadian resources were simply inadequate and exacerbated by the shortage of specie, making imports from Great Britain and Ireland necessary.

In 1813 the Assembly of Upper Canada prohibited the distillation of liquor to preserve grain, though not before ensuring that whiskey had been bought for issue to the troops.[25] Complicating matters was a shortage of salt—essential for preserving meat—which before the war had been shipped from Oswego in New York. Despite small amounts that were smuggled into the province and imports from outside, Upper Canada was in salt deficit throughout the war.[26] Between June 1812 and September 1813 the monthly food demand at Kingston rose from 15 barrels of flour and 9 barrels of pork to 765 and 445 barrels respectively; and although the allowance of meat for troops in garrison was smaller than for those in the field, it included generous amounts of peas, butter, and rice.[27] But the Canadian population was unwilling to sell what little it had, and though the Kingston commissariat sought the imposition of martial law in August 1813, it was not until November that de Rottenburg imposed a modified form of it to purchase provisions and forage forcibly at prices fixed by magistrates.[28] Long before Surgeon William Dent reached Kingston in August 1814 with the 3rd (East Kent) Regiment, the country around was exhausted. "The whole Army now regret very much our ever having left France," he lamented; "the people are very uneasy and everywhere imposition is attempted to be practiced on us."[29]

Fortunately trade with northern New York, Vermont, and Maine continued to the great benefit of the British, most flagrantly along the Champlain Valley, where cattle were driven under the pretence that they were for the U.S. Army to the south of the St. Lawrence, then taken over the river at night, because, as one man put it, "Men will always run great risks—when great personal profits are expected to be realized."[30] Major-General George Izard, who succeeded to Wilkinson's command in May, complained that the road "to St. Regis is covered with Droves of Cattle and the River with Rafts destined for the enemy" and similarly providing flour. Indeed, "the high roads are found insufficient for the supplies of cattle which are pouring into Canada; like herds of buffalo that press through the forests making paths for themselves . . . Were it not for these supplies the British forces in Canada would soon be suffering from famine, or their government subjected to enormous expense for their maintenance."[31] And the trade was eased by corrupt officialdom; in June 1814 Thomas Ridout contracted with a "Yankee magistrate" to furnish Cornwall with fresh beef. "A major came with him to make the agreement but as he was [foreman] to the Grand jury at the court in which the Government prosecutes the magistrate for high treason & smuggling he turned his back and would not see the paper signed."[32]

Surgeon Dunlop reported dickering with an American militia officer in full uniform who closed the deal with the remark, "they do say it is wrong to supply an innimy [*sic*] and I think so too; but I don't call that man my innimy who buys what I have to sell, and gives such a genteel price for it. We have worse innimies than you Britishers."[33]

According to the Salem *Gazette,* smuggling became "the most lucrative business which is now carried on." Profits were so great that the smugglers "could afford to lose one half by custom house spies, and yet make money faster than those who follow the 'dull pursuits' of regular business."[34] Attempts to restrain it were regularly met with force; two revenue officers were killed and two others wounded in a clash with smugglers at Belfast, Maine; and George Izard declared that nothing "but a Cordon of Troops" along the New York and Vermont borders with Canada could "check the Evil."[35] On 27 August Prevost assured Bathurst that "two-thirds of the British Army in Canada are, at this Moment, eating Beef provided by American Contractors drawn principally from the States of Vermont and New York," while a brigade of artillery recently arrived at Cornwall from southern France was feeding its horses on American-supplied hay.[36] And trade was not confined to victuals; the inhabitants of Vermont were not above trading with Lower Canada in naval stores which the British were having trouble sourcing. American naval personnel intercepted and destroyed two spars intended for the British frigate under construction at Isle-aux-Noix on 28 June 1814, although the "persons who were towing them made their escape on shore."[37] They set a watch for the possible passage of the mainmast down Lake Champlain, but only another four spars were intercepted on the night of 7 July.

It was not the shortage of suitable timber in Lower Canada that led to its import from the United States, but the difficulty of transporting it across the rough country and up the Richelieu River rapids—necessarily a slow and difficult process—and the movement of guns and other naval stores was already stretching available resources.[38] In the early nineteenth century financial and transportation techniques lagged behind those of production. Bonaparte succeeded in Europe, where he could use speed and tactical skill, such as at Austerlitz; he failed in the vast spaces of Russia, which before railways were simply too great for the existing means of communications and supply. In North America, distances were greater than in Europe, the climate harsher, and the terrain substantially more difficult.[39] Logistical problems severely limited the size of force that could operate, and this constraint particularly affected offensive operations, not only because greater support was required to sustain them, but also because the extreme primitiveness of the communications network made providing that support considerably more difficult.[40]

As food demands grew, so did those on transportation: there were never enough waggons or teams to pull them, and as the numbers of the latter increased, so did the demands for forage in a vicious circle. The *bateaux* service needed more bottoms and men to operate them, but militiamen called from their farms for the purpose put food production in Lower Canada at risk. The service needed 4,000 men, and the people grew weary of constant call-ups. Every militiaman mobilized was another mouth to feed and one less to work the fields; British reinforcements only exacerbated the problem, which increased the farther west a man moved.[41] In March 1814 the Assembly of Upper Canada petitioned the Prince Regent for relief, noting that there were only 10,000 men able to bear arms to defend an 800-mile frontier, and that many of these had been embodied in 1812 and 1813, causing considerable hardship throughout the province.[42] The Assembly of Lower Canada made a similar petition, noting that agriculture, transport, and other business had all suffered, as did the militiamen themselves through inadequate supplies and clothing and backlogs in pay.[43] When Drummond assumed command he repealed de Rottenburg's proclamation but soon discovered that the farmers were no more willing to offer up their produce. Despite a vote of censure passed by the Assembly against de Rottenburg in March, by April Drummond also had to resort to forced purchase, deepening resentment among the population and prompting a rash of prosecutions against commissariat officers and agents, though the authorities in Canada received the support of those in London.[44] Furthermore, the Americans understood the importance of mills in turning grain into usable flour, and these became a primary target of raids despite being private property and legally protected, and both sides burned them whenever possible. Militia used to defend them were also thus unavailable for other duties.[45]

"When a march was undertaken in spring, or in autumn, the miry state of the roads presented many obstructions," noted John Douglas. "Nor were the oppressive heats of summer, superadded to the fatigues of long and forced marches, less dispiriting to the soldier."[46] The men suffered badly from chest complaints, including pneumonia, in the spring, though it is doubtful that the usual treatment—bleeding—did them much good. On active service in 1813 ninety-two men of the 104th Regiment died of "natural causes" compared with just twenty-three killed in action and eight who died of wounds.

Of the ninety-two, twenty died at Kingston as a result of the 700-mile march from New Brunswick over fifty-two days, and the others from malaria, dysentery, and other ills suffered in Niagara, not helped by excess of drink.[47] Militia seemed generally healthier than British regulars; nevertheless 83 percent of militia casualties in Upper Canada were from disease and accidents, most occurring during the first twelve months of the conflict, when thousands participated despite severe food shortages, so that 95 percent of casualties were from non-battle causes. A sharp decline in militia participation from 1813 onwards saw an equally dramatic fall in deaths from all causes, so that by 1814 only the most dedicated colonists were still serving. Only in the final six months did battle casualties among Upper Canadian servicemen outnumber deaths from other causes, with nearly one-third of these occurring at the battle of Chippawa.[48]

At least, reported Douglas, the men were spared dysentery, although American reports recorded this as a considerable problem; and in American forces, sick rates were higher among the militia than among regulars, probably because of neglect by inexperienced officers.[49] "For every soldier killed," wrote Samuel D. Brown, "three die of disease."[50] Among the New York militia camped at Buffalo in the autumn of 1812, eight or nine men had died every day from "fever," pleurisy, dysentery, and measles; two or three graves were dug daily, with three or four bodies laid in each, covering an area of 2 acres.[51] The most fatal was dysentery of *"flux or camp distemper,"* which Brown declared "every old woman in the country would cure in three days with a decoction of milk, pine bark and spikenard root." Dr. James Mann believed this could be treated through the diet, with vegetables and milk, although others prescribed ipecac and opium, and still others relied on bleeding and emetics.[52] Surgeon General James Tilton was a firm believer that vomiting was "of excellent use, by opening and squeezing of all the glands of the body, and thus shaking from the nervous system, the contaminating poison before its impressions are fixed." He also noted that more medical officers died than did officers of the line, strong evidence that "infection is more dangerous, in military life, than the weapons of war."[53]

Elias Darnell, serving with Brigadier-General James Winchester in the winter of 1812–13, complained that the troops were denied the "common necessaries of life," and 100 had died by Christmas Eve. "The sufferings of about 800 sick at this time, who are exposed to the cold ground and deprived of every nourishment, are sufficient proofs of our wretched condition!"[54] When typhus then hit the camps, it killed 3 or 4 men a day, with 300 on the sick list, while many went without shoes in only scanty clothing, making frostbite a common condition.[55] Besides, the quality of care for those unfortunate enough to fall sick was unlikely to be high. At Fort Meigs Eleazer D. Wood noted the absence of a head of hospital department:

> Those to whom the important duties of that department had been committed were but a young, inexperienced set of men with nothing but the title of Surgeon to recommend them, or to give them claims to employment, and the principal part of whom had been picked up here and there among the militia wherever a person could be found with a lancet in his pocket, or who had by some means or other *obtained the title of doctor.*[56]

Robert B. McAfee noted in the summer of 1813 that "a most fatal epidemic prevailed in the camp, which carried off from three to five and sometimes as many as ten in a day. It was computed that near 200 fell a sacrifice to it, within the space of six weeks." He blamed "bad water" and "the flat marshy, putrescent condition of that region of country, [which] was well calculated to destroy an army of men, who were alike unused to such a climate, and to the life of a soldier."[57]

For the garrison at Fort George it was also a long summer, and by August nearly a third of the division—1,200 men—were suffering from one ailment or another. Mann, the senior medical officer, attributed the large sick list to the unhealthy location, unsanitary conditions (even as these were understood in 1813), constant alarms, and frequent inebriation, and thought that lack of alcohol helped explain the generally better condition of British as opposed to American troops.[58] This apparent superiority, however, may have been as much due to better-quality bread as to excess or lack of booze. If the British gained extra roughage from grit and gravel, it was as nothing to what sometimes went into American bread. Dr. James Ross at Sackets Harbor in September found it was "made from flour of sprouted or grown wheat and damaged flour, in which from negligence, lime, soap, and other extraneous and even feculent ingredients, have been discovered." Ross was horrified to discover that the bakers drew their water from the lake near where the latrines drained into it, and it was "impregnated with, and contains a diffusion of excrementious matter."[59] At least American meat rations were more generous than British ones, being 20 ounces of beef or 12 ounces of pork per man per day, but the American system of purchasing by the Commissary General of Purchasers proved a total failure, with the graft of the rations contractors especially egregious.[60]

Matters were made worse by the lowering of physical standards for recruits, very quickly dropped in a desperate attempt to meet targets, with the result that many were "habitually intemperate, with constitutions broken down by inebriation and its consequent diseases; whose bloated countenance exhibited false and insidious marks of health."[61] Captain Arthur Sinclair was not impressed by the quality of the army at Sackets Harbor, who

> really make me sick at the stomach to look at them. They remind me very much of the water street Hogs of Norfolk well fed and lazy and muddy as the devil. Really I never saw such looking troops in any Country. Figure to yourself the dirtiest and most slovenly looking blackguards you have ever seen, and you have our army, generally, in your own mind's eye. The fittest of the army, *if they have any,* is the worst in the world. I believe the men are brave but they want officers and discipline.[62]

It was hardly surprising, then, that as Leonard Covington reported, "We bury hundreds."[63]

DESPITE defeat along the Thames, the British retained control in the west of the vast area around Lake Michigan, thanks to possession of the tiny posts of Michilimackinac and Prairie du Chien, which ensured the continuing support of Chippewa, Ottawa, Menominee, Winnebago, Fox, Sac, and Sioux Indians and enabled a very small number of British troops to control an area far greater than that of Britain itself. Here was waged a very strange type of war in a region encompassing the whole of modern Wisconsin and Minnesota, as yet largely untouched by white settlement.[64]

Armstrong reasoned that the British would want to re-establish themselves on the Thames and wished to frustrate any such plans, but he was against the cabinet decision to send the Detroit garrison to recapture Fort Mackinac and remove the British post at St. Joseph. With the loss of Lake Erie these could still be supported by an overland route from York to the Holland River and Lake Simcoe, thence to Georgian Bay on Lake Huron, where the schooner *Nancy* operated; but the journey was difficult and inefficient, requiring the cross-loading of stores.[65] At Sault Ste. Marie the North West Company had bypassed the rapids with locks, and local Canadian knowledge of alternative routes using previously unmapped trails and rivers gave British forces a distinct advantage in *la petite guerre.*[66] The switch in the strategic situation in early 1814 left the American authorities with little alternative to trusting regional commanders and hoping for the best; British power could begin to apply pressure on all frontiers and coasts, and when Captain Richard Bullock at Mackinac requested reinforcement by 200 infantry and 20 gunners to prevent American forces regaining his post, Prevost agreed.[67]

The Americans were determined to regain control of the upper Mississippi region, and in early 1814 William Clark was appointed governor of Missouri Territory, with its capital at St. Louis, theoretically embracing the entire upper Mississippi, including Illinois Territory.[68] He had available five gunboats, about 50 regulars, and 140 militia, with which he set off upriver in May, defeating the Sac Indians at Rock River and taking the key fur post of Prairie du Chien without opposition from Captain Francis Dease and his militia.[69] They then set about building Fort Shelby—named after the governor of Kentucky—consisting of three blockhouses linked by a pallisade.[70] The American cabinet was divided about a Lake Huron adventure; even Jones was reluctant. Nevertheless, on 1 April Chauncey ordered Jesse Elliott to prepare the brigs *Niagara* and *Lawrence* to move into Lake Huron as soon as the ice cleared to permit an expedition.[71] The land component would be under newly promoted Lieutenant-Colonel George Croghan, with the whole under the command of Captain Arthur Sinclair.[72] The operation began on 14 May, when 150 men of the 2nd U.S. Infantry under Captain Charles Gratiot established Fort Gratiot on the banks of the St. Clair River.

By now the British troops scattered along the Niagara frontier were far less effective than those who had seized Fort Niagara and raided Lewiston, Black Rock, and Buffalo; the 8th Regiment at Fort Niagara was plagued by sickness and desertion—actually increased by the men receiving an arrears of pay—and Riall was forced to replace them with the 100th Regiment.[73] On the American side Colonel John B. Campbell arrived with reinforcements, and Sinclair saw an opportunity; he proposed a raid on the Long Point region of the peninsula, which he believed produced half the breadstuff for the British army in the region. Campbell readily agreed and on 14 May led 800 men to raid the undefended village of Port Dover. He burned three flour mills, three sawmills, three distilleries, and—despite Sinclair's protests—some twenty houses as once again Canadian renegades, this time under Major Abraham Markle, settled old scores.[74] Five days later nearby Port Talbot was razed in a similar act while Campbell claimed he could have marched unopposed to Burlington Heights but for want of supplies. Senior officers on both sides were appalled, but these actions would come to back haunt the United States.[75] The Americans claimed it was retaliation for the destruction of Black Rock and Buffalo, but the British pointed out that these places had been destroyed in retaliation for Newark; and although an American court of inquiry later disavowed the destruction of private property, Prevost decided to retaliate. Rather than act locally, however, he requested Cochrane do so along the Atlantic coast.[76]

On 19 June the Lake Erie squadron sailed for Lake Huron, reaching Detroit on 3 July. Thither the schooner *Scorpion* brought news that the British were preparing a large naval force. Henry H. Leavitt joined *Caledonia* for the attack: "I shall never forget the almost overwhelming effect which this imposing array of war vessels produced in my mind when first exhibited to view. The scene was entirely new to me and produced a sensation which I do not have words to describe."[77] Fears of an attack on Detroit coupled with adverse weather prevented a move to Lake Huron before 12 July, whereafter the squadron reached St. Joseph on the 19th to find it abandoned. The Americans burned the fort and took the *Mink* of 45 tons, carrying 230 barrels of flour.[78] Having learned of the presence of the North West Company schooner *Perseverance* at Sault Ste. Marie, an expedition was sent in boats to take her. Andrew H. Holmes—now promoted major—led 280 men of the 24th U.S. Infantry, who landed and destroyed everything: sawmills, stores, houses, vessels; they also slaughtered cattle, burnt horses in the stables, took various sympathizers hostage, and ruined gardens. Nothing was left standing, as they claimed the fur post was a prize of war.[79] At the same time, Lieutenant David Turner USN went searching for *Perseverance* upstream on Lake Superior. Although the Canadians tried to burn her, he managed to put out the fire, but she was wrecked and lost when the Americans tried to bring her down the rapids.[80]

In early spring Prevost had despatched Lieutenant-Colonel Robert McDouall of the Glengarry Light Infantry, originally a native of Stranraer, Ayrshire, to take command at Mackinac with 300 men, including shipwrights and seamen, and two companies of the Royal Newfoundland Regiment—known affectionately as the "sleigh establishment"—plus four small guns and badly needed supplies.[81] They first crossed Lake Simcoe in ice and snow and established Fort Willow, or Willow Creek Depot, where they built thirty *bateaux* at the forks of the Nottawasaga River, which later became Glengarry Landing. In April they moved downstream to the shores of Lake Huron, and on the

25th, with about 90 men, McDouall set out to row the 360 miles to Mackinac in twenty-four *bateaux* deeply laden with military stores and provisions. The journey—made with no protection from the elements—took nineteen days through the northern waters of Lake Huron and its ice fields, yet in spite of severe weather, no personnel and only one *bateau* was lost.[82] When they arrived they received reinforcement from a large party of Indians led by Robert Dickson; on 22 June they learned of the loss of Prairie du Chien. McDouall noted that the Americans stood to gain complete control of the fur trade, since the "furs brought down from the distant regions of the North-West . . . are what constitute the principal part, both as to quality and value, of those exported from Montreal."[83]

McDouall immediately prepared an expedition of some 100 men to march 700 miles across the wilderness of Wisconsin and retake Prairie du Chien. The backbone of the force was provided by 63 Canadian "Mississippi Volunteers" raised by two leading fur traders from among their employees and associates, a group of zealous partisans whose local knowledge was invaluable.[84] McDouall appointed the heavy-drinking fur trapper Major William McKay of the Michigan Fencibles to command with local rank of lieutenant-colonel. The volunteers were armed and equipped with only sketchy uniforms available out of the stores. Thomas G. Anderson, fur trader–cum–captain, described his as a red coat, "a couple of epaulettes and an old rusty sword with a red cock feather adorning my round hat."[85] Many Indians of the north-western tribes were at Mackinac, and about 130 volunteered to join the party; but, apparently having reservations about the martial qualities of their white comrades, they requested that an army officer command the expedition and that one of their "Father's big guns" accompany them. McDouall agreed to give them a 3-pounder which he had brought "chiefly for the novelty of the thing amongst the Indians."[86] With the gun went Sergeant James Keating RA and "twelve smart fellows." For McDouall, who would die a major-general, this was almost certainly the most important operational decision of his career.[87]

Departing on 28 June, the party arrived on 4 July at Green Bay, where the number of Indians was doubled, amounting to some 140 voyageurs and troops and around 500 Menominees, Sioux, Puants, Winnebagos, Follesevoines, and Sacs. Travelling by boats which they often had to manhandle up the Wisconsin River, the British-Indian force reached the Mississippi flood plain above Prairie du Chien on 17 July while McDouall was left fretting at Mackinac over dwindling supplies; the Indians consumed 1,600 pounds daily, and he had no confidence in Lieutenant Newdigate Poyntz RN, whom he found overbearing and whom he desperately wanted Yeo to replace. Eventually Yeo agreed to send the very able Lieutenant Miller Worsley RN.[88]

On arrival at Fort Shelby McKay found that Clark had returned to St. Louis, leaving Captain Joseph Perkins and 61 regulars of the 7th U.S. Infantry with about 130 rangers and militia to man the fort, supported by a gunboat, the *Governor Clark.* Although McKay regarded the Indians as "perfectly useless," they did alarm the Americans, and when Perkins refused to surrender, their own labouriously transported 3-pounder, expertly handled by Sergeant Keating, proved decisive.[89] The Americans had a 6-pounder and a 3-pounder in the fort and at least as much on the gunboat, plus some 1-pounder swivel guns. Keating skilfully deployed his gun where he could target the gunboat from cover, and two-thirds of the eighty-six rounds he fired struck home, forcing it to flee downstream and abandon the occupants of the fort to their fate.[90] On 19 July, following an unsuccessful day of tunnelling and a desultory exchange of fire, McKay was about to use the rest of his little gun's ammunition as heated shot when a white flag appeared above the fort.[91] Perkins blamed the defeat on the loss of the gunboat and shortage of ammunition and water. Although the Americans had no dead, they had 5 wounded and were very afraid of the Indians. McKay "was the first to observe the singular fact that" although the Americans' flag "was completely riddled with balls, the representation of the American eagle was untouched."[92]

McKay related that he was pleased with his men but angry with the Indians: "They despise the idea of receiving orders from an officer that does not hold a blanket in one hand and a piece of pork in the other to pay them to listen to what he may have to say," and he was forced to great lengths to prevent a massacre of the fort's inmates. A group of Canadians then escorted the prisoners to St. Louis.[93] On 22 July at Rock River rapids a group of Sac, Renards, Fox, and Kickapoos under Black Hawk attacked a party of six American keelboats sent to relieve the fort, three of which were armed. Following this action McKay was forced to suspend his usual contempt for the Indians: he reported that even the women jumped on board one of the barges wielding hoes, "some breaking heads, others breaking casks, some trying to cut holes in the bottom to sink her." It was, he said, "one of the most brilliant actions fought by Indians only, since the commencement of the war."[94] The Indians lost 2 men and a woman killed and the Americans at least 10 dead (British reports claimed 100), as well as two 3-pounders and three mortars; the barge was burnt. The survivors made off, reaching St. Louis on 6 August, the same day the United States signed a treaty with many of the Indians in which it promised to confirm the boundaries that had existed between the two sides before the war.[95]

Sinclair's fleet had by now arrived off Mackinac, but the Americans dithered, giving McDouall early warning of their intentions as they loitered off Dowsman's Farm. In early July Croghan had set out from Detroit with a force of around 750 men, but it was not until 4 August that this impressive force was landed at the far end of the island from the fort, as Croghan intended a slow advance covered by ships' guns either to force McDouall to attack or to give his supporting Indians an opportunity to desert. With Worsley and the *Nancy* in Georgian Bay and McKay at Prairie du Chien, McDouall was isolated. "I knew that they would land upwards of 1,000 men," he reported to Prevost, "and after manning the guns at the fort, I had only a disposable force of 140 [regulars] to meet them."[96] Nevertheless, leaving just 25 men in the fort, he led a sortie comprising the rest to do so, occupying a prime piece of high ground. There he built a redoubt in which he deployed some 300 regulars and militia supported by around 350 Indians, giving strict instructions to hold their fire for maximum effect.[97] At 1 P.M., recalled Usher Parsons, the Americans "began to disembark. At two a firing commenced from the vessels which cleared the shore. At three o'clock the troops were formed at a short distance from the shore and at quarter past three firing commenced with field pieces, and shortly after musketry."[98] But the Americans declined to meet the British directly and tried to ease past some Indian resistance on their forest perimeter. As the American ships moved to outflank him on his left, McDouall moved to an intermediate position to protect his line of retreat to the fort, and as he did so the Indians under their chief, Thomas, opened an effective fire on the Americans, inflicting heavy casualties. By 4:30 P.M. they were in full retreat to their boats, leaving behind 13 dead, including Andrew H. Holmes, 51 wounded, and 2 prisoners.[99]

Meanwhile Sinclair had detached *Lawrence* and *Caledonia* and some of Croghan's troops to Fort Erie and had himself gone with *Niagara, Scorpion,* and another schooner, *Tigress,* in search of *Nancy,* which Worsley had taken to the mouth of the Nottawasaga River in July. Worsley sailed for Mackinac on 1 August but was intercepted by a messenger from McDouall sent on 28 July, warning him to hide out upriver, where he might build a blockhouse, which he did at a place now known as Schooner Town.[100] When Sinclair arrived on 14 August, he engaged the blockhouse, Seaman David Bunnell recalling that the Americans played upon them "warmly with our guns."[101] Worsley, who commanded 23 British, 9 *Canadiens,* and 23 Indians under Lieutenant

12.1. *Attack on Mackinac, 1814,* painting by Peter Rindlisbacher.

Robert Livingstone of the Indian Department, replied with a 6-pounder and two 24-pounder carronades set up onshore; but they faced eighteen 32-pounder carronades on *Niagara* and two long 12-pounders, while Sinclair's schooners each carried a 12-pounder and two long 24-pounders, and he had 500 men. They fought from 9 A.M. until 4 P.M., when, "finding my little crew were falling all around me," Worsley later wrote to his father, "I immediately formed a resolution to blow both [the blockhouse and the *Nancy*] up, which I did." He had prepared a powder train linking the two; an American shell ignited both, taking with it *Nancy*, some 303 barrels of flour and pork, candles, and hundreds of pairs of shoes. Worsley and his men took cover in the woods and escaped, "to the great astonishment of the enemy," carrying valuable arms and supplies and covering 36 miles with their wounded and dying "before we came to any house. We lost everything we had except what we stood up in."[102]

Sinclair decided that as the British had nothing left afloat on Lake Huron, he could now return to the milder climes of Lake Erie, and accepted Croghan's advice not to bother fortifying or garrisoning the Nottawasaga River entrance. Instead he departed, leaving only the two schooners to deal with any remaining trappers and Indians.[103] But as Bunnell noted, the British "were not so simple as to let two small vessels rule the lake, but took advantage of this blunder by our commander, to be revenged for the loss of their navy."[104] On 18 August Worsley slipped out into Georgian Bay with eighteen seamen in two *bateaux* and began picking his way along the island-dotted eastern shore, covering 380 miles in six days, "exposed to great hardships and privations of every description having only what we could shoot or catch by fishing to subsist on."[105] Acting on an Indian report, he spotted the two schooners sailing between islands near Fort St. Joseph, and, seeing no chance of passing them in the narrow channel, he decided to hide the *bateaux*, assisted by Livingstone, who had accompanied him in his canoe from the Nottawasaga River.[106] Instead he went to consult McDouall, who immediately provided a detachment of the Royal Newfoundland Regiment under Lieutenant Andrew Bulger with a 6- and a 3-pounder in two more *bateaux*. When it was learned that the Americans were accompanied by some Indians in canoes, he was also granted a group of loyal Indians under Dickson.[107]

On 3 September Worsley discovered by canoe reconnaissance that *Tigress* was at anchor 6 miles away and separated from her sister. The British managed to row to within 10 yards before being seen; though fired upon, they quickly boarded and captured her. The Americans lost one killed, four wounded, and three missing (reported killed and thrown overboard) to two dead and seven wounded, including Bulger. The remaining twenty-three Americans were taken as prisoners to Mackinac. *Scorpion* was 10 miles away, and amid a thunderstorm, her crew thought they heard gunfire. Worsley sent Livingstone by canoe to reconnoitre the *Scorpion,* which he reported as blissfully unaware of the situation, and the following morning the British held their position, pretending *Tigress* was still American, "and the better to carry on the deception, the American pendant was kept flying. On the 5th instant, we discovered the enemy Schooner beating up to us. The soldiers I directed to keep below, or to lie on the deck to avoid being seen; everything succeeded to our wish; the Enemy came to anchor about two miles away."[108] In fact, there was unease onboard *Scorpion* as David Bunnell recalled. He communicated his suspicions

> to the rest of the crew, and they only laughed at me. They said "the English have no vessels on this lake, and what have we to fear?" While we were discussing the subject, the Tigress having got across our bow, fired a twenty-four pounder, and immediately boarded us with twenty soldiers, twelve sailors and about one hundred Indians. We were all taken prisoner without firing a gun.[109]

Five officers and thirty-one men were taken.[110] "Thus you see," wrote Worsley to his father, "after a series of hardships I have got two schooners both finer vessels than the *Nancy* and have providentially escaped unhurt."[111] They would be renamed *Confiance* and *Surprise,* proof that American power had been extinguished on Lake Huron.

At around the same time, the Americans made one final attempt to wrest control of the area west of Lake Michigan from the British, where Fort McKay—the former Fort Shelby—was now under the command of Captain Thomas G. Anderson.[112] Towards the end of August Major Zachary Taylor led 330 men to attack the Indians in the Rock River area—a difficult task, as around 1,000 Indians were gathered there, and the ground offered numerous ambush sites. The British at Prairie du Chien sent a sortie of 30 men under Lieutenant Duncan Graham with Sergeant Keating and his 3-pounder to support them, and this addition proved decisive against the American boats, which were driven off on 29 August, forcing Taylor to retreat on 5 September.[113] He stayed briefly in an improvised fort at the mouth of the Des Moines River, but in October burnt it and retreated to St. Louis, ending American hopes of regaining the area before the war ended.[114]

13

The Niagara Frontier

The Yankees did invade us,
To kill and to destroy,
And to distress our country,
Our peace for to annoy,
Our countrymen were filled
With sorrow, grief and woe,
To think that they should fall
By such an unnatural foe.

Come all ye bold Canadians,
Enlisted in the cause,
To defend your country,
And to maintain your laws;
Being all united,
This is the song we'll sing:
Success unto Great Britain
And God Save the King!
—Anon., "The Bold Canadian"

LATE IN April the British government sought to reinforce Prevost with 10,000 new troops after their defeat of the French in the Peninsula, and on 9 May the first of these, the 4th Battalion, The Royal Scots, left Portsmouth and the 97th (Queen's Own Germans) Regiment left Cork.[1] The government was also able to provide Prevost with a much-needed £100,000 in specie to relieve the financial pressure in Canada. In the meantime, Drummond proposed to Prevost in April that he could destroy Sackets Harbor with 4,000 men, for which purpose he needed only 800–1,000 reinforcements from Lower Canada. Despite Prevost's cautious nature—suited to the early stages of the war but a hindrance now the time had arrived to attack—Drummond was in a position to launch an attack against Oswego by early May.[2]

Lieutenant-Colonel George A. Mitchell of the 3rd U.S. Artillery arrived there on 30 April with a small detachment to find its fort rotten, with few guns, and set about repairing the defences.[3] With Chauncey's squadron not due to be ready until July, Yeo had temporary control; sailing from Kingston on 4 May and arriving at Oswego the following morning with 900 troops, the British found the Americans in no position to make an effective defence, but adverse winds drove them off. That evening Captain William Holtaway RM had a premonition of his death and asked Lieutenant J. C. Morgan RM to look after his accounts. "I complied with his desire," recalled Morgan, "and endeavoured to rally his spirits; but it was to no avail, he felt assured of his fate and prepared to meet it as if it had been his inevitable doom."[4] Next morning conditions improved, and Lieutenant-Colonel Victor Fischer led ashore through waist-deep water six companies of the Régiment De Watteville, one of the Glengarry Light Infantry, and one from the 2nd Battalion, Royal Marines, with supporting detachments of gunners and sappers. Although the landing was disputed, the enemy soon retreated, leaving the British to destroy the barracks and stores and carry away 2,400 barrels of pork, salt, and flour and seven heavy guns. But among the eighteen dead was Holtaway, and among the seventy-four wounded was William Mulcaster; American losses were six killed, thirty-eight wounded, and twenty-five missing. Most of the Americans' heavy ordnance had already been shifted to Oswego Falls 12 miles away, so the attack was only a partial success.[5]

Throughout the spring the rivalry between the two navies on Lake Ontario continued apace. On 1 May Chauncey launched *Superior* (64)—built in just eighty days. Then at the end of the month came disaster; Chauncey was determined to move stores up to Sackets Harbor and chose to do so by boat, defying the British naval threat by keeping close inshore, which he did on 28 May, using 130 men of the 1st U.S. Rifle Regiment under Major Daniel Appling and a similar number of pro-American Indians as escort moving along the shore. Anchored at Sandy Creek on the 29th, Captain Stephen Popham RN, leading 200 seamen and Royal Marines, was sent to attack the Americans in boats from the blockading squadron. But when Popham landed near the creek, the British were ambushed by a detachment of riflemen. They lost 19 killed and 28 wounded, and a further 133 sailors and marines, 2 Royal Navy captains and 4 lieutenants, and 2 Royal Marine lieutenants captured, for the loss of one rifleman and one Indian killed.[6] It was a humiliating defeat that was all the more costly because the British could not afford to lose seamen. The strategic consequences were felt soon afterwards, as Yeo had to release his blockade on Sackets Harbor and Oswego, thus enabling the Americans to complete the ships needed to contest control of the lake.[7] In early June he reported that he was already short of 280 seamen and that when HMS *St. Lawrence* was ready he would need 680 more. On 11 June Chauncey launched *Mohawk* (42), making the total number of vessels about equal but giving 251 American guns to 222 British, with a total broadside advantage of 4,188 to 2,752 pounds; the Americans also had a manpower superiority—some 3,300 men to the British 1,500.[8]

Despite this setback there was better news for Prevost. On 3 June Bathurst outlined that substantial reinforcements were on the way, although Prevost did not receive this letter until the second week of July. The 4th Royal Scots would be joined at Quebec by the Nova Scotia Fencibles from Newfoundland, the 90th (Perthshire Volunteers) Regiment from the West Indies, and the 1st/6th (1st Warwickshire) and 1st/82nd (Prince of Wales' Volunteers) Regiments from Bordeaux, to be followed by "twelve of the most effective Regiments" from Wellington's army, plus three Royal Artillery companies—some 13,000 men in total—while other forces would harass the American coast. The primary objective remained the security of Canada, but Prevost should also consider the "ultimate security" of British possessions in North America, necessitating offensive operations with a view to the complete destruction of Sackets Harbor and the American naval establishments on Lakes Erie and Champlain. He was also to retain Fort Niagara and look to re-take Detroit and Michigan for the material benefit of the Indians.[9] However, these expectations were somewhat unreasonable; Bathurst in London was focused more clearly on the negotiating table than on military and naval realities in North America, where the situation along the Niagara and on Lakes Ontario and Champlain was more important. In reply, the ever-cautious Prevost wrote that as soon as all the promised troops arrived he would implement his instructions; but there were as yet no resources spare to attempt to regain Lake Erie, without which there appeared little prospect of winning control of Michigan, and in the meantime and until complete naval control of Lakes Ontario and Champlain was gained, he would have to confine himself to defensive operations.[10]

With Armstrong having first stripped Brown of shipping by sending most of the Lake Erie squadron to support Croghan's attempt to recover Mackinac, it seems Brown's whole campaign was something of an afterthought to

Armstrong's desire to help his western friends by giving troops who would otherwise be unoccupied something to do. Then just as things were about to get under way Armstrong had a change of heart; he decided that because the British had shipped no supplies on Lake Erie that winter, they must be concentrating on the Niagara Peninsula and making that the western limit of their campaign. He now decided that American naval forces due to operate on Lake Huron could be better employed to support Brown, who had only a very tenuous supply line with which to invade Canada and thus by definition could not go very far; and in May he questioned the use of naval force on Lake Huron.[11] Time was rapidly running out for the Americans to make offensive moves along the frontier; the United States had to achieve local superiority somewhere, and as the bulk of British forces were deployed around Montreal, Madison's cabinet favoured the western theatre.[12] When news of the British attack on Oswego reached Washington, the president called an extraordinary cabinet meeting for 7 June, at which Armstrong's ambitious four-pronged plan of 30 April was agreed.[13] But it was a confused plan at the mercy of events and chance: it was doubtful whether sufficient supplies could be mustered and whether the army and navy would cooperate; and even if it succeeded in clearing the Niagara Peninsula of the British, it was unclear how this plan might further Madison's war aims.[14]

Crucially, the cabinet was under the impression that Chauncey's squadron would be available to support Brown, and Armstrong would lead Brown to believe he would be available to do so no later than 15 July. But Chauncey was fixated with engaging Yeo's squadron and had no intention of being deflected from this task to assist the army.[15] Brown assumed command on the Niagara frontier on 6 June, and four days later Armstrong finally sent vague instructions for an offensive in the Niagara region which took two weeks to reach the frontier. "Why not take Fort Erie & its garrison," Armstrong suggested, "push forward a corps to seize the bridge at Chippeway, & be governed by circumstances in either stopping there, or going further."[16] On 22 June Izard received the campaign plan for the Right Division of the U.S. Army, which was to establish a post on the St. Lawrence to support armed galleys that were supposed to interdict British communications; but Armstrong did not tell Izard that as a secondary mission he was supposed to demonstrate towards Montreal and divert Prevost's attention.[17] Unfortunately Izard's command was suffering from indiscipline and desertion among his 5,000 mostly raw troops, and he would have to take his time; apart from a raid in July that took nine prisoners, he remained south of the river until August.[18]

In Montreal Alicia Cockburn—wife of Lieutenant-Colonel Francis Cockburn, the admiral's youngest brother, who was commanding the Canadian Fencibles—reported to her brother that an attack was expected:

> All is bustle however in the neighbouring Camp—Guns—Drums—Bugles—Horse—Foot—Brigadiers—Grenadiers—& Fuzileers—Right—Left—here—there—march—halt—wheel—double-quick—tumble down—tumble up—fire away—thus they 'keep moving' and a most moving scene it is, but I think if I commanded, I would move it *a little nearer the enemy.*[19]

Although the advance across the Niagara was to be the American main effort for the region in 1814, Brown had fewer than 3,400 effectives supported by around 600 friendly Indians under the Seneca chief Sagoyewatha ("He Keeps Them Awake")—Red Jacket—with which to make his attack.[20] Brigadier-General Peter B. Porter had enlisted Seneca support following Bisshopp's raid on Black Rock the previous year, thus paving the way for civil war with their Iroquois brethren to the west.[21] Brown was a man underestimated by many: both Wilkinson and Scott regarded him contemptuously as an amateur, but he was, in fact, fast, aggressive, and something of a disciplinarian.[22] The 2,400 regulars were mostly New Englanders who had volunteered for regular service in large numbers despite the general lack of enthusiasm for the war in that section.[23] They were organized in two brigades under Scott and Ripley and supported by an artillery battalion of 300 serving as infantry, together with 480 Pennsylvania volunteers under Porter, who succeeded Amos Hall after the latter resigned in disgust at the failure to secure arms or pay for his men.[24]

Most of the Pennsylvanians assigned to the operation were reluctant to cross the border, but Corporal John Witherow was among those who did, and was extremely impressed by the training the regulars were performing under Scott.[25] Scott had spent the spring intensively training his brigade at a "camp of instruction," something that has since been mythologized, not least by Scott himself: how the young brigadier, through discipline and drill, turned ragtag recruits into soldiers capable of defeating the British on the open field. However, it was not basic training for raw recruits, as many writers have assumed, but rather advanced battle training for experienced soldiers.[26] In only one matter was he thwarted: he could not find enough blue uniforms for his men. They had been shipped in plenty of time for once but had been diverted to Plattsburgh and Sackets Harbor, although enough were found from one source or another to clothe the 21st U.S. Infantry. Eventually Commissary-General Callender Irvine had to have 2,000 uniforms hastily run up and sent to Buffalo, but, there being insufficient blue cloth, short grey jackets were substituted.[27]

Despite the small size of the American force, they faced only 2,500 British troops, who were still awaiting reinforcements from Europe and were mostly stationed around Fort George. Drummond was very nervous about the Niagara frontier, but Prevost remained sanguine; in contrast to America's muddled approach, British preparations were generally successful thanks to a measure of understanding, however imperfect, between army and navy.[28] By the beginning of July there were 600 effectives of the 41st Regiment at Fort Niagara with 1,500 from 1st Royal Scots and the 100th Regiments garrisoning various posts along the shore, supported by a detachment of 19th Light Dragoons, two troops of Provincial Light Dragoons, the flank companies of the Lincoln Militia, and a dwindling company of militia artillery. A reserve of some 500 men of the 103rd Regiment was at Burlington, and some 1,000 men of the 8th Regiment and Glengarry Light Infantry were now at York.[29]

Since the depredations of the winter, Buffalo had recovered quickly in the typical manner of the frontier: by May it boasted three taverns, four stores, twelve shops, twenty-three houses, and thirty to forty other commercial and farm structures, with a thriving lumber and brickmaking business.[30] The Americans were now able to effect a landing quite easily at a point below Fort Erie on the morning of 3 July. Major Thomas Buck of the 8th Regiment with three guns and 137 men had been, according to his orders from Riall, set up "to resist an attack short of an Invasion in force."[31] Most of his officers thought it wise to surrender, and he offered no serious resistance before doing so—"rather too soon perhaps to satisfy the claims of military etiquette," thought Porter, although the detachment of 19th Light Dragoons set off to warn Riall of the American approach.[32]

The alarm sounded on the Canadian side that Sunday was well remembered by Private George Ferguson; he had permission from his commanding officer to leave Fort George and preach at a chapel between Queenston and Chippawa, where "there came an express for a Militia officer who was in the congregation that the American army had crossed at Black Rock. This threw the congregation into confusion—the people ran to secure their effects—one running here and another there. I felt calm and tranquil, and my trust was in the Lord Jehovah."[33] John Norton was camped with some 300 warriors near the Falls, where he was preparing to reconnoitre the American shore when he received a summons from Lieutenant-Colonel Thomas Pearson, commanding the flank companies of the 100th Regiment, who despite the abundant rumours reacted calmly and posted piquets, retiring to join the Indians at Chippawa that evening.[34] On the morning of 4 July American prisoners in Dartmoor hung out a flag with the motto: "All Canada or Dartmoor for Life."[35] That morning Pearson met Riall with five companies of 1st Royal Scots and most of a squadron of 19th Light Dragoons. Riall wanted to attack the Americans while they were preoccupied at Fort Erie, being still unaware of its fall, but he decided he was too weak to do so and chose to wait for the 1st/8th Regiment marching from York, which did not arrive until the following morning.[36] Scott's 1st Brigade was sent forward by Brown 4 miles to Frenchman's Creek, which was covered by Pearson.[37] He was reinforced by a Royal Scots company and a strong detachment of 19th Light Dragoons under Lieutenant William Horton, together with two 24-pounders under Captain James Maclachlan RA.[38] The creek was flooded and the bridge planking torn up, and the British retired, pausing at each subsequent creek for the next 14 miles.[39]

By the afternoon the Americans had reached Ussher's Creek, the last before Chippawa, where Scott's left flank guard, Captain Turner Crocker's company of 9th U.S. Infantry, emerged upstream of the bridge and, seeing the British guns apparently isolated, forded the chest-deep water to reach an area of open ground to the north. Seeing them unsupported, Horton's dragoons immediately charged across the open field. As the Americans on the far bank watched in horror, Crocker kept his cool: his company fired a volley, then retreated to shelter in a farmhouse, bringing down eight horses and wounding four dragoons; but the British guns escaped.[40] In the evening Scott saw the British assembled on the far bank of the Chippawa River and retired 2 miles to make camp with his right flank resting on the Niagara River, where he was joined at 11 P.M. by Brown with Ripley's brigade and more artillery, and next morning by some Indians and the Pennsylvanians. Having marched some 15 miles in continuous rain, the Americans were cold and tired and lay down to rest on the waterlogged ground.

Early on 5 July outposts to the north and south-west of the American camp came under fire and lost several men, with desultory sniping continuing throughout the morning.[41] With the arrival of the 1st/8th Regiment and the 1st and 2nd Lincoln Regiments of Militia, Riall now decided to attack, although he believed his 1,400 regulars, 200 militia (2nd Lincolns were detailed to provide rear security), and 300 Indians were outnumbered two to one.[42]

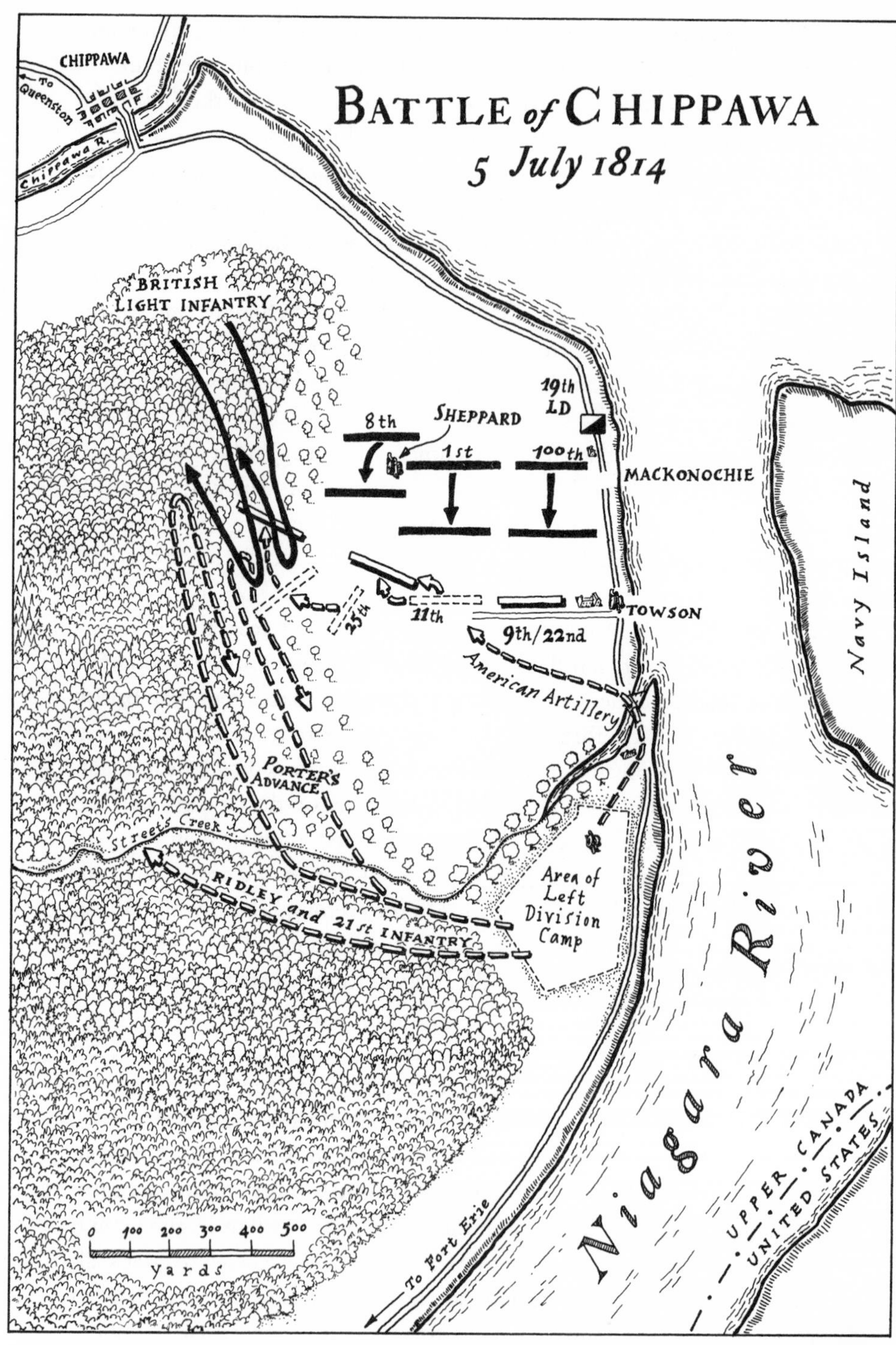

BATTLE of CHIPPAWA
5 July 1814
CHIPPAWA
To Queenston
Chippawa R.
BRITISH LIGHT INFANTRY
8th
SHEPPARD
1st
100th
19th LD
MACKONOCHIE
Navy Island
25th
11th
TOWSON
9th/22nd
American Artillery
PORTER'S ADVANCE
Streets Creek
RIDLEY and 21st INFANTRY
Area of Left Division Camp
Niagara River
UPPER CANADA
UNITED STATES
To Fort Erie
0 100 200 300 400 500
yards

The new commanding officer of the 100th Regiment was Lieutenant-Colonel George Hay, eighth marquess of Tweedale, who had ridden into camp only to be struck down by fever. The twenty-six-year-old twice-wounded Peninsula veteran was summoned to see Riall, but replied "that I was in the cold fit of ague and I expected the hot fit in a short time." Riall thoughtfully postponed the conference for an hour.[43] In the afternoon of 5 July Porter's militia brigade was sent to drive off the British forces that had been raiding American piquets. Captain Samuel White recalled that, having marched 18 miles "without rations, it is not to be wondered at that not much alacrity was showed by the men to become of the party," and, seemingly true to form, his men broke and fled when they realized the entire British force was moving across the bridge towards them.[44] The British deployed onto open ground bounded on their right by dense woods and their left by the Niagara River, but without the space to form a single line, so that the 1st/8th Regiment reinforced the right flank.

As they advanced, Private Ferguson recalled the rumour that the American front rank was composed of desperate men—"deserters and Europeans"; another rumour ran that the Americans outnumbered the British five to one, to which Riall supposedly replied: "O, they are a set of cowardly untrained men—scape gallows or state prison men who will not stand the bayonet."[45] His hubristic confidence may have been born of previous experience against American troops, mainly militia, and he expected the forces opposite to wilt before resolute action in the same manner as on previous occasions. But Hay already had his doubts about Riall after the general informed him that he intended to march straight down the river road and attack: when Hay pointed out that the Americans would probably be massed in strength in the woods and attack the British on the march, Riall ignored him; and this was exactly what happened, although Pearson's light infantry fortunately cleared that threat.[46]

Riall soon discovered, however, that this American army was no disorganized rabble. As Scott's brigade, consisting of the combined 9th/22nd, 11th, and 25th U.S. Infantry—all experienced units but dressed in grey, which Riall appears to have mistaken for militia—advanced to meet him on open ground, forsaking the relative security of its position behind a narrow creek in order to do so, it came under artillery fire.[47] Although Drummer Jarvis Hanks of the 11th U.S. Infantry recalled that the "balls and grape, mostly passed over our heads and into the bend of the river," Riall supposedly exclaimed in admiration at their steadiness: "Why, these are regulars by God!" although there were no British witnesses to verify this oft-quoted exclamation.[48] He ordered the 1st Royal Scots and 100th Regiment to advance at about 4:30 P.M. directly at the American front. Some fifteen minutes later they approached to within about 60 yards, when Scott ordered his men to fire, which the British returned, soon engulfing both lines in dense clouds of smoke.[49] A severe firefight ensued in which both sides suffered greatly—a "scene of carnage," recalled Lieutenant John Stevenson of the 100th Regiment.[50] However, the British had also to endure American artillery firing canister under the able direction of Captain Nathan Towson, while their own gunners, some way behind and unable to intervene effectively, had to watch helplessly. They were further disadvantaged by flanking fire from the 11th U.S. Infantry from the woods, while the 25th U.S. Infantry under twenty-five-year-old Kentuckian Major Thomas S. Jesup became engaged with the 1st/8th Regiment, preventing them from intervening in the main fight.[51]

Both lines stood and fired; reloaded and fired; reloaded and fired. The British, getting the worst of the exchange, could not close to use the bayonet, but they refused to retire and continued firing.[52] Private Ferguson was hit in the arm, although he "knew nothing of it until my piece fell out of my hand, and I saw the blood running down in a stream." Reluctantly he went to the rear, where waggons waited to evacuate the wounded, and had his arm bandaged with his own handkerchief. Although Ferguson was desperate for water, the officer tending him could offer only rum, and decent teetotaler that he was he accepted without enthusiasm, "to find partial relief—the only time I ever experienced any benefit from spirituous liquors."[53] After twenty-five minutes of this pounding, Riall, his own coat pierced by a bullet, was forced to order a withdrawal, which was completed in good order without American pursuit.[54] The battle cost 95 British and 16 Indians killed, with 321 reported wounded and 46 missing; American casualties totalled around 300, including 53 dead, in what was the most sanguinary encounter of the war so far. Among the wounded was Colonel John B. Campbell, who died six weeks later.[55] But significantly, British regulars had been beaten for the first time in a stand-up fight of roughly matching strength, and Scott's subsequent long career would see him take credit for a victory that perhaps really belonged to Brown.[56] The Americans exulted; the stain of Crysler's Farm and so many previous defeats had been erased, and even captured British officers were effusive in their praise. "We had never seen those grey-jackets before," said one, and "supposed it was only a line of Militia-men, [but] it became clear enough we had something besides Militia-men to deal with."[57]

For two days an uneasy calm settled over the area, before the Americans advanced in an attempt to outflank Riall's position, forcing him to retire on Fort George followed by a trail of refugees. On 10 July the Americans occupied Queenston, where they began to receive reinforcements.[58] Prevost reacted with dismay to the news of Chippawa, informing Bathurst on 12 July that he would have to act defensively until the British could attain naval supremacy on Lakes Ontario and Champlain, something which he did not anticipate before September.[59] The next day Drummond ordered reinforcements forward and requested further support: the 2nd/89th and flank companies of the 104th Regiments were detailed to York, while the Incorporated Militia Battalion of Upper Canada was sent to Fort George, then on to join Riall, who, having left a strong garrison of the 41st and 100th Regiments in Fort George, withdrew the remainder of his force to Twenty-Mile Creek to avoid being trapped between Brown and Chauncey; there he was joined by Lieutenant-Colonel Hercules Scott and the 103rd Regiment.[60]

Brown hoped Chauncey would sail from Sackets Harbor to support him and bring heavy guns with which to assail Forts George and Niagara, but Chauncey was laid up in bed with a fever; his new ship was still not ready, and the American squadron dared not leave port. Brown wrote in frustration on 13 July: "For God's sake let me see you."[61] Secretary Jones thought the lake service had been struck by paralysis and instructed Stephen Decatur to take over, but suspended the order when he learned of Chauncey's illness. Chauncey for his part took offence at Brown's tone, and, as the chances of effective cooperation receded, so did any realistic chance of significant American success in the region.[62] In the meantime, Brown drilled his men and sent out strong patrols that clashed frequently with Riall's screen of militia; the reaction of the population and steady drain of casualties led to American reprisals with the burning of property, and the whole campaign took on a distinctly bitter tone. On 18 July the village of St. Davids, consisting of about forty houses, was put to the torch, much to Brown's disgust; he dismissed the officer responsible, Lieutenant-Colonel Isaac W. Stone, despite the latter's denial of responsibility.[63]

Following a failed reconnaissance towards Fort George on 15 July and the refusal of the British to be drawn forward into contact, Brown decided that without heavy guns Forts George and Mississauga could not be taken. Meanwhile Drummond's suspension of habeas corpus and the confiscation of property of those who deserted to the enemy culminated in the trial for treason at Ancaster—the "bloody Assize"—of fifty citizens for serving with the enemy.

Although only nineteen of the accused were in custody, fifteen of them were convicted of high treason, and on 20 July eight of these men were hanged. The other seven were banished, but of those, three died of typhus while still in captivity, and one escaped.[64] On 22 July Brown pulled back to Queenston only to find it occupied by some Canadian militia, who were loudly abused by "King Joe" Willcocks and his men.[65] That day Drummond reached York with the 2nd/89th Regiment and received Riall's dispatch, and immediately reported the desperate supply situation, which necessitated evacuating civilians and putting Indian families on half-rations.[66] Riall was uncertain what to do and was anxious for Drummond's arrival, but Drummond sent Riall detailed instructions to demonstrate against Queenston and not to engage the enemy until he arrived.[67]

With Riall defending the forts, Brown summoned a council of war at which it was agreed to bypass them and make a risky move towards Burlington Heights. A confident Brown discounted that he might not win the battle that he knew must follow such a move, and regarded the risk as entirely logistical. On 24 July he suddenly retired to Chippawa, his numbers reduced to 2,644 effectives to divest himself of excess baggage; he planned to bring supplies from Fort Schlosser, then continue his advance across country towards Burlington.[68] However, Brown had not counted on British reaction to his moves; on hearing of his withdrawal Riall immediately sent Pearson south to shadow him. Pearson's 2nd or Light Brigade comprised the Glengarry Light Infantry and Incorporated Militia of Upper Canada, and he also had under command a detachment of 19th Light Dragoons and 1st Militia Brigade under Lieutenant-Colonel Love Parry, supported by two 6-pounders and a 5.5-inch howitzer—a total of around 1,100 men. They marched through the ruins of St. Davids at dawn on 25 July and halted at Lundy's Lane, a road which ran east–west from the Portage Road at the village of the same name—named after a Pennsylvania Loyalist who had settled there in 1786—about one mile north of Niagara Falls; there he was joined by John Norton and his warriors. At this point the British were outnumbered by the Americans to their south, but Riall arrived that afternoon with the 1st Brigade under Hercules Scott, comprising the 1st/8th and 103rd Regiments, the 2nd Militia Brigade, and the reserve 1st Royal Scots under Lieutenant-Colonel John Gordon.[69]

That same morning Drummond arrived at Fort George from York on the schooner *Netley* with the 2nd/89th Regiment under Lieutenant-Colonel Joseph Morrison in the *Star* and *Charwell* (formerly the *Moira*), and sent them on to Riall.[70] He also organized a force of 500 men supported by a party of

Indians under Colonel John Tucker of the 41st Regiment to sortie from Fort Niagara, while armed seamen in boats gave support from the river under Captain Alexander Dobbs RN.[71] Tucker soon scattered the New York militia and found Lewiston abandoned, and Drummond ordered him to return to Fort Niagara with part of his force; the rest, including the Indians, crossed the river at about 3 P.M.[72] This force might have accomplished more had Tucker remained on the American bank and threatened Black Rock and Buffalo, but when Brown gained news of this movement, although he knew it meant his supply base at Fort Schlosser was threatened, he boldly decided that the best way to turn round the British advance was to advance himself towards Queenston, and he sent for Winfield Scott.[73] At about the same time, Drummond sent Morrison on to Lundy's Lane with some 800 men comprising his own 2nd/89th Regiment and the light companies of the 1st Royal Scots, 1st/8th, and 41st Regiments, Maclachlan's 24-pounder detachment, and a Royal Marine Artillery rocket section, plus a large body of Indians.[74]

Late in the afternoon Winfield Scott arrived at Lundy's Lane and, deciding the British on the hill opposite were of similar numbers, deployed his men into line and prepared to attack. As the Americans approached, but before they debouched from the woods to his front, a now nervous Riall ordered a retreat. Drummond, arriving shortly afterwards, countermanded this order and put his 1,600 men into line along the hill that dominated the junction between Lundy's Lane and the Portage Road with the 24-pounders, 6-pounders, and Congreve rocket detachment deployed forward of the crest of the rise.[75] When Scott's men emerged from the wood at about 7 P.M., he was shocked to find the British in strength and ready to stand, and at first considered retreating, but chose instead to deploy his brigade and stand fast.[76] As it did so it came under heavy fire from the British guns, which hit the 22nd U.S. Infantry especially hard. Nonetheless the Americans formed line and opened fire on the British to their front, despite the extreme range, supported by Towson's guns, although, unlike at Chippawa, they had little effect.[77]

The British guns, in contrast, were this time ideally situated to wreak fearful damage, and Americans fell steadily to roundshot and shell (there being little shrapnel available in the Niagara Peninsula). Scott's brigade stood its ground and endured this punishment for some forty-five minutes until Scott decided he had to advance; but he cancelled this order after about 100 yards, leaving the American line still some 400 yards distant of the British.[78] During this time word reached Brown's camp near Chippawa, accompanied by the unmistakable sounds of battle, which carried to Buffalo 20 miles away, that

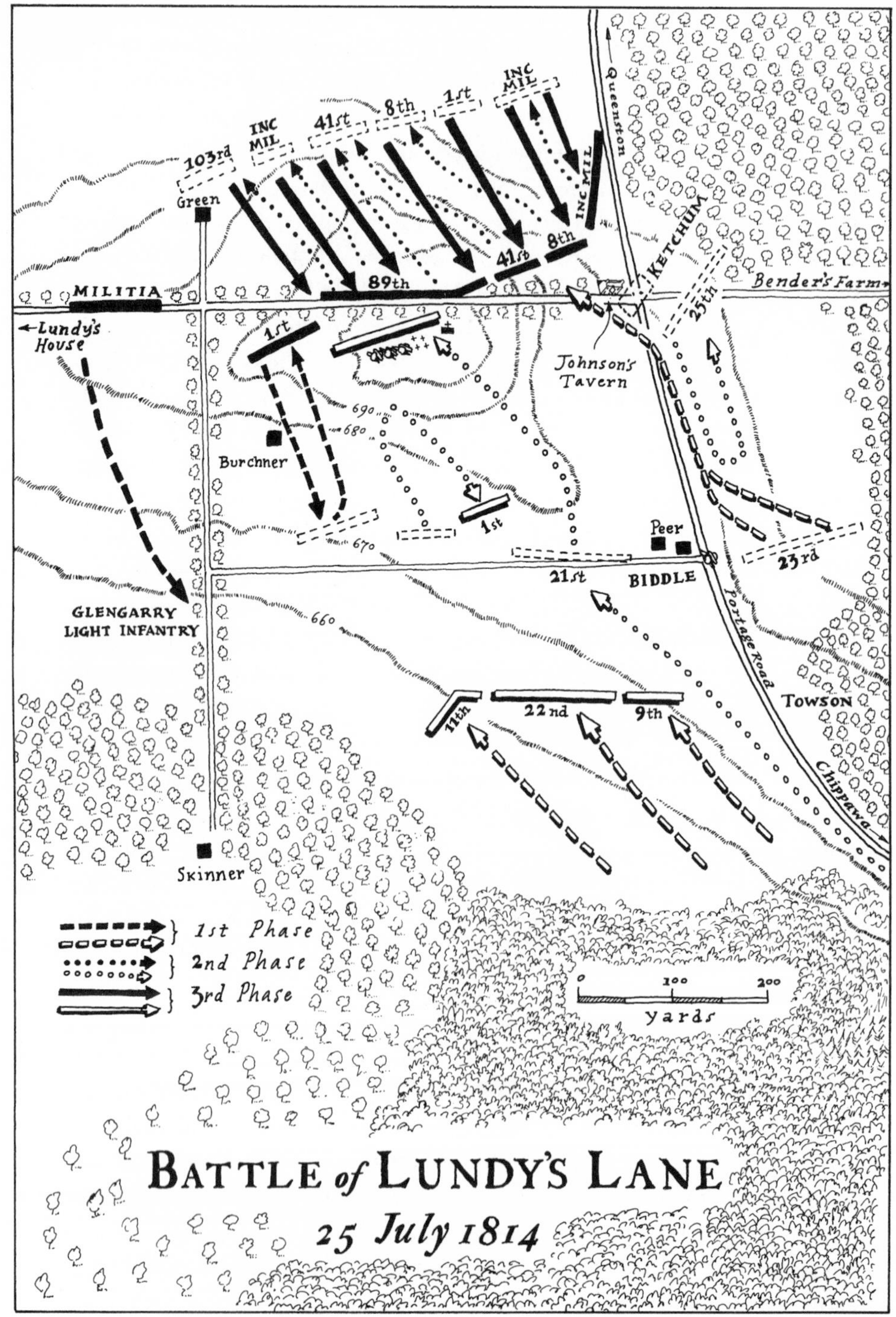
103rd
INC MIL
41st
8th
1st
INC MIL
INC MIL
Green
89th
41st
8th
MILITIA
Queenston
KETCHUM
Bender's Farm
25th
←Lundy's House
1st
Johnson's Tavern
690
680
Burchner
1st
670
Peer
21st
BIDDLE
23rd
GLENGARRY LIGHT INFANTRY
660
Portage Road
TOWSON
11th
22nd
9th
Chippawa
Skinner
1st Phase
2nd Phase
3rd Phase
0
100
200
yards
BATTLE of LUNDY'S LANE
25 July 1814

Scott was engaged with some 1,100 British; ever bold, Brown immediately set his men marching towards the gunfire.[79] A few miles to the north the British column under Hercules Scott, marching towards the battle from Twelve-Mile Creek via Beaver Dams, could also hear "the roar of Artillery and of Musketry pealing in Our front, sometimes rattling in heavy surges—sometimes scant, as if the troops pressed were retiring."[80] The noise was phenomenal, Elihu H. Shepard noted, recalling that it "is difficult to bring the imagination to realize the tremendous roar of the Falls of Niagara, the thunder of the artillery, the crash of musketry, and the shouts of battle."[81]

The Canadian 1st Militia Brigade and the Glengarry Light Infantry on Drummond's right noted that the American advance exposed their left flank and, together with some of Norton's Indians, moved forward to engage them; Drummond ordered three companies of 1st Royal Scots to support them.[82] Seeing the danger, Scott ordered the 11th U.S. Infantry on his left to wheel and face the threat, and they returned the skirmishers' fire with volleys that had little effect on the scattered Canadians and Indians. But worse, Scott's ineffective firing for so long from extreme range had the inevitable effect that his men were now running short of ammunition, as well as having suffered severe casualties from the British guns.[83] However, with twilight descending, Jesup, commanding the 25th U.S. Infantry on Scott's right, had found a track that enabled him to advance his regiment under cover to attack the British left flank. Led by Captain Daniel Ketchum's company, equipped and drilled to act as skirmishers, they fired a volley that took the Incorporated Militia and the Light Company of the 1st/8th Regiment stationed there by surprise and then advanced, overrunning the two easternmost companies of Incorporated Militia and seriously wounding their commanding officer, Lieutenant-Colonel William Robinson. The remaining militia fired and retreated to form a new line, leaving Drummond's left exposed. Major Robert Lisle's 19th Light Dragoons also retired as Jesup pressed on towards the Portage Road, where they formed up at right angles to Lundy's Lane. Jesup again selected Ketchum's company to secure the road junction and reconnoitre, and Ketchum's men soon began to capture small groups of British and Canadians and individuals using the road. Riall had been wounded in the right arm and was riding slowly back with his orderly when he too was taken, followed shortly afterwards by an aide of Drummond's sent to fetch back Lisle's dragoons; Lieutenant William H. Merritt was captured on his way to report the situation to Drummond.[84]

With a dozen officers and over 100 soldier prisoners to contend with, Jesup could not attack the British guns, whose muzzle flashes he could see in the

13.1. *Battle of Niagara* (Battle of Lundy's Lane, 25 July 1814), ca. 1820, engraving by William Strickland, first published in *Portfolio*.
Source: W. H. Coverdale Collection of Canadiana, C-040721, Library and Archives Canada.

dark. He therefore chose to send Ketchum to the rear with the prisoners and shortly afterwards received word that the rest of the brigade had been cut to pieces. Drummond had reason to feel satisfied, having maintained his position against what he believed to be Brown's entire force, although Hercules Scott had not yet arrived, despite quickly marching the 12 miles that separated them. By 8:30 P.M. Scott's brigade was reduced to around 600 men, and the fight subsided in the darkness, with only Maclachlan's gunners in action. Drummond, however, was taking no chances, and retired and re-oriented his line slightly, leaving the guns forward of the infantry. But as the 25th U.S. Infantry groped their way towards the rear, Brown arrived with the rest of the American force and prepared to renew the battle just as the British guns finally ceased firing. Hercules Scott's men arrived at about the same time, to be greeted by a cheer from the British line, and the three 6-pounders under Captain James Mackonochie RA were sent forward to join Maclachlan.[85]

Brown ordered Ripley's 2nd Brigade to deploy forward of Scott's 1st, and both Brown and Ripley decided that the hill where the British guns were stationed was the key to the British position. He deployed the 1st U.S. Infantry to form line facing the British infantry and draw their attention and ordered the 21st U.S. Infantry, commanded by Colonel James Miller, to attack the hill.[86] But before they could do so the 1st U.S. Infantry, though woefully under strength, advanced towards it. As the smoke was now clearing and the moon rising, the British guns opened fire, and the 1st wisely retired to the base of the hill. Yet the attack was not in vain; it had drawn the attention of the gunners away from the genuine threat now emerging on their left.[87] At about 9:15 P.M. the 21st U.S. Infantry suddenly appeared, having moved silently in the lee of the hill in a two-rank line with their bayonets at the "charge," unimpeded—indeed undetected—by British skirmishers; they halted at an old rail fence barely 30 yards from the guns. John Norton was conversing with two officers when they noticed the Americans, and as he approached them he "observed the Moon glimmer faintly on the plates of their Caps, the form of which denounced them to be our Enemies—before I could speak, they fired."[88]

Maclachlan was among the twenty or so casualties as the Americans pushed down the rail fence and charged; the remaining gunners either fled or surrendered. Morrison's 2nd/89th Regiment, formed just north of the lane behind the guns, was thrown into confusion as some of the artillery horses stampeded in panic through the line. Drummond, who was close by, ordered Morrison to counter-attack, and he quickly complied, opening a sharp fire at the 21st U.S. Infantry. But the British advance was hindered by guns, trees, waggons, and gravestones as they crossed the cemetery to their front, and the Americans returned their fire. The two regiments had faced each other at Crysler's Farm, but this time it was the British who withdrew first, though in good order; they returned to the attack supported by three companies of 1st Royal Scots and the Light Company of the 41st Regiment. A second firefight ensued in which Morrison was among the wounded. Once again the British retired as the 21st held its ground; once more they returned to renew the fight, and this time Drummond was among the wounded, as a ball entered under the right ear and lodged in the back of his neck. Despite losing a great deal of blood, he remained in action as the Light Company of the 41st under Captain Joseph Glew briefly regained the guns but was unable to bring them away to safety for lack of horses.[89] Once more the British withdrew, this time not to return; and with contact between the two armies now broken, Miller and his men awaited support from the main American line.[90]

The first unit to arrive was the 1st U.S. Infantry. However, while the 21st had been performing its sterling service in securing the British gun line, the other regiment of Ripley's brigade, the 23rd U.S. Infantry, had advanced in column on its left. It was just at the point of deploying into line when it was ambushed. Private Amasiah Ford recalled that "out of 32 in the first platoon, only eight of us escaped the desperate slaughter."[91] Among the dead was Major Daniel McFarland, the commanding officer, and the regiment was thrown into confusion. Only Ripley's presence enabled the remaining officers to regain control, and they now climbed the hill to join their sister unit, shortly joined by four 6-pounders and two 5.5-inch howitzers. Jesup and the 25th U.S. Infantry had also returned to the fray, and Porter's militia brigade was beginning to arrive as Brown also appeared. Unsure what the British intended, he seems to have prevented the removal of the British guns, but, going forward to reconnoitre, he was nearly captured. Realizing that the British were about to renew the attack, he quickly ordered Porter to deploy to Ripley's left.[92] He was only just in time.

Drummond knew that he had to recapture his guns or he would be unable to face the Americans on the open field, but his army was in a jumbled confusion, with many disordered units, and it was imperative that they reform and counter-attack at the earliest opportunity. He seems to have formed them into a single line divided into two wings—a difficult task in the darkness. Meanwhile, "the ridiculous mistakes which could only occur fighting an army speaking the same language were laughable though serious—Who goes there?—A friend—To whom?—To King George. If the appellants, as you would call them, were of that persuasion [*sic*], all was well, but when a friend to Madison, then there was a difference of opinion."[93] Both sides benefitted from windfalls as messages and prisoners fell into their hands, but there were also frequent "friendly fire" incidents on both sides. It took Drummond some thirty minutes to prepare to launch the counter-attack. But his failure to protect his guns with light infantry was now compounded by failure to use them ahead of his attack.

At about 10 P.M. the British and Canadian line moved forward. On the right were two companies of Incorporated Militia and the Light Company of the 41st Regiment; the 1st Royal Scots and 2nd/89th Regiments formed the centre, and the right flank comprised two more companies of Incorporated Militia and the Light Company of the 1st/8th Regiment. By now the Americans had also reorganized themselves and were ready, but they too had neglected to post skirmishers to their front. Both sides were in perfect silence as the British approached to within 30 yards, or even as close as 10. The Americans had orders to fire second so that the British would be illuminated by their muzzle flashes, but as the first volley crashed along the line it caused horrific casualties, greatly reducing their own effectiveness and also knocking out so many American gunners as to effectively neutralize their artillery. But it did not break their line, and another fierce firefight began while Drummond and Ripley rode up and down behind their respective lines, exhorting and encouraging their men, Drummond shouting "Stick to them, my fine fellows," matched by the more practical American cry of "Level low and fire at their flashes."[94] Some twenty-five minutes later Drummond saw that the Americans remained unshaken and gave the command for the British line to withdraw, which it did, maintaining good order.[95]

Ripley knew they would be back, and as his men closed their gaps he ordered Porter's men up to extend his line to the left. At about 10:45 P.M. the British renewed the attack, closing once more in the darkness to a range of some 30 yards. A "sheet of fire" marked the resumption of the fight, "more severe, and . . . longer continued than the last."[96] And this time the Americans began to waver; Porter's brigade was disordered and fired only irregularly before starting to withdraw, and the 23rd U.S. Infantry in the centre also started to give way. At this point Winfield Scott tried to intervene with his brigade with an assault on the British line in column, but in the dark it immediately came under fire from both lines, suffering heavy casualties, and the survivors fled. The firefight continued and then gradually died down, the

British being too exhausted to press the attack with the bayonet. Significantly, Lieutenant John Le Couteur would never forget, Drummond "rode up to the 103rd [Regiment]. 'My lads *will you* charge the Americans?' He *put a question* instead of *giving the order*—they fired instead of charging."[97] Drummond had inflicted heavy casualties on the Americans but was still no nearer to reclaiming his guns: he ordered a third attack.

Shortly before 11:30 P.M. the British and Canadians once more advanced in a repetition of the tactics that had so far proved unsuccessful. But having re-formed his brigade, Winfield Scott also chose to attack once more. This time the result was even worse for the battered remnants of his command, crossing the front of Lieutenant-Colonel William Drummond's 104th Regiment, which poured volleys into the Americans until they retreated: only two officers and about thirty men of the 22nd U.S. Infantry marched into camp that night.[98] Soon afterwards Brown was wounded by a musket ball in the thigh, and his aide was killed. Brown was then wounded again but refused to depart the field as he watched the third British attack come in.[99] Once more, heavy firing commenced, but in the dark the British did not close, and Porter decided to attack; he forced them to give way and took a number of prisoners, while on the right the 25th U.S. Infantry also performed well. Winfield Scott appeared beside Jesup and was knocked unconscious; then Jesup received his fourth wound of the action, but still he held his position.[100] However, the fight would be decided in the centre, and here the British seemed finally to break through: the 2nd/89th Regiment at last got amongst the guns, where a vicious hand-to-hand fight ensued. But as the British troops on the flanks pulled back, the centre was also forced to give way, and at around midnight the Americans were left once more in possession of the heights. Drummond's third attack had failed, although his report written three days later tried to obfuscate this result by claiming that the guns were re-captured, along with an American 5.5-inch howitzer and a 6-pounder, and "in limbering up our Guns at one period, one of the Enemy's Six pounders was put, by mistake, upon a limber of ours, and one of our six limbered on one of his, by which means the pieces were exchanged, and thus, we have gained only one Gun."[101]

Ripley waited for around thirty minutes until he was sure the British would not return, and ordered Porter's brigade to take off the guns; but lack of horses or harness allowed them to take away only one.[102] A conference of senior American officers agreed to collect the wounded, then to withdraw the exhausted and battered American force to camp, all of which was accomplished without incident. The British and Canadians withdrew down the hill and slept on their arms, amid rumours that the Americans would attack again. But once it was known the Americans had gone, they relaxed until it began to grow light towards 5 A.M. to reveal the horror of the night's work. Hundreds of men lay sprawled dead, dying, or horribly wounded and groaning for water. The Americans lost 173 killed, 571 wounded, and 117 missing, some 45 percent of those engaged;[103] British losses were officially stated as 84 killed—Lieutenant H. N. Moorsom of the 104th, "a very intelligent and promising young officer," according to Drummond, was killed by one of the last shots fired—559 wounded, including Drummond; and 193 missing, including Riall, although it seems likely this last figure was overstated, and amounting to losses of about 30 percent of those engaged. Certainly the hardest hit was the 2nd/89th Regiment, which suffered 252 casualties from 425, including 13 from 18 officers. The 1st Royal Scots lost 170; the Incorporated Militia of Upper Canada suffered 142 casualties, and the 1st/8th Regiment 74.[104]

It was the bloodiest battle of the war, but precious little glory was gained in return for the price paid in agony by the American wounded, who were taken to a tented hospital at Williamsville near Buffalo, where only

> the Groans, of the wounded & agonies of the Dying are to be heard. The Surgeons, wading in blood, cutting of[f] arms, legs & trepanning heads to rescue their fellow creatures from untimely deaths—to hear the poor creatures, crying—Oh, Dear! Oh Dear! Oh My God! My God! Do, Doctor, Doctor! Do cut of[f] my leg! my arm! my head! To relieve me from misery! I cant live! I cant live![105]

As with other branches of medical science, the art of surgery was crude indeed, amounting to little more than an attempt, if possible, to extract the bullet or shell fragment, followed by cleaning and dressing of wounds; internal surgery was practically impossible.[106] Wounds in the arm or leg would receive similar treatment, with splinting of broken bones if not complicated; but amputation was usually necessary, with precious little anaesthetic. Amputation was also likely for the reason that it converted a difficult wound into a relatively simple one, and made life easier for massively overworked medical staff. But antisepsis was unheard of, and little attention was paid to hygiene of either persons or buildings; so it is unsurprising that expected mortality rates were 9 percent for simple fractures, 42 percent for compound or open fractures, and up to 50 percent for gunshot wounds.[107] American surgeon William E.

Horner "had sole attendance and dressing of one hundred and seventy-three sick and wounded. My fingers became so sore from incessant dabbing in water and pus that I could seize nothing without pain."[108]

On the British side William Dunlop was among those left to pick up the pieces as the miserable British wounded were brought into Fort George, where he had the assistance of only a sergeant, in charge of a hospital with 320 patients, noting: "There is hardly on the face of the earth a less enviable situation than that of an Army Surgeon after a battle—worn out and fatigued in body and mind, surrounded by suffering, pain and misery, much of which he knows it is not in his power to heal or even to assuage." Among the melancholy scenes he witnessed was the wife of an American prisoner who came to nurse her husband, "lying on a truss of straw, writhing in agony, for his sufferings were most dreadful." Dunlop watched as the poor woman took her man's head in her lap and wept until,

> awakened by a groan from her unfortunate husband, she clasped her hands, and looking wildly around, exclaimed, "O that the King and President were both here this moment to see the misery their quarrels lead to—they surely would not go to war without cause that they could give as a reason to God at the last day, for thus destroying the creatures that He hath made in his own image."[109]

Later the wounded were transferred to York, but the general hospital was too small to accommodate them and the many sick, so other buildings, including a church, had to be taken over; but men evacuated to York were debilitated by the journey and less likely to recover.[110] At least the methods of transport were marginally better than those found in Europe, where the wounded were frequently jolted and bounced to death in any available unsprung country waggons that could be pressed into service. In America they were more variously carried on litters made of blankets strung between poles, or by water, as well as by waggons and sleighs.[111] As for the dead, there were so many that many had to be burned rather than buried. Shadrach Byfield recalled that one Indian persisted in trying to throw a wounded American onto the fire, despite being repeatedly restrained by Byfield's mates. Eventually they lost patience with the obstinate native: they shot him, and threw him onto the fire.[112]

On the morning of 26 July, acting in direct contravention of Brown's orders, Ripley drew off the American force to the Black Rock ferry site. He realized that although the British might expect reinforcement, the Americans could not, and retreated as soon as his men had thrown excess stores into the river, destroying Street Mills and the bridge at Chippawa. In his superb account, Donald Graves regards Lundy's Lane as a tactical victory for the Americans, but concludes that their failure to secure its fruits in terms of position and the captured British guns rendered it an operational success for the British.[113] But regardless of the balance of success, the U.S. Army had finally shown the determination, fortitude, and resilience that had been so conspicuously lacking during the first two years of war.[114] The same could not be said of the local New Yorkers, however; and both Brown and Porter were indignant at the lack of support from the frontier's inhabitants; only 300 of 1,000 men called out bothered to show up. Persons who failed to show up for militia service, wrote Porter, should lose their right to vote.[115] But despite the pride they could take in their performance in the field, once again the overall American effort was too little, too late: they had been unable to overwhelm the British defences even though these were yet to be reinforced from Europe. Not until 5 August did Chauncey appear off Fort George ready to contest the lake; it was typical of the war as a whole that both sides held control on the water at the wrong time to assist offensive operations along the lakeshore.[116]

With barely 2,100 effectives available at the end of July, Ripley favoured withdrawal across the river, but Brown insisted that Fort Erie be held as a bridgehead, and while the Americans worked feverishly to improve their toehold on Canadian territory Drummond decided not to follow up immediately, but instead withdrew 7 miles to Queenston; he released his sedentary militia to ease the logistic burden and withdrew the 41st, 2nd/89th, and 100th Regiments to the forts to shorten his supply line and await reinforcements.[117] When he did begin his pursuit, he knew that with only 3,000 men he was too weak for sustained operations against prepared positions at Fort Erie, although it was still less a fort than a fortified bridgehead. The unfinished earthworks were eminently vulnerable, and had he followed up closely after the battle and forced the Americans to fight again he might have made his success complete. Instead this backward step would doom the British to six weeks of intense and bloody frustration.[118]

Drummond hoped to draw the defenders out by cutting off their supplies, and he sent a force of 580 men to destroy the depots at Buffalo and Black Rock, hoping this would provoke a response. The force, comprising six companies of the 41st, the Light Company of the 2nd/89th, and flank companies of the 104th Regiments, under Colonel Tucker of the 41st, crossed the river unopposed on the night of 2–3 August. Tucker, whose nickname was "Brigadier Shindy," was not well respected and did nothing for four hours; then he advanced without advance or flank guards.[119] At Conjocta (also known as Conjocheta or Scajaquada) Creek the British met a strong detachment of the 1st U.S. Rifle Regiment out from Black Rock under Major Ludowick Morgan, who had taken down the bridge and occupied a breastwork on the far bank.[120] After taking casualties, the 41st Regiment broke, but the remainder of Tucker's force advanced towards the riflemen, who kept up such an effective fire that the attackers could find no other means to cross, even though the creek was fordable a mile upstream. The men, according to Tucker, "displayed an unpardonable degree of unsteadiness," prompting him to retreat after three hours without achieving his objectives, having lost eleven killed, seventeen wounded, and four missing, against two Americans killed and eight wounded.[121] Among the British wounded was Shadrach Byfield, who had to have his left arm amputated in a "tedious and painful" operation.[122] On the American side Lieutenant Jonathan Kearsley noted that "the skill in planning and the firmness in the execution of the riflemen defeated the designs of the British and saved the entire American army."[123]

14

Burning the White House

Fell traces of the conqueror's car,
And ruins of barbarian war,
The wither'd tree and blacken'd wall
Of marble nodding to its fall,
Canvass and bust, to ruin, doom'd.
The lore of ages half consum'd,
Models of art by Genius plann'd,
Scath'd by incendiary brand,
And undistinguish'd ravage swore,
The Goth or Briton had been there.

—Anon., "The Curse of Liberty"

As SUMMER approached, pressure increased along the New England coast. On 13 June Lieutenant James Garland RN led 200 men to attack vessels at Wareham, at the head of Buzzard's Bay, where they destroyed ten and a cotton warehouse worth $20,000, and escaped without loss after taking some local hostages, who were released once their boats reached safety.[1]

A few days later boats from HMS *Bulwark* (74) raided the Saco River in Maine, while at New York Robert Fulton's latest invention was launched, the long-awaited "Turtle Boat." This cumbersome vessel, measuring some 30 feet by 16, was heavily armoured with iron plates and was to be used to launch "torpedoes" against the blockading squadron. In fact, she did manage to get underneath *Ramillies,* where her crew bored a hole in the copper sheathing but then broke the bolt that was to fix the torpedo.

After this narrow escape Hardy kept his vessels moving and notified the Americans that prisoners of war would be aboard all his ships and blown up with them.[2] Subsequently word that the turtle boat had run aground on Long

Island in a storm reached Captain George Burdett RN of *Maidstone.* On 24 June 1814 he departed the blockade of New London and attacked it, after landing a party of marines, who drove off the local militia with a single volley, then planted charges. "And in half an hour I had the gratifying spectacle of seeing her explode with a heavy crash; when the smoke cleared away there was not a vestige of her to be seen but the splinters."[3] Besides, it would take far more than one man's inventiveness to break the Royal Navy's stranglehold; the element of surprise elicited by the super-frigates had long gone, and the U.S. Navy simply had too few ships to compete effectively. On 11 July Hardy's Maine expedition sailed into Passamaquoddy Bay and prepared to attack Fort Sullivan on Moose Island, defended by 80 regulars and about 250 militia under Major Perley Putnam, who yielded without offering resistance; the British force then occupied Eastport and Robbinston opposite St. Andrews.[4]

A 3rd Battalion of Royal Marines including a company of Marine artillery had formed at Portsmouth in March and would soon be arriving, giving Cockburn, who besides being an admiral was also a colonel of the Royal Marines, a powerful addition to his landing forces.[5] In early July Cockburn was able to report to Cochrane that Tangier Island was secure against any possible attack and that Barney's flotilla was so far out of reach as to pose no threat. It could be ignored until sufficient land forces were available to destroy it.[6] In early July *Albion* sent a cutter ashore under a flag of truce to obtain water and purchase provisions. It was met by a colonel of militia and several other officers who refused, and one of their number could not restrain himself. Captain Jabo poured forth a stream of invective and offensive vitriol that was an outrageous insult against both its recipient and the etiquette of a truce: knowing full well that the defenceless British lieutenant was in no position to respond, Jabo threatened to string him up like a scarecrow. On his return the lieutenant inquired among the former slaves if any of them knew Jabo, and one had indeed previously been owned by him. That night, having received permission from Cockburn, the lieutenant led twenty Royal Marines and some Colonials to seek him out. They landed near a militia encampment and found their man in a house some 8 miles away, "shivering in his shirt" with his newly-wed wife beside him. The normally kind-hearted lieutenant seized his man without compunction together with his overseer and bundled them off, hotly pursued by the militia. Jabo was well treated on the *Albion,* being accorded the privileges of his rank, but he behaved cravenly in marked contrast to his previous arrogance. When Cockburn received a special plea on his behalf from the local militia commander, noting that Jabo was not a regular officer and highlighting the distress caused to his wife, Cockburn replied that he could not consent that Jabo was a non-combatant, and although he released the overseer, Jabo was sent to Britain.[7]

James Scott, who was now serving as the admiral's aide-de-camp, noted that Cockburn had long "fixed an eye of peculiar interest upon Washington. It had been the concentrated object of his thoughts and actions; every measure he adopted was more or less remotely connected, conceived, and carried into execution, as affording preliminary steps to the final accomplishment of the grand ultimatum of his exertions."[8] It would seem his ships' captains were also acutely aware of his fixation with the enemy capital, as Captain Robert Rowley RN of the troopship HMS *Melpomme* (22) declared: "I hope to God we shall be successful and lessen the dignity and pomp of a misjudged and impolitic people."[9] Other British servicemen who fought in the Chesapeake expressed ambivalence about fighting Americans at all because they realized the close kinship between Britons and Americans.[10] On 15 July, when *St. Lawrence* and *Loire* returned with fourteen prizes, Cockburn was also joined by three troopships bringing the 3rd Battalion, Royal Marines, together with additional escorts and a bomb vessel and news that Cochrane was following with another 20,000 men. On 17 July Cockburn compiled a comprehensive report to his superior in which he outlined his appreciation and plan. He highlighted in detail the potential for landing at Benedict, Maryland, and the speedy seizure of Washington, pointing out the probable strength of seaward defences at Annapolis and Baltimore, which might be outflanked by land, and noting that only Norfolk appeared to have significant defensive strength.[11] He underscored his confidence in a second, private letter: "I most firmly believe that within forty eight Hours after the Arrival in the Patuxent . . . the City of Washington might be possessed without Difficulty or Opposition," and also explained that American guides would not be difficult to obtain provided that sufficient money was available.[12]

Although British forces had threatened Washington through much of 1813, the American government took no effective action to fortify or defend the capital in the spring of 1814. Armstrong believed Baltimore was more important militarily and the capital safe; he ignored the psychological attraction of a British assault on their enemy's capital and never considered the British prisoners brought before him as anything but foragers. And Madison was not prepared to overrule him.[13] At last Armstrong was persuaded to take some action: on 2 July a new military district was formed—No. 10—covering Maryland, the District of Columbia, and parts of eastern Virginia, with Brigadier-General William H. Winder in command. Winder had been recently exchanged following his capture at Stoney Creek and did not meet with Armstrong's approval, but Madison insisted for political reasons: Winder was the nephew of Levin Winder, the Federalist governor of Maryland and an arch war-critic.[14] But Armstrong did not assign any staff to the new military district, leaving Winder to do much of the work himself, and he also discouraged Winder from calling out the militia until a British attack was imminent. As Winder became increasingly bogged down in minutiae, he failed to plan an integrated defence for Washington and Baltimore.[15] In theory he had 15,000 militia available for the defence of the capital, but in reality the necessary requisitions were unfilled. By 1 August he had only around 1,000 regulars and a few hundred militia ready, and there were no prepared lines of defence. Armstrong, resentful at Madison's interference, did nothing to help.[16]

On 18 July Cochrane issued a general order to "lay waste" towns along the American coast but to spare the lives of unarmed inhabitants, until such time as the Americans gave compensation for the destruction they had wrought in Upper Canada.[17] This order was issued partly with a view to its effect on American opinion, and was accompanied by a secret memorandum exempting places that furnished supplies or that might be later occupied and where lenity and forbearance might prove wiser. A tribute might be levied for the sparing of private property, but on no account were harbours, magazines, shipping, or government property to be spared. This policy was subsequently approved by the Admiralty. Meanwhile Cockburn swept through the Maryland and Virginia waterside communities inside the Potomac: Leonardstown on 19 July—whence the 36th U.S. Infantry promptly withdrew, leaving stores to be destroyed—Nominy Ferry (20 July), St. Clement's Creek (23 July), Machodoc Creek (26 July), Hamburgh (28 July), Chaptico (30 July), all received a visit with prizes taken.[18] Significantly, Captain Joseph Nourse RN of the newly arrived frigate HMS *Severn* (38) gained Benedict with ease on 23 July, despite drawing more water than the other ships that had previously attempted it, and found the district as deserted and defenceless as the lower reaches. Her sailing master produced a fine river plan compiled as a result of an expedition into the now virtually abandoned Calvert and St. Mary's Counties. Previously Nourse had told Cochrane:

> In one of our expeditions an American told us he guessed we were the advance guard of a considerable force intended to land at Benedict and march to Washington. I wish with all my heart that the force was ar-

> rived, for Jonathan I believe is so confounded that he does not know when or where to look for us . . . It would require but little to burn Washington and I hope soon to put the torch to it myself.[19]

British intelligence was aided by a few runaway slaves but also by an American named Hopewell who was prepared to betray his country because he believed the war unjust.

On 1 August the people of Britain celebrated in gala fashion the centenary of the succession of the House of Brunswick, or Hanover, to the throne; it also marked the anniversary of Nelson's great victory of the Nile and was, in fact, a mammoth celebration of peace; for "the Corsican ogre" Bonaparte had finally been returned to the Mediterranean in exile on Elba, where it was fervently hoped he would remain. Castlereagh was carefully studying his plans for the crucial conference that would settle post-war Europe, the Congress of Vienna, making pageantry and celebration the order of the day.[20] Only the continuing war with America gave pause for thought. On 2 August the British landed on the Virginia shore from the Yocomico River and destroyed ordnance stores. For once, the local militia rallied and formed on the heights at Kinsale to make a fight of it the following day. Cockburn then moved to the Coan River on the 6th and 7th, crossing to the St. Mary's River on 11 August.[21] For Lieutenant William Stanhope Lovell RN, who served under Nourse on the *Severn,* the raids were,

> to use an American expression, "scaring the militia" . . . Some of the Americans used to say, "What did King George send you here from the old country to come and scare us for? We don't go to yours to frighten you, I guess. Your confounded sarpents come and anchor in our waters; then send their barges, full of armed men, who are pulling about day and night, landing here and there, scaring us and our families very considerably—tarnation seize them." Our reply used to be, "You must ask your President, Jim Madison, he invited us."[22]

At Nominy a bottle of poisoned whiskey and glasses were discovered inviting the visitors to slake their thirst, an act well outside the acceptable bounds of warfare. It was not the first such incident, and although Brigadier-General John P. Hungerford of the Virginia militia ordered an inquiry, its conclusion of American innocence convinced nobody on the British side. "Such criminal devices must at once excite our pity and contempt for the authors and executors of them," noted Scott.[23] Operations in the Potomac were wound up with a visit to St. Mary's Creek on the 10th and 11th. Three days later Cochrane joined Cockburn, and the latter pressed the case for a descent on Washington.[24]

Hardy had by now returned to join the squadron off New London. Rear-Admiral Henry Hotham suspected that the small nearby port of Stonington, Connecticut, was harbouring Fulton's torpedoes, regarded by the Royal Navy as an infernal and illegal weapon, as were submarines. When pilot Joshua Penny was overheard making boastful remarks about attacking British ships with torpedoes, he soon found himself seized by Royal Marines and clapped in irons. When Hardy received a request for Penny's release from the local militia commander, his reply was astonishing in the detail it contained of British intelligence on both civilian and military activity ashore. He rejected the request because information he had received from ashore flatly contradicted the American's protestation of innocence: "Having been so well acquainted with the conduct of this man for the last six weeks, and the purpose for which he has been so employed in hostilities against his Britannic Majesty, I cannot avoid expressing my surprise that the inhabitants of east Hampton should have attempted to enforce on you a statement so contrary to fact."[25] Hardy was directed to take HM Ships *Ramillies* (74), *Pactolus* (44), and *Dispatch* (22) and the bomb-ship *Terror* and destroy Stonington, where he arrived on 9 August. The women and children were sent away, but the men stayed behind to defend their home, and would show how much the United States had lost by not securing the support of New England for the war.[26]

That evening many shells and rockets fell in the town, but there was no loss of life as the defenders hauled an 18-pounder and a 6-pounder to the end of the peninsula near the town and built a breastwork; when they opened fire, they drove off some barges and a launch that were approaching the shore. The following morning Hardy ordered *Pactolus* and *Dispatch* to anchor near the town, but the former grounded and was unable to support the smaller vessel, which was struck by the town's 18-pounder, losing two men killed and twelve wounded. However, the gun ran out of ammunition and had to be spiked, although later that day some more ammunition was found, and the gun was brought back into action. An anonymous Connecticut militiaman described how the men "were driven by expediency of making cartridges with clothing from their bodies; and when the match rope failed, they fired the cannon with a small gun snapped over the vent."[27] By the evening a large number of militia had gathered, and although the bombardment continued on the 11th and 12th, it proved a singular failure: one American died of wounds, but fewer than fifty buildings were damaged and only a handful destroyed.[28] Private Henry Chesebrough later told his grand-daughter how he and a friend were watching the bombardment when he predicted a close shot. "They stepped apart, as the cannon ball passed between them, [it] penetrated the door where they had just been standing and crashed through a china closet causing a great clatter of broken dishes, and went out the back of the house."[29]

On board *Tonnant* Cockburn learned the details of the army being sent in support, which was somewhat reduced from an originally promised 13,000 men. The 1st/4th (The King's Own) and 1st/44th (East Essex) Regiments and 85th (Bucks Volunteers) Light Infantry—some 2,800 men—were due at Bermuda, having come direct from Bordeaux, and the 21st Regiment (Royal North British Fusiliers) from the Mediterranean, giving a total of 4,500 including the 3rd Battalion, Royal Marines, and bluejackets.[30] The military commander, Major-General Robert Ross, was a Peninsula veteran recently severely wounded at the battle of Orthes, and would probably have been regarded as still unfit for active service by modern standards. With the long war against France finally over, his letters to his wife, Elizabeth, were full of assurances to mollify her fears for his well-being.[31] Cochrane sailed from Bermuda for the Chesapeake on 1 August with Rear-Admiral Sir Pulteney Malcolm, bringing Ross and his command on the 4th.[32] To fifteen-year-old Midshipman Robert Barrett the troops appeared to be "eager souls, panting for fame and opportunity to sustain the laurels they had gained in so many bloody fields of Spain and Portugal."[33]

On arrival at the Chesapeake Cochrane consulted Cockburn, and the initial decision was to continue pressing Barney's flotilla up the Patuxent. The considerable reduction in his force encouraged Cochrane's natural caution, despite the evidence of American weakness, and Cockburn had to use all his powers of persuasion to obtain permission for an attack on Washington. According to his deputy adjutant-general, Major Harry Smith, Ross was also "very cautious in responsibility—awfully so, and lacked that dashing enterprise so essential to carry a place by *coup de main*."[34] Washington was as far inland as Antwerp, and the soldiers had misgivings; but Cockburn knew his enemy and drove the project forward. Ross was a forceful and experienced commander, and he and Cockburn soon struck up a rapport; they went ashore the following day, and when he saw the ease with which Cockburn's men operated, Ross was won over.[35] Cochrane agreed to forgo his earlier intention of an attack north of Rhode Island but would not yet approve a direct assault on Washington, although the need to destroy Barney's gunboats lent justification to Cockburn's proposals. The fleet entered the Patuxent and anchored off Benedict. This position offered two possible routes to Washington, the most interesting running parallel with the Patuxent to Upper Marlborough, whence it was just 15 miles via Bladensburg to the capital. As the troops marched north, the navy could support them from the river, offering the opportunity of retreat if it proved necessary.[36] On the evening of 16 August the now enlarged squadron entered the Chesapeake. The vast spread of sail could mean only one thing to observers on shore, and the best riders were quickly dispatched to warn Washington and the government that they finally faced what they had been dreading all summer: invasion![37]

On the morning of 17 August in the Chesapeake a final conference was held on board *Tonnant.* A small squadron led by Captain James Alexander Gordon RN of the frigate HMS *Seahorse* (38) would destroy the Potomac defences, and Captain Sir Peter Parker RN—a twenty-six-year-old baronet, cousin of Lord Byron and described as "the handsomest man in the navy"—commanding the frigate HMS *Menelaus* (38) with two schooners in support, would sail up the Chesapeake above Baltimore to interrupt communications with Philadelphia and New York.[38] The rest of the force would follow the *Severn* up to Benedict beginning at dawn on 18 August. Resembling a regatta in peacetime, as it entered the Patuxent the fleet tacked against wind and tide. "The river at its mouth," recalled George Laval Chesterton of the Field Train, Royal Artillery,

> was scarcely two miles wide . . . Thus, in a narrow fresh-water river, the banks whereof were skirted with trees, and enriched with verdure to the very margin, was beheld a powerful fleet, consisting of several line-of-battle ships, frigates, troop-ships, bomb-vessels, sloops, brigs, schooners and transports—together with numerous diminutive tenders; the whole decorated with the ensigns of their nation—red, white or blue.[39]

The first navigational hazard was Point Patience, 7 miles upstream, where the channel narrowed to less than a mile and the strong tidal stream forced the fleet to anchor. Since the heavier ships would find it hard going farther on, Cochrane wisely transferred the troops to the frigates and lighter vessels, and his flag to the frigate HMS *Iphigenia* (36). But in the afternoon, with the flood tide beneath them, they advanced beyond St. Leonard's Creek, and the larger ships stopped there while the lighter vessels went on to Sandy Point, where Ross's assistant adjutant related his curious impression that the fleet was not sailing on water but stalking through some primeval forest—so thick were the magnificent trees lining the banks. Indeed, so narrow was the passage that sea room permitted only single file; nevertheless, by dusk the ships had anchored close to Benedict town. Little sign of human presence had been noted, despite numerous white cottages dotting the shoreline, but news soon reached Washington of the fleet's movements, and William Jones ordered Barney to move his flotilla as far upstream as possible; should the British approach the capital, he was to destroy them and move with his men to assist in its defence.[40]

On 18 August Winder was making desperate attempts to increase his force while Armstrong remained unsure if Washington was the target, preferring the idea that it was a feint for a move on Baltimore. Winder thought Annapolis the likely objective, but into this comic-opera came all sorts of senior government officials taking inappropriate roles: James Monroe, the secretary of state, was convinced the British were coming to Washington, and as a former colonel of cavalry he set out next day with a small party of horsemen towards Benedict to reconnoitre for himself. He found that although the British were passing through well-wooded country, there were no abatis to impede them. What he saw alarmed him further: four battalions spread amid so many transports required considerable planning, and now, throughout the night and following morning, they were free to disembark and shake out after their long sea voyage, which they completed by 3 P.M. on 19 August.[41] On the afternoon of 20 August, with each man carrying three days' rations consisting of 3 pounds of pork and 2 1/2 pounds of biscuit, the troops began to advance towards Nottingham about 20 miles upstream in three columns, supported by a flotilla of small craft on the river.

The 1st or Light Brigade consisted of the 85th Light Infantry and the Light Companies of the 4th, 21st, and 44th Regiments, the Colonial Marines, and a company of Royal Marines; the 2nd Brigade comprised the 4th and 44th Regiments, and the 3rd Brigade the balance of the Royal Marines and the 21st Fusiliers. But the British were unused to the stifling, humid weather; having spent weeks inactive at sea, they were not in the best condition in their woollen uniforms and heavy packs in the hottest summer in memory, and Ross halted them after 6 miles on the first day. A violent thunderstorm that night did little for their comfort, and they were glad to get moving early next morning. At about 5 P.M. on 21 August they reached Nottingham to find Cockburn already there but their prey gone, as Barney had moved his flotilla farther upstream. Cockburn was not to be put off, however; next day he led a force of boats and tenders upstream above Pig Point, where

> I plainly discovered Commodore Barney's broad pendant in the headmost vessel (a large sloop), and the remainder of the flotilla extending in a long line astern of her. Our boats now advanced towards them as rapidly as possible but on nearing them we observed the sloop bearing the broad pendant to be on fire, and she blew up very soon afterwards. I now saw clearly that they were all abandoned and on fire with trains to their magazines, and out of the 17 vessels which comprised this formidable and so much vaunted flotilla, 16 were in quick succession blown to atoms, and the 17th (in which the fire had not taken), we captured.[42]

So ended Barney's flotilla; the British also found thirteen merchant schooners and brought those that were serviceable away, destroying the rest.

Winder did nothing in response. Although he hoped to gather sufficient forces to meet a British advance, and had now gathered around 2,000 men, including 300 regulars at Bladensburg under Brigadier-General Tobias Stansbury, he did not send any light troops to harass and slow the British.[43] As they marched out of Baltimore on 21 August, Private John Pendleton Kennedy and his buddies of the 5th Maryland Volunteer Infantry, recruited from the best society in town, were waved off by crowds: "the populace was cheering and huzzaing at every corner, as we hurried along in brisk step to familiar music, with banners fluttering in the wind and bayonets flashing in the sun." Among his kit he had packed a pair of dress shoes, "which I had provided with the idea, that, after we had beaten the British Army and saved Washington, Mr. Madison would very likely invite us to a ball at the White House, and I wanted to be ready for it."[44] On Monday, 22 August, there was a general exodus from the capital; by Tuesday evening very few women and children remained there.[45] Winder was indecisive and reluctant to commit his badly trained force; he withdrew to Old Fields, about 8 miles from Washington and the same from Bladensburg, where his embarrassment was intensified that evening by a visit from Madison and some of his cabinet, although he was also reinforced by Barney with 400 sailors.[46]

Ross had arrived direct from Bordeaux without supporting artillery or cavalry and was unsure about risking his brigade against the defences of Washington. Because of a lack of draught horses for the artillery, only one 6-pounder and two 3-pounders were brought ashore, and thirty to forty Royal Artillery drivers mounted on stray horses formed an ad hoc troop of cavalry.[47] Foraging expeditions set out:

> with a few picked men, acting alternately as a boat's crew or a predatory band, we literally scoured the country; visited farmhouses even so late as midnight; aroused—and doubtless not a little terrified—their sleeping inmates, and insisted upon the pick of the poultry, yards or pigsty, upon our own terms . . . We paid where payment was practicable, but were not over-scrupulous in helping ourselves.[48]

It was Cockburn, with his now extensive experience after over a year of coastal operations, who insisted Washington would offer no effective resistance.[49] Ross had marched his small force the 25 miles from Benedict to Upper Marlborough along the Patuxent to try out the land, ready to re-embark if necessary, and on 23 August he agreed with Cockburn to advance to Melwood, on the road to Washington, and bivouac there. Cockburn sent Scott to inform Cochrane of the intention to attack, but Scott returned with a note from Cochrane suggesting that "the sooner the army gets back the better."[50] It took some persuasion on his part to convince Ross that with Washington just 16 miles away, it was too late to turn back now. Although it was not a formal order, Cockburn also knew that in ignoring Cochrane's note he was risking his entire career against success, and that even should they succeed he would not endear himself to Cochrane.[51]

Meanwhile Winder had retreated in disarray towards Washington as panic gripped the American high command; Stansbury, who had been in a strong position to the east of Bladensburg with orders to hold fast, was disgruntled at the thought that Winder was hazarding Maryland troops, and after a council of war decided to cross the eastern branch of the river and take a position on the slope beyond. The river was 40 yards wide here and only 3 feet deep, crossed by a wooden bridge; although Stansbury later claimed he ordered the bridge destroyed, it was not. He was joined by 1,000 reinforcements under Colonel Joseph Sterrett, including the 5th Maryland.[52] Madison and his party arrived, the tiny figure of the president made absurd by a pair of duelling pistols buckled to his waist. He retained faith in Armstrong despite

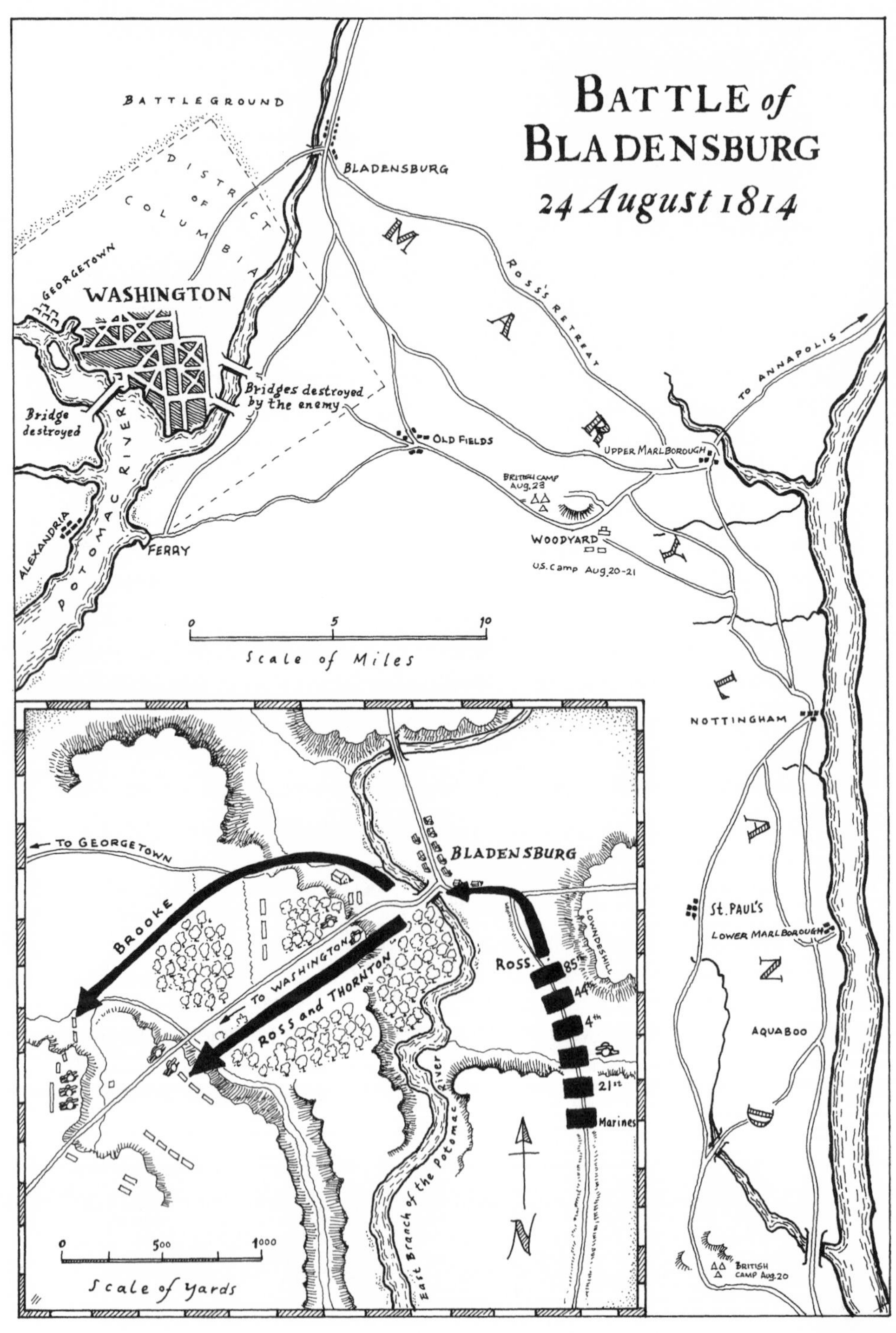

BATTLE of BLADENSBURG
24 August 1814
BATTLEGROUND
DISTRICT OF COLUMBIA
BLADENSBURG
GEORGETOWN
WASHINGTON
MARYLAND
ROSS'S RETREAT
TO ANNAPOLIS
Bridges destroyed by the enemy
Bridge destroyed
OLD FIELDS
UPPER MARLBOROUGH
BRITISH CAMP Aug. 23
WOODYARD
U.S. Camp Aug. 20-21
ALEXANDRIA
POTOMAC RIVER
FERRY
Scale of Miles
0
5
10
NOTTINGHAM
St. PAUL'S
LOWER MARLBOROUGH
AQUABOO
BRITISH CAMP Aug. 20
TO GEORGETOWN
BLADENSBURG
BROOKE
TO WASHINGTON
ROSS and THORNTON
LOWNDES HILL
ROSS.
85th
44th
4th
21st
Marines
East Branch of the Potomac River
N
0
500
1000
Scale of Yards

the latter's informing him that any clash between regulars and militia would see the militia beaten.

As the morning of the 24th broke hot and oppressive, the British were enthusiastic for the fray, but marching hour upon hour with just one short break in the mid-summer heat soon drained them. With the 85th Light Infantry in the van they approached Bladensburg, chosen partly to deceive the Americans and partly to avoid having to cross the bridges of the eastern Potomac. Towards noon Lieutenant George Gleig confided in his diary that "we could perceive heavy clouds of dust rising, and in half an hour more we saw the Yankeys drawn up on the heights above the village." Having marched some 14 miles under a scorching sun, "we were so tired that literally it was with difficulty we could drag one leg after the other."[53] Colonel Arthur Brooke of the 44th Regiment noted in his diary that many men "in striving to keep up fell down from actual fatigue and breathed their last": as many as eighteen died from heat exhaustion.[54] They were greeted by an American force drawn up on the heights above the town in prepared positions, and the subsequent decision to attack immediately with 2,600 or so men was extravagantly dramatic, even rash, against some 6,300 Americans assembled and now dug in, supported by twenty-six guns, including twenty 6-pounders.[55]

Stansbury had arranged his men quite effectively to begin with, posting the Baltimore artillery and riflemen to cover the river crossing, and was then joined by the Annapolis militia under Colonel William Beall, who arrived at the double and took up a position behind his lines. But when Monroe appeared at about 11:30 A.M., he began rearranging them without consulting the general. When he had finished, the artillery and riflemen were left to face the initial assault alone, with no support closer than 500 yards away. And Winder's instructions were hardly more encouraging; helping Captain Benjamin Burch place three of his five 6-pounders, Winder informed him: "When you retreat, take notice you must retreat by the Georgetown Road."[56]

When Colonel William Thornton, commanding the vanguard Light Brigade, proposed an immediate attack, Harry Smith was horrified; he recommended further reconnaissance and a feint to the left.[57] But Ross agreed with Thornton, and the Light Brigade threw down their packs and moved through some woods, then dashed across the bridge or forded the stream, although the advance brought heavy casualties, including Thornton, who was replaced by Major Timothy Jones. Captain the Honourable John James Knox of the 85th "was never under such a heavy fire of cannon and small arms since I listed," and soon three field officers were shot down and eight or nine other men were sent sprawling, so that "before we had been under fire for a quater of an hour, thinks I to myself, thinks I, by the time this action is over the devil is in it if I am not either a walking Major or a dead Captain."[58] Captain Charles Furlong later told his diary:

> As soon as the enemy perceived the head of our column halt to draw breath for a moment, they set up three cheers, thinking, I dare say, that we were panic-stricken by their appearance. We were immediately ordered to advance, which we effected by the 85th and us (the flank companies of the Twenty-First) under a heavy fire from their guns, but with little mischief, as their shots went generally clean over our heads. After passing the river we formed line, and advanced to their centre and left flank. They immediately opened a most destructive fire from all quarters, which we sustained with firmness, and in our turn discharged a volley at them and rushed forward with the greatest impetuosity up the hill.[59]

Private Henry Fulford of the Maryland militia described the effects of the American fire: "They took no notice of it; their men moved like clockwork, the instant part of a platoon was cut down, it was filled up by men in the rear without the least noise and confusion whatever."[60]

Soon after the firing commenced, Barney and 400 sailors joined the defenders, blocking the Washington road with five large naval guns. The Americans were now disposed in three lines, but none was in a position to support the others, and only Barney's men offered any effective resistance. Ross had two horses shot from under him as the Light Brigade was ordered to hold its position until the 4th and 44th Regiments could join them. Captain Mortimer Timpson RM recalled that they "suffered severely . . . As our men hurried over the bridge to get into Action, we found the Americans drawn up on the Heights. After a short but severe fire, the Americans gave way."[61] When rockets began exploding around the Americans, their first line was quickly broken, and the militia fled, ignoring Winder's earlier instructions and running in all directions.[62] Although the second line appeared prepared to stand firm, Winder ordered a withdrawal, and it simply melted away.[63] "The drafted militia ran away at the first fire," recalled John Pendleton Kennedy, "and the Fifth Regiment was driven from the field with the bayonet. We made a fine scamper of it. I lost my musket in the melée while bearing off a comrade."[64] Hezekiah Niles called it a "lamentable and disgraceful affair," and the rout was memorialized in a satirical piece called *The Bladensburg Races.* The militia, he said, "generally fled without firing a gun, and threw of[f] every incumbrance of their speed!"[65] Private Fulford considered himself lucky to escape alive, but Anna M. Thornton, who witnessed the flight, was highly critical: "Never was there such a complete discomfiture of an army—the poor creatures were marched to their deaths on that dreadful hot day before the engagement began & then retreated 12 or 13 miles without halting."[66] "The rapid flight of the enemy," said Ross laconically, "and his knowledge of the country, precluded many prisoners being taken."[67]

On the other hand, Charles Ball, an escaped slave who served on a gunboat and witnessed Bladensburg, "could not but admire the handsome manner in which the British officers led on their fatigued and worn-out soldiers. I thought then, and think yet, that General Ross was one of the finest-looking men that I ever saw on horseback."[68] Cockburn, on a white charger, resplendent in gold-laced hat and epaulettes, had busied himself supervising the Royal Marine Artillery and, ignoring Scott's warnings that he was making a mark for enemy sharpshooters, had a bullet pass between his legs and the flap of his saddle, which cut the stirrup leather in two. Amazingly, the round missed both Cockburn and his horse, but when he dismounted a marine standing beside him was killed by a roundshot.[69] When Scott involuntarily ducked, Cockburn scolded him: "Don't bob your head, Scott; it looks bad."[70] Less fortunate was Barney, who led his seamen in a rearguard defence of the 18-pounder and 12-pounder batteries, trying to stem the tide as the rest of the force disintegrated; Barney's horse was shot from under him, and as he tried to get up, he was struck in the thigh. When Cockburn was brought to his side, he sighed weakly: "Well admiral, you have got hold of me at last."[71]

With victory the now exhausted British sank to the ground where they were; they had lost 64 killed and 185 wounded against 26 American dead and 51 wounded, but the road to the capital of the United States lay open.[72] Lieutenant David Dennear of the Royal Artillery Drivers recalled that the Americans "retreated in the direction of Washington but our troops being so much fatigued from the heat of the weather and marching, we were not able to pursue them, therefore rested on the field of action til sunset."[73] Cockburn and Ross moved forward with the 3rd Brigade but did not arrive before dark. Ross repeatedly sounded a parley by his drums, and a flag of truce was sent, "saying that such of the inhabitants as remained quiet in their houses, their property should be respected, and nothing but the public buildings and stores touched"; but nobody was forthcoming.[74] Washington had been ignominiously abandoned; the president, statesmen, and government officers, to say nothing of the troops supposed to defend it, had simply vanished. Monroe, Armstrong, and Winder had sought to turn the Capitol into a citadel, but this plan collapsed with the discipline of the troops as the situation degenerated into *sauve qui peut.*

When Madison arrived at the Executive Mansion at around 4:30 P.M., he found that his wife, Dolley, had left half an hour earlier, and he made a similar hasty retreat towards Virginia. Dolley later wrote to her sister that she refused to leave without first securing Washington's portrait, which was screwed to a wall. "The process was found too tedious for these perilous moments. I have ordered the frame to be broken and the canvas taken out."[75] It was taken by Jacob Barker, a ship-owner and fellow Quaker, and Robert G. L. de Peyster, "assisted by two colored boys . . . and we fell into the trail of the army."[76] When Cockburn and Ross, accompanied by their staffs and a small escort, reached the open space surrounding the Capitol, recalled Corporal David Brown of the 21st Fusiliers, "part of the enemy, being Concealed in one of the houses, fired upon our approach, which killed two of our Corporals and General Ross got his horse shot from under him."[77] Cockburn, who had been in many similar situations along the Chesapeake, immediately ordered Scott to force entry into the houses flanking the Capitol as the snipers fled from their rear. These buildings had been appropriated to war use, and private status could not now save them; the American propensity to burn the property of British citizens throughout the war was now revisited upon them. The public buildings would be put to the torch.[78]

In 1814 the city had been the seat of government for fourteen years, but little progress had been made in development across its marshy area in accordance with the expansive plans of 1791 by Major Pierre Charles L'Enfant; the work of surveying under the capable surveyor-general, Major Andrew Ellicott, was still incomplete.[79] The most recent census gave the population of Washington and nearby Georgetown as 13,156, including some 2,599 slaves, and the capital was known to these residents by numerous uncomplimentary names: "City of Magnificent Distances," "Wilderness City," and "City of Streets without Houses"; the well-heeled preferred to live in Georgetown and nearby Alexandria.[80] On the night of 24 August a huge glow in the sky revealed that the Washington Navy Yard was already alight, sparked by its commandant, Captain Thomas Tingey USN, who decided he could not afford to allow its precious stores to fall into British hands.[81] Only one building was spared, the Marine Corps commandant's house, overlooked for no apparent reason; but the following day the British ensured that this structure survived the wholesale destruction of other government property, which included the new frigate *Columbia* and the sloop *Argus,* supposedly because of the respect earned by the U.S. Marine Corps from the Royal Marines. It is now the oldest government building in Washington.[82]

Thus with the sky already bright, men of the 3rd Brigade deployed in front of the Capitol; they fired a volley to deter any remaining sharpshooters, then advanced to complete its destruction. Not that this was an easy task. The Capitol consisted of two wings, for the House and the Senate, with a makeshift wooden building joining them. Stories of a "Redcoat Congress" voting for the destruction appear to be apocryphal.[83] Instead, the burning was organized by Lieutenant George de Lacey Evans, the deputy quartermaster-general, and pyrotechnics expert Lieutenant George Pratt RN. After several attempts, the task was achieved with the aid of Congreve's trusty rockets, and soon flames were surging up through the doors and windows. But the activity brought no pleasure to the men, who set about it in silence. Seaman William Jarvis Neptune was among those watching: "The fierce blazings, ships and stores—the thundering report of exploding magazines—the crash of falling houses—and the loud roar of bursting cannon, gave dreadful note to the progress of destruction."[84] But that did not mean there was no satisfaction in paying out the Americans in their own coin. As Colonel Arthur Brooke recalled, "Certainly on the whole it [was] an affair as fine a thing as any done during this war, and a sore rub to the Americans than can ever be forgotten."[85] The Library of Congress went the same way, apart from one small memento retained by Cockburn—*An Account of the Receipts and Expenditure of the United States for the Year 1810,* which included such information as the payment of bounties on pickled fish, and pension payments to Monsieur L'Enfant for planning services. Cockburn took it for no other reason than to prove his presence in Madison's office; he later inscribed it on the inside cover as a gift to his "eldest brother Sir James Cockburn of Langton, Bart, Governor of Bermuda."[86] Stephen Pleasonton, a State Department clerk, related how he had recovered valuable papers from his office a week before the British raid—including the original Constitution; these were taken to safety at Leesburg, Virginia, 35 miles away. Armstrong had "observed to me that he thought we were under unnecessary alarm as he did not think the British were serious in their intention of coming to Washington."[87] It was as well that Pleasonton ignored him, for the flames from the

Capitol ignited four more buildings to the north where congressional papers had been moved.

The glare and the roar of flammable material invoked among the unfortunate inhabitants a feeling of shock and awe. Mordecai Booth, a civilian clerk to the Washington Naval Yard commander, was instructed to secure waggons and remove the powder from the magazine to a secure location as the British approached.[88] As he set out on a two-week adventure, the Capitol in flames was a sight "so repugnant to my feelings, so dishonorable, so degrading to the American character and at the same time so awful [it] almost palsied my faculties."[89] "Never shall I forget," wrote Dr. James Ewell, "the tortured feelings when beholding that noble edifice wrapped in flames which, bursting through the windows and mounting far above its summits, with a noise like thunder, filled all the saddened night with a dismal gloom."[90] Daniel Sheldon had left the city three hours earlier, but his journey "during almost the whole of the night was illuminated by the flames of the public buildings which at the distance of twenty eight miles, where I stopped at one o'clock in the morning, were most dismally and distinctly visible."[91] And Mary Hunter recalled: "You never saw a drawing room so brilliantly lighted as the whole city was that night. Few thought of going to bed—they spent the night gazing on the fires and lamenting the disgrace of the city."[92] And some Britons, at least, shared their discomfiture. Captain Furlong felt that although they represented "the pride of the Americans, I must confess I felt sorrow when witnessing such magnificent buildings demolished."[93]

At about 10:30 P.M. Ross and Cockburn collected around 150 men and moved up Pennsylvania Avenue, en route reassuring an anxious resident that private property would be respected. Cockburn sent a message in advance to offer Dolley Madison safe passage, unaware that she had long since left. In the dining room the British found the table set for the celebratory dinner the Americans had been anticipating. Ross noted in his journal:

> So unexpected was our entry and capture of Washington; and so confident was Maddison [*sic*] of the defeat of our troops, that he had prepared a supper for the expected conquerors; and when our advanced party entered the President's house, they found a table laid with forty covers. The fare, however; which was intended for *Jonathan* was voraciously devoured by *John Bull;* and the health of the Prince Regent and success to his Majesty's arms by sea and land, was drunk in the best wines.[94]

14.1. *Capture of the City of Washington,* hand-coloured engraving from *Rapin's History of England* (London: Albion, 1815). Anne S. K. Brown Military Collection, Brown University Library.

It is clear from later letters to his wife that Ross had hesitated to take the risk but was pleased to have got away with it, and he was frankly indebted to Cockburn for the success of the expedition.[95] Scarcely able to believe their good fortune, they tucked in, enjoying excellent Madeira and other fine wines as Scott mused on the irony of the situation, blessing his absent hosts, who in different circumstances would have been toasting the champions of republican freedom. A swift visit to the various apartments saw men change their shirts—Scott exchanged his sweaty one for one belonging to no less a personage than the chief magistrate of the United States.[96] Roger Weightman, a Washington book dealer, accompanied Cockburn as guide, and Weightman himself sought to remove a valuable souvenir; but Cockburn sat Weightman down and insisted he drink a toast to "Jemmy," as Cockburn referred to Madison, then gave him a few odds and ends of no consequence before turning the place over to Pratt and his pyrotechnicians; Cockburn selected a cushion from Dolley's chair to remind him of her "seat."[97] "I shall never forget," recalled Harry Smith as they departed, "the destructive majesty of the flames as the torches were applied to beds, curtains, etc. Our sailors were artists at the work."[98]

As Margaret Bayard Smith noted on her return to the city, Cockburn and all his officers and men had been perfectly polite to the citizens, and all provisions taken were paid for; he "deserves praise and commendation for his own good conduct and the discipline of his sailors and Marines."[99] Also joining the president's residence in flames was the nearby Treasury, although its contents—legitimate war booty—had long been removed by the retreating Americans.[100] As Cockburn was returning along Pennsylvania Avenue at around midnight, he decided to stop off and pay a call on the offices of the *National Intelligencer.* Cockburn was not Attila the Hun, although Americans might be forgiven for thinking so, such was the impression created by this semi-official voice of the administration under its English editor Joseph Gales. "Dear Josey," as Cockburn called him, took great pains to portray Cockburn in the worst possible light.[101] But barely had he begun to arrange its destruction when two women appeared to plead that it be spared lest their building should burn too. He arranged instead for a team of seamen to pull it down and build a huge bonfire with its papers and contents, saying, as the printer's type was consigned to the flames: "Be sure that all the c's are destroyed so the rascals can't abuse my name anymore."[102] When another group of attractive women appeared, apparently abandoned by their menfolk, and started chatting gaily, Cockburn was delighted with their friendliness. "Now did you expect to see me such a clever fellow?" he inquired. "Were you not prepared to see a savage, a ferocious creature, such as Josey represented me? But you see I am quite harmless; don't be afraid, I will take better care of you than Jemmy did!" When the destruction was complete, they were entertained to refreshments, and when Scott was asked by the hostess the name of the delightful officer accompanying him, "Why," he replied, "that is the vile monster Cock-burn," stressing the two syllables in the American fashion to electrifying effect.[103]

The following morning Cockburn was awake at dawn and rode along Pennsylvania Avenue a second time towards Georgetown, where the War and Navy offices and their records were situated. The government rope-walk, with its stores of cordage, hemp, and tar, went up like a torch amid great clouds of black smoke, a sight which persuaded the Virginia militia at the southern end of the Potomac bridge to set fire to that as well. Cockburn spent much of the day at the house of Dr. James Ewell, where he established his temporary headquarters. Ewell was a prominent citizen to whom the destruction was as abhorrent as to anyone, but he took pains to mediate with the British commanders to limit the destruction. He was politely received by Ross and Cockburn, who ensured his personal safety, and Ewell found both to be magnanimous and charming gentlemen.[104] At Greenleaf Point, on the eastern branch of the Potomac, the fortifications had already been destroyed by the Americans, but the magazine remained. A work party of four officers and 200 men was sent to remove the powder and dispose of it amid mounting heat and cumulus clouds threatening a storm; they found a deep well nearby and rolled the barrels in, but in their haste to complete the tasks, barrels and loose powder were left above the waterline. A chance spark was all it took to cause a catastrophic explosion. Captain Timpson found himself "shot up into the air like a rocket: I went up some distance, & then fell on my face while a quantity of rubbish . . . fell on the back of my head at the same moment, I felt a sensation as if my head had been suddenly split open & shut again, & for some time lay senseless."[105] Around him lay 12 dead and another 30 horribly wounded, whose broken bodies were removed to a makeshift hospital set up near the Capitol.

Then came the storm, or, as Scott recalled it, the tornado: "trees were uprooted, plantations destroyed, and houses blown down, the conflict of winds setting at nought the industry and power of man."[106] Roof tiles were showered all over the ground, and the only protection for those caught in the open was to lie flat; a mounted officer turning a street corner found both himself and his horse laid prone. But the storm was brief, and as Cockburn sat in Dr. Ewell's dining room late in the afternoon, satisfied that every vestige of government property had been laid waste, he knew there was no point in prolonging his stay, and Ross concurred. Rumours suggested that another American force was gathering at Georgetown, and Ross's men were not in fit condition to fight a second general action. Security demanded that they give no indication of an immediate withdrawal, and word was passed quietly to commanding officers. A curfew imposed at 8 P.M. helped to shroud the move, and even Ewell, who humanely offered to care for the injured from Greenleaf Point, had no idea of the purpose of the activity around him. Cockburn later wrote to offer his thanks "for the kindness and uncommon care and solicitude with which you appear to have tended our wounded when left in Washington, and I beg you to believe with what readiness and pleasure I would meet any wish of yours . . . I beg my best respects to Mrs. Ewell and my acknowledgments of her for all she has said respecting the British officers."[107] The British lit camp fires as usual and appeared to follow their customary routine, but at 9 P.M. they marched silently away, having occupied Washington for less than twenty-four hours, and returned without incident to their boats at Nottingham. The city was looted by the local poor following their departure; two British soldiers caught stealing received 100 lashes, and another was shot.[108]

In nine days the British marched a force of barely 4,000 men 50 miles into the enemy homeland, defeated a field force three times its size, destroyed the public buildings of the enemy capital—property valued at $1.5 million—and returned safely through that same hostile territory, bringing with them 200 guns, 500 barrels of powder, and 100,000 musket cartridges.[109] As Cockburn himself pointed out, this feat "for the extent of the ground passed over, the importance of its objects, and the mischief done the enemy—ashore and afloat—in so short a space of time is scarcely perhaps to be paralleled."[110] Not surprisingly, the men were very tired, and their letters home were full of self-congratulation. "We completely defeated them," wrote Private William Kirke of the 4th Regiment to his father, and "destroyed twenty thousand stands of small arms and two hundred pieces of cannon," while Midshipman Samuel Davies told his family they had been "surrounded by twenty thousand soldiers but they would not engage us the dam [*sic*] rascals."[111]

Ross had been less than enthusiastic about the destruction of Washington, but Cochrane heartily endorsed it. Elsewhere, however, the destruction generated much ill feeling and recrimination among both Americans and also some Britons who regarded these actions as excessive. The Radical member of Parliament for Bedford, Samuel Whitbread, told the House of Commons that he "could not but lament that the gallant Ross was obliged to concur in a transaction so discordant to every example of the civilized world."[112] But as James Scott pointed out—and his own later career revealed him as a kind, fair-minded, and independent man—those who complained were ignorant of the facts: "war itself is barbarous, and though the issue may be regretted, the disregard by the Americans to the various parleys sounded by the General before our entrance, and the fire of concealed enemies, were the causes of the destruction of the Capitol and public buildings."[113] War is an obscenity, and the concept of "civilized warfare" is an oxymoron. The United States had started the war, and American forces had rained destruction on British communities; America could not then reasonably complain if the fates of war brought its effects home.

15

Baltimore and Fort Erie

On the shore dimly seen through the mists of the deep,
Where the foe's haughty host in dread silence reposes,
What is that which the breeze, o'er the towering steep,
As it fitfully blows, half conceals, half discloses?
Now it catches the gleam of the morning's first beam,
In full glory reflected new shines in the stream,
'Tis the star spangled banner, O! long may it wave
O'er the land of the free and the home of the brave.

—Francis Scott Key, "Defense of Fort McHenry"

On 28 August Madison and Monroe returned to Washington, and the president gave Monroe acting powers at the War Department. When Armstrong arrived the next day, Madison suggested a temporary retirement from the city. At Baltimore, Armstrong resigned, and Monroe became both secretary of state and secretary of war.[1] News of the capture of Washington spread quickly through the United States in late August and early September, causing consternation and something close to panic. Ross's force was now expected to turn on Baltimore, with 45,000 people the third-largest city in the republic, while both Philadelphia and New York made desperate efforts to improve their own defences. Tompkins' organization of the New York City defences involved mobilizing thousands of labourers and culminated in a grand review of 6,000 militia on 31 August, with another 14,000 awaiting call-up; by the end of September 17,000 militia were stationed in and around the state, supplemented by naval personnel and New Jersey militia.[2]

Before sending Major Harry Smith home with dispatches following the capture of Washington, Ross assured him that he would have nothing to do with an assault on Baltimore. He had already written to his wife: "I trust all our differences with the Yankees will shortly be settled. That wish is, I believe, very prevalent with them. They feel strongly the disgrace of having had their capital taken by a handful of men and blame very generally a government which went to war without the means or abilities to carry it on."[3] Cockburn, however, was very much in favour of a swift move against Baltimore, and to begin with it appeared that Cochrane agreed: he wrote to Bathurst on 28 August that "Baltimore may be destroyed or laid under a severe contribution."[4] But six days later in a letter to the First Lord of the Admiralty he appeared to have changed his mind: "As soon as the army is re-embarked, I mean to proceed to the northward and try to surprise Rhode Island."[5] Ultimately it was British procrastination that saved Baltimore, seemingly the product of personality clashes within the British high command that allowed the city some three weeks grace to improve its defences. These had been put in train in earnest the previous year, when the town was twice threatened by the British fleet and its commerce cut off, frightening away some of its merchants and citizens. Unlike other large cities, its defence rested in the hands of those citizens, rather than the Maryland or federal governments.[6]

Although Cochrane and Cockburn had always got on reasonably well, their characters were very different, and it may be that Cochrane was smarting after Cockburn's "blind eye" assault on Washington, evidenced by his failure to grant Cockburn the customary honour of selecting the officer to relay home dispatches, one that traditionally brought promotion and would surely have been granted to Scott.[7] It also appears that Ross was less inclined than Cockburn to strike hard against the Americans along their coast; he may have been less susceptible to Cochrane's blandishments when actually operating onshore, but once seated at Cochrane's table aboard *Tonnant* he may have been inclined to give more credence to the opinions of the senior admiral. Decisions were finally taken on 4 September, with Cockburn ordered to take *Albion,* loaded with prize material, to Bermuda, then to join Cochrane at a secret location to the north; the transports would proceed immediately to this rendezvous near Block Island, leaving Hardy as senior officer in Chesapeake Bay. Cockburn had made a mere 8 miles when he was signalled to return to *Tonnant* and there informed that Cochrane had changed his mind, and he was to assault Baltimore after all.

The reasons for this sudden change of heart are unclear, but may have been related to the return of the Gordon and Parker expeditions. The former—comprising *Seahorse* and another frigate, HMS *Euryalus* (36), with a rocket-vessel, three bomb ketches, and a dispatch boat—had turned into a minor epic, yielding twenty-one prizes.[8] Progress had been slower than expected, as Gordon's boats had to be warped the entire distance upstream and frequently grounded, during which advance the "strictest discipline was observed in the guard boats, no landing or plundering was permitted; the numerous flocks of geese swam undisturbed in the river; the bullocks and sheep browsed unmolested, the poultry yards were respected, and any act that might irritate the inhabitants was most industriously avoided."[9] As soon as Fort Washington came under fire from the approaching British on the evening of 27 August, Captain Samuel T. Dyson USN, the garrison commander, who was drunk at the time, blew up the inner buildings and retreated, leaving the British to take possession the following morning. The following day they advanced unopposed to Alexandria, which immediately sued for terms.[10] Gordon agreed to destroy only public works as long as all ordnance, shipping, and merchandise were surrendered, and in his twenty-one prize ships he stuffed 12,000 barrels of flour, 1,000 hogsheads of tobacco, 150 bales of cotton, and $5,000 worth of sugar, wine, and other commodities from the town.[11] The return proved more problematic than the approach, as Commodore Rodgers had been ordered to proceed overland from Baltimore to harass the withdrawal, and he was able to erect shore batteries along the Potomac which, supported by militia, put the squadron under heavy fire. One of the bomb ketches grounded, and Gordon had to shift ballast in all his ships to list them so that their guns could fire high enough to reach the American battery. When this moved, Gordon sent a shore party to assail it, and it was briefly defended with gallantry by the Virginia militia, who lost eleven killed and eighteen wounded before being driven off. It was 6 September before Gordon managed to get past them, the British having lost seven killed and thirty-five wounded, but they brought away all the booty.[12]

The other diversion met with failure. Parker had learned from a freed slave that some 200 militia were camped a mile or so inland from his position, and at 11 P.M. on 30 August he landed with a party of 124 men armed with bayonets and pikes to attack the camp. Discovering that the American force had now moved near to Chestertown, Maryland, they covered 4 or 5 miles before coming up to the new position, where they found the Americans in line, commanded by Lieutenant-Colonel Philip Reed of the 21st Maryland Militia. The British charged and were repulsed, losing Parker and 13 others killed and 27 wounded.[13] The battle of Caulk's Field, as it became known, also cost another 40 British sailors, who presumably took the opportunity to desert. The retreating British were about to abandon Parker's body when, recalled Frederic Chamier, a "shout of displeasure arose from the men, they swore he should never be left behind to be buried by strangers." They labouriously carried his body back to the *Menelaus,* where hardened tars "wept like children over his coffin."[14]

On 6 September James Monroe wrote to Cochrane to point out that the destruction of Newark and at Long Point had been unauthorized and that the U.S. government would be happy to come to some reciprocal agreement regarding the affair; he also pointed out that the British had used Indian allies—never ones to respect private property—and had been raiding the Chesapeake region since 1813. In response to this letter the British government finally suspended the retaliation policy on 2 November, but by that date the campaigning season had finished.[15] Meanwhile on 7 September the decision was taken to continue operations against Baltimore. Cochrane had written to Bathurst on 28 August to say that his force was inadequate for such operations, but once Ross and Cockburn returned, he agreed to make a demonstration against the city that might be turned, if things went well, into an attack.[16] What finally prompted the decision is unclear, but it was probably intelligence brought by *Menelaus,* for before Parker's death he had succeeded in sending the tender *Jane* all the way up the Patapsco River, sounding the channel and examining the forts, "and a boat which came to us from the harbour with an officer in her, mistaking us for a friend, only escaped by a momentary calm between the lands."[17]

However, to approach the city was by no means easy. In 1814 it lay about 12 miles upriver from the waters of the Chesapeake while Whetstone Point, the narrow entrance to its harbour, was guarded by Fort McHenry, built by French engineers and completed around 1800.[18] Above the fort flew an outsized flag; its garrison of 1,000 men included 600 regulars and a detachment of Barney's sailors, plus militia and volunteers under Major George Armistead.[19] News of events farther south and the British delay in moving against it had given the inhabitants time to prepare, and citizen work parties had dug trenches and fortifications. There were also nearly 14,000 men available for its defence, mostly militia but including over 1,000 sailors under Rodgers. Overall command was given by Baltimore's Committee of Vigilance and Safety to Major-General Samuel Smith, a sixty-two-year-old Revolutionary War veteran now deeply involved in political intrigue, who refused to yield to Winder when he arrived from Washington.[20] Smith had taken precautions to protect the seaward approach, sealing the north-west branch of the Patapsco with barges; Cockburn favoured a direct approach against Fort

McHenry in tenders and ships' boats, but was overruled. The troops would land at North Point to the east and march round the city while frigates and bomb vessels would provide fire support.[21]

By the evening of 9 September the fleet was once more anchored off the Patuxent; the next morning it pressed north under full sail, making a magnificent and disturbing sight to shore-based onlookers. The residents of Annapolis feared they would be the target of that terrible fleet, and breathed relief as it swept by.[22] When the Americans saw ship movement towards North Point on the afternoon of 11 September, Smith sent Brigadier-General John Stricker with 3,200 men and six 4-pounders to block the British near the Meeting House, where Bear and Cheese Creeks formed a choke point. On the morning of 12 September the ships anchored off North Point and disgorged launches, pinnaces, barges, and cutters full of men to make an unopposed landing, with Cockburn reprising his role as colonel of Royal Marines, leading some 600 seamen and Royal and Colonial Marines among a total force of 4,500.[23] Stricker, fearing a night attack, had deployed 140 cavalry and 150 riflemen forward as a screen. Suddenly a party of some 50 British appeared ahead of the main body, led by Cockburn and Ross. Unsupported by the main force, Cockburn recalled "there was . . . nothing left for it but to dash forward against them, returning their fire as quickly as possible to induce them to suppose our whole force to be at hand."[24] Lieutenant Gleig was

> drawing near the scene of the action, when another officer came at full speed towards us, with horror and dismay in his countenance, and calling aloud for a surgeon. Every man felt within himself that all was not right, though none was willing to believe the whispers of his own terror. But what at first we could not guess at, because we dreaded it so much, was soon realized; for the aide-de-camp had scarcely passed, when the general's horse, without its rider, and with the saddle and housing stained with blood, came plunging onwards.[25]

The charge had succeeded; the Americans turned and ran, but in the ensuing exchange of fire one of the last "straggling shots" had struck Ross. He died while being carried to the boats some two hours later.[26] It was a terrible blow to the expedition, recalled Captain John Robyns RM, and the death of "an officer who was an ornament to his profession, enjoying the fullest confidence of the Army for his skill, judgement and bravery," probably saved the city.[27] Corporal Brown of the 21st Fusiliers could not "mention or depict the sorrow every soldier in the army felt at the loss of their gallant general";[28] nor would Lieutenant Gordon Gallie MacDonald RN later forget "the gloom such an appearance cast, seeing so gallant an officer dying and his servant leading a magnificent black horse, the animal actually appearing conscious of the loss."[29] Cockburn later wrote to Cochrane, "my gallant and highly valued friend, the Major General received a musket ball through his arm into his breast, which proved fatal to him . . . Our country, Sir, has lost one of its best and bravest soldiers."[30]

Command of the army devolved upon Colonel Arthur Brooke, who pressed on towards the American main force of some 3,000 men drawn up behind a paling fence, and who opened a sharp bombardment.[31] The approaching British deployed and then calmly lay down to eat their lunch. As they did so a detachment of the 21st Fusiliers and Royal Marines moved to turn the Americans' left flank, where a bloody encounter ensued as the 51st Maryland Militia put up a stout resistance to the 4th Regiment under Major Alured Faunce.[32] When they had finished their luncheon, the troops started forward along the whole line. Gleig told his diary that they sprang over some palings "and advanced in a cool orderly manner, notwithstanding the showers of grape with which the enemy played us, till we got within 150 yards of them, when they gave us a volley from right to left of their line. To this we returned a hearty cheer, and giving them back a volley, rushed on at double quick."[33] The bluejackets in the centre crossed an open space some 600 yards deep. Lieutenant Scott recalled:

> A roar of musketry opened out; it fell like a hailstorm around us; not a shot was returned until we were within 20 yards of the enemy, when they received a tremendous discharge—our troops rushing on, scaled the palings. Their fire now became deadly on the flying foe, and would have told tenfold more severely but for the shelter afforded them by the trees . . . It now became a regular chase and numerous Americans were taken prisoner.[34]

It was all over in less than an hour, but once more the defeat of the Americans could not be followed up for want of cavalry, and the weary victors camped on the field while the Meeting House was turned into a temporary hospital. The British had lost 46 killed (including Ross) and 295 wounded; American losses were 24 killed, 139 wounded, and 50 prisoners.[35]

The following morning the army moved forward towards Baltimore and came within 1 1/2 miles by 10 A.M. as the bomb vessels commenced a bombardment of Fort McHenry. Cochrane was impressed by the American defences, which included 24 block ships sunk across the harbour between Fort McHenry and Lazaretto Point, on which was mounted a small battery with gunboats cruising behind. The British had a total of seventeen vessels, including five bomb- and rocket-boats. At first they stayed out of range of the fort's guns but later came in closer before being forced back. This bombardment continued with little respite until 1 A.M. on the 14th. But firing at such long range made it impossible to cut the fuses accurately, and what resulted was probably the greatest fireworks display the city has ever witnessed. Armistead estimated that between 1,500 and 1,800 10- and 13-inch shells were fired at the fort, with around 400 landing within the ramparts, leaving four dead and twenty-four wounded.[36] The Reverend James Stevens, a Methodist preacher, described to his sister the consternation the bombardment caused:

> I do not feel able to point out the distress and confusion half as it was with us—to see the wagons, carts and drays, all in haste moving the people, and the poorer sort with what they could carry and their children on their backs flying for their lives while I could plainly see the British Sail which was engaged in a severe fire on our fort for 24 Hours. I could see them fire and the Bombs lite and burst on the Shore at which explosions the whole town and several miles out would shake.[37]

Scott was sent to report to Cochrane and returned to find Cockburn in high spirits and ready to launch an assault on the 14th. But the orders he brought from the commander-in-chief "dispelled his animated smile of confidence and he handed it to Brooke; it was evident there was a breakdown."[38] Cochrane was against pressing the assault because, although he later claimed to be confident of success, he did not think the likely casualties to be worth the prize, and reminded his superiors in London that he had to keep in mind "the ulterior operations of this force"; a veiled reference to plans for the expedition to New Orleans.[39]

A council of war was convened that lasted until midnight. Although Cockburn remained convinced that a successful assault was still possible, Brooke refused to attempt it alone: "All my hopes were in a moment blasted," he confided to his diary. "If I took the place, I should have been the greatest man in England. If I lost, my military character was gone for ever."[40] The eventual consensus among military officers was to comply with Cochrane's instructions not to proceed "unless *positively* certain of success." The decision provoked mixed reactions: Gordon of *Seahorse* agreed, for example, but Corporal Brown was among many soldiers dismayed at the lack of a chance to avenge Ross's death.

> Although the position of the enemy was almost immediate death to attack and they were nearly five times our numbers, still the British soldiers were not to be daunted for every soldier seemed eager for the attack and to be as quick as possible . . . I cannot express the discontent and murmuring that every soldier felt when he found they were to retreat, though every man knew it was a great saving of their lives.[41]

Meanwhile Cochrane had transferred his flag to HMS *Surprise* (38), a frigate of shallow draught suitable for directing operations against Fort McHenry, but which also happened to be commanded by his son, Thomas, rather than the experienced Nourse of the *Severn* or gallant Gordon of the *Seahorse;* a move that smacked of nepotic favouritism.[42] It served to reinforce Cochrane's natural pessimism and indecision once battle was joined; he had been alarmed when Scott reported the enemy's suspected strength at 15,000–20,000 militia. On the far side of the peninsula on which Fort McHenry stood was Fort Covington, and while the council of war was contemplating withdrawal it was too late to cancel a promised diversionary raid against the latter by some 1,200 Royal Marines and seamen commanded by Lieutenant Charles Napier RN.[43] Cochrane had taken close personal interest in its planning; the boats would move quietly up the Patapsco and up the Ferry Branch to open fire when the main force recommenced its bombardment of Fort McHenry. But the Americans were alerted by the noise of movement, and the British were engaged from the shore-based Battery Babcock and Fort Covington. At about 2 A.M. Napier decided to abort the mission and retired under heavy fire.[44] The last shots were fired at around 7 A.M., after which an eerie stillness descended on the river to reveal British corpses floating on the current.

The action was observed by Francis Scott Key, a lawyer who had gone to visit Cochrane to obtain the release of Dr. William Beanes, a Maryland doctor and close friend of Madison, who had been involved in arresting stragglers—some 111 were reported following the march on Washington—and he in turn had been detained by the British.[45] Key wrote a poem inspired by the action called "Defense of Fort McHenry" and gave it to his brother-in-law, Judge Joseph H. Nicholson, who recognized that the poem fitted the popular drinking song of the London Anacreonitic Society, "To Anacreon in Heaven," written by Ralph Tomlinson and John Stafford Smith and published in 1779, the year of Key's birth. Nicholson took the poem to a printer, and broadside copies, the song's first known printing, appeared in Baltimore on 17 September. Three days later the *Baltimore Patriot* and *The American* printed the song, with the note "Tune: Anacreon in Heaven." It very quickly became popular, with seventeen newspapers from Georgia to New Hampshire printing it. In 1889 the U.S. Navy began singing it at flag-raising ceremonies, followed by the Army, and it was officially adopted as the national anthem of the United States in 1931.[46]

On the 15th the British marched back to their boats and re-embarked without setting eyes on an American, although stragglers were subjected to occasional potshots. One American fired down from a tree against which two sailors were resting, grazing one of them, recalled Midshipman John Bluett RN. The American then begged for quarter when he realized the matelots were armed with pistols.

> Devil burn me if I do says Denis; it was just such a . . . as you killed our Genl. [Ross]—besides you've had your shot it's our turn now. I'll bet you a pint of grog Jack I bring him down the first shot. [D]one says the other, if you miss I'll try; they both missed and then agreed that as they had had their turn, it would not be fair to kill the fellow: they therefore made him come down, and drawing their cutlasses placed him between them, and marched him arm to arm into the camp.[47]

The 85th Light Infantry formed the rearguard, recalled Gleig, and "halted to cover the embarkation of the rest of the army, and during this halt we employed ourselves in chasing and killing pigs, of which a great number were running about. We had a very nice fry made which we had just finished when the order was given to fall in, and off we marched to the boats and embarked immediately."[48]

Cockburn regarded the expedition as a military failure, but Cochrane, Melville, and the British government judged it by different criteria. Cochrane described it as a demonstration and stressed the defeat of the American army at the Meeting House and the alarm and despondency created in the Baltimore

15.1. *John Bull and the Baltimoreans,* engraving by William Charles. *Source:* Library of Congress, Prints and Photographs Division.

area.[49] At least some concerned with the enterprise prospered: Colonel Brooke not being a literary man, Lieutenant de Lacey Evans was deputed to write the dispatch, "which was pronounced one of the most beautiful ever written. Not failing therein to speak highly of himself and as the Irish say 'Small blame to him' (he was both poor and clever) he rose within a twelve-month by fortuitous circumstances from being a lieutenant to be lieutenant-colonel gaining the last step at Waterloo."[50]

Before quitting Baltimore, Cochrane learned that another 7,000 troops would soon be arriving, and he was already forming plans for an attack against New Orleans before setting sail for Halifax on 19 September, giving orders for Cockburn to create a diversion for this expedition with a close blockade along the coasts of South Carolina and Georgia; Cockburn then returned to Bermuda to prepare and refit, activities which took until mid-November.[51] Meanwhile on 4 October another landing was made by a force made up from the 21st Fusiliers, 44th Regiment, and Royal Marines in pursuit of a force of American militia said to be at Northumberland Courthouse, Virginia; but this could not be located, and the invasion force withdrew to Jamaica in the middle of the month to prepare for future operations. From then until the end of the war the blockade continued in the Chesapeake area under Rear-Admiral Malcolm.[52]

On 29 July Prevost had been able to report the arrival at Quebec of the 4th Royal Scots and the 97th Regiment from Ireland and of Major-General Manley Power's brigade from Bordeaux, comprising the 3rd (East Kent), 5th (Northumberland), 1st/27th (Inniskilling), and 58th (Rutlandshire) Regiments, together with a brigade of artillery; a week later Major-General James Kempt's brigade reached Montreal, comprising the 9th (East Norfolk), 37th (North Hampshire), 57th (West Middlesex), and 81st Regiments, also accompanied by a brigade of artillery.[53] But on 5 August Prevost insisted that time was still needed to prepare this force and the naval squadron before operations in the Champlain Valley could begin, and

> not withstanding every exertion it will be impossible to collect the whole force in the neighbourhood of this place [Montreal], before the end of the present Month. The circumstance is the less to be regretted as our Fleets on the lakes cannot attain a sufficient strength to co-operate with the Divisions of the Army . . . before the 15th of next

> Month, and without their Aid and protection, nothing could be undertaken affording a reasonable hope of substantial advantage.[54]

Thus Prevost outlined the necessary support of the Royal Navy on Lake Champlain for his hopes of success. Plattsburgh was a simpler objective than Sackets Harbor, although Bathurst assumed that expeditions were being organized against both, not realizing that Chauncey was effectively blockading Kingston. Still, Prevost's chances regarding Plattsburgh were increased when on 12 August Armstrong directed Izard to "carry the war as far to the westward as possible," and Izard set out for Sackets Harbor with 4,000 men two weeks later.[55]

In front of Fort Erie and with his supplies reduced by Chauncey on Lake Ontario, Drummond, furious at his failure to lever the Americans out of Canada, issued a severe censure to the troops in a general order that forbade "crouching, ducking or laying down when advancing under fire," against riflemen or not; and he sent the 41st Regiment back to the forts to be replaced by the Régiment De Watteville.[56] But the critical failure was Drummond's desultory advance; his light troops did not draw up to Fort Erie until 3 August to drive in the American piquets and enable him to examine the defences, five days after Brown made the decision to hold it. What Drummond saw was far from reassuring: the Americans had been strengthening the fort since its capture, and it now covered some 30 acres with an 800-yard line of defensive works roughly parallel to the lake just east of the fort and a battery near the shore, with another battery on a sand mound called Snake Hill in the south-western corner of the position.[57] Most of the perimeter was protected by a ditch and abatis, and besides the guns forming its defences, the approaches were covered by batteries at Black Rock and by three U.S. Navy schooners on the lake under Lieutenant Augustus Conklin USN, making it an "ugly Customer."[58] On 5 August Brigadier-General Edmund P. Gaines arrived to assume command from the wounded Brown while the British camped in woods about 2 miles to the north, and Eleazer Ripley loyally reverted to command of his brigade in the Snake Hill area.[59]

Drummond had decided not to risk an assault on the fort until he had weakened it and had sent to Fort George for heavy guns. British siege doctrine was well established by 1814, but Drummond lacked experienced engineer officers, there being only nineteen in all British North America. There was little activity while his young and very inexperienced engineer, Lieutenant George Philpott RE, completed the battery armed with three

24-pounder guns, a 24-pounder carronade, and an 8-inch mortar.[60] At least the annoying fire from the American schooners was stopped. A force of seventy-five seamen and Royal Marines, aided by the Lincoln Militia, cut 8 miles of trail through the woods, then carried a captain's gig they had already brought 20 miles overland from Frenchman's Creek, together with five *bateaux,* to the lakeshore. After dark on 12 August they rowed towards the vessels in silence and, when challenged, claimed they were provisioners. But once close in they had to fight and captured *Somers* and *Ohio,* although *Porcupine* managed to cut her cable and drift out of danger. The British lost two dead and four wounded against one American killed and seven wounded.[61] But on 13 August when the British battery opened fire, the range was immediately found to be too great; William Dunlop noted in disgust that barely one shot in ten reached the American ramparts, and those that did rebounded like tennis balls.[62]

After two days of rather pointless bombardment Drummond decided to attack, a consideration reinforced by his serious underestimation of the strength of the garrison.[63] He chose to launch an elaborate night assault with three converging columns: one against Snake Hill and two from the battery towards the north side of the fort itself, due to commence at 2 A.M. on 15 August.[64] The largest column, under Lieutenant-Colonel Victor Fischer, consisted of 1,300 men from the 1st/8th Regiment and the Régiment De Watteville, the Light Companies of the 2nd/89th and 100th Regiments, plus some dragoons; it was to attack Snake Hill with fixed bayonets and their flints removed to prevent a negligent discharge from revealing their roundabout approach.[65] It would also force them "to use the Bayonet with the effect which that valuable weapon has been ever found to possess in the hands of British soldiers," although William Dunlop was unimpressed by such tactics: "In the British Army one would suppose that the only use of a musket was understood to be that it would carry a bayonet at the end of it."[66] A diversionary attack by Indians would be made in the centre of the perimeter while two columns would attack in the north: one under Lieutenant-Colonel William Drummond of the 104th Regiment comprising some 300 sailors, Royal Marines, and light infantry would attack the small stone fort; and another on the far left, with 650 men under Lieutenant-Colonel Hercules Scott of the 103rd Regiment, would attack the entrenchments running from the fort to the lake shore.[67]

However, the Americans had by now been strongly reinforced with elements of the 9th, 11th, 17th, 19th, 21st, 22nd, and 23rd U.S. Infantry and by New

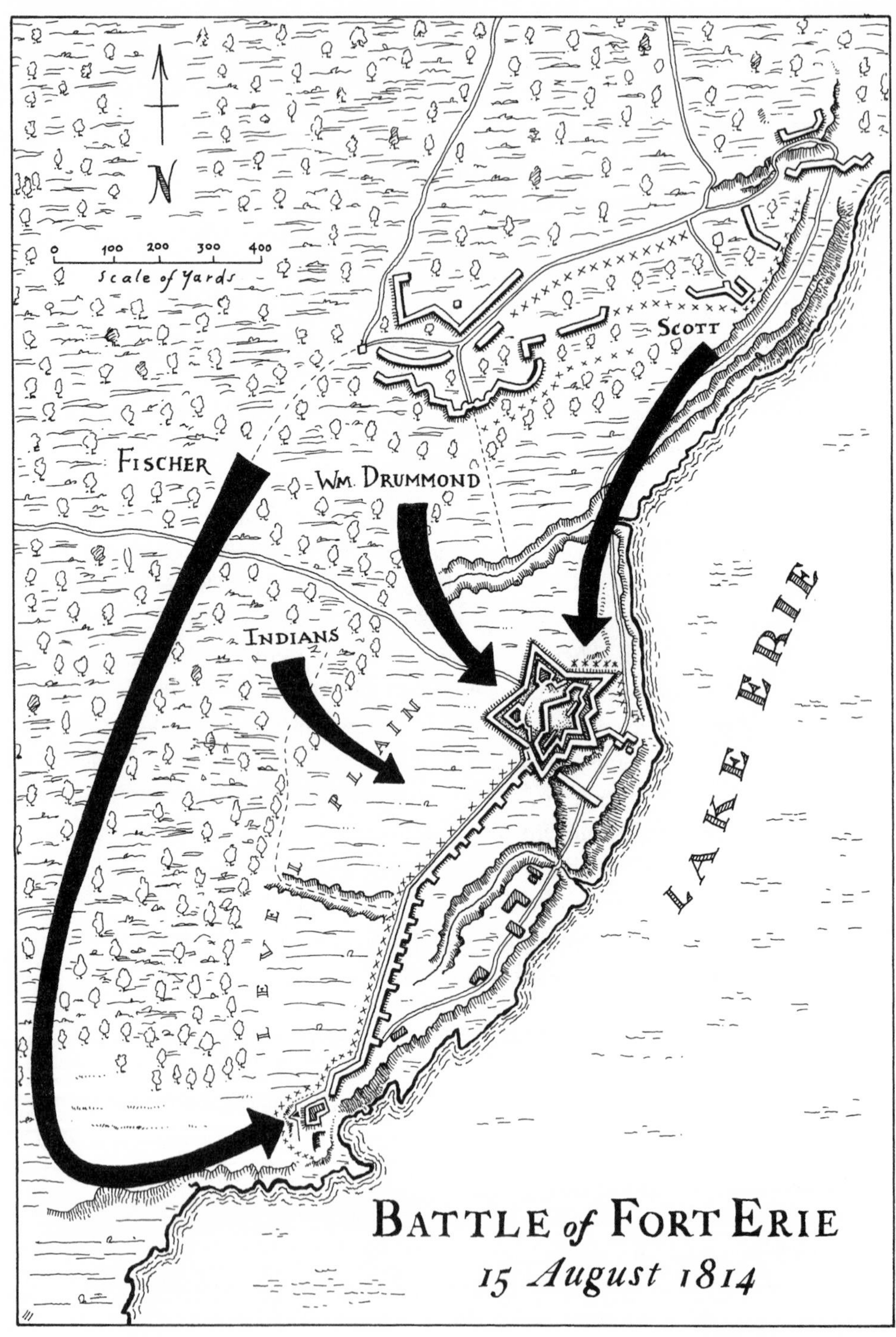

N
0 100 200 300 400
Scale of Yards
SCOTT
FISCHER
WM. DRUMMOND
INDIANS
LEVEL PLAIN
LAKE ERIE
BATTLE of FORT ERIE
15 August 1814

York and Pennsylvania militia with a dozen 6-pounders, two 12-pounders, and an 18- and 24-pounder, all reasonably well entrenched and protected by abatis.[68] Skirmishing around the fort continued as the Americans tried to slow down the siege process; Ludowick Morgan's 1st U.S. Rifles were augmented by Captain Benjamin Birdsall's two companies of 4th U.S. Rifles, who went into the woods on 6, 10, and 12 August, the last sortie marked by the death of Morgan. Then during the following two days British fire artillery increased, and when rocket fire began on 14 August, Gaines decided an attack was imminent. At about 4 P.M. a mortar shell struck a small U.S. magazine, making a spectacular explosion that did little real damage but persuaded Drummond that the bombardment was more effective than was really the case. At about 12:30 A.M. the following morning the British fire slackened, and ceased entirely an hour later, effectively alerting the Americans to impending assault.

Things went wrong from the beginning: the Indians failed to make their demonstration; Fischer's column was thirty minutes late getting into position; the forlorn hope, comprising the De Wattevilles and part of the 1st/8th Regiment's Light Companies, stumbled upon an American piquet and was then attacked by the Americans, losing some 150 men as prisoners in just twenty minutes;[69] and, finally, the main body could not penetrate the abatis between the hill and the lake, discovering to their disgust that their 16-foot scaling ladders were 9 feet too short, and they fell back in confusion under heavy fire without penetrating the American position. A few men tried a flanking movement by wading through the shallows of the lake, but these were captured, and the remainder fled.[70]

The two columns attacking the north side of the fort met with initial success, marching forward to the sound of Fischer's battle, but because of Lieutenant-General Drummond's over-complicated plan, Fischer had been driven off before they could attack. The centre column under Lieutenant-Colonel Drummond managed to get into the north-east bastion of the fort, although the left-hand column under Hercules Scott was repulsed from the shore battery and Scott killed following two brave assaults.[71] Having bloodily repulsed the first attack at the bastion, American gunners under the command of Captain Alexander J. Williams "instantly mounted our parapet and rent the air with loud huzzas, calling upon our brave foe to try it again."[72] The British did try again, twice more, before Lieutenant-Colonel Drummond himself sprang through an embrasure, and the position was taken after a violent mêlée.[73] But there the British were held, unable to break into the fort itself or advance before dawn, and unsupported by Lieutenant-General

Drummond's reserve under the hapless Colonel Tucker. During one rush the gallant Lieutenant-Colonel Drummond was shot and killed.[74]

Then, as William Dunlop was following up behind the assault force at the breach, "just as I was scrambling over some dead bodies, an explosion took place. At first I thought it was a shell had burst close to me, for the noise was not greater if so great, as that of a large shell; but the tremendous glare of light and falling of beams and rubbish soon demonstrated that it was something more serious."[75] Lieutenant John Le Couteur had just mounted a scaling ladder and got over the palisade when he remembered "seeing a black volume rise from the earth and I lost my senses."[76] On the American side Lieutenant David B. Douglass recalled that there was a sudden hush, as if everything was being sucked into a vacuum; then

> an unnatural tremor beneath our feet, like the first heave of an earthquake, and almost at the same instant, the center of the bastion burst up with a terrific explosion and a jet of flame, mingled with fragments of timber, earth, stone, and bodies of men, rose to a height of one or two hundred feet, in the air, fell in a shower of ruins, to a great distance all around.[77]

When Le Couteur came to, "a horrid sight presented itself. Some three hundred men lay roasted, mangled, burned, wounded, black, hideous to view . . . I found my hand in a mass of blood and brains—it was sickening."[78]

The explosion of a magazine in the bastion enabled the Americans, now reinforced from Snake Hill, to drive the demoralized remnant out of the position. An anonymous American witness later claimed that the magazine detonation was detrimental to the Americans, as "it caused the precipitate retreat of [the British] reserve, which should have been intercepted in a few moments more, and in all probability made prisoners."[79] Whether true or not, it was a very severe setback, the most "unfortunate business that happened [to] us during the war," according to William H. Merritt.[80] The British posted casualties of 59 dead, including Colonels Drummond and Scott, 309 wounded, and no fewer than 539 missing, with the 103rd losing 424 men, including 14 out of 18 officers, and the two flank companies of the 104th losing 54 out of 77 men engaged.[81] Drummer Jarvis Hanks "counted 196 bodies lying in the ditch and about the fort"; the youngster was transfixed by the sight of "legs, arms and heads lying, in confusion, separated, by the concussions, from the trunks to which they had long been attached."[82] The explosion "was tremendous," reported Gaines; "it was decisive." He later reported that 222 dead British had been found on the position, while total American losses came to 84.[83]

Since Chippawa the British had lost 2,300 men for no tangible gain, and although Drummond tried to blame the failure on "the present disgraceful, and unfortunate, conduct of the troops," and in particular the foreigners of the Régiment De Watteville, this reasoning cut little ice with Prevost, while Bathurst was appalled by the losses, which he ascribed to poor leadership.[84] For the most part the men fought bravely against a vigilant and valiant enemy. It seems fairer to blame the failure on the plan of attack; an anonymous officer of the 41st Regiment damned the order to remove the flints from the muskets. "Alas! If this absurd order had not been issued I have no sort of doubt that we should have carried the fortress."[85] Indeed, Drummond was an inexperienced commander who had never directed siege operations, and while the preliminary bombardment was clearly inadequate, surprise was also totally lacking.[86] Fortunately for Drummond, he received some 1,200 reinforcements from Burlington and York to replace some of these grievous losses.

On 17 August Prevost reported that his reinforcements from Bordeaux were complete with the arrival of Major-General Frederick Robinson's brigade, bringing the total number of regulars in the Canadas to some 29,000 excluding militia.[87] British sea power had enabled this strategic shift, and British sea power would be necessary to ensure the delivery of some 45 tons of supplies daily to maintain them.[88] However, most of these reinforcements were earmarked for operations in the Champlain Valley, and they could do little to improve Drummond's fundamentally weak position: although the siege continued, the American naval blockade on Lake Ontario against which he railed repeatedly ensured that his men remained short of provisions, ammunition, and equipment—especially tents—just as the weather turned cool and rainy. The continued delay in launching the mighty *St. Lawrence* led Prevost to write to Bathurst on 27 August that "all hopes of using our Squadron on Lake Ontario, before the first week in October have vanished."[89] So grave a threat did this ship pose that Chauncey hired a renegade Canadian, Bill Johnson, to try to blow her up before she was launched. Although nothing came of this plan, it would not have been a difficult task: Captain R. E. Armstrong of the Nova Scotia Fencibles reported nervously that *St. Lawrence* was guarded by only six sentries. "Notwithstanding I am convinced I could burn her with fifty determined fellows. We are of course very anxious to get her launched and out of our hands."[90]

The Americans by contrast took great heart from their successful defence of the fort, although for six weeks Lieutenant-Colonel Thomas Aspinwall of the 9th U.S. Infantry "seldom got more than 3 or four hours daily repose, and never undressed or even pulled off my boots."[91] Both sides were plagued by supply shortages, but things were probably worse for the British: on 18 August Drummond's commissary officer reported that food stocks were down to four weeks rather than the six to seven previously thought.[92] Drummond desperately called for a company of sappers and miners, camp stores, food, and tents and for Yeo's assistance: without tents the men lived in scrapes and shelters, poor protection from two weeks of appalling weather that started on 28 August, during which time the Americans grew increasingly aggressive. But on that day a shell crashed through the roof of Gaines's room, badly wounding him. Though not fully recovered from his own injuries, Brown was forced to resume command.[93]

Lieutenant Philpott constructed a second battery some 800 yards from the fort, but this proved ineffective when it opened fire on 29 August, as it had to restrict its bombardment to conserve ammunition. Still, Drummond urged Yeo to get out onto Lake Ontario and secure his position.[94] Fortunately for the Americans, Drummond was now reluctant to renew the assault without express instructions, and the persistent heavy rain in early September further dampened his division's spirits and raised sickness levels, so that trenches "filled with Water, & the chilling blasts of Autumn began to be felt."[95] On 2 September Ripley and a council of officers were in favour of evacuation, but Brown would not accept this. His main difficulty was that the British had completed a third battery south-east of the second one and only 400 yards from the fort, well capable of causing immense damage. Furthermore, Drummond had amassed 200 rounds per gun, and with Kempt's brigade now reaching Kingston the commander there, Major-General Richard Stovin, was able to forward as reinforcements 1,200 men of the 6th and 82nd Regiments, both Peninsula veteran units, retaining the 97th Regiment until Drummond should call for them.[96]

Artillery fire was exchanged daily, and skirmishing continued that served little purpose, but on 4 September Porter led a sortie to attack the second battery; fighting lasted for about six hours, until a heavy downpour "tended to cool both parties."[97] During this fight Joseph Willcocks was shot in the chest and killed, an event which caused great rejoicing in the British lines. Despite this coup, however, Drummond felt overwhelmed with difficulties and four days later warned Prevost of the

> possibility of my being compelled by sickness or suffering of the troops, exposed as they will be to the effects of the wet and unhealthy Season which is fast approaching, to withdraw them from their present Position to one which may afford them the means of cover. Sickness has, I am sorry to say, already made its appearance in several of the corps, particularly the 82nd.[98]

Although Yeo finally launched *St. Lawrence* on 10 September, neither Drummond nor Prevost had any faith in the navy's ability to cooperate with land operations, intent as both sides were on defeating the other's fleet. Drummond continued to complain of lack of ammunition and reinforcement as he lost heart, and on 15 September he restricted his guns to one round each per hour. The following day his new second-in-command, Major-General Louis de Watteville, urged him to abandon the siege and withdraw, a proposal which he seems to have accepted.[99] But as the batteries were starting to pack up on 17 September, suddenly the Americans came boiling out of the fort to attack them.

Having first set up his command post at Buffalo, with Ripley in charge of the fort, Brown crossed over at the behest of his senior officers, who had no confidence in Ripley. Finding the garrison "impatient," he had decided to attack the No. 3 Battery and was encouraged by the improved response of the militia; 1,500 men had volunteered to cross into Canada under Porter.[100] He committed 2,000 men to this raid against one brigade of British, hoping to be away again before they could bring up reserves from their main camp. Inexplicably Drummond took no precautions despite warnings from American deserters that a raid was in the offing. His engineers left standing the dense woods within pistol shot of No. 3 Battery, and all through 16 September American fatigue parties were able to open a path to this point.[101] At midday, in heavy rain that masked their movement and lulled the British sentries, Porter led 1,600 regulars and militia through the woods running from Snake Hill to outflank the British position on the extreme right of the line to No. 3 Battery, and caught them unprepared. The battery was taken almost immediately, the guns spiked, and the magazine blown up.[102] Now covered by a very heavy bombardment from the fort itself, the column moved on to attack the No. 2 Battery, this time aided by a column of 400 regulars sallying from the fort under Colonel James Miller. At this stage Porter's column was counter-attacked by two companies of the 82nd Regiment under Captain Robert Patteson, who poured a concentrated fire into the American ranks, which were so tightly packed that few could use their weapons. Seeing an officer, Patteson demanded his surrender, but as some of the Americans began to lay down their muskets, Patteson was shot dead. Enraged by this apparently dishonourable act, his men charged in with the bayonet and slaughtered many Americans as the fighting became general, and Porter and Miller began to lose control as their commands intermingled.[103] The No. 2 Battery, where the British were protected by trenches, fell only after very heavy fighting, so that "constant use of the bayonet was the only mode of assailing them," recalled Sergeant Jesse P. Harmon; and by now the British reserves had arrived.[104] These included seven more companies of the 82nd and three of the 6th Regiment under Major Henry Adolphus Proctor, who made a fine charge to drive the Americans back.[105] A soldier of the 21st U.S. Infantry described a savage encounter in which "man to man and steel to steel, across carriages and at the mouth of the guns, every inch of ground was disputed, and both American and Briton fell to mingle in one common dust."[106]

Seeing that things were not going entirely well, Brown sent Ripley forward with the reserve, but Ripley lost his way in the tangled undergrowth and was badly wounded. More fighting took place around No. 1 Battery before the Americans retired, harassed by Indians and the Glengarry Light Infantry.[107] With Drummond already committed to retiring, the Americans lost 72 killed—including the invaluable engineer Eleazer D. Wood—with 432 wounded and missing in what was essentially an unnecessary operation, although Brown could not know that; British losses were 115 killed, 178 wounded, and 316 missing, over half coming from the 1st/8th and the Régiment De Watteville.[108] In the fierce fighting one American, Private Eber D. Howe, recalled one encounter with the enemy: "Many of them threw away their arms and in their attempts to run would fling themselves full length upon the ground, quite willing and anxious to be prisoners."[109] Three of Drummond's six siege guns were disabled and their ammunition destroyed. Ignoring his own errors, Drummond wrote to Prevost that

> the sickness of the troops has increased to such an alarming degree, and their situation has really become one of such extreme wretchedness from the torrents of rain which have continued to fall for the last 13 days, and from the circumstance of the Division being entirely destitute of camp equipage, that I feel it my duty no longer to persevere in a vain attempt to maintain the blockade.[110]

The British buried the dead of both sides and, further delayed by rain, finally pulled out of their lines on 21 September to retreat towards Chippawa as the summer campaign season finally drew to a miserable close.[111]

FOLLOWING her launch on 10 September *St. Lawrence* was ready to sail from Kingston by mid-October. With this development, Chauncey relinquished his blockade and returned to port. The Royal Navy planned to build two more ships to carry 120 guns each, together with a 55-gun frigate, whose frame had been shipped across the Atlantic, and other vessels. On 11 October Drummond warned Prevost bluntly:

> Should the 90th Regiment (or some strong Regt.) and the requisite supply of provisions and Stores, not come up in the [Lake Ontario] Squadron, and should any disaster happen to this Division (in consequence) and above all should Commodore Chauncey (as is probable) decline an Action, His Majesty's Naval Commander will in My Opinion have much to answer for.[112]

Drummond's stinging rebuke of Yeo's lack of cooperation with the army was remarkably similar to Brown's complaints about Chauncey, coming to a head as Yeo's and Prevost's differences grew increasingly bitter and personal. In mid-October Yeo finally sailed for the first time since July, taking provisions and stores to the troops in the Niagara area.[113] On the peninsula there was a brief stand-off in the middle of the month before Drummond finally withdrew to Fort George, sending parts of his force to Burlington and York for the winter.[114] In fact, the 90th Regiment, like a number of others brought across the Atlantic, spent the war entirely without incident; it served three months in garrison at Kingston and on 13 October moved to Fort Niagara, which it occupied until 22 May 1815.[115]

Meanwhile Brown was waiting for Izard's reinforcements from Plattsburgh, who completed their arduous trek on 12 October, their combined forces now totalling 7,000.[116] The more aggressive Brown wished to attack Drummond immediately, but Izard, the superior officer, chose not to risk casualties by attacking a strong defensive position. Angered at Izard's inaction, Brown marched his division back to Sackets Harbor and, seeing no purpose in retaining Fort Erie except as a trophy, prepared it for demolition.[117] Izard finally decided on a plan to lure Drummond away from his defensive position. Intelligence indicated that a quantity of grain was stored at Cook's Mills on Lyons Creek, a tributary of the Chippawa. Izard sent a brigade under Brigadier-General Daniel Bissell with about 1,200 men to capture it. On 18 October skirmishing between his riflemen and a detachment of Glengarry Light Infantry led Bissell to believe that a sizeable British force was opposing him across the creek.[118] In fact, Drummond had sent about 750 men under Lieutenant-Colonel Christopher Myers of the 100th Regiment to protect Cook's Mills, which Lieutenant Le Couteur recalled involved marching "knee deep in mud in a pitch dark night—over rough and smooth—an exquisite enjoyment for those who have never tried it."[119]

On the morning of the 19th, Myers attacked and drove the lead American units back across Lyons Creek. The British crossed the creek, but Bissell managed to hold them off and immediately planned a counter-attack. The Americans surged across the creek, and Myers retreated in orderly fashion, losing one man dead and thirty-five wounded to twelve Americans killed and fifty-four wounded.[120] The Americans then took Cook's Mills and burned about 200 bushels of wheat. Despite this success, when it became apparent that Drummond was not going to move from his defences, Izard withdrew back to Fort Erie. On 5 November Izard blew it up in a pyrotechnic display worthy of Guy Fawkes' Night, then retired to the American shore.[121] Drummond moved to the remains of the fort but chose not to rebuild it, and thus the fighting along the Niagara Frontier came to an end, the hardest-fought and bloodiest campaign of the war, summed up by American Surgeon William E. Horner: "there was never a campaign in which the belligerents came to a better understanding of what they might expect in battle at each other's hands; and where leaders, though under the excitement of a state of war, left with more military respect for one another."[122] Drummond blamed lack of men and supplies for his operational failures, but his own tardiness and lack of drive, especially in the aftermath of Lundy's Lane, were at least as much to blame for the disappointments of the year. Nevertheless, the campaign represented strategic success: the final American attempt to invade Canada had failed.[123]

16

Plattsburgh

Sir George Prevost with all his host march'd forth from Montreal, Sir,
Both he and they as blithe and gay as going to a ball, Sir.
The troops he chose were all of those that conquer'd Marshal Soult, Sir,
Who at Garonne (the fact is known) scarce brought them to a halt, Sir.

With troops like these, he thought with ease to crush the Yankee faction:
His only thought was how he ought to bring them into action.
Your very names, Sir George exclaims, without a gun or bay'net,
Will pierce like darts thro' Yankee hearts, and all their spirits stagnate . . .

—Miner Lewis, "The Battle of Plattsburgh"

By summer 1814 four vessels of the U.S. Navy—*Congress, Constellation, John Adams,* and *United States*—carrying a total of 144 guns were pinned uselessly in port. But with an optimism that defied its situation, the U.S. government continued to build ships: the frigate *Guerrière* (44) was launched at Philadelphia in June and Rodgers and his crew from *President* sent to man her; a sister ship, *Java,* was launched in August at Baltimore, but neither would have the chance to make its power felt. Nor would the first American 74s: *Independence,* launched in June at Charlestown, Massachusetts; and *Washington,* launched at Portsmouth, New Hampshire, in October. Besides, both were top heavy and needed so many major alterations that they ultimately served only as receiving ships. Six sloops were also finished during the war, and several more were on the stocks, but these and three of the sloops languished uselessly for want of guns and crews.[1]

As the destruction of Washington was progressing, so were British preparations for the occupation of eastern Maine as pressure on New England came to a head. With Moose Island occupied, the decision was made in late summer to take control of Maine from the New Brunswick border to the Penobscot River, the area to the south of this stream being deemed too populous for successful operations with the 2,500 troops available to Major-General Sherbrooke. He had decided that an occupation of northern Maine was impractical because of its isolation from any large settlements, but that the same object could be achieved by occupying the Penobscot coast "with a respectable force, and to take that river (which was the old frontier of the state of Massachusetts), as our boundary."[2] This move would serve to reopen coastal trade with New England because the place of origin of American products would not concern British customs officials in an occupied port such as Castine, as long as it was legally cleared for shipment to a port in British North America.[3] Naval command rested on Rear-Admiral Edward Griffith, who had spent most of the war in command of Halifax. The force, comprising *Dragon* with the frigates HMS *Endymion* (40) and *Bacchante* (38), the sloop *Sylph* (18), and ten transports, arrived on 31 August at the mouth of the Penobscot River, where it was joined by the *Bulwark,* the frigate *Tenedos,* the sloop *Peruvian* (18), the brig *Rifleman* (18), and the schooner *Picton* (10) and proceeded up the bay. The first objective was the fort at Castine, which was blown up as the British approached. The town was occupied without resistance by a force comprising the 29th (Worcestershire), 62nd (Wiltshire), and 98th Regiments, supported by two rifle companies of the 7th/60th Regiment—raised among German prisoners of war specifically for service in North America[4]—with a detachment of Royal Artillery. The battalion companies of the 29th Regiment were then sent under Major-General Gerard Gosselin to occupy Belfast on the opposite shore, and 700 men of the combined flank companies, commanded by Lieutenant-Colonel Henry John, were sent under Barrie of the *Dragon* to take the more important town of Hampden, where the corvette *Adams* (28) was trapped, having been grounded at Isle au Haut on the 17th and forced to throw off all her stores in order to refloat.[5] Some 600 militia had gathered near Bangor, and Captain Charles Morris USN of the *Adams,* with 200 seamen and marines and about 40 regulars from Castine, had formed a battery with guns taken from the ship.[6]

The British landed early on the morning of 2 September some 3 miles downstream in heavy fog, and as they approached the militia fled. Morris set fire to *Adams,* and when she exploded it was "truly terrific—resounding between the high banks of the Penobscot like the loudest thunder."[7] Moses Smith also watched as "Masts, yards, rigging, sails, planks, and everything moveable were thrown into the air in wild confusion."[8] The British then advanced upriver to take Hampden and receive the surrender of Bangor, taking twelve other vessels, twenty-two guns, three stands of colours, and 190 prisoners. When Hardy occupied Eastport in July, the citizens had presented him with an address on his departure acknowledging "the liberal and honourable conduct observed by you towards them . . . the order and discipline of the Navy and Army, and . . . freedom from insult in what we hold most dear, our families and domestic firesides." Now, however, there was much destruction and pillage, and when a deputation approached Barrie, he is alleged to have replied: "My business is to burn, sink and destroy. Your town was taken by storm, and by the rules of war we ought both to lay your village in ashes and put the inhabitants to the sword. But I will spare your lives, though I mean to burn your houses." Fortunately Sherbrooke ordered that there was to be no more fire-setting than absolutely necessary.[9]

On 9 September the battalion companies of the 29th Regiment under Lieutenant-Colonel Andrew Pilkington were sent to occupy Machias, "the only place occupied by the Enemy's Troops between this and Passamaquoddy Bay." They arrived the following evening and thrashed through the woods behind the fort, only to find on 11 September that the defenders had fled; the town fell without a fight, and another twenty-four guns were taken. Two days later, as Pilkington prepared to advance, he received a letter of capitulation from the senior American militia officers:

> We propose a capitulation and offer for ourselves and on behalf of the officers and Soldiers of the Brigade within the County of Washington to give our Parole of honor that we will not directly or indirectly bear Arms, or in any way serve against His Britannic Majesty King George . . . upon condition we have your assurance that . . . we shall have the safe and full enjoyment of our Private property, and be protected in the exercise of our usual occupations.[10]

In two weeks the whole of eastern Maine—some 100 miles of seaboard and the country behind it—had fallen into British hands until the war's end for the loss of one man killed and eight wounded.[11] Subsequently the male population quietly swore allegiance to the Crown, happy to resume their interrupted trade with Nova Scotia and New Brunswick, which was opened by proclamations from Griffith and Sherbrooke, who appointed a military governor for the territory and a customs official for Castine.[12] Thereafter Swedish vessels ran huge quantities of British goods up to Hampden for distribution throughout New England; neutral Swedish and Spanish ships also operated on Lake Champlain, and continued trade with Canada drained the United States of specie as smuggling continued to thrive.[13]

Elsewhere in New England the effect of the blockade led Nantucket Island to seek a separate peace. The population relied on the sea, especially whaling, for economic support; the poor soil provided little by way of produce and no fuel to ease the harshness of a north Atlantic winter. On 23 July 1814 the inhabitants, having been "universally opposed" to the war, petitioned Cochrane that the forthcoming winter would see them facing starvation, as the American government was unable to help them, and requested permission to import food and fuel from the mainland.[14] Cochrane directed Rear-Admiral Henry Hotham to investigate, and on 21 August Hotham sent Captain Vincent Newton RN of HM Sloop *Nimrod* (18) to inspect the situation; he reported that conditions were in fact worse than the petitioners claimed, with only two weeks' supply of food and fuel to hand. A town meeting elected representatives who visited Hotham on board HMS *Superb* (74) and signed a unilateral declaration of neutrality, asserting that any supplies they might later be able to spare would be available for British ships. On 8 September Hotham wrote to the committee to say that Cochrane wanted assurances that they would cease paying taxes to the U.S. government, and at the end of the month a town meeting voted to do so for the war's duration. On receiving this assurance the British government released Nantucket men held as prisoners of war, including those at Dartmoor.[15]

By war's end the Halifax squadron had captured 12 U.S. warships and burned 3 others—55 percent of America's naval strength—for the loss of 6; of the 714 U.S. merchant ships processed by the Court of Vice-Admiralty, 494 were taken by Royal Navy vessels, which burned at least 200 more. The Royal Navy also took 92 of the 93 American privateers adjudicated before the Halifax Court of Vice-Admiralty.[16] American merchant ships had been virtually driven from the ocean, and at no other time in history has the United States been so effectively isolated. Imports of gunpowder dropped to one-sixth of the pre-war level, although this shortfall was compensated by the development of the DuPont works in Delaware; and, fortunately for the United States, the blockade was not as effective as it would have been in 1776 or might have been later, when nations became reliant on such commodities as rubber and tin.[17] Finally, in January 1815 Cochrane withdrew his system of retaliation from towns he knew disapproved of the war, mostly in New England, and directed his subordinates to bear down hard on those which harboured the privateers that still plagued British shipping.[18]

Successful privateer captains included Thomas Boyle of the *Comet* (8) and later the *Chasseur* (16), whose favourite cruising ground was the Bristol Channel, and who in 1814 was bold enough to declare a blockade of the British coast in retaliation for the British blockade of the United States.[19] One notable success was *General Armstrong* (9), commanded by Captain Samuel C. Reid, which took almost £250,000 worth of prizes before being cornered at Faial in the Azores by a British squadron under Captain Robert Lloyd RN of HMS *Plantagenet* (74), including HMS *Rota* (38) and HM Brigs *Carnation, Calypso,* and *Thais* (all 18s). The squadron had been assembled to carry troops and supplies to Jamaica for Cochrane's forthcoming operations in Louisiana, and although it succeeded in capturing the privateer following a bloody stand-off in the neutral port on 26 September 1814, success came at a severe cost: 36 killed and 28 wounded to just 2 Americans killed and 7 wounded.[20] Rather than departing for Jamaica immediately, as he had been ordered, Lloyd sent home two of the brigs with the severely wounded, delaying the squadron's departure by at least three weeks, a result which converted into a major American success. Equally the ever-inventive Richard Fulton remained undeterred. On 29 October at New York he launched the first ever steam frigate, *Demologus* (renamed *Fulton the First* in March 1815 following his death on 24 February), capable of firing 32-pound heated shot from her carronades and making 3–4 knots against the wind. Her 156-foot-long hull was constructed of timbers 5 feet thick, enlarged to 11 feet around the engine; and it was perhaps as well for the Royal Navy that she never achieved readiness.[21] She blew up in 1829 after an accident in her magazine, but although Molson's *Swiftsure* was said to have carried 8,000 men by the end of the war, and the Pittsburgh-built *New Orleans* had been operating on the Mississippi since January 1812, the full impact of steam on naval warfare lay in the future.[22]

In July Bathurst urged Prevost to press the war with all possible vigour right up to the conclusion of peace and to undertake offensive operations as soon as reinforcements arrived; he reiterated on 22 August that moves should be made against American naval forces in the Lake Ontario and Lake Champlain areas.[23] Prevost intended to restrict offensive operations to the western shore of Lake Champlain, as the eastern side was such a rich source of smuggled supplies, but despite urging from London, taking control of Lake Champlain could not be anticipated before 15 September. Although the British had made useful territorial gains for use as bargaining counters during peace negotiations, Prevost decided the Champlain region offered the best prospect of further gains. Control of the lake would be essential to any British advance, and Prevost hoped that HMS *Confiance* (36), being built at Isle-aux-Noix, would be of help once she was ready.[24] But on land the Americans appeared weak. When Armstrong ordered Izard to Sackets Harbor in August, the force remaining to Brigadier-General Alexander Macomb, in command of forces around Lake Champlain, amounted to around 3,400, of whom Macomb reported only some 1,500 were effectives. Thus the entire region was left dangerously exposed while the New England authorities continued to resist federal control.[25]

Even then Prevost's objectives remained limited and did not extend, as some American historians have claimed without evidence, as far as Albany or even New York City. Rather, his instructions were "not to expose His Majesty's Forces to being cut off by too extended a line of advance."[26] Instead he was to gain a foothold on Lake Champlain sufficient to force its demilitarization at the peace conference. But his natural caution was reinforced by a lack of naval strength, and he would not hold the advantage on Lake Ontario until it was once more too late in the season.

For the proposed operation three brigades were available: the 1st Brigade, under Major-General Robinson, comprising the 3rd/27th, 39th (Dorsetshire), 76th, and 88th (Connaught Rangers) Regiments; the 2nd, under Major-General Thomas Brisbane, drawn from troops stationed in Lower Canada—the 2nd/8th, 13th, 49th, and De Meuron Regiments, and the Voltigeurs Canadiens; and Power's 3rd Brigade, comprising the 3rd, 5th, 1st/27th, and 58th Regiments, each supported by a Royal Artillery brigade of five 6-pounders and one 5.5–inch howitzer, together with 309 officers and men of 19th Light Dragoons to give the division a total strength on paper of 10,351 regulars and militia.[27] Thus they were not all Peninsula veterans, and this figure does not take into account the sick or personnel detached for one reason or another; so the actual invasion strength was far lower. Besides, the Peninsula veterans were not at all happy soldiers. After almost six years of continuous campaigning across burning plains and freezing mountains they had expected to return to the British Isles, and their mood was not lightened to embark on a fresh campaign, noted Lieutenant William Grattan, especially when

> the poor faithful Spanish and Portuguese women, hundreds of whom had attached themselves to our soldiers, and who had accompanied them

> through all their fatigues and dangers, were from stern necessity obliged to be abandoned to their fate . . . these faithful and heroic women [and their children] were now, after these trials, to be seen standing on the beach [at Bordeaux], while they witnessed with bursting hearts the filling of those sails and the crowding of those ships, that were to separate them for ever from those to whom they had looked for protection and support.[28]

Once in Canada Kempt's veterans remained at Montreal as army reserve, destined for Kingston and a possible attack on Sackets Harbor, which the continued delay in launching *St. Lawrence* frustrated.

Prevost had been disturbed all summer by Yeo's siphoning of manpower, naval stores, and guns to Kingston for use on Lake Ontario, and shortage of crew for this and the other vessels on Lakes Ontario and Champlain hampered the deployment of *Confiance*—named after the French ship Yeo had captured much earlier in his career. She was launched on 25 August but was far from being combat ready, and her impact was reduced by the fact that the Americans had launched *Eagle* (20) ten days earlier.[29] *Confiance* carried twenty-seven long 24-pounders and six carronades, which would enable her to defeat *Saratoga* (eight long 24s and eighteen larger carronades) at long range, while the other vessels in the rival squadrons were roughly equal and cancelled each other out. However, hopes of naval efficiency were not helped by changes in senior personnel. Captain Peter Fisher RN had arrived to take command on Lake Champlain on 24 June while Pring remained as his deputy, but on 2 September Fisher was summarily replaced by Captain George Downie RN, despite being the more experienced officer, and Fisher duly complained that "the manner in which I am removed without the least previous communication can only carry with it the impression to the Army now assembled on this frontier, and with whom we are expected to co-operate, that I must be either unfit or unworthy in your [Yeo's] estimation to retain it."[30] Fisher's brief tenure and abrupt replacement further disrupted the Royal Navy's command and hampered the development of inter- and intraservice cooperation, and Yeo's reasoning for the change has never been satisfactorily explained, although he apparently held that Fisher had too violent a temper to hold independent command.[31]

Command within the army was no more harmonious: Prevost had chosen to quibble over dress regulations with the generals newly arrived from Europe, complaining about "a fanciful variety inconsistent with the rules of service" to veteran officers who knew better, and complained to London.[32] As William Grattan noted: "Provided we brought our men into the field well appointed, and with sixty rounds of good ammunition each, [the Duke] never looked to see whether their trowsers were black, blue, or grey, and as to ourselves [the officers], we might be rigged out in all the colours of the rainbow if we fancied it."[33] Unsurprisingly, fusty orders of this sort to veteran troops provoked resentment, and went a long way to damage their confidence in Prevost. Fortunately for the United States, Prevost also decided that now was the time to take the field personally, subordinating de Rottenburg as second-in-command. He soon found himself in conflict with his brigade commanders, who resented being instructed in the minutiae of campaign management by a man whom they regarded as a penpusher with little practical experience, and who were annoyed that Prevost's adjutant-general, Edward Baynes, had been promoted major-general despite his lack of field experience.[34] It would have been far better for all concerned had one of these officers been appointed commander of the expedition, for, as Robinson later wrote in his journal, the army moved without a clear plan and with no effort to gather intelligence, Prevost apparently believing that "it was throwing money away to attempt it."[35]

On 1 September, the same day Downie arrived, the army crossed the frontier. The timing was certainly inauspicious; the following morning Downie ordered Pring to take the gunboats out in support of the army, and that day Macdonough brought his three warships and supporting gunboats into Plattsburgh Bay. The army made slow progress along appalling roads, reaching Beekmantown Corners on the 5th within eight miles of Plattsburgh and camping on the farm of Miner Lewis. Most of the region's inhabitants fled, and there was little opposition apart from some 700 New York militia under Brigadier-General Benjamin Mooers, who skirmished and destroyed bridges to impede the invaders. Early on the morning of 6 September the British advanced in two columns: the left-hand column, under Brisbane, made its way along the lake road; the right-hand column, under Power, went along the Beekmantown Road driving some American militia and 250 regulars before it, turning Macomb's position at the Deer Creek bridge on the lake road, where he had built abatis manned by riflemen. To begin with, some militia rallied to their support but dissolved into flight when some New York dragoons wearing red coats appeared behind them,[36] so that Macomb was forced to retreat.[37] At Beekmantown Lieutenant-Colonel James Wellington and Ensign J. Chapman of the 3rd Regiment were killed by a sniper, Samuel Terry of Peru,

Clinton County, New York.[38] The Americans retired across the river, broke up the bridges, and, "except a few brave men, fell back most precipitately in the greatest disorder, notwithstanding the British troops did not deign to fire on them, except by their flankers and advanced patrols . . . So undaunted was the [British force], that he never deployed in his whole march, always pressing on in column."[39]

When the British reached Plattsburgh that evening, the Régiment De Meuron got separated from the column and entered the town itself. For subaltern Frédéric de Graffenreid it was

> the first time I had been under fire, and as we ran along the coast, the [American] fleet served us generously with grape shot, which caused us a few losses . . . The town was completely deserted, the inhabitants having fled at our approach. There were plenty of provisions, and in a number of houses dinner had just been served, so I helped myself and also to the excellent cigars that I found there![40]

Prevost asked Robinson if he could attack immediately, but Robinson demurred: his men had been marching all day without food, and the fords across the river had not yet been identified. He also wanted naval support from the lake against the American fortifications, but the American lake squadron was anchored offshore.[41] The Americans "didn't seem to worry much about their own houses," noted de Graffenreid, "which they doused liberally with both cannon and grape shot, although without causing us much damage," as over the following days the American squadron kept up a fire on the town that included heated shot. When they set some buildings on fire, recalled Captain J. H. Wood RA, "a flag of truce was sent in, proposing to extinguish it, which they declined, and kept up their fire, warmer than before."[42]

Prevost, who had always maintained that naval control of the lake was essential, wrote to Downie on the morning of 7 September while the latter was some 15 miles away, giving details of the American squadron and requesting that it be dealt with if Downie deemed it possible; he also stated that his own actions were dependant on Downie's decision, berated Downie for not getting into position sooner, and impugned Downie's motives by expressing the hope that the navy's delay resulted from "nothing but the state of the wind."[43] Downie replied that he would engage as soon as *Confiance* was ready but that this would take a day or two, to which Prevost replied that he was in urgent need of the fleet's support and that he was waiting for it, and he sent further letters seemingly designed to rush the much younger and junior Downie into action.[44] Although Downie pointed out that his duty was not to commit his forces before they were ready, Prevost warned about the dangers of delay as New York militia and Vermont volunteers arrived to strengthen the defences.[45] Downie would have to defeat the American squadron, consisting of the ship *Saratoga* (26), the brig *Eagle* (20), the schooner *Ticonderoga* (17), the sloop *Preble* (7), and ten gunboats, with total manpower of almost 900.[46] Against this he deployed *Confiance,* the brig *Linnet* (16), the sloops *Chubb* (11) and *Finch* (10), and eleven gunboats, but Prevost's claims that American deserters were reporting that their squadron was inefficiently manned did not reassure Downie, who hoped to use a company of the 39th Regiment to supplement his few sailors. Thus, while the two fleets were broadly equal in numbers and firepower, the British were clearly inferior in manpower. And though Prevost insisted that he never promised to support Downie with shore fire, Pring and others later reported that Downie expected such.[47]

Not until the evening of 9 September did Downie write to say he would enter Plattsburgh Bay the following day, but he was then held up by contrary winds, while Captain Wood complained that there was a "great deficiency of arrangement and decision."[48] On the morning of the 11th Downie wrote to say that he would be arriving, and Prevost planned to launch his assault simultaneously. Plattsburgh was divided by the Saranac River, and the Americans had three strong redoubts and two blockhouses to the south of it crossing the neck of a small peninsula between the river and the lake.[49] Covered by fire from the new batteries, Brisbane's brigade would make a diversionary attack at the two stripped-plank bridges while Robinson led a force—comprising his own 3rd/27th and 76th Regiments with Power's brigade and the Light Companies of the 39th and 88th Regiments, two squadrons of 19th Light Dragoons, and an artillery detachment of two 6-pounders and Congreve rockets—to a ford farther up the Saranac to cross the river and assault the American works with scaling ladders. Robinson's force waited from an hour before dawn but was told by Prevost not to march off before 10 A.M.; as Robinson went to Prevost's headquarters to receive his final orders, he heard Downie's guns in action.[50]

Yeo later claimed that Prevost's urging of Downie to attack an American squadron in an anchorage of its own choosing put him at a grave disadvantage; had Prevost stormed the American position the American squadron would have been forced to put out into the lake, where the British could have met it on equal terms.[51] Instead Downie tried to sail into the bay in a light

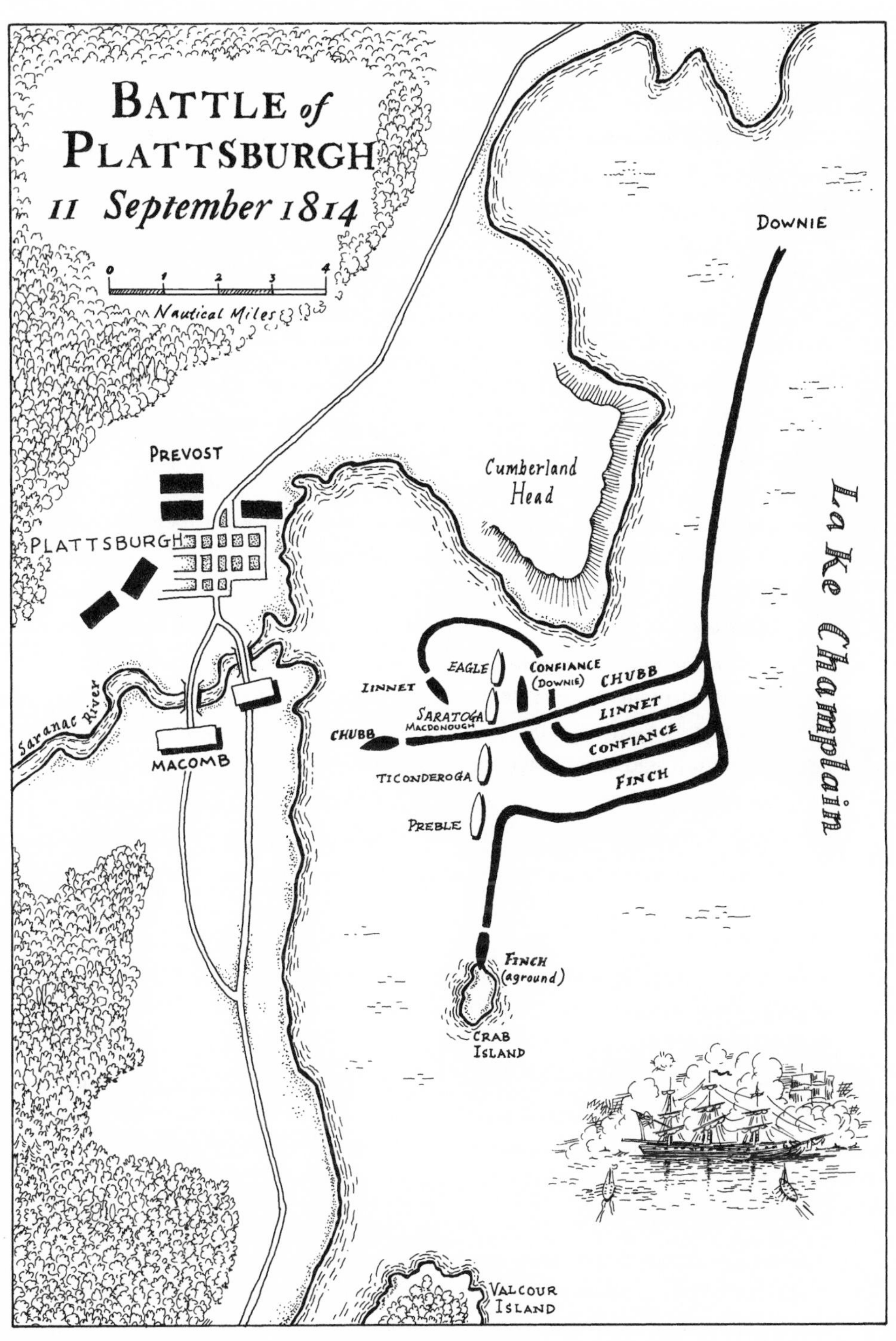

Battle of Plattsburgh
11 September 1814
0
1
2
3
4
Nautical Miles
Prevost
Plattsburgh
Saranac River
Macomb
Downie
Cumberland Head
Lake Champlain
Linnet
Eagle
Confiance (Downie)
Chubb
Saratoga Macdonough
Chubb
Linnet
Confiance
Ticonderoga
Finch
Preble
Finch (aground)
Crab Island
Valcour Island

and variable breeze and to place *Confiance* alongside *Saratoga,* but he was unable to get closer than about 300 yards. *Saratoga* waited until *Confiance* was anchored to return fire, and then, with her guns double-shotted, she delivered a destructive broadside. *Linnet* anchored to engage *Eagle,* aided by *Chubb,* while *Finch* and most of the British gunboats took on *Ticonderoga, Preble,* and the American gunboats. But the battle soon turned against the British: Downie was cut down and killed by a gun knocked loose from a carriage, and the two British sloops were lost, with *Finch* being disabled and drifting onto Crab Island, where she came under fire from a shore battery manned by American sick. *Chubb* also drifted out of control and was taken by a midshipman from *Saratoga.* The only British success was the forcing inshore of *Preble* by gunboats.

By 10:30 A.M. it was clear that all British hopes now rested on *Confiance. Eagle* had been under fire from both *Linnet* and *Confiance* and had the springs of her cable shot away. Her captain cut the cable and anchored between *Confiance* and *Ticonderoga,* which left *Saratoga* exposed to fire from *Linnet.* Both *Confiance* and *Saratoga* suffered dreadfully with Macdonough's starboard battery in no state to reply, but at this point Macdonough's seamanship saved the day. He managed to wind his ship round on an anchor and hawsers to bring his larboard battery to bear, the guns stuffed to the muzzle with hand spikes and fired into the throng of British sailors trying to turn *Confiance.* "Where it had been black with men the moment before, scarcely one man could now be seen," noted seaman Asa Fitch.[52] With *Confiance* having received 105 shot through her hull, Lieutenant James Robertson RN, who had taken over from Downie, recalled that "the Ship's Company declared they would no longer stand to their Quarters, nor could their officers with their utmost exertions rally them," and she was forced to strike her colours.[53] *Saratoga* then sprung round on her anchors to engage *Linnet,* which struck colours fifteen minutes later. The British gunboats fled, leaving Macdonough with a famous victory that cost 52 killed and 58 wounded to British losses of 80 killed and 100 wounded.[54] "Although the bombs were bursting in all directions," wrote American seaman Jonathan Stevens, later "they seemed as harmless as tho' it was only a game at ball or some amusement."[55] After the victory John Edsall, who served on *Saratoga,* found "the English sailors had brought with them large canteens of liquor and were singing and carousing merrily with our seamen."[56]

As soon as the British squadron appeared, Prevost had ordered his land assault to begin; but the guides for Robinson's column took the wrong road,

16.1. Battle of Plattsburgh. *Battle of Lake Champlain, Opening Salvos,* painting by Peter Rindlisbacher.

causing a one-hour delay, although this did not prevent them from rushing the shallow ford defended by American volunteers and militia while the regulars defended the bridge site. The British "dashed down a very steep and high bank and forded the river like so many fox hounds," Robinson reported, "driving the Doodles before them."[57] Captain Mackenzie Kennedy watched the 76th Regiment fording the Saranac as

> an orderly bugler was sounding a call in the middle of the river, when a shot knocked off his head-dress, which was carried down the stream. This accident, however, did not disturb him, for, still continuing to sound, he employed one of his hands in disengaging his forage cap from the strap of his knapsack, and placed it on his head as if nothing had happened.[58]

Robinson soon had four battalions across and was ready to launch his final assault, one that appeared straightforward compared to any against the French, when suddenly he received the order from Baynes to retire: it took him completely by surprise, and Power was "equally astonished."[59] But as soon as Prevost realized that the naval squadron had been beaten, he had cancelled the operation, and had it not been for the hour's delay it is probable that the British would have already secured victory on the ground. Instead, Robinson's men had to retire, losing three officers and thirty-one men of the Light Company of the 76th Regiment, who, out in front, failed to receive word to do so. Their commander, Captain Purchas, was shot while waving a white waistcoat at the end of his sword in surrender, and Macomb would later convert his fortunate escape into a military victory for his own men.[60] The Meurons watched the battle from *Platzbourg,* recalled Lieutenant Charles de Goumoëns; the regiment "was supposed to mount its own attack during the naval combat. But the order was never given by General Prevost who thus committed a grave error as the Swiss could have taken the Fort and from there bombarded the American fleet, and thus prevented them from occupying the grounded British fleet."[61]

Prevost certainly achieved greater celerity in retreat than he ever had in advance. That evening the baggage was sent to the rear and the batteries dismantled, and before daylight the following day the troops were marching back to Canada, having destroyed excess ammunition and stores.[62] American losses on the ground were 38 killed, 64 wounded, and 20 missing. Officially British losses were 37 dead, 150 wounded, and 55 missing, although many more took the opportunity to desert.[63] On 15 September Macomb reported that over 300 had already come in, with more arriving daily, disgusted by the retreat and tempted by American offers of high pay.[64] Pring reached the British lines on 16 September under his parole and, reported Captain Wood, represented Macdonough as being "most delicate, honorable and kind. Thus [the Americans] are making themselves respected by their generosity of character, as well as their gallantry."[65]

Prevost tried to place the blame for defeat entirely on the naval action, alleging to Bathurst:

> The disastrous and unlooked for result of the Naval Contest by depriving me of the only means by which I could avail myself of any advantage I might gain, rendered a perseverance in the attack of the Enemy's position highly imprudent as well as hazardous. Under the circumstances I had to determine whether I should consider my own fame in gratifying the ardor of the troops in persevering in the attack, or consult the more substantial interests of my country by withdrawing the Army which was yet uncrippled for the security of the provinces.[66]

Certainly it is true that once the lake was lost he had little option but to withdraw, as he could not rely on tenuous road communications, which could easily have been cut now that control of the lake was lost.[67] Yet it is difficult to resist the conclusion that a more confident and aggressive commander would have quickly overrun Macomb's small force and forced the American squadron out of Plattsburgh Bay, either to confront the British in open waters or even to seek refuge elsewhere.[68] As Captain Wood noted later, the "unnecessary precipitancy of our retreat, or more properly speaking, our *flight* . . . is spoken of with disgust and indignation"; it caused needless loss of precious stores and men.[69] But Prevost was not a commander to take risks, and a sudden abundance of experienced troops could not transform him into a dynamic and effective field commander. Yeo did not agree that the naval battle was "unlooked for," and became convinced that Prevost had hurried Downie into a doomed venture. What was worse, argued Yeo, was the decision to break off the land assault.

> Had His Excellency taken the Batteries even after the Action it must have led to the recapture of our Vessels; if not those of the Enemy as it is Notorious, and a fact, that the Enemy's Vessels were so cut up and disabled as to be incapable of taking possession of our Ship and Brig for

> upwards of three hours after the Action; and as the wind was directly on Shore, our Ships could have run under the Works had they been in our possession.[70]

In due course, he would lay charges.

In the meantime, anglophone civilians angry at Prevost's cozy relationship with the *Canadiens* and the Catholic Church, were sending vicious reports back to London, such as this by Alicia Cockburn, who claimed that by using deception Prevost had "contrived to blind the eyes of Ministers," but

> his infamous behaviour can no longer be concealed . . . Had any man with common abilities been at the head of this Government, unbiased by the invidious counsels of fools and sycophants, we must long ago have taught the Yankees submission, & been at Peace. Such is the *decided opinion of every military man* in the Province, whether his rank be high or low, so glaring are the state of affairs at this moment.[71]

Many reports were even sillier than this, and Liverpool decided that the army had lost confidence in Prevost. On 30 October Wellington pointed out to Bathurst that it was "very obvious to me that you must remove Sir George Prevost. I see he has gone to war over trifles with the general officers I sent him, which are certainly the best of their rank in the army."[72] It suited the politician to take Prevost's detractors at their word and to blame the soldier for failures on the lakes, although in fact his own inability to provide adequate support during the first two years of the war was the ultimate cause of failure to secure offensive success now.[73] Wellington later wrote in Prevost's support to his former quartermaster-general, Major-General Sir George Murray, who was being sent out to replace Prevost with the local rank of lieutenant-general, saying that he admired "all that has been done by the military in America, as far as I understand it generally. Whether Sir George Prevost was right or wrong in his decision at Lake Champlain is more than I can tell; but of this I am very certain, he must equally have retired . . . after our fleet was beaten, and I am inclined to believe he was right."[74]

ON THE FAR side of the Atlantic the peace negotiations had been slowly getting under way at Ghent. Although the American peace commissioners arrived in June, they had to wait until August for the British to appear.

The two commissions presented a striking contrast: whereas the American one consisted of experienced and highly regarded political figures, the British were represented by relative unknowns, with no discretion to act independently, and Castlereagh was clearly repeating a mistake made in 1783 by Lord Shelburne. The American War was an embarrassment, diverting forces from Europe, and Castlereagh was preparing for the much more important Congress of Vienna, called to settle the peace of Europe.[75] Few Europeans were interested in the obscure American War; as Jonathan Russell noted, the "Great Congress at Vienna" overshadowed "the little congress at Ghent."[76] Britain was concluding over twenty years of conflict in Europe, and, as in the case of the origins of the war, her negotiations with the United States for its conclusion must be seen through this prism. After 1688 the rise of a modern financial system with central banking and harmonized national debt had provided the stability and strength to maintain long-term British dominance through the Royal Navy over all potential rivals. Britain was now economically exhausted, as evidenced by the massive national debt created by the Great War, the repayment of which would remain at well over 30 percent of government expenditure as late as the 1880s.[77] Having secured a dominant position in world trade, shipping, and finance, her statesmen were keen for the country to be left alone across her formal and informal empire for the serious business of making money.

The British commission was led by Admiral Lord James Gambier, best known for his bombardment of Copenhagen in 1807, but who had served during the War of Independence as commander-in-chief at Newfoundland and twice as an Admiralty lord.[78] His position on the commission confirmed to the British public that precious naval rights would not be compromised, a principle reinforced by the presence of William Adams LL.D., a well-known maritime law expert but of no other significance. The third member, Henry Goulburn, would go on to have a distinguished political career (and a town in New South Wales named after him), but at this stage he was an unproven young man serving as under-secretary for war and the colonies, and his delegation was under strict Foreign Office control.[79] A final gesture of indifference was the appointment of Anthony St. John Baker, who had made himself loathed while serving as an attaché in Washington, as secretary to the commission. Although Liverpool was anxious to be rid of the war, since a difficult conflict of indeterminate cost and duration would be a clog on British diplomacy in Europe at a time when all Castlereagh's objectivity and authority were never more needed, the British government was in no great hurry to negotiate; things were going well militarily in Europe and America, and America appeared threatened with financial ruin, insurrection, and slave revolt. In addition, Canadians insisted that there should be no peace unless Canada was secure from her predatory southern neighbour, and other voices regarded America as Britain's future trade rival who needed reining in.[80]

The variance between the status of the negotiating teams was mirrored in their opening positions. The Americans began with the instructions sent to Russia at the end of 1813, modified by those issued to Clay and Russell on their appointment. The only sine qua non was guaranteed to kill all discussion: the British must abandon impressment. And Monroe's suggestion that the British cede all or part of Canada was absurd, given the military situation.[81] Fortunately the question of impressment was partially solved before the first meeting on 8 August, the Americans having received word from Monroe that they could drop it as a sine qua non; and with the end of the war in Europe there was no point pressing an issue on which the British would not budge.[82] Goulburn declared that the British wished to discuss Indian lands, the Canadian boundary, and the American privilege of landing and drying fish on British shores, which had been granted since the end of the War of Independence. This move alarmed the Americans, who regarded the last issue as an established right, and as the Americans knew that they could not guarantee Indian lands, the following day both sides agreed to consult their governments.[83]

In this manoeuvre the British were trying to make up for repeated previous failures towards the Indians, but at the same time pursuing a long-standing policy of using them as a buffer. When Brock first met Tecumseh he had been instructed by Prevost to inquire what the Indians wanted in case of either victory or defeat, and the answer amounted to land rights.[84] Prevost backed these in his advice to Bathurst and suggested that British peace conditions should include a suitable Indian boundary.[85] Canadian merchants also supported this view, being afraid that driving the Indians from the country west and south of the Great Lakes would ruin the fur trade, and they urged that the return of territory north of the Ohio and west of the Sandusky should be a sine qua non of any treaty, although this would require the Americans to reverse every treaty they had signed with the northern Indians since 1784.[86] The merchants would have liked to reclaim the boundary that stood at the end of the War for Independence, but Prevost preferred the line established by the Treaty of Greenville in 1795, and Bathurst was hoping that a successful war would restore all of Michigan country to the Indians.[87] With matters thus complicated, Castlereagh issued instructions on 14 August to suggest that an

Indian barrier state be established in the Old Northwest, with its boundaries based on the Greenville line; that the Americans yield Fort Niagara and Sackets Harbor and eliminate naval forces on the Lakes; and that they cede land in eastern Maine to facilitate communications between Halifax and Quebec.[88] But the commissioners then exceeded their authority by presenting these proposals as a sine qua non, though officials in London saw it only as one possible means of protecting the Indians.[89]

These suggestions were completely unrealistic from the American point of view: the Greenville line had been superseded long ago, Harrison had obtained huge acreages of land now filled with pioneers, and, with Tecumseh's death, effective Indian resistance was over. The American commissioners knew how essential peace was for their country, but they also knew they could not alienate territory to get it. On 24 August the Americans flatly rejected these terms and prepared to leave.[90] Goulburn, who was taking the political lead on the British side, was not worried and also prepared for the short journey back across the Channel. But the British government was optimistic about events in North America and did not want to break off negotiations, hoping to be able to overwhelm the Americans with news of crushing victories.[91] In early September the British delivered another note, but once more the Americans refused to compromise on armaments on the lakes or on the Indian situation. At the same time, and with an eye to the proposed expedition against New Orleans, Britain sought to deny the legality of the Louisiana Purchase. But this ploy remained ambiguous, as Bathurst wrote to Ross on 6 September in regard to enlisting support among the French and Spanish populations: "You must give them clearly to understand that Great Britain cannot pledge herself to make the independence of Louisiana, or its restoration to the Spanish Crown, a *sine qua non* of peace with the United States."[92]

It was apparent to all that Britain's diplomatic freedom of action was hindered by the American imbroglio, and continental sympathy steadily mounted for the United States; French ports remained open to her privateers.[93] The shipping interest in particular wanted the war to end, as privateers were again starting to make inroads into British merchant shipping, mainly because since the end of the war in Europe, impatient ship-owners had begun eschewing the convoy system.[94] A resolution was passed at Glasgow on 10 September complaining that

> the number of American privateers with which our channels have been infested, the audacity with which they have approached our coasts, and

> the success with which their enterprise has been attended, have proved injurious to our commerce, humbling to our pride, and discreditable to the directors of the naval power of the British nation, whose flag of late waved over every sea and triumphed over every rival.[95]

As a consequence of such actions, insurance rates between Liverpool and Halifax rose to 30 percent, and the *Morning Chronicle* complained that with American privateers operating around the British Isles "we have been insulted with impunity."[96]

Among the most successful privateers that year was the *Prince de Neufchâtel,* belonging to the estate of Madame Flory Charreton, a wealthy Parisienne living in New York. Built there in 1813, she was armed and fitted as a privateer in Cherbourg, her captain, John Ordronaux, having previously commanded the French privateer *Marengo.* In early March she entered the English Channel and took nine prizes and in June made another dash against the Channel shipping, sending six prizes into Le Havre between the 4th and 10th. In September she took eight brigs, two sloops, and a cutter, acting "in sight of Lundy." She also captured the ship *Harmony* (4) and an English privateer; but the latter was allowed to escape, for, just at the moment of taking possession, a suspicious sail hove in sight which proved to be a large warship, and she was compelled to flee, one among seventeen successful escapes. A prize crew was placed in the *Harmony* to make for the United States, but a few days later she was recaptured. Then, instead of returning to a French port after her final cruise as had been her custom, she made directly for Boston, where she refitted and put to sea again early in October.[97]

On 14 September Liverpool commented to Bathurst that he would settle for retaining Fort Niagara and Michilimackinac, with any "reasonable article" for the Indians, although this stipulation fell some way short of full protection. He thought the Americans would settle for the pre-war situation and that delaying matters by throwing Sackets Harbor into the equation might allow time for favourable news to arrive from North America. Above all, negotiations should continue.[98] But the British people were increasingly weary of war. A great victory in Europe could not be celebrated fully until there was peace in North America; more pertinently, taxes could not come down until there was peace in North America. Landowners in particular baulked at continued high taxation; both they and the shipping interest urged the government not to try to humiliate the Americans, as doing so would only prolong hostilities now or postpone them to a later date.[99] Furthermore, it was clear that sharp differences of opinion had arisen in the vital Congress of Vienna. The American commissioners duly rejected an article in favour of the Indians, even though the British abandoned the demand for exclusive military possession of the Great Lakes; then news arrived of the burning of Washington, and Liverpool instructed the commissioners at Ghent to gain some territory around the lakes and in northern Maine, where many Loyalists still lived.[100] "We need not, therefore," wrote Liverpool to Bathurst on 30 September, "be in any great haste about our reply. Let them feast in the mean time upon Washington."[101]

The British claim to eastern Maine was that possession gave right, *uti possedetis;* but the Americans, demonstrating diplomatic shrewdness, refused to countenance it. The British had territorial interests all over the world; at this stage the Americans had them only at home. Britain was deeply entangled in European affairs, unlike the Americans, and territorial integrity was one thing all Americans agreed upon. During early October the British government softened its line regarding Indian lands. On 8 October Gambier delivered a note restoring the Indians to the position of 1811. Initially John Quincy Adams opposed this move, but his fellows brought him around, and the Americans agreed. It was a turning point and, after all, a small enough concession now that Tecumseh was dead. Ultimately the British would let down their allies once more.[102] Then, just as things seemed darkest for the Americans, came news of Ross's death and the sparing of Baltimore. Goulburn lamented that the failure to capture Baltimore "will be considered by the Americans as a victory, and not as an escape," and peace might otherwise have been achieved within a month. Now, "the result of our negotiations may be very different."[103]

British officials were already exasperated by American intransigence and refusal to make any concessions. Their doctrine, wrote Liverpool to Wellington, "will always be to keep what they acquire, but never to give up what they lose."[104] But British reaction to Prevost's repulse from Plattsburgh was far more significant than the news of Baltimore, which was but a minor setback, and to the continuing toll from privateers. On 11 October *Prince de Neufchâtel* encountered *Endymion,* under Captain Henry Hope RN, which was returning to blockade duties off New York. The privateer had sailed with 80 men but now, depleted by prize crews, had only 37; she tried to escape, but as night approached the two ships were becalmed a quarter-mile from each other. Under the cover of darkness, the British attacked with 111 men in five barges under Lieutenant Abel Hawkins RN. The operation was well planned, and all five boats attacked simultaneously from five directions. In the remarkable and desperate battle that followed, the crew of the privateer drove off their attackers, of whom 49 were killed (41 in a boat that was sunk, from which only 2 men were saved), 37 wounded, and 30 taken prisoner. Of the 37 defenders, 7 were killed and 24 wounded.[105]

In western Upper Canada starting on 22 October an American invasion force of about 700 men under Brigadier-General Duncan McArthur advanced rapidly along the Thames. McArthur intended to devastate the Thames and Grand River settlements and the region around the head of Lake Ontario which supplied British forces on the Niagara frontier. On his aggressive march to Oxford County, McArthur burned houses, barns, and mills. The Oxford Militia commander decided to join with the Norfolk Militia to defend the Grand River area, but when a traitor informed McArthur about this Canadian plan, he decided to move his men across the Grand River through Norfolk County to Lake Erie. McArthur reached the Grand River and on 6 November, after an unsuccessful attempt to force a crossing, attacked a body of some 150 Canadians comprising elements of the 1st and 2nd Norfolk, 1st Oxford, and 1st Middlesex Regiments of Militia, at Malcolm's Mills (Oakland). The Canadians put up a brief resistance but were overwhelmed and routed. The Americans continued their destructive foray on their withdrawal to Detroit.[106]

However, despite these minor successes the fundamental situation remained bleak for the Americans: when Congress ignominiously assembled in special session on 19 September 1814—forced to convene at the only government building left standing in Washington, the Post and Patent Office—it faced financial and political crisis. It could no longer rely on loans to pay for war, as banks in Philadelphia and Baltimore had suspended specie payments, with all banks outside New England soon forced to followed suit, while New Englanders were buying British government bills at a discount and sending specie to Canada to pay for smuggled goods. Treasury Secretary George W. Campbell reported the need for $50 million but had no idea how to raise it, and was replaced by Alexander J. Dallas of Philadelphia.[107] Though an able man, Dallas could do little in the circumstances, and the financiers who had underwritten the war thus far would no longer do so.[108] Dallas was forced to announce in November that the government could not pay the interest on its debt; taxes would have to rise, and even then it was difficult to imagine how the country could fight on for much longer.[109] Worse was to come when Monroe announced in October that conscription would have to be introduced to raise sufficient troops to fight the British reinforcements now arriving in North America, a measure that prompted fierce resistance, especially from New England representatives.[110]

Financial crisis was compounded by looming political crisis as New England opposition to the war threatened to develop into actual disunion.[111] In October, Governor Caleb Strong of Massachusetts called a special session of the state legislature and recommended the calling of a convention of neighbouring states, "the affinity of whose interests is closest," to discuss defence and revision of the federal constitution.[112] Bathurst hoped to promote a separate peace with New England and wrote to Sherbrooke in November and December about sending a secret emissary to Strong, instructing Sherbrooke "to concert measures with the commanders of H.M.'s naval forces to mitigate in every possible manner the pressure of war in favour of such states as shall have satisfactorily shewn a disposition to conclude an armistice with his Majesty."[113] But attacks farther south continued; in November Lieutenant William Lovell RN went up the Rappahannock River on *Severn* to attack 600 militia who had some field pieces at Farnham Church. "We took the town of Rappahannock, driving the enemy out of it, who ran away so fast that they dropped their colours, which we took. On one side of them, under the American eagle, was the motto, 'Death or Victory'; on the other, 'Down with the tyrants' . . . We then attacked the militia at Farnham Church, and captured two of their field pieces."[114]

Nothing eventually came of Sherbrooke's approach to New England, but agreement was reached to call a convention; Massachusetts would send twelve delegates to Hartford, Connecticut, which agreed to send seven delegates, while Rhode Island would send four. But New Hampshire was split on the issue, and Vermont declined, although two unofficial delegates came from the former and one from the latter.[115] The Hartford Convention that met from 15 December 1814 to 5 January 1815 proved more petulant than revolutionary as the extremists failed to take control, although by meeting in secret it raised fears of treachery.[116] Eventually it recommended only that individual states should be responsible for their own defence, for which they should receive a portion of federal taxes collected from within the state. It also recommended seven amendments to the U.S. Constitution that reflected their disgust with events since 1800, and the dominance of Virginia politicians such as Jefferson and Madison; but it was the final throw of the Federalists and would mark the beginning of their eclipse as a political force.[117] And American prospects for the new year were not good:

delighted though the public was at the salvation of Baltimore, success at Plattsburgh, and the regular army's brave showing on the Niagara front, it was also smarting in the wake of Washington's destruction, and the talk was of more and more British Peninsula veterans arriving to harass the coasts and borderlands, with eastern Maine already firmly occupied and trade having ground to a halt.[118]

17

New Orleans

Well, in eighteen and fourteen we took a little trip
along with Colonel Jackson down the mighty Mississip.
We took a little bacon and we took a little beans,
And we caught the bloody British near the town of New Orleans.

We fired our guns and the British kept a'comin'.
There wasn't nigh as many as there was a while ago.
We fired once more and they began to runnin'
down the Mississippi to the Gulf of Mexico.
—Jimmy Driftwood, "The Battle of New Orleans"*

JACKSON'S CREEK victories, like those of Harrison and Perry in the far Northwest, were too remote to have any strategic influence on the war against Britain: Canada remained firmly in British hands, and in those terms the Creek war was an irrelevant sideshow.[1] But the British continued to expect assistance from that quarter for their expedition to New Orleans, fed by faulty intelligence from their agent, Captain George Woodbine RM, who did not know that the Choctaws, Chickasaws, and Cherokees were already siding with the United States.[2] Despite instructions to the contrary, Jackson sought to impose a severe peace on all the Creeks in place of the conciliatory terms suggested by the War Department, including upon those who had sided with the United States, claiming that they had "forfeited all right to the Territory we have conquered."[3]

On 9 August Jackson forced the Creeks to sign the Treaty of Fort Jackson, which compelled them to relinquish more than 23 million acres, or more than half of their homeland, and to move farther west.[4] His superiors were infuriated, but the frontiersmen roared their approval, and Jackson's massive land grab ensured that his reputation began to take on legendary status. And it was as well for the U.S. government that an efficient general officer was now in position to defend the Gulf Coast. Two days later he left Fort Jackson to descend the Coosa and Alabama Rivers, and in eleven days reached Mobile, 400 miles away. On 27 August he heard of a British presence at Pensacola and immediately set about mobilizing militia from the governors of the region; reports left him in no doubt that the British intended to attack Mobile and New Orleans, despite the supposed strict secrecy in which their plans were being hatched.[5] The British expectation of capturing a weak and badly organized Gulf coast did not take account of Jackson's energy and drive. At Mobile he sent 160 regulars under Major William Lawrence to garrison Fort Bowyer at the mouth of Mobile Bay. Although it was not a strong fort, with only 12- and 9-pounders and a couple of larger pieces, Lawrence put it into the best possible state of defence.[6]

From the very beginning of the war the British Cabinet had been aware of the strategic possibilities offered by control of the Mississippi delta and its colossal hinterland.[7] As early as April 1812, even before war was declared, Cochrane had noted that the place "where the Americans are most vulnerable is New Orleans and in Virginia," and accordingly had proposed schemes which were fully discussed before he left London to assume command at Halifax.[8] With the end of the war in Europe, the government contemplated sending a large force from the south of France in early summer, but this plan was abandoned because of continuing difficulties in Europe and tension with Russia.[9] But Major Nicolls and his party landed at the mouth of the Apalachicola on 13 August to find that the British agent had gone to Pensacola to work with the Creeks taking refuge there; Captain Percy followed on, and, finding the Spanish nervous of American attack, Nicolls put his Royal Marines in the fort and issued a highblown appeal to the inhabitants of Louisiana for help "in liberating from a faithless imbecile government, your paternal soil." He even urged the people of Kentucky to rise against the United States on behalf of the British.[10]

On 3 September Percy dispatched Captain Nicholas Lockyer RN of HM Sloop *Sophie* (18) to Barataria, about 60 miles south-west of New Orleans, to try to enlist the help of the pirates and smugglers based there under their colourful leader Jean Lafitte.[11] Before 1810 the Baratarians were sailors and fishermen of little consequence who made a modest living avoiding government duties and smuggling through French and Spanish domains.[12] The prohibition on importing slaves—imposed in Louisiana four years before it was imposed nationally—prompted the previously small-time Baratarian smugglers to become big-time bootleggers of slaves.[13] Between 1804 and 1810 the population of New Orleans had doubled, mostly with French refugees fleeing the slave revolt in Haiti via Cuba, or Guadeloupe and Martinique, recently seized by Britain.[14] In the summer of 1810 Lafitte became the Baratarians' agent in New Orleans, and as an efficient businessman fluent in English, French, Spanish, and Italian, with "a conscience as elastic as any politician could wish for," he was soon chosen as their leader.[15] With his brothers, Pierre and Dominique, he held sway over a successful business enterprise protected in the bay by a battery of heavy guns.

The Lafittes were unscrupulous scoundrels, in no way patriotic Americans, who took defenceless American prizes as happily as any others and never applied for letters of marque to attack British shipping.[16] The gang threw in their lot with the Americans only because they realized that the offer the British were making was, in fact, an ultimatum; the British were finally enforcing Spanish authority in the area on behalf of their ally after the Baratarians had taken letters of marque from the revolutionary party at Cartagena, the first city in New Granada to declare independence from Spain.[17] The Baratarians openly sold their loot in New Orleans, in flagrant disregard of U.S. laws and neutrality, and by 1813 Lafitte and his gang were outlaws fighting a minor war with Governor William C. Claiborne and the federal authorities.[18] Mawkish sentimentalists may try to justify their behaviour, but piracy involved almost unmitigated and revolting cruelty.[19] With his brother Pierre now in gaol, Jean Lafitte must have viewed the British offer as a great stroke of luck; he promised to give them an answer within two weeks, and they departed. But Lafitte also realized that his freebooting lifestyle depended upon continued U.S. control of the Gulf. The British approach enabled him to offer Claiborne his services in return for "an act of oblivion for himself and all his adherents."[20] This proposal was forwarded to Jackson, who regarded the Baratarians to be "hellish banditti," and on 16 September, led by Master-Commandant Daniel Todd Patterson USN and Colonel Robert Ross, the Americans carried out the long-planned break-up of the pirate settlement; they encountered little resistance, taking several privateers and prizes and around eighty prisoners.[21]

On the same day that the Americans took action against the pirates, Percy sailed from Pensacola to attack Fort Bowyer with HM Ships *Hermes* (22) and *Carron* (20) and the sloops *Sophie* and *Childers* (18), carrying Nicolls with

60 Royal Marines, 12 Royal Marine Artillerymen, and 130 Indians. They arrived in the vicinity of Mobile Bay, where Nicolls landed 9 miles from the fort the following day. But because of contrary winds, Percy could not pass the Mobile Bar before the 15th, when the Americans saw them approaching under full sail, although only *Hermes* and *Sophie* managed to get into position before the wind failed. They anchored close to the fort and opened fire at about 4 P.M. After heavy firing *Hermes* had her bowsprit shot away, swung round towards the fort, and grounded. She suffered heavily from American fire until Percy eventually got her around to bring the larboard broadside to bear. When she tried to get away shortly after 6 P.M., her sails and rigging were so badly shot up that she could not make it, and she once more grounded. Her crew was taken off in boats, and she was fired at 7:20 P.M., later blowing up. The British had lost 32 killed and 37 wounded, including Nicolls in the leg and head, being blinded in the right eye; the Americans lost only 4 killed and 5 wounded.[22] More importantly, the Americans had dealt a severe blow to Cochrane's plans for taking control of the region and capturing New Orleans.

On 6 September Cochrane and Bathurst had sent Ross instructions, although he would not get to read them, and in the middle of the month reinforcements set out from Plymouth under Major-General John Keane. Shortly afterwards it was also decided to send the 40th (2nd Somersetshire) Regiment—another Peninsula veteran unit—as additional reinforcement. As Sergeant William Lawrence recalled, it "can better be imagined than I can describe in what sort of spirit we began this other war, scarcely having slipped out of one field before we were launched into another."[23] But an accident to one of their transports delayed them, and they did not depart Cork until 2 November. The 43rd (Monmouthshire) Regiment (Light Infantry) was on the way, however. "Shipboard is the place of all others for arguments," noted Captain John Cooke. In spite of its nominal Welsh affiliation, the regiment was made up mostly of Scots and Irish, and their Celtic arguments were usually parochial in nature.

> I have often joined in and enjoyed much mirth and laughter at some of the vehement and feudal like arguments and discussions between the Caledonian and Hibernian companions of "voyages and travel": . . . The highlanders accused the lowlanders of being neutrals, and worse than *common Englishmen;* the lowlanders retorted on the highlanders, calling them the bare-a[rsed] cattle stealers from the mountains; the Hibernians protested that the Scots were renegades from the green isle, and vice

versa . . . Every legend, fable of historical record was ripped up before and after the Norman conquest.[24]

By now news of the brief occupation of Washington had reached London, and the expedition was becoming ever more elaborate. Originally a force of 2,200 men sent to Bermuda under Major-General John Lambert was expected to enable Ross to continue operations in the Chesapeake area, but news of Ross's death arrived on 17 October together with Cochrane's plans to sail into the Gulf.[25] Lambert was ordered to proceed directly to Jamaica, and Major-General Sir Edward Pakenham, Wellington's brother-in-law, was chosen to command the land component instead and to follow the instructions sent earlier to Ross.[26] Pakenham had served under the Duke in Spain and had proved himself in battle; he "might not be the brightest genius," said Wellington, "but my partiality does not lead me astray when I tell you he is one of the best we have."[27] Pakenham was confident and refused to see the impossibility of his position. The aim was to gain command of the mouth of the Mississippi, which would deprive the back country of maritime access, and to obtain some important possessions for use as a bargaining counter. The details of whether or not to proceed to New Orleans were originally to be left to the discretion of Ross and Cochrane, but the decision would obviously now fall to Cochrane alone.[28] Had Fort Bowyer fallen in September, it is likely that the Mobile approach would have been taken. Ross had explicit instructions to refuse joint operations that he considered militarily unfeasible, but pending Pakenham's arrival his temporary replacement, the very inexperienced Major-General John Keane, had no such instructions.[29]

The original plans seemed sound but were constantly undermined and changed; thus the whole expedition came about in piecemeal fashion, without effective central planning or control, relying to a great extent on the judgement and decisions of naval officers, who both grossly overestimated the willingness and ability of the Indians to provide support and grossly underestimated American powers of resistance; all of which was conducted without proper military consultation, leaving Pakenham to do all he reasonably could in the circumstances.[30] As the plan unfolded by accretion and wishful thinking, Cochrane gained the first intimation that events might not run smoothly. In late September and October Jackson continued to prepare to resist a British assault and chose to safeguard Mobile and Fort Bowyer by seizing Pensacola, despite instructions from Monroe forbidding such a move.

On 23 October, the day he left Mobile, Monroe wrote to Jackson to say that nothing should be done to risk war with Spain.[31] But it seems from the tardy way these dispatches were prepared and sent that this order was not to be taken seriously: the government wanted an attack on Pensacola, but it should be Jackson's personal responsibility.[32]

This shrewd move would ensure that there was no flocking of Indians to British colours, but it would nevertheless entail a gamble. Jackson, with three regular regiments, some Mississippi dragoons, and a large party of Choctaw Indians, first went north to meet reinforcements, and met up with Brigadier-General John Coffee, who brought 2,000 Tennesseans with him. Aware that he was acting without authorization, Jackson wrote to Monroe that he would end the Indian war by cutting off all foreign influence, and that once he had ensured the region's safety he could set off for New Orleans, to which he had already ordered the movement of 5,500 Kentuckians and Tennesseans. On 6 November 1814 he led his forces across the international boundary, reaching Pensacola that evening.[33] Following their abortive attack on Fort Bowyer, the British had returned to the Apalachicola River, where they received a letter from the Spanish governor of Pensacola warning of imminent American attack. Arriving at Fort Barrancas on 31 October, they found the place in a state of ruin, and the governor would not cooperate in strengthening it. Gordon of the *Seahorse* was forced to make a hurried departure in the face of Jackson's advance, after which the British blew up the fort and departed in disgust.[34]

Despite his wounds, Nicolls remained in the vicinity and built a small fort at the mouth of the Apalachicola River at Prospect Bluff. From there he sent small parties to harass the Georgia frontiers, where by the war's end he attracted to the British side almost 2,000 people, including Seminole and Creek Indians and many escaped slaves.[35] However, by seizing Pensacola itself Jackson had ensured that the British would have to make a direct assault on New Orleans and could not outflank it.[36] Built in 1718, New Orleans lay 105 miles upstream from the mouth of the Mississippi and could be approached either by the river or, by shallow-draught vessels, via Lakes Borgne to the east and Pontchartrain to the north. The country between was cut by numerous rivers, creeks, and bayous, making for a difficult approach whichever route was chosen. In 1814 New Orleans lay 4 miles from Lake Pontchartrain; its still largely French-speaking population of 24,552 included 10,824 slaves, and the city was considered distinctly unreliable by the U.S. authorities.[37] "The War of the U.S. is very unpopular with us," wrote John Windship, a transplanted New Englander, in early 1814. Although the French and Spanish residents were called up for militia service, they "absolutely refused to be marched" and "declared themselves liege subjects of France or Spain."[38]

Originally the British plan was to mount the expedition from Barbados following a diversionary attack against Georgia and South Carolina to draw away the defence. But not only did the Admiralty fail to mount this diversion; in the interests of economy it shifted the advance base to Jamaica, much closer to New Orleans, thus effectively giving away the whole show. Cochrane had also recommended purchasing *schuyts*—shallow-draught vessels designed for the Dutch Frisian coast—but instead the Admiralty hired or purchased local small craft of too great draught at West Indian ports, further scuppering security. Equally, Cochrane's requests for warm clothing for the West Indian regiments were ignored.[39]

British troops from the Chesapeake arrived at their rendezvous in Negril Bay, Jamaica, at the beginning of November, and Keane's force from Britain some three weeks later, bringing the total number of troops to hand to over 6,000. Cochrane appears to have begun to have doubts, especially with news of the failure at Fort Bowyer and the absence of Indian support; but despite complaining to the Admiralty that everyone in Jamaica seemed to know all about the expedition to New Orleans and the shortage of flat-bottomed and shallow-draught vessels for negotiating the difficult waters that lay all around the city, he decided to proceed all the same. Accompanied by Keane on the *Tonnant* he set out on 27 November for the Gulf of Mexico and arrived on 8 December at the Chandeleur Islands, near the entrance to Lake Borgne, where he was joined three days later by the bulk of the fleet under Malcolm. On 5 December he had issued a proclamation offering belated support to the Creeks. Addressed to "the Great and Illustrious Chiefs of the Creek and Other Indian Nations," it asked for assistance and offered "the restoration of those lands of which the People of Bad Spirit have basely robbed them."[40] When some pro-British chiefs came aboard, Edward Codrington, who received news of his promotion to rear-admiral on 9 October, thought them poor creatures to have for allies; Cappachamico, Hopsi (or Ferryman), and the Prophet Francis (Hillis Hadjo) wore one layer of clothes over another and had tied several pairs of trousers around their waists without climbing into the legs. When they then discarded their impressive native headdress in favour of gold-laced cocked hats and sergeants' jackets, he thought they looked like "dressed up apes."[41]

Jackson returned on 19 November to Mobile, where he left the three regular regiments; three days later he left for New Orleans, inspecting possible landing sites along the way. He arrived on 2 December, dirty and emaciated from long illness, but immediately began organizing the defences with great energy.[42] After making detailed reconnaissances and finding what Marquis James called "neither land nor water, but a geological laboratory where land [was] being made," he decreed that all bayous leading from the Gulf to the city be obstructed and batteries erected at given points.[43] The Mississippi River approach was guarded by twenty-eight 24-pounders at Fort St. Philip, some 60 miles downriver from the city, while at English Town, 18 miles away, there was supposed to be another battery of nine guns, although this was not in use. He also began improving the city's defences, including the eastern approaches between the lakes by way of the Gentilly Road, which formed a defile where it ran narrowly between a bayou and swamps.[44] Given the nature of the ground, any British attack would have to be made on a narrow frontage, and it would be difficult to achieve surprise or speed; Jackson could also hope to hinder any approach via Lake Borgne with gunboats stationed there.[45]

Many panegyrics have been written about Jackson's masterful defence, and while his forceful and skilful leadership was indeed hugely important, these accounts overlook the geographical inconsistencies and British blunders—obstinacy being a prime factor—that turned defeat into disaster once Jackson had blunted the initial advance. It is likely that had the British gained the assistance of the Lafitte brothers they would have chosen the route via Lake Barataria, which seemed the best approach; but instead Cochrane and Keane decided to disembark at Bayou Bienvenu, 15 miles from the city at the western end of Lake Borgne. Many waterways pointed wet fingers towards the city, and route selection through vast acreages of marsh and swamp was only one difficulty; but once Bayou Bienvenu had been chosen, involving a 62-mile journey to the debarkation point, defeat was practically assured, since the troops would have to be transported using the shallow-draught boats that were in such short supply. Only 2,000 men—half the force—could be carried in one lift, and such a calculation takes no account of the stores and provisions they would need; thus the possibilities of a rapid build-up and of achieving surprise were reduced to nothing.[46] Even reaching the landing site brought little relief; tall reeds obstructed movement, and only after engineers had cut a path through these "trembling prairies" could the guns be dragged across the soggy ground on matted reeds.[47] And before any of this could be achieved, the American gunboats had to be cleared away.

On the night of 12 December the fleet's barges and pinnaces were deployed with 1,000 seamen and marines under Lockyer and went in search of the gunboats. Upon sighting this force on the morning of 13 December, the American flotilla commander, Lieutenant Thomas ap Catesby Jones USN, at first thought they were disembarking troops and only some hours later realized they were coming for his five Jeffersonian gunboats, numbered 5, 23, 156, 162, and 163.[48] He tried to sail away, but the British rowed patiently after him in over forty ship's boats armed with forty-three guns. They closed in on the morning of the 14th after a thirty-six-hour chase. About 10 A.M. the British paused for breakfast, then fifty minutes later rowed directly towards the Americans into a storm of round- and grapeshot. Around noon they boarded the American flagship and turned her guns on the other boats, and by 12:40 P.M. all five had been captured, together with an armed sloop that sought to join the fray. British losses were 19 killed and 75 wounded, including Lockyer, to 6 Americans killed and 35 wounded, including ap Catesby Jones; but the lake was secured.[49]

The news of the loss of the gunboats came as a great shock to the city. On 16 December, still awaiting his Tennessee and Kentucky reinforcements, Jackson placed the city under martial law and also called out the Louisiana militia despite suffering severe anxiety over supplies, particularly arms and ammunition.[50] On 17 December Claiborne issued a proclamation suspending court proceedings against Lafitte's pirates if they would serve the United States; Judge Dominick Hall promptly agreed to release those Baratarians who agreed to enlist and granted Jean, who had been in hiding, a pass to enter the city.[51] Lafitte was by now desperate; his headquarters had been raided and burned, his ships had been sequestered, and his fortune was all but gone. If Louisiana fell to the British he and his men would be lucky to escape with their lives; but if the Americans won, his lawyers told him, and if he could play some dramatic part in their victory, they might contrive a pardon and the possibility of recovering his treasure.[52] On 18 December he called on Jackson and said that he had a substantial cache of powder and ammunition and 1,000 men willing to fight. Reluctantly, Jackson agreed to accept his services.[53]

Fortunately for Jackson, his position improved on 22 December, when Coffee arrived with 1,250 men, soon followed by Major-General William Carroll with 2,500, a squadron of Mississippi dragoons and some Baratarian pirates. Jackson still awaited 2,500 Kentuckians, but he did have parts of the 3rd, 7th, and the newly raised 39th and 44th U.S. Infantry with some artillerymen.[54] Although Jackson still did not know where the British were planning to land, they were severely hampered by the lack of boats. Cochrane decided to land first on a swampy deserted point near the mouth of the Pearl River: the Isle-aux-Poix, "which we christened 'Lobs-scouse Island,'" recalled Corporal

Brown of the 21st Fusiliers, "it being our chief diet during our stay there," but where the men suffered from heavy frosts and strong winds.[55] At the same time, they reconnoitred Bayou Bienvenu to within 6 miles of the city, guided by Spanish fishermen and unhampered by the Louisiana militia, which arrived only after they had finished. On 22 December they had assembled a force of 1,800 organized as a light brigade under Colonel William Thornton, comprising the 4th Regiment, 85th Light Infantry, and 3rd/95th Rifles, which set off in the fleet boats and reached the bayou the following morning, where they captured the American outpost after some trouble in the shallow waters. They were able to land 5 miles upstream unobserved by the Americans, putting them some 3 miles from the Mississippi in reed-covered country deeply cut by numerous ditches.[56] The engineers quickly bridged these and cut a path, enabling the troops to advance to the plantation of Brigadier-General Jacques Villeré of the Louisiana militia, where they captured his son and militia company, although the son, Major Gabriel Villeré, soon escaped and took the word to Jackson.[57] They then moved to cut the main road to the city, some 7 miles distant. Had they pressed on immediately, the city would probably have fallen; but the men were very tired and the extent of American defences unknown, and Keane believed a prisoner called Joseph Ducros who exaggerated the defenders' numbers, and instead the British made camp.[58]

At noon on 23 December Jackson heard of the British approach and with characteristic decisiveness moved immediately. Leaving Carroll's Tennesseans to cover Gentilly Road, and supported by the schooner *Carolina* (14) in the river, he led 900 regulars, 550 mounted riflemen, and 650 Louisiana and Mississippi militia, including 200 free African-Americans, to attack the British at 8 P.M.[59] Already many of the British were asleep, and, as Seaman G. Raymond noted, the *Carolina* "did a deal of mischief on that night. The troops had not been landed above two hours, and were just in the act of cooking some victuals, when this vessel opened a galling fire, and a large party of volunteers and regulars attacked in front."[60] The confused struggle in darkness was made more so by gunsmoke and a light fog, and many men fired on friends or blundered into enemies and were captured. In hand-to-hand fighting conducted mostly in small groups, the Americans were finally driven off around midnight, when British reinforcements began to appear. British losses were 46 killed, 167 wounded, and 64 missing to 24 Americans killed, 115 wounded, and 74 missing.[61]

Next morning Thornton wanted to press on, but the cautious Keane chose to await the rest of the army, not realizing that his force, now 4,700 strong, greatly outnumbered Jackson's 1,900. Jackson, meanwhile, retired 2 miles to a shallow canal stretching about 1,000 yards from the river to a cypress swamp and began digging in. Much of the open ground in front of this position was inundated, although after a week the river began to fall and this ground to dry out. But the British were occupied in the gruelling business of bringing forward more men and supplies, and Keane's failure to press forward gave Jackson time to prepare his position, while his sharpshooters ensured the British were under constant pressure.[62] On the 25th, as gales and sleet continued, one boat containing 37 men and 2 officers of the 14th (The Duchess of York's Own) Regiment of (Light) Dragoons was surprised and captured as the oarsmen were taking a breather in the creek. But British morale was improved by the arrival of Pakenham, who was accompanied by Colonel Alexander Dickson, Wellington's Peninsula artillery commander.[63]

The first task was to remove the *Carolina,* which was achieved from a prepared battery on 27 December with heated shot: she went on fire and blew up, while her sister, *Louisiana* (22), which had come up in support, had to warp herself out of range.[64] Next morning the British advanced in two columns under Keane and Major-General Sir Samuel Gibbs, who had arrived with Pakenham, driving in the American piquets to within some 800 yards of the main position, which Pakenham was surprised to find so close by and already studded with emplacements.[65] The American gunners and *Louisiana*—which fired over 700 rounds that day—gave the columns and Pakenham serious pause for thought.[66] The troops lay on the ground to avoid the worst effects of the fire before Pakenham withdrew 2 miles and brought up additional guns, including two 18-pounders that had been labouriously floated and dragged to the plantation; but he wanted eight more, and the strain on British communications now became apparent, as did the lack of suitable clothing and equipment. "It is difficult to express how much the black troops suffered from the excessive cold," noted Colonel Dickson, "which they are so little accustomed to, and also so improvided with warm clothing to protect them from [it]. Several have died from mere cold and the whole appear quite torpid and unequal to any exertion; I am convinced that little or no benefit will be derived from these troops while exposed to such cold."[67]

In some places the Bayou Bienvenu was so narrow that boats could not be rowed but had to be pushed along with oars in the muddy banks. Herculean efforts brought up the British guns by 31 December, but only the smallest amount of ammunition could be provided, and all the while the American position was improved with cotton bales as well as earth. Jackson extended his line a quarter of a mile into the swamp to prevent its being turned, and ordered the construction by some 900 slaves of two more lines before the city. Most importantly, he added new batteries of guns to his main line, some manned by sailors from *Carolina,* to include a 32-pounder, three 24-pounders, an 18-pounder and numerous smaller pieces, together with a flanking battery on the far bank of the river with a 24-pounder and two 12-pounders under Brigadier-General David Morgan, although this position was left to start rather late and was never completed.[68] British batteries built of sugar casks were set up that night, but they were far from satisfactory, although two columns of infantry were formed to exploit any breaches that might appear. But when dawn broke misty on 1 January 1815, the British could not see the Americans drawn up behind their earthworks in parade order for a review, and it took until 10 A.M. to clear sufficiently.[69] A three-hour bombardment produced no effect, and the British ammunition supply was used up; Dickson blamed the hastily erected batteries, but essentially failure was due to accurate American counter-fire that dismounted five British guns and disabled eight more, so that Pakenham had to give the humiliating order to withdraw. That evening the assault was abandoned and the guns dragged back through the mud, with British losses totalling 23 killed and 41 wounded to 11 Americans killed and 23 wounded.[70]

Pakenham decided to wait for reinforcements under Lambert that included Peninsula veterans of the 7th Regiment (Royal Fusiliers) and 43rd Light Infantry.[71] They were expected at any time and in fact arrived that day in the fog-bound anchorage. As the road forward was improved and ammunition and supplies brought up, Pakenham also had the Villeré canal improved to bring boats that would enable troops to cross the river and attack the flanking batteries. Meanwhile Jackson received reinforcements in the form of 2,250 Tennesseans and Kentuckians under Brigadier-General John Thomas who were, it seemed, "the worst provided body of men, perhaps, that ever went 1,500 miles from home to help a sister state."[72] They were lamentably equipped, having only one camp kettle to over 80 men and no other cooking equipment, tents, or blankets, while their clothes were so ragged they had to hold them together with their hands, and only a third were armed. Jackson was incredulous: "I have never in my life," he reportedly said, "seen a Kentuckian without a gun, a pack of cards and a jug of whiskey."[73] The Louisiana legislature had to vote $6,000 to relieve their distress, and private sources raised another $12,000. But the city could find arms for only 500 of them; Jackson ordered those with arms to join Morgan, although only 250 managed to do so.[74]

Lambert's force finally reached the British main position on 6 January, but digging the canal meant another day's delay, and operations did not begin until the night of 7th, with the main assault scheduled for the following morning.[75] That afternoon the 7th Fusiliers and 43rd Light Infantry were reviewed within artillery range of the Americans. "A more foolish measure was possibly never perpetrated," complained the 7th's historian,

> for beside giving extra time to the Americans to consolidate their works, it exposed the increased strength of the British. But with the infatuation that marked the operations from first to last the greatest display of pomp was resorted to. The music played, the sun shone brilliantly, and every member of the two regiments was in the highest spirits of his chance of being led forward to attack.[76]

Almost a month had now passed since the fleet arrived at the mouth of Lake Borgne, and over two weeks since Jackson first heard of the British arrival at Bayou Bienvenu; two weeks in which he had received reinforcements and established and fortified his position. He now had some 3,500 men, with another 1,000 in reserve, holding a line some 1,500 yards across anchored on river and swamp, consisting of a parapet 5 feet high punctuated by batteries of heavy guns, in front of which lay a ditch 10 feet wide and 4 feet deep, commanding a wide open field of fire.[77] Throughout the war American militia had proven no match for British regulars in the open; but when defending fortified positions they had a clear record going back to Bunker Hill in 1775 and repeated on numerous occasions since. Jackson's one weak point was the batteries on the far side of the river, which had been sited to fire in front of the main position and not for local defence. A line to protect them had been started but was held only by some 450 Louisiana militia, and he learned only on the morning of 7 January that the British were extending the canal. Although he ordered 400 Kentuckians to reinforce the position, he had no boats to send them by water, so they had to march back to the city to cross the river.[78]

The British plan was for a night move by boat to attack the batteries across the river by Thornton's light brigade. For this boats had to be dragged out of the Villeré canal through the cut in the levee and into the river; simultaneously a frontal assault in two columns would be launched against Jackson's line supported by six 18-pounders, the main effort to be made on the right towards the Tennessee and Kentucky militia with 2,200 men of the 4th, 21st,

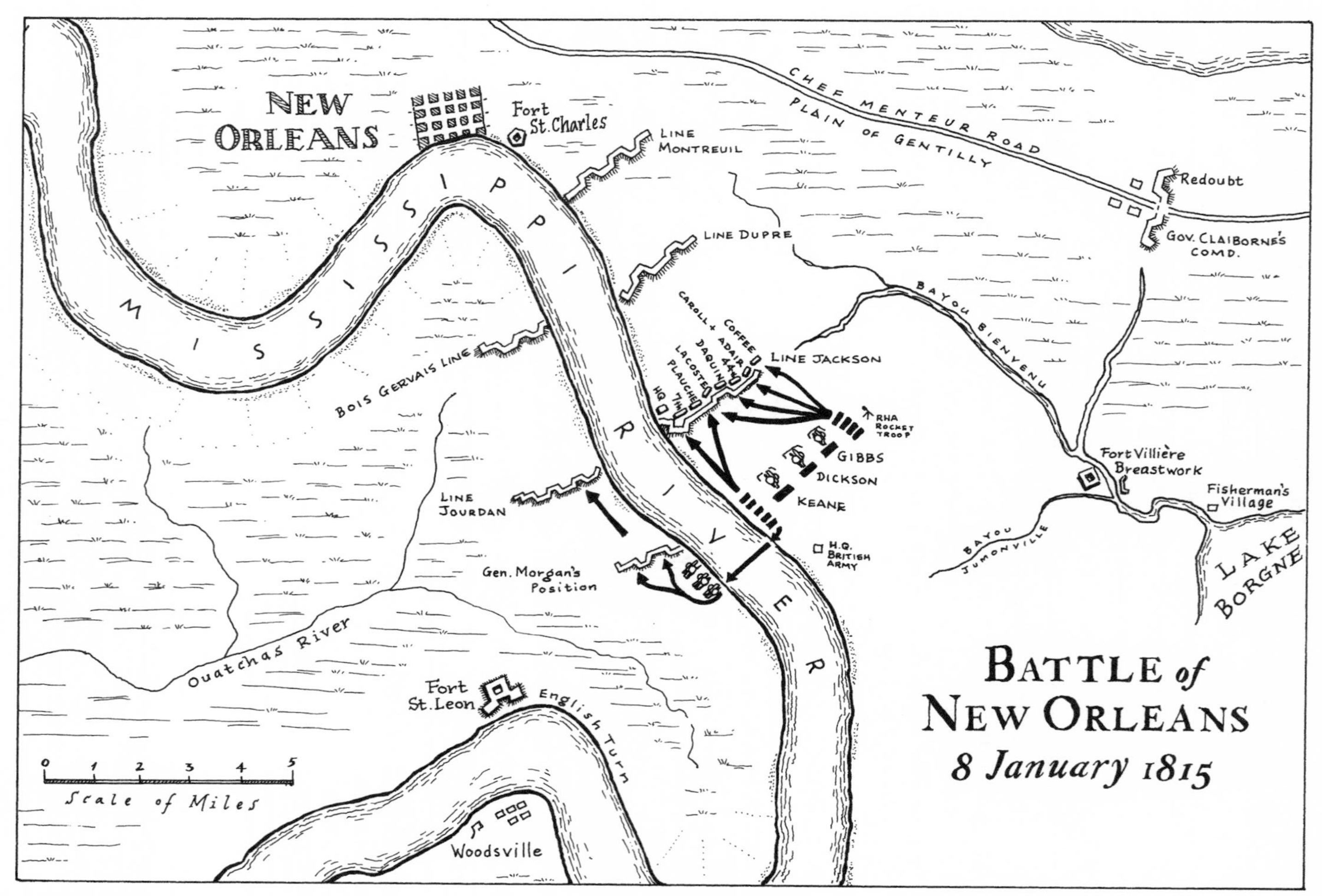

Battle of New Orleans
8 January 1815
New Orleans
Fort St. Charles
Line Montreuil
Chef Menteur Road
Plain of Gentilly
Redoubt
Gov. Claiborne's Comd.
Line Dupre
Bayou Bienvenu
Line Jackson
Coffee
Caroll + Adair
44th
Daquin
Lacoste
Plauche
7th
HQ
RHA Rocket Troop
Gibbs
Dickson
Keane
H.Q. British Army
Fort Villière
Breastwork
Fisherman's Village
Bayou Jumonville
Lake Borgne
Mississippi River
Bois Gervais Line
Line Jourdan
Gen. Morgan's Position
Ouatchas River
Fort St. Leon
English Turn
Woodsville
0 1 2 3 4 5
Scale of Miles

and 44th Regiments with three companies of 3rd/95th Rifles under Gibbs.[79] Lieutenant-Colonel the Honourable Thomas Mullins of the 44th Regiment, a captain holding a brevet lieutenant-colonelcy, was especially unhappy about the plan: his unit was to lead, carrying fascines to throw in the 4-foot ditch, followed by a second wave with scaling ladders to climb the American earthworks, and he believed his regiment was being sacrificed to earn glory for others.[80] On the left another column of 1,200 men would advance under Keane, comprising the 93rd (Sutherland) Highlanders, newly arrived from garrisoning the Cape of Good Hope, supported by two companies of the 95th and two of the 43rd Light Infantry.[81] Meanwhile the 1st West India Regiment would skirmish in the swamp. Keane was to keep the 7th Fusiliers and remainder of the 43rd, another 1,200 men, in reserve.[82] "Those men will storm anything," said Pakenham, "but, indeed, so can the others, and when we are in New Orleans, I can depend upon Lambert's reserve."[83]

Many of the British troops had been shipped directly from Europe and were due for discharge at the end of their seven years' service, something they pointed out to their officers the night before the attack. At daybreak the fields in front of the American position were covered by a heavy mist. Into this the artillery of both sides opened a rapid fire, which began before the river crossing was completed; the passage of the boats out of the canal had taken longer than expected. The British columns advanced into the smoke and mist as along the American line, safe and snug behind their parapet, drummers beat "Yankee Doodle." Gibbs's column marched almost directly towards an 18-pounder battery and was raked by others from both sides, together with fire from the American infantry. Pakenham's insistence that they advance in column of companies maximized the effect of American fire, and Gibbs was mortally wounded. Vincent Nolte, a civilian who witnessed the attack, saw that the cypress woods were filled with riflemen who were protected by thick bushes, and dealt death from behind them to the British platoons whose officers were falling fast but saw no enemy.[84]

On the right the British were soon driven back in disorder, as Sergeant John Cooper of the 7th Fusiliers recalled:

> At the word "Forward!" the two lines approached the ditch under a murderous discharge of musketry; but crossing the ditch and scaling the parapet were found impossible without ladders. These had been prepared but the regiment that should have carried them [the 44th] left them behind, and thereby caused, in a few minutes, a dreadful loss of

17.1. Coffee's Tennesseans at New Orleans. *Battle of New Orleans,* wood engraving by Andrews after H. Billings from *Ballou's Pictorial,* 1856. Anne S. K. Brown Military Collection, Brown University Library.

> men and officers; while the enemy suffered little, being ensconced behind the parapet.[85]

Crucially, Mullins had led his regiment past the redoubt where the assault stores were kept and failed to oversee their collection, while his pessimism affected his men. It was half an hour before anybody realized this astonishing blunder; they went back the 500 yards to collect their equipment but returned only after the battle had started, and Mullins was not with them.[86] But on the left the light companies drove the defenders out of Jackson's forward redoubt, although they could go no farther. The 93rd Highlanders charged forward to the strains of "Monymusk" played by their pipers,[87] and Lieutenant C. H. Gordon described how within 150 yards of the American lines

> a most destructive and murderous fire was opened on our Column of round, grape, musquetry, rifle and buckshot along the whole course and length of their line in front, as well as on our left flank. Not daunted, however, we continued our advance which in one minute would have carried us into their ditch, when we received a peremptory order to halt—this was indeed the moment of trial. The officers and men being as it were mowed down by ranks.[88]

The column twice re-formed and tried to resume the advance, and Lieutenant-Colonel Robert Dale was killed.

Colonel Dickson described how when Gibbs's column stopped, Pakenham was watching from some distance behind and

> galloped up to the head of the column exclaiming "Lost from want of Courage," and was trying to encourage the troops on, which he succeeded in doing for a few yards, when he was wounded in the thigh and his horse killed, and Major [Duncan] Macdougall [Pakenham's aide-de-camp], having extricated and raised him from the ground, he was in the act of mounting Macdougall's horse when he was hit again, and fell into Macdougall's arms ejaculating a few words, which were the last he spoke, and he expired as he was conveyed to General Gibbs's house.[89]

The troops fell back 250 yards as Lambert brought forward the reserve, and held their position.

The men were ordered to lie down, but great damage was caused by the guns, and Keane was among those severely wounded. "For *five* hours the enemy plied us with grape and roundshot," recalled Captain John Cooke; "some of the wounded lying in the mud or on the wet grass, managed to crawl away; but every now and then some unfortunate man was lifted off the ground by round shot, and lay killed or mangled."[90] Sergeant Cooper recalled that a man on his right

> was smashed to pieces by a cannonball. I felt something strike my cap; I took it off, and found sticking to it a portion of his brains, about the size of a marble. A young man on my left got a wound on the top of his head, and ran to the surgeon behind us; he was dressed and sent into his place again. Close to him, another man had his arm so badly fractured near the shoulder that it was taken out of the cup. A few yards behind sat a black man, with all the lower part of his face shot away; his eyes were gone and the bones of his brow all jagged and dripping blood. Near him, in a ditch, lay one of the 43rd, trying to hold in his bowels.[91]

Arsène Lacarrière Latour, Jackson's chief engineer, deemed it "my indispensable duty to do justice to the intrepid bravery displayed in that attack by the British troops, especially by the officers."[92]

They lay there all day until finally ordered to retire. Major Joseph Hutchison of the 7th Fusiliers noted that "on assembling the troops when out of fire, only fifteen men were found serviceable out of 85 of which the company was composed one hour before. I received seven shots through my clothes & cape."[93] Only on the far bank did the British enjoy any success; there Thornton quickly drove off "the Kentucky reinforcements, in whom so much reliance had been placed [and who] ingloriously fled, driving after them, by their example, the remainder of the forces."[94] The Kentuckians abandoned their unfinished line and forced the gunners to spike their pieces and run. Jackson was afraid that this setback might enable the British to turn his position, but losses had been so severe that Lambert, now in charge with Gibbs dying and Pakenham dead—together with 289 others; 1,262 wounded, including Keane; and a further 484 missing—decided that it was pointless to continue.[95]

Following a reconnaissance by Colonel Dickson, who had reported that 2,200 men would be required on that flank, Lambert had decided to withdraw from the captured batteries, and a six-hour truce was agreed for gathering the wounded and burying the dead. As part of the truce, in a tacit admission of error, Jackson insisted that there be no reinforcement of the right bank. Jackson placed the blame wholly on the Kentucky militia for the failure there, and nobody at the time charged him with negligence for failing to make sufficient provision to defend that quarter.[96] During the truce Sergeant Cooper recalled that an American soldier, "looking at the long rows of slain, exclaimed 'I never saw the like of that!' One of our party sneeringly said, 'That's nowt, man; if you'd been wi' us in Spain, you would ha' seen summat far war!' "[97] Surgeon William P. Lawrence of the Tennessee militia noted that "I could have walked on the dead bodies of the British for one quarter of a mile without stepping on the ground."[98] Total American casualties of 71 were given as 13 dead, 39 wounded, and 19 missing. But James Roberts, a private in the Tennessee militia who responded to Jackson's appeal for slave volunteers on the promise of freedom, later insisted that 50 blacks were killed but not mentioned in Jackson's official report. Indeed, more than 10 percent of Jackson's force were African-Americans, and when Jackson later reneged on his promise to free them, Roberts was incensed: "Such monstrous deception and villainy could not, of course, be allowed to disgrace the pages of history, and blacken the character of a man who wanted the applause and approbation of his country."[99]

Over the following week Lambert made preparations to retreat, and on the night of 18 January he quickly withdrew to the fleet, which had failed to fulfil its instructions to bombard Fort St. Philip and create a diversion, starting only on 9 January to little effect and ending on the 17th, killing two Americans and wounding another seven.[100] Sergeant Lawrence of the 40th Regiment, which reached Dauphin Island on 10 January, noted that the battery captured on the far bank was constructed of barrels of brown sugar, and

> some terms having been hinted at, when the black regiments had eaten a quantity of the fortifications, which they seemed to be very fond of, and we had put some into our haversacks as likely to be useful to sweeten our cocoa, we returned to our boats, and dropping down the river to a piece of land called Dolphin [Dauphin] Island, there encamped again.[101]

On Dauphin Island the officers of the 7th Fusiliers, 43rd Light Infantry, and 14th Light Dragoons launched a spirited campaign with fir cones against those of the 85th Light Infantry, 93rd Highlanders, and 95th Rifles. The exercise lasted several days and was watched by the whole army. Such juvenile behaviour was a symptom of relief and recovery of which a modern psychologist might approve.[102] The last unit to leave was the 7th Fusiliers, which re-embarked on 27 January, by which time the road was "in a most deplorable state," recalled Major Hutchison, "& in many places impassable. Three or four men in search of better footing, leaving the rushes, sank to rise no more."[103] But because of adverse winds the fleet could not pull away until 4 February, and at no stage did Lambert appreciate how nervous Jackson was about his own position; far from contemplating a counter-offensive, he was calling for reinforcement by 5,000 regulars and confined his operations to harassment of British working parties and the encouragement of deserters.[104]

For the British the battle was an unmitigated disaster. Mullins was later tried for this failure and for misbehaviour under fire; he was found guilty and cashiered. But J. W. Fortescue in his *History of the British Army* insisted that Mullins had been made a scapegoat, and that the man who should have been tried "and shot was Sir Alexander Cochrane. The callous manner in which he deliberately placed the troops in a most dangerous situation and then worked his faithful blue-jackets to death to keep them there—all with the principal object of filling his own pockets—cannot be too strongly condemned."[105] Fortescue was echoing the sentiments of the Duke of Wellington, who was singularly unimpressed when he received news of the death of his brother-in-law; he was highly critical of the Royal Navy and regarded the campaign as having been conducted entirely with a view towards plunder, concluding that "this evil design defeated its own end."[106] Pakenham and Gibbs also came in for official criticism, although they were in no position to answer for themselves; and Colonel Arthur Brooke was also censured for having been present but not taken over command from Mullins, although he insisted that he had already handed over to Mullins and was waiting to go on leave, largely because he felt disgraced after Baltimore.[107] Yet the whole operation was tragically unnecessary and in a later age with more modern communications would not have occurred: the two warring nations had signed a peace treaty on Christmas Eve.

18

The Peace of Christmas Eve

> Such men as thou, who wade across the world
> To make an epoch, bless, confuse, appal,
> Are in elemental ages' chart
> Like meanest insects on obscurist leaves
> But incidents and grooves of Earth unfolding;
> Or as the broken rod that stirs the fire
> Because it must.
>
> —Thomas Hardy, *The Dynasts*

A FEATURE of war without strategy is that it tends to be played out in a series of "hands," the scores of which cancel each other out, as in bridge. The failure of British forces to secure a crushing victory in 1814 thus became a sufficient inducement to settle for peace. Britain had been at war for twenty-two years and was desperately weary of it; the prospect of its dragging into another year was one to be avoided. It is difficult to measure accurately the costs of the American War to Britain, because they are bound up in general expenditure on the Great War in Europe, but an estimate may be made based on the increased borrowing undertaken during the period. The budget presented in June 1812, immediately before the outbreak of war, called for £22.4 million and rose in 1813 to £46.8 million, then declined slightly in 1814, with war in Europe now over, to £40.5 million; on this basis we may conclude that the American War as a whole added some £25 million to the national debt.[1] Indeed, shortly after peace was concluded Liverpool wrote to Canning: "I do not believe it would have been possible to have continued [income tax] for the purpose of an American war."[2] In America the cost was proportionally greater, at some $105 million; the national debt rose from $45 million in 1812 to $127 million by the end of 1815, although through discounts and paper money the government received only $34 million worth of specie.[3]

Thus it was in nobody's interest to continue fighting, though for a while the British continued to press for Fort Niagara, Mackinac, and part of northern Maine. The Americans firmly rejected this demand and argued instead for a mutual restoration of territory. On 3 November the British Cabinet met amid some thought of continuing the war in order to retrieve the disaster of Plattsburgh, but there were more important considerations; tensions within occupied France remained a problem, highlighted by the warm reception accorded *Wasp* at L'Orient.[4] The government also believed that Wellington in Paris was under threat from several Bourbon princes and took seriously talk of assassination plots, even if the Duke did not. There seemed to be only two options available to withdraw him honourably: to appoint him as Castlereagh's deputy at Vienna or to command in Canada. Liverpool chose the latter, partly as a means of galvanizing the Ghent negotiations. On 4 November he wrote to Castlereagh, "we should not be justified in allowing [him] to incur the risk to which he might be exposed by his continuance at Paris . . . The point of [his] quitting Paris being decided, I [feel] that he should accept the command of America," although he was in no great hurry actually to send the Duke across the Atlantic.[5] On the same day Wellington wrote to Bathurst that the British public were "very impatient about the want of success in America, and I expect they will never be quiet until I go there." But he argued the greater need for his presence in Europe, and continued, "I believe I should not be able to go to Quebec until April [1815]."[6]

This arrangement suited Liverpool, whose overriding desire was that Wellington should leave Paris, as shown by his reply on 13 November. If Wellington was "still of the opinion that [command in Canada] is not the best ground on which you can rest your departure from Paris, and any other reason should appear to you to have fewer inconveniences attending it, we have no objection to you availing yourself of that reason, whatever it may be."[7] When formally offered the post, Wellington answered bluntly that his presence in Canada would be of little use without naval control of the Great Lakes, and that Britain was not justified in asking for territorial concessions.[8] Five days later Liverpool wrote to Castlereagh: "I think we have determined, if all other points can be satisfactorily settled, not to continue the war for the purpose of obtaining or securing any acquisition of territory."[9] With a rift opening between Britain and Russia at Vienna and little chance of improving the military situation in North America, Britain was prepared to forgo territorial gain. In concluding the war on these terms, the prime minister was taking into account domestic opposition to continued taxation—especially among

18.1. *A Hundred Years' Peace: The Signature of the Treaty of Ghent between Great Britain and the United States of America, December 24th, 1814,* painting by A. Forestier, ca. 1915. *Source:* A. Forestier collection, C-005996, Library and Archives Canada.

the merchants of Liverpool and Bristol, who were keen to get back to doing business with America—and foreign policy considerations of far greater significance. The wisdom of this course was amply confirmed by Bonaparte's escape from Elba the following spring: had Wellington gone to North America, his remit would clearly have been to preside over a diplomatic settlement, not to wage war;[10] and of course he could not have been at Waterloo. And with regard to North America, at this point the British government was considering chiefly how soon it could recall troops.[11]

The delegations at Ghent met again on 1 December for the first time since 19 August, with the Americans increasing in confidence. However, another three weeks would elapse before agreement was finally reached while the British right to navigation of the Mississippi and the American right to land fish were argued over. The lack of power in the British team caused the Americans some frustration, as the British had constantly to refer back to London for instructions.[12] At first the British argued that the landing right had been forfeited by the war, but New Englander Adams was not prepared to accept this claim. However, this issue prompted a rift within the American commission: Kentuckian Henry Clay cared nothing for New England fishing rights but was keen to deny the British access to the Mississippi. Eventually these issues were resolved by simply ignoring them in the final treaty.[13] There was little left to add but an announcement to end the war, and the Treaty of Ghent, also known as the Peace of Christmas Eve, was duly signed on 24 December 1814.[14]

However, peace was not so simply achieved in the days before the telegraph. And since on three previous occasions America had insisted on modifications after its envoys had signed treaties, this time Britain insisted that the treaty could not become effective until both parties had ratified it, and sent Anthony Baker to get Madison's signature on it, being quite prepared to sign an independent peace with New England separatists the minute Madison reneged. News of American ratification, accomplished by the Senate on 17 February, did not reach London until 13 March, four days after Bonaparte's escape from Elba. This allowed troops due to go to America to deploy to Belgium instead, forming the basis of Wellington's victorious army at Waterloo.[15]

OVER THE winter the naval building race continued; the British began constructing two gunboats at Chippawa and two massive 120-gun ships-of-the-line at Kingston. Prevost informed Bathurst that the future safety of Canada depended on ascendancy on the lakes and requested that an admiral be assigned to command the service. The government did not accept this suggestion, but it did decide it was time to recall Yeo: on 12 December Captain Sir Edward Owen RN was ordered to take over command on the lakes, and told that he must do better than Yeo had done at communicating with the Admiralty. Yeo finally departed on 23 March 1815 and reported his arrival at Liverpool on 23 May, but did not face any criticism; his role in Barclay's defeat on Lake Erie and his failure to get to grips with Chauncey were forgotten at a time when the Royal Navy was being massively reduced, and he was given command of a squadron fighting the slave trade off the west coast of Africa.[16]

On 14 January 1815 Cockburn arrived at Cumberland Island, Georgia, where he found landings already completed by 700 men of the 3rd Battalion, Royal Marines, and the 2nd West India Regiment under Barrie of *Dragon*, opposed by men of the 1st U.S. Rifles and a company of the 42nd U.S. Infantry, who were unable to prevent them from seizing the battery. The Royal Marines smartly pushed the enemy, who, "injudiciously quitting the fort for the woods, was successively driven from three positions and at length from the forest itself, which with the barracks, artillery etc. Fell into our hands."[17] "While scrambling over the fallen timber," recalled William Lovell, two men of the 2nd West India Regiment "stumbled upon a rifleman who fired at them and missed. One of them put his musket to his shoulder and was going to shoot him when the other cried out 'Ta'am, why you poil king cartridge? Tick him Ta'am, tick him!' which between the two they immediately accomplished."[18]

Cockburn immediately followed up by seizing St. Mary's, the frontier town of Georgia, and taking large quantities of military stores before withdrawing to the island on the 23rd.[19] "They promised that private property & person would be respected," complained Thomas H. Miller, "which promise they broke in a short time by plundering the stores and private houses, breaking up the church floors & doing all the most shameful acts they could."[20] Cochrane and Lambert decided to try to salvage something from the disastrous New Orleans expedition with an attack on Mobile and Fort Bowyer. On 7 February the Americans were able to capture a raiding party of 18 from HMS *Dauntless* (26) in the Chesapeake, when ice helped trap their longboat and jolly boat.[21] But that night 600 men were landed 3 miles east of Fort Bowyer, and batteries were erected to bombard it. These were completed on the 11th, and the fort surrendered for a loss to the British of 13 killed and 18 wounded.[22] But news of the peace treaty was spreading in early February as Cochrane sailed once more into the Chesapeake, his plans being to organize two bodies of Indians and former slaves supported by British soldiers to harass the interior of Georgia and capture Fort Stoddert, again with the aim of diverting American attention from Canada. But two days later Cochrane was forced to suspend operations, leaving Mobile in American hands to become the only U.S. conquest of the war.[23] On Cumberland Island Cockburn began developing a base from which he launched raids up the nearby creeks and inlets. The number of escaped slaves seeking refuge with him eventually reached some 2,000, far exceeding expectations, and the island became "the scene of one of the most extraordinarily effective mass military emancipations ever seen in the United States."[24]

Cockburn was unimpressed by the peace terms: "That Jonathan should have been so easily let out of the cloven stick in which I thought we so securely had him," he wrote disappointedly, "I sincerely lament. The terms of the treaty are tolerably disgraceful to him for all his vaunting, and this in some measure makes up for their not being quite so honourable to us as might have been obtained by a little more firmness, and a little longer continuation of the war with our present unfettered means."[25] Meanwhile James Monroe had come up with yet another plan for the conquest of Canada, but it would never come to fruition.[26] And warfare at sea continued sporadically for some months; the Admiralty issued instructions that hostilities would continue until ratification of the treaty had been exchanged, and even then it was difficult for news to reach widely spread units.[27] In late January Captain Charles Napier RN on *Euryalus* off Norfolk Island issued a challenge to Captain Gordon USN of *Constellation,* which had spent the entire war cooped up. Gordon accepted, but news of peace prevented this meeting.[28] Elsewhere, despite his inability or unwillingness to get his frigate out of New London, Stephen Decatur remained the darling of his nation, and he was granted command of the *President.* In one of his final acts before his resignation on 1 December 1814, Navy Secretary Jones ordered a squadron led by *President* on a commerce-raiding cruise in the East Indies.

The sloops *Hornet* (18) and *Peacock* (18) and the storeship *Tom Bowline* managed to slip out of New York in January, planning to rendezvous at Tristan da Cunha, in the South Atlantic, and to head for the Indian Ocean to attack British shipping there.[29] Decatur's former subordinate James Biddle, who now had command of *Hornet,* was contemptuous of him, and delighted with the order to escort *Tom Bowline* to the rendezvous at Tristan da Cunha.[30] Before news of the treaty reached America, Decatur tried to take advantage of conditions that had blown the British blockading squadron off Sandy Hook, putting to sea from New York in *President* on the evening of 14 January. George N. Hollis, a fourteen-year-old midshipman, recalled that in the storm she grounded on a sand-bar, "and we thumped there for two or three hours."[31] She managed to get off and ran along the shore of Long Island. Until now the British squadron had kept *President* bottled up with a consummate display of seamanship, led by Captain John Hayes RN—known throughout the service as "Magnificent" Hayes after saving a ship of that name from almost certain destruction on a lee shore through another piece of brilliant seamanship—in the razee HMS *Majestic* (56). Though repeatedly blown off station by winter gales, Hayes was careful to take post on the point of bearing from Sandy Hook that he judged likely to be the enemy's track in the prevailing weather. As a result, when he was blown out to sea once more by a blizzard on the morning of 13 January, and found a fresh west-north-west wind blowing the following morning, preventing a return to the Hook, he nevertheless successfully spotted the American when she emerged, and gave chase.[32]

Throughout the 15th *Endymion* gradually reduced *President*'s lead despite Decatur's comprehensive measures to lighten his ship, throwing provisions, boats, spare stores, and anchors overboard. By 3 P.M. *Endymion* was able to open fire, and for two hours a running fight continued until the pursuer was forced to break off with severe damage to her sails and rigging. But she had delivered serious damage that put 6 feet of water in *President*'s hold, enabling HM Ships *Pomone* (38) and *Tenedos* to come up with the American. When the British asked Decatur if he surrendered, he replied, "I surrender to the squadron," recalled Hollis. "They either pretended to or did misunderstand him & gave us another broadside while our men were standing defenseless about the deck."[33] This tragedy left the Americans with twenty-five dead and sixty wounded while the crew of *Endymion* suffered eleven dead and fourteen wounded.[34]

Constitution, on the other hand, enjoyed a final run of success. When war broke out, the United States found itself short of salt, and following the Treaty of Paris ending war in Europe the price of salt from Cape Cod, one of its principal sources, rose from 50¢ to $8 a bushel. The British blockaded Massachusetts in an effort to prevent Cape Cod salt from reaching Boston or New York, though wily sailors sometimes managed to slip through. In December the three heavy frigates HM Ships *Acasta* (50), *Leander* (58), and *Newcastle* (50) were on blockade duty off Boston. *Newcastle* sent four barges to Rock Harbor and threatened to burn down the salt works at Orleans, where a skirmish was fought with the local militia in which two British sailors were killed; after Jackson's victory, the locals could not resist calling the defence of their little salt works "the Battle of Orleans."[35] More significantly, while the three were off station, *Constitution* under Captain Charles Stewart USN managed to escape. She then defied Admiralty forces sent to take her. In February she happened across HM Sloops-of-war *Cyane* (33) and *Levant* (21) about 60 leagues off Madeira. The British were armed with nearly all carronades; the American, carrying thirty-two long 24-pounders plus many other guns, held the advantage. But the British gamely engaged her, hoping to do enough damage to end her cruise. It was a forlorn hope: after a forty-minute engagement both were taken. *Constitution* lost three killed and twelve wounded to a total British loss of nineteen killed and forty-two wounded.[36] The colourfully named Pardon Mawley Whipple was aboard *Constitution* and upon boarding the *Levant* noted: "The mizzen mast for several feet was covered with brains and blood; teeth, pieces of bone, fingers and large pieces of flesh were picked up from the deck."[37] Subsequently *Constitution* managed to evade the three heavy frigates, in what William James described as "the most blundering piece of business" by the Royal Navy recorded in his naval history of the Napoleonic Wars, and returned to New York in the middle of May.[38]

On 26 February Thomas Boyle of the privateer *Chasseur,* the "Pride of Baltimore," enjoyed his most spectacular success when he took the *St. Lawrence* (15), formerly the *Atlas* of Philadelphia, taken by Cockburn at Ocracoke Inlet on 12 July 1813 and converted into a packet.[39] *Chasseur* was not expecting to fight, but when it became inevitable her superior manpower told, enabling her to use musketry at close quarters. After a sharp action that saw six British killed and seventeen wounded but also cost the Americans five dead and eight wounded, Boyle felt it necessary to explain to his owners that "I should not willingly, perhaps, have sought a contest with a King's vessel, knowing that is not our object; but my expectations at first were a valuable vessel and a valuable cargo also. When I found myself deceived, the honor of the flag entrusted to my care was not to be disgraced by flight."[40]

On 23 March James Biddle of *Hornet* was about to anchor off the north of Tristan da Cunha when he spotted a sail which turned out to be HM Sloop *Penguin* (18) under Commander James Dickinson RN, which came up for action. In twenty minutes the action was over: the British fired high, as usual, and the two ships collided, taking *Hornet*'s mizzen-shroud, stern davits, and spanker boom, but also snapping *Penguin*'s bowsprit and bringing her foremast down on her port guns, rendering them useless. *Hornet,* with superior firepower in the form of two extra 32-pounder carronades, was able to pound *Penguin;* one 32-pound round, noted William James, "carried away *six legs,* killed the powder boy of the division, capsized the opposite gun on the starboard side and 'sunk in sullen silence to the bottom.' "[41] Dickinson snapped to his first lieutenant, James McDonald: "The fellows are giving it to us like hell! We must get on board!" But when he tried to give the order, he "found the men rather backward—and so, you know, we concluded to give it up."[42] The killed included Dickinson and thirteen others and twenty-eight wounded for an American loss of two killed and nine wounded; *Penguin* was so badly shot up that the Americans had to scuttle her the following day.[43] *Hornet* then joined up with *Peacock,* and the two Americans continued to cruise, blissfully unaware that peace had been declared nearly four months earlier. On 27 and 28 April they chased a strange sail to discover it was HMS *Cornwallis* (74), carrying Rear-Admiral Sir George Burlton but commanded by Captain Thomas Bayley RN, who in turn now gave chase. The Americans split up, with *Peacock* going north-east and *Hornet* south-east, and, correctly deducing that *Peacock* was faster, Bayley set off after *Hornet* around the Cape of Good Hope. Every loose item was thrown overboard except for one long gun, and she eventually escaped into San Salvador harbour and finally returned to New York on 30 July, somewhat chastened.[44] *Peacock* was left to cruise alone.

American prisoners were still being returned at this late stage, among them many of the 1,000 African-Americans who represented an important element in privateer crews and did not want to sail in any ship bound for a southern U.S. port, despite the appalling conditions in which they were kept.[45] The exchange system had broken down as the British accumulated a surplus of prisoners, held at Halifax and in various hulks around Britain, but then concentrated at Dartmoor. In July 1813 there were 490 Americans held there, and by early 1815 a total of around 6,000.[46] In a curious episode in December 1814 six Americans who had served on *Pelican* arrived at Dartmoor, having decided in September to serve no longer, despite having made no previous objection to doing so and having taken part in the defeat of *Argus* a year earlier. They were seized and tried by the other American prisoners, who sentenced 2 to hang; but the authorities got wind of the situation, and they were moved to Plymouth, where they re-volunteered for the Royal Navy.[47] Never a pleasant place, Dartmoor was now thoroughly vile from overcrowding and from the constant Devonshire mist, drizzle, and damp, with water running down the bare stone walls. More than 250 men had already died of smallpox and pneumonia when the glad news of peace arrived on 31 December. Repatriation, however, had to await news of ratification. By the time this came, on 14 March, smallpox was rampant again, and although the authorities were willing to free the men, there was further delay while the Americans gathered the ships necessary to convey them. The men's impatience could hardly be contained, and on 6 April they complained about the shortage of bread. During the months of waiting the men were wont to play ball in the prison yard; normally, if a random ball sailed over the wall, the sentry would toss it back, but one day the sentry refused. Several prisoners threatened to dig under the wall to retrieve it, and when the sentry still refused, they started digging. When he learned what was happening, the prison commander, Captain Thomas Shortland RN, panicked; believing a mass breakout was imminent, he ordered all prisoners into the compound, where he had stationed squads of soldiers at eight points, and ordered them to fire. David Bunnell, who was among the prisoners, recalled that "the soldiers, being more humane than their tyrannical commander, fired high for the express purpose of missing us";

but this tactic did not stop the tragic and wholly unnecessary loss of 7 killed and 54 wounded.[48]

Meanwhile *Peacock* continued her cruise under Captain Lewis Warrington USN, taking four British ships before learning of peace on 30 June. Having encountered East India Company Ship *Nautilus* (10) under Lieutenant Charles Boyce EIC, while flying no colours, she then hoisted them once within hailing distance, whereupon Warrington demanded that the Briton haul down her own. When the Briton refused, *Peacock* fired a broadside into her and after a fifteen-minute action forced her to strike, with Boyce, who lost a leg, and his first lieutenant among the many badly wounded. The master-intendant said that peace really had been declared and that he could prove it, whereupon *Peacock* began a leisurely four-month cruise home, and with this episode the war finally ended.[49]

The reception of the treaty in each country was determined by the timing of the arrival of the news. For the British public it came after a period of heightened expectation of an important victory, and was deflated by the release of parliamentary papers displaying the embarrassing retreat of the commissioners at Ghent. There was a mixed reaction to the terms in the British press; the *Courier, Naval Chronicle,* and *Annual Register* all welcomed them, and Harry Smith recalled that most soldiers did too, realizing that "neither fame nor any military distinction could be acquired in this species of milito-nautico-guerrilla-plundering-warfare."[50] The *Morning Chronicle* welcomed peace but lamented the terms, and *The Times* bitterly resented them; but essentially Britain was content to be rid of a pointless and expensive war that was quickly forgotten.[51] The year 1814 had proved to be a major disappointment: Britain's overconfidence had turned into hubris, and American arms had pricked the bubble. But Castlereagh—if not Bathurst or Liverpool—got precisely the peace he wanted: the *status quo ante bellum.*[52]

In Canada a clamour of criticism had been mounting against Prevost's conduct of affairs for some time, led by Bishop Mountain, who showered Bathurst with complaints, being particularly peeved by the bishopric bestowed on his Catholic counterpart Plessis, thus effectively establishing the Roman religion, "a religion which every man of unfettered judgement admits to be equally unfavourable to morality, to industry, and to improvement."[53] Now this antipathy finally erupted into open and acrimonious debate. Newspapers detailed Prevost's alleged military and political blunders in a series of anonymous articles in the *Montreal Herald,* subsequently published in pamphlet form as *The Letters of Veritas* and *Nerva,* that twisted fact and rumour to suit the anglophone faction that now hated Prevost.[54] With de Rottenburg's assistance Prevost ferreted out the authors, who proved to be a pair of local disgruntled Tories; but he could not stifle the growing contempt of the anglophone élite, exemplified by Wystius Ryland, clerk of the Executive Council of Lower Canada, who wrote: "There he sits, like an idiot in a skiff, admiring the rapidity of the current which is about to plunge him into the abyss!"[55]

On 1 March 1815 Prevost learned of the ratification of the peace treaty but was dismayed the following day by the arrival of his replacement, Sir George Murray, with the news that he was to return to London forthwith to explain his conduct of the Plattsburgh campaign. When he left on 3 April he followed the route taken by the 104th Regiment in its epic march of February 1813, and in August Yeo was participating in a court-martial that "honourably acquitted" the survivors of the naval defeat on Lake Champlain and blamed Prevost for it.[56] Prevost protested the publication of this finding and requested a court-martial of his own to give him an opportunity to justify himself. Yeo was quite prepared to lay formal charges, and the Prince Regent summoned Prevost for trial on 15 January 1816; but Prevost died at age forty-nine just ten days before the court-martial was due to convene, worn out by worry and humiliation.[57] His undefended reputation has suffered accordingly, as disillusionment among his contemporaries meant he gained little credit for his quiet solid achievements. For although he was strategically inflexible and proved a hopeless field commander, as commander-in-chief facing overwhelming odds in the early years of the war he performed well; his sound political and administrative abilities formed the basis of success, meeting a series of seemingly insurmountable crises over two years with a mixture of careful planning, improvisation, and brilliant timing.[58] At Ghent Goulburn told John Quincy Adams that nothing had saved Canada "but the excellent dispositions and military arrangements" of Prevost.[59]

For Americans, news of peace followed the political trauma that culminated in the Hartford Convention and news of victory at New Orleans. It was therefore unsurprising that few Americans actually considered the implications, and that these should be constantly played down over the years as various war heroes sought to exploit their positions politically.[60] Madison's self-congratulatory proclamation that the peace treaty was "highly honorable to the United States, and terminates, with particular felicity, a campaign signalized by the most brilliant successes," was a singular piece of political spin from a man who led to war a nation totally unprepared for it, and had recently been a bewildered refugee in back-country Virginia while his capital burned behind him.[61] But whereas the War for Independence uplifted its participants, the War of 1812 depressed most of those who took part on the American side. As John Strachan put it, "I wish that those who are so ready stirring up wars would traverse the field of battle after an engagement or visit hospitals the next day—and they would receive a lesson that might be very beneficial to them in the future."[62] Certainly it achieved precisely none of the objectives for which America went to war: the United States had allowed the whole issue of impressment and neutral rights to pass unaddressed. The administration had even lost interest in Florida; in April 1814 Monroe denied support from Washington, and the American occupation of East Florida withered as the "Patriots" were forced to evacuate Fernandina and negotiate amnesty with the Spanish governor in St. Augustine.[63]

All that remained now was for the construction of a reassuring myth which might transform Madison's futile and humiliating adventure that had aimed to conquer Canada into one of defending the republic.[64] But America had enjoyed the more glamourous if less tangible successes, and by publicizing them in the national consciousness during the first half of the nineteenth century, it turned weary survival into colourful victory. Indeed, only the sterling performance of the U.S. Navy and the marked improvement in the army—in spite of, rather than because of, the government—ensured that Madison escaped the disaster he had brought upon his country. Instead Republican papers simply ignored the evidence and, like the Worcester *National Aegis,* declared that "*we have triumphed*—let snarling discontents say what they will—*we have gloriously triumphed!*"[65] Such claims were plainly ridiculous even if, thanks to its effective commissioners, the United States might claim to have won the peace; although at least one American commentator has noted that this outcome owes much not only to Castlereagh's statesmanship and generosity of spirit, but also to his marksmanship. For had he not shot Canning in the backside in 1809 the Americans might have faced a much more hard-headed Canningite delegation and punitive demands instead.[66]

In the final analysis, American military efforts proved sufficient to sustain U.S. diplomacy, but only by discarding its basic tenets as they stood in 1812. So for America the results of the war were largely psychological, and this was perhaps fitting, since attitudes of mind had generated it in the first place.[67] Because the Treaty of Ghent conveniently coincided with the cessation of hostilities in Europe and ended U.S. entanglement in European affairs, it was perhaps easy to portray the war as a second one for independence, a useful illusion, as Herbert Agar later noted:

> Perhaps it is well that no one told America that her new freedom depended not on the Treaty of Ghent, but on the Treaty of Paris which had been signed on May 30, 1814, after Napoleon's abdication at Fontainebleau. It was not the little war against England which won for America the blessing of being left alone; it was the enormous war against Europe's conqueror.[68]

At least after 1812 the British took the United States seriously as a naval power, an honour accorded to few others.[69]

A weary Britain was willing to end the war in order to focus on the European diplomatic situation, where it had much larger fish to fry.[70] During the recent conflict Britain had expanded its economic and territorial horizons to include such areas as South America, and now it had no desire to attack another major power or to control any part of Europe.[71] Its strategy had been, and would continue to be, based on the power of economic warfare conferred by its navy, and should not be wasted in chasing sterile battlefield glories. With peace seemingly restored by Bonaparte's defeat in April 1814, British post-war planning relied on the limited maritime strategy that had proved so effective since 1803. Its security would be compromised if any single power dominated the Continent, and in particular the obvious invasion base in the Low Countries around the Scheldt estuary. Therefore it looked to create a peaceful European equilibrium, building into the settlement at Paris the security of what became Belgium.[72] As would become evident after Bonaparte's final defeat at Waterloo, Britain needed that stable settlement based on nation-states to ensure long-term peace, and this objective overrode any desire to gain trifling advantages on the Canadian frontier or to retrieve prestige against the United States: Castlereagh sought to replace local aims in North America with global ones.[73]

Therefore the Treaty of Ghent deliberately excluded all mention of the strategic question of belligerent rights in wartime, which would prove to be a key element in post-war British strategy against the United States; there was no future cause for war and need not be one. Castlereagh could see that the Americans would always hold the upper hand in local issues, so the British were happy to limit naval forces on the Great Lakes and to keep their side of any agreements. The only exceptions were the islands in Passamaquoddy Bay claimed by both sides. Their fate was to be decided by commissioners from each country, and if they disagreed, their reports would be referred to a third power for arbitration. Commissioners were also appointed to settle the details of the American-Canadian border arising from inadequate geographical knowledge at the time of the Paris Treaty of 1783.[74] Some American writers have claimed that had it not been for the victory at New Orleans the British would have disavowed the peace of the Treaty of Ghent and attempted to retain the city, but this claim has no basis. The British government fully expected success at New Orleans—and beyond—long before it signed the peace treaty, and could have held out for far tougher conditions on that basis if it regarded such an outcome as desirable.[75] But the war did have important consequences in North America. The United States may have been thwarted in its desire to conquer Canada, but it did nothing to restrain American expansionism: the British clause for the protection of the western Indians soon became inoperable, in part as a result of the locally famous battle of the Sink Hole, fought on 24 May 1815 between local militia and Black Hawk's band near Fort Howard on the Missouri bank of the Mississippi; and peaceful relations were not restored between Indians and the United States in Illinois until May 1816.[76]

Indeed, although Winston Churchill later described Plattsburgh as "the most decisive engagement of the war," it was not.[77] Plattsburgh helped convince the British to come to terms but had little wider significance: the battles of Lake Erie and the Thames were the only truly decisive engagements, effectively ending the concept of an Indian buffer state. In Wisconsin Territory Captain Andrew Bulger of the Royal Newfoundland Regiment was commanding at Fort McKay in late 1814 and early 1815, having been sent there following Zachary Taylor's abortive attack in September because McDouall wanted a regular in command pending reinforcements.[78] He was planning to adopt an aggressive defence in the spring of 1815, and the Indians were already on the war-path. Towards the end of his stay he was disturbed by Indian hostility, and when the Treaty of Ghent restored the fort to the Americans, he bitterly concluded: "Our negotiators, as usual, have been egregiously duped: as usual they have shown themselves professionally ignorant of the concerns of this part of the empire."[79] Various Indian chiefs "expressed a determination not to abide by the treaty; and there even appeared that acts of hostility would be directed against ourselves."[80] The Americans would make their own peace with the Indians, and the Treaties of Portage des Sioux with several of the tribes opened the way for westward migration by their gradual removal.[81] In the south-east Lieutenant-Colonel Edward Nicolls also protested at the running of boundary lines set by the Treaty of Fort Jackson, which was a violation of Article IX of the Treaty of Ghent; but to no avail. The defeat of the

Indians in the north-west and south-east facilitated America's western expansion, and no European treaty was going to impede it.[82]

The war also signalled major changes within American politics; in fact, it proved to be a narrow escape from a near-death experience for the young republic. Since at least the beginning of the French Revolution the rift between Republicans and Federalists had been growing, until it seemed that the republic might split. The war brought moderates of both sides together to ensure that the great experiment would not fail. Although the re-imposition of British rule had never been on the cards, choosing to regard the conflict with Britain as a "second war of independence" helped usher in the "Era of Good Feelings" that followed.[83] However, both Republican foreign policy and domestic harmony had foundered on war, and talk of a new kind of diplomacy availed little in the crucible of international realpolitik. The European war of 1793–1801 exacerbated domestic partisan schisms; that of 1803–1815 buffeted Jefferson and Madison from policy pillar to partisan post. Jefferson's federal state could effect little in an Atlantic world ruled by the superpowers of the day. Afterwards "National" Republicans such as Henry Clay urged greater federal effort in national security—a more robust army and navy and extensive coastal fortification system—a policy that had long been mooted by Federalists but resisted by Republicans before 1812.[84] Indeed, it did not matter that the war vindicated so many Federalist policies; it represented the beginning of the end of the Federalist party. And both political parties were effectively redundant now that Republicans had instituted everything they professed to loathe: a strong government, a strong military, high taxes, booming cities, and finance capitalism, producing a restless country that doomed the Jeffersonian agricultural arcadia, expanding manufacturing in three years as much as it had in the previous twenty. Now the United States would seek to get rich, whereas before the nation had been satisfied with self-sufficiency.[85]

In asserting itself on the world stage in a fight against a major power, the United States certainly took the first step towards the self-confidence that has since been its hallmark. "I must acknowledge that the war has been useful," wrote Albert Gallatin. "The character of America stands now as high as ever on the European continent, and higher than ever it did in Great Britain."[86] Being American no longer meant being simply anti-British or anti-French, however. The war left Americans with a greater sense of antagonism towards the British than towards the French; far more than the Revolution, it planted a seed of enduring anglophobia.[87] A new assertive and ambitious United

States emerged, and, as embodied by Jackson, highly nationalistic; for the war vindicated the United States to itself as a nation. American victories at the end gave enough cause for celebration to strengthen a still feeble Union, and it created a pantheon of new heroes.[88] The war helped elevate four men to the presidency: James Monroe, John Quincy Adams, Andrew Jackson, and William Henry Harrison would all make much of their exploits and would actively drive the country westwards in a progress culminating in the war against Mexico and the subsequent taming of the West. Ironically, the Staffordshire potteries, and others in Liverpool and Sunderland, took the opportunity to make up for business lost during the war by exploiting the new "colonial" nationalism in the United States. Over the next two decades they sold large quantities of ceramics celebrating American successes and heroes, or scenic views such as Niagara Falls, as their aggressive design and marketing techniques enabled them to substantially increase their work-forces.[89]

IN 1816 James Monroe became president, and John Quincy Adams became secretary of state. A thorough-going expansionist, Adams began by settling some outstanding details of dispute with the British. First came the signing of the Rush-Bagot Agreement in 1817, which limited warships on the Great Lakes to those necessary to enforce customs regulations, averted a threatened arms race, and set a precedent in international relations on naval arms control.[90] Next came the Convention of 1818, which not only recognized American fishing rights off the coasts of Labrador and Newfoundland and secured the withdrawal of the British garrison on Moose Island—the last foreign force to occupy any part of the United States—but also established the 49th parallel as the northern boundary of the Louisiana Purchase from the Lake of Woods to the Rockies and provided for joint occupation of the disputed Oregon Territory for ten years—an agreement subsequently renewed until 1845.[91] In 1821, with the ratification of the Adams-Onís Treaty, Spain formally relinquished all claims to Florida, East and West. Two years later the adoption of what later became known as the Monroe Doctrine stated that the American continent was not to be considered by the European powers for future colonization, and that the United States would regard European intervention in New World affairs as a manifestation of unfriendliness; it also assured European powers that it would not involve itself in their internal affairs or interfere with existing colonies. While within the United States this policy would come to symbolize hostility to despotism and be considered as sacrosanct as the Constitution, in

Latin America it would become redolent of Yankee domination; and in Europe it had no immediate effect, because then and for a long time afterwards it was clear that the United States lacked the power to match the words.

It was not the Monroe Doctrine but British diplomacy, backed by the irresistible might of the Royal Navy, that prevented the "Holy Alliance" of France, Russia, Prussia, and Austria from intervening to restore Latin America to Spain.[92] For Britain, Canada had proved its loyalty and its value and was clearly worth defending, but that defence would always rely on assistance that could be forthcoming only via the superiority of the Royal Navy. And for Britain's superior power to take full effect would require an enormous mobilization of resources, something to be avoided if possible. Thus the aftermath of the war created a pattern that would hold for the next fifty years. In the post-war period British strategy would have to deal with two strands: actual American naval forces, and the U.S. claim to have won the war. The latter was of considerable significance.

American literature created a widespread impression, in Britain as well as in America, that the United States had won. British literature—far less impressive in scale—refuted these claims, but it also significantly altered the strategic perceptions of its target audience. Captain Edward Brenton RN concluded that Britain had the power to convulse the continent of America, and was among the first to point out that the United States had failed to achieve any of its war aims.[93] This assessment was echoed by William James, the leading British naval analyst of the war, who devoted his life to correcting the misstatements and propaganda of early American writers. By establishing that the Royal Navy had nothing to fear from the U.S. Navy or from another conflict with it, James's analysis significantly affected relations between the two countries, which returned to resolving disputes through diplomacy as they had until 1812: he reinforced British confidence as to who could most effectively back up this diplomacy with the threat of force if necessary.[94]

In fact by the late 1820s the U.S. Navy had been significantly reduced to a small force with inadequate infrastructure to support it. In the same period Halifax and Bermuda had been continuously upgraded, as they would continue to be until the end of the American Civil War.[95] These developments maintained the threat to American coastal cities and commerce so evident during the war. Thus the massive American investment of $8.25 million on coastal fortifications between 1815 and 1829 constituted an expensive admission of naval weakness. Worse still from the American point of view, the U.S.

Army lacked sufficient troops to man these fortifications and also mount offensive operations against Canada.[96] Moreover, the fortifications were soon rendered obsolete by steel plate and rifled guns, as evidenced by British assaults on Russian fortifications during the Crimean War (1854–1856). The Royal Navy's mastery of the seas and its ability to project power, not only onto enemy coasts but deep inland, so amply demonstrated during the War of 1812, created fear among Americans for decades afterwards.[97] Indeed, it proved an effective deterrent worldwide: between 1815 and 1914 no major power dared attack Britain.

Along the border Murray, recognizing that Lake Ontario was the key to the defence of Upper Canada, recommended granting land to discharged regulars. For the first time British emigrants, particularly from among the Scots and Irish and from discharged soldiers, were encouraged to settle the area.[98] But no such consideration was given to those slaves who had escaped their bondage and hoped to make a new life in British North America; they were simply dumped in Nova Scotia and left to fend for themselves, with no thought whatever for their provision and welfare, although ironically they were given some clothing in the form of American uniforms captured during the expedition to Castine. Long after the war Americans pushed hard for the return of or compensation for lost slaves, forming another strand in Anglo-American relations.[99] And the 1817 agreement limiting armaments on the Great Lakes was soon obsolescent. Americans believed the march of history implied convergence with British North America and applauded the Canadian rebellions of 1837 as the advent of republicanism, while the abolition of the Corn Laws in Britain in 1846, which threw the Canadian provinces onto the world market, seemed another step towards continental union. But peace survived because "Manifest Destiny" had been effectively diverted south and westwards.[100]

On 14 April 1846 an American military patrol engaged a Mexican force south of the Nueces River in the newly annexed state of Texas, resulting in the Mexican-American War, which secured a vast area for the United States, including west Texas, New Mexico, Arizona, Nevada, Utah, and California. An 1812 veteran, Zachary Taylor, particularly distinguished himself in this adventure and, in so doing, eased his path to the White House as the eleventh president in 1848, affording more striking evidence of how closely soldiering and politics have been intertwined in the United States. For decades it remained true that participation in one of the great American successes, such as the battle of the Thames, was worth thousands of votes to governors, legislators, and judges, although they were insufficient to gain Winfield Scott entry to the White House in 1852.[101]

The Treaty of Ghent had also restored Fort Astoria to the United States, and President James K. Polk had briefly considered claiming Oregon as far north as 54° 40', but with war looming against Mexico he offered to settle with Britain along the 49th parallel. At first the British refused, but when the Hudson Bay Company moved its western headquarters from the Columbia River to Vancouver Island, they agreed to an Oregon Treaty that divided the territory along the 49th parallel from the Rockies to the straits of Vancouver, and left Vancouver Island in British hands.[102] Thus the "longest undefended border in the world" was defined. In 1867 the United States purchased Alaska from Russia for $7,200,000, although it did not seem a bargain to most people at the time. One argument in favour of the deal was that it would help promote the annexation of Canada, which remained a long-standing objective among some political factions, strengthened by Britain's perceived hostility during the American Civil War.[103]

Between 1883 and 1892 a sea change occurred in American perceptions of the war as a result of a "navalist" rewriting of its history, led by Theodore Roosevelt, Admiral Alfred Mahan, and Henry Cabot Lodge, although the move was not limited to naval historians. The revised interpretation was resisted by Henry Adams, who failed to prevent its triumph. The main lessons drawn, often with an overt political agenda, were the dangers of inadequate war preparation, the futility of land operations and therefore of armies, and the consequent need for control of the seas. This change in attitude to the War of 1812 went a long way to explain the expansion that would eventually lead to the United States' overtaking Britain as the world's dominant naval power.[104]

Meanwhile, one might have expected the American Civil War to have refocused American military thinking, but as Richard A. Preston shows in *The Defense of the Undefended Border,* until 1940 anglophobia remained a central motivating factor in the United States, and Canada a target for conquest. Between the world wars the United States developed three major war plans: one against Japan, one against Mexico, and War Plan Red, against the United Kingdom. (Germany was colour-coded black, but there never was a War Plan Black.) In 1935 secret congressional hearings for air bases to launch surprise attacks on Canada, based on War Plan Red, were mistakenly published by the Government Printing Office and reported by the *New York Times* and the *Toronto Globe.* The story was re-discovered in 1975 and again in 1991 before being dug up once more in 2005. The existence of such a plan was treated with a sense of disbelief and laughing up the sleeve.[105] But War Plan Red was not funny: it was detailed, amended and acted upon, and, as Preston makes clear, it was no defence plan. The United States would start the war, and even if Canada declared neutrality the United States would still invade and conquer it, planning to "hold in perpetuity" all territory gained and to abolish the Dominion government. The plan was approved in May 1930 by the secretary of war and the secretary of the Navy in expectation of "consequent suffering to the [Canadian] population and widespread destruction and devastation of the country." In October 1934 the secretaries approved the strategic bombing of Halifax, Montreal, and Quebec City "on as large a scale as practicable."[106] A second amendment, also approved at cabinet level, directed the U.S. Army to use poison gas from the outset as a supposedly "humanitarian" action that would cause Canada to surrender quickly, and thus save American lives.[107] Even as late as 1939, as the free world was mobilizing to fight fascism, the U.S. Army War College and the Naval War College set as their planning priority "Overseas Expeditionary Force to Capture Halifax from Red-Crimson Coalition."[108] This enduring hostility to Britain and Canada within the U.S. military was a legacy of the War of 1812 and was finally extinguished only by the Second World War, which ushered in the "special relationship."

Canadian nationalism had also been strengthened by the War of 1812, and the move towards Confederation was accelerated by Anglo-American tensions created during the American Civil War and the ill-fated Fenian incursions in 1866 by U.S.-based Irish nationalists. These tensions and its own increasing self-reliance helped bring into existence the Dominion of Canada on 1 July 1867, a new and independent nation with its own currency and its own prime minister, to the north of the United States.[109] The one really decisive and lasting result of the War of 1812 was the complete British victory in Canada that secured Canadian independence. It would reverberate through history to 1914 and again to 1939, when, in Britain's darkest hours of need, Canada stood proudly by its side.

Abbreviations

Notes

Select Bibliography

Index

Abbreviations

The following abbreviations are used in the notes.

AC	U.S. Congress, *Annals of Congress,* collected in *The Debates and Proceedings of the Congress of the United States* (Washington, D.C.: Gales and Seaton, 1853)
AHR	*American Historical Review*
AN	*American Neptune*
AO	Archives of Ontario, Toronto
AR	*Alabama Review*
ASP: FR	U.S. Congress, *American State Papers, I: Foreign Relations,* 6 vols. (Washington, D.C.: Gales and Seaton, 1832–1859)
ASP: MA	U.S. Congress, *American State Papers, V: Military Affairs,* 7 vols. (Washington, D.C.: Gales and Seaton, 1832–1861)
ASP: NA	U.S. Congress, *American State Papers, VI: Naval Affairs,* 4 vols. (Washington, D.C.: Gales and Seaton, 1834–1861)
BECHS	Buffalo and Erie County Historical Society, Buffalo
BHC	Burton Historical Collection, Detroit
BL	British Library, London
BNYPL	*Bulletin of the New York Public Library*
CHJ	*Cambridge Historical Journal*
CHR	*Canadian Historical Review*
CMH	*Canadian Military History*
DAB	*Dictionary of American Biography,* 20 vols. (London: Oxford University Press, 1928–1937)
DCB	*Dictionary of Canadian Biography,* 13 vols. (Toronto: University of Toronto Press, 1966–1994)
DHC	E. A. Cruikshank, ed., *Documentary History of the Campaigns upon the Niagara Frontier in 1812–1814,* 9 vols. (Welland, Ont.: Tribune Press, 1896–1908)
DNB	*Oxford Dictionary of National Biography,* 60 vols. (Oxford: Oxford University Press, 2004)

ABBREVIATIONS

DRIC	E. A. Cruikshank, ed., *Documents Relating to the Invasion of Canada and the Surrender of Detroit* (1896; reprint, Manchester, N.H.: Ayer Company Publishers, 1979)
DRINP	E. A. Cruikshank, ed., *Documents Relating to the Invasion of the Niagara Peninsula . . . 1814* (Niagara-on-the-Lake, Ont.: Niagara Historical Society, 1920)
EIHC	*Essex Institute Historical Collections*
FCHQ	*Filson Club Historical Quarterly*
FHQ	*Florida Historical Quarterly*
GHQ	*Georgia Historical Quarterly*
HJ	*Historical Journal*
HSP	Historical Society of Pennsylvania, Philadelphia
ICRO	Ipswich and East Suffolk County Record Office
IMH	*Indiana Magazine of History*
IMHJ	*Indiana Military History Journal*
IS	*Inland Seas*
JAH	*Journal of American History*
JAS	*Journal of American Studies*
JEH	*Journal of Economic History*
JER	*Journal of the Early Republic*
JES	*Journal of Erie Studies*
JMilH	*Journal of Military History*
JModH	*Journal of Modern History*
JSAHR	*Journal of the Society of Army Historical Research*
JUSI	*Journal of the United Services Institute*
LAC	Library and Archives Canada (formerly National Archives Canada), Ottawa
LC	Library of Congress, Washington, D.C.
LHQ	*Louisiana Historical Quarterly*
LL	Lilly Library, University of Indiana, Bloomington
MA	*Military Affairs*
MCH	*Military Collector and Historian*
MHM	*Maryland Historical Magazine*
MHR	*Michigan Historical Review*
MM	*Mariner's Mirror*
MPHC	*Michigan Pioneer and Historical Collections*
MVHR	*Mississippi Valley Historical Review*
NAM	National Army Museum, London
NC	*Naval Chronicle*
NHSP	*Niagara Historical Society Publications*
NLS	National Library of Scotland, Edinburgh
NM/MN	*Northern Mariner/Marin du nord*
NMM	National Maritime Museum, Greenwich
NOQ	*Northwest Ohio Quarterly*
NWR	*Niles' Weekly Register*
NYHSQ	*New York Historical Society Quarterly*
NYSL	New York State Library, Albany

ABBREVIATIONS

OAHSP/Q	*Ohio Archaeological and Historical Society Publications/Quarterly*
OH	*Ontario History*
OHSPR	*Ontario Historical Society Papers and Records*
PBHS	*Publications of the Buffalo Historical Society*
PFB	B. L. Lossing, *The Pictorial Field-Book of the War of 1812 . . .* (New York: Harper Brothers, 1869)
PMHB	*Pennsylvania Magazine of History and Biography*
PMHS	*Proceedings of the Massachusetts Historical Society*
PRONI	Public Record Office of Northern Ireland, Armagh
RKHS	*Register of the Kentucky State Historical Society*
RMM	Royal Marines Museum, Southsea
SBD	W. C. H. Wood, ed., *Select British Documents of the Canadian War of 1812*, 3 vols. (Toronto: Champlain Society, 1920–1928)
THQ	*Tennessee Historical Quarterly*
TNA	The National Archives (formerly Public Record Office), Kew
UCA	United Church of Canada/Victoria University Archives, Toronto
USNA	National Archives, Washington, D.C.
USNIP	*United States Naval Institute Proceedings*
VH	*Vermont History*
VQ	*Vermont Quarterly*
WHSC	*Wisconsin Historical Society Collections*
WLC	William L. Clements Library, University of Michigan
WMQ	*William and Mary Quarterly*
WRM	The Welch Regiment Museum, Cardiff

Notes

For full citations of book-length works, see the Select Bibliography.

Introduction

Epigraph: Mackay, *Memoirs of Extraordinary Popular Delusions,* 1: 1–2.

1. William Kingsford, *History of Canada,* 8: 579.

2. Donald E. Graves, "Introduction," in Hitsman, *Incredible War,* xvii–xviii. See Henry Adams, *History,* vols. 5–9. On Adams and his work, see Wills, *Henry Adams and the Making of America;* and Gordon S. Wood, "A Century of Writing Early American History: Then and Now Compared; or How Henry Adams Got It Wrong," *AHR* 100 (1995), 678–696.

3. Perkins, *Prologue to War,* 55. See also Lawrence S. Kaplan, "France and Madison's Decision for War, 1812," *MVHR* 50 (March 1964), 652–671. For biographies of Madison see Irving Brant's *James Madison* (six volumes in total or a later abridged version); Ketcham, *James Madison;* McCoy, *The Last of the Fathers;* Rakove, *James Madison and the Creation of the American Republic;* Rutland, *James Madison* and *James Madison and the American Nation.* See also Madison, *Writings.*

4. Some American writers have acknowledged this, notably Hickey, *War of 1812,* 300.

5. Ryerson, *The Loyalists of America and Their Times,* 379; Stacey, *The Military Problems of Canada,* 57; idem, "The War of 1812 in Canadian History," *OH* 50 (1958), 1539. See also George Sheppard, "'Deeds Speak': Militiamen, Medals, and the Invented Traditions of 1812," ibid., 82 (1990), 207–232.

6. John Strachan, "An Exhortation Pronounced after the Sermon . . .," York, 22 December 1812, in *Report of the Loyal and Patriotic Society of Upper Canada,* app.

7. See Sheppard, "'Deeds Speak.'"

8. Pitch, *The Burning of Washington,* 234.

9. James became a naval historian by chance, as a result of being detained at Philadelphia as an enemy alien when war broke out. Astonished by the contemporary exaggerated reports of American naval victories, after the war he set out to correct them, though he overcompensated with a virulent anti-Americanism. For details of his career see Andrew Lambert's introduction to the Conway Press reissue of James's *Naval Occurrences of the War of 1812.* See also Holden Furbre, ed., "How William James Came to Be a Naval Historian," *AHR* 38 (1932–33), 74–85. Roosevelt wrote his *Naval War of 1812* at just twenty-three and gained a major reputation on the back of it by refuting much of what James had written. See William S. Dudley, "Naval Historians and the War of 1812," *Naval History* 4 (1990), 52–57. See also Kenneth L. Moll, "A. T. Mahan, American Historian," *MA* 27 (1963–64), 131–140; Keith S. Dent, "The British Navy and the Anglo-American War of 1812 to 1815" (Master's thesis, University of Leeds, 1949), 2–5.

10. Numerous books on the war include it in the title, among these recent publications by Walter R. Borneman, *1812: The War That Forged a Nation;* and A. J. Langguth, *Union 1812: The Americans Who Fought the Second War of Independence.* But as the leading American authority on the war points out, it is at best "an exaggeration"; Hickey, *Don't Give Up the Ship!* 46.

11. See Stanley, *Canada Invaded.*

12. Various members of Madison's cabinet seemingly discussed his avowal to use Canada as a bargaining chip when it seemed America might just keep it; Stuart, *United States Expansionism and British North America,* 59–60, 63–64.

13. Hickey, *War of 1812,* 1–3. This is the most thorough and balanced account of the politics of the war.

14. Glenn Tucker, *Poltroons and Patriots,* 1: 152.

15. To the British he remained General Bonaparte throughout the war; Britain never recognized his claim to the title "emperor," which he took in 1804.

16. Watson, *The Reign of George III,* 14–16, 18, 288–290.

17. Perkins, *Prologue to War,* 97–99.

18. Blanchard, *Discovery and Conquest of the Northwest,* 257; Silverstone, *Divided Union,* 90.

19. Horsman, *War of 1812,* ix–x, 3–4.

20. *Monthly Review; or, Literary Journal Enlarged,* March 1808, 310; Perkins, *Prologue to War,* 6–8, 11.

21. Horsman, *Causes,* 189–195.

22. For a long time, life in the Royal Navy of the period was regarded as unremittingly harsh, thanks largely to John Masefield's *Sea Life in Nelson's Time.* More recent scholarship has shown that it was not entirely without compensations, and that once a man had been in the service for a year or more, he was considerably less likely to run. See Pope, *Life in Nelson's Navy;* and Lavery, *Shipboard Life and Organization* and *Nelson's Navy.*

23. Hickey, *War of 1812,* 11.

24. C. D. Hall, *British Strategy,* 1–6; Cookson, *The British Armed Nation,* 2–7.

25. Geoffrey J. Marcus, *Heart of Oak,* 121; Rodger, *Command of the Ocean,* 492–493. Good examples of such memoirs are Leech, *Thirty Years from Home;* and Pemberton's *Autobiography of Pel. Verjuice.*

26. Byrn, *Crime and Punishment in the Royal Navy,* 108–109; McKee, *A Gentlemanly and Honorable Profession,* 233–354; Langley, *Social Reform in the United States Navy,* 133–145; Durand, *James Durand,* 18, 23–24; Leech, *Thirty Years from Home,* 234–237.

27. Rodger, *Command of the Ocean,* 497–502.

28. Carr, *The Coming of War,* 11.

29. Perkins, *Prologue to War,* 68–69.

30. See Julius W. Pratt, *Expansionists of 1812,* for the former thesis and Roger H. Brown, *The Republic in Peril,* for the latter.

31. For a study of the religious sentiment of the period see Gribbin, *The Churches Militant.*

32. Warren H. Goodman, "The Origins of the War of 1812: A Survey of Changing Interpretations," *MVHR* 28 (1941–42), 177. There are a number of academic volumes addressing the causes of the war, each placing a subtly different emphasis on the individual strands that made up the decision. For an overview, see Clifford L. Egan, "The Origins of the War of 1812: Three Decades of Historical Writing," *MA* 38 (April 1974), 72–75.

33. Carr, *The Coming of War,* 354.

34. Mackesy, *War without Victory,* 225.

35. The term "carronade" originated with the Carron company of Scotland, which first manufactured this type of gun in the 1780s, and was sometimes called a "smasher" because of the effect its original 68-pound shot had on timber. Carronades were sometimes referred to as "columbiads" by the Americans, although these were really an intermediate type of weapon; Roosevelt, *Naval War of 1812,* 36; Emanuel Raymond Lewis, "The Ambiguous Columbiads," *MA* 28 (1964–65), 111–122.

36. For detailed coverage of rigging and rates, see Lee, *Masting and Rigging of English Ships of War.*

37. See Mahon and Danysh, *Army Lineage Series,* 3–121.

38. For an excellent overview of the subject and a detailed examination of the drill books on which these tactics were based, see Muir's *Tactics,* 51–104; for a North American perspective, see Graves, *Red Coats and Grey Jackets,* 47–54; idem, *Field of Glory,* 162–182.

39. Muir, *Tactics,* 86–89.

40. AO, F 43, Ridout Family Papers, Thomas Ridout to his father, 3 July 1811.

41. See Donald E. Graves, "'Dry Books of Tactics': U.S. Infantry Manuals of the War of 1812 and After," *MCH* 38 (1986), 50–61, 173–177; Graves and John C. Fredriksen, "'Dry Books of Tactics' Re-Read: An Additional Note on U.S. Infantry Manuals of the War of 1812," *MCH* 39 (Summer 1987), 64–65; Graves, "From Steuben to Scott: The Adoption of French Infantry Tactics by the U.S. Army, 1807–1816," in International Commission on Military History, *Acta* 14 (1991), 223–235.

42. Nosworthy, *Battle Tactics of Napoleon and His Enemies,* 71–73, 77–79; Elting, *Amateurs to Arms!* 9–10.

43. See Spencer C. Tucker, "The Carronade," *USNIP* 99 (August 1973), 65–70.

44. Hughes, *British Smooth-Bore Artillery,* 56.

45. See Congreve, *Details of the Rocket System;* Richard R. Hobbs, "Congreve War Rockets, 1800–1825," *USNIP* 94 (1968), 80–88; Ralph Robinson, "The Use of Rockets by the British in the War of 1812," *MHM* 40 (March 1945), 1–6; A. D. McCaig, "'The Soul of Artillery': Congreve's Rockets and Their Effectiveness in Warfare," *JSAHR* 78 (Winter 2000), 252–263; C. E. Franklin, "Uniforms of the British Rocket Troops in the Napoleonic Wars," *JSAHR* 81 (Autumn 2003), 191–215; Eric I. Manders and George A. Snook, "Rocket Section, Royal Marine Artillery—1814," *MCH* 18 (Winter 1966), 122–123.

46. Hughes, *Firepower,* 166.

47. See Donald E. Graves, "Field Artillery of the War of 1812: Equipment, Organization, Tactics and Effectiveness," *Arms Collecting* 30, no. 2 (1992), 39–48; idem, "American Ordinance of the War of 1812: A Preliminary Investigation," ibid., 31, no. 4 (1993), 111–120.

48. University of Southampton, Wellington Papers, WP 1/478, Wellington to Croker, 8 August 1815, printed with Croker's name suppressed in Wellesley, *Despatches of Wellington,* 8: 231–232.

49. Muir, *Salamanca 1812,* 74–75.

1. "Canada! Canada! Canada!"

1. Elze, *Lord Byron,* 125–126.

2. MacCarthy, *Byron,* 159.

3. *Leicester Journal,* 25 July 1812.

4. Horsman, *Causes,* 14.

5. Kaiser, *Politics and War,* 246–249, 255–261; Kennedy, *Rise and Fall of the Great Powers,* 170–175; Harvey, *Collision of Empires,* 66–71; Paul W. Schroeder, "Napoleon's Foreign Policy: A Criminal Enterprise," *JMilH* 54 (1990), 147–162; Dorothy Mackay Quynn, "The Art Confiscations of the Napoleonic Wars," *AHR* 50 (1944–45), 437–460. Opinion on Bonaparte in continental Europe remains ambiguous: see Geyl, *Napoleon, For and Against;* and Alexander, *Napoleon.* See also Ribbe, *Le Crime de Napoléon.*

6. Schom, *Trafalgar,* 8–9, 16.

7. Gardiner, *Naval War of 1812,* 9.

8. *ASP: FR,* 1: 520–525; Bemis, *Jay's Treaty;* Jerald A. Combs, *The Jay Treaty;* and Estes, *The Jay Treaty Debate.* See also Phillips and Reede, *Neutrality.*

9. For a biography of Adams see McCullough, *John Adams.* Jefferson has had innumerable biographers, and will doubtless have many more. A useful recent and concise volume is Bernstein, *Thomas Jefferson.* See also Cunningham, *In Pursuit of Reason;* Malone, *Jefferson and His Time;* Mapp, *Thomas Jefferson;* Peterson, *Thomas Jefferson and the New*

Nation. For studies of the Federalist party, see Donald R. Hickey, "The Federalists and the War of 1812" (Ph.D. diss., University of Illinois, 1972); Kerber, *Federalists in Dissent;* Fischer, *Revolution of American Conservatism;* Banner, *To the Hartford Convention.* On Republicanism see McCoy, *The Elusive Republic;* Banning, *The Jeffersonian Persuasion;* Stuart G. Brown, *The First Republicans;* and Cunningham, *The Jeffersonian Republicans.*

10. For an analysis of the political origins of America's military establishment, see Kohn, *Eagle and Sword;* James R. Jacobs, *Beginnings of the U.S. Army,* chaps. 1–9; Sprout and Sprout, *Rise of American Naval Power,* 13–53; Smelser, *The Congress Founds the Navy;* Donald R. Hickey, "Federalist Defense Policy in the Age of Jefferson, 1801–1812," *MA* 45 (1981), 63–70; Toll, *Six Frigates,* chaps. 1–4; and William G. Anderson, "John Adams and the Creation of the American Navy" (Ph.D. diss., SUNY–Stony Brook, 1975). For an analysis of how the European wars affected American commerce, see Clauder, *American Commerce.* For the "Quasi-War" see Gardner W. Allen, *Our Naval War with France;* DeConde, *The Quasi-War;* Stinchcomb, *The XYZ Affair;* Michael A. Palmer, *Stoddert's War;* and idem, "The Quasi-War and the Creation of the American Navy, 1798–1801" (Ph.D. diss., Temple University, 1981).

11. See Ferling, *Adams vs. Jefferson.*

12. For biographies of Gallatin see Balinky, *Albert Gallatin;* Ewing, *America's Forgotten Statesman;* and Ray Walters, *Albert Gallatin.*

13. See Smelser, *The Democratic Republic;* Peterson, *Thomas Jefferson and the New Nation;* Johnstone, *Jefferson and the Presidency;* and Spivak, *Jefferson's English Crisis.* For Republican defence policies see Crackel, *Mr. Jefferson's Army;* J. R. Jacobs, *Beginnings of the U.S. Army,* chaps. 10–14; Sprout and Sprout, *Rise of American Naval Power,* 53–85; Sidney Forman, "Why the United States Military Academy Was Established in 1802," *MA* 29 (1965–66), 16–28. For a revisionist defence of Jefferson's naval policy, see Julia H. McLeod, "Jefferson and the Navy: A Defense," *Huntington Library Quarterly* 8 (1945), 153–184. On the Barbary War see Toll, *Six Frigates,* chaps. 5–9; Wheelan, *Jefferson's War;* and William M. Fowler Jr., "The Navy's Barbary War Crucible," *Naval History* 19, no. 4 (2005), 55–59.

14. Meinig, *The Shaping of America,* 4–23.

15. Schom, *Trafalgar,* 37.

16. Perkins, *First Rapprochement,* 138–143; Burt, *United States, Great Britain, and British North America,* 185–197.

17. For the most recent biography of Cobbett see Ingrams, *Life and Adventures of William Cobbett.* See also Cobbett's *Autobiography;* G. D. H. Cole, *Life of William Cobbett;* Spater, *William Cobbett;* and Gaines, *William Cobbett and the United States.*

18. Carr, *The Coming of War,* 222, 226–227; Perkins, *Prologue to War,* 29; Bailey, *Diplomatic History of American People,* 116, 126; Alice B. Keith, "Relaxations in the British Restrictions on the American Trade with the West Indies, 1783–1802," *JModH* 20 (1948), 1–18.

19. Quoted in Hecksher, *The Continental System,* 104. This is a most comprehensive examination of economic warfare in the period. See also Crouzet, *L'Economie Britannique et le blocus continental.*

20. In 1810 there were only 269 cotton mills and 153 iron furnaces in the United States, most of them very small; Perkins, *Prologue to War,* 53–56, 96.

21. The standard work on impressment of Americans is Zimmerman, *Impressment of American Seamen.* For more recent research on the subject see Scott Thomas Jackson, "Impressment and Anglo-American Discord, 1787–1818" (Ph.D. diss., University of Michigan, 1976); and David Scott Thompson, "'This Crying Enormity': Impressment as a Factor in Anglo-American Foreign Relations" (Master's thesis, Portland State University, 1993). See also Michael A. Lewis, *Social History of the Navy,* 85–140, 434–439.

22. Lavery, *Nelson's Navy,* 117–123.

23. Thomas Barclay to Vice-Admiral Sir Thomas Mitchell, 22 November 1803, in Rives, *Selections from Correspondence of Thomas Barclay,* 154; Geoffrey J. Marcus, *Heart of Oak,* 117–119. For a biography of Merry see Lester, *Anthony Merry Redivivus.*

24. Adam Smith, *Wealth of Nations,* 1: 112.

25. Watson, *The Reign of George III,* 472.

26. In 1802 Congress revised the Naturalization Act of 1798, which set the residence requirement for American citizenship at fourteen years. This was federal law, however, and individual states often awarded citizenship more freely; Glover, *Britain at Bay,* 67–68.

27. Admiral Pellew, commander-in-chief of the Mediterranean Fleet, reported on 12 December 1812 that there were 482 Americans serving with him, and of these 109 (22 percent) had volunteered to continue their service (TNA, ADM 1/425); on 28 May 1813 he sent 115 back to Britain as prisoners with a full nominal roll (TNA, ADM 1/426). Costello, *Nelson's Yankee Boy,* presents a fictionalized first-hand account of Americans being pressed into the Royal Navy, 1–16.

28. Uriah Phillips Levy, *Defense of Uriah Phillips Levy,* 6. Levy encountered Cochrane in Paris in 1823 and thanked him. See also "Uriah Phillips Levy," in J. R. Marcus, *Memoirs of American Jews,* 1: 76–116; *DAB,* 6: 203–204.

29. Zimmerman, *Impressment of American Seamen,* 266–267.

30. TNA, ADM 1/130, "Statement of Thomas Brown and Robert Clark, 2 May 1806," Ins 259.

31. TNA, ADM 1/138, p. 505, Gambier to Pole, 11 July 1808.

32. Pope, *Life in Nelson's Navy,* 109–113.

33. Morison and Commager, *Growth of the American Republic,* 1: 401.

34. See Harvey Strum, "The Leander Affair," *AN* 43 (1983), 40–50. For a personal account see Basil Hall, *Fragments of Voyages and Travels,* 46–49.

35. Ashton, *Economic History,* table xiv, 252.

36. See G. S. Graham, *Sea Power and British North America,* chap. 11, "The Fight for the West India Carrying Trade"; J. H. Rose, "British West India Commerce a Factor in the Napoleonic Wars," *CHJ* 3 (1930), 34–46.

37. LC, Monroe Papers, Monroe to Secretary of State, 1 July 1804. For a biography of Monroe, see Ammon, *James Monroe.*

38. William S. Dudley, *Naval War of 1812,* 1: 17–21; Herbert W. Briggs, *The Doctrine of Continuous Voyage,* 11–40; Horsman, *Causes,* 71–75; Carr, *The Coming of War,* 228–229; Perkins, *First Rapprochement,* 86–89, 177–180; idem, *Prologue to War,* 79–82; idem, "Sir William Scott and the Essex," *WMQ,* 3d ser., 13 (April 1956), 169–183.

39. Emsley, *British Society and the French Wars,* 116.

40. Glover, *Britain at Bay,* 13, 17–19.

41. Stephen, *War in Disguise,* 123. Stephen had worked in the West Indies and was familiar with the conditions of trade during the long naval war with France; his was far from being an extreme jingoistic view. He was very religious, belonging to the Clapham Sect, and devoted a large part of his life to fighting slavery. He defended the taking of prizes in war as the only means by which seamen could hope "to wrest the means of comfortably sustaining [honour]"; for the common sailor, "the natural motives of dislike to the naval service, are in their breasts far more effectually combated by the hope of prize money, than by all other inducements" (106–107).

42. Perkins, *Prologue to War,* 77–79.

43. Carr, *The Coming of War,* 229–231; Horsman, *Causes,* 63–82.

44. Thomas Barclay to Anthony Merry, 26 and 27 April, 13 May 1806, in Rives, *Selections from Correspondence of Thomas Barclay,* 230–233, 240–241; Perkins, *Prologue to War,* 107.

45. Laughton, *Letters and Papers of Lord Barham,* 3: 118.

46. TNA, FO 5/51, Holland and Auckland to Lord Howick, 20 October 1806; Anthony Steel, "Impressment in the Monroe-Pinkney Negotiation, 1806–7," *AHR* 57 (1951–52), 357. See also A. D. Harvey, "The Ministry of All the Talents: The Whigs in Office, February 1806 to March 1807," *HJ* 15 (1972), 619–649. On Pinkney see Horace H. Hagan, "The Greatest American Lawyer," *Case and Comment* 22 (1916), 87–96.

47. See Donald R. Hickey, "The Monroe-Pinkney Treaty of 1806: A Reappraisal," *WMQ,* 3d ser., 44 (January 1987), 65–88; Brant, *James Madison: Secretary of State,* 366–373.

48. Perkins, *Prologue to War,* 89–139; Anthony Steel, "Anthony Merry and the Anglo-American Dispute about Impressment, 1803–6," *CHJ* 9 (1949), 331–358; idem, "Impressment in the Monroe-Pinkney Negotiations, 1806–7," *AHR* 57 (1952), 352–369; Charles R. Ritcheson, "Thomas Pinckney's London Mission, 1792–1796, and the Impressment Issue," *International History Review* 2 (1980), 523–541; George Selement, "Impressment and the American Merchant Marine, 1782–1812," *MM* 54 (1973), 409–418.

49. Hickey, *War of 1812,* 16. For an examination of Jefferson's conviction that Britain posed a greater threat than Bonaparte, see Lawrence S. Kaplan, "Jefferson, the Napoleonic Wars, and the Balance of Power," *WMQ,* 3d ser., 14 (April 1957), 196–217.

50. Heckshher, *The Continental System,* 88–97.

51. For a biography see Denis Gray, *Spencer Perceval,* especially 169–173.

52. Horsman, *Causes,* 96–97. For biographies of Canning see Hinde, *George Canning;* Marriott, *George Canning and His Times;* Charles Petrie, *George Canning;* and Rolo,

George Canning. See also A. Aspinall, "The Canningite Party," *Transactions of the Royal Historical Society,* 4th ser., 17 (1934), 177–226; and Bradford Perkins, "George Canning, Great Britain and the United States, 1807–1809," *AHR* 63 (1957–58), 1–22.

53. For a biography of Barron, see William Oliver Stevens, *An Affair of Honor.*

54. TNA, ADM 1/5383, "Proceedings of the Court Martial of Jenkin Ratford, William Ware, Daniel Martin and John Strachan"; ADM 1/497, pp. 581–582, "Letter Referring to the Court Martial of Jenkin Ratford, William Ware, Daniel Martin and John Strachan." Some American scholars continue to assume that these men had been impressed, e.g., Robert E. Cray, "Remembering the USS Chesapeake: The Politics of Maritime Death and Impressment," *JER* 25 (2005), 445–474.

55. TNA, CO 42/160, p. 24, Canning to Monroe, 2 August 1807; Rodger, *Command of the Ocean,* 566; Silverstone, *Divided Union,* 75–80. Spencer C. Tucker and Frank T. Reuter have written a detailed account of this affair, *Injured Honor.* They find no evidence that it was part of British government policy, but it is highly unlikely that they would. There is no doubt that the British were prepared to go to war to defend the right of impressment, and it seems quite likely that this was a deliberate warning of that intent; and the incident certainly did nothing to hamper Berkeley's career, as he was subsequently appointed to command off the coast of Portugal in support of Wellington at Lisbon. Both Barron and Humphreys, however, saw their careers ruined. See also Emmerson, *The Chesapeake Affair of 1807;* C. E. S. Dudley, "The *Leopard* Incident, 1807," *History Today* 19 (1969), 468–474; Edward E. Gaines, "George Cranfield Berkeley and the *Chesapeake-Leopard* Affair of 1807," in Bales, *America in the Middle Period;* Burt, *United States, Great Britain, and British North America,* 241–243; Carr, *The Coming of War,* 239–241; Dye, *Fatal Cruise of the Argus,* 43–70; Perkins, *Prologue to War,* 140–142, 190–197. For a biography of Berkeley see Brian M. De Toy, "Wellington's Admiral: The Life and Career of George Berkeley, 1753–1818" (Ph.D. diss., Florida State University, 1997).

56. J. H. Rose, "Canning and Denmark, 1807," *English Historical Review* 11 (1896), 8–92; A. N. Ryan, "The Causes of the British Attack on Copenhagen in 1807," ibid., 68 (1953), 37–55.

57. Michael Roberts, "The Leadership of the Whig Party in the House of Commons from 1807 to 1815," *English Historical Review* 50 (1935), 620–638.

58. Horsman, *Causes,* 115–122: Perkins, *Prologue to War,* 197–200; Watson, *The Reign of George III,* 464–466. See also François Crouzet, "Bilan de l'économie britannique pendant les guerres de la Révolution et de l'empire," *Revue Historique* 234 (1965), 71–110; idem, "Groupes de pression et politique de blocus: Remarques sur les origines des Ordres en Conseil de novembre 1807," ibid., 228 (1962), 45–72.

59. See Richard Glover, "The French Fleet, 1807–1814: Britain's Problem and Madison's Opportunity," *JModH* 39 (1967), 233–252.

60. See Jennings, *The American Embargo;* Louis M. Sears, *Jefferson and Embargo;* idem, "British Industry and the Embargo," *Quarterly Journal of Economics* 34 (1919–20), 88–113; Spivak, *Jefferson's English Crisis;* G. W. Daniels, "American Cotton Trade with Liverpool

under the Embargo and Non-Intercourse Acts," *AHR* 21 (1915–16), 276–287; Jeffrey A. Frankel, "The 1807–1809 Embargo against Great Britain," *JEH* 42 (1982), 291–308; and Herbert Heaton, "Non-Importation, 1806–1812," *JEH* 1 (1941), 178–198.

61. *AC,* Tenth Cong., 2d sess. (1808), 1798–1804. For a compelling view of Jefferson's disregard for civil liberties, see Leonard W. Levy, *Jefferson and Civil Liberties,* chap. 6. See also Donald G. Alcock, "The Best Defense Is . . . Smuggling? Vermonters during the War of 1812," *Canadian Review of American Studies* 25 (1995), 73–92; Richard F. Casey, "North Country Nemesis: The Potash Rebellion and the Embargo of 1807–09," *NYHSQ* 64 (1980), 31–49; Harvey Strum, "A Gross and Unprovoked Outrage: Niagara Incident," *IS* 48 (1992), 28–90; idem, "Smuggling in the War of 1812," *History Today* 29 (August 1979), 532–537; idem, "Smuggling in Maine during the Embargo and the War of 1812," *Colby Library Quarterly* 19 (1983), 90; John D. Forbes, "Boston Smuggling, 1807–1815," *AN* 10 (April 1950), 144–154; H. N. Muller III, "Smuggling into Canada: How the Champlain Valley Defied Jefferson's Embargo," *VH* 38 (Winter 1970), 5–21; and Reginald C. Stuart, "Special Interests and National Authority in Foreign Policy: American-British Provincial Links during the Embargo and the War of 1812," *Diplomatic History* 8 (1984), 311–328.

62. Carr, *The Coming of War,* 252; Jennings, *The American Embargo,* chaps. 7–9.

63. Ritcheson, "Thomas Pinckney's London Mission," 531–534; Glover, *Britain at Bay,* 200–204; De Toy, "Wellington's Admiral," 576–588.

64. Horsman, *Causes,* 104–109.

65. Egan, *Neither Peace nor War,* 97; Carr, *The Coming of War,* 257; Horsman, *Causes,* 141–142; Perkins, *Prologue to War,* 71–72.

66. Emsley, *British Society and the French Wars,* 137, 153–154; Horsman, *Causes,* 124–136.

67. Watson, *The Reign of George III,* 466; Dorothy Burne Goebel, "British Trade to the Spanish Colonies, 1783–1826," *AHR* 43 (1937–8), 288–320.

68. Reilly, *The British at the Gates,* 24.

69. Gardiner, *Naval War of 1812,* 9.

70. Perkins, *Prologue to War,* 236–237.

71. Canning to Bathurst, 24 March 1809, in Bickley, *Report on Manuscripts of Bathurst,* 86–87; Horsman, *Causes,* 142. For biographies of Castlereagh see C. J. Bartlett, *Castlereagh;* Derry, *Castlereagh;* and Webster, *The Foreign Policy of Castlereagh.* See also C. K. Webster, H. Temperley, and E. Cooke, "The Duel between Castlereagh and Canning in 1809," *CHJ* 3 (1930), 83–95. Its significance for subsequent events is discussed by Stephen Jay Gould, "George Canning's Left Buttock," in *Bully for Brontosaurus,* 21–31.

72. Carr, *The Coming of War,* 264–275; Perkins, *Prologue to War,* 69–70; Watson, *The Reign of George III,* 466–467.

73. Vandal, *Napoléon et Alexandre 1er,* 2: 441–445.

74. Horsman, *Causes,* 175–177; Perkins, *Prologue to War,* 287. This argument was convincingly made by George R. Taylor in two articles: "Agrarian Discontent in the Mississippi Valley Preceding the War of 1812," *Journal of Political Economy* 39 (1931), 471–505;

and "Prices in the Mississippi Valley Preceding the War of 1812," *Journal of Economic and Business History* 3 (1930–31), 148–163. See also Margaret Kinard Latimer, "South Carolina—A Protagonist of the War of 1812," *AHR* 61 (1955–56), 914–929.

75. Stuart, *United States Expansionism and British North America,* 81.

76. Sugden, *Tecumseh,* 43, 86–90. For Wayne's campaign see Gaff, *Bayonets in the Wilderness;* and Milo M. Quaife, ed., "General James Wilkinson's Narrative of the Fallen Timbers Campaign," *MVHR* 16 (1929–30), 81–90. For an overview of American Indian policy, see Horsman, *Expansion and American Indian Policy.* For overviews of British-Indian relations, see Robert S. Allen, *His Majesty's Indian Allies;* idem, "His Majesty's Indian Allies: Native Peoples, the British Crown and the War of 1812," *MHR* 14 (Fall 1988), 1–24; Calloway, *Crown and Calumet;* Reginald Horsman, "The British Indian Department and the Resistance to General Anthony Wayne, 1793–1795," *MVHR* 49 (1961–62), 269–290; idem, "British Indian Policy in the Northwest, 1797–1812," *MVHR* 45 (1958–59), 51–66; Cecil K. Byrd, "The Northwest Indians and the British Preceding the War of 1812," *IMH* 38 (1942), 427–476.

77. Horsman, *Matthew Elliott,* 157–173; idem, "Western War Aims, 1811–1812," *IMH* 53 (1957), 1–18; idem, "The Role of the Indian in the War," in Mason, *After Tippecanoe,* 60–77; Julius W. Pratt, *Expansionists of 1812,* 60–125. See also Dice R. Anderson, "The Insurgents of 1811," in American Historical Association, *Annual Report* 1 (1911), 165–176; Christopher B. Coleman, "The Ohio Valley in the Preliminaries of the War of 1812," *MVHR* 7 (1920–21), 39–50, reprinted in *OAHSQ* 3 (1924), 39–50; Robert L. Fisher, "The Western Prologue to the War of 1812," *Missouri Historical Review* 30 (1936), 267–268; and Ellery L. Hall, "Canadian Annexation Sentiment in Kentucky prior to the War of 1812," *RKHS* 27 (1930), 372–378.

78. TNA, CO 42/136, Lieutenant-General Sir James Craig to Sir Francis Gore, 6 and 28 December 1807; *DCB,* 5: 205–214; *DNB,* 13: 945–947. John Sugden's *Tecumseh* is the easily the best biography. See also Herbert C. W. Goltz Jr., "Tecumseh, The Prophet and the Rise of the Northwest Indian Confederation" (Ph.D. diss., University of Western Ontario, 1973), 135–258. Allan W. Eckert's *A Sorrow in Our Heart* is a biography that succeeds better as fiction by an author who also wrote a play based on his hero. See also Edmunds, *Tecumseh and the Quest for Indian Leadership;* idem, "Tecumseh, the Shawnee Prophet, and American History: A Reassessment," *Western Historical Quarterly* 14 (1983), 261–276. Edmunds has also written the only worthwhile biography of Tenskwatawa, *The Shawnee Prophet.*

79. For biographies see Horsman, *Matthew Elliott; DCB,* 5: 301–303.

80. LAC, RG 10 M2 R627, McKee to William Halton, 11 June 1807; Horsman, *Causes,* 158–166; Perkins, *Prologue to War,* 95–96; H. C. W. Goltz Jr., "The Indian Revival Religion and the Western District, 1805–1813," in Pryke and Kusilek, *The Western District,* 18–32. For biographies of Clay, see Mayo, *Henry Clay;* and Remini, *Henry Clay.*

81. LC, Madison Papers, vol. 38, Jefferson to Madison, 17 August 1809.

82. LC, Rodney Papers, Clay to Caesar A. Rodney, 6 August 1810.

83. *AC,* Eleventh Cong., 1st sess. (1810), 579–580; Horsman, *Causes,* 182.

84. Heckshér, *The Continental System,* 140; Perkins, *Prologue to War,* 240–246; Carr, *The Coming of War,* 280–281; Bonnel, *La France, Les Ftats-Unis,* 34–36, 290–303; Hickey, *War of 1812,* 22, 42–43.

85. See Isaac Joslin Cox, "The Pan-American Policy of Jefferson and Wilkinson," *MVHR* 1 (1914–15), 212–239; Clifford L. Egan, "United States, France and West Florida, 1803–1807," *FHQ* 47 (January 1969), 227–252. See also Anthony W. Rasporich, "Quasi-Alliance with France in 1812: An Ideological Study, 1789–1812" (Master's thesis, Queen's University, 1964).

86. Rutland, *James Madison,* 215; *ASP: FR,* 3: 7–98.

87. Cox, *The West Florida Controversy,* 312–436; idem, "The American Intervention in West Florida," *AHR* 17 (1911–12), 290–313; Margeurite B. Hamer, "John Rhea of Tennessee," *East Tennessee Historical Society Publications* 3 (1932), 35–44; Alfred Hasbrouck, "Our Undeclared War with Spain," *Journal of the American Military History Foundation* 2 (1938), 115–125; James A. Padgett, ed., "The West Florida Revolution of 1810, as Told in the Letters of John Rhea, Fulwar Skipwith, Reuben Kemper and Others," *LHQ* 21 (January 1938), 76–202; Thomas M. Owen, ed., "West Florida and Its Attempt on Mobile, 1810–1811," *AHR* 2 (July 1897), 699–705. For an analysis of Republican thinking in the run-up to war, see Roger H. Brown, *The Republic in Peril;* Watts, *The Republic Reborn;* and John Matthew Phillips, "Republican Politics and the War of 1812" (Ph.D. diss., University of Cambridge, 2002).

88. Watson, *The Reign of George III,* 470.

89. Bryant, *Age of Elegance,* 50–52. How much this owed to Bonaparte's Continental System is unclear. Heckshér argues that its effects were mild and undercut by smuggling, but at least one more recent study suggests that it did considerable damage to the British economy: François Crouzet, "Wars, Blockades and Economic Change in Europe, 1792–1815," *JEH* 24 (1964), 567–588.

90. TNA, ADM 1/501, pp. 100–102, Bingham to Sawyer, 21 May 1811; W. S. Dudley, *Naval War of 1812,* 1: 40–50; Gardiner, *Naval War of 1812,* 21.

91. Horsman, *Causes,* 220–222; Perkins, *Prologue to War,* 274–276, 279. See also Margaret B. Tinksom, "Caviar along the Potomac: Sir Augustus John Foster's Notes on the United States, 1804–1812," *WMQ,* 3d ser., 8 (1951), 69–107.

92. Phillips and Reede, *Neutrality,* 158–166; Heckshér, *The Continental System,* 205–213; Watson, *The Reign of George III,* 470–471.

93. Carr, *The Coming of War,* 302; J. C. A. Stagg, "James Madison and the 'Malcontents': The Political Origins of the War of 1812," *WMQ,* 3d ser., 53 (1976), 567–569.

94. For biographies of Harrison see Cleaves, *Old Tippecanoe;* Goebel, *William Henry Harrison;* and Beverly W. Bond Jr., "William Henry Harrison and the War of 1812," *MVHR* 13 (1926–27), 499–516. On Prophetstown see Timothy D. Willig, "Prophetstown on the Wabash: The Native Spiritual Defense of the Old Northwest," *MHR* 23 (Fall 1997),

115–158. For the events leading to and the battle of Tippecanoe, see Sugden, *Tecumseh,* 193–236; Gilpin, *War of 1812 in Old Northwest,* 14–19; Adam Walker, *Journal of Two Campaigns,* 1–30; Pirtle, *The Battle of Tippecanoe;* Reginald Horsman, "American Policy in the Old Northwest, 1783–1812," *WMQ,* 3d ser., 18 (April 1961), 48–53; Marshall Smelser, "Tecumseh, Harrison, and the War of 1812," *IMH* 65 (March 1969), 25–44, with particular reference to Kentucky; Joe C. Creason, "The Battle of Tippecanoe, November 7, 1811," *FCHQ* 36 (1962), 308–319; Florence G. Watts, ed., "Lieutenant Charles Larabee's Account of the Battle of Tippecanoe," *IMH* 57 (September 1961), 225–247; Isaac Naylor, "The Battle of Tippecanoe, as Described by Judge Isaac Naylor, a Participant—A Recently Discovered Account," *IMH* 2 (December 1906), 163–169; John Tipton, "John Tipton's Tippecanoe Journal," ibid., 170–184; Richard G. Carlson, ed., "George P. Peter's Version of the Battle of Tippecanoe," *VH* 45 (Winter 1977), 38–43; and J. Wesley Whicker, ed., "Shabonee's Account of Tippecanoe," *IMH* 17 (December 1921), 353–363. For the aftermath and the controversy about the militia's performance, see Robert S. Lambert, "The Conduct of the Militia at Tippecanoe: Elihu Stout's Controversy with Colonel John P. Boyd, January 1812," *IMH* 51 (September 1955), 237–250.

95. *True American* (Trenton, N.J.), 2, 9, and 16 December 1811 and 6 January 1812; *Essex Register* (Salem, Mass.), 21 December 1811; *New-Hampshire Patriot* (Concord, N.H.), 24 December 1811; *Reporter* (Lexington, N.H.), 23 November 1811, 14 March 1812.

96. Carr, *The Coming of War,* 304; F. P. Prucha, "Andrew Jackson's Indian Policy: A Reassessment," *JAH* 56 (1969–70), 527–539. Jackson's complicated and contradictory nature led his first biographer, James Parton, to declare that he was "a traitor and a patriot. He was one of the greatest of generals and wholly ignorant of the art of war"; *Life of Andrew Jackson,* 1: vii. There have been innumerable biographies and studies of him since. For a good recent account see Brands, *Andrew Jackson;* and for a focus on his early life see Buchanan, *Jackson's Way.* See also Ratner, *Andrew Jackson and His Tennessee Lieutenants;* and Charles Grier Sellers Jr., "Andrew Jackson versus the Historians," *MVHR* 44 (1957–58), 615–634.

97. See Swanton, *Social Organization and Social Usages;* Saunt, *A New Order of Things;* Debo, *The Road to Disappearance;* Joel W. Martin, *Sacred Revolt;* and Doster, *Creek Indians and Florida Lands.* See also Michael D. Green, *The Politics of Indian Removal,* chaps. 1 and 2; and J. Leitch Wright Jr., *Creeks and Seminoles,* chaps. 1–3.

98. Sugden, *Tecumseh,* 243–251; Richter, *Facing East from Indian Country,* 229 and 296 n. 76.

99. Jackson to Blount, 4 June 1812, in Jackson, *Correspondence,* 1: 225. Tom Kanon, "The Kidnapping of Martha Crawley and Settler-Indian Relations Prior to the War of 1812," *THQ* 64 (2005), 2–23. For Blount, see Mary Clark, "Willie Bount: Governor of Tennessee, 1809–1815," in Charles W. Crawford, *Governors of Tennessee;* and Elizabeth H. Peeler, "The Policies of Willie Bount as Governor of Tennessee, 1809–1815," *THQ* 1 (1942), 309–327; William A. Walker Jr., "Martial Sons: Tennessee Enthusiasm for the War of 1812," *THQ* 20 (1961), 20–37.

100. *Knoxville Gazette,* 25 May 1812. See also John G. Biel, ed., "The Savage Preface to 1812," in *Yearbook of the Society of Indiana Pioneers* (Indianapolis: Society of Indiana Pioneers, 1956).

101. Though the post was usually referred to as Fort Malden, its correct name was Fort Amherstburg; Antal, *A Wampum Denied,* 26. *NWR* 2 (13 June 1812), 256. Jeffersonian Republican and anglophobe Niles began his *Weekly Register* in September 1811 to support congressional militants demanding war with Britain. His prejudices became near obsessions and were pushed to the extreme. For a biography of the paper and the best work on Niles himself, see Luxon, *Niles' Weekly Register.* See also Schmidt, *Hezekiah Niles and American Economic Nationalism;* Donald R. Avery, "The Newspaper on the Eve of the War of 1812: Changes in Content Patterns" (Ph.D. diss., Southern Illinois University at Carbondale, 1982). For a look at the War Hawks' use of Indian depredations to further their cause, see Tom Kanon, "James Madison, Felix Grundy, and the Devil: A Western War Hawk in Congress," *FCHQ* 75 (2001), 453–455.

102. There is some debate over who exactly was a War Hawk. For a variety of opinions, see Roger H. Brown, "The War Hawks of 1812: An Historical Myth," *IMH* 60 (June 1964), 137–151; Alexander DeConde, "The War Hawks of 1812: A Critique," ibid., 152–154; Clifford L. Egan, "The Path to War in 1812 through the Eyes of a New Hampshire 'War Hawk,'" *Historical New Hampshire* 30 (1975), 147–177; Harry W. Fritz, "The War Hawks of 1812," *Capitol Studies* 5 (Spring 1977), 25–42; Ronald L. Hatzenbuehler, "The War Hawks and the Question of Congressional Behavior in 1812," *Pacific Historical Review* 65 (February 1976), 1–22; Reginald Horsman, "Who Were the War Hawks?" *IMH* 60 (June 1964), 121–136; Norman K. Risjord, "The War Hawks and the War of 1812," ibid., 155–158; idem, "1812: Conservatives, War Hawks, and the Nation's Honor," *WMQ,* 3d ser., 18 (April 1961), 196–210; and Stagg, "James Madison and the 'Malcontents,'" 557–585. For biographies of Calhoun see Irving H. Bartlett, *John C. Calhoun;* Coit, *John C. Calhoun;* Niven, *John C. Calhoun and Price of Union;* and Wiltse, *John C. Calhoun.* For Grundy see Parks, *Felix Grundy.*

103. *AC,* Twelfth Cong., 1st sess. (1812), 373–377; Charles M. Wiltse, "The Authorship of the War Report of 1812," *AHR* 49 (1943–44), 253–259. For Porter see Joseph A. Grande, "The Political Career of Peter Buell Porter, 1787–1829" (Ph.D. diss., Notre Dame University, 1971); and *DAB,* 8: 99–100.

104. Watson, *The Reign of George III,* 550–551; Horsman, *Causes,* 156–157, 225–229, 237–239; J. W. Pratt, *Expansionists of 1812,* 12–13.

105. See Lawrence S. Kaplan, "France and Madison's Decision for War, 1812," *MVHR* 50 (1964–65), 652–671; idem, "France and the War of 1812," *JAH* 57 (1971–72), 36–47.

106. Gribbin, *The Churches Militant,* 62–64, 78, 89, 103. See also Lawrence D. Cress, "Cool and Serious Reflection: Federalist Attitudes toward War in 1812," *JER* 7 (1987), 123–145; James M. Upton, "The Shakers as Pacifists in the Period between 1812 and the Civil War," *FCHQ* 47 (1973), 267–269.

107. J. W. Pratt, *Expansionists of 1812,* 126–152; Silverstone, *Divided Union,* 93; Norman K. Risjord, "1812: Conservatives, War Hawks and the Nation's Honor," *WMQ,* 3d ser., 18 (1961), 196–210.

108. *AC,* Twelfth Cong., 1st sess. (1812), 441–445, 525–546; Perkins, *Prologue to War,* 47–48. See Bruce, *John Randolph of Roanoke;* Kirk, *Randolph of Roanoke;* and Risjord, *The Old Republicans.* For a study of fears regarding the status of slaves see Matthew Mason, "'Nothing Is Better Calculated to Excite Divisions': Federalist Agitation against Slave Representation during the War of 1812," *New England Quarterly* 75 (2002), 531–561. Nova Scotia did not become part of Canada until 1949.

109. Patrick C. T. White, *A Nation on Trial,* 66.

110. See Ronald L. Hatzenbuehler and Robert L. Ivie, "Justifying the War of 1812: Towards a Model of Congressional Behaviour in Early War Crises," *Social Science History* 4 (1980), 453–477.

111. Clay to Thomas Bodley, 18 December 1812, in Clay, *Papers,* 842; Reginald Horsman, "On to Canada: Manifest Destiny and United States Strategy in the War of 1812," *MHR* 13 (Fall 1987), 1–24; J. C. A. Stagg, "James Madison and the Coercion of Great Britain: Canada, the West Indies, and the War of 1812," *WMQ,* 3d ser., 38 (1981), 3–34; and Tennyson, *Canada and the Commonwealth Caribbean.*

112. Channing, *History of the United States,* 4: 481–482. Zimmerman quotes 5,987 as "the more conservative figure for the years 1803 to 1812" (*Impressment of American Seamen,* 267). But this is merely the figure reported to the U.S. peace commissioners in 1814 as the number of applications for release from the Royal Navy received by the U.S. consulate in London between 1803 and 31 December 1811. A true figure would require removing all those applications made by British seamen with false protections and from American volunteers masquerading as pressed men; then add those pressed in the six months leading to the outbreak of war and all those pressed who never lodged formal complaints. An accurate figure will probably never be found. See Perkins, *Prologue to War,* 84–94; Glover, *Britain at Bay,* 71.

113. TNA, FO 5/104, p. 107, Unsigned Memorandum, "Impressment of American Seamen," 21 February 1812.

114. Gallatin, *Writings,* 1: 336.

115. Matthew Mason, "The Battle of the Slaveholding Liberators: Great Britain, the United States, and Slavery in the Early Nineteenth Century," *WMQ,* 3d ser., 59 (2002), 668–669.

116. Henry Adams, "Count Edward de Crillon," *AHR* 1 (1895–96), 52. See also Donald R. Hickey, "The Federalists and the Coming of the War, 1811–1812," *IMH* 75 (1979), 70–88.

117. W. F. Galpin, "The American Grain Trade to the Spanish Peninsula, 1810–1814," *AHR* 28 (October 1922), 25. See also G. E. Watson, "The United States and the Peninsular War, 1808–1812," *HJ* 19 (1976), 859–876.

118. USNA, RG 59/M30/R20, "Dispatches from United States Ministers to Great Britain, 1791–1906," Russell to Secretary of State, 14 January 1812; Milne to George Hume,

9 April 1812, in Edgar E. Hume, ed., "Letters Written during the War of 1812 by the British Naval Commander in American Waters (Admiral Sir David Hume)," *WMQ,* 2d ser., 10 (1930), 286; Albion and Pope, *Sea Lanes in Wartime,* 108. For Russell see Twila Muriel Linville, "The Public Life of Jonathan Russell" (Ph.D. diss., Kent State University, 1971).

119. In his study "American Sanctions against Great Britain, 1808–1812" (Ph.D. diss., University of Glasgow, 1972), Graham Watson highlights the indifference of British politicians to the problems created by American policy in connection with the Peninsular War. The two parliamentary inquiries into the Orders in Council in 1808 and 1812 raised only the problems facing British industry.

120. Perkins, *Prologue to War,* 369–372, 382–383; Carr, *The Coming of War,* 310–317. Horsman quickly dismisses the Crillon affair (*Causes,* 324–325). It is detailed in Samuel Eliot Morison, "The Henry-Crillon Affair," in *By Land and by Sea,* 265–286, originally published in *PMHS* 69 (1947–1950), 207–231. Both men's careers are dealt with exhaustively by Ernest Cruikshank in *Political Adventures of John Henry.*

121. Patrick, *Florida Fiasco,* 55–65.

122. Gardiner, *Naval War of 1812,* 23.

123. Carr, *The Coming of War,* 325–326; Mayo, *Henry Clay,* 509–513; Glenn Tucker, *Poltroons and Patriots,* 1: 66–67; Perkins, *Prologue to War,* 398. For a biography of Worthington see Alfred Byron Sears, *Thomas Worthington.*

124. For biographies of Brougham see Aspinall, *Lord Brougham and the Whig Party;* Garratt, *Lord Brougham;* Hawes, *Henry Brougham;* and New, *Life of Henry Brougham to 1830.*

125. Emsley, *British Society and the French Wars,* 160; Cookson, *The Friends of Peace,* 67–68; S. G. Checkland, "American versus West Indian Traders in Liverpool, 1793–1815," *JEH* 18 (1958), 141–160.

126. *The Times,* 2 February 1812. *The Times* was strongly anti-American but by no means represented the full range of British opinion. *The Examiner,* for example, took a broadly neutral view, while Cobbett's *Political Register* verged on being wholly pro-American. See Kenneth Ross Nelson, "Socio-Economic Effects of the War of 1812 on Britain" (Ph.D. diss., University of Georgia, 1972), 2–3.

127. See Gillen, *Assassination of the Prime Minister;* Gray, *Spencer Perceval,* 450–454.

128. For biographies of Liverpool, see Gash, *Lord Liverpool;* Charles Petrie, *Lord Liverpool and His Times;* and Yonge, *Life and Administration of Robert Banks.* On the crisis in Parliament, see Michael Roberts, "The Ministerial Crisis of May–June 1812," *English Historical Review* 51 (1936), 466–487.

129. *Leicester Chronicle,* 4 July 1812.

130. *Aris' Birmingham Gazette,* 3 August 1812.

131. James D. Richardson, *Compilation of Messages and Papers of the Presidents,* 1: 499–505. See also R. Bryan McAuley, "President James Madison and the War Congress of 1812" (Master's thesis, Southwest Texas State University, 1995).

132. Jackson, *Correspondence,* 1: 221–222.

133. See Heidler and Heidler, *Encyclopedia of War of 1812,* app. 1, pp. 571–574; Hatzenbuehler and Ivie, *Congress Declares War;* Ronald L. Hatzenbuehler, "Party Unity and the Decision for War in the House of Representatives, 1812," *WMQ,* 3d ser., 29 (1972), 367–390; idem, "The War Hawks and the Question of Congressional Leadership in 1812," *Pacific Historical Review* 45 (February 1976), 1–22; Leland R. Johnson, "The Suspense Was Hell: The Senate Vote for War in 1812," *IMH* 65 (December 1969), 247–267; Rudolph M. Bell, "Mr. Madison's War and Long Term Congressional Voting Behavior," *WMQ,* 3d ser., 36 (1979), 373–395; William R. Barlow, "Congress during the War of 1812" (Ph.D. diss., Ohio State University, 1961); Harvey J. Strum, "New York Federalists and Opposition to the War of 1812," *World Affairs,* Winter 1980, 169–187; idem, "New Jersey Politics and the War of 1812," *New Jersey History* 105 (Fall/Winter 1987), 37–69; Donald Yocovone, "Connecticut against the Tide: Federalism and the War of 1812," *Connecticut Historical Society Bulletin* 40 (1975), 1–7. For Pennsylvania's attitude to and subsequent role in the war see Sapio, *Pennsylvania and the War of 1812;* and Martin Kaufman, "War Sentiment in Western Pennsylvania: 1812," *Pennsylvania History* 31 (1964), 436–448.

2. Soldiers, Sailors, Immigrants, and Indians

Epigraph: Mary R. Archer, ed., "Journal of Major Isaac Roach, 1812–24," *PMHB* 17, no. 3 (1893), 132.

1. Croker, *Key to the Orders in Council,* 8. For biographies of Croker see Brightfield, *John Wilson Croker; DNB,* 14: 273–278. See also Croker, *The Croker Papers;* and C. I. Hamilton, "John Wilson Croker: Patronage and Clientage at the Admiralty, 1809–1857," *HJ* 43 (2000), 48–77.

2. Charles Petrie, *Lord Liverpool and His Times,* 170.

3. For biographies of Bathurst see Thompson, *Earl Bathurst and the British Empire; DNB,* 4: 354–355. For Melville and his father, Henry, see Fry, *The Dundas Despotism; DNB,* 17: 292–294.

4. Bryant, *Age of Elegance,* 109. There are many biographies of King George IV, as he later became, or aspects of his life. Recent studies include David, *Prince of Pleasure;* Hibbert, *George IV;* and Parissien, *George IV.*

5. BL, Liverpool Papers, 38386, pp. 195–196, [James Stephen?,] "Observations upon the Present War with the United States," 18 June 1812. See also Frank L. Owsley Jr., " Role of the South in the British General Strategy in the War of 1812," *THQ* 31 (1972), 22–38.

6. BL, Liverpool Papers, 38363, pp. 12–16, "Observations upon American Affairs," 16 September 1812.

7. For a well-illustrated study of the uniforms and equipment of both forces, see Katcher and Fosten, *The American War, 1812–14.* For further detail on British forces, see Chartrand, *British Forces in North America;* and Richard J. Koke, "The Britons Who Fought on the Canadian Frontier: Uniforms of the War of 1812," *NYHSQ* 45 (April 1961), 141–194. For details of daily life in the British Army, see Reid, *British Redcoat (2) 1793–1815.*

8. Fardy, *Before Beaumont Hamel*, 77–78; Eric I. Manders and René Chartrand, "Fencible Regiments and the 104th Foot in British North America, 1803–1817," *MCH* 27 (Spring 1975), 30–32.

9. Squires, *The 104th Regiment of Foot*, 43–45; Philippart, *Royal Military Calendar*, 1: 205–206. See Robert Henderson, "His Majesty's Canadian Regiment of Fencible Infantry, 1803–1816," *Military Illustrated* 37 (June 1991), 18–25; and 38 (July 1991), 27–33.

10. Brock to Duke of York [6 January 1806], in Tupper, *Life and Correspondence of Brock*, 33; Petre, *The Royal Berkshire Regiment*, 83–84.

11. For biographies of Brock, see Edgar, *General Brock;* Nursey, *The Story of Isaac Brock;* Read, *Life and Times of Major-General Isaac Brock;* Bagamudré, *Isaac Brock;* Fryer, *Bold, Brave and Born to Lead;* Ernest A. Cruikshank, "The Military Career and Character of Major-General Sir Isaac Brock," *New York State Historical Proceedings* 8 (1909), 67–90; Wesley B. Turner, "The Career of Isaac Brock in Canada, 1802–1812" (Master's thesis, University of Toronto, 1961); idem, *British Generals in the War of 1812*, chap. 3; *DCB*, 5: 109–115; *DNB*, 7: 749–750. For details of Fort George see Robert S. Allen, "A History of Fort George, Upper Canada," *Canadian Historic Sites: Occasional Papers in Archaeology and History* 11 (1974), 61–93.

12. The unit saw some action early in the war but then moved to garrison duties in Lower Canada; A. S. White, "Garrison, Reserve and Veteran Battalions," *JSAHR* 38 (1958), 156–157. See also Dunnigan, *The British Army at Mackinac;* and René Chartrand, Brian Dunnigan, and Dirk Gringhuis, "10th Royal Veteran Battalion, Fort Mackinac, 1812," *MCH* 23 (1971), 47–48, 82.

13. See G. F. G. Stanley, "The Contribution of the Canadian Militia during the War," in Mason, *After Tippecanoe*, 28–48.

14. Hitsman, *Incredible War*, 277.

15. See Ernest A. Cruikshank, "The 'Chesapeake' Crisis as It Affected Upper Canada," *OHSPR* 24 (1927), 281–322.

16. LAC, CO 42/347, Gore to Castlereagh, 7 October 1808.

17. *Quebec Mercury*, 31 August 1808.

18. Brock to Gordon Brock, 6 September 1807, in Tupper, *Life and Correspondence of Brock*, 64.

19. LAC, CO 42/136, Gore to Craig, 5 January 1808.

20. Hitsman, *Incredible War*, 5–6; Meinig, *The Shaping of America*, 43–66.

21. LAC, RG 9 I B1, vol. 2, 1812, Miscellaneous.

22. Stanley, *War of 1812*, 49–60.

23. Malcomson, *Brilliant Affair*, 35–66.

24. For de Rottenburg, see Turner, *British Generals in War of 1812*, chap. 5; *DCB*, 6: 660–662; Philippart, *Royal Military Calendar*, 1: 322–323; Glover, *Peninsular Preparation*, 128.

25. For biographies, see Brenton, *Some Account of Public Life of Prevost;* and Turner, *British Generals in War of 1812*, chap. 2; *DCB*, 5: 693–698; *DNB*, 45: 278–279; Philippart, *Royal Military Calendar*, 1: 131–132.

26. Ouellet, *Economic and Social History of Quebec,* 234–242; *DCB,* 6: 523–529, 586–598. See also Maxwell Sutherland, "The Civil Administration of Sir George Prevost 1811–1815: A Study in Conciliation" (Master's thesis, Queen's University, 1959). Officially, Plessis had been "Superintendent of the Romish Church" since 1806, but by ostentatiously urging Catholic loyalty to the Crown during the war he subsequently gained British government recognition as Roman Catholic bishop of Quebec, and was admitted to the Legislative Council in 1817; *DCB,* 6: 586–598.

27. See Eric I. Manders, Brian Dunnigan, and René Chartrand, "41st Regiment of Foot, 1779–1815," *MCH* 32 (Winter 1980), 166–167.

28. University of Virginia, John Hartwell Cocke Collection, Arthur Sinclair to Cocke, 25 August 1813; USNA, RG 45/M125/R40, Isaac Chauncey to William Jones, 5 November 1814; Gilpin, *War of 1812 in Old Northwest,* 45.

29. Hitsman, *Incredible War,* 32. For Baynes see Philippart, *Royal Military Calendar,* 2: 136–137.

30. TNA, WO 1/537, pp. 75–106, "Memorandum [on the defence of Canada]," 31 March 1841.

31. Stanley, *War of 1812,* 70.

32. LAC, MG 24 L8, Jacques Viger, "Ma Saberdache." See also H. R. Holmden, ed., "Baron de Gaugreben's Memoir of the Defense of Upper Canada," *CHR* 2 (March 1921), 58–68. On Kingston's importance see G. F. G. Stanley, "Kingston and the Defence of British North America," in Tulchinsky, *To Preserve and Defend,* 83–101; and Stephen D. Mecredy, "Some Military Aspects of Kingston's Development during the War of 1812" (Master's thesis, Queen's University, 1982).

33. Useful material on waterborne logistics can be found in Frederick C. Drake, "The Niagara Peninsula and Naval Aspects of the War of 1812," in Turner, *Military in Niagara Peninsula,* 5. A solid analysis of British lines of communication to the west is C. P. Stacey's "Another Look at the Battle of Lake Erie," *CHR* 39 (1958), 41–51.

34. See *DCB,* 8: 630–634.

35. Robert Malcomson, "'Nothing More Uncomfortable than Our Flat-Bottomed Boats': Bateaux in British Service during the War of 1812," *NM/MN* 13, no. 4 (2003), 17–28; Barbuto, *Niagara, 1814,* 13; Stanley, *War of 1812,* 71–73. On Molson and his steamboat see G. H. Wilson, "The Application of Steam to St. Lawrence Valley Navigation, 1809–1840" (Master's thesis, McGill University, 1961).

36. LAC, RG 8 I C1218, p. 308, Prevost to Bathurst, 15 July 1812.

37. Hitsman, *Incredible War,* 26, 30–31.

38. Robert Malcomson, "'Not Very Much Celebrated': The Evolution and Nature of the Provincial Marine, 1755–1813," *NM/MN* 9, no. 1 (2001), 25–37; Tom Malcomson, "Muster Table for the Royal Navy's Establishment on Lake Ontario during the War of 1812," *NM/MN* 9, no. 2 (2000), 41–67; William A. B. Douglas, "The Anatomy of Incompetence: The Provincial Marine in Defence of Upper Canada before 1813," *OH* 71 (March 1979), 3–25; C. P. Stacey, "The Ships of the British Squadron on Lake Ontario,

1812–14," *CHR* 34 (December 1953), 311–323. For biographical details of Woolsey see Leon N. Brown, "Commodore Melancthon Taylor Woolsey: Lake Ontario Hero of the War of 1812," *Oswego Historical Society Journal* 5 (1941), 14–21; James F. Cooper, "Melancthon Taylor Woolsey," *Graham's Magazine* 26 (1845), 14–21; Malcomson, *Lords of the Lake,* 17–20, 27–28.

39. LAC, MG 11 A21 NB, Hunter to Liverpool, 27 June 1812. For biographical details of Sherbrooke see Arthur Patchett Martin, *Life and Letters of Robert Lowe, Viscount Sherbrooke; DCB,* 6: 712–716; *DNB,* 50: 284–285; Philippart, *Royal Military Calendar,* 1: 133.

40. LAC, CO 42/90, Proclamation, 3 July 1812, contained in Sherbrooke to Bathurst, 2 August 1812; Bowler, *War of 1812,* 62; Facey-Crowther, *The New Brunswick Militia,* 30–31; Squires, *The 104th Regiment of Foot,* 108. See also Walter R. Copp, "Nova Scotian Trade during the War of 1812," *CHR* 18 (1937), 141–155.

41. Hitsman, *Incredible War,* 31–32; Donna Neary, Reginald L. Campbell, and René Chartrand, "100th Regiment of Foot (The Prince Regent's County of Dublin Regiment), 1812–1815," *MCH* 27 (Fall 1975), 118.

42. Lomax, *History of the 41st,* 49–50.

43. This unit began as The New Brunswick Regiment of Fencible Infantry, but when it volunteered en masse for service anywhere in the world it was taken into the line in 1810.

44. Glenn A. Steppler, "British Military Artificers in Canada, 1760–1815," *JSAHR* 60 (Autumn 1982), 150–163. For a contemporary report on the area's defence capability in time of war, see D. A. Muise, ed., "A Descriptive and Statistical Account of Nova Scotia and Its Dependencies," *Acadiensis* 2 (Autumn 1972), 82–93.

45. For a detailed description of raising the regiment see H. Winston Johnston, *The Glengarry Light Infantry,* chap. 2. For George Macdonell see George Raudzens, "'Red George' Macdonell, Military Saviour of Upper Canada?" *OH* 62 (December 1970), 199–212; W. S. Buell, "'Red George'—One of the Macdonells," *CHR* 4 (June 1923), 150–159; *DCB,* 9: 484–485; H. W. Johnston, *The Glengarry Light Infantry,* 219, 242–244. For Alexander Macdonell see ibid., 239–240; *DCB,* 7: 544–551.

46. Boss, *Stormont, Dundas and Glengarry Highlanders,* 29; H. W. Johnston, *The Glengarry Light Infantry,* 217–219.

47. LAC, RG 8 I, vol. 1218, Prevost to Bathurst, 26 May 1812. See Marvin Pakula, John F. Graham, and John R. Elting, "The Glengarry Light Infantry Fencible Regiment, 1812–1816," *MCH* 13 (Winter 1961), 113.

48. TNA, CO 42/146, pp. 197–202, Prevost to Liverpool, 20 April 1812; Eric I. Manders and René Chartrand, "Lower Canada Select Embodied Militia Battalions 1812–1815," *MCH* 31 (Fall 1979), 127.

49. For biographies of de Salaberry, see *DCB,* 6: 341–345; and Wohler, *Charles Michel de Salaberry.*

50. Hitsman, *Incredible War,* 36–39; Martin F. Auger, "French Canadian Participation in the War of 1812: A Social Study of the Voltigeurs Canadiens," *CMH* 10, no. 3 (2001), 23–41.

51. For a study of the conflict between civil and military administration, see William M. Weekes, "The War of 1812: Civil Authority and Martial Law in Upper Canada," *OH* 68 (Autumn 1956), 147–161.

52. *SBD*, 3: 545. For a biography of Merritt, see Jebediah Merritt, *Biography of Honourable William H. Merritt; DCB*, 9: 544–548.

53. AO, MU8559.2, Noah Freer, Captain and Quarter Master General's Office, Quebec, "Ideas on the Defence of the Canadas, Grounded upon the Present Strength, and Such Resources in Men, as the Populations of the Two Provinces May Offer," 8 May 1812.

54. See Ann Carlos, "The Causes and Origins of the North American Fur Trade Rivalry: 1804–1810," *JEH* 41 (1981), 777–794.

55. For histories of the North West Company see Marjorie W. Campbell, *The North West Company;* and Davidson, *The North West Company.*

56. Gray to Prevost, 13 January, 1812, "Memoranda on the Defensive Strength and Equipment of the North West Company"; and Gray to Prevost, 29 January 1812, in *DRIC*, 8–11, 11–12, 14–15. See also J. W. Pratt, "Fur Trade Strategy and the American Left Flank during the War of 1812," *AHR* 40 (1935), 246–273.

57. Horsman, *Causes*, 213–214.

58. Gough, *Fighting Sail*, 5–7.

59. Speech of Tecumseh, in *MPHC*, 25: 275–276.

60. Sugden, *Tecumseh*, 5–8, 24, 51, 86, 95–96.

61. John McDonald, "The Tragical Death of Wawillowa," *Western Christian Advocate*, 22 April 1836.

62. "Big Knives" or "Long Knives" became the Indian term for Americans during the Revolutionary War after Virginian Colonel John Gibson decapitated the distinguished Mingo chief Little Eagle in combat. Indians at first used the term in relation to Virginians, then for Americans in general; Butterfield, *Historical Account of Expedition against Sandusky*, 32–33.

63. LAC, RG 8 I C676, Claus to Brock, 16 June 1812; Sugden, *Tecumseh*, 43, 171–174, 185–190, 238, 265.

64. Berton, *Invasion of Canada*, 28, 81–85. For biographies see Ernest A. Cruikshank, "Robert Dickson, Indian Trader," *WHSC* 12 (1892), 13–53; Louis A. Tohill, "Robert Dickson, British Fur Trader on the Upper Mississippi," *North Dakota Historical Quarterly* 3 (1928–29), 5–49, 83–128, 182–203; idem, "Robert Dickson, the Fur Trade and the Minnesota Boundary," *Minnesota History* 6 (1925), 330–342; *DCB*, 6: 209–211.

65. Robert S. Allen, *His Majesty's Indian Allies*, 125–128, 224; Dowd, *A Spirited Resistance*, 123–147, 181–201. See also George C. Chalou, "The Red Pawns Go to War: British-American Indian Relations, 1812–1815" (Ph.D. diss., Indiana University, 1971).

66. Matthew Irwin to John Mason, 16 October 1812, in C. F. Carter, *Territorial Papers*, 10: 411–415; R. S. Allen, *His Majesty's Indian Allies*, 121–122, 219–221.

67. LAC, RG 8 I C673, p. 171, Brock to Prevost, 11 December 1811.

68. LAC, CO 42/23, Prince Regent's Instructions to Prevost, 22 October 1811; Prevost to Brock, 14 December 1811, in Tupper, *Life and Correspondence of Brock,* 133.

69. Berton, *Invasion of Canada,* 88–92; Meddert, *Raw Recruits and Bullish Prisoners,* 27–35; Sugden, *Tecumseh,* 274–275, 279. For Hull see Samuel C. Clarke, "William Hull," *New England Historical and Genealogical Magazine* 47 (1893), 141–153, 305–314; Alec R. Gilpin, "General William Hull and the War on the Detroit in 1812" (Ph.D. diss., University of Michigan, 1950).

70. TNA, CO 43/23, Liverpool to Prevost, 15 May 1812.

71. Hitsman, *Incredible War,* 286.

72. Christopher Lloyd, *Captain Marryat and the Old Navy,* 117. See also Pocock, *Captain Marryat; DCB,* 7: 585–586.

73. Officially the regiment's title was 1st (Royal) Regiment of Foot, and it became 1st Regiment of Foot (The Royal Scots) from 2 November 1812. But it was, like most units of the period, strongly Irish. When it arrived in the West Indies on 20 June the composition was 287 Scots, 352 English, 505 Irish, and 56 assorted foreigners. It was accompanied by 85 women and 78 children; Leask and McCance, *Regimental Records of Royal Scots,* 262.

74. See *DCB,* 5: 346–347; Philippart, *Royal Military Calendar,* 1: 356.

75. Brock to Savery Brock, 18 September 1812, in Tupper, *Life and Correspondence of Brock,* 316; Higginson, *Major Richardson's,* 5. For Richardson see *DCB,* 8: 743–748.

76. Dunlop, *Recollections of the American War,* 63; *DCB,* 7: 260–264.

77. Brinckman, *Historical Record of the Eighty-ninth,* 16.

78. R. L. Rogers, *History of Lincoln and Welland Regiment,* 2–3. Both the 1st and 2nd Regiments of Lincoln Militia had artillery companies, and following the outbreak of war the Incorporated Artillery Company and Royal Militia Artillery were raised in Upper and Lower Canada respectively, together with the Mississippi Volunteer Artillery in the far west. The Loyal Company of Artillery was formed in Saint John, New Brunswick, in 1793 and claims to be the third-oldest artillery unit in the Commonwealth today. Two companies of drivers were also formed: Captain Isaac Swayze's Troop of Provincial Royal Artillery Drivers in Upper Canada and the Corps of Provincial Royal Artillery Drivers in Lower Canada. See Nicholson, *Gunners of Canada,* 45–51; and Jose M. Bueno and René Chartrand, "Upper Canadian Militia and Provincials, 1812–1815," *MCH* 28 (Spring 1976), 14–16.

79. See John Norton, *Journal;* J. M. Murray, "John Norton," *OH* 37 (1945), 7–16; *DCB,* 6: 550–553; Charles M. Johnston, "William Claus and John Norton: A Struggle for Power in Old Ontario," *OH* 57 (June 1965), 101–108.

80. See Benn, *Iroquois in War of 1812;* David J. Glenney, "An Ethnohistory of the Grand River Iroquois and the War of 1812" (Master's thesis, University of Guelph, 1973); G. F. G. Stanley, "The Significance of the Six Nations Participation in the War of 1812," *OH* 55 (1963), 215–231.

81. Malcomson, *Brilliant Affair,* 48–52.

82. Benn, *Iroquois in War of 1812,* 30, 42–43. See also *DHC,* 3: 105–113.

83. Perkins, *Prologue to War,* 284, 347. For Jefferson's view of war see Stuart, *The Half-Way Pacifist.*

84. Andrew Jackson, *Correspondence,* 1: 222.

85. LC, Jefferson Papers, reel 46, Jefferson to William Duane, 4 August 1812; Jefferson, *Writings,* 9: 366. See Reginald L. Horsman, "On to Canada: Manifest Destiny and United States Strategy in the War of 1812," *MHR* 13 (Fall 1987), 1–24.

86. Samuel Eliot Morison, "Dissent in the War of 1812," in Morison, Merk, and Friedel, *Dissent in Three American Wars,* 5. See also Michael A. Bellesiles, "Experiencing the War of 1812," in Flavell and Conway, *Britain and America Go to War,* 207–208. For a study of conflicting naval policy see Symonds, *Navalists and Anti-Navalists;* and Peter J. Kastor, "Toward 'the Maritime War Only': The Question of Naval Mobilization, 1811–1812," *JMilH* 56 (1997), 455–480.

87. See *Testimony Taken before the Committee of Grievances and Courts of Justice;* Frank A. Cassell, "The Great Baltimore Riot of 1812," *MHM* 70 (Fall 1975), 241–259; Paul A. Gilje, "The Baltimore Riots of 1812 and the Breakdown of the Anglo-American Mob Tradition," *Journal of Social History* 13 (Summer 1980), 547–564; idem, " 'Le Menu Peuple' in America: Identifying the Baltimore Rioters of 1812," *MHM* 81 (Spring 1986), 50–66; Donald R. Hickey, "The Darker Side of Democracy: The Baltimore Riots of 1812," *Maryland Historian* 7 (1976), 1–14; idem, *War of 1812,* chap. 3.

88. For Stricker see John Stricker, "General John Stricker," *MHM* 9 (1914), 209–218.

89. George, *Terror on the Chesapeake,* 14–20; Pitch, *The Burning of Washington,* 1–12; Glenn Tucker, *Poltroons and Patriots,* 1: 136–144. For biographies of Lee, see Royster, *Light Horse Harry Lee and the Legacy of the American Revolution;* and Thomas E. Templin, "Henry 'Light Horse Harry' Lee: A Biography" (Ph.D. diss., University of Kentucky, 1975).

90. *Connecticut Courant,* 25 August 1812. See also John E. Talmadge, "Georgia's Federalist Press and the War of 1812," *Journal of Southern History* 19 (1953), 488–500.

91. Hickey, *War of 1812,* 56–71; G. Tucker, *Poltroons and Patriots,* 1: 136–144; Harvey Strum, "New York's Antiwar Campaign," *Peace and Change* 7 (1982), 7–18.

92. For Eustis see G. W. Porter, "A Sketch of the Life and Character of the Late William Eustis," *Lexington Historical Society Proceedings* 1 (1890), 101–109.

93. Brant, *James Madison: Commander-in-Chief,* 53; Burt, *United States, Great Britain, and British North America,* 46; Stagg, *Mr. Madison's War,* 193.

94. Madison, *Writings,* 8: 210.

95. See William B. Skelton, "High Army Leadership in the War of 1812: The Making and Remaking of the Officer Corps," *WMQ,* 3d ser., 51 (1994), 253–274; Jeffrey Kimball, "The Fog and Friction of Frontier War: The Role of Logistics in American Offensive Failure during the War of 1812," *Old Northwest* 5 (Winter 1979–80), 323–343.

96. Major J. Mitchell, "British Troops in America," *JUSI,* 1836, 85; Graves, *Field of Glory,* 171.

97. See Spencer C. Tucker, *The Jeffersonian Gunboat Navy;* and Gene A. Smith, *"For the Purposes of Defense";* idem, " 'For the Purposes of Defense': Thomas Jefferson's

Naval Militia," *AN* 53 (1993), 30–38; idem, "A Means to an End: Gunboats and Jefferson's Theory of Defense," *AN* 55 (1995), 111–121; Dean R. Mayhew, "Jeffersonian Gunboats in the War of 1812," *AN* 32 (1982) 108–113.

98. Barnes, *Naval Actions in the War of 1812,* 10; Perkins, *Prologue to War,* 50–51. There are numerous biographies of the *Constitution,* the most relevant being Tyrone G. Martin, *Undefeated.* See also Lardas and Bryan, *American Heavy Frigates;* Canney, *Sailing Warships;* and Theodore M. Prudden, "Her Thunder Shook the Mighty Deep," *USNIP* 90 (January 1964), 74–83.

99. Brant, *James Madison: Commander-in-Chief,* 125–126. For a study of the Navy Department see Edward K. Eckert, *Navy Department in War of 1812.*

100. *AC,* Twelfth Cong., 1st sess. (1812), 803–846, 859–1001.

101. Armstrong to Eustis, 2 January 1812, in *DHC,* 3: 30.

102. USNA, RG 45/M149/R10, Hamilton to Rodgers and Hamilton to Decatur, 21 May 1812; M125/R24, Rodgers to Hamilton, 3 and 19 June, and Decatur to Hamilton, 8 June 1812; William S. Dudley, *Naval War of 1812,* 1: 52–59, 117–124; Brant, *James Madison: The President,* 402–404. For biographies of Decatur, all rather uncritical, see Allison, *Stephen Decatur;* Charles L. Lewis, *The Romantic Decatur;* Spencer C. Tucker, *Stephen Decatur;* De Kay, *Rage for Glory;* and Alexander Slidell Mackenzie, *Life of Stephen Decatur.* For a biography of Rodgers see Paullin, *Commodore John Rodgers.* For Bainbridge see Long, *Ready to Hazard;* and Dearborn, *Life of William Bainbridge.*

103. Perkins, *Prologue to War,* 361; Stagg, *Mr. Madison's War,* 90–91, 147–149; idem, "James Madison and the Coercion of Great Britain: Canada and the West Indies and the War of 1812," in Tennyson, *Canada and the Commonwealth Caribbean,* 39–47; Hatzenbuehler and Ivie, *Congress Declares War,* 31–33; Julius W. Pratt, *Expansionists of 1812,* 145–147.

104. Henry Adams, *History,* 6: 168, 206, 392, 395–396.

105. *AC,* Seventh Cong., 1st sess. (1802), 13–17; Balinky, *Albert Gallatin,* 167–179; idem, "Gallatin's Theory of War Finance," *WMQ,* 3d ser., 16 (1959), 73–82; William Barlow and David O. Powell, "Congressman Ezekiel Bacon of Massachusetts and the Coming of the War of 1812," *Historical Journal of Western Massachusetts* 6 (Spring 1978), 28–41. For Lewis, see *DAB,* 6: 222.

106. Barbuto, *Niagara, 1814,* 99; L. D. Cass, *Citizens in Arms,* 150–152; Huston, *The Sinews of War,* 102–112; Mahon, *War of 1812,* 3–4; Leonard D. White, *The Jeffersonians,* 211–223, 265–283. See also John K. Mahon, "The Principal Causes of the Failure of the United States Militia System during the War of 1812," *IMHJ* 4 (1979), 15–21; Cress, *Citizens in Arms;* idem, "The Standing Army, the Militia and the New Republic: Changing Attitudes toward the Military in American Society" (Ph.D. diss., University of Virginia, 1976); Jonathan David Hills, "The Militia's Relationship with the Regular Army in the War of 1812 with Particular Reference to the Militias of Ohio and New York" (Ph.D. diss., University of Sunderland, 2001).

107. Marguerite M. McKee, "Services of Supply in the War of 1812," *Quartermaster Review* 6 (1927), 45–55; Risch, *Quartermaster Support of the Army,* 81–180; Stagg, *Mr. Mad-*

ison's War, 155–161; L. D. White, *The Jeffersonians,* 224–232; René Chartrand, "The U.S. Army's Uniform Supply 'Crisis' during the War of 1812," *MCH* 40 (Summer 1988), 62–65; idem, *Uniforms and Equipment,* 24–34, 84–86; Kochan and Rickman, *The United States Army,* 12–16, 23–24.

108. Mahan, *Sea Power,* 1: 300–310.

109. Risch, *Quartermaster Support of the Army,* 136–142.

110. Dr. W. M. Ross in James Wilkinson, *Memoirs,* 3: 111; John Armstrong to Jacob Brown, 19 June 1812, in *DRINP,* 36; William B. Skelton, "High Army Leadership in the Era of the War of 1812: The Making and Remaking of the Officer Corps," *WMQ,* 3d ser., 51 (1994), 253–274.

111. For a biography see Erney, *Public Life of Henry Dearborn; DAB,* 5: 175.

112. TNA, CO 42/148, Foster to Castlereagh, 21 April 1812; *DHC,* 3: 53.

113. William Hull, *Memoirs,* 17.

114. *Aurora* (Philadelphia), 13 June 1812.

115. USNA, RG 107/M221/R43, Dearborn to Eustis, 10, 13, 28, and 30 July 1812; M6/R5, Eustis to Dearborn, 26 July 1812; R6, Eustis to Dearborn, 1 August 1812.

116. Winfield Scott, *Memoirs,* 1: 35–36. For biographies, see Timothy D. Johnson, *Winfield Scott;* and idem, "Young Fuss and Feathers: Winfield Scott's Early Career, 1808–1841" (Ph.D. diss., University of Alabama, 1989); see also Eisenhower, *Agent of Destiny;* Elliot, *Winfield Scott; DAB,* 8: 505–511.

117. See Charles E. Walker, "The Other Good Guys: Army Engineers in the War of 1812," *Military Engineer* 69 (May–June 1978), 178–183.

118. H. Adams, *History,* 2: 389. See J. C. A. Stagg, "Soldiers in Peace and War: Comparative Perspectives on the Recruitment of the United States Army, 1802–1815," *WMQ,* 3d ser., 57 (2000), 79–120.

119. There were to be ten infantry regiments, each with 72 officers, 144 NCOs, and 1,800 privates organized into two battalions of nine companies. This arrangement was changed on 26 June to twenty-five regiments of one-battalion strength, with two of artillery and one of light dragoons; *AC,* Twelfth Cong., 1st sess. (1812), 108; H. Adams, *History,* 6: 149–153; Hickey, *War of 1812,* 76–77.

120. *AC,* Twelfth Cong., 1st sess. (1812), 2111–12. The best source available shows that fewer than 2,100 men joined the regular ranks in the first four months of 1812, and over the next four months the number rose to only 8,140, far below establishment; "Enlisted Men in the United States Army," in Stagg, *Mr. Madison's War,* 620–621.

121. LC, Madison Papers, reel 14, Joseph Wheaton to Madison, 10 December 1812. For a study of pre-war common militia units, see Mark Pitcavage, "Ropes of Sand: Territorial Militias, 1801–1812," *JER* 13 (1993), 481–500. See also Robert L. Kerby, "The Militia System and the State Militias in the War of 1812," *IMH* 73 (June 1977), 102–124.

122. *ASP: MA,* 1: 319–320; *AC,* Twelfth Cong., 1st sess. (1812), 2235–37, 2267–69.

123. *National Intelligencer,* 17 October 1811. See Kreidberg and Henry, *History of Military Mobilization,* 23–59; Coffman, *The Old Army,* 34–41. For a biographical study of publisher

Joseph Gales and the *National Intelligencer,* see Howard F. Mahan, "Joseph Gales, the National Intelligencer, and the War of 1812" (Ph.D. diss., Columbia University, 1958).

124. Hickey, *War of 1812,* 75–76.

125. Campbell to Worthington, 17 June 1812, quoted in Stagg, *Mr. Madison's War,* 163. See also *AC,* Twelfth Cong., 1st sess. (1812), 723–801.

126. Hickey, *War of 1812,* 259–260; Horsman, *War of 1812,* 31, 33.

127. For a biography, see Irwin, *Daniel D. Tompkins.* For a history of the war in New York see Guernsey, *New York City and Vicinity during War of 1812–15;* William A. Griswold, "A Reasoned Approach to the Defense of New York Harbor for the War of 1812," *Journal of America's Military Past* 30 (Winter 2004), 26–42; and William J. Joseph, "New York in the War of 1812" (Ph.D. diss., Columbia University, 1957).

128. See J. C. A. Stagg, "Between Black Rock and a Hard Place: Peter B. Porter's Plan for an Invasion of Canada in 1812," *JER* 19 (1999), 385–422.

129. USNA, RG 107/M6/R/5, Eustis to Dearborn, 16 June 1812.

130. Hitsman, *Incredible War,* 53–54.

131. LAC, RG 8 I C676, p. 150, Brock to Prevost, 12 July 1812. For a study of the unpreparedness of the New York militia see Philip R. Shriver, ed., "Broken Locks and Rusty Barrels: A New York Militia Company on the Eve of the War of 1812," *New York History* 67 (1986), 353–357. See also Wilbur E. Apgar, "New York's Contribution to the War Effort of 1812," *NYHSQ* 29 (1945), 203–212; Allan J. Ferguson, ed., "Militia Service in 1812: Noadiah Hubbard's Memorandum Book," *MCH* 33 (Spring 1981), 38–39. A useful discussion of the state of transportation on the U.S. side of the border is Landon, *Bugles on the Border,* 7–9.

132. Tompkins, *Public Papers,* 3: 21.

133. J. W. Redway, "General Van Rensselaer and the Niagara Frontier," *Proceedings of the New-York State Historical Association* 8 (1909), 15; Malcomson, *Brilliant Affair,* 62–66. For biographies, see *DAB,* 19: 210–211; Bernard, *Discourse on the Life, Services and Character of Stephen Van Rensselaer;* Kilian Van Rensselaer, "The Van Rensselaers of Van Rensselaerwyck," *NYHSQ* 39 (1945), 17–37; and William Bertrand Fink, "Stephen Van Rensselaer: The Last Patroon" (Ph.D. diss., Columbia University, 1950).

134. Bonney, *Legacy of Historical Gleanings,* 1: 196–199.

3. Brock—Saviour of Canada

Epigraph: James L. Hughes, "The Battle of Queenston Heights," in *Raise the Flag and Other Patriotic Canadian Songs and Poems,* 15.

1. A. Galloway, "Firing the First Shot as Told by the Man Who Fired It," *PBHS* 5 (1902), 23.

2. Julius W. Pratt, *Expansionists of 1812,* 153.

3. TNA, CO 42/147, pp. 1–3, 15–18, Prevost to Liverpool, 25 June and 6 July 1812; Sean Mills, "French Canadians and the Beginning of the War of 1812: Revisiting the

Lachine Riot," *Histoire sociale* 38, no. 75 (2005), 37–57; Edgar, *Ten Years of Upper Canada,* 129–131; *The Letters of Veritas,* 9–11.

4. Malcomson, *Lords of the Lake,* 32–33, 34; Shepard, *Autobiography of Elihu H. Shepard,* 33. For biographies of Brown, see Hoard, *Major General Jacob Jennings Brown;* Frank B. Latham, *Jacob Brown and the War of 1812;* and John D. Morris, *Sword of the Border.* On Forsyth see "Lieutenant Colonel John Forsyth," *North Country Notes,* November 1974. In 1849 a county of North Carolina was named after him.

5. "Dispatch from Col. Lethbridge to Major General Brock," *OHSPR* 18 (1913), 59; Philippart, *Royal Military Calendar,* 2: 76–78; Robert Malcomson, "The Capture of the Schooner *Julia/Confiance,*" *AN* 51 (1991), 83–90. For a study of the state of the militia in Upper Canada in 1812 see Sheppard, *Plunder, Profit, and Paroles,* 40–67.

6. USNA, RG 107/M6/R6, Eustis to Hull, 24 June 1812.

7. Gilpin, *War of 1812 in Old Northwest,* 32–33, 40; McAfee, *History,* 51–54; Stagg, *Mr. Madison's War,* 194–198; L. B. Hamlin, ed., "Selections from the Gano Papers," *Quarterly Publication of the Historical and Philosophical Society of Ohio* 15 (January–June 1920), 54–68. For biographical details of Miller see Robert J. Holden, "General James Miller, Collector of the Port of Salem, Massachusetts, 1825, 1849," *EIHC* 104 (1968), 253–302; Heitman, *Historical Register,* 1: 710. For Cass see his memoir, *Life of General Lewis Cass;* and for McArthur see Clarence Henley Cramer, "Duncan McArthur: The Military Phase," *OAHSQ* 46 (April 1937), 128–147; and idem, "The Career of Duncan McArthur" (Ph.D. diss., Ohio State University, 1931). Two out of three of Ohio's representatives to Congress opposed the war on the basis that the frontier, indeed the nation, was unprepared. See also William Ray Barlow, "Ohio's Congressmen and the War of 1812," *Ohio History* 72 (July 1963), 175–198; Jeffrey P. Brown, "The Ohio Federalist, 1803–1815," *JER* 2 (1982), 261–282; and W. C. Wilkinson, "Private John Jones in the War of 1812," *IMHJ* 7 (1982), 4–11.

8. Hull to Eustis, 24 June 1812, in *MPHC,* 40: 398.

9. Berton, *Invasion of Canada,* 117–119; Verchères de Boucherville, *War on the Detroit,* 78; *DRIC,* 232; *MPHC,* 40: 399; Gilpin, *War of 1812 in Old Northwest,* 53–54. For Rolette, see *DHC,* 2: 57–59.

10. W. K. Beall, "Journal of William K. Beall, July–August 1812," *AHR* 17 (July 1912), 784–787; F. Cleary, "Defence of Essex in the War of 1812," *OH* 10 (1913), 73; Adam Walker, *Journal of Two Campaigns,* 48; Robert Lucas, *Journal,* 19; *DHC,* 2: 351.

11. USNA, RG 107/M221/R46, Hull to Eustis, 9 July 1812; Meddert, *Raw Recruits and Bullish Prisoners,* 37–38; *PFB,* 260–261; Stanley, *War of 1812,* 93–98.

12. John Hunt, *Memoirs,* 13.

13. William Hull, *Memoir,* 54; Gilpin, *War of 1812 in Old Northwest,* 75–76. See also Fred C. Hamil, "Michigan in the War of 1812," *MH* 44 (1960), 257–291; William Ray Barlow, "The Coming of the War of 1812 in Michigan Territory," *MH* 53 (1969), 247–267; Mark Pitcavage, "'Burthened in Defense of Our Rights': Opposition to Military Service in Ohio during the War of 1812," *Ohio History* 104 (1995), 142–162.

14. TNA, CO 42/147, p. 35, Hull's Proclamation, 12 July 1812; Berton, *Invasion of Canada,* 124–131; Bowler, *War of 1812,* 52–53; *DRIC,* 58; Gilpin, *War of 1812 in Old Northwest,* 73–79. See also Colin G. Calloway, "Beyond the Vortex of Violence: Indian-White Relations in the Ohio Country, 1783–1815," *NOQ* 64 (Winter 1992), 16–26.

15. LAC, RG 8 I C676, St. George to Brock, 8 July 1812; Antal, *A Wampum Denied,* 46, 52; Philippart, *Royal Military Calendar,* 3: 104–105. Joseph Watson, Hull's aide, said 367 Canadians enrolled on the U.S. side, and other estimates are even higher; William Hull, *Report of Trial,* 151. For a study of disloyalty in Upper Canada, see Sheppard, *Plunder, Profit, and Paroles,* 152–170.

16. For Proctor, see *DCB,* 6: 616–618; Antal, *A Wampum Denied,* 67–70, 84–85; idem, "Myths and Facts Concerning General Proctor," *OH* 79 (September 1987), 251–262; Philippart, *Royal Military Calendar,* 2: 79.

17. Proctor to Brock, in *MPHC,* 15: 119–120; Brock to Prevost, 29 July 1812, in *SBD,* 1: 399; John Richardson, *Richardson's War of 1812,* 58; Lomax, *History of the 41st,* 53–54; A. C. Whitehorne, *History of The Welch Regiment,* 91–92. According to Richardson, Brock personally released Dean from confinement, and, as "his voice betrayed strong emotion, he warmly approved his conduct and declared that he was indeed an honour to the profession of a soldier."

18. LAC, MG 40 G4, file 1, "Notes to Richardson's War of 1812," p. 45. Cochran records that Dean was captured again in 1813 and later deserted the service.

19. Cass to Hull, 17 August 1812, in Verchères de Boucherville, *War on the Detroit,* 240–242; W. Hull, *Report of Trial,* 105. See G. J. Evelyn, "A Feather in the Cap? The Affair at the River Canard, 16th July 1812," *MCH* 39 (Winter 1987), 169–171; Woodbridge N. Ferrs, "Lewis Cass, Michigan's Hero of the War of 1812," *Michigan Historical Collections* 39 (1915), 270–274.

20. Antal, *A Wampum Denied,* 51.

21. Beall, "Journal," 802; McAfee, *History,* 64.

22. Ohio Historical Society, Columbus, Denny Papers, box 1, folder 1, James to Isabella Denny, 17 July 1812. The strength of the 4th Infantry was 264 on 28 July, to which was added a detachment of 1st Infantry. Militia numbers were reported as 1,592 on 24 June, so it is unlikely more than 1,400 remained at this point, although reinforcements did arrive later; BHC, B. F. C. Witherall Papers, "Morning Report, 28 July 1812 (signed by Adjutant John Eastman)"; Hull to Eustis, 24 June 1812, in Dearborn, *Defense of Dearborn,* 10.

23. Hitsman, *Incredible War,* 65–70. Michilimackinac (sometimes spelt with two "l"s), Mackinac Island, and Fort Mackinac may be used interchangeably, but should not be confused with the modern Mackinac City on the north-east of the Michigan peninsula adjacent to Mackinac Island.

24. For Roberts see *DCB,* 5: 713–714. For Fort St. Joseph see Abbott, Mount, and Mulloy, *History of Fort St. Joseph.*

25. John Richardson, *Richardson's War of 1812,* 22–25.

26. TNA, CO 42/147, pp. 110, 111–113, Roberts to Baynes, 17 July 1812 (and enclosure); USNA, RG 98/M2/R2, P. Hanks to Hull, 4 August 1812; "Observations of Toussaint Pothier on Michilimackinac," "Articles of Capitulation," Askin to Claus, 18 July 1812, and Hanks to Hull, 4 August 1812, in *DRIC,* 64–69; Berton, *Invasion of Canada,* 13–14, 103–113; Dunnigan, *British Army at Mackinac,* 5–15; Gilpin, *War of 1812 in Old Northwest,* 88–91; Robert S. Allen, *His Majesty's Indian Allies,* 128–132, 214–217.

27. Malcomson, *Lords of the Lake,* 34.

28. LAC, RG 8 I C676, p. 232, Roberts to Brock, 17 July 1812; Louise P. Kellogg, "The Capture of Mackinac in 1812," in *Proceedings of the State Historical Society of Wisconsin at Its Sixtieth Annual Meeting Held October 24, 1912* (Madison: The Society, 1912), 135–141. For a discussion of the importance of British possession of Mackinac, see Malcomson, *Lords of the Lake,* 81–83, 284–285.

29. Brock to Edward Baynes, 29 July 1812, in *DRIC,* 106.

30. Berton, *Invasion of Canada,* 141–146, 163; Stanley, *War of 1812,* 104–106.

31. Verchères de Boucherville, *War on the Detroit,* 81–84.

32. For Muir see *DCB,* 6: 529–531.

33. TNA, CO 42/147, pp. 153–155, Hull to Eustis, 4 August 1812; *DRIC,* 115.

34. Porter to Meigs, 29 July 1812, in Knapp, *History of Maumee Valley,* 129.

35. Berton, *Invasion of Canada,* 146–148; Gilpin, *War of 1812 in Old Northwest,* 95–98; J. Hunt, *Memoirs,* 18; R. Lucas, *Journal,* 46–49; John Richardson, *Richardson's War of 1812,* 26–34. See also Dalliba, *Narrative of the Battle of Brownstown;* Henry Brush, "Expedition of Captain Henry Brush, with Supplies for General Hull, 1812 etc.," in Samuel Williams, *Two Western Campaigns.*

36. Hull to Eustis, 7 August 1812, in Brannan, *Official Letters,* 36.

37. TNA, CO 42/147, p. 156, Hull to Eustis, 8 August 1812; *DRIC,* 126; Dalliba, *Narrative of the Battle of Brownstown,* 10.

38. Proctor to Brock, 11 August 1812, in *DRIC,* 135; Verchères de Boucherville, *War on the Detroit,* 84–106; Hull to Eustis, 13 August 1812, in Brannan, *Official Letters,* 47; Ohio Historical Society, Columbus, James Miller Papers, James to Ruth Miller, 27 August 1812; BHC, James Taylor Papers, Taylor to James Eubank, 12 August 1812; Antal, *A Wampum Denied,* 80–81; Berton, *Invasion of Canada,* 158–163; Gilpin, *War of 1812 in Old Northwest,* 102–103; Lomax, *History of the 41st,* 56; Sugden, *Tecumseh,* 295–297; Adam Walker, *Journal of Two Campaigns,* 59–63. See also Van Horne testimony and Munson testimony in W. Hull, *Report of Trial,* 68, 131.

39. Hull to Eustis, 13 August 1812, in *DRIC,* 139–141; Brannan, *Official Letters,* 36–38; Gilpin, *War of 1812 in Old Northwest,* 95–104; McAfee, *History,* 77–82; *SBD,* 1: 456–457.

40. A story much loved by Canadian historians has Tecumseh supposedly turn to his men and hold out his hand, saying: "Ho-yo-o-e! This is a man"; Tupper, *Life and Correspondence of Brock,* 261. It was told to Tupper by James FitzGibbon, an officer of the 49th who was not at Fort Malden at the time but claimed to have heard it from an eyewitness; AO, Tupper Papers, FitzGibbon to Tupper, 27 September 1845.

41. Brock to Prevost, 17 August 1812, in *SBD,* 1: 467.

42. Burton, Stocking, and Miller, *City of Detroit,* 1: 984–985; Antal, *A Wampum Denied,* 39. Built by the British as Fort Lernoult during the Revolutionary War, Fort Detroit should not be confused with the earlier French post, Fort Pontchartrain, torn down long before.

43. *SBD,* 3: 554.

44. Laws, *Battery Records of Royal Artillery,* 154; Nicholson, *Gunners of Canada,* 59.

45. John Richardson, *Richardson's War of 1812,* 50; *DRIC,* 192.

46. Prevost to Bathurst, 24 August 1812, in *SBD,* 1: 491–492; Gilpin, *War of 1812 in Old Northwest,* 110–112, 114–115.

47. In early June 1812 the 41st Regiment mustered 32 officers and 880 men spread all over Canada. There was probably a total of 300 regulars at Fort Malden including gunners; Lomax, *History of the 41st,* 49; Dixon to Bruyeres, 8 July 1812, in *SBD,* 1: 351.

48. Sheldon, *Early History of Michigan,* 401.

49. *DHC,* 3: 186; Gellner, *Recollections,* 6. Brock gave his force as 330 regulars, 400 militia, and 600 Indians (not including officers), although the prize list recorded 131 NCOs and 1,112 privates—1,360, not including Indians, and Brock had indicated to Muir a commissariat requirement for 2,000. Thus his force was probably larger than Hull's; *SBD,* 1: 462, 493, 497.

50. W. Hull, *Report of Trial,* 40, 109, app. 2, p. 15; J. F. Clarke, *History of the Campaign of 1812,* 450; Stanley, *War of 1812,* 107–109. For a civilian view of events at Detroit, see Mary M. Crawford, ed., "Mrs. Lydia Bacon's Journal, 1811–12," *IMH* 40 (December 1944), 367–386; 41 (March 1945), 59–79.

51. Verchères de Boucherville, *War on the Detroit,* 298; John Richardson, *Richardson's War of 1812,* 54; R. Lucas, *Journal,* 63–64; Livingstone to Woodward, 16 August 1812, in *MPHC,* 8: 636.

52. WRM, Acc. No. 1822, "The War in Canada 1812–14," 11; AO, F775 MU2102, Brock to Hull and Hull to Brock, 16 August 1812, Terms of Capitulation of Detroit, 16 August; Brock to Prevost, 17 August 1812, in *SBD,* 1: 465–470; McAfee, *History,* 419; Sugden, *Tecumseh,* 301–304; F. Palmer, *Early Days in Detroit,* 880–885.

53. Snelling, *Remarks on "General Hull's Memoir of the Northwestern Army,"* 7; Harrison to Eustis, 3 September 1812, in Harrison, *Messages and Letters,* 2: 110; Berton, *Invasion of Canada,* 174–183; *PFB,* 314. See also Hatch, *Chapter in History of War,* 30–53.

54. John Richardson, *Richardson's War of 1812,* 33. The colour now resides at the regimental museum in Cardiff Castle.

55. James A. Padgett, "The Letters of James Taylor to the Presidents of the United States," *RKHS* 34 (July 1936), 272. The fall of Detroit was viewed with incredulity but prompted renewed American nationalism. See Robert John Dodge, "Nationalism and the Fall of Detroit—1812," *NOQ* 40 (Summer 1968), 1118–26.

56. TNA, CO 42/147, pp. 175–183, Brock to Prevost, 17 August 1812; *SBD,* 1: 474; Baynes to Brock, 10 September 1812, in *DHC,* 3: 250; "Return of Ordnance and Ordnance Stores

Taken at Detroit," in *DRIC,* 154; Tupper, *Life and Correspondence of Brock,* 284–286, 304–305, 497; Edgar, *Ten Years of Upper Canada,* 246; Brannan, *Official Letters,* 38–39, 40–42, 56–60; Glenn Tucker, *Poltroons and Patriots,* 1: 167; Verchères de Boucherville, *War on the Detroit,* 187; *PFB,* 253.

57. Gilpin, *War of 1812 in Old Northwest,* 124; Milo M. Quaife, "General Hull and His Critics," *OASHQ* 47 (1938), 168–182.

58. Skeen, *Citizen Soldiers,* 79–80. For a discussion of Ohioan insubordination see Le Roy, *Weakness of Discipline.* For its wider implications in Ohio see Mark L. Bender, "The Failure of General William Hull at Detroit in 1812 and Its Immediate Effects upon the State of Ohio" (Master's thesis, Kent State University, 1971). For prisoner accounts see Fairchild, *Journal of an American Prisoner;* Marshal S. Durkee, "Land to Old Soldiers—Old Fourth Regiment," in *House Reports,* No. 322, 27th Cong., 2d sess. (1841–1843), 1: 1–7; and M. M. Crawford, "Mrs. Lydia B. Bacon's Journal." Hull faced court-martial two years later headed by, of all people, Dearborn. He was charged with treason and cowardice and denied access to War Department records necessary for his defence. Though acquitted of treason, he was found guilty of cowardice and sentenced to death, commuted on account of his former services. His remaining years were spent in a futile effort to clear his name, later taken up by his daughter, Maria Campbell, and grandson, James Freeman Clarke. See their *Revolutionary Services and Civil Life of General William Hull;* and W. Hull, *Report of Trial* and *Memoirs.*

59. S. Williams, *Two Western Campaigns,* 32; Gilpin, *War of 1812 in Old Northwest,* 119–120.

60. *SBD,* 1: 538, 550.

61. The best study of prisoners in the war is Anthony G. Dietz, "The Prisoner of War in the United States during the War of 1812" (Ph.D. diss., American University, 1964). See 258–259.

62. TNA, CO 42/147, pp. 185–187, Brock to Prevost, 17 August 1812 (enclosure); Return of Ordnance Stores Taken at Detroit, in *SBD,* 1: 495–496.

63. Antal, *A Wampum Denied,* 104–106.

64. Brant, *James Madison: Commander-in-Chief,* 73–74; Linda Maloney, "The War of 1812: What Role for Sea Power?" in Kenneth J. Hagan, *In Peace and War,* 57–61; K. J. Hagan, *The People's Navy,* 882–884; Eckert, *Navy Department in War of 1812,* 30–37.

65. Kellogg, *British Régime in Wisconsin and the Northwest,* 285–287; Milo M. Quaife, ed., "The Fort Dearborn Massacre," *MVHR* 1 (1914–15), 561–573; idem, "The Story of James Corbin, a Soldier at Fort Dearborn," *MVHR* 3 (1916–17), 219–226; idem, *Chicago and the Old Northwest,* 416–419; Black Hawk, *Life,* 17–18. See Bert Anson, *The Miami Indians;* Edmunds, *The Potawatomis, Keepers of the Fire;* and idem, "The Illinois River Potowatomi in the War of 1812," *Journal of the Illinois State Historical Society* 62 (1969), 341–362.

66. Mentor L. Williams, ed., "John Kinzie's Narrative of the Fort Dearborn Massacre," *Journal of the Illinois State Historical Society* 48 (1953), 349; Heald to Eustis,

23 October 1812, in *DRIC,* 225–227. See also Helm, *The Fort Dearborn Massacre;* Van Horne, *Narrative;* John D. Barnhart, ed., "A New Letter about the Massacre at Fort Dearborn," *IMH* 41 (June 1945), 187–199; Paul A. Hutton, "William Wells: Frontier Scout and Indian Agent," *IMH* 74 (1978), 183–222; Harvey Lewis Carter, "A Frontier Tragedy: Little Turtle and William Wells," *Old Northwest* 6 (1980), 3–18; Simon Pokagon, "The Massacre of Fort Dearborn at Chicago," *Harper's New Monthly Magazine* 98 (March 1899), 649–656.

67. Berton, *Invasion of Canada,* 191–198; Sugden, *Tecumseh,* 298–299, 306–308; George W. Geib, "Fort Wayne: Imperial Outpost, 1811–1819," *IMHJ* 10 (October 1985), 16–19; Milo M. Quaife, ed., "A Diary of the War of 1812," *MVHR* 1 (September 1914), 272–278.

68. Zachary Taylor to William Henry Harrison, 10 and 13 September 1812, in Harrison, *Messages and Letters,* 2: 124, 134. See also David C. Bennett, "Fort Harrison under Seige—1812," *Journal of America's Military Past* 25 (Fall 1998), 19–28; John Gibson, "Some Letters of John Gibson," *IMH* 1 (1905), 128–131; Gilpin, *War of 1812 in Old Northwest,* 137–139; McAfee, *History,* 153–154; *PFB,* 317–318, 334; George W. Geib, "Fort Wayne in the British and Indian War: The Siege of 1812," *IMHJ* 2 (October 1977), 12–15. For biographies of Taylor see Bauer, *Zachary Taylor;* Holman Hamilton, *Zachary Taylor, Soldier of the Republic;* and Kevin Burnett, "Tippecanoe and Taylor Too," *Journal of the West* 31 (1992), 44–50.

69. Gerald O. Haffner, ed., "The Pigeon Roost Massacre: An Eyewitness Account," *Indiana History Bulletin* 53 (November–December 1976), 158–161; Isaac Naylor, "An Account of the Pigeon Roost Massacre," *Indiana Historical Society Publications* 2 (1886), 128–131; "Narrative of the Reverend George Knight Hester and His Wife Benee (Briggs) Hester," *IMH* 22 (June 1926), 131–158; and John Brown Dillon, *History of Indiana,* 492–493.

70. Muir to Proctor, 26 and 30 September 1812, in *MPHC,* 15: 148–149, 151–154; Antal, *A Wampum Denied,* 124–126; Black Hawk, *Life,* 12–13. On the Sacs see William T. Hagan, *Sac and Fox Indians.*

71. Howard Peckham, ed., "An Eyewitness Account of the Siege of Fort Wayne," *IMH* 4 (December 1948), 415. See also John P. Hedges, "Early Recollections of John P. Hedges," *IMH* 8 (December 1912), 171–173; Thomas M. Hopkins, *Reminiscences of Col. John Ketcham,* 11–18; Jeff L. Patrick, ed., "'We Lay There Doing Nothing': John Jackson's Recollection of the War of 1812," *IMH* 88 (1992), 116–20; Edgar B. Wesley, ed., "A Letter from Colonel John Allen," *OAHSQ* 36 (July 1927), 332–339; Irene McCreery, ed., "A Memorial to Major William G. Oliver," *NOQ* 29 (Spring 1957), 89–96; and George W. Geib, "Fort Wayne in the British and Indian War: The Siege of 1812," *IKHJ* 2 (October 1977), 12–15.

72. R. M. Campbell, "The Copus Hill Tragedy," *JAH* 16 (1922), 50–54; William Eugene Ellis, "The Copus Battle Centennial," *OAHSP* 21 (1912), 379–395.

73. Brock to Prevost, 28 September 1812, in Tupper, *Life and Correspondence of Brock,* 320; TNA, CO 42/147, pp. 207–211, Prevost to Liverpool, 5 October 1812; CO 43/40, p. 366, Bathurst to Brock, 16 November 1812.

74. See Kate L. Gregg, "The War of 1812 on the Missouri Frontier," *Missouri Historical Review* 33 (1938), 3–22, 184–202, 326–348.

75. Bathurst to Wellington, 12 October 1812, in Wellesley, *Despatches, Correspondence and Memoranda of Wellington,* 7: 442.

76. USNA, RG 107/221/R43, Dearborn to Eustis, 28 July 1812.

77. For discussion of this criticism, see J. M. Hitsman, "Sir George Prevost's Conduct of the Canadian War of 1812," *Canadian Historical Association* 41 (1962), 34–43; and Turner, *British Generals in War of 1812,* 24–57.

78. TNA, CO 42/147, pp. 94–101, Bathurst to Prevost, 10 August 1812.

79. TNA, CO 42/147, pp. 23–26, 31–33, 41, 45–53, 197–200, Prevost to Liverpool, 18 and 30 July, 3 August 1812, and Prevost to Bathurst, 24 September 1812 and enclosures. Bowler, *War of 1812,* 66–67. For continuing difficulties over specie see TNA, CO 42/156, pp. 133–134, 195–203, Prevost to Bathurst, 10 and 18 March 1813; C. S. Howard, "Financing the War of 1812," *Canadian Banker* 58 (1951), 115–118; and Stevenson, *War of 1812 in Connection with the Army Bill Act.* For difficulties of supply see William M. Weekes, "The War of 1812: Civil Authority and Martial Law in Upper Canada," in Zaslow, *Defended Border,* 191–204.

80. Mahan, *Sea Power,* 1: 297; William S. Dudley, *Naval War of 1812,* 1: 296–302, 304–306. For biographical details see James L. Mooney, "Isaac Chauncey," in Rutland, *Madison and American Nation;* Fletcher Pratt, *Preble's Boys,* 170–178; *DAB,* 3: 40–41.

81. Malcomson, *Lords of the Lake,* 42–48; Skaggs and Altoff, *A Signal Victory,* 37–39. For biographical information see F. Pratt, *Preble's Boys,* 170–198; *DAB,* 2: 40–41; Spiller, Dawson, and Williams, *Dictionary of American Military Biography,* 1: 167–170. See also William S. Dudley, "Commodore Isaac Chauncey and U.S. Joint Operations on Lake Ontario, 1813–14," in Cogar, *New Interpretations in Naval History,* 139–155.

82. Malcomson, *Brilliant Affair,* 71–72, 85–86. For Sheaffe see *DCB,* 8: 793–796; Philippart, *Royal Military Calendar,* 2: 31–32; Turner, *British Generals in War of 1812,* chap. 4.

83. See René Chartrand, "Canadian Voyageurs during the War of 1812," *JSAHR* 72 (Autumn 1994), 184–186.

84. Shepard, *Autobiography of Elihu H. Shepard,* 35–37.

85. Hitsman, *Incredible War,* 88–91, 105–108. For Vincent see *DCB,* 7: 888–889; Philippart, *Royal Military Calendar,* 2: 75.

86. Brock to Savery Brock, 18 September 1812, in Tupper, *Life and Correspondence of Brock,* 315.

87. Hitsman, *Incredible War,* 88.

88. See R. Bruce Taylor, ed., "Garrison Orders and Proceedings of Fort Niagara, Etc.," *Quarterly Journal of the New York State Historical Association* 8 (January–April 1927), 62–80, 152–178.

89. Van Rensselaer, *Narrative of Affair of Queenstown,* 10. Written to rebut eight allegations made in John Armstrong's *Notices of the War of 1812,* it is self-serving but provides supporting documentation; Malcomson, *Brilliant Affair,* 80–84.

90. Bonney, *Legacy of Historical Gleanings,* 1: 216.

91. LAC, RG 8 I 677 81, Brock to Prevost, 13 September 1812.

92. Malcomson, *Brilliant Affair,* 107–109.

93. Dearborn to Stephen Van Rensselaer, 26 September 1812, in *DHC,* 3: 295. For Smyth see *DAB,* 17: 373–374.

94. Everest, *War in Champlain Valley,* 88.

95. Stephen Van Rensselaer to Dearborn, 8 October 1812, in *DHC,* 4: 40.

96. Brock to Savery Brock, 18 September 1812, in Tupper, *Life and Correspondence of Brock,* 315.

97. Hitsman, *Incredible War,* 108; Mahon, *War of 1812,* 93.

98. W. S. Dudley, *Naval War of 1812,* 1: 328. On Elliott's background see Lawrence J. Friedman and David Curtis Skaggs, "Jesse Duncan Elliott and the Battle of Lake Erie: The Issue of Mental Stability," *JER* 10 (1990), 493–499; Alan Westcott, "Commodore Jesse D. Elliott: A Stormy Petrel of the Navy," *USNIP* 54 (1928), 773–781; McKee, *A Gentlemanly and Honorable Profession,* 293, 295, 297; Guttridge and Smith, *The Commodores,* 127, 130, 165–166, 220–234, 316, 318.

99. Mary R. Archer, ed., "Journal of Major Isaac Roach, 1812–24," *PMHB* 17, no. 3 (1893), 133.

100. Berton, *Invasion of Canada,* 225–227; W. S. Dudley, *Naval War of 1812,* 1: 327–333; Malcomson, *Brilliant Affair,* 114–117; Skaggs and Altoff, *A Signal Victory,* 42–44. See also Elliott, *Correspondence,* in which Elliott rather petulantly argued with Captain Nathan Towson about who had the hardest task.

101. For a detailed breakdown of opposing forces, see apps. E and I in Malcomson, *Brilliant Affair,* 255–258, 272–273.

102. Van Rensselaer, *Narrative of Affair of Queenstown,* 72.

103. Museum of Liverpool Life, Liverpool, 1974.29.2, Letters from Thomas Evans, 1812. In fact there were no troops from these states present; Evans must have seen some riflemen from a New York militia company; Malcomson, *Brilliant Affair,* 125 n. 4.

104. Van Rensselaer, *Narrative of Affair of Queenstown,* 61.

105. The administration wanted to appoint Brigadier-General James Winchester, a regular; but Harrison, the local favourite, was appointed after Kentucky leaders made him a militia major-general despite not being a citizen of the state, then pressured the administration until he was given command of the whole theatre; Hickey, *War of 1812,* 85.

106. Van Rensselaer, *Narrative of Affair of Queenstown,* 24–25.

107. TNA, WO 44/245, Quebec, 1812, G. Ridout to father, 14 October 1812.

108. Malcomson, *Brilliant Affair,* 123–142. See Harman P. Hinton, "The Military Career of John Ellis Wool, 1812–1863" (Ph.D. diss., University of Wisconsin, 1960). Wool composed a lengthy rebuttal of what he saw as inaccuracies in Solomon Van Rensselaer's version of the battle, including the decision to take the heights. See "Major General John Ellis Wool to W. L. Stone on the Battle of Queenston Heights, October, 1812," *BNYPL* 9 (April 1905), 120–122.

109. USNA, RG 59/M588/R7, Smith to Proctor, 18 October 1812.

110. AO, F44, John Beverley Robinson Papers, "Account of the Battle of Queenston Heights"; *DHC,* 4: 103; Robinson, *Life of Sir John Beverley Robinson,* 33; *DCB,* 9: 668–679.

111. Armstrong, *Notices,* 1: 207.

112. See *DCB,* 5: 520–523.

113. For a discussion of the legend, see Robert Malcomson, "The Last Words of Isaac Brock," in *Brilliant Affair,* 231–233.

114. *DHC,* 4: 146. Three different men have been named as Brock's assailant, but according to Ludwig Kosche the testimony of Private Robert Walcot comes nearest to Jarvis' account; "Relics of Brock: An Investigation," *Archivaria* 9 (1979–80), 100–102. However, Guy St. Denis has shown that Walcot could not have been responsible, and indeed, that no individual can be realistically credited with the deed. See "Robert Walcot: The Man Who Could Not Possibly Have Shot General Brock," *JSAHR* 83 (2005), 281–290.

115. John H. Land, ed., "Tales of the War: Queenston Heights," *Wentworth Historical Society Journal and Transactions* 6 (1915), 63. See also Janet Carnochan, ed., "Col. Daniel MacDougal and Valuable Documents," *NHSP* 23 (1912), 36.

116. Van Rensselaer, *Narrative of Affair of Queenstown,* 26.

117. Malcomson, *Brilliant Affair,* 155–165. Runchey's company were thirty mostly fugitive slaves from the United States and "expert axemen." See Steve Pitt, "To Stand and Fight Together," *Rotunda,* Spring 1997, 8–13; W. M. Gray, *Soldiers of the King,* 185–186.

118. J. Willson, "A Rifleman at Queenston," *PBHS* 9 (1906), 374.

119. Thompson Mead Account in *Albany Argus,* 30 March 1813, in *DHC,* 4: 90.

120. See the account of Lieutenant-Colonel John Chrystie in Armstrong, *Notices,* 1: 207–219.

121. Haythornthwaite, *Weapons and Equipment,* 71.

122. Winfield Scott, *Memoirs,* 1: 60–61.

123. TNA, WO 44/245, Quebec, 1812, G. Ridout to his father, 14 October 1812. See also James Crooks, "Recollections of the War of 1812," *NHSP* 28 (1916), 37; Janet Carnochan, ed., "Letters of 1812," *NHSP* 31 (1919), 6–10.

124. Willson, "A Rifleman at Queenston"; Frank H. Severance, ed., "Documents Relating to the War of 1812: The Letter-Book of Gen. Roger Hale Sheaffe," *PBHS* 17 (1914), 275–277.

125. TNA, CO 42/148, pp. 17, 19, Return of killed, wounded, and prisoners of war by Evans, 13 October 1812; Stephen Van Rensselaer to Dearborn, 20 October 1812, in *DHC,* 4: 143; Berton, *Invasion of Canada,* 232–250; Robert Louis Rogers, *History of Lincoln and Welland Regiment,* 7. See also Carol Whitfield, "The Battle of Queenstown Heights," *Canadian Historical Sites: Occasional Papers in Archaeology and History* 11 (1974), 9–59.

126. W. Scott, *Memoirs,* 1: 71–81.

127. Malcomson, *Brilliant Affair,* 215–219; R. Arthur Bowler, "Propaganda in Upper Canada in the War of 1812," in *War along the Niagara,* 83–86. See also Symons, *The Battle of Queenston Heights.*

128. TNA, CO 42/352, Sheaffe to Bathurst, 20 October and 31 December 1812; Severance, "Documents: Letter-Book of Sheaffe," 280–283.

129. TNA, CO 42/150, pp. 143–146, Prevost to Bathurst, 21 April 1813.

130. LC, Madison Papers, reel 14, Ezekiel Bacon to Albert Gallatin, 13 October 1812.

4. Frigates and Privateers

1. For a study of British anti-American sentiment and its effect on strategic planning, see C. J. Bartlett, "Gentlemen versus Democrats: Cultural Prejudice and Military Strategy in Britain in the War of 1812," *War in History* 1 (July 1994), 140–159.

2. For a study of these contrasting strengths see Tunstall, *Naval Warfare in the Age of Sail.*

3. William S. Dudley, *Naval War of 1812,* 1: 96n, 504; Lavery, *Nelson's Navy,* 289; Michael A. Lewis, *Social History of the Navy,* 270–276.

4. Roosevelt, *Naval War of 1812,* 16–20, 246.

5. Gardiner, *Naval War of 1812,* 12, 22.

6. Keith S. Dent, "The British Navy and the Anglo-American War of 1812 to 1815" (Master's thesis, University of Leeds, 1949), 44–48, 61, 63, 65–68.

7. James Henderson, *The Frigates,* 139.

8. American 44s were not cut-down 74s as sometimes claimed. See Joshua Humphreys, "Report, 23 December 1794," in *ASP: NA,* 18: 8. For a biography see *DAB,* 9: 376–377. See also Tyrone G. Martin, "Joshua Humphreys' Real Innovation," *Naval History* 8 (March–April 1994), 32–37.

9. For a full study of U.S. naval armaments in the period, see Spencer C. Tucker, *Arming the Fleet.*

10. Roosevelt, *Naval War of 1812,* 32–34; Chapelle, *History of American Sailing Navy,* 127–128, 130–132, 165. The speed of a sailing vessel is generally limited by its length at the water line (LWL), maximum speed under similar conditions varying as the square root of LWL. Thus a ship measuring 100 feet does 10 knots while one of 144 feet should achieve 12 knots, although myriad other considerations also affect performance.

11. Mahan, *Sea Power,* 1: 315–318; Irving Brant, "Timid President? Futile War?" *American Heritage* 10 (October 1959), 46–47, 85–89; Linda Maloney, "The War of 1812: What Role for Sea Power?" in Kenneth J. Hagan, *In Peace and War,* 46–62. See also James E. Valle, "The Navy's Battle Doctrine in the War of 1812," *AN* 44 (Summer 1984), 171–178.

12. TNA, ADM 8/100, List Book 1812–1813; ADM 2/1374, pp. 357–363, "Conduct to Be Observed towards the United States," 9 May 1812; ADM 1/502, pp. 143–144, Foster to Sawyer, 15 June 1812; Boileau, *Half-Hearted Enemies,* 18–21; Hitsman, *Canada,* 70. For Sawyer see Marshall, *Royal Naval Biography,* 1: 337–339; Peter Padfield, "Criticism," *MM* 59 (1973), 453–454. On the development of Halifax see Harry Piers, *The Evolution of Halifax Fortress, 1749–1928,* 1–7; Walter R. Copp, "Military Activities in Nova Scotia during the War of 1812," *Nova Scotia Historical Society Collections* 24 (1938), 57–58, 74.

13. Mahan, *Sea Power,* 1: 388–389, 400–401; Horsman, *War of 1812,* 58–59; Richard Glover, "The French Fleet, 1807–1814: Britain's Problem and Madison's Opportunity," *JModH* 39 (1967), 248–252.

14. *Nova Scotia Royal Gazette,* 1 July 1812; TNA, ADM 1/502, pp. 207, 209, 221, Sawyer to Croker, 18 July and 6 August, Sawyer to Allen, 5 August 1812; W. S. Dudley, *Naval War of 1812,* 1: 202–203, 491–494, 536–537, 565–570, 637–638; Mahan, *Sea Power,* 1: 410.

15. TNA, WO 744/95, "Minutes of the Privy Council Meeting," 21 August 1812; ADM 1/502, p. 280, Sawyer to Croker, 7 September 1812. The practice did not guarantee protection, however, and carried both risks and restrictions; Morison, *Maritime History of Massachusetts,* 205–206; Cranwell and Crane, *Men of Marque,* 32–33; Garitee, *Republic's Private Navy,* 50–53; Fairburn, *Merchant Sail,* 2: 837–845.

16. *AC,* Twelfth Cong., 2d sess. (1812), 121, 1146, 1153, 1163–64. See also Donald R. Hickey, "American Trade Restrictions during the War of 1812," *JAH* 68 (1981), 517–538; Brian M. De Toy, "Wellington's Lifeline: Naval Logistics in the Peninsula," [Papers of the] *Consortium of Revolutionary Europe* 7 (1995), 363–364; G. E. Watson, "The United States and the Peninsular War, 1808–1812," *HJ* 19 (1976), 865–872.

17. Lawrence S. Kaplan, "France and the War of 1812," *JAH* 57 (1970–2), 38.

18. Wade G. Dudley, *Splintering the Wooden Wall,* 69–82; W. S. Dudley, *Naval War of 1812,* 1: 202–203; Joseph A. Goldenberg, "The Royal Navy's Blockade in New England Waters, 1812–1815," *International History Review* 6 (1984), 424–427; Hickey, "American Trade Restrictions"; idem, *War of 1812,* 167–171; Faye Kert, "Taking Care of Business: Privateering and the Licensed War of 1812," in Starkey, van Heslinga, and de Moor, *Pirates and Privateers,* 135–143; Joshua M. Smith, "The Rogues of Quoddy: Smuggling in the Maine–New Brunswick Borderlands, 1783–1820" (Ph.D. diss., University of Maine, 2003), 301–305, published as *Borderland Smuggling.*

19. BL, Liverpool Papers, 38250, Cockburn to Croker, 6 November 1812, and Clancarty to Liverpool, 24 November 1812; Hickey, *War of 1812,* 117.

20. Hansard, *Parliamentary Debates* 24: 576–578; TNA, ADM 1/502, pp. 195, 221–223, Sawyer to Croker, 18 July and 6 August 1812; ADM 2/163, pp. 9, 47, Order in Council, 20 August 1812, and "Instructions to Transport Board"; CO 43/49, p. 239, Goulburn to Harrison, 26 September 1812.

21. Barry J. Lohnes, "British Naval Problems at Halifax during the War of 1812," *MM* 59 (1973), 319. See also idem, "The War of 1812: The British Navy, New England and the Maritime Provinces of Canada" (Master's thesis, University of Maine, 1971).

22. HSP, Roberts Papers, John Binns to James Roberts, 13 November 1812.

23. Little, *Life on the Ocean,* 194.

24. See W. S. Dudley, *Naval War of 1812,* 1: 166–170.

25. Garitee, *Republic's Private Navy,* 47–64. This is a comprehensive study of Baltimore privateering based on his Ph.D. dissertation, "Private Enterprise and Public Spirit: Baltimore Privateering in the War of 1812" (American University, 1973).

26. G. M. Footner, *Tidewater Triumph,* 101–102.

27. See Gillmer, *Pride of Baltimore.*

28. See Norway, *History of Post Office Packet Service.*

29. Forester, *Naval War of 1812,* 68–72.

30. Log-Book of the *Rossie,* 12 July—22 October 1812, *NWR* 3 (7 November 1812); W. S. Dudley, *Naval War of 1812,* 1: 248–260, 617–624; Cranwell and Crane, *Men of Marque,* 63–74; Kenneth Scott, "The Privateer 'Yankee' in the War of 1812," *AN* 21 (January 1961), 16–22; Wilfred Harold Munro, "The Most Successful American Privateer: An Episode of the War of 1812," *Proceedings of the American Antiquarian Society* 23 (April 1913), 12–62; Noah Jones, *Journals of Two Cruises aboard the Privateer Yankee,* 61–156. For biographies of Barney see Hulbert Footner, *Sailor of Fortune;* and Louis A. Norton, *Joshua Barney.*

31. *The Times,* 30 December 1812, 1 January 1813; *Morning Chronicle,* 22 August, 17 and 18 September, 31 December 1812, 1 January 1813; Warren to Croker, 26 February 1813, *NC* 29 (January—June 1813), 198.

32. C. Dowling, "The Convoy System and the West Indian Trade, 1803–1815" (D.Phil. diss., Oxford University, 1961), 83–84, 162–166; Faye Kert, "The Fortunes of War: Commercial Warfare and Maritime Risk in the War of 1812," *NM/MN* 8, no. 4 (1998), 2; idem, "Cruising in Colonial Waters: The Organization of North American Privateering in the War of 1812," in Starkey, van Heslinga, and de Moor, *Pirates and Privateers,* 141–154. The figures given in W. G. Dudley, *Splintering the Wooden Wall,* 138–142, are from old and unreliable sources. For a discussion on the importance of marine insurance to enable the shipping industry to withstand the shocks of war, see Crowhurst, *Defence of British Trade,* chap. 3.

33. TNA, ADM 1/502, pp. 249, 303–304, 337, "A List of American Privateers Taken and Destroyed by His Majesty's Ships and Vessels on the Halifax Station between the 1st July and 25th August 1812," and Warren to Croker, 5 and 17 October 1812; W. S. Dudley, *Naval War of 1812,* 1: 223–226.

34. *NC* 29 (January–June 1813), 257, 509.

35. Mahan, *Sea Power,* 2: 242; Kert, *Prize and Prejudice,* 78–79.

36. Dent, "British Navy," 80.

37. Perkins, *Castlereagh and Adams,* 37; Kenneth Ross Nelson, "Socio-Economic Effects of the War of 1812 on Britain" (Ph.D. diss., University of Georgia, 1972), 100–107.

38. On convoy practice, see Lavery, *Nelson's Navy,* 305–310; Geoffrey J. Marcus, *Heart of Oak,* 202–203; Pope, *Life in Nelson's Navy,* 236–241.

39. On first receiving news of the war, Richard S. Smith sailed for Gothenburg in the schooner *Champlin* to serve as consul and to warn the forty-odd American ships hiding there before they could be taken by the British. He then spread the news to several other ports and saved several merchantmen. Alfred W. Crosby, "Richard S. Smith, Baltic Paul Revere of 1812," *PMHB* 86 (January 1962), 42–48.

40. USNA, RG 45/M125/R24, Rodgers to Hamilton, 21 June 1812; TNA, ADM 1/502, pp. 155–156, "Account of H.M.S. Belvidera," 23 June 1812; W. S. Dudley, *Naval War of*

1812, 1: 154–160; William James, *Naval History,* 6: 122; idem, *Naval Occurrences,* 37–39; Roosevelt, *Naval War of 1812,* 43–44.

41. *NC* 28 (1812), 104.

42. TNA, ADM 1/502, pp. 144–145, 148–149, Sawyer to Croker, 28 June and 5 July 1812; pp. 150–153, Byron to Sawyer, 27 June 1812.

43. Dent, "British Navy," 126–127.

44. For biographies of Broke see Padfield, *Broke and the Shannon;* "Biographical Memoir of Sir Philip Bowes Vere Broke," *NC* 33 (1815), 1–22; Brighton, *Admiral Broke; DCB,* 7: 106–107; *DNB,* 2: 294–295; Marshall, *Royal Naval Biography,* 2: pt. 1, pp. 367–381; J. Henderson, *The Frigates,* 144; Forester, *Naval War of 1812,* 25–28.

45. Letter from British officer at Halifax, 15 October 1812, *NC* 28 (July–December 1812), 426; Coggeshall, *History of American Privateers,* 6; Forester, *Naval War of 1812,* 20–22; Hickey, *War of 1812,* 9; Mahan, *Sea Power,* 1: 401–404. See also Roy Manser, "Royal Navy, Officers' Undress Uniform, 1812," *MCH* 20 (Spring 1968), 19–20; idem, "Royal Navy, 1814," *MCH* 21 (Spring 1969), 19–20.

46. For biographies of Hull, see Bruce Grant, *Isaac Hull;* Maloney, *The Captain from Connecticut;* and Isaac Hull, *Commodore Hull: Papers.*

47. Forester, *Naval War of 1812,* 37–39.

48. Moses Smith, *Naval Scenes,* 27.

49. Charles Morris, *Autobiography,* 50–53; H. D. McHenry, "Kedging the Constitution," *USNIP* 52 (1926), 1509–12.

50. Fletcher Pratt, *Preble's Boys,* 58.

51. Anon., "How the 'Constitution' Escaped," *USNIP* 53 (1927), 623–629.

52. Quoted in Oliver H. Perry to Paul Hamilton, 26 July 1812, in W. S. Dudley, *Naval War of 1812,* 1: 200; see also pp. 161–165; USNA, RG 45/M125/R24, Hull to Hamilton, 27 July 1812; TNA, ADM 1/502, pp. 144–153, Byron to Sawyer, 27 June 1812; Maclay, *History of United States Navy,* 1: 334–343; Gardiner, *Naval War of 1812,* 35–37; Roosevelt, *Naval War of 1812,* 47–50; Brighton, *Admiral of the Fleet Wallis,* 26–27.

53. For a study of Boston's role in the war, see Watkins, *Defence of Boston.*

54. Forester, *Naval War of 1812,* 44–45.

55. USNA, RG 45/M125/R24, Hull to Hamilton, 2 August 1812.

56. Coggeshall, *History of American Privateers,* 25–27.

57. William James gives the crew strengths as 244 to 460 and says that of 7 Americans sent below, one accidentally stayed with his gun; *Naval Occurrences,* 52.

58. F. Pratt, *Preble's Boys,* 62.

59. Denison, *Old Ironsides and Old Adams,* 18.

60. TNA, ADM 1/502, pp. 270–272, Dacres to Sawyer, 7 September 1812; W. S. Dudley, *Naval War of 1812,* 1: 237–245; Gardiner, *Naval War of 1812,* 40–43; W. James, *Naval History,* 142–157; idem, *Naval Occurrences,* 48–54; Mahan, *Sea Power,* 1: 330–335; Nicolas, *Historical Record of Royal Marine Forces,* 197–198; Roosevelt, *Naval War of 1812,* 51–56;

Linda A. M. McKee, "'Constitution' versus 'Guerriere,'" *USNIP* 88 (August 1962), 72–79; Tyrone G. Martin, "Isaac Hull's Victory Revisited," *AN* 47 (Winter 1987), 14–21.

61. Lilla M. Hawes, ed., "Letters of Henry Gilliam, 1809–1817," *GHQ* 38 (March 1954), 61.

62. A. W. Evans, "A Journal of the Constitution, 1812, by Amos A. Evans, Surgeon," *PMHB* 19 (1895), 376.

63. Forester, *Naval War of 1812,* 53.

64. Patriotic songs were a significant feature of the period, and, with lack of success on land, American ones were usually naval in character. See Jennifer Clark, "The War of 1812: American Nationalism and Rhetorical Images of Britain," *War and Society* 12 (1994), 1–26.

65. *Reporter* (Lexington, Ky.), 6 January 1815: L. H. Bolander, *"Constitution,"* in J. T. Adams, *Dictionary of American History,* 2: 29.

66. For a brief biography of Chauncey before the war, see F. Pratt, *Preble's Boys,* 170–177.

67. W. S. Dudley, *Naval War of 1812,* 1: 531–533, 577–579. See also Linda A. M. McKee, "Captain Isaac Hull and the Portsmouth Navy Yard, 1813–1815" (Ph.D. diss., St. Louis University, 1968).

68. F. Pratt, *Preble's Boys,* 63–65.

69. For a biography of Porter see Long, *Nothing Too Daring.* On the building of *Essex* see P. C. F. Smith, *The Frigate Essex Papers.* See also Charles C. Bassett, "The Career of the Frigate Essex," *EIHC* 87 (1951), 9–40, 155–177.

70. Leask and McCance, *Regimental Records of Royal Scots,* 262–264; Roosevelt says there were 197 soldiers on board, but this number probably includes the crew (*Naval War of 1812,* 45).

71. USNA, RG 45/M125/R24, Porter to Hamilton, 15 August; R25, Porter to Hamilton, 3 September 1812; W. James, *Naval History,* 127–129; idem, *Naval Occurrences,* 40–41; Roosevelt, *Naval War of 1812,* 46–47; Anthony G. Dietz, "The Use of Cartel Vessels during the War of 1812," *AN* 28 (July 1968), 165–194.

72. Long, *Nothing Too Daring,* 63–67; W. S. Dudley, *Naval War of 1812,* 1: 170–176, 216–220, 443–447; Forester, *Naval War of 1812,* 55–56; F. Pratt, *Preble's Boys,* 220–221; Tracy, *The Naval Chronicle,* 101–102. See also Anthony G. Deitz, "The Use of Cartel Vessels during the War of 1812," *AN* 28 (July 1968), 165–194.

73. M. A. Lewis, *Social History of the Navy,* 379.

74. TNA, ADM 2/1376, p. 33, Croker to Warren, 3 August 1812; W. James, *Naval History,* 224; Dent, "British Navy," 138–139; Mahan, *Sea Power,* 1: 390. For biographies, see Walter Vernon Anson, *Life of Admiral Sir John Borlase Warren; DCB,* 6: 802–804; *DNB,* 57: 485–489.

75. C. J. Bartlett, "Gentlemen versus Democrats: Cultural Prejudice and Military Strategy in the War of 1812," *War in History* 1 (1994), 147; Forester, *Naval War of 1812,* 61–62.

76. Russell to Monroe, 17 September 1812, in *ASP: FR,* 3: 594–595.

77. Padfield, *Broke and the Shannon,* 103.

78. TNA, ADM 1/502, p. 306, Warren to Croker, 5 October 1812; Mahan, *Sea Power,* 1: 391.

79. Warren to Monroe, 30 September 1812, and Monroe to Warren, 27 October 1812, in *ASP: FR,* 3: 595–577; Perkins, *Castlereagh and Adams,* 11–19; John Quincy Adams, *Memoirs,* 2: 401–404.

80. W. James, *Naval History,* 224.

81. See W. F. Galpin, "The American Grain Trade to the Spanish Peninsula, 1810–1814," *AHR* 28 (October 1922), 24–44.

82. Forester, *Naval War of 1812,* 63–66.

83. Copp, "Military Activities," 143–146.

84. TNA, ADM 1/502, pp. 306–307, Warren to Croker, 5 October 1812; ADM 1/503, pp. 9–102, 110, 119, 29 December 1812, 25 January and 26 February 1813.

85. TNA, ADM 1/503, pp. 51–52, Governor Beckwith to Warren, 22 November 1812.

86. TNA, ADM 2/1375, pp. 320–324, Croker to War Office, 18 December 1812. See Vernon, *Early Recollections of Jamaica,* 66–124.

87. TNA, ADM 1/502, pp. 49–50, Warren to Croker, 29 December 1812; ADM 1/503, pp. 110–111, 119, Warren to Croker, 25 January and 26 February 1813; ADM 2/1376, pp. 1–6, Croker to Liverpool West India Association, 12 January 1813.

88. TNA, ADM 2/1375, pp. 252–259, Croker to Warren, 18 November 1812.

89. TNA, ADM 2/1375, p. 365, Croker to Warren, 9 January 1813; W. S. Dudley, *Naval War of 1812,* 2: 14; Mahan, *Sea Power,* 2: 151.

90. NMM, Robert Saunders-Dundas Papers, Melville to Hope, 13 November 1812; TNA, ADM 2/1375, pp. 276–278, 337–338, Croker to Warren, 27 November and 26 December 1812; Ralfe, *Naval Biography,* 3: 217–218.

91. Dent, "British Navy," 241–245.

92. W. S. Dudley, *Naval War of 1812,* 1: 209–212; 2: 631–632; Brighton, *Admiral Broke,* 22–24. Originally a French privateer *La Brave,* HMS *Barbadoes* was wrecked off Sable Island along with two other vessels on 28 September 1812, but her cargo of £12,000 destined for Halifax Dockyard was salvaged by attaching a buoy to each of the cases.

93. For Yeo see *DCB,* 5: 874–877; *DNB,* 60: 792–794; "Memoir of the Public Services of Sir James Lucas Yeo," *NC* 24 (July–December 1810), 265–285; W. James, *Naval History,* 73–77; John W. Spurr, "Sir James Lucas Yeo: A Hero of the Lakes," *Historic Kingston* 30 (1981), 30–45. For Yeo's service in American waters see "Ships in Sea Pay," J. H. Dent to Hamilton, 14 November 1812, and Yeo to Sterling, 22 November and 11 December 1812, in W. S. Dudley, *Naval War of 1812,* 1: 181, 582–586, 594–595; 2: 413; also TNA, ADM 1/5434, Court Martial of Sir James Lucas Yeo for the loss of HMS *Southampton,* 13 February 1813.

94. TNA, ADM 1/503, pp. 57, 59, Croker to Warren, 22 November 1812, and Warren to Croker, 2 January 1813; *Narrative of the Capture of the U.S. Brig Vixen.*

95. *NC* 28 (July–December 1812), 343.

96. *The Examiner,* 13 September 1812.

97. *The Times,* 7 October 1812; Forester, *Naval War of 1812,* 56; Nelson, "Socio-Economic Effects," 24–29, 31–36.

98. ICRO, Saumarez Papers, HA 93 877/13, Broke to Louisa Broke, 29 September 1812; Roosevelt, *Naval War of 1812,* 135. In an echo of the prisoner incident following the capture of Detroit, twelve of the *Guèrriere's* crew were threatened with hanging in retaliation for six British men found fighting against His Majesty's ships; Edgar Erskine Hume, ed., "Letters Written during the War of 1812 by the British Naval Commander in American Waters," *WMQ,* 2d ser., 19 (1930), 288.

99. Forester, *Naval War of 1812,* 58–59.

100. For a brief biography of Jones's early career, see F. Pratt, *Preble's Boys,* 67–75.

101. The weather gauge was defined as the situation of one ship being to windward of another, when in action or company. It gave several immediate advantages: the smoke of battle cleared more quickly from that side of the ship and blew onto the enemy, but most importantly it gave the holder the ability to choose the timing and range at which an action would be fought.

102. TNA, ADM 1/502, p. 341, Beresford to Warren, 18 October 1812, and Whinyates to Warren, 23 October 1812; Forester, *Naval War of 1812,* 78–80; Gardiner, *Naval War of 1812,* 44–45; W. James, *Naval History,* 159–163; idem, *Naval Occurrences,* 71–75; Long, *Sailor-Diplomat,* 41–42; Mahan, *Sea Power,* 1: 412–415; Roosevelt, *Naval War of 1812,* 57–60, gives much higher British casualty figures.

103. W. S. Dudley, *Naval War of 1812,* 1: 536–541, 579–583; Loftus, *My Youth by Sea and Land,* 1: 248–251, 257–262.

104. F. Pratt, *Preble's Boys,* 77–79.

105. Carden, *A Curtail'd Memoir,* 269. For the story of *Macedonian* during and after the war see De Kay, *Chronicles of the Frigate "Macedonian."*

106. Padfield, *Broke and the Shannon,* 108.

107. Leech, *Thirty Years from Home,* 128. See also idem, "We Must Fight Her," *USNIP* 99 (March 1973), 90–93.

108. Carden, *A Curtail'd Memoir,* 263.

109. W. S. Dudley, *Naval War of 1812,* 1: 548–553; Gardiner, *Naval War of 1812,* 46–49; W. James, *Naval History,* 164–176; idem, *Naval Occurrences,* 77–79; Mahan, *Sea Power,* 1: 416–422; Nicolas, *Historical Record of Royal Marine Forces,* 1987–89; Roosevelt, *Naval War of 1812,* 61–64.

110. Shaw, *Short Sketch of the Life of Elijah Shaw,* 61.

111. F. Pratt, *Preble's Boys,* 103; Tracy, *The Naval Chronicle,* 141.

112. The prize master was Lieutenant William H. Allen USN; see Dye, *Fatal Cruise of the Argus,* 80–100; Roosevelt, *Naval War of 1812,* 65–66.

113. *The Times,* 20 March 1813; Nelson, "Socio-Economic Effects," 36–43.

114. *The Times,* 17 and 18 May 1813; *NC* 29 (January–June 1813), 288, 472; Tracy, *The Naval Chronicle,* 114–115; W. James, *Naval History,* 6.

115. *The Times,* 12 July 1814.

116. Forester, *Naval War of 1812,* 101–104; Rodger, *Command of the Ocean,* 567.

117. TNA, ADM 2/1375, pp. 365–373, Croker to Warren, 9 January 1813; ADM 2/1377, pp. 14–16, Warren to Cockburn, 17 May 1813; W. S. Dudley, *Naval War of 1812,* 2: 183–184.

118. Perrin and Lloyd, *Keith Papers,* 3: 323; Rodger, *Command of the Ocean,* 568; T. G. Martin, "Isaac Hull's Victory Revisited"; Leech, *Thirty Years from Home,* 143, 149; Gardiner, *Frigates,* 129–130.

119. W. S. Dudley, *Naval War of 1812,* 1: 237–247, 548–553, 639–649; 2: 69–75, 213–224, 232–237, 631–632; Canney, *Sailing Warships,* 122–123; Gardiner, *Naval War of 1812,* 26–27, 40–53; Hepper, *British Warship Losses,* 141–147; Rodger, *Command of the Ocean,* 568–569.

5. Winter on the Lakes

1. Proclamation by Sheaffe, 9 November 1812, in *DHC,* 4: 188. See also W. M. Weeks, "The War of 1812: Civil Authority and Martial Law in Upper Canada," *OH* 48 (1956), 147–161.

2. Malcomson, *Lords of the Lake,* 64–66.

3. Glegg to Powell, 10 January 1813, in *DHC,* 1: 34.

4. Dearborn to Smyth, 21 October 1812, in Brannan, *Official Letters,* 103–104; *DHC,* 4: 151; Eustis to Smyth, 6 November 1812, ibid., 184.

5. TNA, CO 42/148, p. 112, Smyth "Proclamation," 10 November 1812; *DHC,* 4: 193.

6. USNA, RG 107/M6/R6, Eustis to Smyth, 25 November 1812; Black Hawk, *Life,* 19.

7. Clinton was the Republican mayor of New York City, a fact which presented the Federalists with a dilemma of whether or not to support him: they did so without officially endorsing him for fear of alienating his Republican support. For biographical studies see Hanyan and Hanyan, *De Witt Clinton and the Rise of the People's Men;* Siry, *De Witt Clinton and the American Political Economy;* idem, "The Sectional Politics of 'Practical Republicanism': De Witt Clinton's Presidential Bid, 1810–1812," *JER* 5 (1985), 441–462; Craig R. Hanyan, "De Witt Clinton and Partisanship: The Development of Clintonianism from 1811 to 1820," *NYHSQ* 57 (1972), 211.

8. Norman K. Rijsord, "Election of 1812," in Schlesinger, Israel, and Hansen, *History of American Presidential Elections,* 1: 249–296; Hickey, *War of 1812,* 105.

9. For Macdonough see Burdick, *Captain Thomas Macdonough;* Skaggs, *Thomas Macdonough,* especially 63–68; Macdonough, *Life of Commodore Thomas Macdonough;* and Edward K. Eckert, "Thomas Macdonough: Architect of a Wilderness Navy," in Bradford, *Command under Sail,* 147–169.

10. Mahan, *Influence of Sea Power,* 1: 362; USNA, RG 45/M125/R25, Chauncey to Hamilton, 24 September, 21 October, 5 November 1812. See also Orlando B. Wilcox, "Sacket's Harbor and the War of 1812," *Jefferson County Historical Society Transactions* 1 (1886–87), 23–31, 97–100.

11. William S. Dudley, *Naval War of 1812,* 1: 273–274.

12. Malcomson, *Lords of the Lake,* 17–22, 26–27, 44–49. For a description of *Oneida* see Chapelle, *History of American Sailing Navy,* 229–230; also Richard F. Palmer, "James Fenimore Cooper and the Navy Brig Oneida," *IS* 40 (1984), 90–99.

13. TNA, CO 42/148, pp. 3, 57–59, Prevost to Bathurst, 26 October and 21 November 1812; CO 42/150, pp. 47–49, Prevost to Bathurst, 8 February 1813.

14. Malcomson, *Lords of the Lake,* 48–53; C. P. Stacey, "The American Attack on Kingston Harbour," *Canadian Army Journal* 5 (1951), 2–14; idem, "Commodore Chauncey's Attack on Kingston Harbour, November 10, 1812," *CHR* 32 (1951), 126–138; J. M. Hitsman, "Alarum on Lake Ontario, Winter 1812–13," in Zaslow, *Defended Border,* 45–55. See also George R. Dolan, "The Past and Present Fortifications at Kingston," *OHSPR* 12 (1914), 72–80; Jane Ermington, "British American Kingstonians and the War of 1812," *Historic Kingston* 32 (January 1984), 35–45; idem, "Friends and Foes: The Kingston Elite and the War of 1812: A Study in Ambivalence," *Journal of Canadian Studies* 20 (1985), 58–79.

15. USNA, RG45/M125/R25, Chauncey to Hamilton, 17 November and 9 December 1812; W. S. Dudley, *Naval War of 1812,* 1: 336–353; Mahan, *Influence of Sea Power,* 1: 362, 366; 2: 59.

16. Gray to Prevost, 3 December 1812, in *DHC,* 4: 272; and TNA, CO 42/150, pp. 108–111, Gray to Prevost, 12 March 1813. See also W. A. B. Douglas, "The Anatomy of Naval Incompetence: The Provincial Marine in Defence of Upper Canada before 1813," *OH* 71 (1979), 3–25.

17. Prevost proposed that his brother, an unemployed post captain, be made superintendent of the establishment; TNA, CO 42/147, p. 215, Prevost to Bathurst, 17 October 1812; NMM, Warren Papers, Warren to Melville, 7 October, 11 and 18 November, and 31 December 1812; Letterbook, Prevost to Gray, 19 December 1812, and Gray to Prevost, 12 March 1813.

18. Malcomson, *Sailors of 1812,* 22–23; idem, *Lords of the Lake,* 37.

19. Tupper, *Life and Correspondence of Brock,* 84; Graves, *Merry Hearts,* 224; *DCB,* 6: 660–662.

20. TNA, CO 42/147, pp. 193–196, 215–219, Prevost to Bathurst, 22 September and 17 October 1812; WO 1/96, Prevost to Duke of York, 7 October 1812.

21. Myer, *Life and Letters of Beaumont,* 50; TNA, CO 42/148, Prevost to Bathurst, 21 and 28 November 1812; John C. Frederiksen, ed., "The Letters of Captain John Scott, 15th U.S. Infantry: A New Jersey Officer in the War of 1812," *New Jersey History* 107 (Fall/Winter 1989), 61–82.

22. Ingersoll, *History of Second War,* 1: 102. See also Meigs, *Life of Charles Jared Ingersoll.*

23. TNA, CO 42/148, p. 67, "General Orders," 27 November 1812; *PFB,* 375–376.

24. Nicholson, *Gunners of Canada,* 63.

25. Most of the American documentary evidence of Smyth's abortive operation can be found in the sixty-five documents submitted under the collective title "On the Manner

in Which the War Has Been Conducted," in *ASP: MA,* 1: 490–510. See also Dearborn to Smyth, 21 October 1812, in Brannan, *Official Letters,* 103–104; Smyth to Dearborn, 4 and 14 December 1812, ibid., 105–109; TNA, CO 42/352, Sheaffe to Bathurst, 20 October and 31 December 1812; CO 42/354, p. 5, Sheaffe to Prevost, 23 November 1812; CO 42/148, pp. 105–108, Sheaffe to Prevost, 30 November 1812, and Bisshopp to Sheaffe, 1 December 1812; Frank H. Severance, ed., "Documents Relating to the War of 1812: The Letter-Book of Gen. Roger Hale Sheaffe," *PBHS* 17 (1914), 316–319; USNA, RG 107/M222/R6, Winder to Smyth, 7 December 1812. For Bisshopp see R. S. Allen, ed., "The Bisshopp Papers during the War of 1812," *JSAHR* 61 (1983), 26–29; *DCB,* 5: 82–83.

26. Smyth to New York Committee, 4 December 1812, in Brannan, *Official Letters,* 97; *PFB,* 430–431; Stanley, *War of 1812,* 134–138.

27. Winfield Scott, *Memoir,* 1: 31; Berton, *Invasion of Canada,* 257–263; Mahon, *War of 1812,* 84–85. See also Skeen, *Citizen Soldiers,* 102–105; Frank H. Severance, ed., "The Case of Brigadier-General Alexander Smyth as Shown by His Writings," *PBHS* 18 (1914), 213–235.

28. Antal, *A Wampum Denied,* 156–157.

29. For biographies of Winchester see Durham, *James Winchester;* John H. DeWitt, "General James Winchester, 1752–1826," *Tennessee Magazine* 1 (1915), 79–105, 183–205; David E. Harrell, "James Winchester, Patriot," *THQ* 17 (1958), 301–317. See also "The Expeditions of General Samuel Hopkins up the Wabash in 1812: The Letters of Captain Robert Hamilton," *IMH* 43 (1947), 393–402; Glenn Tucker, *Poltroons and Patriots,* 1: 233–234. For a study of Kentucky in the war see Hammack, *Kentucky in Second American Revolution.* For a study of militia service in the west see Rowe, *Bulwark of the Republic,* especially chap. 3.

30. USNA, RG 107/M6/R6, Eustis to Harrison, 17 September 1812; Winchester to Meigs, 22 September 1812, in Knapp, *History of Maumee Valley,* 137–138; Brant, *James Madison: Commander-in-Chief,* 82–85; Clift, *Remember the Raisin!* 176; Gilpin, *War of 1812 in Old Northwest,* 131–132; Stanley, *War of 1812,* 145.

31. See Robert J. Holden, "Ninian Edwards and the War of 1812: The Military Role of a Territorial Governor," in *Selected Papers in Illinois History, 1980: Inaugural Illinois History Symposium of the Illinois State Historical Society* (Springfield, 1980); Reynolds, *My Own Times,* 81–103.

32. Harrison, *Messages and Letters,* 2: 211, 253–265; *PFB,* 346–348; E. A. Cruikshank, "Harrison and Proctor," *Royal Society of Canada Proceedings,* 3d ser., 4 (1910), 145–146; Holliday, *Battle of the Mississinewa;* idem, "The Battle on the Mississinewa," *Indiana Historical Bulletin* 45 (December 1968), 152–166; Ashley Brown, "The Expedition of John B. Campbell of the 19th U.S. Infantry in Nov. 1812 from Franklintown [*sic*] to the Mississinewa Indian Villages," *NOQ* 8 (January 1936), 1–6; idem, "A Chapter in the Warfare against the Indians in Illinois in the Year 1812," *Illinois State Historical Society Journal* 24 (1931), 342–343; John R. Niebaum, "The Pittsburgh Blues," *Western Pennsylvania Historical Magazine* 4 (January 1916), 114–117; John C. Frederiksen, "The Pittsburgh Blues and

the War of 1812: The Memoir of Private Nathaniel Vernon," *Pennsylvania History* 56 (July 1989), 199–201; "Firelock," "Recollections of an Old Campaigner: The Battle of Mississinewa," *Literary Cabinet* 1 (November 1833), 148–149; Reynolds, *My Own Times,* 81–83; and Glen G. Clift, ed., "War Diary of William B. Northcutt," *RKHS* 56 (April–October 1956), 165–189, 253–269, 325–344.

33. *AC,* Twelfth Cong., 2d sess. (1812).

34. *Weekly Register* (Baltimore), 5 December 1812.

35. *AC,* Twelfth Cong., 2d sess. (1812), 498.

36. LC, Madison Papers, reel 26, [Eustis] to Madison, 3 December 1812; Brant, *James Madison: Commander-in-Chief,* 114–168; Stagg, *Mr. Madison's War,* 270–303.

37. For a biography of Armstrong see Skeen, *John Armstrong Jr.;* also his study "John Armstrong and the Role of the Secretary of War in the War of 1812" (Ph.D. diss., Ohio State University, 1966). Skeen's work is an attempt to resurrect Armstrong's reputation. On his appointment see Stagg, *Mr. Madison's War,* 282–284. James Wilkinson accused him of plagiarizing much of his pamphlet from Jomini's *Traité de guerre; Memoirs,* 3: 398.

38. USNA, RG 45/M125/R10, Jones to Chauncey, 27 January 1813. For Jones see Edward K. Eckert, "William Jones: Mr. Madison's Secretary of the Navy," *PMHB* 96 (April 1972), 167–182; idem, "Early Reform in the Navy Department," *AN* 33 (1973), 231–245; idem, "William Jones and the Role of the Secretary of the Navy in the War of 1812" (Ph. D. diss., University of Florida, 1969); Frank L. Owsley Jr., "William Jones," in Coletta, *American Secretaries of the Navy,* 1: 93–98; Charles O. Paullin, "Naval Administration under Secretaries of the Navy Smith, Hamilton and Jones, 1801–1814," *USNIP* 32 (1906), 1289–1328.

39. Dunlop, *Recollections of the American War,* 35–36.

40. Skeen, *John Armstrong Jr.,* 121–133, 135; Stagg, *Mr. Madison's War,* 278–288; Kreidberg and Henry, *History of Military Mobilization,* 42–46.

41. TNA, CO 42/147, pp. 210–214, Bathurst to Prevost, 16 November 1812.

42. Hickey, *War of 1812,* 85, 135.

43. Meddert, *Raw Recruits and Bullish Prisoners,* 59.

44. For a biography of Wood, see Cullum, *Campaigns,* 102–138. For Meigs see Knopf, *Return Johnathan Meigs.*

45. Mahon, *War of 1812,* 132.

46. "Picture of a Soldier's Life," *NWR* 4 (4 May 1813), 166; Mahon, *War of 1812,* pp. 159–161. For the full story of the fort, see Larry L. Nelson, *Men of Patriotism, Courage and Enterprise!;* and Rex L. Spencer, "The Gibraltar of the Maumee: Fort Meigs in the War of 1812" (Ph.D. diss., Ball State University, 1988).

47. Meddert, *Raw Recruits and Bullish Prisoners,* 69–75.

48. McAfee, *History,* 138–145.

49. Harrison, *Messages and Letters,* 2: 156, 177, 185, 211–215.

50. Cullum, *Campaigns,* 101–102n; Clift, *Remember the Raisin!* 40; McAfee, *History,* 185.

51. Darnell, *Journal,* 41.

52. "Nathan Newson Journal," cited in Banta, *The Ohio,* 222.

53. *SBD,* 2: 3; Clift, *Remember the Raisin!* 50–55.

54. Atherton, *Narrative,* 33–42; Armstrong, *Notices,* 1: 199–200; LAC, RG 8 I C678, Proctor to Sheaffe, 25 January 1813; Samuel R. Brown, *Views of Campaigns,* 148; Darnell, *Journal,* 45; Harrison, *Messages and Letters,* 2: 319–326; Antal, *A Wampum Denied,* 163–165; Gilpin, *War of 1812 in Old Northwest,* 164–165.

55. William F. Coffin, *1812,* 203.

56. Sugden, *Tecumseh,* 324–325.

57. TNA, CO 42/150, pp. 76–79, 80–81, Prevost to Bathurst, 27 February 1813, and Macdonell to Baynes, 22 February 1813.

58. On Roundhead see "'Stayegtha' (Roundhead)," in *DCB,* 5: 774–775.

59. W. F. Coffin, *1812,* 204; Sandor Antal in *A Wampum Denied* states that American sentries spotted the British approach, but the victory was nevertheless "one of the most complete of any in the war" (168–182). For an alternative view, see Quimby, *U.S. Army in War of 1812,* 1: 135–136, 198; Clift, *Remember the Raisin!* 63–76.

60. LAC, RG 8 I C678, Proctor to Sheaffe, 25 January 1813; Gellner, *Recollections,* 16; Darnell, *Journal,* 52; John Hunt, *Memoirs,* 43; Atherton, *Narrative,* 46.

61. John Richardson, *Richardson's War of 1812,* 134–136, 302. Robert Richardson to John Askin, 7 February 1813, in Askin, *Askin Papers,* 2: 749–750. John Richardson was one of four gentleman volunteers then serving with the 41st Regiment, all of whom were recommended for advancement by Proctor. But Richardson was the first to be promoted, which displeased Proctor, "whom I find promoted over the faculty here who have invariably shown zeal and ability which he has not." Some three decades later, in researching his book *War of 1812,* Richardson found Proctor's comments and in return was unreserved in his criticism of his former commander; LAC, RG 8 I C678, Proctor to Myers, 23 May 1813; Antal, *A Wampum Denied,* 239.

62. Atherton, *Narrative,* 46–50; Darnell, *Journal,* 52–53; Antal, *A Wampum Denied,* 170–171. For a biography see Gerald F. Williams, "William O. Butler, Kentucky Cavalier" (Master's thesis, University of Kentucky, 1971).

63. WRM, Acc. No. 1822, "The War in Canada 1812–14," p. 23.

64. *Morning Chronicle,* 23 April 1813. Although the capture is generally attributed to Roundhead, Reynolds reckoned it was made by a drunken Indian known as "Brandy Jack"; W. F. Coffin, *1812,* 204.

65. Atherton, *Narrative,* 50–53; Berton, *Invasion of Canada,* 292–299; Harrison, *Messages and Letters,* 2: 360–362; J. Hunt, *Memoirs,* 42; McAfee, *History,* 215–216.

66. Gellner, *Recollections,* 18. Byfield's account is also published in Stuart Sutherland's *Two British Soldiers in the War of 1812.*

67. W. F. Coffin, *1812,* 205–206.

68. Proctor to Sheaffe, 25 January 1813, *SBD,* 1: 7–9; Darnell, *Journal,* 57–60.

69. Knapp, *History of Maumee Valley,* 150–151; Clift, *Remember the Raisin!* 80–91; Darnell, *Journal,* 61; Lewis Bond, "Journal of the Battle and Massacre of River Raisin

January 22 & 23, 1813, and of the War of 1812," in Knopf, *Document Transcriptions,* 10: 204–205. See also Thomas P. Dudley, "Battle and Massacre at Frenchtown, January 22, 1813," *Western Reserve Historical Society Tracts,* no. 1 (August 1870), 1–4; Frank C. Dunn, "Captain Nathaniel G. S. Hart," *FCHQ* 24 (1950), 28–33.

70. Statement of John Todd MD, 2 May 1813, in *ASP: MA,* 1: 372–373; Woodward to Proctor, 2 February 1813, in *MPCH,* 36: 291; Antal, *A Wampum Denied,* 178; Horsman, *Matthew Elliott,* 203–206.

71. "Return of American Prisoners Killed," Winchester to Harrison, 21 January 1813; and Major Elijah McClenahan to Harrison, 26 January 1813, both in Knopf, *Document Transcriptions,* 7: 49–52, 61–62; Berton, *Invasion of Canada,* 300–304; McAfee, *History,* 200–235; John Richardson, *Richardson's War of 1812,* 132–137. See also Vernon L. Beal, "John McDonnell and the Ransoming of American Captives after the River Raisin Massacre," *Michigan History* 35 (September 1951), 331–351; James Russell Harris, "Kentuckians in the War of 1812: A Note on Numbers, Losses, and Sources," *RKHS* 82 (1984), 277–286.

72. TNA, WO 1/96, "Return of Killed and Wounded in the Action at Rivierre au Raisin, 22nd January 1813," Proctor to Sheaffe, 25 January 1813; Gilpin, *War of 1812 in Old Northwest,* 167–170; Harrison, *Messages and Letters,* 2: 328; Armstrong, *Notices,* 1: 201–205; Winchester to Monroe, 11 February 1813, in Cruikshank, "Harrison and Proctor," 163; Right Division Return, 22 January 1813, in *SBD,* 2: 10–12; Lomax, *History of the 41st,* 67–68; A. C. Whitehorne, *History of The Welch Regiment,* 97–100; John C. Parish, ed., "The Autobiography of John Chambers," *Iowa Journal of History and Politics* 6 (April 1908), 266.

73. Antal, *A Wampum Denied,* 191–202. Some early American historians showed commendable balance. "There is no doubt that General [*sic*] Proctor intended to keep his promises but the wounded men were left on the ground with insufficient guard . . . Proctor did protect those who could walk"; Shaler, *Kentucky,* 162–163; *NWR* 4 (10 April 1813), 97. See also John N. Cronbie, ed., "The Papers of Major Daniel McFarland," *Western Pennsylvania Historical Magazine* 51 (April 1968), 101–125; Dennis Carter-Edwards, "The War of 1812 along the Detroit Frontier: A Canadian Perspective," *Michigan Historical Review* 13 (1987), 25–50.

74. LC, Proctor Papers, Proctor to Sheaffe, 28 November 1812.

75. Richardson to Askin, 7 February 1813, in Askin, *Askin Papers,* 2: 749–750.

76. *MPHC,* 36: 309–314; Brant, *James Madison: Commander-in-Chief,* 151–152; Hammack, *Kentucky in Second American Revolution,* 47–54; Darnell, *Journal,* 71–76.

77. Prevost to Proctor, 9 February 1813, in *DHC,* 1: 62.

78. Hickey, *War of 1812,* 50, 96–99, 168–171; Sellers, *The Market Revolution,* 28.

79. Kenneth Ross Nelson, "Socio-Economic Effects of the War of 1812 on Britain" (Ph.D. diss., University of Georgia, 1972), 19–21.

80. *AC,* Twelfth Cong., 2d sess.(1812), 75, 97, 907–908, 919–920, 1326–28, 1330–33; "Report to the Secretary of State, 12 July 1813, U.S. Congress," in *ASP: FR,* 2: 646–647; Hickey, *War of 1812,* 118, 122. Astor's involvement is described in Haeger, *John Jacob Astor,*

138–169. For a biography see Kenneth W. Porter, *John Jacob Astor; DAB,* 1: 397–399. For Girard see George Wilson, *Stephen Girard;* W. Tasman, "Stephen Girard (1750–1831): A One-Eyed American Patriot," *Documenta Ophthalmologica* 94 (1997), 39–58; Kenneth L. Brown, "Stephen Girard, Promoter of the Second Bank of United States," *JEH* 2 (1942), 201–220; Donald R. Adams, "The Bank of Stephen Girard, 1812–1831," *JEH* 32 (1972), 841–868. Parish was a German-born financier who made a fortune smuggling gold from Mexico to Paris and invested it in a scheme to develop 200,000 acres of northern New York State. See J. M. Hitsman, "David Parish and the War of 1812," *MA* 26 (1962–63), 171–177; Raymond Walters and Philip G. Walters, "The American Career of David Parish," *JEH* 4 (1944), 149–166. See also Donald H. Kagin, "Monetary Aspects of the Treasury Notes of the War of 1812," *JEH* 44 (1984), 69–88.

81. USNA, RG 107/M6/R45, Armstrong to Swartout, 4 April 1813; Graves, *Field of Glory,* 21.

82. Brant, *James Madison: Commander-in-Chief,* 166; "Register, United States Army," 27 December 1812, in *ASP: MA,* 1: 384–425.

83. Skeen, *John Armstrong Jr.,* 129.

84. Armstrong to Harrison, 5 and 17 March, 21 April 1813, and Harrison to Armstrong, 17 March and 27 April 1813, in Harrison, *Messages and Letters,* 2: 378–380, 387–392, 425, 428; Risch, *Quartermaster Support of the Army,* 159–164, 172; Mahon, *War of 1812,* 132–134, 159.

85. NMM, Warren Papers, Allen to Warren, 7 December 1812.

86. Nichol to Talbot, 12 December 1812, in *DHC,* 4: 299.

87. For details of these units and other foreign corps serving in the British Army, see Chartrand, *Émigré and Foreign Troops.* For a history of the Régiment De Meuron, see Meuron, *Le Régiment Meuron.* See also Linder, *The Swiss Regiment Meuron;* King's College, London, Liddell Hart Centre for Military Archives, Davidson 1/2, 1935 May 2—1957 Apr. 5, "His Majesty's Regiment de Meuron," pamphlet reprinted from *Army Quarterly,* October 1936; and C. C. P. Lawson and J. P. Severin, "De Meuron's Swiss Regiment 1814–1816," *MCH* 9 (Fall 1957), 77; Roy F. Forgit, "The Swiss Connection: Le Regiment Meuron," *Je Me Souviens* 25 (Autumn 2002), 13–20; Robie L. Reid, "Who Were the Meurons?" *The Beaver* 273 (1942–43), 28–29; F. H. N. Davidson, "His Majesty's Regiment de Meuron," *Army Quarterly* 33 (1937); and C. C. P. Lawson and John P. Severin, "De Meuron's Swiss Regiment, 1814–1816," *MCH* 9 (Fall 1957), 77–79. For the Régiment De Watteville, see Herbert Knötel and John R. Elting, "De Watteville's Swiss Regiment, 1814," *MCH* 12 (Winter 1960), 109–110; and John D. P. Martin, "The Regiment de Watteville: Its Settlement and Services in Upper Canada," *OH* 62 (1960), 17–30.

88. Biddulph, *The Nineteenth and Their Times,* 174. See Duke University, William R. Perkins Library, Diary of Lieutenant John Lang, 19th Light Dragoons, 1813–14. The 19th Light Dragoons were converted into the 19th Lancers in 1817, and disbanded in 1821. Though the later 19th Hussars (Queen Alexandra's Own) had no formal relationship to the Dragoons, they inherited their battle honours, including "Niagara." This circumstance

was somewhat ironic given the Indian origins of the 19th Hussars, who were converted from the 1st Bengal European Light Cavalry in 1861.

89. Besides Canadians, English, Scots, Irish, a few Welsh, and 200 Acadians from New Brunswick, Nova Scotia, and Prince Edward Island, by 1812, when their strength reached 1,008, the regiment included Americans from New York, New Jersey, and Pennsylvania; Germans, Italians, Poles, and Swedes, and some Indians and Africans; Squires, *The 104th Regiment of Foot,* 53–54, 85–86.

90. Hitsman, *Incredible War,* 119. See *DCB,* 6: 38–39; *DNB,* 4: 745–746; Philippart, *Royal Military Calendar,* 2: 151.

91. Squires, *The 104th Regiment of Foot,* 112–114.

92. Graves, *Merry Hearts,* 95. He means "The Girl I Left Behind Me," the traditional loath-to-depart tune of the British Army; Winstock, *Songs and Music of the Redcoats,* 70. See also M. A. Pope, ed., "The March of the 104th Foot from Fredericton to Quebec, 1813," *Canadian Defence Quarterly* 7 (July 1930), 490–501.

93. Squires, *The 104th Regiment of Foot,* 121.

94. Ibid., 124, 127–132.

95. Graves, *Merry Hearts,* 104.

96. Squires, *The 104th Regiment of Foot,* 136.

97. See Anon., "Smuggling in 1813–1814: A Personal Reminiscence," *VH* 38 (Winter 1970), 22–26: Neil R. Scott, ed., "Excerpts from John Howe's 'Smuggler's Journal,'" *VH* 40 (Autumn 1972), 262–270; H. N. Muller III, "A 'Traitorous and Diabolical Traffic,'" *VH* 44 (1976), 78–96.

98. René Chartrand, "Canadian Voyageurs during the War of 1812," *JSAHR* 72 (Autumn 1994), 186.

99. USNA, RG 107/M221/R52, Forsyth to Dearborn, 8 February 1813; *PFB,* 578.

100. Macdonell, writing anonymously as "Philalethes," later claimed that he was in fact "acting under something like a certainty of being cashiered by a court-martial, if not indeed sentenced to be shot (for disobedience of orders) in the event of a failure"; "The Last War in Canada," *JUSI,* pt. 1 (March 1848), 427, 436–439.

101. Hitsman, *Incredible War,* 130–132; Boss, *Stormont, Dundas and Glengarry Highlanders,* 13.

102. Boss, *Stormont, Dundas and Glengarry Highlanders,* 17.

103. N. Lord. ed., "The War on the Canadian Frontier, 1812–1814: Letters Written by Sergt. James Commins, 8th Foot," *JSAHR* 18 (Winter 1939), 203.

104. Squires, *The 104th Regiment of Foot,* 145.

105. LAC, RG 8 I C678, pp. 95–96, 100–102, Macdonell to Harvey, 22 and 25 February 1813; Macdonell to Prevost, 23 February 1813, in William James, *Naval History,* 393–394; TNA, CO 42/150, pp. 76–79, 80–81, Prevost to Bathurst, 27 February 1813, and Macdonell to Adjutant General, 22 February 1813; Boss, *Stormont, Dundas and Glengarry Highlanders,* 16–18; Edgar, *Ten Years of Upper Canada,* 175–178; H. Winston Johnston, *The Glengarry Light Infantry,* 94–109.

106. Prevost to Macdonell, 22 February 1813, in "Philalethes," "The Last War in Canada," *JUSI,* pt. 2 (June 1848), 271–283.

107. Hitsman, *Incredible War,* 133 n. 38.

108. Dearborn to Armstrong, 25 February 1813, in *ASP: MA,* 1: 440.

109. TNA, CO 42/148, p. 359, Bathurst to Prevost, 12 March 1813.

110. TNA, ADM 2/1376, pp. 131–133, 205–206, 249–263, 823, Appointment of Sir J. L. Yeo, 19 March 1813, and General Order, 22 April 1813; *SBD,* 1: 240, 250–251; W. S. Dudley, *Naval War of 1812,* 2: 435–437; Mahan, *Sea Power,* 2: 435. See Frederick C. Drake, "Commodore Sir James Lucas Yeo and Governor General George Prevost: A Study in Command Relations, 1813–14," in Cogar, *New Interpretations in Naval History,* 156–171; John B. Irvine, "The Role of Sir James Lucas Yeo in the War of 1812" (Master's thesis, Carleton University, 1958).

111. USNA, RG 107/M221/R58, Vandeventer to Armstrong, 15 March and 1 April 1813; M222/R9, Vandeventer to Armstrong, 5 April 1813.

112. W. S. Dudley, *Naval War of 1812,* 1: 319–320, 324–327, 354, 368–369; 2: 420–423; Skaggs and Altoff, *A Signal Victory,* 44–44. For biographies of Perry see Dutton, *Oliver Hazard Perry;* Fenton, *Oliver Hazard Perry;* Hoyt, *The Tragic Commodore;* Richard Dillon, *We Have Met the Enemy;* and Alexander Slidell Mackenzie, *Life of Commodore Oliver Hazard Perry.* See also John K. Mahon, "Oliver Hazard Perry: Savior of the Northwest," in Bradford, *Command under Sail,* 126–146; Frederick L. Oliver, "Commodore Oliver Hazard Perry of Newport, Rhode Island," *USNIP* 80 (July 1954), 776–783; and Sarah Wallace Perry, "A Sister's Reminiscences of Oliver Hazard Perry," *American Magazine and Historical Chronicle* 4 (Autumn–Winter 1988–89), 19–31.

113. Malcomson and Malcomson, *H.M.S. Detroit,* 42–45.

114. Chauncey to Perry, 1 February 1813, in A. S. Mackenzie, *Life of Commodore Oliver Hazard Perry,* 1: 125.

115. S. R. Brown, *Views of Campaigns,* 41–42; Mahan, *Influence of Sea Power,* 2: 68; Frederick C. Drake, "The Loss of Mastery: The British Squadron on Lake Erie, May–September 1813," *JES* 17 (1988), 55–56.

116. For a biography of Dobbins see Ilisevich, *Daniel Dobbins, Frontier Mariner;* Clarence S. Metcalf, "Daniel Dobbins, Sailing Master, USN," *IS* 14 (Summer 1958), 88–96, and (Fall 1958), 181–191; A. J. Druggan, "Dan Dobbins—The Unsung Hero of the Battle of Lake Erie," *Columbus Dispatch Magazine,* September 1963, 6–21; William Maher Howell, "The Arrival of Dobbins at Erie," *IS* 51 (1995), 32–34; Frank H. Severance, ed., "Career of Daniel Dobbins," *PBHS* 8 (1905), 257–282. See also E. A. Cruikshank, "The Contest for the Command of Lake Erie in 1812–13," in Zaslow, *Defended Border,* 84–90; W. S. Dudley, *Naval War of 1812,* 2: 406–413; Rosenberg, *Building of Perry's Fleet;* Milton W. Shreve, "The Issues at Stake in the Battle of Lake Erie," *JAH* 8 (January–March 1914), 58–82.

117. Hickey, *War of 1812,* 110–113.

6. Spring on the Frontier

Epigraph: This song dates to 1706 and George Farquahar's play *The Recruiting Officer,* and was revived in the 1790s; Winstock, *Songs and Music of the Redcoats,* 29–31.

1. William S. Dudley, *Naval War of 1812,* 2: 642–645.

2. Armstrong to Cabinet, 8 February 1813, in *ASP: MA,* 1: 439; Stagg, *Mr. Madison's War,* 284–286.

3. Malcomson, *Lords of the Lake,* 84.

4. Armstrong to Dearborn, 24 and 26 February, 3 and 9 March 1813, and Dearborn to Armstrong, 3 and 9 March 1813, in *ASP: MA,* 1: 441; Skeen, *John Armstrong Jr.,* 148.

5. HSP, Dallas Papers, Jones to Alexander Dallas, 19 July 1813; LC, Madison Papers, James Monroe to Madison, 27 December 1813; Scholarly Resources, Wilmington, Del., Gallatin Papers, Gallatin to James W. Nicholson, 5 May 1813, and Gallatin to William Few, 9 May 1813.

6. Henry Adams, *History,* 7: 388–389; Dewey, *Financial History of United States,* 133; Studenski and Krooss, *Financial History of United States,* 78–79.

7. For a biography see Jordan, *George Washington Campbell of Tennessee.*

8. Glenn Tucker, *Poltroons and Patriots,* 1: 430–435.

9. Nielson, *Financial History of United* States, 28, 43–49; Act of 2 August 1813, *NWR* 5 (11 September 1813), 17–21.

10. H. Adams, *History,* 7: 30, 33–41; Perkins, *Castlereagh and Adams,* 2, 15–18, 20, 150; Stagg, *Mr. Madison's War,* 270–274, 295–297; idem, "The Politics of Ending the War of 1812," in Bowler, *War along the Niagara,* 94.

11. Brant, *James Madison: Commander-in-Chief,* 219, 221–222, 226, 253; Balinky, *Albert Gallatin,* 194–206; H. Adams, *History,* 7: 26–47, 396–397; Stagg, "The Politics of Ending the War," 97.

12. Hitsman, *Incredible War,* 121–123, 134–136.

13. *ASP: MA,* 1: 441–442; Armstrong, *Notices,* 1: 129 n. 2; Malcomson, *Lords of the Lake,* 87–89.

14. Malcomson, *Lords of the Lake,* 67–69, 94–95.

15. On the York militia in the war, see Hunter, *History of the 12th Regiment,* 9–32.

16. For Pike see Hollon, *The Lost Pathfinder;* idem, "Zebulon Montgomery Pike and the York Campaign, 1813," *New York History* 60 (July 1949), 265–275; *DAB,* 7: 599–600. For Chandler see George F. Talbot, "General John Chandler of Monmouth, Maine, with Extracts from His Autobiography," *Collections of the Maine Historical Society* 9 (1887), 167–205; *DAB,* 3: 613–614. The 21st is one of the few American regiments of the period to have its own history by Hampton, *History of the Twenty-first U.S. Infantry.* For the U.S. 2nd Light Dragoons see Donald E. Graves, "The Second Regiment of United States Light Dragoons, 1812–1814," *MCH* 34 (Fall 1982), 101–108; Hugh C. Barron Jr. and René Chartrand, "U.S. Light Dragoons, 1813–1814," *MCH* 42 (Summer 1990), 67; Samuel D. Harris, "Service of Capt. Samuel D. Harris: A Sketch of His Military Career as a Captain

in the Second Regiment of Light Dragoons during the War of 1812," *PBHS* 24 (1920), 327–342.

17. H. Strum, "Smuggling in the War of 1812," *History Today* 29 (1979), 537. See also Edward Brynn, "Patterns of Dissent: Vermont's Opposition to the War of 1812," *VH* 60 (1972), 10–27.

18. *PFB,* 586–587n.

19. James Fenimore Cooper, *Ned Myers,* 51, 59.

20. Mahon, *War of 1812,* 142.

21. Lieutenant Fraser in the *Philaelphia Aurora,* 10 May 1813; *DHC,* 5: 192.

22. Finan, *Journal of a Voyage to Quebec,* quoted in *DHC,* 5: 206.

23. Talman, *Loyalist Narratives,* 252–253; W. S. Dudley, *Naval War of 1812,* 2: 453–459; Turner, *British Generals in War of 1812,* 96. Sheaffe was later defended by "Truth," "Sir Roger Sheaffe and the Defense of York," *Anglo-American Magazine* 3 (December 1853), 565–566.

24. TNA, CO 42/354, pp. 132–135, Sheaffe to Prevost, 5 May 1813; *SBD,* 2: 89–94; USNA, RG 45/M125/R28, Chauncey to Jones, 28 April 1813; Dearborn to Armstrong, 28 April and 3 May 1813, in *ASP: MA,* 1: 443–444. See also Benn, *Historic Fort York,* 50–64; idem, *The Battle of York;* Berton, *Flames across the Border,* 37–52; H. Winston Johnston, *The Glengarry Light Infantry,* 110–116; Nicholson, *Gunners of Canada,* 67–68; Quaife, *The Yankees Capture York;* Stacey, *Battle of Little York;* Stanley, *War of 1812,* 168–173; Abraham Eustis, "Letter of Major Abraham Eustis, Giving an Account of the Capture of York, now 'Toronto,'" *PMHS* 11 (December 1876), 492–495; and Charles Humphries, "The Capture of York," in Zaslow, *Defended Border,* 251–270. See also "Extracts from the Jarvis Papers," *Women's Canadian Historical Society of Toronto* 5 (1905), 3–9.

25. Trowbridge, *The Trowbridge Genealogy,* 537.

26. Connecticut Historical Society, Hartford, George Howard Journal, Howard to Sarah Howard, 7 May 1813. Other witnesses say his back was crushed. See also the diary of Eli Playter, 27 April 1813, in Firth, *The Town of York,* 300; Eustis, "Letter Giving Account of Capture of York,"; Shepard, *Autobiography of Elihu H. Shepard,* 51.

27. Beaumont, *William Beaumont's Formative Years,* 46. See also Myer, *Life and Letters of Beaumont;* Rodney B. Nelson, *Beaumont;* and Cynthia DeHaven Pitcock, "The Career of William Beaumont, 1785–1853: Science and the Self-Made Man in America" (Ph.D. diss., Memphis State University, 1985).

28. TNA, CO 42/150, Terms of Capitulation, 27 April 1813; W. S. Dudley, *Naval War of 1812,* 2: 446–453. See also M. L. Magill, "William Allan and the War of 1812," *OH* 64 (September 1972), 132–141. Allan commanded the York militia at Queenston and was one of those who negotiated the surrender.

29. Stacey, *Battle of Little York,* 17.

30. AO, F556 MU 5901, Ely Playter fonds, Playter's diary, 30 April 30 1813; Isaac to Jonathan Wilson, 5 December 1813, in Firth, *The Town of York,* 293.

31. Hickey, *War of 1812,* 128; Berton, *Flames across the Border,* 57–61.

32. TNA, CO 42/150, Major W. Allen to Sheaffe, 2 May 1813; CO 42/354, pp. 107, 109, 350–351, Sheaffe to Bathurst, 13 and 15 May 1813, and de Rottenburg to Bathurst, 25 October 1813; Myer, *Life and Letters of Beaumont,* 45–46.

33. Prevost to Bathurst, 20 July 1813, in *DHC,* 6: 256.

34. Dearborn to Armstrong, 13 May 1813, in *DHC,* 5: 229; Malcomson, *Lords of the Lake,* 104–112.

35. TNA, CO 42/150, pp. 143, 156, 171, Prevost to Bathurst, 21 April, 18 and 26 May 1813; Sheaffe to Bathurst, 18 May 1813, in *DHC,* 5: 232; Stanley, *War of 1812,* 177–178. For Strachan see Strachan, *Memoir;* John H. L. Henderson, *John Strachan;* Robertson, *The Fighting Bishop;* and Strachan, *Letterbook.*

36. Turner, *British Generals in War of 1812,* 97–100.

37. Malcomson, *Lords of the Lake,* 115; *DHC,* 5: 192.

38. A. A. Davidson, "The Battle of Tipton's Island," *IMH* 9 (March 1913), 47–49.

39. Cullum, *Campaigns,* 128.

40. LAC, RG 8 I C678, p. 253, Embarkation Return, 23 April 1813.

41. Proctor to Roger Sheaffe, 17 April 1813, in *SBD,* 2: 38.

42. For an account of the fort and its role in the war, see Larry L. Nelson, *Men of Patriotism, Courage and Enterprise!* For the story of Ohio militia garrison duty at Fort Amanda on the Auglaize River, see William Schillinger, "Journal of Ensign William Schillinger," *OAHSQ* 41 (January 1932), 51–82. See also Hugh C. McBarron Jr., René Chartrand, and James L. Kochan, "Regular Infantry Regiments of the Northwest Army, 1813," *MCH* 35 (Spring 1983), 30–31.

43. Lorrain, *The Helm, the Cross and the Sword,* 131; John Richardson, *Richardson's War of 1812,* 148; Knapp, *History of Maumee Valley,* 164.

44. See P. C. Rainwater, ed., "The Siege of Fort Meigs," *MVHR* 19 (September 1932), 261–264.

45. Cullum, *Campaigns,* 389–390.

46. Proctor to Prevost, 14 May 1813, in *SBD,* 2: 34.

47. Todd and Drake, *Sketches of Services of Harrison,* 75.

48. Cushing, *Captain Cushing,* 116–117; Samuel R. Brown, *Views of Campaigns,* 45.

49. Clay's Report to Harrison, 9 May 1813, in Harrison, *Messages and Letters,* 2: 440–442.

50. Howe, *Historical Collections of Ohio,* 2: 870.

51. John Richardson, *Richardson's War of 1812,* 152; Cushing, *Captain Cushing,* 118–119.

52. Howe, *Historical Collections of Ohio,* 2: 867. For the 2nd U.S. Artillery, see Michael N. Morell, "The Artillery Detachment at Fort Meigs, 1813," *MCH* 38 (Summer 1986), 78–79.

53. T. Christian, "Campaign of 1813 on the Ohio Frontier," *Western Reserve and Northern Ohio Historical Society* 23 (1874), 5.

54. Harrison to Armstrong, 5 May 1813, in Harrison, *Messages and Letters,* 2: 432.

55. Cullum, *Campaigns,* 399–400. See also Samuel Rogers, *Autobiography,* 17–18; Neil E. Salich, ed., "The Siege of Fort Meigs, 1813: An Eyewitness Account by Colonel

Alexander Bourne," *NOQ* 17 (October 1945), 139–154; 18 (January 1946), 39–48; "Historical Sketch of the Siege of Fort Meigs," *Analectic Magazine* 13 (June 1819), 508–517; and James T. Eubank, "The Siege of Fort Meigs," *RKHS* 19 (May 1921), 54–62.

56. Sugden, *Tecumseh*, 332.

57. Howe, *Historical Collections of Ohio*, 2: 871.

58. Gellner, *Recollections*, 25.

59. Berton, *Flames across the Border*, 117–125; L. L. Nelson, *Men of Patriotism, Courage and Enterprise!* 67–92; McAfee, *History*, 287–292; Hammack, *Kentucky in Second American Revolution*, 62–68; A. C. Whitehorne, *History of The Welch Regiment*, 100–101.

60. Wisconsin Historical Society, Madison, Tecumseh Papers, Combs to Green Clay, 6 May 1815; Leslie Combs, *Colonel William Dudley's Defeat*, 8–13. For a biography of Combs see *Narrative of the Life of General Leslie Combs*.

61. John Richardson, *Richardson's War of 1812*, 154.

62. L. Combs, *Colonel William Dudley's Defeat*, 8–13; Howe, *Historical Collections of Ohio*, 2: 872–873; Knapp, *History of Maumee Valley*, 170–171. See also Thomas Christian, "The Campaign of 1813 on the Ohio River: Sortie at Fort Meigs, 1813," *RKHS* 67 (July 1969), 260–268.

63. WRM, Acc. No. 1822, "The War in Canada 1812–14," p. 36.

64. Sugden, *Tecumseh*, 334–338.

65. Harrison to Armstrong, 13 May 1813, in Harrison, *Messages and Letters*, 2: 443.

66. LAC, RG 8 I C678, Proctor to Prevost, 14 May 1813, and Militia captains to Proctor, 6 May 1813; Stanley, *War of 1812*, 152–156, 159–161, 210–214; John Richardson, *Richardson's War of 1812*, 159, 214–234; Skaggs and Altoff, *A Signal Victory*, 57.

67. Proctor to Prevost, 11 July 1813, in *SBD*, 2: 253.

68. TNA, CO 42/151, pp. 3–6, Proctor to Prevost, 14 May 1813; also pp. 7, 9, 12–14.

69. "Diary of the Siege of Fort Meigs," *NWR* 4 (4 June 1813), 242–244; McAfee, *History*, 256–277; Gilpin, *War of 1812 in Old Northwest*, 182–189.

70. TNA, ADM 2/1376, pp. 183–185, Establishment of officers and men for the lakes action, 8 March 1813. On Mulcaster see Malcomson, *Lords of the Lake*, 118–120; Henry J. Morgan, *Sketches of Celebrated Canadians*, 226–227.

71. See John C. Spurr, "The Royal Navy's Presence in Kingston, Part I: 1813–1836," *Historic Kingston* 25 (1977), 63–64; and E. A. Cruikshank, "The Contest for the Command of Lake Ontario in 1812 and 1813," *Transactions of the Royal Society of Canada*, 3d ser., 19 (1916), 161–222.

72. TNA, ADM 9/4, No. 1241, "Memorandum of the Services of Captain Robert Barclay"; *DCB*, 7: 45–47; Blanche A. Burt, "Sketch of Robert Heriot Barclay, R.N.," *OHSPR* 14 (1916), 169–178; Robert Holden Mackenzie, *The Trafalgar Roll*, 225; Malcomson and Malcomson, *H.M.S. Detroit*, 20–23; Marshall, *Royal Naval Biography*, 3: 186–187.

73. *SBD*, 2: 298. See also Robert Malcomson, "Controversial Relationships among the British before and after the Battle of Lake Erie," *IS* 46 (1990), 187–197.

74. Stanley, *War of 1812*, 202–203.

75. TNA, ADM 1/503, pp. 178–179, 271, Warren to Croker, 13 March 1813, and Barclay to Warren, 23 March 1813; ADM 2/1376, pp. 131–133, 183–184, 191–195, 249–264, Croker to Goulburn, Navy Board, "Lake Service in Canada," 6 March 1813; Croker to Goulburn, 9 March 1813; Croker to Yeo on appointment, 12 April 1813; Skaggs and Altoff, *A Signal Victory*, 61–68.

76. W. S. Dudley, *Naval War of 1812*, 2: 246.

77. TNA, CO 42/150, p. 150, Prevost to Bathurst, 26 May 1813.

78. Brinckman, *Historical Record of the Eighty-ninth*, 16; Cunliffe, *Royal Irish Fusiliers*, 139.

79. Hitsman, *Incredible War*, 144; Lomax, *History of the 41st*, 108.

80. For Vincent, see *DCB*, 7: 888–889; H. J. Morgan, *Sketches of Celebrated Canadians*, 196.

81. John D. Carroll, *My Boy Life*, 53.

82. Cruikshank, *Battle of Fort George*, 42.

83. USNA, RG 107/M222/R8, Lewis to Armstrong, 5 July 1813. For Boyd, see *DAB*, 1: 526–529. For Winder, "General William H. Winder," *Genealogical Magazine and Historical Chronicle* 21 (1919), 217–219; *DAB*, 10: 382; Graves, *Field of Glory*, 35–36.

84. John C. Fredriksen, ed., "Memoirs of Ephraim Shaler: A Connecticut Yankee in the War of 1812," *New England Quarterly* 57 (September 1984), 414.

85. J. F. Cooper, *Ned Myers*, 66–57.

86. "First Campaign of an A.D.C.," *Military and Naval Magazine* 2 (September 1833), 19.

87. TNA, CO 42/150, pp. 185–187, 189–193, Vincent to Prevost, 28 May 1813, and Prevost to Bathurst, 3 June 1813; W. S. Dudley, *Naval War of 1812*, 2: 460–466; *SBD*, 2: 103–107; USNA, RG 45/M125/R28, Chauncey to Jones, 27 and 18 May 1813; Morgan Lewis to Dearborn and Dearborn to Armstrong, 27 May 1813, in Brannan, *Official Letters*, 161–162; Berton, *Flames across the Border*, 65–70; Boss, *Stormont, Dundas and Glengarry Highlanders*, 32–33; *Historical Record of the King's Liverpool Regiment*, 89–90; H. W. Johnston, *The Glengarry Light Infantry*, 117–126; Malcomson, *Lords of the Lake*, 125–128; Petre, *Royal Berkshire Regiment*, 95–97; R. L. Rogers, *History of Lincoln and Welland Regiment*, 8–9. Boyd's men counted 107 British dead and 175 wounded. See also Cruikshank, *Battle of Fort George*, 45–51; Margaret Coleman, "The American Capture of Fort George, Ontario," *Canadian Historic Sites: Occasional Papers in Archaeology and History* 13 (1977), 3–107; Lynn Morrison, "An Amphibious Doubleheader," *Marine Corps Gazette* 42 (1957), 131–140.

88. One of Burgoyne's pieces is now in the state capitol of Vermont and another in the Bennington Museum; J. P. Earle, "The Bennington Cannon," *New York History* 35 (1937), 12–17. For a biography see Delafield, *Biographies of Francis Lewis and Morgan Lewis.*

89. Stanley, *War of 1812*, 182–184.

90. Prevost to Bathurst, 1 June 1813, in *DHC*, 5: 292.

91. Hitsman, *Incredible War*, 147.

92. Most accounts state that Jacob Brown was in command of the American defences, but recent research suggests otherwise. For a full account see Wilder, *Battle of Sackett's Harbour.*

93. Graves, *Merry Hearts,* 116.

94. M. K. Ritchie and C. Ritchie, eds., "A Laker's Log," *AN* 17 (July 1957), 206. This article reproduces some of Johnston's correspondence, part of the Johnston family papers within the Halsey Papers held by the Hertfordshire County Record Office, Hertford (refs. 16221–16356), and also reproduced in W. S. Dudley, *Naval War of 1812,* 2: 444–446.

95. Brenton to Noah Freer, 30 May 1813, in *DHC,* 5: 281–282.

96. Armstrong, *Notices,* 1: 143–146; William F. Coffin, *1812,* 132–139; Leask and McCance, *Regimental Records of Royal Scots,* 285; Malcomson, *Lords of the Lake,* 129–140, 142–143; Squires, *The 104th Regiment of Foot,* 148.

97. TNA, WO 1/96, p. 59, Prevost to Duke of York, 1 June 1813; J. M. Hitsman, "Sir George Prevost's Conduct of the Canadian War of 1812," *Canadian Historical Association Report,* 1962, 40; Malcomson, *Sailors of 1812,* 29.

98. N. Lord. ed., "The War on the Canadian Frontier, 1812–1814: Letters Written by Sergt. James Commins, 8th Foot," *JSAHR* 18 (Winter 1939), 204.

99. TNA, CO 42/150, pp. 175–181, 183, Baynes to Prevost, 30 May 1813; USNA, RG 107/M221/R50, Brown to Armstrong, 1 June 1813; W. S. Dudley, *Naval War of 1812,* 2: 467–479; H. W. Johnston, *The Glengarry Light Infantry,* 127–133; Lynn Montross, "America's Most Imitated Battle," *American Heritage* 7 (April 1956), 37–101; Richard A. Preston, "The First Battle of Sacket's Harbor," *Historic Kingston* 2 (1963), 3–7.

100. LAC, MG24 F-18, David Wingfield, "Four Years on the Lakes of Canada"; David Ellison, ed., "David Wingfield and Sackett's Harbour," *Dalhousie Review* 52 (Autumn 1972), 412; Graves, *Merry Hearts,* 117.

101. Jacob Brown, "Letter to Daniel B. Tompkins: Battle of Sacket's Harbor," *Boston Public Library Bulletin* 8 (February 1903), 72–76; Wilder, *Battle of Sackett's Harbour,* 111–125; John D. Morris, *Sword of the Border,* 40–50, 52–55.

102. W. S. Dudley, *Naval War of 1812,* 2: 493. For an overview of shipbuilding at Sackets Harbor, see Joseph M. Thatcher, "A Fleet in the Wilderness: Shipbuilding at Sackets Harbor," in Bowler, *War along the Niagara,* 53–59.

103. J. Mackay Hitsman, "Spying at Sacket's Harbor, 1813," *IS* 15 (Summer 1959), 1–21; Malcomson, *Lords of the Lake,* 146.

104. Skaggs, *Thomas Macdonough,* 68–70.

105. Penley, *Narrative,* 18; George Taylor to Richard Stovin, 3 June 1813, in *SBD,* 2: 221–223. See also E. A. Cruikshank, "From Isle aux Noix to Châteauguay: A Study of Military Operations on the Frontier of Lower Canada in 1812 and 1813," *Proceedings of the Royal Society of Canada* 7 (1914), 129–173.

106. D. Holden, "Maine Troops on Lake Champlain and the Loss of the Eagle and Growler, May–June 1813," *Moorsfield Antiquarian* 2 (May 1838), 37; TNA, CO 42/150, pp. 212–214, "Capture of the Eagle and Growler by Major George Taylor of the 100th," Taylor to Florin, 3 June 1813 and enclosure; W. S. Dudley, *Naval War of 1812,* 2: 488–492.

107. LAC, RG8 I C679, pp. 50, 61, Taylor to Scovin, 3 June 1813, and de Rottenburg to Glasgow, 5 June 1813; TNA, CO 42/150, p. 61, Prevost to Bathurst, 4 July 1813; Everett, *History of Somerset Light Infantry,* 138; Whitton, *History of Prince of Wales's Leinster Regiment,* 21–22; Mahan, *Sea Power,* 2: 358; Everest, *War in Champlain Valley,* 108–109. The last provides a study of the effects of war on the people and governments of Vermont, New York, and Lower Canada. See also Dennis M. Lewis, *British Naval Activity on Lake Champlain.*

108. W. S. Dudley, *Naval War of 1812,* 2: 479–480; Dobbins, *Battle of Lake Erie,* 25–32; Mahan, *Sea Power,* 2: 62–63, 69–73; Skaggs and Altoff, *A Signal Victory,* 49–50.

109. TNA, WO 1/96, p. 60, Prevost to Duke of York, 3 June 1813. See also Cyrenius Chapin's *Review of Armstrong's Notices of the War of 1812,* 8–15.

110. John C. Fredriksen, ed., "Plow-Joggers for Generals: The Experiences of a New York Ensign in the War of 1812," *IMHJ* 11 (October 1986), 19; idem, "The Memoirs of Jonathan Kearsley: A Michigan Hero from the War of 1812," *IMHJ* 10 (May 1985), 5–6.

111. Lord, "War on Canadian Frontier: Letters by James Commins," 205.

112. Fredriksen, "Memoirs of Ephraim Shaler," 418. For Harvey see *DCB,* 7: 374–384.

113. See James Elliott, *Billy Green and Battle of Stoney Creek;* Mabel W. Thompson, ed., "Billy Green, the Scout," *OH* 44 (October 1952), 173–181; "An Old Diary: Entries of D. Slater's Diary," *Wentworth Historical Society Transactions* 5 (1908), 31–33.

114. Livingston, *Portraits of Eminent Americans,* 392.

115. "Military Journal of William H. Merritt," in *SBD,* 3: 579.

116. Shepard, *Autobiography of Elihu H. Shepard,* 56.

117. Berton, *Flames across the Border,* 72–78; Stanley, *War of 1812,* 188.

118. TNA, CO 42/151, pp. 20–24, Vincent to Prevost, 6 June 1813; Chandler to Dearborn, 18 June 1813, and Dearborn to Armstrong, 6 June 1813, in *ASP: MA,* 1: 445, 448; John C. Frederiksen, ed., "Colonel James Burn and the War of 1812: The Letters of a South Carolinian Officer," *South Carolina Historical Magazine* 90 (October 1989), 299–312; *Historical Record of the King's Liverpool Regiment,* 92; H. W. Johnston, *The Glengarry Light Infantry,* 134–137.

119. See E. A. Cruikshank, "The Battle of Stoney Creek and the Blockade of Fort George," *Niagara Historical Society Transactions* 11 (1898), 15–31; Charles M. Johnson, *Battle for the Heartland;* Joseph H. Smith, "The Battle of Stoney Creek," *Wentworth Historical Society Papers and Records* 10 (1922), 101–242; Stanley, *Battle in the Dark;* Herbert F. Wood, "The Many Battles of Stoney Creek," in Zaslow, *Defended Border,* 56–60; "Battle of Stoney Creek," *Grimsby Historical Society Proceedings* 1 (1950), 57–59.

120. Malcomson, *Lords of the Lake,* 149.

121. AO, Plenderleath Papers, 1912–1914, Misc. 1912, FitzGibbon to Somerville, 7 June 1813; Tupper Papers, FitzGibbon to Tupper, 25 June 1848. Vincent wrote a report that downplayed Harvey's role, and Harvey, suspecting this and ignoring the proper channels, wrote one of his own to ensure that his version of events was brought to Prevost's attention; TNA, CO 42/151, p. 211, Vincent to Prevost, 6 June 1813; LAC, RG 8 I C679,

pp. 38–39, Harvey to Baynes, 6 June 1813. For biographies of FitzGibbon see Ruth Mackenzie, *James FitzGibbon;* Mallory, *The Green Tiger;* FitzGibbon, *A Veteran of 1812;* F. L. Jones, "A Veteran of 1812: FitzGibbon," *Canadian Army Journal* 9 (1955), 59–68; *DCB,* 9: 264–267; H. W. Johnston, *The Glengarry Light Infantry,* 222–224.

122. Benn, *Iroquois in War of 1812,* 109–111.

123. See E. A. Cruikshank, "A Study of Disaffection in Upper Canada in 1812–15," in Zaslow, *Defended Border,* 208–221; A. H. U. Colquhoun, "The Career of Joseph Willcocks," *CHR* 7 (December 1926), 287–293; *DCB,* 5: 854–859; and Donald E. Graves, "Joseph Willcocks and the Canadian Volunteers: A Study of Political Disaffection during the War of 1812" (Master's thesis, Carleton University, 1982).

124. LAC, RG 8 I C679, pp. 74–75, Evans to Harvey, 10 June 1813; Petre, *Royal Berkshire Regiment,* 110.

125. TNA, CO 42/151, pp. 16–18, 46–48, Prevost to Bathurst, 14 June and 3 July 1813.

126. That she took a cow along as cover is a myth, but she probably used the need to milk one to get past the American sentries. And though she died aged ninety-three in 1868, she never revealed the source of her information, yet Boerstler himself did not know he was to march on Beaver Dams until 23 June; Raddall, *Path of Destiny,* 248.

127. "Boerstler's Narrative of the Expedition," in *DHC,* 6: 130; Memoir of Laura Secord, 18 February 1861, in *SBD,* 2: 164–165; Berton, *Flames across the Border,* 83–84; Chapin, *Review of Armstrong's Notices,* 10; Cruikshank, *Fight in the Beechwoods,* 10, 14; idem, "Laura Secord's Walk to Warn Fitz Gibbon," *NHSP* 36 (1924), 64–74; Sarah Anne Curzon, "The Story of Laura Secord," in Zaslow, *Defended Border,* 306–310; George Ingram, "Laura Secord's Walk Revisited," *OH* 57 (June 1965), 85–97; John S. Moir, "An Early Record of Laura Secord's Walk," *OH* 51 (Spring 1959), 105–108; Wallace, *Story of Laura Secord.* For biographies see Ruth Mackenzie, *Laura Secord;* and *DCB,* 9: 405–407.

128. For Ducharme see *DCB,* 8: 244–246.

129. Mary R. Archer, ed., "Journal of Major Isaac Roach, 1812–24," *PMHB* 17, no. 3 (1893), 149; Ducharme account, 5 June 1826, in Charles M. Johnson, *Valley of the Six Nations,* 201.

130. "Boerstler's Narrative," 133; Cruikshank, *Fight in the Beechwoods,* 17; Ducharme quoted in C. M. Johnson, *Valley of the Six Nations,* 201.

131. TNA, CO 42/151, pp. 52–53, 58, C. Bishopp to Vincent, 24 June 1813; "Boerstler's Narrative," 130–137; FitzGibbon to de Haren, 24 June 1813, and Boerstler to Dearborn, 25 June 1813, in *SBD,* 2: 159–162; Dearborn to Armstrong, 25 June 1813, in Brannan, *Official Letters,* 173–174; Dewar and Hutchinson, *The Battle of Beaverdams;* Keefer, *Beaver Dams;* Berton, *Flames across the Border,* 83–84; R. Mackenzie, *James FitzGibbon,* 35–38; Petre, *Royal Berkshire Regiment,* 101–103.

132. FitzGibbon to Kerr, 30 March 1818, in *DHC,* 6: 120.

133. Benn, *Iroquois in War of 1812,* 114–122.

134. Malcomson, *Lords of the Lake,* 150–153.

135. Cruikshank, "Battle of Stoney Creek and Blockade of Fort George," 33–38; *PFB,* 627.

136. LAC, RG 8 I C679, p. 194, de Rottenburg to Proctor, 1 July 1813, and Proctor to Prevost, 4 July 1813; Antal, *A Wampum Denied,* 247–248.

137. LAC, RG 8 I C679, p. 210, de Rottenburg to Prevost, 9 July 1813.

138. Ibid.; Porter to Dearborn, 13 July 1813, in *DHC,* 3: 223–225; Cruikshank, "Battle of Stoney Creek and Blockade of Fort George," 40–42; Armstrong, *Notices,* 1: 147; Lomax, *History of the 41st,* 77; *PFB,* 627; Stanley, *War of 1812,* 197–199; Hezekiah Salisbury, "A Guardsman of Buffalo," *PBHS* 9 (1906), 367–370. The border war also pitted Six Nations Indians into a civil conflict as different groups supported the two sides. See chaps. 5 and 6 of Benn, *Iroquois in War of 1812.*

139. Armstrong to Dearborn, 19 June and 6 July 1813, in *ASP: MA,* 1: 449, 451; Barbuto, *Niagara, 1814,* 105–108.

7. Raids and Blockades

Epigraph: "Impromptu," in Brighton, *Admiral Broke,* 90.

1. Rodger, *Command of the Sea.*

2. Michael J. Crawford, *Naval War of 1812,* 15–32.

3. Anon., "A Chase and Escape," *Army and Navy Chronicle* 5 (November 1837), 282–284.

4. Geoffrey J. Marcus, *Heart of Oak,* 44–45.

5. TNA, ADM 2/1380, p. 178, Croker to Cochrane, 31 May 1814; Mahan, *Sea Power,* 2: 311–312.

6. Loftus, *My Youth by Sea and Land,* 1: 294.

7. TNA, ADM 2/1376, pp. 179–181, 231, Croker to Warren, 26 March and 28 April 1813; ADM 1/504, pp. 278, 351, Warren to Croker, 13 November 1813, and "Proclamation," 16 November 1813; ADM 2/1377, pp. 14–16, Warren to Cockburn, 17 May 1813; ADM 1/503, p. 109, "Proclamation of Blockade, 6 February 1813"; CO 43/49, pp. 262–263, Bathurst to Croker, 26 November 1812; CO 43/50, pp. 39–40, Bathurst to Croker, 23 March 1813; William S. Dudley, *Naval War of 1812,* 2: 75–81, 260–263; Mahan, *Sea Power,* 2: 126–127.

8. W. S. Dudley, *Naval War of 1812,* 1: 470–472, 525–526; Forester, *Naval War of 1812,* 88–89.

9. William James, *Naval Occurrences,* 84, 103–104.

10. W. S. Dudley, *Naval War of 1812,* 1: 639–649; Forester, *Naval War of 1812,* 92–95; Gardiner, *Naval War of 1812,* 50–53; William James, *Naval History,* 187–196; idem, *Naval Occurrences,* 85–87; Mahan, *Sea Power,* 2: 1–7; Roosevelt, *Naval War of 1812,* 67–73; Tracy, *The Naval Chronicle,* 156–159.

11. "Medical Report," *NC* 29 (1813), 416–417.

12. James Henderson, *The Frigates,* 149–150.

13. For a biography of Lawrence see Gleaves, *James Lawrence.*

14. Christopher Lloyd, *Captain Marryat and the Old Navy,* 153–154.

15. TNA, ADM 1/503, pp. 244–247, Wright to Warren, 26 March 1813; USNA, RG 45/M125/R27, Lawrence to Jones, 19 March 1813; W. S. Dudley, *Naval War of 1812,* 2: 68–75; Forester, *Naval War of 1812,* 98–100; Gardiner, *Naval War of 1812,* 54–56; W. James, *Naval History,* 279; idem, *Naval Occurrences,* 99–100, 291–293; Mahan, *Sea Power,* 2: 7–9; Roosevelt, *Naval War of 1812,* 93–97. See also Harden Craig, ed., "Notes on the Action between 'Hornet' and 'Peacock,' " *AN,* 73–77.

16. Padfield, *Broke and the Shannon,* 129.

17. W. S. Dudley, *Naval War of 1812,* 2: 59.

18. TNA, ADM 1/503, p. 296, Warren to Croker, 8 March 1813.

19. Christopher Martin, *Damn the Torpedoes!* 37. See this for a biography of Farragut, and Farragut's own memoir, *The Life of D. G. F.* See also Jean Lee Latham, *Anchors Aweigh;* Charles L. Lewis, *David Glasgow Farragut;* and William Oliver Stevens, *David Glasgow Farragut.*

20. Morison, *Maritime History of Massachussets,* 203.

21. David Porter, *Journal of a Cruise,* 2: 76–87; W. S. Dudley, *Naval War of 1812,* 2: 684–710; Long, *Nothing Too Daring,* 79–81; Gardiner, *Naval War of 1812,* 82.

22. TNA, ADM 2/1380, pp. 367–379, Croker to Hillyar, 16 February and 12 March 1813, and Lords of Admiralty to Hillyar, 12 March 1813; W. S. Dudley, *Naval War of 1812,* 2: 710–714.

23. NMM, Warren Papers, Burdett to Warren, 9 February 1813; W. S. Dudley, *Naval War of 1812,* 2: 318–319; Roosevelt, *Naval War of 1812,* 97.

24. Mahon, *War of 1812,* 111.

25. TNA, ADM 1/503, pp. 94–98, Warren to Croker, 20 February 1813; ADM 2/1376, pp. 83–87, 265–267, Croker to Warren, 10 February and 20 March 1813.

26. "Statement of British Naval Forces on North American Station, 1810–13," in Vane, *Correspondence, Despatches of Castlereagh,* 8: 292; W. S. Dudley, *Naval War of 1812,* 2: 11–19.

27. Cockburn's confidence in his own luck was not universally admired. Lieutenant-Colonel Charles Napier described it as "the very thing to be feared; it is worse than 1,000 Yankees"; W. F. P. Napier, *Life and Opinions of General Napier,* 1: 229. For biographies see Pack, *Man Who Burned the White House;* Morriss, *Cockburn and British Navy in Transition; DNB,* 12: 335–337.

28. R. J. Barret, "Naval Recollections of the Late American War," *JUSI,* pt. 1 (April 1841), 455–467.

29. NMM, Warren Papers, Warren to Melville, 18 November 1812 and 18 November 1813.

30. Ibid., Warren to Cockburn, 15 February 1813. See also William L. Calderhead, " 'U.S.F. Constellation' in the War of 1812—An Accidental Fleet-in-Being," *MA* 40 (1976), 79–83.

31. NMM, Warren Papers, Warren to Melville, 19 March 1813; TNA, ADM 1/503, p. 239, Warren to Croker, 20 April 1813; James Scott, *Recollections,* 3: 97. See Frank A. Cassell, "Baltimore in 1813: A Study of Urban Defense in the War of 1812," *MA* 33 (December 1969), 349–361.

32. LC, Cockburn Papers, Cockburn to Burdett, 5 March 1813. See also Rodney C. Foytik, "Aspects of Military Life of Troops Stationed around the Norfolk Harbor, 1812 to 1814," *The Chesopiean* 22 (1984), 12–20.

33. Field, *Britain's Sea Soldiers,* 290–291; Pack, *Man Who Burned the White House,* 147–148.

34. NMM, Warren Papers, Cockburn to Warren, 23 March 1813.

35. W. S. Dudley, *Naval War of 1812,* 2: 339–340; TNA, ADM 1/503, pp. 278–279, Warren to Croker, 28 May 1813; Joseph Allen, *Battles of the British Navy,* 2: 420–422; Pack, *Man Who Burned the White House,* 150; Roosevelt, *Naval War of 1812,* 97–98.

36. J. Scott, *Recollections,* 3: 91–92.

37. LC, Cockburn Papers, Daschkoff to Cockburn (in French), 2 April 1813. See also Bashkina et al., *United States and Russia,* 933–934, 937; F. A. Golder, "The Russian Offer of Mediation in the War of 1812," *Political Science Quarterly* 31 (1916), 360–391.

38. Perkins, *Castlereagh and Adams,* 20–21; Bowers, *Naval Adventures,* 1: 280–283.

39. LC, Cockburn Papers, Cockburn to Beresford, 7 March 1813; USNA, RG 107/M221/R53, Haslet to Armstrong, 24 March 1813; Glenn Tucker, *Poltroons and Patriots,* 1: 288; McMaster, *History,* 4: 123.

40. Marine, *British Invasion of Maryland,* 29. See also Christopher T. George, "Harford Country in the War of 1812," *Harford Historical Bulletin* 76 (1998), 1–61.

41. TNA, ADM 1/503, pp. 328–330, 278–279, Cockburn to Warren, 29 April 1813, and Warren to Croker, 28 May 1813; Auchinleck, *History,* 265; Petrides and Downs, *Sea Soldier,* 180–181; J. Scott, *Recollections,* 3: 97–98; Tracy, *The Naval Chronicle,* 177–179. See Frank A. Cassell, "Slaves of the Chesapeake Bay Area and the War of 1812," *Journal of Negro History* 57 (1972), 144–155; Christopher T. George, "Mirage of Freedom: African Americans in the War of 1812," *MHM* 91 (Winter 1996), 426–450.

42. *NC* 30 (July–December 1813), 163–164.

43. Chamier, *Life of a Sailor,* 1: 201. In 1833 following Cockburn's appointment to command the North American Station, a dispute occurred between James Scott, Cockburn's ADC, and Chamier after the latter accused Cockburn of human rights abuses concerning the burning of civilian houses during the Chesapeake campaign in *Life of a Sailor,* published the previous year. Chamier had been only a midshipman, but a fierce argument in the pages of *JUSI* so aroused Scott that he challenged Chamier to a "hostile meeting," which fortunately never took place. Cockburn regarded "the precocious" Chamier as so unimportant that by 1837 he had looked at neither the book nor the correspondence in the journal; Van der Voort, *The Pen and the Quarter-deck,* 68–70; Morriss, *Cockburn and British Navy in Transition,* 2.

44. W. F. P. Napier, *Life and Opinions of General Napier,* 1: 225. Napier went on to earn fame as the conquerer of Scinde in India. For biographies see this and W. F. Butler, *Sir Charles James Napier;* and for a modern assessment see Falwell, *Eminent Victorian Soldiers,* 62–101; also *DNB,* 40: 156–162.

45. Cockburn to Warren, 3 May 1813, in W. S. Dudley, *Naval War of 1812,* 2: 341–344.

46. Petrides and Downs, *Sea Soldier,* 183.

47. Marine, *British Invasion of Maryland,* 32–33. For more on the Congreve rocket see Graves, *Congreve and Rocket's Red Glare.*

48. J. Scott, *Recollections,* 3: 100–102; TNA, ADM 1/503, pp. 281–282, 331–334, Cockburn to Warren, 29 April 1813, Miller to Warren and Warren to Miller, 10 May 1813; W. S. Dudley, *Naval War of 1812,* 2: 341–344; George, *Terror on the Chesapeake,* 29–34; W. James, *Naval History,* 330; G. Tucker, *Poltroons and Patriots,* 1: 292–293.

49. *NWR* 4 (4 May 1813), 165, cited in J. Scott, *Recollections,* 3: 103n, also 94–95n, 98–99n, etc.

50. See Wilmer, *Narrative Respecting the Conduct of the British;* and Jared Sparks, "Conflagration of Havre de Grace," *North American Review* 5 (July 1817), 157–163.

51. J. Scott, *Recollections,* 3: 102.

52. G. Tucker, *Poltroons and Patriots,* 1: 291–295.

53. NMM, Warren Papers, Cockburn to Warren, 2 May 1813; Auchinleck, *History,* 267; Chamier, *Life of a Sailor,* 1: 205.

54. *NC* 30 (July–December 1813), 165, 167; J. Scott, *Recollections,* 3: 110–112.

55. Ingersoll, *Historical Sketch,* 1: 198; TNA, ADM 1/503, pp. 278–280, 334–342, Cockburn to Warren, 3 and 6 May 1813, and Warren to Croker, 28 May 1813; *ASP: MA,* 1: 359–363, 365–367.

56. See Robin F. A. Fabel, "The Laws of War in the 1812 Conflict," *JAS* 14 (August 1980), 199–218; Pack, *Man Who Burned the White House,* 155.

57. University of Virginia, Nicholas Papers, John Hollins to Wilson Cary Nicholas, 8 April 1813.

58. Forester, *Naval War of 1812,* 108–109; W. S. Dudley, *Naval War of 1812,* 2: 277–283.

59. *The Times,* 6 January 1813.

60. McClellan, *Joseph Story and American Constitution,* 248; Ingersoll, *History of Second War,* 2: 40; *AC,* Thirteenth Cong., 1st sess. (1814), 55, 485, 2777–79.

61. USNA, RG45/M149/R11, General Orders, 29 July 1813; W. F. Galpin, "The American Grain Trade to the Spanish Peninsula, 1810–1814," *AHR* 28 (October 1922), 40.

62. TNA, FO 5/88, pp. 15–16, [Castlereagh?] to Anthony Baker, 3 February 1813.

63. Hickey, *War of 1812,* 123–125.

64. Forester, *Naval War of 1812,* 73–74; Gardiner, *Naval War of 1812,* 65–71. See also William L. Calderhead, "Naval Innovation in Crisis: War in the Chesapeake 1813," *AN* 36 (1976), 206–221.

65. Crowhurst, *Defence of British Trade.*

66. Warren was censured by the Admiralty for this, and the episode provoked a motion in the House of Lords; TNA, ADM 1/504, p. 87, Capel to Warren, 11 May 1813; W. S. Dudley, *Naval War of 1812,* 2: 104–106; Mahon, *War of 1812,* 110.

67. USNA, RG 45/M149/R8, Jones to Navy Captains, 22 February 1813.

68. TNA, ADM 2/1377, pp. 140–149, 264–267, Croker to Griffith, Keats, and Keith, 9 July 1813, and Croker to Otway, 13 August 1813; ADM 1/504, pp. 111–112, Warren to

Croker, 4 September 1813; W. S. Dudley, *Naval War of 1812,* 2: 250–255, 300–301; Roosevelt, *Naval War of 1812,* 99.

69. Whitehill, *New England Blockaded,* 19. For biographies of Hardy see Broadley and Bartelot, *Nelson's Hardy;* Gore, *Nelson's Hardy and His Wife; DNB,* 8: 1242–46.

70. See W. M. P. Dunne, "The Inglorious First of June: Commodore Stephen Decatur on Long Island Sound," *Long Island Historical Journal* 2 (Spring 1990), 201–220; Douglas S. Jordan, "Stephen Decatur at New London: A Study in Strategic Frustration," *USNIP* 93 (October 1967), 61–63; W. S. Dudley, *Naval War of 1812,* 2: 134–139. Inexplicably in his account Roosevelt identifies *Hornet* as *Wasp; Naval War of 1812,* 176.

71. TNA, ADM 2/1377, pp. 21–22, 88, Croker to Warren, 25 May and 19 June 1813 (see also pp. 159, 163–164, 167); NMM, Warren Papers, Warren to Melville, 22 July 1813. See Whipple, *Letters from Old Ironsides.*

72. Padfield, *Broke and the Shannon,* 139–140.

73. Roosevelt, *Naval War of 1812,* 221–223.

74. Lambert, *War at Sea in the Age of Sail,* 198.

75. TNA, ADM 1/505, pp. 380, 387–394, Warren to Croker, 10 May 1814 and enclosure; Howard A. Douglas, *Treatise on Naval Gunnery,* 154–156; Pullen, *The Shannon and the Chesapeake,* 42.

76. USNA, RG 45/M125/R29, Broke to captain of the *Chesapeake,* [1] June 1813; Brighton, *Admiral Broke,* 52–55; Pullen, *The Shannon and the Chesapeake,* 53–55.

77. ICRO, Saumarez Family Records, Broke Papers, HA93 877/25, Letter from William Stack, Captain's Cox'n, 1841.

78. Bentley, *Diary of William Bentley,* 2: 172–173.

79. Pullen, *The Shannon and the Chesapeake,* 57.

80. ICRO, Saumarez Family Records, Broke Papers, HA93 877/122, Quarter Bill of HMS *Shannon,* October 1813.

81. H. Hayman, "The Shannon and Chesapeake (Unpublished Notes by an Eyewitness)," *JUSI,* n.s., 2 (1891), 11.

82. Pemberton, *Autobiography of Pel. Verujuice,* 199–200.

83. Padfield, *Broke and the Shannon,* 27–30; W. S. Dudley, *Naval War of 1812,* 2: 126–134; D. L. Dennis, "The Action between the *Shannon* and the *Chesapeake,*" *MM* 45 (1959), 36–45.

84. Hayman, "Shannon and Chesapeake," 14.

85. TNA, ADM 1/503, pp. 322–325, Broke to Thomas Capel, 6 June 1813; *NC* 33 (January–June 1813), 1–20; USNA, RG 45/M125/R29, Bainbridge to Jones, 3 June 1813, and Budd to Jones, 15 June 1813; Padfield, *Broke and the Shannon,* 160–182, 240–244; idem, "The Great Sea Battle," *American Heritage* 20 (December 1968), 29–65; Brighton, *Admiral Broke,* 62–76; W. S. Dudley, *Naval War of 1812,* 2: 126–134; Gardiner, *Naval War of 1812,* 57–61; W. James, *Naval History,* 285–299; Lambert, *War at Sea in the Age of Sail,* 198–200; Pullen, *The Shannon and the Chesapeake,* 59–63; Roosevelt, *Naval*

War of 1812, 100–107; Poolman, *Guns off Cape Ann,* 81–118; Waldron K. Post, "The Case of Captain Lawrence," *USNIP* 63 (1936), 969–974; Hugh D. Purcell, "Don't Give Up the Ship!" *USNIP* 91 (May 1961), 82–94; Nathaniel Spooner, "The Naval Battle between the Chesapeake and the Shannon," *PMHS* 23 (February 1885), 374–379; and D. L. Dennis, "The Action between the Shannon and the Chesapeake," *MM* 45 (1959), 36–46.

86. Phyllis Kihln, ed., "The Chesapeake and the Shannon, June 1, 1813," *Connecticut Historical Society Bulletin* 30 (July 1965), 85; TNA, ADM 51/2861, Log of HMS *Shannon* for the period 26 May–8 June 1813; ADM 37/4402, Muster Book of HMS *Shannon* for 1 May–30 June 1813; Brighton, *Admiral Broke,* 240–257; H. A. Douglas, *Treatise on Naval Gunnery,* 100–101, 275–278, 549–552; Pullen, *The Shannon and the Chesapeake,* 136–137.

87. New York Historical Society, New York City, R. H. King Papers, Diary of Admiral R. H. King.

88. C. Roche, "Dockyard Reminscences: An Account of the Action between the 'Chesapeake' and the 'Shannon,'" *Collections of the Nova Scotia Historical Society* 18 (1919), 66.

89. Padfield, *Broke and the Shannon,* 188–190; Brighton, *Admiral of the Fleet Wallis,* 95–103; Pullen, *The Shannon and the Chesapeake,* 66–67; Boileau, *Half-Hearted Enemies,* 25–26. *Chesapeake* was later taken to Britain, where she was broken up and her timbers used in building a flour mill, known as Chesapeake Mill, at Wickham in Hampshire. As a result of his spending five days in command Wallis would, by a quirk of fate, rise to the rank of admiral of the Fleet, and, having been officially entered on the rolls of the Royal Navy at age four, spent ninety-six years on active service! For biographies see Brighton, *Admiral of the Fleet Wallis;* and Heine, *96 Years in the Royal Navy.* For a description of Halifax during wartime see J. S. Martell, "Halifax during and after the War of 1812," *Dalhousie Review* 23 (1943), 289–304. See also David Sutherland, "Halifax Merchants and the Pursuit of Development, 1783–1850," *CHR* 59 (1978), 1–17.

90. Thomas Beamish Akins, "The History of Halifax City," *Collections of the Nova Scotia Historical Society* 8 (1895), 24.

91. *Morning Chronicle,* 9 July 1813.

92. *Political Register,* 17 July 1813.

93. Walter Vernon Anson, *Life of Admiral Warren,* 184.

94. Padfield, *Broke and the Shannon,* 205–208; Pullen, *The Shannon and the Chesapeake,* 76–78.

95. G. Tucker, *Poltroons and Patriots,* 1: 268–270; Robert E. Cray Jr., "The Death and Burials of Captain James Lawrence: Wartime Mourning in the Early Republic," *NYH* 83 (2002), 133–164; Purdon, *Memoirs of the Services of the 64th Regiment,* 40. The Crowninshields were a major merchant and privateering dynasty. See also Bowdoi B. Crowninshield, "An Account of the Armed 'Ship' *America* of Salem," *EHIC* 37 (1901), 1–76; John H. Reinhochl, "Post Embargo Trade and Merchant Prosperity: Experiences of the Crowninshield Family," *MVHR* 42 (1955–56), 229–249; Howard Corning, "John Crowninshield

and the Building of the Privateer 'Diomede,'" *Proceedings of the American Antiquarian Society* 53 (October 1953), 163–218; William Dismore Chapple, "Salem and the War of 1812," *EIHC* 59 (October 1923), 49–74.

96. Hickey, *War of 1812,* 156.

97. Cox was court-martialled and dishonourably discharged in 1814. He was exonerated in 1952. See Arthur Lansen, "Scapegoat of the *Chesapeake-Shannon* Battle," *USNIP* 79 (1953), 528–531. See also Robert L. Fowler, ed., "The Chesapeake and Lieutenant Ludlow," *Magazine of American History* 25 (April 1891), 269–292; Purcell, "Don't Give Up the Ship!"

98. NMM, Warren Papers, Cockburn to Warren, 16 June 1813. For biographies of this remarkable engineer, militant free-trader, and ardent revolutionary, see Colden, *Life of Robert Fulton;* Dickinson, *Robert Fulton, Engineer and Artist;* Hutcheon, *Robert Fulton;* William Barclay Parsons, *Robert Fulton and the Submarine;* Philip, *Robert Fulton;* Sale, *The Fire of His Genius;* and Sutcliffe, *Robert Fulton and the "Clermont."* See also Hanson W. Baldwin, "Fulton and Decatur," *USNIP* 62 (1936), 231–235; David Whittet Thomson, "Robert Fulton's Torpedo System in the War of 1812," *USNIP* 68 (1942), 1206–17; idem, "Robert Fulton and the French Invasion of England," *MA* 18 (1954), 57–63; E. Taylor Parks, "Robert Fulton and Submarine Warfare," *MA* 25 (1961–62), 177–182; W. S. Dudley, *Naval War of 1812,* 2: 111–114.

99. Guernsey, *New York City and Vicinity during War of 1812–15,* 1: 279–281.

100. TNA, ADM 1/504, pp. 51–53, Hardy to Warren, 26 June 1813, and Warren to Croker, 22 July 1813; W. S. Dudley, *Naval War of 1812,* 2: 160–164; De Kay, *Battle of Stonington,* 34–37; Loftus, *My Youth by Sea and Land,* 2: 4; Lovell, *From Trafalgar to the Chesapeake,* 167–171, 190; J. Scott, *Recollections,* 3: 173–174.

101. W. S. Dudley, *Naval War of 1812,* 2: 357–6, 373–381; Hulbert Footner, *Sailor of Fortune,* 259–266; Mahon, *War of 1812,* 117–119; Roosevelt, *Naval War of 1812,* 111–112.

102. Peters, Mont, and Sanders, *Public Statutes of United States,* 2: 816; W. S. Dudley, *Naval War of 1812,* 2: 355; Tracy, *The Naval Chronicle,* 170–171. Architect Benjamin Latrobe assisted Mix, and his correspondence with Captain Charles Stewart of the *Constellation* shows the latter's involvement in the attempt; Fulton to Latrobe and Latrobe to Fulton, 22 and 23 April 1813; Latrobe to Mix, 7 May 1813; and Latrobe to Fulton, 6 June 1813, in Latrobe, *Correspondence and Miscellaneous Papers,* 3: 440–444, 445–457, 456, 467–469; W. S. Dudley, *Naval War of 1812,* 2: 354–356; George, *Terror on the Chesapeake,* 39, 180.

103. Weiss, *The Merikens,* 2; Matthew Mason, "The Battle of the Slaveholding Liberators: Great Britain, the United States, and Slavery in the Early Nineteenth Century," *WMQ,* 3d ser., 59 (2002), 670–671.

104. Lovell, *From Trafalgar to the Chesapeake,* 153.

105. J. Scott, *Recollections,* 3: 118–120, 122–130.

106. TNA, WO 1/96, Prevost to Torrens, 12 August 1813. On the Independent Companies see Alistair J. Nichols, "'Desperate Banditti': The Independent Companies of Foreigners, 1812–1814," *JSAHR* 79 (2001), 278–294; J. Mackay Hitsman and Alice Sorby, "Misnamed Canadian Chasseurs," *JSAHR* 40 (1962), 105; Albert W. Haarmann and Eric

I. Manders, "The Independent Companies of Foreigners at Hampton, Virginia, June 1813," *MCH* 38 (Winter 1986), 178–179; John R. Elting, "Those Independent Companies of Foreigners," *MCH* 40 (Fall 1988), 124–125.

107. TNA, CO 43/23, pp. 97–111, Bathurst to Beckwith, 18 March 1813.

108. TNA, ADM 2/1376, pp. 146–148, 358–362, Croker to Henry Goulburn, 17 March 1813, and Croker to Warren, 20 March 1813.

109. Pack, *Man Who Burned the White House,* 105.

110. LC, Cockburn Papers, Lumley to Cockburn, 12 June 1813. See William R. Wells II, "U.S. Revenue Cutters Captured in the War of 1812," *AN* 58 (1998), 225–241.

111. USNA, RG 107/M221/R57, Taylor to Armstrong, 17 March 1813.

112. J. Jarvis, "A Narrative of the Attack on Craney Island on the 22nd June, 1813," *Virginia Historical Register* 1 (July 1848), 134. See also Parker Rouse Jr., "The British Invasion of Hampton in 1813: Reminiscences of James Jarvis," *Virginia Magazine of History and Biography* 76 (1968), 318–336.

113. TNA, ADM 1/503, p. 371, Warren to Croker, 24 June 1813; NMM, Warren Papers, Warren to Melville, 23 June 1813; USNA, RG 107/M221/R57, Taylor to Armstrong, 23 June 1813; Anon., "Reminiscences of the Last War," *United States Nautical Magazine* 2 (February 1846), 341–344; W. S. Dudley, *Naval War of 1812,* 2: 359–361; W. F. P. Napier, *Life and Opinions of General Napier,* 1: 217; Nicolas, *Historical Record of Royal Marine Forces,* 243–244; Petrides and Downs, *Sea Soldier,* 190–194, 196; J. Scott, *Recollections,* 3: 141–145; Tracy, *The Naval Chronicle,* 180–181; Joe Mosier, "'Now My Brave Boys, Are You Ready?!': A Joint American Force Turns Back the British at Craney Island," *Day Book* 2, no. 4 (1996), 1–7, 11.

114. Kate M. Rowland, ed., "Thomas Mason Armistead Letters, 1813–1818," *WMQ,* 2d ser., 23 (April 1915), 230.

115. Jarvis, "Narrative," 141; George, *Terror on the Chesapeake,* 40–48. See also Hallahan, *Battle of Craney Island;* John D. Richardson, *Defense of Craney Island;* T. Crabbe, "Account of the Defense of Norfolk and Craney Island in the Year 1813, in Which He Participated," *United States Nautical Magazine* 2 (1846), 341–344.

116. USNA, RG 107/M221/R57, Crutchfield to Armstrong, 25 June 1813; W. S. Dudley, *Naval War of 1812,* 2: 361–365; W. James, *Naval History,* 339; Field, *Britain's Sea Soldiers,* 291–292; Petrides and Downs, *Sea Soldier,* 196; *PFB,* 681–684.

117. TNA, ADM 1/503, pp. 775–779, Beckwith to Warren, 28 June 1813; W. S. Dudley, *Naval War of 1812,* 2: 362–363; Myers to Taylor, 2 July 1813, in T. H. Palmer, *Historical Register,* 2: 67–69. See also Parker Rouse Jr., "Low Tide at Hampton Roads," *USNIP* 95 (July 1969), 79–86; idem, "British Invasion of Hampton: Reminiscences of James Jarvis"; Robert Anderson, "Action at Hampton, 1813," *USNIP* 31 (October 1923), 351–352; idem, "Operations at and around Hampton during the War of 1812," *USNIP* 37 (January 1929), 1–11.

118. W. F. P. Napier, *Life and Opinions of General Napier,* 1: 221–222. The 102nd Regiment was taken into the line in 1808, having formerly been the New South Wales Corps,

and had a long history of disciplinary problems, earning the nickname the "Rum Corps" while serving in Australia. See Maurice Hill, "A Short History of the New South Wales Corps, 1789–1818," *JSAHR* 13 (1934), 135–140; and Robert J. Marrion and Reginald L. Campbell, "102nd Regiment of Foot, 1814," *MCH* 33 (Summer 1981), 75.

119. W. F. P. Napier, *Life and Opinions of General Napier,* 1: 223. He was also sharply critical of Cockburn's handling of military matters (218).

120. J. Scott, *Recollections,* 3: 153–155.

121. Elting, *Amateurs to Arms!* 80; Clowes, *The Royal Navy,* 94; George, *Terror on the Chesapeake,* 48–51; Pack, *Man Who Burned the White House,* 158.

122. TNA, CO 42/151, p. 71, Beckwith to Warren, 5 July 1813.

123. Sherbrooke to Prevost, 20 July 1813, in *SBD,* 2: 713; Loftus, *My Youth by Sea and Land,* 2: 43–45.

124. J. Scott, *Recollections,* 3: 156–157; Nicolas, *Historical Record of Royal Marine Forces,* 248.

125. John Lovett to Joseph Alexander, 17 July 1813, in Bonney, *Legacy of Historical Gleanings,* 1: 304.

126. TNA, ADM 1/504, pp. 11–14, 31, 36, 47, Lloyd to Warren and Rattray to Warren, 14 July 1813; Warren to Croker, 12 July, 29 July, and 14 August 1813; W. S. Dudley, *Naval War of 1812,* 2: 184–187; *PFB,* 668–691.

127. W. S. Dudley, *Naval War of 1812,* 2: 381–383; George, *Terror on the Chesapeake,* 62–64; Marine, *British Invasion of Maryland,* 54–56; W. F. P. Napier, *Life and Opinions of General Napier,* 1: 215–216, 220; Bryon, *St. Michaels, the Town That Fooled the British;* Norman H. Plummer, "Another Look at the Battle of St. Michaels," *Weather Gauge* 31 (Spring 1995), 10–17.

128. Penny, *Life and Adventures of Joshua Penny,* 43–59; W. S. Dudley, *Naval War of 1812,* 2: 245–250. Large numbers of French and American prisoners were also kept there. For other first-hand accounts of Melville Island see James Fenimore Cooper, *Ned Myers,* 99–136; also Penley, *Narrative;* [Dr. Amos G. Babcock], *Journal of a Young Man of Massachusetts;* Samuel White, *History of American Troops;* and, for a French prisoner's account, Deveau, *Diary of a Frenchman.* For general studies see Brian Cuthbertson, "Melville Island Prison during the War of 1812," *Journal of the Royal Nova Scotia Historical Society* 6 (2003), 40–64; H. Meredith Logan, "Melville Island: The Military Prison at Halifax," *Annual Journal of the United Services Institute of Halifax* 6 (1933), 12–34; Marjorie Major, "Melville Island," *Nova Scotia Historical Quarterly* 6 (1974), 253–272; Boileau, *Half-Hearted Enemies,* 73–95; W. S. Dudley, *Naval War of 1812,* 1: 227–229, 233–237, 473–474, 476–489. For prisoner accounts of Jamaica see Paul A. Gilje, ed., "A Sailor Prisoner of War during the War of 1812," *MHM* 85 (Spring 1990), 58–72; and Egerton, *Journal of an Unfortunate Prisoner.*

129. Marine, *British Invasion of Maryland,* 56–57; Pack, *Man Who Burned the White House,* 161–162.

8. Tecumseh's Tragedy

Epigraph: Tecumseh quoted in Dee Brown, *Bury My Heart at Wounded Knee,* 1.

1. Nitchie was a corruption of the Ojibway *nii-jii,* meaning "friend" or "comrade"; Graves, *Field of Glory,* 385.

2. USNA, RG 107/M221/R8, Porter to Armstrong, 27 July 1813; Graves, *Field of Glory,* 38–41.

3. Graves, *Merry Hearts,* 146.

4. Viger, *Reminiscences,* 14; *DCB,* 8: 900–913.

5. Walter R. Copp, "Military Activities in Nova Scotia during the War of 1812," *Nova Scotia Historical Society Collections* 24 (1938), 57–58, 84; Philippart, *Royal Military Calendar,* 3: 300.

6. Meuron, *Le Régiment Meuron,* 207.

7. Squires, *The 104th Regiment of Foot,* 155.

8. De Rottenburg to Prevost, 7 July 1813, in *DHC,* 6: 199; LAC, RG 8 I C680, pp. 22–24, 68, de Rottenburg to Prevost, 5 and 17 September 1813; R. S. Allen, ed., "The Bisshopp Papers during the War of 1812," *JSAHR* 61 (1983), 25.

9. William S. Dudley, *Naval War of 1812,* 2: 523–525; Malcomson, *Lords of the Lake,* 161–162; Whitton, *History of Prince of Wales's Leinster Regiment,* 23–24.

10. LAC, RG 8 I C679, p. 291, "Instructions to Colonel Murray"; Mooers to Tompkins, 8 August 1813, in Tompkins, *Public Papers,* 3: 107; William F. Coffin, *1812,* 190; Hitsman, *Incredible War,* 161.

11. UCA, "Memoir of Reverend George Ferguson," 54.

12. LAC, RG 8 I C679, p. 340, Everard to Prevost, 3 August 1813; USNA, RG 107/M221/R50, Bankhead to Armstrong, 2 August 1813. For a study of wartime Burlington see Karen Campbell, "Propaganda, Pestilence and Prosperity: Burlington's Camptown Days during the War of 1812," *VH* 64 (1996), 133–158.

13. Francis D. McTeer and Frederick C. Warner, eds., "The British Attack on Burlington," *VH* 29 (April 1961), 83; Everest, *War in Champlain Valley,* 116–118.

14. TNA, CO 42/150, pp. 208–209, Prevost to Bathurst, 7 June 1813; CO 42/151, pp. 95–98, Prevost to Bathurst, 1 August 1813; ADM 1/504, pp. 160–162, Prevost to Glasgow, 4 July 1813, and Everard to Warren, 21 July 1813.

15. Mahan, *Sea Power,* 2: 51–53.

16. Hertfordshire County Record Office, Hertford, Halsey Collection, 16295 (a) and (b), Johnston to mother, 25 July 1813.

17. Strachan to Baynes, 2 August 1813, in *SBD,* 2: 193; W. S. Dudley, *Naval War of 1812,* 2: 525–529; Mahon, *War of 1812,* 155.

18. TNA, CO 42/151, pp. 106–108, Prevost to Bathurst, 8 August 1813.

19. TNA, ADM 1/504, pp. 168–169, Yeo to Warren, 10 August 1813; CO 42/151, pp. 141–142, Prevost to Bathurst, 25 August 1813; Roosevelt, *Naval War of 1812,* 267–283; Brannan,

Official Letters, 195–198; Malcomson, *Lords of the Lake,* 168–173; James Fenimore Cooper, *Ned Myers,* 81–83. See also Emily Cain, *Ghost Ships;* and Daniel A. Nelson, "Ghost Ships of the War of 1812," *National Geographic* 3, no. 163 (1983), 289–313.

20. USNA, RG 45/M125/R30, Chauncey to Jones, 13 August 1813; Yeo to Prevost, 11 August 1813, in *DHC,* 7: 7; W. S. Dudley, *Naval War of 1812,* 2: 534–541; Malcomson, *Lords of the Lake,* 175–180; J. F. Cooper, *Ned Myers,* 75–78; Roosevelt, *Naval War of 1812,* 131–135; Robert J. Williamson, "The First Encounter: Fighting for Naval Supremacy on Lake Ontario, 7–10 August 1813," *CMH* 11, no. 3 (2002), 15–30.

21. Malcomson, *Lords of the Lake,* 185; Mahon, *War of 1812,* 156.

22. Cushing, *Captain Cushing,* 116–117.

23. Speech of Tecumseh, 18 September 1813, *NWR* 5 (6 November 1813), 174–175; Sugden, *Tecumseh's Last Stand,* 19; TNA, ADM 1/5445, pp. 73–74, Barclay to Yeo, 1 June 1813; ADM 1/503, p. 142, Prevost to Warren, 24 June 1813; W. S. Dudley, *Naval War of 1812,* 2: 483–485.

24. TNA, CO 42/151, p. 84, Prevost to Bathurst, 20 July 1813; ADM 1/2736, Yeo to Croker, 16 July 1813 (enclosure); Robert Malcomson, "The Barclay Correspondence: More from the Man Who Lost the Battle of Lake Erie," *JES* 20 (1991), 18–35; idem, "Controversial Relationships among the British before and after the Battle of Lake Erie," *IS* 46 (Fall 1990), 187–197; idem, *Lords of the Lake,* 159–161.

25. Sugden, *Tecumseh,* 341–342.

26. See *DCB,* 6: 209–211.

27. Proctor to Prevost, 9 August 1813, in *SBD,* 2: 45–47; John Norton, *Journal,* 340–341.

28. Sugden, *Tecumseh,* 347–348.

29. Bruce Bowlus, "A 'Signal Victory': The Battle for Fort Stephenson, August 1–2, 1813," *NOQ* 63 (Summer–Autumn 1991), 43–57.

30. See Thomas W. Parsons, "George Croghan in the War of 1812," *NOQ* 20 (Autumn 1948), 192–202; Charles Richard Williams, "George Croghan," *OAHSP* 12 (October 1903), 375–409.

31. Harrison to Croghan, 29 and 30 July, and Croghan to Harrison, 30 July 1813, in Harrison, *Messages and Letters,* 2: 496, 502–503; McAfee, *History,* 323. See also Elizabeth D. Putnam, "The Life and Services of Joseph Duncan, Governor of Illinois, 1834–1838," *Illinois State Historical Society Transactions* 26 (1919), 110–111.

32. Lucy E. Keeler, "The Croghan Celebration," *OAHSP* 16 (January 1907), 82–84; Proctor to Prevost, 9 August 1813, in *SBD,* 2: 46.

33. John Richardson, *Richardson's War of 1812,* 179–180; Gellner, *Recollections,* 22–23. A fascine was a bundle used for lining trenches asnd ditches.

34. John C. Fredriksen, "The Pittsburgh Blues and the War of 1812: The Memoir of Private Nathaniel Vernon," *Pennsylvania History* 56 (July 1989), 206. See also David D. Anderson, "The Battle of Fort Stephenson: The Beginning of the End of the War of 1812 in the Northwest," *NOQ* 33 (Spring 1961), 81–90; Glen G. Clift, "War of 1812 Diary of Willam B. Northcutt," *RKHS* 66 (1958), 325–344.

35. See *Proceedings of a Court Martial . . . of Lieutenant Benoit Bender*, 29, 32, 76, 111, 115–116, 120–123. Personal rivalries surfaced among two factions of the officers of the 41st in which Captain Peter Chambers made insinuations against Lieutenant Benoit Bender, who demanded a court-martial; Antal, *A Wampum Denied,* 259–260; Stanley, *War of 1812,* 158–160.

36. Berton, *Flames across the Border,* 140–146; A. C. Whitehorne, *History of The Welch Regiment,* 102–103.

37. LAC, RG 8 I C679, p. 476, Prevost to Proctor, 22 August 1813; Croghan to Editor, *Liberty Hall,* 27 August 1813, in Harrison, *Messages and Letters,* 2: 527–529; Hallaman, *British Invasions of Ohio,* 28–35.

38. Proctor to Prevost, 9 August 1813, in *SBD,* 2: 46; Gilpin, *War of 1812 in Old Northwest,* 202–207; Brannan, *Official Letters,* 181–186.

39. Black Hawk, *Life,* 68.

40. Hitsman, *Incredible War,* 168.

41. Antal, *A Wampum Denied,* 261.

42. W. S. Dudley, *Naval War of 1812,* 2: 529–533; Skaggs and Altoff, *A Signal Victory,* 76–84.

43. David Curtis Skaggs, "Joint Operations during the Detroit–Lake Erie Campaign, 1813," in Cogar, *New Interpretations in Naval History,* 127–128.

44. Usher Parsons, *Battle of Lake Erie,* 5. For biographies of Parsons, see Goldowsky, *Yankee Surgeon;* Fredriksen, *Surgeon of the Lakes.*

45. Noah Brown, "The Remarkable Statement of Noah Brown," *JAH* 8 (January–March 1914), 106.

46. See Frederick C. Drake, "A Loss of Mastery: The British Squadron on Lake Erie, May–September, 1813," *JES* 17 (1988), 45–75; idem, "Artillery and Its Influence on Naval Tactics: Reflections on the Battle of Lake Erie," in Welsh and Skaggs, *War on the Great Lakes,* 17–29.

47. USNA, RG 45/M125/R28, Chauncey to Jones, 7 May 1813; C. P. Stacey, "Another Look at the Battle of Lake Erie," *CHR* 39 (1958), 45. On shortage of transport craft see TNA, ADM 1/5445, pp. 34–35, "Narrative of Proceedings . . . Court Martial of Captain Barclay, 9 September 1814."

48. Barclay to Prevost, 16 July 1813, and Proctor to Prevost, 18 and 26 August 1813, in *SBD,* 2: 258, 261, 264–265.

49. Skaggs and Altoff, *A Signal Victory,* 53, 59.

50. TNA, CO 42/151, pp. 78–81, 138–144, Barclay to Prevost (extract), 16 July 1813, and Prevost to Bathurst, 20 July 1813; CO 43/23, p. 118, Bathurst to Prevost, 13 August 1813; ADM 1/504, pp. 140–143, Prevost to Warren, 24 June 1813, and Warren to Croker, 21 August 1813.

51. TNA, CO 42/151, p. 150, Prevost to Yeo, 14 September 1813; ADM 1/505, pp. 188–189, 201–202, Yeo to Warren, 14 November 1813, and Warren to Croker, 27 January 1814.

52. Snider, *Leaves from War Log of the Nancy,* xii, xlii.

53. TNA, CO 42/151, p. 152, Gilmor to Couche, 5 September 1813.

54. Barclay to Yeo, 1 and 12 September 1813, and narrative of Barclay in "Lake Erie Court Martial Papers," in *SBD,* 2: 268, 274, 304; Robert Gilmor to Edward Couche, ibid., 291.

55. Among reasons put forward for Barclay's lapse are bad weather, repair and resupply, and even a story of romantic liaison popularized by Amelia Harris, a highly embellished version of which appeared in Snider's *Story of the Nancy;* "Statement of Stephen Champlain," *PBHS* 8 (1905), 391–392. The best descriptions of crossing the bar are in Mills, *Oliver Hazard Perry,* 86–91; Rosenberg, *Building of Perry's Fleet,* 50–52; and Walter Rybka, "The Camel: Nautical Beast of Burden," *Niagara League News* 6 (May 1995), 1–3; Dobbins, *Battle of Lake Erie,* 48–51; Drake, "Loss of Mastery," 64–65; W. S. Dudley, *Naval War of 1812,* 2: 543–549; Skaggs and Altoff, *A Signal Victory,* 85–86.

56. TNA, ADM 1/505, p. 87, "Statement of His Majesty's Naval Force Employed on Lake Erie in Upper Canada"; Robert Malcomson, "The Crews of the British Squadrons at Put-in-Bay: A Composite Muster Roll and Its Insights," *IS* 51 (1995), 16–34, 43–56; Stacey, "Lake Erie," 41–51; W. S. Dudley, *Naval War of 1812,* 2: 549–552.

57. Skaggs and Altoff, *A Signal Victory,* 74–76, 107–112; Antal, *A Wampum Denied,* 283.

58. Skaggs and Altoff, *A Signal Victory,* 76–84; Joseph T. Wilson, *The Black Phalanx,* 79. See also Altoff, *Deep Water Sailors, Shallow Water Soldiers;* idem, *Amongst My Best Men,* 33–41; David C. Skaggs, "Creating Small Unit Cohesion: Oliver Hazard Perry at the Battle of Lake Erie," *Armed Forces and Society* 23 (1997), 635–668.

59. Skaggs and Altoff, *A Signal Victory,* 119–128.

60. Relations broke down between Perry and Elliott soon afterwards, and contention between them came to a head when the prize money was distributed in 1818, a year before Perry's death. Thomas Brownell, sailing master of the US Brig *Ariel,* then wrote a searing indictment of Elliott. See "Affidavit of Captain Thomas Brownell Relating to Captain J. D. Elliott's Conduct in the Battle of Lake Erie," *New York Genealogical and Biographical Record* 68 (January 1937), 1–2. Elliott later defended himself in *Speech of Commodore Jesse D. Elliott, U.S.N.* The controversy lay largely dormant for twenty years until taken up by James Fenimore Cooper surrounding the critical word "enabled" in Perry's official report, while Alexander Slidell Mackenzie took up Perry's defence, all summarized in Ralph J. Roske and Richard W. Donley, "The Perry-Elliot[t] Controversy: A Bitter Footnote to the Battle of Lake Erie," *NOQ* 34 (Summer 1962), 111–123; and Hugh Egan, "Enabling and Disabling the Lake Erie Discussion: James Fenimore Cooper and Alexander Slidell Mackenzie Respond to the Perry-Elliott Controversy," in William S. Dudley and Michael J. Crawford, *The Early Republic and the Sea.* See also Gerard T. Altoff, "The Perry-Elliott Controversy," *NOQ* 60 (1988), 135–152; Allan Belovarac, "A Brief Overview of the Battle of Lake Erie and the Perry-Elliott Controversy," *JES* 17 (1988), 3–6; David W. Francis, "Politics, Sectionalism and the Naval Officer Corps: The Perry-Elliott Controversy," *IS* (2003), 200–217; Lawrence J. Friedman and David C. Skaggs, "Jesse Duncan Elliott and

the Battle of Lake Erie: The Issue of Mental Stability," *JER* 10 (1990), 493–516; David C. Skaggs, "Aiming at the Truth: James Fenimore Cooper and the Battle of Lake Erie," *JMilH* 59 (1995), 237–255; Michael Palmer, "A Failure of Command, Control and Communication," ibid., 7–26.

61. Edgar, *Ten Years of Upper Canada,* 324.

62. Bunnell, *Travels and Adventures,* 117.

63. Emerson, *The Perry's Victory Centenary,* 137; Skaggs and Altoff, *A Signal Victory,* 128–134.

64. TNA, CO ADM 1/505, p. 192, Barclay to Yeo, 12 September 1813, and Lt. George Inglis to Barclay, 10 September 1813. See also R. H. Barclay, "Commodore Barclay's Account of the Battle of Lake Erie," *JAH* 8 (January–March 1914), 123–128.

65. Skaggs and Altoff, *A Signal Victory,* 141–148.

66. TNA, CO 42/152, pp. 49–54, Inglis to Barclay, 10 September 1813, and Barclay to Yeo, 12 September 1813; *SBD,* 2: 274–277. See also Howard H. Peckham, "Commodore Perry's Captive," *Ohio History* 72 (July 1963), 220–227.

67. TNA, ADM 1/504, pp. 387–388, Inglis to Barclay, 10 September 1813; Tracy, *The Naval Chronicle,* 201–203. See also Robert Malcomson, "George Inglis: Insights about the Man Who Hauled Down the British Flag at Put-in-Bay," *JES* 24 (1995), 71–80.

68. Perry to William Jones, 13 September 1813, in *ASP: NA,* 1: 295; Yeo to Warren, 10 October 1813, in *SBD,* 2: 287–288; Berton, *Flames across the Border,* 157–168; E. A. Cruikshank, "The Contest for the Command of Lake Erie," in Zaslow, *Defended Border,* 96–104; W. S. Dudley, *Naval War of 1812,* 2: 553–560; Roosevelt, *Naval War of 1812,* 146–152; Richard F. Snow, "The Battle of Lake Erie," *American Heritage* 27 (February 1976), 14–21, 88–90.

69. Brunson, *A Western Pioneer,* 130. See also Richard J. Cox, ed., "An Eyewitness Account of the Battle of Lake Erie," *USNIP* 104 (February 1974), 67–74; and John C. Fredriksen, ed., "A Grand Moment for Our Beloved Commander: Sailing Master William V. Taylor's Account of the Battle of Lake Erie," *JES* 17 (Fall 1988), 113–124; Malcomson and Malcomson, *H.M.S. Detroit,* 94–111.

70. TNA, ADM 1/505, pp. 196–197, "A List of Killed and Wounded in His Majesty's Ships and Vessels Undermentioned in Action with an American Squadron on Lake Erie Upper Canada, 10th September 1813." See also Frank Allaben, ed., "The Battle Described by the Victorious American Leader," *JAH* 8 (January–March 1914), 109–116; "The Log Book of the 'Lawrence,'" ibid., 117–121; "Commander Barclay's Account of the Battle of Lake Erie," ibid., 123–128; "The Court Martial of Commander Barclay," ibid., 129–146; Usher Parsons, "Surgical Account of the Naval Battle on Lake Erie, on the 10th of September, 1813," *New England Journal of Medicine and Surgery* 7 (October 1817), 313–316 (reproduced in slightly different form in W. S. Dudley, *Naval War of 1812,* 2: 561–565); Marjorie C. Brazier, ed., "An After Word to the Battle of Lake Erie," *IS* 3 (Spring 1977), 180–183.

71. Chapelle, *History of American Sailing Navy,* 269.

72. Perry to Harrison, 10 September 1813, in *PFB,* 530. See also Douglas E. Clanin, ed., "The Correspondence of William Henry Harrison and Oliver Hazard Perry, July 5, 1813–July 31, 1815," *NOQ* 60 (Autumn 1988), 153–180.

73. *Nancy* was built in 1790 and taken up by the Navy in 1813. See Canadian Ministry of Natural Resources, *HMS Nancy and the War of 1812;* E. A. Cruikshank, "An Episode in the War of 1812: The Story of the Schooner 'Nancy,'" *OHSPR* 9 (1910), 75–126; W. H. Breithaupt, "Some Facts about the Schooner 'Nancy' in the War of 1812," *OHSPR* 23 (1926), 5–8; and Snider, *Leaves from War Log of the Nancy.*

74. *SBD,* 2: 289.

75. TNA, ADM 1/2736, pp. 134–135, Yeo to Warren, 10 October 1813; ADM 1/2737, pp. 2–3, Yeo to Warren, 14 November 1813; NMM, Melville Papers, Warren to Melville, 9 November 1813.

76. Howard Peckham, "Commodore Perry's Captive," *Ohio History* 72 (1963), 220–227; Marshall, *Royal Naval Biography,* 3: pt. 1, p. 194; Strachan, *Letterbook,* 85; Malcomson, *Lords of the Lake,* 228–229.

77. Blanche A. Burt, "Sketch of Robert Heriot Barclay, R.N.," *OHSPR* 14 (1916), 177.

78. Barclay to Yeo, 6 September 1813, in *SBD,* 2: 293; Proctor to Freer, 6 September 1813, ibid., 269–270; TNA, ADM 1/5445, p. 41.

79. *SBD,* 2: 306. See W. A. B. Douglas, "'The Honor of the Flag Had Not Suffered': Robert Heriot Barclay and the Battle of Lake Erie," in Welsh and Skaggs, *War on the Great Lakes,* 30–40; and Robert Buckie, "'His Majesty's Flag Has Not Been Tarnished': The Role of Robert Heriot Barclay," *JES* 17 (1988), 85–102.

80. Antal, *A Wampum Denied,* 297–309.

81. Proctor to Francis de Rottenburg, 12 September 1813, in *SBD,* 2: 273. See Dennis Carter-Edwards, "The Battle of Lake Erie and Its Consequences: Denouement of the British Right Division and Abandonment of the Western District to American Troops, 1813–1815," in Welsh and Skaggs, *War on the Great Lakes,* 41–55.

82. TNA, CO 42/151, p. 152; Stanley, *War of 1812,* 202–204; C. O. Ermatinger argues in mitigation of Proctor's plight in "The Retreat of Proctor and Tecumseh," *OHSPR* 17 (1919), 11–21.

83. For biographies of Shelby see Wrobel and Grider, *Isaac Shelby;* and Paul W. Beasley, "The Life and Times of Isaac Shelby, 1750–1826" (Ph.D. diss., University of Kentucky, 1968). See also Carl E. Pray Jr., "The Contributions of Governor Shelby and the People of Kentucky to the Freedom of Michigan in the War of 1812," *Michigan History Magazine* 29 (October–December 1945), 522–540; Thomas D. Clark, "Kentucky in the Northwest Campaign," in Mason, *After Tippecanoe,* 78–98.

84. Johnson was a congressional War Hawk who voted in favour of conflict, then resigned his seat in order to fight. See Leland W. Meyer, *Life and Times of Richard M. Johnson of Kentucky;* James A. Padgett, ed., "The Letters of Richard M. Johnson of Kentucky," *RKHS* 38 (July–October 1940), 186–201, 323–329. See also Young, *Battle of the*

Thames; Anderson, *Short History of Life of John Anderson* (about a Michigan soldier who served in this unit); and R. B. McAfee, "Book and Journal of Robt. B. McAfee's Mounted Company, in Col. Richard M. Johnson's Regiment," *RKHS* 26 (1928), 4–23, 107–136, 236–248.

85. McAfee, *History,* 331–332; Mahon, *War of 1812,* 178.

86. Sugden, *Tecumseh,* 360.

87. TNA, WO 71/243, Courts Martial Proceedings: Papers 1815 Oct.–Dec., p. 6. For contrasting views of Proctor's decision to retreat and how he broke the news to his allies see Antal, *A Wampum Denied,* chap. 13; and Sugden, *Tecumseh's Last Stand,* chap. 3.

88. TNA, WO 71/243, p. 381, Speech of Tecumseh, 18 September 18131; *NWR* 5 (6 November 1813), 175; John Richardson, *Richardson's War of 1812,* 205–206.

89. TNA, CO 42/151, pp. 217–218, Proctor to Prevost, 21 September 1813.

90. Horsman, *War of 1812,* 110; Hitsman, *Incredible War,* 173.

91. Perry to Jones, 24 and 27 September 1813, in Brannan, *Official Letters,* 214–215, 220–221; Harrison, *Messages and Letters,* 2: 251.

92. TNA, WO 71/243, pp. 6–46, Testimony of Lt.-Col. Augustus Warburton; Samuel R. Brown, *Views on Lake Erie,* 45–49. For contrasting views on Proctor's decision to retreat see Katherine B. Coutts, "Thamesville and the Battle of the Thames," and Victor Lauriston, "The Case for General Proctor," in Zaslow, *Defended Border,* 114–120, 121–129; Antal also defends Proctor's conduct on the retreat, *A Wampum Denied,* 315–328.

93. Antal, *A Wampum Denied,* 334–336.

94. WRM, Acc. No. 1822, "The War in Canada 1812–14," p. 63.

95. John Richardson, *Richardson's War of 1812,* 230; Lomax, *History of the 41st,* 83.

96. TNA, WO 71/243, pp. 13, 51–52, 67, 160–161, 257, Warburton testimony, Evans testimony, Evans cross-examination, Caldwell cross-examination, Hall cross-examination.

97. Stanley, *War of 1812,* 209.

98. USNA, RG 107/M222/R8, Harrison to John Armstong, 9 October 1813; Harrison, *Messages and Letters,* 2: 565.

99. Lowell H. Harrison, ed., "Nat Crain and the Battle of the Thames," *FCHQ* 63 (July 1990), 350. See also James A. Padgett, ed., "Joseph Desha: Letters and Papers," *RKHS* 51 (1953), 301–304.

100. Gellner, *Recollections,* 26.

101. Adam Walker, *Journal of Two Campaigns,* 135; Antal, *A Wampum Denied,* 340–346; Lomax, *History of the 41st,* 84–85, 108–112; A. C. Whitehorne, *History of The Welch Regiment,* 104–106.

102. Sugden, *Tecumseh,* 373–374.

103. John C. Fredriksen, ed., "Kentucky at the Thames: A Rediscovered Narrative by William Greathouse," *RKHS* 83 (1985), 103.

104. Stuart S. Sprague, "The Death of Tecumseh and the Rise of Rumpsey Dumpsey," *FCHQ* 59 (1985), 455–461. For a complete discussion on Tecumseh's death see Sugden,

Tecumseh's Last Stand, 136–181; also D. Duffy, "Fate of Tecumseh," *The Beaver* 73 (1993), 20–23. James Knaggs was among those witnesses convinced that Johnson killed Tecumseh (F. Palmer, *Early Days in Detroit,* 149), as was Garrett Wall (Mann Butler, *History of Commonwealth of Kentucky,* 547–548); and Benjamin Witherell ("Reminiscences of the Northwest," *WHC* 3 [1856], 302) supported Potawatomi chief Shabonee in "Death of Tecumseh," *Wisconsin Historical Review* 4 (1857–58), 375–376. Darius B. Cook interviewed an Ottawa chief after the battle who also attributed the shot to Johnson ("The Death of Tecumseh," *Century Magazine* 30 [June 1885], 332); but Alfred Brunson suggests that a soldier named David King was responsible ("Death of Tecumseh," *Wisconsin Historical Review* 4 [1857–58], 369–374; idem, *A Western Pioneer,* 135–148), a thesis supported by James Davidson ("Who Killed Tecumseh," *Historical Magazine* 10 [July 1866], 204–207). Another Kentucky private, Obediah Butler, claimed to have shot him with a pistol (M. Butler, *History of Commonwealth of Kentucky,* 203–204), while Terrance Kirby attributed the death to Colonel Whitley in his colourful if dubious *Life and Times.*

105. Quoted in Clark, "Kentucky in the Northwest Campaign," 94. See also "Memoranda and Notes by the Late Alfred T. Goodman," *Western Reserve Historical Society Tracts* 36 (January 1977), 1–4.

106. Harrison to Jonathan Meigs, 11 October 1813, in Brannan, *Official Letters,* 239–240; Berton, *Flames across the Border,* 198–204; W. S. Dudley, *Naval War of 1812,* 2: 565–576.

107. "War of 1812: Reports and Correspondence from the Canadian Archives at Ottawa," *NOQ* 2 (October 1930), 13.

108. Milo M. Quaife, ed., "A Narrative of the Northwest Campaign of 1813 by Stanton Sholes," *MVHR* 15 (1928–29), 525; Antal, *A Wampum Denied,* 346–349.

109. Lomax, *History of the 41st,* 86; Evelyn Crady Adams, "The Imprisonment of British Officers in the Frankfort Penitentiary during the War of 1812," *RKHS* 49 (July 1951), 231–233; Ralph Robinson, "Retaliation for the Treatment of Prisoners in the War of 1812," *AHR* 49 (October 1943), 65–70.

110. For Barclay see *DCB,* 6: 33–36. For the most complete study of British prisoners of war see Anthony G. Dietz, "The Prisoner of War in the United States during the War of 1812" (Ph.D. diss., American University, 1964). See also Hickey, *War of 1812,* 178–180; Meddert, *Raw Recruits and Bullish Prisoners,* 108–122; John Richardson, *Richardson's War of 1812,* 243–293; and Thomas Franklin Waters, "An Episode of the War of 1812," *Proceedings of the Massachusetts Historical Society* 48 (June 1915), 496–504.

111. Elma E. Gray, *Wilderness Christians,* 237–245; Samuel R. Brown, *Views of Campaigns,* 45; J. Norton, *Journal,* 314.

112. Antal, *A Wampum Denied,* 356; McAfee, *History,* 433; Milo M. Quaife, "General Shelby's Army in the Thames Campaign," *FCHQ* 10 (1936), 154.

113. Armstrong, *Notices,* 1: 176; Russell, *History of the War,* 274–275; Hitsman, *Incredible War,* 176; Quisenberry, *Kentucky in the War of 1812,* 101–109.

114. For a comparison of Harrison's performance with that of the unfortunate Hull, see Steven J. Rauch, "The Eyes of the Country Were upon Them: A Comparative Study

of the Campaigns of the Northwestern Army Conducted by William Hull and William Henry Harrison, 1812–1813" (Master's thesis, Eastern Michigan University, 1992).

115. Antal, *A Wampum Denied,* 371–377; Fortescue, *History of British Army,* 9: 335–336; Lomax, *History of the 41st,* 89–90; A. C. Whitehorne, *History of The Welch Regiment,* 206. Proctor later published his *Defence of Major General Proctor* without giving the verdict of the court. For a discussion of the fairness of the court-martial, see Stuart Sutherland's note 43 in Hitsman, *Incredible War,* 343–344. Strongly criticized by Richardson among many others, Proctor's reputation never recovered. But at least one staunch critic, Victor Lauriston, went from calling him "the most pathetic mockery in Canadian military history" to acknowledging him as the most neglected of the British commanders. See his "The Case for General Proctor," *Kent Historical Society Papers* 7 (1951), 7–17.

116. W. S. Dudley, *Naval War of 1812,* 2: 579–582; Malcomson, *Lords of the Lake,* 188–193; Roosevelt, *Naval War of 1812,* 135–136.

117. Malcomson, *Lords of the Lake,* 195–200.

118. For Mulcaster, see Henry J. Morgan, *Sketches of Celebrated Canadians,* 226–227.

119. Leila S. Barnett, ed., "Commodore Sinclair and the 'Nautical School,'" *DAR Magazine* 54 (October 1920), 556.

120. TNA, ADM 1/504, p. 325, Yeo to Warren, 29 September 1813; USNA, RG 45/M125/R31, Chauncey to Jones, 1 October 1813; Mahan, *Influence of Sea Power,* 2: 106–109; Malcomson, *Lords of the Lake,* 200–208; Roosevelt, *Naval War of 1812,* 136–139. See also Robert J. Williamson, "The Burlington Races Revisited: A Revised Analysis of an 1813 Naval Battle for Supremacy on Lake Ontario," *CMH* 8, no. 4 (1999), 7–15.

121. W. S. Dudley, *Naval War of 1812,* 2: 582–591.

122. Malcomson, *Lords of the Lake,* 211.

9. Crysler's Farm

Epigraph: "How Happy the Soldier," in Winstock, *Songs and Music of the Redcoats,* 85.

1. Winfield Scott, *Memoir,* 1: 94n.

2. LC, Nicholson Papers, Randolph to Nicholson, 25 June 1807.

3. Quimby, *U.S. Army in War of 1812,* 1: 303.

4. For biographies see Hay and Werner, *The Admirable Trumpeter;* and James R. Jacobs, *Tarnished Warrior.* See also Brant, *James Madison: Commander-in-Chief,* 203–209; Stagg, *Mr. Madison's War,* 336–347.

5. Ellery, *Memoirs of General Swift,* 96–97.

6. James R. Jacobs, *Beginning of the U.S. Army,* 344–352.

7. James Wilkinson, *Memoirs,* 3: 341.

8. Stagg, *Mr. Madison's War,* 331–343; Skeen, *John Armstrong Jr.,* 145–163.

9. *DAB,* 4: 212–213; W. Scott, *Memoir,* 1: 51–52; Everest, *War in Champlain Valley,* 111–114.

10. Crackel, *Jefferson's Army,* 175; Skeen, *John Armstrong Jr.,* 160.

11. Graves, *Field of Glory,* 30–33. This is a superb account of the whole campaign on which this chapter leans heavily.

12. Minutes of Council of War, 26 August 1813, in Armstrong, *Notices,* 2: app. 8; Armstrong to Madison, 23 July 1813, Armstrong to Wilkinson, 5 August 1813, Wilkinson to Armstrong, 21 and 26 August 1813, in *ASP: MA,* 1: 463, 465; Wilkinson to Armstrong, 24 August 1813, in J. Wilkinson, *Memoirs,* 3: 29; Wilkinson to Tompkins, 21 August 1813, in *DHC,* 7: 46; Tompkins to McClure, 27 August 1813, ibid., 75.

13. Horsman, *War of 1812,* 124.

14. LAC, RG 8 I C680, pp. 212, 235, Vincent to de Rottenburg, 11 August 1813, and de Rottenburg to Prevost, 14 October 1813.

15. Dunlop, *Recollections of the American War,* 13–14.

16. Graves, *Field of Glory,* 95–96.

17. Guitard, *Militia of Battle of Chateauguay,* 10–18, 29–30.

18. On de Wattville see *DCB,* 7: 896–899; Philippart, *Royal Military Calendar,* 2: 112.

19. Purdy to Wilkinson, n.d., in *ASP: MA,* 1: 461.

20. Graves, *Field of Glory,* 53–54.

21. Penley, *Narrative,* 11; USNA, RG 94, Journal of General George Izard, 21 October 1813.

22. Hampton to Armstrong, 25 September 1813, in *ASP: MA,* 1: 459.

23. Armstrong to Hampton, 28 September 1813, ibid., 460.

24. J. Wilkinson, *Memoirs,* 3: 377.

25. Ibid., app. 12, "Council of War, 20 Sep. 1813."

26. Armstrong to Wilkinson, 18 September 1813, in *ASP: MA,* 1: 468.

27. Armstrong to Wilkinson, 20 September 1813, ibid.

28. Pringle, *Lunenburgh,* 101–102.

29. Ellery, *Memoirs of General Swift,* 114–115; Graves, *Field of Glory,* 63–64, 69–71.

30. J. Wilkinson, *Memoirs,* 3: 193, 197, 353–356, 366, 369.

31. Malcomson, *Lords of the Lake,* 212–214.

32. Skeen, *John Armstrong Jr.,* 163.

33. Hampton to Armstrong, 4 October 1813, in *ASP: MA,* 1: 460; Walton, *Records of Vermont,* 486.

34. NYSL, Richard Bishop Diary, 21 October 1813. For Izard, see George Edward Manigault, "The Military Career of General George Izard," *Magazine of American History,* June 1888, 462–478; *DAB,* 9: 523–524; and John C. Fredriksen, ed., "The War of 1812 in Northern New York: General George Izard's Journal of the Châteauguay Campaign," *New York History* 76 (1995), 173–200.

35. WLC, War of 1812 MSS, Neef to Bell, 20 December 1813.

36. John C. Fredriksen, "A New Hampshire Volunteer in the War of 1812: The Experiences of Charles Fairbanks," *Historical New Hampshire* 40 (1985), 168. See also Fairbanks, *The Old Soldier's History.*

37. Boss, *Stormont, Dundas and Glengarry Highlanders,* 19.

38. King to Armstrong, n.d., in *DHC,* 8: 112.

39. See Charles-Casimir Pinguet, "Deux Lettres écrites dans les tentes de Châteauguay," *Les Soirées Canadiennes,* March 1864, 94–96.

40. Philalethes, "The Last War in Canada," *JUSI,* pt. 2 (June 1848), 274–275; Victor Suthren, "The Battle of Châteauguay," *Canadian Historical Sites: Occasional Papers in Archaeology and History* 11 (1974), 114–120. For orders of battle of both sides, see Graves, *Field of Glory,* apps. B and C.

41. Hampton to Armstrong, 1 November 1813, in *ASP: MA,* 1: 461; E. A. Cruikshank, "From Isle au Noix to Châteauguay: A Study of Military Operations on the Frontier of Lower Canada in 1812 and 1813," *Transactions of the Royal Society of Canada* 2 (1914), 83.

42. Purdy to Wilkinson, n.d., in *ASP: MA,* 1: 479.

43. Hampton to Armstrong, 1 November 1813, in *ASP: MA,* 1: 461.

44. Michael O'Sullivan, "An Eye Witness's Account," *Montreal Gazette,* 9 November 1813; Suthren, "Battle of Châteauguay," 123–127.

45. USNA, RG 94, Journal of George Izard, 26 October 1813.

46. WLC, War of 1812 MSS, Neef to Bell, 20 December 1813; Robert Morrison, "What an Eye-Witness Said of the Engagement and What Followed It," *Montreal Gazette,* 11 May 1895; Suthren, "Battle of Châteauguay," 126–128.

47. Fredriksen, "New Hampshire Volunteer," 170; idem, "War of 1812 in Northern New York: Izard's Journal," 198; Bilow, *Chateaugay,* 72.

48. Suthren, "Battle of Châteauguay," 130.

49. Fredriksen, "New Hampshire Volunteer," 170. Two British accounts are in *SBD,* 2. Major Michael O'Sullivan emphasizes the topography (401–412); Private Robert Morrison is very anti-French (423–429).

50. De Salaberry to [Baynes ?], 1 November 1813, in *SBD,* 3: 396; TNA, CO 42/151, pp. 163–172, 210–213, Prevost to Bathurst, 8 and 30 October 1813; Francis A. Carman, "Châteauguay and De Salaberry: An Account of the Famous Campaign from De Salaberry's Own Letters," *Canadian Magazine* 13 (1913), 23–28; Guitard, *Militia of Battle of Chateauguay,* 84–87; Suthren, "Battle of Châteauguay," 130–136; and Lighthall, *Account of Battle of Chateauguay.*

51. Berton, *Flames across the Border,* 222–228.

52. Wool to Dawson, 26 March 1860, in Harman P. Hinton, "The Military Career of John Ellis Wool, 1812–1863" (Ph.D. diss., University of Wisconsin, 1960), 31; Suthren, "Battle of Châteauguay," 137–138; Guitard, *Militia of Battle of Chateauguay,* 87–89; Graves, *Field of Glory,* 103–111.

53. USNA, RG 107/M221/R53, Hampton to John Armstrong, 1 November 1813.

54. Henry Adams, *History,* 8: 98–101, 221; J. T. Adams, *New England in the Republic,* 286: Hickey, *War of 1812,* 266–267. See also Sharp, *Sharp's Motion.*

55. J. Wilkinson, *Memoirs,* 3: 43–47, 50, 58, 81–82, 98–103, 117–120, 123–125, 165–166, 199–200, 209, 224, 240–241, 266–267, 281, 425; Graves, *Field of Glory,* 72–81.

56. Graves, *Field of Glory,* 80.

57. Ibid., 80–81; idem, *Soldiers of 1814,* 26–27. See also Lester W. Smith, ed., "A Drummer Boy in the War of 1812: The Memoirs of Jarvis Frary Hanks," *Niagara Frontier* 7 (Summer 1960), 53–62; BECHS, "Biography of Jarvis Hanks, Eleventh Infantry."

58. USNA, RG 107/M222/R9, Wilkinson to Armstrong, 19 October 1813.

59. Malcomson, *Lords of the Lake,* 217–218.

60. Graves, *Field of Glory,* 82–84.

61. TNA, ADM 1/505, p. 185, Mulcaster to Yeo, 2 November 1813; *DHC,* 8: 123; William S. Dudley, *Naval War of 1812,* 2: 596–597; Graves, *Field of Glory,* 120–122; Malcomson, *Lords of the Lake,* 219–220.

62. USNA, RG 45/M125/R32, Chauncey to Jones, 11 November 1813; Malcomson, *Lords of the Lake,* 214–220.

63. Graves, *Field of Glory,* 124–127.

64. J. Wilkinson, *Memoirs,* 3: 202; Ellery, *Memoirs of General Swift,* 116; *PFB,* 649–651; Graves, *Field of Glory,* 127–134; Shepard, *Autobiography of Elihu H. Shepard,* 65–66. For details of this fort see Burns, *Fort Wellington;* Frederick Curry, "Little Gibraltar," *OHSPR* 33 (1939), 39–44.

65. LAC, RG 8 I C1221, p. 183, Prevost to Yeo, 12 October 1813.

66. Hitsman, *Incredible War,* 188–189. For Morrison see William Patterson, "A Forgotten Hero in a Forgotten War," *JSAHR* 78 (1990), 7–21.

67. LAC, RG 8 I C681, p. 29, de Rottenburg to Prevost, 11 November 1813.

68. Graves, *Field of Glory,* 139–140. For Macomb see Everest, *Military Career of Alexander Macomb;* and George H. Macomb, *Memoir.*

69. Council of War at the White House, 8 November 1813, in J. Wilkinson, *Memoirs,* 3: app. 24.

70. Extract of a letter from a gentleman, 23 November 1813, *Kingston Gazette,* 1 March 1814.

71. Fredriksen, "War of 1812 in Northern New York: Izard's Journal," 198; *DAB,* 5: 523; James Mann, *Medical Sketches,* 116, 119, 126–127, 144. USNA, RG 107/M221/R9, Hampton to Wilkinson, 8 November 1813; WLC, War of 1812 MSS, Neef to Bell, 20 December 1813; NYSL, Richard Bishop Diary, 9 November 1813; Fredriksen, "New Hampshire Volunteer," 171.

72. Brinckman, *Historical Record of the Eighty-ninth,* 18–19; Graves, *Field of Glory,* 147–148. For orders of battle of both sides, see apps. D, E, and F. On the Provincial Light Dragoons see Paul Fortier, "Fraser's Troop: Incorporated Provincial Light Dragoons in Upper Canada during the War of 1812," *Campaigns* 47 (1984), 42–48. Crysler was a captain of militia at the time. See Graham Neale, "Colonel John Crysler of Crysler's Farm," *Journal of the Orders and Medals Research Society* 21 (Autumn 1982), 50–54; *DCB,* 8: 194–195.

73. "Extract from an Officer of Rank with Colonel Morrison's Army, 13 November," *Quebec Mercury,* 23 November 1813.

74. J. Wilkinson, *Memoirs,* 3: 82, 130, 163, 203; *ASP: MA,* 1: 477–478; NYSL, Gardner Papers, Gardner to Parker, 15 November 1813.

75. Fredriksen, "War of 1812 in Northern New York: Izard's Journal," 306.

76. LAC, RG 8 I C681, pp. 31, 41, Dennis to Scott and Cochrane to Scott, 11 November 1813; J. Wilkinson, *Memoirs,* 3: 319; W. Scott, *Memoir,* 1: 108; Pringle, *Lunenburgh,* 61, 204.

77. Graves, *Field of Glory,* 152–161.

78. Ellery, *Memoirs of General Swift,* 116; J. Wilkinson, *Memoirs,* 3: 201.

79. See J. C. A. Hériot, "Major General, the Hon. Frederick George Heriot," *Canadian Antiquarian and Numismatic Journal* 2, no. 8 (1911), 50–75; *DCB,* 7: 397–400.

80. The greatcoat was an essential item of kit in Canada, and because of "constant wear for seven months of the year" was supposed to be replaced every two years instead of the normal three, although there were always shortages. See Robert Henderson, "'Not Merely an Article of Comfort': British Infantry Greatcoats during the War of 1812," *JSAHR* 75 (1997), 23–36.

81. Graves, *Field of Glory,* 44–45, 200–201.

82. Ibid., 187, 191–192, 195–203, 207–218.

83. NYSL, Gardner Papers, Gardner to Parker, 15 November 1813.

84. Brinckman, *Historical Record of the Eighty-ninth,* 21; Cunliffe, *Royal Irish Fusiliers,* 142; John C. Fredriksen, ed., "Reynold M. Kirby and His Race to Join the Regiment: A Connecticut Officer in the War of 1812," *Connecticut History* 32 (1991), 70–72.

85. Letter of Lieutenant-Colonel John Harvey, 12 November 1813, quoted in Edgar, *Ten Years of Upper Canada,* 252.

86. G. J. Jackson, *Bath Archives,* 2: 392.

87. Graves, *Field of Glory,* 219–227.

88. For a biography of Pearson see Graves, *Fix Bayonets!*

89. Wailes, *Memoir of Leonard Covington,* 28–30.

90. John C. Fredriksen, ed., "'A Poor but Honest Sodger': Colonel Cromwell Pearce, the 16th U.S. Infantry and the War of 1812," *Pennsylvania History* 52 (1985), 145. See also idem, "Lawyer, Soldier, Judge: Incidents in the Life of Joseph Lee Smith of New Britain, Connecticut," *Connecticut Historical Society Bulletin* 51 (Spring 1986), 103–121; William James, *Full Account of Military Occurrences,* 2: 333.

91. Graves, *Field of Glory,* 228–234.

92. Narrative of Lieutenant John Sewell, 49th Foot, 11 November 1860, quoted in Ronald Way, "The Day of Crysler's Farm," *Canadian Geographic Journal* 62 (1961), 208.

93. Samuel D. Harris, "Service of Capt. Samuel D. Harris: A Sketch of His Military Career as a Captain in the Second Regiment of Light Dragoons during the War of 1812," *PBHS* 24 (1920), 329.

94. Sewell Narrative, quoted in Way, "Crysler's Farm," 208; Graves, *Field of Glory,* 236–250; Brinckman, *Historical Record of the Eighty-ninth,* 22; Cunliffe, *Royal Irish Fusiliers,* 142–143.

95. "Biographical Notice of Lieutenant W. W. Smith," *Analectic Magazine* 8 (July 1816), 52–54; Ellery, *Memoirs of General Swift,* 117.

96. J. Wilkinson, *Memoirs,* 3: 91.

97. John C. Fredriksen, ed., "A Georgian Officer in the War of 1812: The Letters of William Clay Cumming," *GHQ* 71 (Winter 1987), 682; M. Myers, *Reminiscences,* 41–42.

98. Berton, *Flames across the Border,* 234–240; Graves, *Field of Glory,* 252–255.

99. LAC, RG 8 I C681, p. 59, Corrected Return of the Killed Wounded and Missing, 12 November 1813; TNA, WO 17/263, Monthly Return of the 49th Foot, 25 November 1813; WO 25/218, Return of the Casualties of the Canadian Fencibles, 25 December 1813; Petre, *Royal Berkshire Regiment,* 105–107.

100. *NWR* 5 (18 December 1813); Boyd to Wilkinson, 12 November 1813, Return of the Killed and Wounded, 11 November 1813, in Boyd, *Documents and Facts,* app.; Way, "Crysler's Farm," 82; NYSL, "Gardner Letter." The figures given in Boyd for light dragoons and artillery are seventeen killed and forty wounded, but elsewhere they were reported as eighteen dead, and the American return did not break down losses by brigade, a fact which may indicate post-action confusion and inaccuracy; Harris, "Service of Capt. Samuel D. Harris," 330; John C. Fredriksen, ed., "Plow-Joggers for Generals: The Experiences of a New York Ensign in the War of 1812," *IMHJ* 11 (October 1986), 24; Graves, *Field of Glory,* 268–271, 281.

101. G. J. Jackson, *Bath Archives,* 1: 393–394.

102. Graves, *Soldiers of 1814,* 28.

103. Wilkinson to Hampton, 12 November 1813, in Brannan, *Official Letters,* 263.

104. TNA, CO 42/152, p. 23, McGregor to Prevost, 6 November 1813; Pearse, *History of 31st Foot Huntingdonshire Regt and 70th Foot Surrey Regt.,* 305.

105. Graves, *Field of Glory,* 285.

106. Dunlop, *Recollections of the American War,* 30.

107. Prevost Family, London, Anne Prevost Diary, 7 January 1814.

108. M. K. Ritchie and C. Ritchie, eds., "A Laker's Log," *AN* 17 (July 1957), 209.

109. Dr. Lovel, quoted in J. Mann, *Medical Sketches,* 119; Fredriksen, "Reynold M. Kirby," 73; idem, "'Poor but Honest Sodger,'" 148; HSP, Carr Diary, 17 November 1813; Graves, *Soldiers of 1814,* 28; W. James, *Full Account of Military Occurrences,* 2: 7.

110. Graves, *Field of Glory,* 293–298. Boyd later published a pamphlet defending his conduct: *Documents and Facts Relative to Military Events during the Late War.*

111. Fredriksen, "Reynold M. Kirby," 75.

10. Drummond's Winter Offensive

Epigraph: "The British Bayoneteers," to the tune "The British Grenadiers," in Winstock, *Songs and Music of the Redcoats,* 111.

1. See Hawkins, *Letters, Journals and Writings,* 2: 626–711. For a biography see Pound, *Benjamin Hawkins.*

2. *Clarion* (Nashville), 23 May 1812; "Crawley Deposition," in Andrew Jackson, *Correspondence,* 1: 225–226. For a somewhat fanciful account of Tandy Walker's rescue of Crawley, see George F. Mellon, "A Blacksmith Hero," *Southeastern Native American Exchange* 1 (Winter 1993), 6–9. For a study of Jackson's attitude to the "Indian problem," see Remini, *Andrew Jackson and His Indian Wars.*

3. For Hawkins' involvement, see William Eustis to Willie Blount, 22 June 1812, in U.S. Congress, *American State Papers, II: Indian Affairs,* 1: 813; Hawkins to Andrew Jackson, 18 May 1812, in Andrew Jackson, *Papers,* 2: 307 n. 5. See also Ross Hassig, "Internal Conflict in the Creek War of 1812–1814," *Ethnohistory* 21 (1974), 251–271.

4. Richard K. Murdock, ed., "A British Report on West Florida and Louisiana, November 1812," *FHQ* 43 (July 1964), 36–51.

5. A. Jackson, *Correspondence,* 1: 242–243, 252–253, 256–268; Parton, *Life of Andrew Jackson,* 1: 360–373; William A. Walker Jr., "Martial Sons: Tennessee Enthusiasm for the War of 1812," *THQ* 20 (March 1961), 20–37.

6. See Cusick, *The Other War of 1812;* also J. H. Alexander, "The Ambush of Captain John Williams, USMC: Failure of the East Florida Invasion, 1812–1813," *FHQ* 56 (January 1978), 280–296; Frederick T. Davis, ed., "United States Troops in Spanish East Florida, 1812–13," *FHQ* 9 (July–October 1930), 259–278, and 10 (July 1931), 24–34; John C. Fredriksen, ed., "A Georgian Officer in the War of 1812: The Letters of William Clay Cumming," *GHQ* 71 (Winter 1987), 672–679; Paul Kruse, "Secret Agent in East Florida: General George Matthews and the Patriot War," *Journal of Southern History* 18 (May 1952), 193–217; and J. C. A. Stagg, "James Madison and George Matthews: The East Florida Revolution of 1812 Reconsidered," *Diplomatic History* 30 (2006), 23–55.

7. Elizabeth Howard West, ed., "A Prelude to the Creek War of 1813–14: In a Letter of John Innerarity to James Innerarity," *FHQ* 18 (April 1940), 247–266.

8. Halbert and Ball, *Creek War,* 125–142; Owsley, *Struggle for the Gulf Borderlands,* 30–33. See also O'Brien, *In Bitterness and in Tears;* Leland L. Lengel, "The Road to Fort Mims: Judge Harry Toulmin's Observations on the Creek War, 1811–1813," *AR* 29 (January 1976), 16–36; and Frank Heiman Akers Jr., "The Unexpected Challenge: The Creek War of 1813–1814" (Ph.D. diss., Duke University, 1975).

9. Griffith, *McIntosh and Weatherford,* 111.

10. Halbert and Ball, *Creek War,* 147–164; Owsley, *Struggle for the Gulf Borderlands,* 15–17, 35–41; idem, "The Fort Mims Massacre," *AR* 24 (July 1971), 192–204; James F. Doster, "Letters Relating to the Tragedy of Fort Mims: August–September, 1813," *AR* 14 (October 1961), 269–285.

11. TNA, CO 23/60, pp. 110, 111, Creek and Seminoles to Charles Cameron, 11 September 1813; Archivo General de Indias, Seville, Spain, Papeles Procedentes de Cuba, Report of Marinque, 8 January 1814, legajo 1795.

12. Floyd to Pinckney, 4 December 1813, in Brannan, *Official Letters,* 283–284; Peter A. Brannon, "Journal of James A. Tait for the Year 1813," *GHQ* 8 (September 1929), 229–239.

13. Richard H. Faust, "Another Look at General Jackson and the Indians of the Mississippi Territory," *AR* 28 (July 1975), 202–217. For Tennessee's part in the war, see Sistler and Sistler, *Tennesseans in the War of 1812.* Carolinians also took part; see John K. Mahon, "The Carolina Brigade Sent against the Creek Indians in 1814," *North Carolina Historical Review* 28 (1951), 421–425. For individual accounts, see Crockett, *Narrative of the Life of David Crockett,* 71–124; and Mary H. McCowen, ed., "The J. Hartsell Memoirs: The Journal of a Tennessee Captain in the War of 1812," *East Tennessee Historical Society Proceedings* 11 (1939), 93–115, and 12 (1940), 118–146. See also Beatrice Merle Smith, "Sam Houston in Tennessee" (Master's thesis, University of Tennessee, 1932). For Georgia operations, see Stephen F. Miller, *Memoir of General David Blackshear;* and John Floyd, "Letters of John Floyd, 1813–1838," *GHQ* 33 (September 1949), 229–246.

14. Aaron M. Boom, "John Coffee, Citizen Soldier," *THQ* 22 (September 1963), 223–237. See also John H. DeWitt, "Letters of General John Coffee to His Wife, 1813–1815," *Tennessee Historical Magazine* 2 (December 1916), 264–295; and William R. Garrett and John M. Bass, eds., "Letters from John Coffee," *American Historical Magazine* 6 (April 1901), 174–190.

15. Owsley, *Struggle for the Gulf Borderlands,* 15–17, 42–66.

16. LC, Jackson Papers, reel 7, Jackson to John Armstrong, 16 December 1813.

17. Hickey, *War of 1812,* 148–149.

18. Horsman, *War of 1812,* 222; *PFB,* 771–773; Neal Smith, "Battle of the Holy Ground," *Alabama Historical Reporter* 1 (July 1880), 2–3.

19. A. Jackson, *Correspondence,* 1: 444–454; Floyd to Pinckney, 27 January 1814, in Brannan, *Official Letters,* 296–297.

20. For a study of American military punishments see John S. Hare, "Military Punishments in the War of 1812," *MA* 4 (Winter 1940), 225–239. See also Ernest W. Peterkin and Detmar H. Finke, "Regulations Prescribing the Uniform for the Southern Department, 24 January 1813," *MCH* 42 (Fall 1990), 82–89.

21. LC, Jackson Papers, reel 62, General Orders [14 March 1814]; Parton, *Life of Andrew Jackson,* 1: 504–512.

22. A. Jackson, *Correspondence,* 1: 489–494; William R. Garrett, ed., "Report of General Andrew Jackson to Governor Willie Bount: 'Battle of Tehopiska or the Horseshoe,'" *American History Magazine* 4 (1899), 291–296; *PFB,* 777–781. See also C. J. Coley, "The Battle of Horseshoe Bend," *Alabama Historical Quarterly* 14 (January 1952), 129–134; Thomas W. Cutrer, ed., "The Tallapoosa Might Truly Be Called the River of Blood: Major Alexander McCulloch at the Battle of Horseshoe Bend, March 27, 1814," *AR* 43 (January 1990), 35–39; Tom Kanon, "'A Slow, Laborious Slaughter': The Battle of Horseshoe Bend," *THQ* 58 (1999), 2–15; Finley McIlwaine, "The Horseshoe," *Tennessee Valley Historical Review* 2 (Fall 1973), 2–11; Owsley, *Struggle for the Gulf Borderlands,* 79–81.

23. Quoted in letter of Anne Royall, 15 December 1817, in Royall, *Letters from Alabama,* 91–92.

24. A. Jackson, *Correspondence,* 1: 4–5.

25. Charles Petrie, *Lord Liverpool and His Times,* 178.

26. Hickey, *War of 1812,* 165–167.

27. Webster, *British Diplomacy,* 126.

28. Hickey, *War of 1812,* 283–285.

29. Perkins, *Castlereagh and Adams,* 21–23; Engelman, *The Peace of Christmas Eve,* 29, 42, 46, 55, 67, 81–82, 86; Brant, *James Madison: Commander-in-Chief,* 159–182. For Bayard see Borden, *The Federalism of James A. Bayard.* For Adams see John Quincy Adams, *Memoirs;* idem, *Diary;* Bemis, *John Quincy Adams and American Foreign Policy;* and Nagel, *John Quincy Adams.*

30. J. C. A. Stagg, "The Politics of Ending the War of 1812," in Bowler, *War along the Niagara,* 101; Halvdan Koht, "Bernadotte and Swedish-American Relations, 1810–1814," *JModH* 16 (1944), 265–285. Ghent, the port and capital of East Flanders, was incorporated into the Kingdom of the United Netherlands under the Peace of Paris in 1814. It passed to Belgium on the establishment of that kingdom in 1830.

31. Scott to Wilkinson, 11 October 1813, in Brannan, *Official Letters,* 241–244; Edgar, *Ten Years of Upper Canada,* 228, 237–239.

32. Proclamation, 16 October 1813, in Brannan, *Official Letters,* 244–246; Quimby, *U.S. Army in War of 1812,* 1: 350–351, 360.

33. Examination of the Mabee Brothers, 2 November 1813, in *DHC,* 7: 183–184; Bostwick to Gregg, 14 November 1813, in *DHC,* 8: 181–182; J. J. Poole, "The Fight at Battle Hill," in Zaslow, *Defended Border,* 131.

34. USNA, RG 107/M221/R55, McClure to Armstrong, 13 December 1813; *ASP: MA,* 1: 486–487; William S. Dudley, *Naval War of 1812,* 2: 623–624.

35. The *New York Evening Post* published correspondence between them on 29 November 1814. See also the letter to the *Buffalo Gazette,* 21 December 1813, in *DHC,* 4: 9–10.

36. *Buffalo Gazette,* 14 June 1814.

37. USNA, RG 107/M221/R55, McClure to John Armstrong, 13 December 1813; Berton, *Flames across the Border,* 251–256.

38. BL, F.232: 20997, p. 12, "Excerpts from Letters from Lieut. and Adjutant William MacEwen to His Wife, Canada 1813–14."

39. Whitton, *History of Prince of Wales's Leinster Regiment,* 24–25.

40. TNA, CO 42/152, p. 84, Murray to Vincent, 12 December 1813; CO 42/156, pp. 103–104, Wilkinson to Prevost, 28 January 1814; *The Letters of Veritas,* 93; *Report of the Loyal and Patriotic Society of Upper Canada,* 379–382. See also McClure's apologia, *Causes of the Destruction of the American Towns on the Niagara Frontier and the Failure of the Campaign in the Fall of 1813.*

41. LAC, RG 8 I C1712, p. 56, Prevost to de Rottenburg, 11 November 1813; C681, p. 29, de Rottenburg to Prevost, 11 November 1813; C1171, p. 106, General Order, 20 November 1813; Hitsman, *Incredible War,* 194.

42. See D. Massy Griffin, "Forging an 1812 General: The Early Life of Sir Gordon Drummond," *OH* 98 (1996), 297–313; Turner, *British Generals in War of 1812*, chap. 6; *DNB*, 16: 954–955; *DCB*, 8: 236–239; Philippart, *Royal Military Calendar*, 1: 134.

43. TNA, CO 42/151, p. 230, Prevost to Bathurst, 30 October 1813; CO 42/156, pp. 11–14, Prevost to Bathurst, 6 January 1814. For Riall, see *DCB*, 7: 744–746; *DNB*, 46: 628–629; Philippart, *Royal Military Calendar*, 2: 70.

44. William Hamilton Merritt, *Journal*, 52–53.

45. Bibliothèque et Archives Nationales du Québec, Montreal, Maurice Nowlan Papers, Nowlan to Agathe Nowlan, 18 December 1813.

46. Whitton, *History of Prince of Wales's Leinster Regiment*, 28–34. In 1818 the 100th Regiment was disbanded, and the 102nd briefly assumed its number before it too was disbanded. In 1858 the 100th was re-raised in Canada, with many of its recruits coming from descendants of the original regiment who had settled in the country with land grants. The battle-honour "Niagara" was passed to the new regiment (41–43).

47. UCA, "Memoir of Reverend George Ferguson," 56.

48. USNA, RG 107/M221/R55, McClure to John Armstrong, 22 December 1813; "Capture of Fort Niagara by Lieutenant Henry Driscoll," in *DHC*, 9: 19.

49. TNA, CO 42/156, p. 26, "Return of Killed and Wounded in an Assault on Fort Niagara, 19 December 1813"; LAC, RG 8 I C681, p. 249, Murray to Drummond, 19 December 1813; Lewis Cass to Armstrong, 12 January 1814, in *ASP: MS*, 1: 488; Dunnigan, *Forts within a Fort*, 44–49; Lomax, *History of the 41st*, 94–98.

50. *DHC*, 9: 19.

51. Tompkins to John Armstrong, 24 December 1813, in Tompkins, *Public Papers*, 3: 407.

52. Brinckman, *Historical Record of the Eighty-ninth*, 26; Leask and McCance, *Regimental Records of Royal Scots*, 287; *Historical Record of The King's Liverpool Regiment*, 94–95.

53. David Brayman, "A Pioneer Patriot," *PBHS* 9 (1906), 364. See also Samuel Blakeslee, "Narrative of Samuel Blakeslee: A Defender of Buffalo," *PBHS* 8 (1905), 419–439.

54. USNA, RG 107/M222/R8, McClure to Armstrong, 20 December 1813.

55. Tompkins to Hall and to McClure, 24 December 1813, in Tompkins, *Public Papers*, 3: 402–404.

56. Heidler and Heidler, *Old Hickory's War*, 222–223.

57. TNA, CO 42/156, pp. 19–22, Riall to Drummond, 19 December 1813; *PFB*, 633–635. See also William Dorsheimer, "Buffalo during the War of 1812," *PBHS* 1 (1879), 185–229; Amos Hall, "Militia Service of 1812–14 as Shown by the Correspondence of Major General Amos Hall," *PBHS* 5 (1902), 26–62; Frank H. Severance, ed., "Papers Relating to the Burning of Buffalo and to the Niagara Frontier during the War of 1812," *PBHS* 9 (1906), 311–401.

58. *Kingston Gazette*, 1 February 1814; *DHC*, 9: 112; Bowler, *War of 1812*, 73–74.

59. TNA, CO 43/23, pp. 144–145, Bathurst to Prevost, 5 March 1814.

60. Cass to [Armstrong], 12 January 1814, in *ASP: MA*, 1: 487.

61. Tompkins to Armstrong, 2 January 1814, in Tompkins, *Public Papers,* 3: 408; Edward Bernard Hein, "The Niagara Frontier and the War of 1812" (Ph.D diss., University of Ottawa, 1949), 201.

62. Letter to *Argus* (Albany), 26 December 1813.

63. Benn, *Iroquois in War of 1812,* 150.

64. TNA, CO 42/23, Bathurst to Prevost, 15 December 1813.

65. For a description of garrison life, see Dr. Lowry, "Fort Niagara, 1814," *NHSP* 30 (1917), 38–39.

66. The failure of the 1813 military plan prompted an investigation and report by Armstrong submitted to Congress on 2 February 1814 as No. 127, "Causes of the Failure of the Army of the Northern Frontier," published in *ASP: MA,* 1: 439–488.

67. Wellington to Bathurst, 22 February 1814, in Wellesley, *Despatches, Correspondence and Memoranda,* 11: 525–526; TNA, CO 43/23, pp. 287–289, Bathurst to Prevost, 5 March 1814.

68. TNA, CO 42/157, pp. 91–92, 95–102, Drummond to Prevost, 27 and 28 April 1814, Prevost to Drummond, 30 April 1814, and Drummond to Bathurst, 3 July 1814; CO 43/23, pp. 291, 306, Bathurst to Prevost, 14 April and 11 July 1814; W. Kingsford, *History of Canada,* 8: 529.

69. See Mary A. Dunn, "The Career of Thomas Barclay" (Ph.D. diss., Fordham University, 1974).

70. Museum of Liverpool Life, 4.88, Extracts from the Diary of Marshall McDermott, Esq. This was later reproduced in the journal of The King's Regiment (Liverpool). Despite claiming that the march was made in 1812–13, the article acknowledges that "all other Regimental records give the date of this march as February 1814"; "The Winter March of the 2nd Bn. in 1812/1813," *The Kingsman* 43 (1956), 27–8, 34.

71. Drummond to Prevost, 10 March and 15 April 1814, in *SBD,* 1: 46; 3: 93–94.

72. TNA, CO 42/355, pp. 4, 49, 82–83, Drummond to Bathurst, 18 January, 5 April, and 28 May 1814; CO 42/156, p. 225, "Address to Prince Regent," March 1814; CO 42/161, p. 40, "Address to Prince Regent, by House of Commons, Upper Canada," 14 March 1814; Hitsman, *Incredible War,* 204–205.

73. Drummond to Prevost, 22 December 1813, in *SBD,* 2: 500–505.

74. TNA, CO 42/1556, pp. 77–78, 83, Drummond to Prevost, 21 January and 19 February 1814, and Prevost to Drummond, 29 January 1814; *SBD,* 3: 38–39.

75. Brannan, Butler to Harrison, 7 March 1813, and Butler to Holmes, 10 March 1813, in *Official Letters,* 313–317.

76. See Ermatinger, *Life of Colonel Talbot;* Turner, *War of 1812,* 86; Stanley, *War of 1812,* 193; Louis L. Babcock, *War on Niagara Frontier,* 127–129. For an overview of the war in south-west Ontario, especially following the battle of the Thames, see Stott, *Greater Evils.*

77. AO, 971.034, Loyal and Patriotic Society Book, 1817, pp. 246–247.

78. USNA, RG 107/M221/R51, Holmes to Butler, 10 March 1814; J. I. Peek, "The Fight at Battle Hill," in Zaslow, *Defended Border,* 130–142.

79. Bathurst to Prevost, 2 November 1813, in *House of Lords Sessional Papers,* 4: 332.

80. TNA, CO 43/50, pp. 214, 219, Bathurst to Admiralty, 1 and 11 January 1814; CO 43/23, p. 270, Bathurst to Prevost, 20 January 1814; ADM 2/1379, pp. 30, 100, Croker to Cochrane and Croker to Yeo, 24 January 1814.

81. Tracy, *The Naval Chronicle,* 203–206; H. F. Pullen, "The March of the Seamen," and John R. Stevens, "Story of H.M. Armed Schooner *Tecumseth,*" Occasional Papers, Nos. 8–9 (Halifax: National Maritime Museum of Canada, 1961); Malcomson, *Lords of the Lake,* 240.

82. TNA, CO 43/23, pp. 140–142, Bathurst to Prevost, 20 January 1814; ADM 2/1379, pp. 130–135, Croker to Yeo, 29 January 1814; Malcomson, *Warships of the Great Lakes,* 115–118; Mahon, *War of 1812,* 257.

83. LAC, RG 8 I C219, pp. 191–192, "Statement of the Navy on Ontario," 26 January 1814; Graves, *Merry Hearts,* 158; Malcomson, *Lords of the Lake,* 230–231, 263; Zaslow, *Defended Border,* 169–171.

84. Malcomson, *Lords of the Lake,* 237–239; Townsend, *HMS St. Lawrence,* 10–11. Various sources put her as being pierced for as many as 122 guns and mounting 102 or 112, but this is how she is rated in a statement of the force of the Lake Ontario squadron dated 14 October 1814, and during her brief active career in October–November 1814 she actually mounted 104; TNA, ADM 106/1997, "Dockyards, Canada." See Robert Malcomson, "HMS *St. Lawrence:* Commodore Yeo's Unique First-Rate," *Freshwater* 6 (1991), 27–36; idem, "HMS *St. Lawrence:* The Freshwater First-Rate," *MM* 83 (1997), 419–433.

85. NMM, Warren Papers, Warren to Melville, 26 October 1813; BL, Liverpool Papers, 38255, Warren to Liverpool, 16 November 1813. Baring Brothers acted as America's bankers in London. For a study of the family's long-standing American connections see Hidy, *House of Baring in American Trade and Finance.*

86. TNA, CO 42/158, p. 8, Croker to Bathurst, 10 January 1814; ADM 2/1379, p. 131, Bathurst to Prevost, 20 January 1814; Malcomson, *Lords of the Lake,* 241–242.

87. TNA, ADM 2/1379, p. 171, Griffith to Croker, 9 February 1814; USNA, RG 45/M149/R11, Jones to Macdonough, 17 March and 18 April 1814; *NWR* 6 (5 March 1814), 150.

88. *AC,* Thirteenth Cong., 2d sess. (1814), 124; Barbuto, *Niagara, 1814,* 106; Fredriksen, *Green Coats and Glory,* 43.

89. J. C. A. Stagg, "Enlisted Men in the United States Army, 1812–1815: A Preliminary Survey," *WMQ,* 3d ser., 43 (1986), 616–645; Graves, *Soldiers of 1814,* 8–10; Lerwill, *Personnel Replacement,* 39.

90. USNA, RG 107/M222/R8, Hampton to Armstrong, 31 December 1813; Skeen, *John Armstrong Jr.,* 137–141; Brant, *James Madison: Commander-in-Chief,* 253.

91. On Macomb see Macomb, *Memoir;* Everest, *Military Career of Alexander Macomb;* and Milo M. Quaife, "Detroit Biographies: Alexander Macomb," *Burton Historical Collection Leaflet,* no. 10 (1931). For Gaines see Silver, *Edmund Pendleton Gaines.* For Ripley see Baylies, *Eleazor Wheelock Ripley;* and E. W. Ripley, "Memoirs of General Ripley," *Portfolio* 14 (1815), 108–136. For Izard, see John C. Fredriksen, "A Tempered Sword Untested:

The Military Career of General George Izard," *Journal of America's Military Past* 25 (Winter 1999), 5–16.

92. Jeffrey Phillip Kimball, "Strategy on the Northern Frontier: 1814" (Ph.D. diss., Louisiana State University, 1969), 175.

93. James Wilkinson, *Memoirs,* 3: app. 49; James R. Jacobs, *Tarnished Warrior,* 301–302.

94. Graves, *Field of Glory,* 310–312.

95. LAC, RG 8 I C682, Secret Information, 7 February 1814; *DHC,* 9: 176; T. W. Leavitt, *History of Leeds,* 39; Brinckman, *Historical Record of the Eighty-ninth,* 28.

96. TNA, CO 42/156, pp. 134–139, Prevost to Bathurst, 12 March 1814; Hough, *History of St. Lawrence and Franklin Counties,* 501–502, 641, 651–652, 654–655.

97. Stanley, *War of 1812,* 226.

98. Richard A. Preston, ed., "The Journals of Sir F. P. Robinson, G.C.B.," *CHR* 37 (December 1956), 353. For Robinson see *DNB,* 47: 329–330; Philippart, *Royal Military Calendar,* 2: 65–66.

99. Sinclair to Jones, 27 May 1814, in *DRINP,* 23. See also Kent, *Norfolk Spies in 1812;* Berton, *Flames across the Border,* 215–218; W. S. Dudley, *Naval War of 1812,* 2: 520–522.

100. "On a Claim for Pay for Services as a Spy in the War of 1812," in *ASP: MA,* 4: 281–282.

101. USNA, RG 107/M221/R58, Wilkinson to Armstrong, 20 March 1814; M6/R7, Armstrong to Izard, 24 March 1814.

102. Field, *Britain's Sea Soldiers,* 294.

103. J. Woods, "A Citizen Complains," *North Country Notes,* September 1964.

104. LAC, RG 8 I C1219, p. 201, Prevost to Bathurst, 31 March 1814; Nicolas, *Historical Record of Royal Marine Forces,* 253–254. It seems probable that the designation of the 13th as a light infantry regiment in 1822 was as a result of its service in North America, where it was commanded by Lieutenant-Colonel William Williams, formerly of the 60th Regiment, who trained the 13th extensively in light infantry tactics as being appropriate to the forests of the country; Everest, *War in Champlain Valley,* 139, 143–145.

105. Jesse P. Harmon, "War of 1812," *VQ* 21 (January 1953), 47. See also Wilmond Parker, ed., "Letters of the War of 1812 in the Champlain Valley," *VQ* 12 (April 1944), 104–124.

106. LC, Wilkinson Papers, Wilkinson to Dr. Bule, 31 March 1814; D. C. L. Gosling, "The Battle at la Colle Mill," *JSAHR* 47 (1969), 169–174; Thomas Carter, *Historical Record of the Thirteenth Regiment,* 69; Everett, *History of Somerset Light Infantry,* 139; Everest, *War in Champlain Valley,* 142–143.

107. J. R. Jacobs, *Tarnished Warrior,* 306–307. Volume 3 of Wilkinson's *Memoirs* provides surprisingly full coverage of the evidence at his trial.

108. Izard, at Plattsburgh, commanded the Right Division, whose district extended into Vermont; but Brown's command was also sometimes referred to as the 1st Division or the Army of the Niagara; Graves, *"Where Right and Glory Lead!"* 18.

109. Armstrong to Brown, 28 February 1813, in Armstrong, *Notices,* 2: 213; Kimball, "Strategy on the Northern Frontier," 118–123.

110. USNA, RG 107/M221/R51, Brown to Armstrong, 21 March 1814.

111. Ibid., Armstrong to Brown, 8 April 1814.

112. Armstrong to Madison, 30 April 1814, in *DHC,* 9: 320; Hitsman, *Incredible War,* 216.

113. Skeen, *John Armstrong Jr.,* 177–178; Graves, *Field of Glory,* 18–21.

114. See Crisman, *History and Construction of the Schooner Ticonderoga;* W. S. Dudley, *Naval War of 1812,* 2: 603–606.

115. TNA, CO 42/156, pp. 293–297, Prevost to Bathurst, 18 May 1814; Muller, *The Proudest Day,* 237–242.

116. *The Times,* 15 April 1814.

117. Guillaume de Bertier de Sauvigny, "The American Press and the Fall of Napoleon in 1814," *Proceedings of the American Philosophical Society* 98 (1954), 337–376.

118. *Military Register,* 21 May 1814; *National Intelligencer,* 15 August 1814.

119. HSP, Jones Papers, Nicholson to William Jones, 20 May 1814.

11. Atlantic and Pacific

1. For a biography of Allen see Dye, *Fatal Cruise of the Argus,* 3–100, 110–119, 134–145.

2. For a biography of Maples see ibid., 150–258; for her cruise, 264–275. See also Uriah Phillips Levy, *Defense of Uriah Phillips Levy,* 5–8.

3. James Fenimore Cooper stated the American crew was drunk with wine smuggled aboard; *History of the Navy,* 2: 190–191.

4. W. H. Watson to B. W. Crowninshield, 2 March 1815, in Brannan, *Official Letters,* 485–487; William James, *Naval History,* 343–345; idem, *Naval Occurrences,* 134–136; Mahan, *Sea Power,* 2: 216–219; Roosevelt, *Naval War of 1812,* 114–118. See also Wilbur E. Apgar, "The Last Cruise of the U.S. Brig *Argus,*" *USNIP* 65 (1939), 653–660; Victor H. Paltsits, ed., "Cruise of the U.S.S. Brig Argus in 1813: Journal of Surgeon James Inderwick," *BNYPL* 21 (June 1917), 395–405; Dye, *Fatal Cruise of the Argus,* 274–280; idem, "The Fatal Cruise of the *Argus:* Two Captains in the War of 1812," *NM/MN* 5, no. 4 (1996), 99–100; Ira Dye and J. Worth Estes, "Death on the *Argus:* American Malpractice versus British Chauvinism in the War of 1812," *Journal of the History of Medicine and Allied Sciences* 44 (April 1989), 179–195; William S. Dudley, *Naval War of 1812,* 2: 217–224, 274–276.

5. *The Times,* 18 August 1813.

6. Dye, *Fatal Cruise of the Argus,* 286–289.

7. TNA, ADM 103/207, p. 563, "General Entry Book, Plymouth," Record 2; Charles Andrews, *The Prisoners' Memoirs,* 82.

8. Cranwell and Crane, *Men of Marque,* 114, 164.

9. TNA, ADM 1/504, pp. 152–154, McCreery to Gordon, 6 September 1813; USNA, RG 45/M125/R31, Tillinghurst to Hull, 9 September 1813; W. S. Dudley, *Naval War of*

1812, 2: 232–242; Mahan, *Sea Power,* 2: 187–192; Roosevelt, *Naval War of 1812,* 119–121; Frederic Stanhope Hill, *The "Lucky Little Enterprise" and Her Successors;* Picking, *Sea Fight off Monhegan.*

10. W. James, *Naval History,* 317–318.

11. For accounts of Astor's role in colonizing Oregon see Flandrau, *Astor and the Oregon Country;* Franchère, *Adventures at Astoria* and *A Voyage to the North West Coast of America;* Ronda, *Astoria and Empire;* Dorothy Wides Bridgwater, "John Jacob Astor Relative to His Settlement on the Columbia River," *Yale University Library Gazette* 24 (October 1949), 47–69; Roberta Mildred Keeling, "John Jacob Astor and the Settlement of Astoria" (Master's thesis, Southwest Texas State University, 1940); Anne Simpson Scott, "John Jacob Astor and the Settlement of the North West" (Master's thesis, Arkansas State College, 1961). See also Brannon, *Last Voyage of the Tonquin.*

12. Gough, *Royal Navy and Northwest Coast of America,* 8–28; Hussey, *Voyage of the "Racoon";* Coues, *New Light on Early History of Greater Northwest,* 2: 781–916; W. S. Dudley, *Naval War of 1812,* 2: 714; Ross, *Adventures of First Settlers on Oregon or Columbia River,* 255–272; Stanley, *War of 1812,* 162–165; T. C. Eliot, "Sale of Astoria, 1813," *Oregon Historical Quarterly* 33 (1932), 43–50; Harold Sands, "Canada's Conquest of Astoria: How Montrealers Peacefully Secured the American Fort on the Pacific Coast," *Canadian Magazine* 42 (1914), 464–468; Vernon D. Tate, "Spanish Documents Relating to the Voyage of the *Racoon* to Astoria and San Francisco," *Hispanic American Historical Review* 18 (1938), 183–191. See also B. M. Gough, "The Royal Navy on the Northwest Coast of North America, 1810–1910" (Ph.D. diss., University of London, 1969).

13. Leland, *Oration Pronounced at Dorchester,* 10; J. Smith, "Rogues of Quoddy: Smuggling in the Maine–New Brunswick Borderlands, 1783–1820" (Ph.D. diss., University of Maine, 2003), 284–288.

14. J. Smith, "Rogues of Quoddy," 292, 294–302, 305–311.

15. Stanley, *War of 1812,* 361, 363; Facey-Crowther, *The New Brunswick Militia,* 33. See also Temperly, *New Brunswick Journals of Gubbins.*

16. Hickey, *War of 1812,* 152–153; W. S. Dudley, *Naval War of 1812,* 2: 394–396.

17. Brant, *James Madison: Commander-in-Chief,* 230; Henry Adams, *History,* 7: 369–373.

18. C. D. Hall, *British Strategy,* 198–200; G. E. Watson, "The United States and the Peninsular War, 1808–1812," *HJ* 19 (1976), 870–875; Wade G. Dudley, *Splintering the Wooden Wall,* 105, 112; Hickey, *War of 1812,* 172–174; Faye Kert, "The Fortunes of War: Commercial Warfare and Maritime Risk in the War of 1812," *NM/MN* 8, no. 4 (1998), 4, 10.

19. Morison, *Maritime History of Massachusetts,* 205–206.

20. Mahan, *Sea Power,* 2: 220; Kert, *Prize and Prejudice,* 19–22; idem, "The Fortunes of War," 1–16.

21. Crowhurst, *Defence of British Trade,* 204.

22. H. H. Brindley, ed., "Loss of the Lapwing, Post Office Packet," *MM* 16 (January 1930), 18–47; Cranwell and Crane, *Men of Marque,* 187–197.

23. *The Times,* 31 August 1813; Bowers, *Naval Adventures,* 1: 274–275.

24. Maclay, *History of American Privateers,* 274–277; Coggeshall, *History of American Privateers,* 168–169; Marryat, *Frank Mildmay,* chap. 20.

25. Coggeshall, *History of American Privateers,* 219–225; Donald A. Petrie, *The Prize Game,* 86–90, 96–99; idem, "The *Scourge,* the *Rattle Snake,* and the *True Blooded Yankee,*" *Log of Mystic Seaport* 50 (Summer 1998), 2–10.

26. Gardiner, *Naval War of 1812,* 28.

27. Ibid., 71.

28. Hansard, *Parliamentary Debates,* 29: 649–650. Garitee claimed a minimum of 1,300 taken, and a contemporary Baltimore newspaper claimed 1,750 (*Republic's Private Navy,* 243). Recently Donald A. Petrie even claimed 2,500 British ships were lost; *The Prize Game,* 1.

29. Nova Scotia was not seriously threatened by the war and played a military role of only minor significance, although it did provide a significant source of privateers. See John Leefe, "The Atlantic Privateers," *Nova Scotia Historical Quarterly* 8 (1978), 1–17, 109–124. See also Louis A. Holman, ed., "The Log of a Canadian Privateer," *Canadian Magazine* 31 (1908), 435–440.

30. For a description of Portsmouth's privateering heritage, see Winslow, *Wealth and Honour.* See also Arthur P. Wade, "The Defenses of Portsmouth Harbor, 1794–1821," *Historical New Hampshire* 33 (1978), 25–51; and Emma C. Watts, "New Hampshire in the War of 1812," *Granite Monthly* 30 (1901), 357–366.

31. Kert, *Prize and Prejudice,* 78–79; Snider, *Under the Red Jack,* 9–52; Janet E. Mullins, "The Liverpool Packet," *Dalhousie Review* 14 (July 1934), 193–202; John Leefe, "A Bluenose Privateer of 1812," *Nova Scotia Historical Quarterly* 3 (1973), 1–20.

32. Faye M. Kert, "Cruising in Colonial Waters: The Organisation of North American Privateering in the War of 1812," in Starkey, van Heslinga, and de Moor, *Pirates and Privateers,* 143–145. See also D. J. Starkey, "The Fortunes of War: Privateering in Atlantic Canada in the War of 1812" (Master's thesis, Carleton University, 1986).

33. Canney, *U.S. Coast Guard and Revenue Cutters,* 12.

34. McNutt, *The Atlantic Provinces,* 137. See also George Francis Dow, "Records of the Vice-Admiralty Court at Halifax, Nova Scotia: The Condemnation of Prizes and Recaptures of the Revolution and the War of 1812," *EIHC* 45 (1909), 28–48, 161–184, 221–244, 309–332; 46 (1910), 69–80, 150–160, 257–272, 317–324; 47 (1911), 20–24, 189–196, 236–249.

35. Gardiner, *Naval War of 1812,* 28; Kert, "Cruising in Colonial Waters," 152.

36. TNA, ADM 2/1378, pp. 146–151, Croker to Warren, 4 November 1813.

37. NMM, Warren Papers, Warren to Melville, 3 February 1814.

38. For a discussion of these qualities, see Cranwell and Crane, *Men of Marque,* 31–41.

39. TNA, ADM 1/505, pp. 44–45, 277–278, Warren to Croker, 30 November and 30 December 1813 and enclosure.

40. RMM, "Journal of Captain John Robyns RMLI, 1796–1834."

41. W. James, *Naval Occurrences,* 160–162.

42. Roosevelt, *Naval War of 1812,* 159–161. For a biography of Stewart, see Berube and Rodgaard, *A Call to the Sea.*

43. Hardy to Joseph Hardy, 1 May 1813, in Broadley and Bartelot, *Nelson's Hardy,* 162.

44. Rodger, *Command of the Ocean,* 570; Ingersoll, *Historical Sketch,* 2: 53–54; Douglas S. Jordan, "Stephen Decatur at New London: A Study in Strategic Frustration," *USNIP* 93 (October 1967), 60–65; Joseph A. Goldenberg, "Blue Lights and Infernal Machines: The British Blockade of New London," *MM* 56 (1975), 385–397.

45. TNA, ADM 2/933, pp. 91–95, Lords of Admiralty to Cochrane, 25 January 1814. See Cochrane, *The Fighting Cochranes,* 229–271; *DNB,* 12: 301–302; Marshall, *Royal Naval Biography,* 1: 257–266.

46. For an assessment of Warren's performance see Gwyn, *Frigates and Foremasts,* 138–144.

47. TNA, ADM 1/505, pp. 309, 318, 322, 420–421, 434, 440, Warren to Croker, 7 March 1814; Cochrane to Croker, 7 and 31 March and 1 April 1814.

48. Morriss, *Cockburn and British Navy in Transition,* 96–97.

49. Whitehill, *New England Blockaded,* 26.

50. Ibid.

51. Proclamation of James Madison, 29 June 1814, in Savage, *Policy of United States toward Maritime Commerce,* 287–288.

52. Nettels, *Emergence of a National Economy,* 385, 396, 399; Wade, *The Urban Frontier,* 39–71; Hickey, *War of 1812,* 214–215, 222–224, 227.

53. H. Adams, *History,* 7: 263–264; Mahan, *Sea Power,* 2: 176–208.

54. TNA, ADM 1/508, p. 579, Cochrane Proclamation, 2 April 1814. See Joseph A. Goldenberg, "The Royal Navy's Blockade in New England Waters, 1812–1815," *International History Review* 6 (1984), 424–439.

55. TNA, ADM 2/1381, pp. 56–57, Cochrane to Croker, 28 November 1814; WO 1/141, pp. 88–89, Cochrane to Bathurst, 31 December 1814; Weiss, *The Merikens,* 6.

56. TNA, ADM 1/506, pp. 273–277, 280, Coote to Capel, 9 April 1814, and Capel to Talbot, 13 April 1814; USNA, RG 45/M221/R57, Smith to Armstrong, 9 April 1814; *PFB,* 888; W. James, *Naval History,* 473.

57. TNA, ADM 1/506, pp. 47–48, 203, Cochrane to Croker, 27 April and 10 May 1814.

58. Mahan, *Influence of Sea Power,* 2: 118.

59. Lavery, *Nelson's Navy,* 194–206; Michael A. Lewis, *Social History of the Navy,* 270–276; Pope, *Life in Nelson's Navy,* 116.

60. *Reporter* (Lexington, Ky.), 7 August 1813.

61. Hickey, *War of 1812,* 171.

62. TNA, ADM 1/506, pp. 26, 38–39, 44–45, 242, 244–247, Cochrane to Croker, 25 and 28 April 1814, and Cochrane to Sherbrooke, 30 May 1814.

63. LAC, MG 11 A23, New Brunswick Joint Address, 3 March 1814, and Bathurst to Sherbrooke, 6 June 1814; Vane, *Memoirs and Correspondence of Castlereagh,* 2: 69.

64. TNA, ADM 2/1380, p. 80, Croker to Cochrane, 29 April 1814.

65. W. S. Dudley, *Naval War of 1812,* 2: 397–398; Michael J. Crawford, *Naval War of 1812,* 6–15.

66. LC, Cockburn Papers, Cochrane to Cockburn, 24 April 1814.

67. W. F. P. Napier, *Life and Opinions of General Napier,* 1: 369–370.

68. John M. Weiss, "The Corps of Colonial Marines, 1814–15: A Summary," *Immigrants and Minorities* 15 (1996), 80–90.

69. TNA, ADM 1/507, pp. 68–70, Captain Ross to Cockburn, 29 May 1814. For an American view see Whitelaw, *Virginia's Eastern Shore,* 815–817.

70. Pack, *Man Who Burned the White House,* 167–168.

71. M. J. Crawford, *Naval War of 1812,* 33–37, 53–59.

72. For Barrie see *DCB,* 7: 50–51; Marshall, *Royal Naval Biography,* 2: pt. 2, pp. 729–735; John W. Spurr, "The Royal Navy's Presence in Kingston. Part I: 1813–1836," *Historic Kingston* 25 (1977), 63–77.

73. TNA, ADM 1/507, pp. 81–86, Barrie to Cockburn, 19 June 1814; M. J. Crawford, *Naval War of 1812,* 76–82; George, *Terror on the Chesapeake,* 68–72; Mahan, *Sea Power,* 2: 336–340; J. Scott, *Recollections,* 3: 240–241; Shomette, *Flotilla,* 36–55; idem, *Tidewater Time Capsule,* 64–68; D. G. Shomette and Fred W. Hopkins Jr., "The Search for the Chesapeake Flotilla," *AN* 43 (1983), 5–19.

74. WLC, Barrie Papers, Cockburn to Barrie, 3 June 1814.

75. NLS, Cochrane Papers, 2333, Cockburn to Cochrane, 25 June 1814; TNA, ADM 1/507, pp. 79, 81, Barrie to Cockburn, 11 and 19 June 1814; M. J. Crawford, *Naval War of 1812,* 84–91; Marine, *British Invasion of Maryland,* 60–70.

76. TNA, ADM 1/506, p. 455, Cochrane to Croker, 18 July 1814.

77. Donald E. Graves, "Sergeant Major Mayeau's Last Stand, 1814," *MCH* 39 (Fall 1987), 113.

78. LC, Cockburn Papers, Barrie to Cockburn, 19 June 1814; WLC, Barrie Papers, Cockburn to Barrie, 25 June, 11 and 16 July 1814.

79. M. J. Crawford, *Naval War of 1812,* 121–128; George, *Terror on the Chesapeake,* 76–77; Shomette, *Flotilla,* 95–97; Pack, *Man Who Burned the White House,* 172–173.

80. C. J. Bartlett and Gene A. Smith, "A 'Species of Milito-Nautico-Guerrilla-Plundering Warfare,'" in Flavell and Conway, *Britain and America Go to* War, 176.

81. Brynmor Jones Library, University of Hull, Hotham Collection, DDHO 7/99, Henry Hotham Book of Remarks, 1813. See *DNB,* 28: 255–256.

82. Bartlett and Smith, "A 'Species of Milito-Nautico-Guerrilla-Plundering Warfare,'" 176–180.

83. Edgar Erskine Hume, ed., "Letters Written during the War of 1812 by the British Naval Commander in American Waters," *WMQ,* 2d ser., 19 (1930), 291.

84. John K. Mahon, "British Strategy and Southern Indians: War of 1812," *FHQ* 44 (April 1966), 285–302; F. L. Owsley Jr., "British and Indian Activities in Spanish West Florida during the War of 1812," *FHQ* 46 (October 1967), 111–123.

85. TNA, CO 23/60, Cameron to Bathurst, 20 October 1813; NLS, Cochrane Papers, 2346, Cochrane to Cameron and Pigot, 25 March 1814.

86. TNA, ADM 1/506, pp. 394–396, Pigot to Cochrane, 8 June 1814. See Lyle N. McAlister, "Pensacola during the Second Spanish Period," *FHQ* 37 (1959), 281–327; Owsley, "British and Indian Activities in Spanish West Florida."

87. Nicolls' name is often erroneously rendered as Nicholls.

88. See Edward A. Mueller, "'Fighting Nicolls' of the British Royal Marines," *Pensacola History Illustrated* 5 (Summer 1996), 2–23.

89. TNA, ADM 1/506, pp. 390–393, Cochrane to Croker, 20 June 1814; Mahon, "British Strategy and Southern Indians"; Frank L. Owsley Jr., "The Role of the South in the British Grand Strategy in the War of 1812," *THQ* 31 (1972), 22–38.

90. Wrottesley, *Life and Correspondence of Burgoyne,* 1: 304–305.

91. NLS, Cochrane Papers, 2345, Cochrane to Melville, 25 March 1814; 2574, Cockburn to Cochrane, 2 April 1814; Booth Johnson to Cochrane, n.d.; 2265, Cochrane to Sir Thomas Cochrane, 21 November 1814; LC, Cockburn Papers, Cockburn to G. P. Hurlbut, 25 June 1814, and Cockburn to Captain Watts, 18 and 22 July 1814; TNA, ADM 1/506, pp. 478–488, 681–682, Hugh Pigot to Cochrane, 8 June 1814; Cochrane to Croker, 23 July 1814; Instructions to Percy, 5 July 1814; Instructions to Nicolls, 4 July 1814; WO 1/141, pp. 7–14, Cochrane to Bathurst, 14 and 15 July 1814. See John Sugden, "The Southern Indians in the War of 1812: The Closing Phase," *FHQ* 60 (January 1982), 273–312. The case for Cochrane's financial motivation was made strongly by Fortescue (*History of British Army,* 10: 150–151) and affirmed by Carson I. A. Ritchie ("British Documents on the Louisiana Campaign," *LHQ* 44 [1961], 33–43), largely on the basis of accusations made by the Duke of Wellington to the family of his brother-in-law, Edward Pakenham. There is no proof that Wellington knew what he was talking about; Mahon, *War of 1812,* 339–340n.

92. Bathurst to Wellington, 28 January 1814, in Wellesley, *Despatches, Correspondence and Memoranda,* 8: 547; Wellington to Bathurst, 30 October 1814, in Bickley, *Report on Manuscripts of Earl Bathurst,* 302.

93. TNA, WO 1/141, pp. 15–25, Croker to Cochrane, 10 August 1814; WO 1/142, pp. 519, 525–527, Melville to Domett, 23 July 1814, and Domett to Melville, 26 July 1814; WO 6/2, pp. 5–8, Bathurst to Ross, 30 July and 10 August 1814. See also Chartrand and Chappell, *British Forces in West Indies,* 18–21; Robert J. Marrion and John R. Elting, "West India Regiments, 1814–1815," *MCH* 22 (Fall 1970), 87–88; Roger N. Buckley, "The Early History of the West India Regiments, 1795–1815: A Study in British Colonial Military History" (Ph.D. diss., McGill University, 1975).

94. Livingston Hunt, "The Suppressed Mutiny on the 'Essex,'" *USNIP* 59 (1933), 1547–54; M. J. Crawford, *Naval War of 1812,* 772–780.

95. M. J. Crawford, *Naval War of 1812,* 712–716.

96. Ibid., 716–723.

97. Christopher Martin, *Damn the Torpedoes!* 64–65.

98. Royal Navy Museum, Portsmouth, Sampson Family Papers, 1999/9, Lieutenant Charles Sampson to brother, 2 April 1814.

99. C. Martin, *Damn the Torpedoes!* 59.

100. See Hillyar's official report in Parker Kemble, ed., "The U.S.S. Essex vs H.M.S. Phoebe," *USNIP* 57 (February 1937), 199–202; David Porter, *Journal of a Cruise,* 2: 144–158, 175; M. J. Crawford, *Naval War of 1812,* 724–744; W. James, *Naval Occurrences,* 331–344; Samuel B. Johnston, *Three Years in Chili,* 101–146; Roosevelt, *Naval War of 1812,* 160–166; Gerald S. Graham and R. S. Humphreys, *The Navy and South America,* 141–142.

101. TNA, ADM 51/2675, Log of the *Phoebe;* G. S. Graham and R. A. Humphreys, *The Navy and South America,* 132–133, 141–142; Porter to William Jones, 3 July 1814, in Brannan, *Official Letters,* 347–358.

102. Carlos C. Hanks, "A 'Spy' Lands at Babylon," *USNIP* 76 (1950), 778–779; M. J. Crawford, *Naval War of 1812,* 745–747, 760–784.

103. TNA, ADM 1/506, p. 213, Captain Pigot to Cochrane, 25 April 1814; Benjamin Waine, "Account of the Capture of the U.S. Ship Frolic by the Orpheus Frigate, Captain Hugh Pigot, 19 April, 1814," *BNYPL* 7 (August 1903), 278; W. James, *Naval Occurrences,* 166–168.

104. TNA, ADM 1/506, pp. 564–565, Wales to Cochrane, 8 May 1814; W. James, *Naval Occurrences,* 170–172; Roosevelt, *Naval War of 1812,* 172–175; R. W. Mindte, ed., "Another Navy Rodgers," *AN* 19 (July 1959), 213–220.

105. TNA, CO 42/160, pp. 212–222, Minutes of Court Martial, 20–21 January 1815.

106. Codrington, *Memoir,* 1: 310. See also *DNB,* 12: 385–386; Marshall, *Royal Naval Biography* 1: pt. 2, pp. 635–638, 872–873.

107. Duffy, *Captain Blakeley and the Wasp,* 198–201; Fletcher Pratt, "Johnston Blakely, the Carolina Sea Raider," *USNIP* 76 (1950), 996–1007.

108. *Newburyport Herald,* 16 September 1814.

109. TNA, ADM 1/5444, "Proceedings of Court-Martial, 12 August 1814"; Blakeley to Jones, 8 July 1814, in *ASP: NA,* 1: 315; Bowers, *Naval Adventures,* 1: 207, 277–279; Duffy, *Captain Blakeley and the Wasp,* 202–214; W. James, *Naval Occurrences,* 181–183; Roosevelt, *Naval War of 1812,* 178–181.

110. Leech, *Thirty Years from Home,* 197.

111. TNA, CO 42/160, pp. 223–224, Arbuthnot to Sawyer, 1 September 1814; Blakeley to Jones, 11 September 1814, in Brannan, *Official Letters,* 410–413; Duffy, *Captain Blakeley and the Wasp,* 239–249; Roosevelt, *Naval War of 1812,* 182–184.

112. Duffy, *Captain Blakeley and the Wasp,* 261–273; James M. Perry, "The U.S. Sloop of War 'Wasp,'" *USNIP* 87 (February 1961), 84–93.

113. Goldenberg, "Blue Lights," 394–395.

114. TNA, ADM 1/504, p. 342, Coote to Oliver, 22 October 1813.

115. TNA, CO 42/160, p. 109, Petition to the Prince Regent, September 1814.

116. Parkinson, *The Trade Winds,* 226.

117. Hansard, *Parliamentary Debates,* 29: 64–70.

12. The Far Northwest

Epigraph: "The Rogue's March," in Winstock, *Songs and Music of the Redcoats,* 96–98.

1. For a study of women's role in the war see George Sheppard, "'Wants and Privations': Women and the War of 1812 in Upper Canada," *Social History* 28 (May 1995), 159–179.

2. In *The Female Marine and Related Works,* Daniel A. Cohen reproduces five narratives first issued by Nathaniel Coverly Jr. of Boston and speculates that they were written by Nathaniel Hill Wright. Involving the racy adventures of Lucy Brewer as she travels from rural Massachusetts via Boston brothels to the dangerous decks of a naval ship, the stories were originally popular with sailors, prostitutes, and "juveniles."

3. Graves, *Field of Glory,* 180.

4. Everest, *War in Champlain Valley,* 52.

5. LAC, RG 8 I C165, "Return of the Regimental Courts Martial."

6. Graves, *Field of Glory,* 180; Fitz-Enz, *The Final Invasion,* 72–73. See also Anthony F. Gero, "American Deserter Notices in the Northern Theater, 1813 to 1815," *MCH* 38 (Summer 1986), 72–73; idem, "Deserter Reports, 1814–1815, from the New Hampshire Patriot," *MCH* 40 (Summer 1988), 61.

7. See John S. Hare, "Military Punishments in the War of 1812," *Journal of the American Military Institute* 4 (1940), 225–239.

8. B. E. Hill, *Recollections,* 2: 313.

9. LAC, RG 19 E5(a), Loss Claim, Michael Cook. For an idea of the scale of damage see Lawler, *Index of Civilian Loss Claims.*

10. Sinclair to Cocke, 4 July 1813, in Malcomson, *Sailors of 1812,* 39.

11. John D. Carroll, *My Boy Life,* 55.

12. LAC, RG 19 E5(a), Loss Claim, John Crysler.

13. Conant, *Upper Canada Sketches,* 47.

14. Edward Bernard Hein, "The Niagara Frontier and the War of 1812" (Ph.D diss., University of Ottawa, 1949), 139–140.

15. T. G. Ridout to T. Ridout, 4, 16, and 21 September 1813, in *DHC,* 7: 99–100, 137, 153–157; *DCB,* 9: 661–663.

16. Dunlop, *Recollections of the American War,* 58.

17. John Douglas, *Medical Topography of Upper Canada,* 36.

18. BL, F.232: 20997, "Excerpts from Letters from Lieut. and Adjutant William MacEwen to His Wife, Canada 1813–14," pp. 6–9.

19. Dunlop, *Recollections of the American War,* 16.

20. Sheppard, *Plunder, Profit, and Paroles,* 109.

21. Quoted in T. W. Leavitt, *History of Leeds,* 69.

22. Dunlop, *Recollections of the American War,* 59–61.

23. Drummond to Prevost, 15 April and 10 March 1814, in *SBD,* 1: 46; 3: 93–94; Cruikshank, *Battle of Fort George,* 14; William Kirby, *Annals of Niagara,* 228.

24. Sheppard, *Plunder, Profit, and Paroles,* 113–114.

25. Cruikshank, *Battle of Fort George,* 30.

26. Landon, *Bugles on the Border,* 10; idem, *Western Ontario and the American Frontier,* 40.

27. Sheppard, *Plunder, Profit, and Paroles,* 117.

28. Horsman, *War of 1812,* 120.

29. NAM, 7008-11-1, Dent Letters.

30. Marshall Smelser, ed., "Smuggling in 1813–14: A Personal Reminscence," *VH* 38 (Winter 1970), 23. See also Harry F. Landon, "British Sympathizers in St. Lawrence County during the War of 1812," *New York History* 35 (April 1954), 131–138.

31. USNA, RG 107/M221/R62, Izard to Armstrong, 31 July 1814; Everest, *War in Champlain Valley,* 150–152.

32. Edgar, *Ten Years of Upper Canada,* 275, 279.

33. Dunlop, *Recollections of the American War,* 33–35.

34. *Gazette* (Salem, Mass.), 2 September 1814.

35. USNA, RG 107/M221/R62, Izard to Armstrong, 31 July 1814.

36. TNA, CO 42/157, pp. 120–121, Prevost to Bathurst, 27 August 1814; Edgar, *Ten Years of Upper Canada,* 319; Skaggs, *Thomas Macdonough,* 105–107.

37. Michael J. Crawford, *Naval War of 1812,* 537–538; Everest, *War in Champlain Valley,* 152; Hitsman, *Incredible War,* 22, 239, 250. See also H. N. Muller III, "'A Traitorous and Diabolical Traffic': The Commerce of the Champlain-Richelieu Corridor during the War of 1812," *VH* 44 (Spring 1976), 78–96.

38. Hitsman, *Incredible War,* 250.

39. B. Greenhous, "A Note on Western Logistics in the War of 1812," *MA* 34 (1970), 41.

40. Jeffrey Kimball, "The Fog and Friction of Frontier War: The Role of Logistics in American Offensive Failures during the War of 1812," *Old Northwest* 5 (Winter 1979–80), 323–325.

41. Wellington to Bathurst, 22 February 1814, in Wellesley, *Despatches, Correspondence and Memoranda,* 2: 525; Charles Prestwood Lucas, *Canadian War,* 6–7.

42. TNA, CO 42/355, pp. 40–42, Address to House of Assembly, Upper Canada, 14 March 1814.

43. TNA, CO 42/156, pp. 223–227, Petition to Prince Regent by representatives of the Commons of Lower Canada, March 1814.

44. TNA, CO 42/355, pp. 49–50, 73–74, 82–84, Drummond to Bathurst, 5 April, 2 and 28 May 1814; CO 42/40, pp. 386–392, Bathurst to Drummond, 23 August 1814; *The Letters of Veritas,* 79–80.

45. Glenn A. Steppler, "Logistics on the Canadian Frontier, 1812–1814," *MCH* 31 (1979), 8–10. This is based on his master's thesis, "A Duty Troublesome beyond Measure: Logistical Considerations in the Canadian War of 1812" (McGill University, 1974).

46. J. Douglas, *Medical Topography of Upper Canada,* 35–36, 44–46, 58.

47. Squires, *The 104th Regiment of Foot,* 63.

48. See Sheppard, *Plunder, Profit, and Paroles,* chap. 3.

49. J. Douglas, *Medical Topography of Upper Canada,* 105–106; Skeen, *Citizen Soldiers,* 55–56.

50. Samuel R. Brown, *Views of Campaigns,* 113–115. This anecdote is confirmed by John Stagg, who calculates that two and a half times as many Americans died from sickness or accident as were killed or injured in action; "Enlisted Men in the United States Army, 1812–1815: A Preliminary Survey," *WMQ,* 3d ser., 43 (1986), 624.

51. *New York Evening Post,* 25 November 1812, in *DHC,* 2: 218–220. See also Henry Huntt, "An Abstract Account of the Diseases Which Prevailed among the Soldiers, Received into the General Hospital, at Burlington, Vermont, during the Summer and Autumn of 1814," *American Medical Recorder* 1 (1818), 176–179.

52. S. R. Brown, *Views of Campaigns;* James Mann, *Medical Sketches,* 64; Beaumont, *William Beaumont's Formative Years,* 11.

53. P. M. Ashburn, "American Army Hospitals of the Revolution and the War of 1812," *Bulletin of the Johns Hopkins Hospital* 46 (1920), 57. Tilton's *Economical Observations on Military Hospitals* was instrumental in his appointment to the post. For biographical details see Thacher, *American Medical Biography,* 129–141; Allen C. Wooden, "James Tilton, Outstanding Military Medical Administrator," *Delaware Medical Journal* 47 (1975), 429–441; Morris H. Saffron, "The Tilton Affair," *Journal of the American Medical Association* 236 (1976), 67–72.

54. Darnell, *Journal,* 25.

55. McAfee, *History,* 183–184.

56. E. D. Wood, "Journal of the Northwestern Campaign of 1812–13," in Cullum, *Campaigns,* 402–403.

57. McAfee, *History,* 302.

58. J. Mann, *Medical Sketches,* 37. For evidence of American liquor abuse see Verchères de Boucherville, *War on the Detroit,* 187–188, 284–285. See also Michael A. Bellesiles, "Experiencing the War of 1812," in Flavell and Conway, *Britain and America Go to War,* 212–215.

59. James Wilkinson, *Memoirs,* app. 9, "Medical Report, Sackets Harbor, 11 Sep. 1813."

60. Marguerite M. McKee, "Services of Supply in the War of 1812," *Quartermaster Review* 6 (1927), 45–55.

61. J. Mann, *Medical Sketches,* 122. See also Charles G. Roland, "Medical Aspects of War in the West in 1812," in Pryke and Kusilek, *The Western District,* 49–60; Louis Duncan, "The Days Gone By: Sketches of the Medical Service in the War of 1812," *Military Surgeon* 71 (1932), 436–542.

62. Sinclair to Cocke, 4 July 1813, in Malcomson, *Sailors of 1812,* 39.

63. Mississippi Department of Archives and History, Jackson, Covington Papers, Covington to Alexander Covington, 31 July 1813; Gillett, *Army Medical Department,* 167–168.

64. Reginald Horsman, "Wisconsin in the War of 1812," *Wisconsin Magazine of History* 46 (Autumn 1962), 6–8.

65. Greenhous, "Note on Western Logistics," 41.

66. See Robert E. Bieder, "Sault Ste. Marie and the War of 1812: A World Turned Upside Down in the Old Northwest," *IMH* 95 (1999), 1–13.

67. Dunnigan, *British Army at Mackinac,* 17. Bullock was described by John Askin Jr. as a "d—d scoundrel . . . tormenting all about him . . . fit only to drive miscreants and [he] knows very little or pretends to, the difference between gentlemen and blackguards"; John Askin Jr. to John Askin, 26 October 1813, in Askin, *Askin Papers,* 2: 771.

68. Together with Meriwether Lewis, Clark made the famous exploration of the Louisiana Purchase in 1806. In 1807 Jefferson appointed him superintendent for Indian Affairs, and in 1813 Madison gave him additional duties as governor of Missouri Territory. For biographies see Foley, *Wilderness Journey;* and Steffen, *William Clark.* See also Glen E. Holt, "After the Journey Was Over: The St. Louis Years of Lewis and Clark," *Gateway Heritage* 2 (Fall 1981), 42–48; Ann Rogers, "William Clark: A Commemoration," ibid., 9 (Summer 1988), 12–15; Reuben Gold Thwaites, "William Clark: Soldier, Statesman," *Washington Historical Quarterly* 1 (1907), 234–251; Frank E. Stevens, "Illinois in the War of 1812–1814," *Illinois State Historical Society Transactions for 1904,* 62–197.

69. Gilpin, *War of 1812 in Old Northwest,* 246–247.

70. Scanlan, *Prairie du Chien,* 117.

71. Stagg, *Mr. Madison's War,* 390–391.

72. M. J. Crawford, *Naval War of 1812,* 417–424, 512–518; McKee, *A Gentlemanly and Honorable Profession,* 138.

73. LAC, RG 8 I C388, p. 44, Riall to Drummond, 15 March 1814; Graves, *"Where Right and Glory Lead!"* 59–60.

74. USNA, RG 107/M221/R51, John B. Campbell to John B. Walbach, 18 May 1814; Court of enquiry, 20 June 1814, and Narrative of Alexander McMullen, in *DHC,* 1: 16–18 and 2: 369–371; Graves, *Soldiers of 1814,* 63–66; M. J. Crawford, *Naval War of 1812,* 483–490; Thomas Talbot to Riall, 16 May 1814, in *SBD,* 3: 88–92. For Markle see *DCB,* 6: 488–491.

75. USNA, RG 107/M221/R51, Campbell to Armstrong, 18 May 1814; R52, Scott to Armstrong, 19 May 1814; Sinclair to Jones, 27 May 1814, in *DRINP,* 23; "Narrative of Alexander McMullen," in *DHC,* 2: 371; J. A. Bannister, "The Burning of Dover," *Western Ontario Historical Notes* 21 (March 1965), 1–25; Talman, *Loyalist Narratives,* 148; Hitsman, *Incredible War,* 218–219; Graves, *"Where Right and Glory Lead!"* 40–41, 224.

76. TNA, ADM 1/506, p. 462, Prevost to Cochrane, 2 June 1814; E. A. Cruikshank, "The County of Norfolk," in Zaslow, *Defended Border,* 230–235.

77. Henry Howe Leavitt, *Autobiography,* 21.

78. Gough, *Fighting Sail,* 86–90.

79. Franchère, *Adventures at Astoria,* 184; Ida Amanda Johnson, *The Michigan Fur Trade,* 119–121.

80. Gough, *Fighting Sail,* 94.

81. TNA, CO 412/156, p. 294, Prevost to Bathurst, 18 May 1814. For McDouall, see *DCB,* 7: 556–558; Fardy, *Before Beaumont Hamel,* 106; H. Winston Johnston, *The Glengarry Light Infantry,* 247–248.

82. TNA, CO 42/157, pp. 7–9, Prevost to Bathurst, 10 July 1814; Gough, *Fighting Sail,* 69–72.

83. *Quebec Gazette,* 27 August 1814.

84. Morrison, *Superior Rendez-vous Place,* 75; Davidson, *The North West Company,* 208.

85. See Thomas Anderson, "Personal Narrative of Capt. Thomas G. Anderson: Early Experiences in the Northwest Fur Trade and the British Capture of Priarie du Chien, 1814," *WHSC* 9 (1880–81), 136–261; "Prairie du Chien Documents," ibid., 262–281; Brian L. Dunnigan, "The Michigan Fencibles," *Michigan History* 57 (1973), 277–295.

86. McDouall to Drummond, 16 July 1814, in *SBD,* 3: 253–256.

87. B. Greenhous, "1814: An Irish Gunner on the Upper Mississippi," *Irish Sword* 10 (1971–72), 247.

88. Gough, *Fighting Sail,* 80–81. For Worsley see *DCB,* 6: 817–818; Robert Holden Mackenzie, *The Trafalgar Roll,* 220, 227.

89. Milo M. Quaife, "A Forgotten Hero of Rock Island," *Journal of the Illinois State Historical Society* 23 (January 1931), 652–653.

90. "One-Gun" Keating was later commissioned and took command of the Mississippi Volunteer Artillery; Irving, *Officers of British Forces in Canada,* 97.

91. Greenhous, "Irish Gunner," 248–249; Gilpin, *War of 1812 in Old Northwest,* 248–249.

92. Augustus Grignon, "Seventy-Two Years' Recollections of Wisconsin," *WHC* 3 (1857), 278.

93. Douglas Brynmer, "Capture of Fort McKay, Prairie du Chien, in 1814," *WHSC* 11 (1888), 254–270; William McKay, "An Account of the Expedition against Fort Shelby on the Mississippi, Undertaken in 1814, under the Command of Lieutenant Col. McKay, Then Major of the Michigan Fencibles," *Canadian Magazine and Literary Repository* 4 (April–May 1825), 323–326; 400–405; Dirk Gringhuis, René Chartrand, and Brian Leigh Dunnigan, "Michigan Fencibles and Mississippi Volunteers, Canadian Militia, at Prairie du Chien, 1814," *MCH* 25 (Fall 1973), 145–148; Robert S. Allen, "Canadians on the Upper Mississippi: The Capture and Occupation of Prairie du Chien during the War of 1812," *MCH* 31 (Fall 1979), 118–123; Horsman, "Wisconsin in the War of 1812," 10–12.

94. TNA, CO 42/157, pp. 199–202, McKay to McDouall, 27 July 1814; *SBD,* 3: 264–265; *WHC,* 11: 254–271; Black Hawk, *Life,* 25–27.

95. Kappler, *Indian Affairs,* 2: 105–107.

96. McDouall to Prevost, 14 August 1814, in *SBD,* 3: 273.

97. Dunnigan, *British Army at Mackinac,* 22.

98. M. J. Crawford, *Naval War of 1812,* 564; Goldowsky, *Yankee Surgeon,* 76.

99. McDouall to Prevost, 14 August 1814, in *SBD,* 3: 273–277; Berton, *Flames across the Border,* 307–310; Brian Leigh Dunnigan, "The Battle of Mackinac Island," *Michigan History* 59 (Winter 1975), 239–254.

100. Gough, *Fighting Sail,* 104–105.

101. Bunnell, *Travels and Adventures,* 123.

102. Worsley to father, 6 October 1814, in Snider, *Leaves from War Log of the Nancy,* xlvii–xlviii. See also E. A. Cruikshank, "An Episode of the War of 1812: The Story of the Schooner 'Nancy,'" *OHSPR* 9 (1910), 76–129.

103. Gough, *Fighting Sail,* 106–107.

104. Bunnell, *Travels and Adventures,* 123.

105. Quoted in *DCB,* 6: 818.

106. TNA, ADM 1/2738, Worsley to Yeo, 15 September 1814, enclosed in Yeo to Croker, 12 October 1814, pp. 4–10.

107. For Bulger see *DCB,* 8: 111–113.

108. G. F. G. Stanley, "British Operations in the American North-west, 1812–15," *JSAHR* 22 (1943–44), 104.

109. Bunnell, *Travels and Adventures,* 123.

110. TNA, CO 42/157, pp. 195–198, 244–248, 402–403, McDouall to Prevost, 14 August 1814; McDouall to Drummond, 9 September 1814; Bulger to McDouall, 7 September 1814; Prevost to Bathurst, 4 December 1814; *SBD,* 3: 277–281; M. J. Crawford, *Naval War of 1812,* 604–607, 645–650; Gilpin, *War of 1812 in Old Northwest,* 242–245.

111. Worsley to father, 6 October 1814, in Snider, *Leaves from War Log of the Nancy,* xlvii–xlviii. Unfortunately he was later taken ill and suffered severe financial hardship; Gough, *Fighting Sail,* 108–113, 175–176.

112. Anderson insinuates that McKay was continually drunk and that he was left in charge when McKay left for Mackinac, later succeeded by Captain William Bulger. See Thomas Gummersall Anderson, "Personal Narrative," *WHC* 7 (1882), 193–202; "Captain T. G. Anderson's Journal, 1814," *WHC* 9 (1884), 207–251; also the statement by his daughter in Talman, *Loyalist Narratives,* 18–29. He details the daily life in the fort and the constant struggle to maintain discipline, keep his men sober and the Indians happy. Following the American attack on 13 September in which they are victorious, garrison life continues.

113. Greenhous, "Irish Gunner," 251–252; Edgar B. Wesley, ed., "James Callaway in the War of 1812," *Missouri Historical Society Collections* 5 (October 1927), 38–81.

114. Horsman, "Wisconsin in the War of 1812," 13.

13. The Niagara Frontier

Epigraph: The ballad "The Bold Canadian" was written down by Robert Warner (1848–1924), whose grandfather served with the Upper Canada militia and who sang it "when he drew his pension, and on the eve of the great battle dates of the war"; "The Bold Canadian: A Ballad of the War of 1812"; Zaslow, *Defended Border,* 303–305.

1. The 97th was later numbered 96th before being disbanded after the war. It saw no action; Wylly, *History of the Manchester Regiment,* 186.

2. Barbuto, *Niagara, 1814,* 108–109.

3. USNA, RG 107/M221/R51, Mitchell to Brown, 8 May 1814.

4. J. C. Morgan, *Emigrant's Note Book and Guide,* 333.

5. TNA, CO 42/156, pp. 299–303, Drummond to Prevost, 7 May 1814; ADM 1/506, p. 106, General Orders, 12 May 1814; Yeo to Croker, 9 May 1814, in *SBD,* 3: 49, 52–57, 61–63; NYSL, MSS 11225, Left Division Order Book, 8 May 1814; Barbuto, *Niagara, 1814,* 145–146; Brannan, *Official Letters,* 333–334; Michael J. Crawford, *Naval War of 1812,* 463–479; E. A. Cruikshank, "Contest for the Command of Lake Ontario in 1814," *OHSPR* 21 (1924), 118–122; Robert Malcomson, "War of Lake Ontario: A Costly Victory at Oswego, 1814," *The Beaver* 75 (1995), 4–13; idem, *Lords of the Lake,* 266–276; Hitsman, *Incredible War,* 209–210, 345–346; Field, *Britain's Sea Soldiers,* 295–296; H. Winston Johnston, *The Glengarry Light Infantry,* 138–144; Nicolas, *Historical Record of Royal Marine Forces,* 258–259. See also Slosek, *Oswego and War of 1812;* John C. Frederiksen, ed., "The War of 1812 in Northern New York: The Observations of Captain Rufus McIntire," *New York History* 68 (July 1987), 297–324.

6. USNA, RG 45/M125/R37, Melancthon Woolsey to Isaac Chauncey, 1 June 1814, and Chauncey to Jones, 2 June 1814; Drummond to Prevost, 2 June 1814, in *SBD,* 3: 73–75; M. J. Crawford, *Naval War of 1812,* 508–512; J. Evans, "Forgotten Battle of the War of 1812: The Battle of Sandy Creek," *Magazine of American History* 29 (1893), 525; Nat Frame, "The Battle of Sandy Creek and Carrying the Cables of the 'Superior,'" *Jefferson County Historical Society Transactions* 3 (1895), 32–40; Richard Palmer, "Lake Ontario Battles: Part 3, The Battle of Sandy Creek," *IS* 53 (1997), 282–291; Malcomson, *Lords of the Lake,* 278–281; Fredriksen, *Green Coats and Glory,* 50–51; Hitsman, *Incredible War,* 211–212.

7. TNA, CO 42/156, pp. 327–329, 331–332, Popham to Yeo, 20 May and 1 June 1814, and Prevost to Bathurst, 8 June and 12 July 1814; CO 42/157, pp. 19–20, 230–231, Prevost to Bathurst, 12 July 1814; Drummond to Prevost, 2 June 1814, in *SBD,* 3: 73–74; M. J. Crawford, *Naval War of 1812,* 518–523.

8. TNA, CO 42/156, p. 333, "Yeo Report," 2 June 1814; Yeo to Drummond, 3 June 1814, and Drummond to Yeo, 6 June 1814, in *SBD,* 3: 76–79; William James, *Naval History,* 486; "Strength on Ontario," *NWR* 6 (18 June 1814), 267.

9. TNA, CO 43/23, pp. 150–155, Bathurst to Prevost, 3 June 1814 (reprinted in Hitsman, *Incredible War,* app. 1, pp. 289–290); ADM 2/1380, pp. 66–68, 138–142, Croker to Admiral Keith, 27 April, 19 and 26 May 1814. On the Nova Scotia Fencibles see C. P. Stacey, "Upper Canada at War: Captain Armstong Reports," *OH* 44 (1942), 173–181.

10. TNA, CO 42/156, pp. 77–85, Drummond to Prevost, 21 January 1814.

11. M. J. Crawford, *Naval War of 1812,* 458–463.

12. Armstrong to Madison, 30 April 1814, in *DHC,* 9: 320; Graves, *"Where Right and Glory Lead!"* 21–22. Once again, I am indebted to Donald Graves for this chapter.

13. M. J. Crawford, *Naval War of 1812,* 495–498; Stagg, *Mr. Madison's War,* 387–391; Skeen, *John Armstrong Jr.,* chap. 10.

14. Jeffrey Phillip Kimball, "Strategy on the Northern Frontier: 1814" (Ph.D. diss., Louisiana State University, 1969), 159–169; Barbuto, *Niagara, 1814,* 109–114, 151–154, 161–162.

15. Hitsman, *Incredible War,* 216–217; Graves, *"Where Right and Glory Lead!"* 22–23; Malcomson, *Lords of the Lake,* 286–289.

16. M. J. Crawford, *Naval War of 1812,* 499–501, 523–528.

17. Izard to Armstrong, 10 June 1814, and Armstrong to Izard, 11 June 1814, in Izard, *Official Correspondence,* 26–30, 33–34.

18. Barbuto, *Niagara, 1814,* 202–203.

19. LAC, MG24 128, Sandys Papers, Alicia Cockburn to Charles Sandys, 28 June 1814.

20. For biographies see Stone, *Life and Times of Red Jacket;* and John H. Kolecki, "Red Jacket: The Last of the Senecas" (Master's thesis, Niagara University, 1950); *DCB,* 7: 703–704.

21. David J. Glenney, "An Ethnohistory of the Grand River Iroquois and the War of 1812" (Master's thesis, University of Guelph, 1973), 122–124; William Kirby, *Annals of Niagara,* 234–235. See also Frank H. Severance, "Two Dramatic Incidents," *BSHP* 5 (1902), 62; Arthur C. Parker, "The Senecas in the War of 1812," *New-York Historical Society Proceedings for 1915,* 78–90; Alan Taylor, "The Divided Ground: Upper Canada, New York, and the Iroquois Six Nations, 1783–1815," *JER* 22 (Spring 2002), 55–76.

22. Winfield Scott, *Memoir,* 1: 118; James Wilkinson, *Memoirs,* 3: 639, 646, 650, 655; John D. Morris, "General Jacob Brown and the Problems of Command in 1814," in Bowler, *War along the Niagara,* 31–32.

23. J. C. A. Stagg, "Enlisted Men in the United States Army, 1812–1815: A Preliminary Survey," *WMQ,* 3d ser., 43 (1986), 616–645.

24. Mahon, *War of 1812,* 259–260, 266–267. See also John C. Fredriksen, ed., "The Pennsylvania Volunteers in the War of 1812: An Anonymous Journal of Service for the Year 1814," *Western Pennsylvania Historical Magazine* 70 (1987), 123–157.

25. Joseph Walker, ed., "A Soldier's Diary for 1814," *Pennsylvania History* 12 (1945), 299.

26. Elliot, *Winfield Scott,* 146–150; Jeffrey Kimball, "The Battle of Chippawa: Infantry Tactics in the War of 1812," *MA* 31 (1967–68), 171–173; James R. Jacobs and Glenn Tucker, *War of 1812,* 130–131; Mahon, *War of 1812,* 267; Berton, *Flames across the Border,* 280–290; Hickey, *War of 1812,* 185–186; Weigley, *History of the U.S. Army,* 129; Charles F. Heller, " 'Those Are Regulars, by God!' " *Army* 37 (1987), 52–54. For a thorough discussion of Scott's camp see Donald E. Graves, " 'I Have a Handsome Little Army . . .': A Reexamination of Winfield Scott's Camp at Buffalo in 1814," in Bowler, *War along the Niagara,* 44–46; idem, *"Where Right and Glory Lead!"* 25–28.

27. David H. Schneider, "Gray Uniforms on the Niagara," *MCH* 33 (1981), 170–172.

28. Barbuto, *Niagara, 1814,* 162.

29. Hitsman, *Incredible War,* 220; Robert Louis Rogers, *History of Lincoln and Welland Regiment,* 14–15.

30. Joseph A. Whitehorne, *While Washington Burned,* 11.

31. BECHS, Riall Letter Book, "Instructions to Commanding Officer, Fort Erie, 12 May 1814."

32. Porter to Stone, 26 May 1840, in *DHC,* 2: 358; Fortescue, *History of British Army,* 10: 107.

33. UCA, "Memoir of Reverend George Ferguson," p. 58.

34. John Norton, *Journal,* 348–349.

35. Charles Andrews, *The Prisoners' Memoirs,* 96.

36. LAC, RG 8 I C684, p. 51, Riall to Drummond, 6 July 1814.

37. Irving, *Officers of British Forces in Canada,* 29.

38. Laws, *Battery Records of Royal Artillery,* 158–161; Askwith, *List of Officers of Royal Regiment of Artillery,* 27, 34; Graves, *"Where Right and Glory Lead!"* 68–69. The monstrous 24-pounders had been cast as experimental pieces during the previous century and weighed 2,050 pounds without their carriages, the heaviest field pieces used by either side during the war; ibid., 69.

39. Graves, *Red Coats and Grey Jackets,* 67–70; W. Scott, *Memoir,* 1: 124.

40. *DHC,* 1: 44; LC, Thomas S. Jesup Papers, "Memoir of the Campaign on the Niagara," p. 9; Biddulph, *The Nineteenth and Their Times,* 197–198.

41. Mary R. Cate, ed., "Benjamin Ropes's Autobiography," *EIHC* 91 (July 1955), 117–118; Treat, *Vindication,* 33–34; LL, "Narrative of Capt. Joseph Henderson, Twenty-second Infantry"; Graves, *Red Coats and Grey Jackets,* 70–72.

42. William H. Merritt, *Journal,* 56; TNA, CO 42/157, pp. 37–41, Riall to Drummond, 6 July 1814; LAC, WO 55 C1223, Mackonochie to Maclachlan, 11 July 1814, in *DHC,* 1: 35; J. Norton, *Journal,* 349–350; Graves, *Red Coats and Grey Jackets,* 82–83.

43. Lewis Einstein, ed., "Recollections of the War of 1812 by George Hay, Eighth Marquis of Tweedale," *AHR* 32 (October 1926), 71–72.

44. Samuel White, *History of American Troops,* 14; Graves, *Red Coats and Grey Jackets,* 92–96.

45. UCA, "Memoir of Reverend George Ferguson," pp. 59–60; N. Lord, ed., "The War on the Canadian Frontier, 1812–1814: Letters Written by Sergeant James Commins, 8th Foot," *JSAHR* 18 (Winter 1939), 208.

46. Einstein, "Recollections," 72–74; Graves, *Soldiers of 1814,* 69.

47. See John L. Crombie, "The Twenty-second United States Infantry: A Forgotten Regiment in a Forgotten War, 1812–1815," *Western Pennsylvania Historical Magazine* 50 (April 1967), 135–148, and (July 1967), 221–237; Hugh C. McBarron Jr. and James L. Kochan, "22nd U.S. Infantry Regiment, 1812–1813," *MCH* 33 (Winter 1981), 165; "An Eyewitness," "Reminiscences of the Last War," *Illinois Monthly Magazine* 2 (February 1832), 202–207; John C. Fredriksen, ed., "Chronicle of Valor: The Journal of a Pennsylvania Officer in the War of 1812," *Western Pennsylvania Historical Magazine* 67 (July 1984), 243–284.

48. Graves, *Soldiers of 1814,* 32; W. Scott, *Memoir,* 1: 128. Scott appears to be the only source for Riall's famous phrase, and there is no record of it in any British source. The

myth has been embellished ever since and repeated in most American sources; Barbuto, *Niagara, 1814,* 175; Berton, *Flames across the Border,* 324; Elting, *Amateurs to Arms!* 187n; Hickey, *War of 1812,* 185; Mahon, *War of 1812,* 269; Perret, *A Country Made by War,* 123; *PFB,* 806, etc. Elliot in his biography of Scott gives it as "Those are regulars" (*Winfield Scott,* 162). That the grey uniform of West Point cadets was adopted in commemoration of Scott's troops at Lundy's Lane also appears to be apocryphal. The reasons given in 1816 for its selection were simply that it wore well and was considerably cheaper than the blue one. However, its origin is not important, as it serves to perpetuate the memory of the Left Division. For a discussion of the myths surrounding the battle see Graves, *Red Coats and Grey Jackets,* 180–187.

49. Graves, *Red Coats and Grey Jackets,* 105–117.

50. AO, Niagara Historical Society Papers, Stevenson to Addison, July 1814.

51. For a biography of Jesup, see Kieffer, *Maligned General,* 27.

52. *Sketch of Life of Nathan Towson,* 13; W. Scott, *Memoir,* 1: 128; Graves, *Red Coats and Grey Jackets,* 120–124.

53. UCA, "Memoir of Reverend George Ferguson," p. 61.

54. Berton, *Flames across the Border,* 324–326.

55. Official records at the time gave British and American dead as 148 and 58 respectively. See Graves, *Red Coats and Grey Jackets,* 133–135, 173–180; idem, *"Where Right and Glory Lead!"* 80–92. Heidler and Heidler, *Encyclopedia of War of 1812,* 80.

56. Hitsman, *Incredible War,* 223, 347.

57. John F. Horton, ed., "An Original Narrative of the Niagara Campaign of 1814," *Niagara Frontier* 46 (1964), 9.

58. Graves, *"Where Right and Glory Lead!"* 93–96.

59. TNA, CO 42/157, pp. 21–22, Prevost to Bathurst, 12 July 1814.

60. LAC, RG 8 I C684, pp. 59, 131, Drummond to Prevost, 13 July 1814, and Riall to Drummond, 15 July 1814.

61. M. J. Crawford, *Naval War of 1812,* 550–551; *DHC,* 1: 64; Brown to Armstrong, 22 July 1814, in Brannan, *Official Letters,* 379; Malcomson, *Lords of the Lake,* 286–290.

62. Mahon, *War of 1812,* 270–271.

63. Porter to Brown, 16 July 1814; Riall to Drummond, 17 July 1814; and David Secord "Memorial," in *DHC,* 1: 68, 71–72; W. H. Merritt, *Journal,* 58–59; William James, *Full Account of Military Occurrences,* 2: 134; NYSL, MSS 11225, Left Division Order Book, General Order, 19 July 1814; Barbuto, *Niagara, 1814,* 196–197; Graves, *"Where Right and Glory Lead!"* 99–101.

64. TNA, CO 52/355, pp. 103–105, Drummond to Bathurst, 10 November 1814; CO 42/157, pp. 45–48, Drummond to Bathurst, 11 July 1814; Berton, *Flames across the Border,* 295–299; E. A. Cruikshank, "John Beverley Robinson and the Trials for Treason in 1814," *OHSPR* 25 (1929), 191–219; William Renwick Riddell, "The Ancaster 'Bloody Assize' of 1814," in Zaslow, *Defended Border,* 241–250. See also "Benjamin Mallory, Traitor," *OHSPR* 26 (1930), 573–578. Mallory, an American immigrant to Canada, had become a prominent

landholder until he joined the regiment of renegade Canadians. He was convicted of high treason in absentia and his lands were confiscated.

65. William H. Merritt, *Journal,* 60.

66. LAC, RG 8 I C684, p. 201, Drummond to Prevost, 22 July 1814.

67. Harvey to Riall, 23 July 1814, in *DHC,* 1: 82–83; Riall to Drummond, 21 July 1814, in *SBD,* 3: 140; USNA, RG 107/M221/R59, Brown to Armstrong, 22 July 1814.

68. Brown to Armstrong, 25 July 1814, in Brannan, *Official Letters,* 379.

69. Graves, *"Where Right and Glory Lead!"* 107–109.

70. Cunliffe, *Royal Irish Fusiliers,* 148.

71. For Dobbs see Malcomson, *Historical Dictionary,* 147–148; for Tucker see ibid., 565.

72. TNA, CO 42/157, pp. 107–113, Drummond to Prevost, 27 July 1814; *SBD,* 3: 147–151; W. James, *Full Account of Military Occurrences,* 2: 142; Gellner, *Recollections,* 37; *The Letters of Veritas,* 150; Walker, "Soldier's Diary," 300.

73. Hitsman, *Incredible War,* 226; W. Scott, *Memoir,* 1: 137.

74. Graves, *"Where Right and Glory Lead!"* 110–113, 262–263.

75. TNA, CO 42/157, p. 109, Drummond to Prevost, 27 July 1814; W. H. Merritt, *Journal,* 61; T. W. Leavitt, *History of Leeds and Grenville,* 70; J. Norton, *Journal,* 356; BHC, "Diary of Ensign Andrew Warffe, Incorporated Militia of Upper Canada," 25 July 1814; Graves, *"Where Right and Glory Lead!"* 118–122.

76. W. Scott, *Memoir,* 1: 140.

77. *Facts Relating to Campaign on Niagara,* 20–21; *Sketch of Life of Nathan Towson,* 13.

78. TNA, WO 44/250, p. 276, "Return and Distribution of Ordnance, Carriages and Ammunition, 1 April 1814"; Albert Ellis, "Fifty-four Years' Recollections of Men and Events in Wisconsin," *WHC* 7 (1876), 260; Henry Parker, "Henry Leavenworth, Pioneer General," *Military Review* 59 (1970), 58–59; Graves, *Soldiers of 1814,* 34–35; *Facts Relating to Campaign on Niagara,* 21.

79. NYSL, Gardner Papers, "Memoranda of Occurrences and Some Important Facts Attending the Campaign on the Niagara," pp. 18–19; Pennsylvania Historical Society, Philadelphia, Daniel Parker Papers, Brown to Armstrong, 7 August 1814; Horton, "Original Narrative," 14; *Facts Relating to Campaign on Niagara,* 14; Connecticut Historical Society, Hartford, Letter Book of Captain George Howard, 25th Infantry, p. 19; Edward B. Hein, "The Niagara Frontier and the War of 1812" (Ph.D. diss., University of Ottawa, 1949), 323.

80. Graves, *Merry Hearts,* 173.

81. Shepard, *Autobiography of Elihu H. Shepard,* 68.

82. H. Winston Johnston, *The Glengarry Light Infantry,* 145–153.

83. Graves, *"Where Right and Glory Lead!"* 127–137, 142–144.

84. LC, Jesup Papers, "Memoir," pp. 10–11; NYSL, Gardner Papers, Jesup Undated Draft Report; Thomas S. Jesup, "Who Captured General Riall?" *Historical Magazine* 8 (July 1870), 54–55; C. W. Upham, "The Capture of General Riall," *Historical Magazine* 11 (April 1872), 252–253; Horton, "Original Narrative," 21; Biddulph, *The Nineteenth and*

Their Times, 202; W. H. Merritt, *Journal,* 62; T. W. Leavitt, *History of Leeds and Grenville,* 70; Shepard, *Autobiography of Elihu H. Shepard,* 69.

85. Graves, *"Where Right and Glory Lead!"* 139–141, 145–147.

86. See John Elting and H. C. McBarron, "Musicians, 1st U.S. Infantry, Winter Uniforms, 1812–1813," *MCH* 2 (1950), 24–25.

87. USNA, RG 153/K-1, Court Martial of Lt. Col. R. C. Nicholas, 1816; J. G. Jacobs, *Life and Times of Patrick Gass,* 172.

88. J. Norton, *Journal,* 357. The plates on American shakos were perfectly rectangular, while British shako plates were slightly curved with scalloped corners; Chartrand, *Uniforms and Equipment,* 147.

89. Graves, *Merry Hearts,* 174; idem, *"Where Right and Glory Lead!"* 155, 265–270.

90. WLC, War of 1812 MSS, Colonel James Miller to wife, 28 July 1814.

91. Graves, *Soldiers of 1814,* 53–55.

92. LL, War of 1812 Papers, Ripley to Brown, 29 July 1814; *Facts Relating to Campaign on Niagara,* 12–13; Graves, *"Where Right and Glory Lead!"* 153–161.

93. Letter of William Drummond, *Edinburgh Annual Register,* 1814, 354.

94. Cunliffe, *Royal Irish Fusiliers,* 151.

95. Graves, *"Where Right and Glory Lead!"* 166–171.

96. *Facts Relating to Campaign on Niagara,* 14–15; LL, War of 1812 Papers, Hindman to Gardner, 29 July 1814. See also Cate, "Benjamin Ropes's Autobiography," 120; *DHC,* 1: 110; *DRINP,* 375; Graves, *"Where Right and Glory Lead!"* 172–175; Horton, "Original Narrative," 19; LC, Jesup Papers, "Memoir," p. 12; Lord, "War on Canadian Frontier: Letters by James Commins," 209; McLeod, *Brief Review of Settlement of Upper Canada,* 65; J. Norton, *Journal,* 358; Talman, *Loyalist Narratives,* 308.

97. Graves, *Merry Hearts,* 175.

98. Hugh Brady, "The Battle of Lundy's Lane," *Historical Magazine* 10 (September 1866), 272; Graves, *"Where Right and Glory Lead!"* 177–179; LC, Jesup Papers, "Memoir," p. 13; Linn, *Annals of Buffalo Valley,* 420.

99. NYSL, Gardner Papers, "Memoranda," p. 23; Massachusetts Historical Society, Boston, Brown Papers, Brown to brother, 4 August 1814; Austin to Armstrong, 29 July 1814, in *DHC,* 1: 96; Shepard, *Autobiography of Elihu H. Shepard,* 68; Graves, *"Where Right and Glory Lead!"* 179.

100. LC, Jesup Papers, "Memoir," pp. 12–13; W. Scott, *Memoir,* 1: 143.

101. TNA, CO 42/157, pp. 109–110, Drummond to Prevost, 27 July 1814; Berton, *Flames across the Border,* 332–342; *DRINP,* 105–106. Given the different construction of British and American gun trails, this story seems unlikely; the gunners of both sides would be immediately aware that it was a foreign piece; Graves, *"Where Right and Glory Lead!"* 180–181, 302 n. 29.

102. Who controlled or possessed the guns at the end of the fighting remains the most difficult question surrounding the battle. For a discussion of the various interpretations, see "The Problem of the Guns," in Graves, *"Where Right and Glory Lead!"* app. D,

pp. 265–270. See also Carl M. Guelzo, "Lundy's Lane—What to Do with an Objective," *Military Review* 39 (September 1959), 45–51.

103. USNA, RG 107/M221/R59, Brown to Armstrong, 7 August 1814; LC, Brown Papers, Brown to Judge Barker, 7 August 1814; Gardner Papers, "Memoranda," pp. 24–50.

104. Graves, *"Where Right and Glory Lead!"* 182–185, 195–197; Leask and McCance, *Regimental Records of Royal Scots,* 292; *Historical Record of the King's Liverpool Regiment,* 98–100; Biddulph, *The Nineteenth and Their Times,* 205; Squires, *The 104th Regiment of Foot,* 164; Arthur B. Ellis, ed., "Letter of John W. Blake, Describing the Battle of Lundy's Lane," *MHSP* 26 (January 1891), 257–259.

105. Beaumont, *William Beaumont's Formative Years,* 46.

106. For a discussion of surgery of the period, see Howard, *Wellington's Doctors,* chap. 5; Graves, *"Where Right and Glory Lead!"* 199–205; and Richard L. Blanco, "The Development of British Military Medicine, 1793–1814," *MA* 38 (1974), 4–10. For an idea of a typical surgeon's equipment see Alan J. Ferguson, "A Surgeon's Personal Inventory from the War of 1812," *MCH* 34 (Fall 1982), 127–128.

107. See Charles G. Roland, "War Amputations in Upper Canada," *Archivaria* 10 (Summer 1980), 73–85; James Phalen, "Landmarks in Surgery. Surgeon James Mann, U.S. Army: Observations on Battlefield Amputations," *Surgery* 66 (1938), 1072–73.

108. William E. Horner, "Surgical Sketches: A Military Hospital at Buffalo, New York, in the Year 1814," *Medical Examiner and Record of Medical Science* 16 (December 1852), 767.

109. Dunlop, *Recollections of the American War,* p. 54.

110. John Douglas, *Medical Topography of Upper Canada,* 96–97.

111. Howard, *Wellington's Doctors,* 82–83.

112. Gellner, *Recollections,* 38.

113. Graves, *"Where Right and Glory Lead!"* 230–232; Hitsman, *Incredible War,* 229.

114. See John C. Fredriksen, "Niagara 1814: The United States Army Quest for Tactical Parity in the War of 1812 and Its Legacy" (Ph.D. diss., Providence College, Rhode Island, 1993).

115. Brown to Tompkins, 1, 19, and 21 August 1814, in *DRINP,* 54, 67–68; Porter to Tompkins, 9 August 1814, in *DHC,* 2: 431.

116. Kimball, "Strategy," 243–244; Horsman, *War of 1812,* 179–180. For a defence of Chauncey's strategy, see William S. Dudley, "Commodore Isaac Chauncey and U.S. Joint Operations on Lake Ontario, 1813–14," in Cogar, *New Interpretations in Naval History,* 139–155.

117. NLS, George Hay Papers, Martin to Hay, 2 August 1814.

118. Graves, *"Where Right and Glory Lead!"* 211–212; Hitsman, *Incredible War,* 348. In contrast, Wesley B. Turner takes the view that Drummond acted prudently; *British Generals in War of 1812,* 126–127.

119. Graves, *Merry Hearts,* 183–184. "Shindy" was slang for a dance, suggesting he was flighty and unreliable.

120. Ludowick Morgan to Brown, 5 August 1814, in Brannan, *Official Letters,* 383–384.

121. TNA, CO 42/157, pp. 134–137, Drummond to Prevost and enclosure, 4 August 1814; LAC, RG 8 I C685, pp. 31, 34, Harvey to Conran, 2 August 1814, and Tucker to Conran, 4 August 1814; Morgan to Brown, 5 August 1814, in Brannan, *Official Letters,* 383–384; Berton, *Flames across the Border,* 354–358.

122. He subsequently returned to Wiltshire, where he received a pension of 9d a day, later increased to 12d. Fortunately, he was able to return to life as a weaver, despite his disability, following a dream that revealed an instrument enabling a one-handed man to work at his trade; Gellner, *Recollections,* 40–41, 44–45.

123. John C. Fredriksen, ed., "The Memoirs of Jonathan Kearsley: A Michigan Hero from the War of 1812," *IMHJ* 10 (October 1985), 11.

14. Burning the White House

Epigraph: "The Curse of Liberty," in *The Court of Neptune,* 21.

1. NLS, Cochrane Papers, 2332 "Report"; TNA, ADM 1/506, pp. 24–28, Hotham to Cochrane, 13 August 1814; *NWR* 6 (20 August 1814), 428–429.

2. James Scott, *Recollections,* 3: 68–70.

3. TNA, ADM 1/506, p. 451, Burdett to Paget, 29 June 1814; W. B. Rowbotham, ed., "Robert Fulton's Turtle Boat," *USNIP* 62 (December 1936), 178.

4. TNA, ADM 1/506, pp. 16–18, Hardy to Cochrane, 12 July 1814; Robert Fraser, "The New South Wales Corps and Their Occupation of Massachusetts during the Anglo-American War of 1812," *Sabretache* 29 (April–June 1988), 6–8; *PFB,* 889–891.

5. TNA, ADM 2/1380, pp. 10–12, Croker to Cochrane, 4 April 1814.

6. See Donald G. Shomette and Fred W. Hopkins Jr., "The Search for the Chesapeake Flotilla," *AN* 43 (1983), 5–19.

7. J. Scott, *Recollections,* 3: 229–235.

8. Ibid., 242.

9. P. Rowley, ed., "Robert Rowley Helps to Burn Washington, D.C.," *MHM* 82 (Fall 1987), 241.

10. Maryland Historical Society Library, Baltimore, MS 1846, John O'Neill Notebook; W. F. P. Napier, *Life and Opinions of General Napier,* 1: 224–225.

11. NLS, Cochrane Papers, 2333, pp. 179–184, Cockburn to Cochrane, 17 July 1814; Lovell, *From Trafalgar to the Chesapeake,* 130–131; "Admiral Cockburn's Plan," *MHM* 6 (1911), 16–19; Ralph Robinson, "New Light on Three Episodes of the British Invasion of Maryland in 1814," *MHM* 37 (September 1942), 273–290.

12. NLS, Cochrane Papers, 2333, pp. 173–178, Cockburn to Cochrane, 17 July 1814; Michael J. Crawford, *Naval War of 1812,* 137–139, 154–157.

13. McKenney, *Memoirs,* 1: 5.

14. Glenn Tucker, *Poltroons and Patriots,* 2: 497–499.

15. *ASP: MA,* 1: 580–582; Brant, *James Madison: Commander-in-Chief,* 284–287.

16. *ASP: MA,* 1: 539, 543–547, 551; *PFB,* 916–920; Henry Adams, *History,* 8: 120–124; Pitch, *The Burning of Washington,* 18–19; Skeen, *Citizen Soldiers,* 133–134.

17. TNA, ADM 1/506, pp. 460–461, 466–469, 504, 596–597, Cochrane to Croker, 18 and 26 July 1814; Cochrane to Senior Officers, 18 July 1814; Cochrane to James Monroe, 18 August 1814; ADM 2/933, p. 210, Croker to Cochrane, 27 August 1814.

18. NMM, Cockburn Papers, "Memoir of Services," 129–130. Morriss, *Cockburn and British Navy in Transition,* 102.

19. LC, Cochrane Papers, Nourse to Cochrane, 17 September and 23 July 1814.

20. *The Times,* 2 August 1814.

21. TNA, ADM 1/507, pp. 101–118, Cockburn to Cochrane, 19, 21, 24, and 31 July, 4 and 8 August 1814; M. J. Crawford, *Naval War of 1812,* 157–171.

22. Lovell, *From Trafalgar to the Chesapeake,* 131–132; George, *Terror on the Chesapeake,* 173–174; Lord, *The Dawn's Early Light,* 51.

23. J. Scott, *Recollections,* 3: 244; Lovell, *From Trafalgar to the Chesapeake,* 167–168.

24. M. J. Crawford, *Naval War of 1812,* 172–173.

25. De Kay, *Battle of Stonington,* 54–57, 59–60.

26. Horsman, *War of 1812,* 159.

27. John Cotton Smith, *Correspondence and Miscellanies,* 284.

28. TNA, ADM 1/507, pp. 24–28, Hardy to Hotham, 12 August 1814, and Hotham to Cochrane, 13 August 1814. See also Richard K. Murdoch, ed., "British Documents on the Stonington Raid," *Connecticut Historical Society Bulletin* 37 (July 1972), 65–72: *PFB,* 892–896.

29. Grace D. Hewitt, "Reminiscences of the War of 1812," *Connecticut Magazine* 12, no. 1 (1908), 122.

30. Cowper, *The King's Own,* 4–6. For details on uniforms see Robert J. Marrion, "The 21st Regiment of Foot, 1814–1815 (Royal North British Fusiliers)," *MCH* 22 (Spring 1970), 24–25; H. Charles McBarron Jr. and Frederick P. Todd, "British 85th (Bucks Volunteers Light Infantry) Regiment, 1814," *MCH* 7 (Spring 1955), 20–21.

31. See "Major-General Robert Ross," in Benjamin Smyth, *History of the XX Regiment,* 340–350; G. N. Wood, "Burning Washington: The Lighter Side of Warfare," *Army Quarterly* 104 (1973–74), 352–357. See also Christopher T. George, "The Family Papers of Maj. Gen. Robert Ross, the Diary of Col. Arthur Brooke and the British Attacks on Washington and Baltimore in 1814," *MHM* 88 (1993), 300–316.

32. TNA, ADM 2/1380, pp. 142–146, Croker to Cochrane, 19 May 1814, and Cochrane to Croker, 23 July 1814; ADM 1/506, pp. 490–493, Malcolm to Croker, 24 July 1814.

33. R. J. Barrett, "Naval Recollections of the Late American War," *JUSI,* pt. 1 (April 1841), 457. In fact only the 4th had extensive Peninsula experience; the 21st Fusiliers had served in the Mediterranean, the 44th was a new battalion with little experience, and the 85th Light Infantry was regarded by veteran units as "young hands," with "subaltern ideas"; Cooke, *Narrative,* 200.

34. Harry Smith, *Autobiography,* 197. For a biography of Smith see Lehmann, *Remember You Are an Englishman.*

35. J. Scott, *Recollections,* 3: 283–284.

36. TNA, ADM 1/506, pp. 598–599, Cochrane to Croker, 2 September 1814.

37. Pack, *Man Who Burned the White House,* 179–181.

38. Chamier, *Life of a Sailor,* 1: 202; Morriss, *Cockburn and British Navy in Transition,* 103–105. For a biography of Gordon see Perrett, *The Real Hornblower;* and Gordon and Gordon, *Letters and Records of Admiral Gordon.* For Parker and his famous grandfather, Admiral Sir Peter Parker, see Dallas, *Biographical Memoir of Sir Peter Parker.* See also Lillian H. Tucker, "Sir Peter Parker: Commander of the H.M.S. *Menelaus* in the Year 1814," *Bermuda Historical Quarterly* 1 (1944), 189–245; *DNB,* 42: 730–731.

39. Chesterton, *Peace, War and Adventure,* 113–114.

40. Pack, *Man Who Burned the White House,* 182–183.

41. Monroe to Madison, 21 August 1814, in *ASP: MA,* 1: 537; Lord, *The Dawn's Early Light,* 30–31. This remains the best overall account of the campaign.

42. *NC* 33 (January–June 1815), 345; J. Scott, *Recollections,* 3: 277–280.

43. *ASP: MA,* 1: 536–542, 560–575.

44. Tuckerman, *Life of John Pendleton Kennedy,* 71–72, 74–75.

45. Margaret B. Smith, *Forty Years of Washington Society,* 98–99.

46. *ASP: MA,* 1: 553–560; H. Adams, *History,* 8: 131–137.

47. Thomas Carter, *Historical Record of the Forty-fourth,* 53.

48. Chesterton, *Peace, War and Adventure,* 126, 135–136; M. J. Crawford, *Naval War of 1812,* 229–231.

49. TNA, ADM 1/506, pp. 602–605, Cockburn to Cochrane, 22 August 1814.

50. NMM, Cockburn Papers, "Memoir of Services," 134–135.

51. Morriss, *Cockburn and British Navy in Transition,* 105–106; Pack, *Man Who Burned the White House,* 13–14; J. Scott, *Recollections,* 3: 282–284. George de Lacey Evans later claimed the credit for having got the army to agree to take particular issue with the essay published in James Ralfe's *Naval Biography of Great Britain,* 3: 257–307. See Evans, *Facts Relating to Capture of Washington,* 17; also criticisms of this account "by an Old Sub," Sir Charles Napier (not to be confused with the soldier of the same name), in "Recollections of the Expedition to the Chespeake," *JUSI,* pt. 1 (1840), 35.

52. See "Winder's Narrative" and "Stansbury Report," in *ASP: MA,* 1: 552–560; Lord, *The Dawn's Early Light,* 59–63.

53. Barrett, *The 85th King's Light Infantry,* 138. For years bibliophiles conducted a medievalists' debate over whether Gleig wrote *A Narrative of the Campaigns* . . . and its companion, *A Subaltern in America,* as both were first published anonymously and differed on minor points. That Gleig's diary formed the basis for both became apparent when Barrett's book was published, where he analyses the diary at length (129–150). See J. A. Every-Clayton, "Who Wrote *A Subaltern in America,*" *Journal of the War of 1812* 3 (Winter 1998), 10–14.

54. PRONI, D.3004, [General] Sir A. Brooke, MS Diary; Codrington, *Memoir,* 1: 318; Burnett, *Rise and Fall of a Regency Dandy,* 225; Philippart, *Royal Military Calendar,* 3: 77; Pitch, *The Burning of Washington,* 80–81.

55. The most detailed estimate puts American forces actually deployed at Bladensburg as 6,370 from a total available of 7,170, and British forces at 2,635 from 4,370 available; H. B. Eaton, "Bladensburg," *JSAHR* 55 (1977), 12. However, an official return gave total British strength as only 4,185 with 3,591 effectives, so even this may be an overestimate; NLS, Cochrane Papers, 2326, "State of the Troops under the Command of Major Gen. Robert Ross, Head Quarters, Benedict, 20 Aug. 1814."

56. George, *Terror on the Chesapeake,* 95–96; Lord, *The Dawn's Early Light,* 116–117; Skeen, *Citizen Soldiers,* 136.

57. H. Smith, *Autobiography,* 198–199; Philippart, *Royal Military Calendar,* 3: 214–216.

58. Barrett, *The 85th King's Light Infantry,* 153.

59. Buchan, *History of Royal Scots Fusiliers,* 170.

60. Marine, *British Invasion of Maryland,* 114.

61. RMM, 7/9/1–17, Captain Mortimer Timpson Memoir, p. 31; M. J. Crawford, *Naval War of 1812,* 189–201, 215–228.

62. TNA, WO 1/141, pp. 31–34, Ross to Bathurst, 30 August 1814; M. J. Crawford, *Naval War of 1812,* 220–226; *ASP: MA,* 1: 529, 548, 579–580; H. Smith, *Autobiography,* 199–200.

63. George, *Terror on the Chesapeake,* 96–102; Lord, *The Dawn's Early Light,* 120–139; Pitch, *The Burning of Washington,* 74–82; Horatio King, "The Battle of Bladensburg: Burning of Washington in 1814," *Magazine of American History* 14 (November 1885), 438–457. The best accounts of the battle are by Walter Lord and Anthony S. Pitch. Liverpool-born Christopher T. George has produced an anglophobic account that relies heavily on Lord and indulges in endless "maybes," "might haves," and "if onlys." He blames Winder and other military leaders for the loss of Washington, but such speculation serves only to deflect the blame for the loss of Washington from those ultimately responsible: the political leadership of Madison and Armstrong.

64. Tuckerman, *Life of John Pendleton Kennedy,* 79–80.

65. *NWR* 6 (27 August 1814), 442–444; *Federal Republican* (Georgetown), 7 January 1815.

66. W. B. Bryan, ed., "Diary of Mrs. William Thornton: Capture of Washington by the British," *Columbia Historical Society Proceedings* 19 (1916), 177.

67. NA, WO 1/141, pp. 31–34, Ross to Bathurst, 30 August 1814; *The Times,* 28 September 1814; Tracy, *The Naval Chronicle,* 255–258.

68. Charles Ball, *Narrative,* 468.

69. J. Scott, *Recollections,* 3: 290; Lord, *The Dawn's Early Light,* 95–96; Pack, *Man Who Burned the White House,* 14–15.

70. John H. Briggs, *Naval Administrations,* 14.

71. J. Scott, *Recollections,* 3: 291; M. J. Crawford, *Naval War of 1812,* 207–208; Hulbert Footner, *Sailor of Fortune,* 284–285; George, *Terror on the Chesapeake,* 102; Louis A. Norton, *Joshua Barney,* 179–182; Pitch, *The Burning of Washington,* 83–84. The King's Own, 21st Fusiliers, and the 85th Light Infantry all claim to have secured his person

(Buchan, *History of Royal Scots Fusiliers,* 171; Barrett, *The 85th King's Light Infantry,* 155; Cowper, *The King's Own,* 9). He died on 1 December 1818 from bilious fever associated with his wound. The bullet was buried too deeply to be removed; Shomette, *Tidewater Time Capsule,* 94.

72. TNA, WO 1/141, p. 45, Ross to Bathurst, 30 August 1814; Pitch, *The Burning of Washington,* 85; Burrows, *The Essex Regiment,* 39–41; T. Carter, *Historical Record of the Forty-fourth,* 55; Cowper, *The King's Own,* 7–8; Nicolas, *Historical Record of Royal Marine Forces,* 279–281; James R. Arnold, "The Battle of Bladensburg," *Columbia Historical Society Proceedings* 37 (1937), 145–168.

73. René Chartrand, ed., "An Account of the Capture of Washington, 1814," *MCH* 37 (Winter 1985), 185.

74. PRONI, D.3004, [General] Sir A. Brooke, MS Diary.

75. D. T. Madison, ed., "At a Perilous Moment Dolley Madison Writes to Her Sister," *Madison Quarterly* 4 (January 1944), 28; Allen C. Clarke, *Life and Letters of Dolley Madison,* 125–203. In fact, Dolley's original letter no longer exists, and the story was based on a transcript or extracts of the letter that Dolley copied from a book, *The National Portrait Gallery of Distinguished Americans,* published in Philadelphia, 1837–1846. Did she rewrite it later, for a broader audience? See David Mattern, "The Famous Letter: Dolley Madison Has the Last Word," *White House History* 4 (1998), 38–43.

76. Pitch, *The Burning of Washington,* 87. In his memoir Barker disputed Dolley's version but appeared to confirm it later to Benson Lossing (*Incidents in the Life of Jacob Barker of New Orleans,* 114; *PFB,* 935). As she wrote to Mary Latrobe on 3 December 1814, Barker was carrying out her instructions that "I sent out the silver (nearly all) and velvet curtains and General Washington's picture"; Anthony, *Dolley Madison,* 230.

77. David Brown, "Diary of a Soldier 1805–1827," *Journal of The Royal Highland Fusiliers (Princess Margaret's Own Glasgow and Ayrshire Regiment)* 8 (June 1973), 77; TNA, WO 1/141, pp. 34–37, 51–52, Ross to Bathurst, 30 August and 1 September 1814; *The Times,* 29 September 1814; Burnett, *Rise and Fall of a Regency Dandy,* 225.

78. TNA, ADM 1/506, pp. 609–612, Cockburn to Cochrane, 27 August 1814.

79. For a description of the early development of the city see Bowling, *Creating the Federal City.*

80. Warden, *Chorographical and Statistical Description of District of Columbia,* 25–26; Constance M. Green, *Secret City,* 33; Sarah A. Wallace, ed., "Georgetown Is Saved from the British!" *Social Studies for Teachers and Administrators* 43 (1952), 233–237.

81. M. J. Crawford, *Naval War of 1812,* 215–220, 318–323.

82. *ASP: MA,* 1: 578–579; Pitch, *The Burning of Washington,* 100–103.

83. Cockburn supposedly asked the assembled soldier delegates: "Shall this harbour of Yankee democracy be burned?" to which they yelled enthusiastic assent. There is scant evidence for this incident, and the story appears to have originated a month later, when the real Congress reconvened. It is included in Ingersoll's *Historical Sketch* (2: 185) but

does not appear in any contemporary newspaper reports or British accounts; G. Tucker, *Poltroons and Patriots,* 2: 556.

84. Neptune, *Life and Adventures,* 65.

85. George, "Family Papers," 305.

86. Pitch, *The Burning of Washington,* 104–110. The volume was donated to the Library of Congress in 1940 after Dr. A. S. W. Rosenbach, a rare book dealer, authenticated Cockburn's handwriting; Pitch, *The Burning of Washington,* 252.

87. J. C. Hildt, ed., "Letters Relating to the Burning of Washington," *South Atlantic Quarterly* 6 (January 1907), 65.

88. M. J. Crawford, *Naval War of 1812,* 208–214; C. B. Judge, "Naval Powder Goes on a Journey: An Episode of the War of 1812," *USNIP* 69 (1943), 1223–28.

89. R. W. Irwin, ed., "The Capture of Washington in 1814 as Described by Mordecai Booth," *Americana* 28 (January 1934), 19.

90. Ewell, *Concise History of the Capture of Washington,* 687.

91. D. Sheldon, "The Burning of Washington," *Magazine of American History* 27 (June 1892), 467.

92. M. Hunter, "The Burning of Washington," *New York Historical Society Bulletin* 8 (October 1925), 82.

93. Buchan, *History of Royal Scots Fusiliers,* 171.

94. Quoted in B. Smyth, *History of the XX Regiment,* 345. Corporal David Brown recorded in his diary that it was a company of 21st Fusiliers that enjoyed the meal; Buchan, *History of Royal Scots Fusiliers,* 171.

95. See W. A. Maguire, "Major General Ross and the Burning of Washington," *Irish Sword* 14 (Winter 1980), 117–128.

96. J. Scott, *Recollections,* 3: 303–304.

97. Lord, *The Dawn's Early Light,* 123; Pitch, *The Burning of Washington,* 118.

98. H. Smith, *Autobiography,* 200.

99. M. B. Smith, *Forty Years of Washington Society,* 109–116.

100. Pitch, *The Burning of Washington,* 119–124.

101. Gales was born at Eckington, near Sheffield, where his father published the Sheffield *Register.* Father and son fled to the United States in 1795, and Joseph set up the *National Intelligencer* in 1810. See Ames, *History of the National Intelligencer;* Howard F. Mahan, "Joseph Gales, the *National Intelligencer,* and the War of 1812" (Ph.D. diss., Columbia University, 1958).

102. Ingersoll, *Historical Sketch,* 2: 189; Pitch, *The Burning of Washington,* 132–133.

103. J. Scott, *Recollections,* 3: 307–308.

104. Ewell, *Concise History of the Capture of Washington,* 661–691; Pitch, *The Burning of Washington,* 111–113.

105. RMM, 7/9/1–17, Captain Mortimer Timpson Memoir, pp. 32–35; M. J. Crawford, *Naval War of 1812,* 223–226.

106. J. Scott, *Recollections,* 3: 312–313.

107. LC, Cockburn Papers, Cockburn to Ewell, 5 February 1815.

108. Lord, *The Dawn's Early Light,* 196–201, 207–210; Pitch, *The Burning of Washington,* 116, 135–137, 144.

109. NLS, Cochrane Papers, 2329, Estimates, p. 79; Auchinleck, *History,* 365; William James, *Naval Occurrences,* 353–354.

110. NMM, Cockburn Papers, "Memoir of Services," 137.

111. Nottinghamshire County Record Office, Nottingham, DD.MM43, William Kirke to father, 13 November 1814; Burnett, *Rise and Fall of a Regency Dandy,* 225.

112. Hansard, *Parliamentary Debates,* 38: cols. 46–47; Hitsman, *Incredible War,* 243–245. On Whitbread's role in the opposition see Dean Rapp, "The Left-Wing Whigs: Whibread, the Mountain and Reform, 1809–1815," *Journal of British Studies,* 21 (1981–82), 35–56. See also BL, Mic.F.232: 21443, "Letters by Major Norman Pringle, Late of The 21st Royal Scots Fusiliers, Vindicating the Character of the British Army, Employed in North America in the Years 1814–15, from Aspersions Cast upon It in Stuart's 'Three Years in America.'"

113. J. Scott, *Recollections,* 3: 301.

15. Baltimore and Fort Erie

1. Henry Adams, *History,* 8: 155–163; Carl Edward Skeen, "Monroe and Armstrong: A Study in Political Rivalry," *NYHSQ* 57 (1973), 120–147.

2. Armstrong to Izard, 12 August 1814, in Izard, *Official Correspondence,* 69; Tompkins, *Public Papers,* 3: 497–498, 523–529, 543–544, 553–555; *PFB,* 965–960, 969–977.

3. PRONI, D.2004/1A/3/8, Ross to Elizabeth Ross, 1 September 1814; Harry Smith, *Autobiography,* 201.

4. TNA, WO 1/141, pp. 13–14, Cochrane to Bathurst, 28 August 1814; Fortescue, *History of British Army,* 10: 147.

5. NLS, Cochrane Papers, 2345, Cochrane to Melville, 3 September 1814; TNA, WO 1/141, pp. 62–66, Cochrane to Bathurst, 2 September 1814.

6. Frank A. Cassell, "Baltimore in 1813: A Study of Urban Defense in the War of 1812," *MA* 33 (1969), 349–361; idem, "Response to Crisis: Baltimore in 1814," *MHM* 66 (1971), 261–287.

7. Pack, *Man Who Burned the White House,* 199–200.

8. Hugh Neel Williams, *Life and Letters of Admiral Napier,* 41–48; James Scott, *Recollections,* 3: 314–315; Tracy, *The Naval Chronicle,* 260–261.

9. C. Napier, "Narrative of the Naval Operations in the Potomac by the Squadron under the Orders of Captain Sir James A. Gordon in 1814," *JUSI,* pt. 1 (March 1833), 475. See also William A. Hoge, "The British Are Coming . . . up the Potomac," *Northern Neck Historical Magazine* 14 (1964), 1269; Peter Rowley, ed., "Robert Rowley Helps to Burn Washington, D.C.," *MHM* 83 (1988), 247–253. To warp a ship is to haul it along by ropes or warps attached to a fixed object.

10. USNA, RG 45/M125/R39, John Rogers to Jones, 9 September 1814; RG 107/M221/R666, General Orders, 17 November 1814; Dyson to Armstrong, 29 August 1814, and Alexandria Council Report, 7 September 1814, in *ASP: MA,* 1: 589–590.

11. Gordon and Gordon, *Letters and Records of Admiral Gordon,* 179–180; "Alexandria Council Report, 7 September 1814," in *ASP: MA,* 1: 591; Gardiner, *Naval War of 1812,* 152–153.

12. TNA, ADM 1/507, pp. 157–160, Gordon to Cochrane and enclosures, 9 September 1814; NMM, Codrington Papers, "Congratulations to Gordon," 19 September 1814; Michael J. Crawford, *Naval War of 1812,* 237–258; Edward Napier, *Life and Correspondence of Admiral Napier,* 76–86; John P. Hungerford to Monroe, 6 September 1814, in Brannan, *Official Letters,* 490–491; *ASP: MA,* 1: 533–534, 591–596, 124–125; Charles G. Muller, "Fabulous Potomac Passage," *USNIP* 90 (May 1964), 84–91; Pitch, *The Burning of Washington,* 157–160, 170–199.

13. TNA, ADM 1/507, pp. 9–10, 12–14, Crease to Cochrane, 1 September 1814; *Maryland Gazette,* 22 December 1814; M. J. Crawford, *Naval War of 1812,* 213–217; George, *Terror on the Chesapeake,* 116–122; Nicolas, *Historical Record of Royal Marine Forces,* 227–228; *PFB,* 945–946.

14. Chamier, *Life of a Sailor,* 1: 207–213. See also Robert J. Barrett, "Naval Recollections of the Late American War," *JUSI,* pt. 1 (April 1841), 455–467, and pt. 2 (May 1841), 13–23.

15. TNA, ADM 1/507, pp. 213–217, 211, Monroe to Cochrane, 6 September 1814, and Cochrane to Monroe, 19 September 1814; ADM 2/1381, p. 35, Barrow to Cochrane, 2 November 1814.

16. TNA, WO 1/141, pp. 27–30, Cochrane to Bathurst, 28 August 1814; ADM 1/506, p. 171, Cochrane to Croker, 17 September 1814.

17. NLS, Cochrane Papers, 2329, Parker to Cochrane, 30 August 1814; 2345, Cochrane to Melville, 17 September 1814.

18. Pitch, *The Burning of Washington,* 180–186. For details of the fort see Lessem and Mackenzie, *Fort McHenry;* and Sheads and Cole, *Fort McHenry and Baltimore's Harbor Defenses;* S. Sidney Bradford, "Fort McHenry: The Outworks in 1814," *MHM* 54 (June 1959), 188–209; Richard Walsh, "Fort McHenry: The Star Fort: 1814," *MHM* 56 (September 1959), 296–304.

19. The flag, measuring 42 feet by 30 feet, was created by Mary Young Pickersgill and her thirteen-year-old daughter Caroline and consisted of fifteen stripes and fifteen stars representing the states, each star being two feet wide. See Sheads, *Guardian of the Star-Spangled Banner;* idem, "U.S. Sea Fencibles at Fort McHenry: 1813–1815," *MCH* 34 (Winter 1982), 159–163; idem, "Defending Baltimore in the War of 1812: Two Sidelights," *MHM* 84 (Fall 1989), 252–257; Barbara K. Weeks, "'This Present Time of Alarm': Baltimoreans Prepare for Invasion," ibid., 259–266; Frank A. Cassell, "Response to Crisis: Baltimore in 1814," *MHM* 66 (Fall 1971), 261–287; William D. Hoyt Jr., "Civilian Defense in Baltimore, 1814–1815," *MHM* 39 (September–December 1944), 199–224, 293–309, and 40 (March–June 1945), 7–23, 137–232.

20. For biographies see Pancake, *Samuel Smith and the Politics of Business;* Cassell, *Merchant Congressman in the Young Republic;* and *DAB,* 9: 341. See also H. Adams, *History,* 8: 166–168; *PFB,* 947–949; Ralph Robinson, "Controversy over the Command at Baltimore," *MHM* 39 (September 1944), 177–198.

21. J. Scott, *Recollections,* 3: 326–327.

22. Lord, *The Dawn's Early Light,* 247–255; Pitch, *The Burning of Washington,* 189–190. See also Anon., "The War of 1812 Battle of the Patuxent (Two Sides of the Same War)," *Calvert Historian* 9 (1994), 7–20.

23. Pack, *Man Who Burned the White House,* 202; Frederick M. Colston, "The Battle of North Point," *MHM* 2 (1907), 111–125; Robert Henry Goldsborough, "Contemporary Report of the Battle of Baltimore," *MHM* 40 (September 1945), 230–232.

24. NMM, Cockburn Papers, "Memoir of Services," 141.

25. Gleig, *Narrative of the Campaigns,* 173–174.

26. PRONI, Ross Papers, Cockburn to Rev. T. Ross, 17 September 1814; M. J. Crawford, *Naval War of 1812,* 280; J. Scott, *Recollections,* 3: 334; William James, *Naval History,* 189. Tradition has credited the fatal shots to two eighteen-year-old privates killed in the ensuing firefight. See Curtis Carroll Davis, *Defenders' Dozen,* 19–21; B. Wheeler Jenkins, "The Shots That Saved Baltimore," *MHM* 77 (December 1982), 362–364; Pitch, *The Burning of Washington,* 198–199.

27. RMM, "Journal of Captain John Robyns RMLI, 1796–1834."

28. David Brown, "Diary of a Soldier 1805–1827," *Journal of the Royal Highland Fusiliers (Princess Margaret's Own Glasgow and Ayrshire Regiment)* 8 (June 1973), 78.

29. Robert Lingel, ed., "The Manuscript Autobiography of Gordon Gallie MacDonald," *BNYPL* 34 (March 1930), 144.

30. J. Scott, *Recollections,* 3: 334.

31. Numbers on both sides are vague. Total British forces were given as 4,419 troops including Royal Marines but not including sailors numbering around 600. American forces seem to have numbered around 3,185; LC, "State of a Division of the Troops under the Command of Colonel Arthur Brooke, 44th Regiment of Foot, Chesapeake, 17th September, 1814"; Cochrane to Croker, 17 September 1814, in T. H. Palmer, *Historical Register,* 4: 206–210; Marine, *British Invasion of Maryland,* 147–148.

32. Christopher T. George, "The Family Papers of Maj. Gen. Robert Ross, the Diary of Col. Arthur Brooke and the British Attacks on Washington and Baltimore in 1814," *MHM* 88 (1993), 310; Philippart, *Royal Military Calendar,* 3: 339–341.

33. Barrett, *The 85th King's Light Infantry,* 169.

34. J. Scott, *Recollections,* 3: 336–340. See also Joseph S. van Why, ed., "Martin Gillette's Letters about the War of 1812," *Connecticut Historical Society Bulletin* 23 (July 1958), 81–84; and Hanna, *History of Life and Services of Samuel Dewees,* 340–358.

35. TNA, WO 1/141, pp. 75–84, 91–98, Cockburn to Cochrane, 15 September 1814, and Brooke to Bathurst, 17 September 1814; Thomas Carter, *Historical Record of the Forty-fourth,* 58, 168–174; Cowper, *The King's Own,* 19–21; George, *Terror on the Chesapeake,*

138–145; Pitch, *The Burning of Washington,* 200–203; John L. Sanford, "The Battle of North Point," *MHM* 24 (1929), 356–365. See also Earl S. Pomeroy, "The Lebanon Blues in the Baltimore Campaign, 1814: Extracts from a Company Orderly Book," *MA* 12 (1948), 168–174.

36. George, *Terror on the Chesapeake,* 146; Marine, *British Invasion of Maryland,* 167–169; Pitch, *The Burning of Washington,* 205–210; Sheads, *Rocket's Red Glare,* 91–103. See also Robert J. Barrett, "Naval Recollections of the Late American War," *JUSI,* pt. 1 (March 1841), 463; George Armistead, "Official Report on the Bombardment of Fort McHenry," *Patriotic Marylander* 1 (September 1914), 20–23; Dagg, *Autobiography of John L. Dagg,* 14–16; Franklin R. Mullaly, "'The Battle of Baltimore' Fort McHenry: 1814," *MHM* 54 (March 1959), 61–103; Scott S. Sheads, ed., "'Yankee Doodle Played': A Letter from Baltimore, 1814," *MHM* 76 (December 1981), 380–382; idem, "A Black Soldier Defends Fort McHenry, 1814," *MCH* 41 (Spring 1989), 20–21; James Piper, "Defense of Baltimore, 1814," *MHM* 7 (December 1912), 375–384.

37. James Stevens, "A Letter Describing the Attack on Fort McHenry," *MHM* 51 (December 1956), 356.

38. J. Scott, *Recollections,* 3: 336.

39. TNA, ADM 1/507, pp. 172–175, Cochrane to Croker, 17 September 1814.

40. George, "Family Papers," 311.

41. Brown, "Diary of a Soldier"; Gordon and Gordon, *Letters and Records of Admiral Gordon,* 180.

42. NMM, Codrington Papers, Codrington to Mrs. Codrington, 12 November and 10 December 1814.

43. M. J. Crawford, *Naval War of 1812,* 278. For biographies of this officer, not to be confused with the soldier of the same name, see E. Napier, *Life and Correspondence of Admiral Napier;* H. N. Williams, *Life and Letters of Admiral Napier; DNB,* 40: 151–156.

44. George, *Terror on the Chesapeake,* 154–156; W. James, *Naval History,* 320; Marine, *British Invasion of Maryland,* 177–181; Nicolas, *Historical Record of Royal Marine Forces,* 284–285; Pitch, *The Burning of Washington,* 212–215.

45. TNA, WO 1/141, Official Return, 1 September 1814; Glenn Tucker, *Poltroons and Patriots,* 2: 585–590; Lord, *The Dawn's Early Light,* 239–242; Franklin R. Mullaly, "A Forgotten Letter of Francis Scott Key," *MHM* 55 (December 1960), 359–360. For biographies of Key, see Sam Meyer, *Paradoxes of Fame;* and Weybright, *Spangled Banner.* For Beanes see Caleb Clarke Magruder Jr., "Dr. William Beanes, the Incidental Cause of the Authorship of the Star-Spangled Banner," *Records of the Columbia Historical Society* 22 (1915), 207–224.

46. For the full story see Kroll, *By the Dawn's Early Light;* Sonneck, *Report on "The Star-Spangled Banner";* J. Henry Francis, "The Star-Spangled Banner: How and Why It Came to be Written," *West Virginia History* 3 (July 1942), 305–313; William Lichtenwanger, "The Music of 'The Star-Spangled Banner,' from Ludgate Hill to Capitol Hill," *Quarterly Journal of the Library of Congress* 34 (July 1977), 136–170; John A. Kouwenhoven

and M. Patten Lawton, "New Light on 'The Star-Spangled Banner'?" *Musical Quarterly* 23 (1937), 198–200. John Stuart Skinner witnessed the events that led to the poem. Apparently he and Scott Key watched the bombardment of Fort McHenry from their packet, not from the admiral's flagship; John Stuart Skinner, "Incidents of the War of 1812," *MHM* 32 (December 1937), 340–347. See also Tyler, *Memoir of Roger Brooke Taney,* 104–119.

47. Royal Navy Museum, Portsmouth, 1995-48, Bluett Dairy, pp. 35–36.

48. Barrett, *The 85th King's Light Infantry,* 171.

49. NLS, Cochrane Papers, 2574, Liverpool to Cochrane, 28 September 1814, and Melville to Cochrane, 25 October 1814.

50. NAM, 2002-02-729, Memoir by Major Peter Bowlby. De Lacey Evans died a general.

51. Pack, *Man Who Burned the White House,* 206–209.

52. Joseph A. Whitehorne, *The Battle for Baltimore,* 196–197.

53. For Power see Philippart, *Royal Military Calendar,* 2: 115–116. For Kempt see *DNB,* 31: 191–192.

54. Prevost to Bathurst, 5 August 1814, in *SBD,* 3: 345.

55. Barbuto, *Niagara, 1814,* 246.

56. AO, MU 2052, Harvey Papers, District General Order, Fort Erie, 5 August 1814; *DHC,* 2: 427.

57. John F. Horton, ed., "An Original Narrative of the Niagara Campaign of 1814," *Niagara Frontier* 46 (1964), 23–25; Cullum, *Campaigns,* 272.

58. Graves, *Merry Hearts,* 189; USNA, RG 152/K-2, Court Martial of Brig. Gen. E. P. Gaines, 1816; *PFB,* 839.

59. *DAB,* 4: 92–93.

60. Graves, *"Where Right and Glory Lead!"* 214–216; J. A. Whitehorne, *While Washington Burned,* 56–57. See also B. P. Hughes, "Siege Artillery in the 19th Century," *JSAHR* 60 (1982), 129–139.

61. TNA, CO 42/157, p. 134, Drummond to Prevost, 4 August 1814; Dobbs to Yeo, 13 Augsut 1814, in *DHC,* 1: 135; M. J. Crawford, *Naval War of 1812,* 588–591; W. James, *Naval History,* 492; Roosevelt, *Naval War of 1812,* 336–337; William Kingsford, *History of Canada,* 8: 495.

62. TNA, CO 42/157, p. 146, Drummond to Prevost, 13 August 1814; Dunlop, *Recollections of the American War,* 64–67.

63. Cruikshank, *Siege of Fort Erie,* 8; Carl M. Guelzo, "Fort Erie: High Point in a Low War," *Military Review* 38 (January 1959), 9.

64. Drummond to Prevost, 12 August 1814, and Prevost to Drummond, 26 August 1814, in *DHC,* 1: 132, 174.

65. Secret Order, 14 August 1814, in *DHC,* 1: 139–141.

66. LAC, RG 8 I C685, p. 90, Instructions to Lt. Col. Fischer, 14 August 1814; Dunlop, *Recollections of the American War,* 70.

67. LAC, RG 8 I C685, p. 83, "Arrangement for the Attack on Fort Erie, 14 August 1814."

68. J. A. Whitehorne, *While Washington Burned,* 59. See also idem, "The Battle of Fort Erie: Reconstruction of a War of 1812 Battle," *Prologue* 22 (Summer 1990), 129–148.

69. John D. Martin, "The Regiment De Watteville: Its Settlement and Services in Upper Canada," *OHSPR* 57 (1960), 22–23; J. A. Whitehorne, *While Washington Burned,* 61–62.

70. LAC, RG 8 I C685, p. 86, Fischer to Harvey, 15 August 1814; Gaines to Armstrong, 26 August 1814, in Brannan, *Official Letters,* 99–400; John C. Fredriksen, ed., "The Memoirs of Jonathan Kearsley: A Michigan Hero from the War of 1812," *IMHJ* 10 (October 1985), 12–13.

71. Cruikshank, *Siege of Fort Erie,* 156.

72. Anon., "The Siege of Fort Erie," *United States Military Magazine* 2 (March 1840), 65. See also "Reminiscences of the Campaign of 1814 on the Niagara Frontier," *Historical Magazine* 2 (September 1873), 133; J. C. Fredriksen, ed., "Chronicle of Valor: The Journal of a Pennsylvania Officer in the War of 1812," *Western Pennsylvania Historical Magazine* 67 (July 1984), 243–284.

73. J. A. Whitehorne, *While Washington Burned,* 63.

74. Donald E. Graves, "William Drummond and the Battle of Fort Erie," *CMH* 1, nos. 1–2 (1992), 25–43.

75. Dunlop, *Recollections of the American War,* 84; Horton, "Original Narrative," 29–30; Anon., "War of 1812–15: Reminiscences of a Veteran Survivor," *Geneva* (N.Y.) *Gazette,* 29 November 1878.

76. Graves, *Merry Hearts,* 190.

77. Horton, "Original Narrative," 29.

78. Graves, *Merry Hearts,* 190.

79. Anon., "Attack on Fort Erie," *Port Folio* 1 (February 1816), 105; John Norton, *Journal,* 362.

80. William H. Merritt, *Journal,* 69.

81. TNA, CO 42/157, pp. 148–155, Drummond to Prevost, 15 August 1814 and enclosure; *SBD,* 3: 185–188, 190–191, 209–212; E. A. Cruikshank, "Drummond's Night Assault upon Fort Erie, August 15–16, 1814," in Zaslow, *Defended Border,* 154–164; Donald E. Graves, ed., "The Assault on Fort Erie, 15 August 1814: A New Le Couteur Letter from the War of 1812," *Camp Stew* 8 (1996), 1–4; Dunlop, *Recollections of the American War,* 81–87; Hitsman, *Incredible War,* 232; Squires, *The 104th Regiment of Foot,* 166.

82. BECHS, "Biography of Jarvis Hanks, Eleventh Infantry," pp. 27–28.

83. USNA, RG 107/M221/R61, Gaines to Armstrong, 23 August 1814; Ripley to Gaines, 17 August 1814, and McMahon to Jarvis, 22 August 1814, in *DHC,* 1: 156, 167; Brannan, *Official Letters,* 390–392; Edmund P. Gaines, "General Edmund P. Gaines's Official Report of the Battle of Fort Erie, August 15, 1814," *PMHB* 21, no. 2 (July 1897), 263–266; *PFB,* 832–835.

84. LAC, RG 8 I C685, p. 101, Drummond to Prevost, 16 August 1814; TNA, CO 43/23, p. 269, Bathurst to Prevost, 15 October 1814.

85. Anon., "The Assault on Fort Erie, or, Two Ways of Telling a Story," *JUSI,* pt. 3 (September 1841), 429.

86. Hitsman, *Incredible War,* 232.

87. Ibid., 250, 253. For biographical details of Robinson see *DNB,* 17: 11–13.

88. TNA, WO 1/735, pp. 77, 167, 219, 471, Keith to Croker, 17 and 31 May, 2 June 1814; Schonberg to Croker, 22 August 1814.

89. Prevost to Bathurst, 27 August 1814, in *DHC,* 1: 179–180.

90. Townsend, *HMS St. Lawrence,* 12–13; C. P. Stacey, ed., "Upper Canada at War: Captain Armstrong Reports," *OH* 48 (Winter 1956), 40; M. J. Crawford, *Naval War of 1812,* 665–666.

91. Hurd, *History of Norfolk County, Massachusetts,* 864. See also C. Charles Smith, ed., "Memoirs of Colonel Thomas Aspinwall," *MHSP* 3 (1891), 30–81; and Isabell O'Reilly, ed., "A Hero of Fort Erie: The Correspondence of Lt. P. Macdonough," *PBHS* 5 (1902), 63–93.

92. Drummond to Prevost, 18 August 1814, in *SBD,* 3: 194–195. For a study of the problems affecting both sides see Kenneth McIntyre Stickney, "Logistics and Communications in the 1814 Niagara Campaign" (Master's thesis, University of Toronto, 1976).

93. J. A. Whitehorne, *While Washington Burned,* 65–76.

94. Drummond to Yeo, 18 August 1814, in *DHC,* 1: 182; Malcomson, *Lords of the Lake,* 297.

95. J. Norton, *Journal,* 365.

96. Barbuto, *Niagara, 1814,* 265. For Stovin see Philippart, *Royal Military Calendar,* 2: 40.

97. Graves, *Merry Hearts,* 195; AO, Harvey Papers, Harvey to Baynes, 6 August 1814; *DHC,* 1: 194; 2: 445.

98. LAC, RG 8 I C685, p. 179, Drummond to Prevost, 8 September 1814.

99. Hitsman, *Incredible War,* 233; Graves, *"Where Right and Glory Lead!"* 222–223.

100. Brown to Armstrong, 19 August 1814, and "Memoranda," in *DRINP,* 67, 89–91; Brown to Monroe, 29 September 1814, and Return of the Left Division, 31 August 1814, in *DHC,* 2: 211, 442; Horton, "Original Narrative," 34; LC, Jesup Papers, "Memoir," p. 16.

101. Hitsman, *Incredible War,* 234.

102. LAC, CO 42 C128-2, p. 271, De Watteville to Drummond, 19 September 1814; Brown to Tompkins, 20 September 1814; Porter to Brown, 23 September 1814; and Brown to Monroe, 29 September 1814, in *DHC,* 1: 207–208, 211.

103. TNA, CO 42/157, pp. 219–226, Drummond to Prevost, 19 September 1814.

104. J. P. Harmon, "War of 1812," *VQ* 21 (January 1953), 50.

105. Mullaly, *The South Lancashire Regiment,* 94; Jarvis, *Historical Record of Eighty-second Regiment,* 60–61; Charles Lethbridge Kingsford, *Story of The Royal Warwickshire Regiment,* 81–82.

106. Anon., "The Sortie from Fort Erie," *United States Military Magazine* 1 (February 1840), 6.

107. H. Winston Johnston, *The Glengarry Light Infantry,* 154–163.

108. TNA, CO 42/157, pp. 164–167, 219–220, 225–226, Robinson to Prevost, 27 August 1814, and Drummond to Prevost, 19 September 1814; Berton, *Flames across the Border,* 348–356; *Historical Record of the King's Liverpool Regiment,* 101–102; George W. Holley, "The Sortie from Fort Erie 1814," *Magazine of American History* 6 (June 1881), 401–413.

109. Eber D. Howe, "Recollections of a Pioneer Printer," *PBHS* 9 (1906), 401.

110. LAC, RG 8 I C685, p. 261, Drummond to Prevost, 21 September 1814.

111. USNA, RG 107/M221/R59, Porter to Brown, 22 September 1814, and Brown to Secretary of War, 29 September 1814.

112. LAC, RG 8 I C686, p. 19, Drummond to Prevost, 11 October 1814.

113. TNA, CO 42/355, p. 127, Drummond to Bathurst, 20 November 1814.

114. Malcomson, *Lords of the Lake,* 305–309.

115. S. H. F. Johnston, *History of The Cameronians,* 223–224.

116. M. J. Crawford, *Naval War of 1812,* 617–624.

117. Izard to Monroe, 16 October 1814, in *DHC,* 2: 254; Izard to Monroe, 28 September and 2 November 1814, in Izard, *Official Correspondence,* 92, 110.

118. H. W. Johnston, *The Glengarry Light Infantry,* 164–168.

119. Graves, *Merry Hearts,* 208; LAC, RG 8 I C686, p. 34, Drummond to Prevost, 18 October 1814; Harvey to Myers, 18 October 1814, in *DHC,* 2: 258.

120. LAC, RG 8 I C686, p. 70, Myers to Drummond, 19 October 1814; Bissell to Izard, 22 October 1814, in *DRINP,* 270–272; Graves, *Merry Hearts,* 208–210; Lewis Einstein, ed., "Recollections of the War of 1812 by George Hay, Eighth Marquis of Tweedale," *AHR* 32 (October 1926), 77; Heidler and Heidler, *Encyclopedia of War of 1812,* 127–128.

121. USNA, RG 107/M221/R62, Izard to Secretary of War, 8 November 1814.

122. William E. Horner, "Surgical Sketches: A Military Hospital at Buffalo, New York, in the Year 1814," *Medical Examiner and Record of Medical Science* 16 (December 1852), 762. See also Alan J. Ferguson, "Congressional Medals for Service in 1814," *MCH* 34 (Spring 1982), 37–39.

123. Drummond to Prevost, 21 and 24 September, Prevost to Bathurst, 11, 18 October 1814, and Izard to Monroe, 16 October and 8 November 1814, in *DHC,* 1: 225, 228, 245–246, 254–256, 298; Drummond to Prevost, 10 and 15 October, 5 November 1814, in *SBD,* 3: 208–210, 217–218, 239–244; TNA, CO 42/157, p. 200, Prevost to Bathurst, 18 October 1814; Barbuto, *Niagara, 1814,* 309.

16. Plattsburgh

Epigraph: "The Battle of Plattsburgh" is attributed to Miner Lewis of Mooers Forks, N.Y., who wrote out the words on chips of wood as he was logging. Stan Ransom recorded a version on *The Connecticut Peddler: Music from the War of 1812* (Cadyville, N.Y.: BMI, 2001).

1. Hickey, *War of 1812,* 217, 266; Mahan, *Sea Power,* 2: 214.

2. LAC, MG 11 A151, Sherbrooke to Bathurst, 18 September 1814.

3. Hitsman, *Incredible War,* 239.

4. TNA, WO 1/656, pp. 151–152, Duke of York to Bathurst, 2 August 1813.

5. Roosevelt, *Naval War of 1812,* 185–186; Kenrick, *Story of The Wiltshire Regiment,* 44. For Gosselin see Philippart, *Royal Military Calendar,* 2: 64.

6. See George Clark, "Military Operations at Castine, Maine," *Worcester Society of Antiquity* 18 (1899), 18–38; D. C. Harvey, "The Halifax-Castine Expedition," *Dalhousie Review* 18 (1938–39), 207–213; Barry J. Lohnes, "A New Look at the Invasion of Eastern Maine, 1814," *Maine Historical Society Quarterly* 15 (Summer 1975), 4–29; Edgar Erskine Hume, ed., "Letters Written during the War of 1812 by the British Naval Commander in American Waters," *WMQ,* 2d ser., 19 (1930), 294–295.

7. Denison, *Old Ironsides and Old Adams,* 47; Morris to Jones, 20 September 1814, *NWR* 7 (6 October 1814), 62–63; Charles Morris, *Autobiography,* 60–64.

8. Moses Smith, *Naval Scenes,* 49.

9. G. F. G. Stanley, "British Operations in the Penobscot in 1814," *JSAHR* 19 (1940), 171–172, 175.

10. LAC, MG 11 A151, Pilkington to Sherbrooke, 14 September 1814, and Capitulation of Machias, 13 September 1814.

11. TNA, ADM 1/506, pp. 263, 539–540, Griffith to Croker, 25 August and 17 September 1814; ADM 1/507, pp. 128–137, 304–307, Griffith to Croker 3, 9, 11, and 27 September 1814; Parker to Griffith, 14 September 1814; ADM 1/508, pp. 28–32, Barrie to Griffith, 3 September 1814; *PFB,* 896–903; Everard, *History of Thos. Farrington's Regiment,* 344–347.

12. TNA, ADM 1/506, p. 59, Griffith to Croker, 25 August 1814; ADM 1/507, p. 304, Griffith to Croker, 27 September 1814; Hitsman, *Incredible War,* 246–248; Williamson, *History of Maine,* 2: 640–654.

13. William Kirby, "A New England Town under Foreign Martial Law," *New England Magazine* 14 (1894), 685–695; Hickey, *War of 1812,* 225–227; Mahan, *Sea Power,* 2: 297.

14. See Reginald Horsman, "Nantucket's Peace Treaty with England in 1814," *New England Quarterly* 54 (1981), 180–198.

15. TNA, ADM 1/507, pp. 249–261, 453–459, Cochrane to Croker, 5 October 1814; Hotham to Cochrane, 29 August and 9 October 1814; Nantucket Committee to Hotham, "Declaration of Neutrality, 23 August 1814"; WO 1/142, pp. 143–148, 425, 427–429, Messrs Chace, Parker, and Mitchell to Hotham, 15 September and encl., vice versa, 22 September 1814; Charles Andrews, *The Prisoners' Memoirs,* 145; William Ballard, "Castine, October 1 1814," *Bangor Historical Magazine* 2 (1996), 45–51.

16. Gwyn, *Frigates and Foremasts,* 128–149; Boileau, *Half-Hearted Enemies,* 29–30.

17. TNA, ADM 1/506, pp. 274–276, Coote to Capel, 9 April 1814; USNA, RG 45/M221/R57, Jones to Armstrong, 9 April 1814; William James, *Naval History,* 473; Mahon, *War of 1812,* 259.

18. TNA, ADM 1/508, p. 274, Cochrane to Griffith and Hotham, 5 January 1815.

19. For a biography of Boyle see Fred W. Hopkins Jr., *Tom Boyle;* Maclay, *History of American Privateers,* 279–300; Coggeshall, *History of American Privateers,* 162, 358, 362–363, 366, 368–369. See also Frank F. White, ed., "The Comet Harasses the British," *MHM* 53 (December 1958), 295–315; "Log of the Chasseur: Journal of the Private Armed Brig Chasseur, Thomas Boyle Commanding," *MHM* 1 (June–September 1906), 165–180, 218–240; Cranwell and Crane, *Men of Marque,* 125–151, 235–246. For some first-hand descriptions of privateering, see Cuffe, *Narrative,* 7–12; George A. Nelson, ed., "A First Cruise of the American Privateer Harpy," *AN* 1 (April 1941), 116–22; Nicholas, *Twenty Years before the Mast,* 107–140; Little, *Life on the Ocean,* 194–245; Neal, *East by Sea and West by Rail,* 75–115.

20. TNA, ADM 1/508, pp. 453–454, Lloyd to Brown, 28 September 1814; *NWR* 7 (17 December 1814), 253; Roosevelt, *Naval War of 1812,* 187–188; Forester, *Naval War of 1812,* 86. This amounted to something of a redemption for the *General Armstrong,* which had an unhappy earlier history. See Harold A. Mouzon, "The Unlucky *General Armstrong,*" *AN* 15 (January 1955), 59–80; William S. Dudley, *Naval War of 1812,* 2: 62–68.

21. See Chapelle, *Fulton's "Steam Battery";* Hutcheon, *Robert Fulton,* 120–124, 129–238; W. S. Dudley, *Naval War of 1812,* 2: 210–212; David B. Tyler, "Fulton's Steam Frigate," *AN* 6 (October 1946), 253–274.

22. Dickinson, *Robert Fulton, Engineer and Artist,* 260–264; Mahon, *War of 1812,* 252–253; "Letters and Documents by or Relating to Robert Fulton," *BNYPL* 13 (September 1909), 579–580; Louis C. Hunter, "The Invention of the Western Steamboat," *JEH* 3 (1943), 201–220.

23. TNA, CO 43/23, pp. 157–159, 163, Bathurst to Prevost, 11 July 1814, and Prevost to Bathurst, 22 August 1814; CO 42/157, p. 19, Prevost to Bathurst, 12 July 1814.

24. TNA, ADM 1/506, pp. 171–172, Prevost to Cochrane, 11 May 1814.

25. See Allan S. Everest, "Alexander Macomb at Plattsburgh, 1814," *New York History* 44 (October 1963), 307–335.

26. TNA, CO 42/23, pp. 150–155, Bathurst to Prevost, 3 June 1814; Everest, *War in Champlain Valley,* 157, 166. The most tendentious interpretation of these orders is by David Fitz-Enz, *The Final Invasion,* in which he stresses they were "secret"—as if government instructions are ever anything else—and ignoring the fact that they have been in the public domain in London and Ottawa since 1910 and were published in Hitsman's *War of 1812* in 1965.

27. Hitsman, *Incredible War,* 250. For Brisbane, who later became governor of New South Wales and after whom the capital of Queensland was named, see *DNB,* 7: 678–681; Philippart, *Royal Military Calendar,* 2: 90.

28. Grattan, *Adventures with the Connaught Rangers,* 333–334.

29. TNA, CO 42/157, p. 156, Prevost to Bathurst, 27 August 1814; Skaggs, *Thomas Macdonough,* 88–92, 98–105.

30. TNA, ADM 1/2737, pp. 183–184, Fisher to Yeo, 30 August 1814.

31. TNA, ADM 1/237, pp. 179, 181, 206, Fisher to Croker, 15 September 1814, and Yeo to Croker, 17 and 29 September 1814; Skaggs, *Thomas Macdonough,* 100–101, 110–111.

32. William Kingsford, *History of Canada,* 8: 531; *The Royal Inniskilling Fusiliers,* 245–246; Knight, *Historical Records of The Buffs,* 418–419.

33. Grattan, *Adventures with the Connaught Rangers,* 50.

34. Hitsman, *Incredible War,* 254–255.

35. Richard A. Preston, ed., "The Journals of Sir F. P. Robinson, G.C.B.," *CHR* 37 (December 1956), 353. See also C. W. Robinson, ed., "The Battle of Plattsburgh, Upper Champlain, Canada, 1814," *Journal of the Royal United Services Institute* 61 (August 1916), 499–522. Passages from Robinson's journals were altered to exonerate Prevost.

36. Ironically, the 19th Light Dragoons, like most British light cavalry, wore dark blue jackets.

37. Mahon, *War of 1812,* 320–321.

38. Knight, *Historical Records of The Buffs,* 420; *PFB,* 862.

39. Macomb to Armstrong, 15 September 1814, in Brannan, *Official Letters,* 418.

40. Meuron, *Le Régiment Meuron,* 211.

41. TNA, CO 42/157, pp. 187–188, Prevost to Bathurst, 11 September 1814; *PFB,* 859–864.

42. Meuron, *Le Régiment Meuron;* UCA, f1001 W88, "Transaction No. 5 of the Women's Canadian Historical Society of Toronto," 10; J. H. Wood, "Plattsburg 1814: Extracts from Diary of Captain, Afterwards Colonel J. H. Wood R.A."

43. Prevost to Downie, 7 September 1814, in *SBD,* 3: 466.

44. Michael J. Crawford, *Naval War of 1812,* 598; Hitsman, *Incredible War,* 257.

45. Prevost to Downie, 8, 9, and 10 September 1814; Downie to Prevost, 7, 8, and 9 September 1814, in *SBD,* 3: 379–386; Brenton, *Some Account of Public Life of Prevost,* 78–83.

46. See Crisman, *The Eagle.*

47. "Abstract of the Crew of His Majesty's Late Ship *Confiance,*" in *SBD,* 3: 480–481; W. James, *Naval History,* 342; Skaggs, *Thomas Macdonough,* 117–123.

48. Wood, "Plattsburg 1814," 11.

49. Skaggs, *Thomas Macdonough,* 112–114.

50. Hitsman, *Incredible War,* 259–260.

51. TNA, ADM 1/2737, pp. 179, 181, 206–207, Fisher to Croker, 15 September 1814, and Yeo to Croker, 17 and 29 September 1814.

52. A. Fitch, "Incident of the Battle of Lake Champlain," *Vermont Historical Society Notes and News* 11 (September 1959), 6.

53. Robertson to Pring, 12 September 1814, in *SBD,* 3: 374.

54. See British Court Martial testimony, in *SBD,* 3: 400–498; M. J. Crawford, *Naval War of 1812,* 607–617; William James, *Naval Occurrences,* 203–206; *ASP: NA,* 1: 309–313; Mahan, *Sea Power,* 2: 355–382; Nicolas, *Historical Record of Royal Marine Forces,* 263–264; Roosevelt, *Naval War of 1812,* 207–220; Tracy, *The Naval Chronicle,* 250–254.

55. J. Stevens, "Vermont Letters," *Vermont Historical Society Proceedings* 6 (March 1938), 19.

56. John Edsall, *Incidents in the Life of John Edsall,* 129.

57. Bickley, *Report on Manuscripts of Bathurst,* 294; Atkinson, *The Dorsetshire Regiment,* 243–244.

58. Hayden, *Historical Record of the 76th "Hindoostan" Regiment,* 105.

59. Robinson, "Battle of Plattsburgh," 507–518.

60. Hayden, *Historical Record of the 76th "Hindoostan" Regiment,* 105; Macomb to Armstrong, 15 September 1814, in Brannan, *Official Letters,* 418; A. Macomb, "The Battle of Plattsburgh," *Journal of the Military Service Institute* 12 (January 1891), 76–79.

61. Meuron, *Le Régiment Meuron,* 212.

62. TNA, CO 42/161, pp. 152–154, "Stores Lost at Plattsburg."

63. The Buffs lost forty-three killed and wounded, and the 58th lost thirty-seven and between them appear to have borne the brunt of the action; Knight, *Historical Records of The Buffs,* 423; Gurney, *History of the Northamptonshire Regiment,* 184; *The Royal Inniskilling Fusiliers,* 248.

64. USNA, RG 107/M221/R64, Macomb to Monroe, 12 and 15 September 1814; Prevost to Bathurst, 22 September 1814, in *SBD,* 3: 364–366; Everest, *War in Champlain Valley,* 185–190; Hayden, *Historical Record of the 76th "Hindoostan" Regiment,* 105; Knight, *Historical Records of The Buffs,* 423; H. M. Walker, *History of The Northumberland Fusiliers,* 343–344.

65. Wood, "Plattsburg 1814," 13.

66. Prevost to Bathurst, 22 September 1814, in *SBD,* 3: 364–366.

67. TNA, CO 42/157, pp. 209–211, Prevost to Bathurst, 22 September 1814; Wellington to Liverpool, 9 November 1814, in Wellesley, *Despatches, Correspondence and Memoranda,* 9: 425–426.

68. Mahon, *War of 1812,* 327.

69. Wood, "Plattsburg 1814," 15–16.

70. Yeo to Croker, 24 September 1814, in *SBD,* 3: 377; Loftus, *My Youth by Sea and Land,* 2: 125–126. The American ships were in a very bad way; Stahl, *The Battle of Plattsburg,* 118.

71. Cockburn to Sandys, 20 October 1814, and Pring to Yeo, 17 September 1814, in *SBD,* 3: 336–337, 385–391; NMM, Codrington Papers, Codrington to Mrs. Codrington, 28 September and 2 October 1814; *The Letters of Veritas,* 89, 108, 110, 118–119, 121–122; LAC, RG 8 I C680, p. 362, "Heriot on Canada War"; Brenton, *Some Account of Public Life of Prevost,* 146–175.

72. WLC, Goulburn Papers, Bathurst to Henry Goulburn, 1 September 1814; Wellington to Bathurst, 30 October 1814, in Bickley, *Report on Manuscripts of Bathurst,* 302; G. S. Graham, "Views of General Murray on the Defense of Upper Canada, 1815," *CHR* 34 (1953), 158n; Dudley Mills, "The Duke of Wellington and the Peace Negotiations at Ghent in 1814," *CHR* 2 (1921), 22.

73. TNA, ADM 1/1381, p. 74, Croker to Yeo, 12 December 1814; CO 42/161, pp. 71, 170–179, 180–184, Prevost to Bathurst, 11 and 24 May 1815, and "Prevost vs. Kay," *Quebec*

Gazette, 30 March 1815; NMM, Codrington Papers, Codrington to Mrs. Codrington, 28 September and 2 October 1814; Brenton, *Some Account of Public Life of Prevost,* 146–175; *The Letters of Veritas,* 89, 108, 110, 118–119, 121–122; *SBD,* 3: 385–391, 393; Mahan, *Sea Power,* 2: 367–373; Fortescue, *History of British Army,* 10: 126–133.

74. Wellington to Murray, 22 December 1814, in Wellesley, *Dispatches of Wellington,* 12: 224.

75. Engelman, *The Peace of Christmas Eve,* 88–89, 92–95, 106, 112–114. See Stephen R. Graubard, "Castlereagh and the Peace of Europe," *Journal of British Studies* 3 (1963–64), 79–87.

76. Brown University, Russell Papers, Russell to John L. Lawrence, 7 October 1814.

77. Beeler, *British Naval Policy,* 53.

78. DNB, 21: 352–354; DCB, 6: 252–253; John Marshall, *Royal Naval Biography,* 1: 74–86; Ralfe, *Naval Biography,* 1: 82–90.

79. For biographies see Jenkins, *Henry Goulburn; DNB,* 23: 62–66. See also Wilbur D. Jones, ed., "A British View of the War of 1812 and the Peace Negotiations," *MVHR* 45 (December 1958), 481–487.

80. BL, Liverpool Papers, 38365, "Heads of a Reply to American Commissioners," n.d., "Memo on the United States," fol. 153; 382259, pp. 91–102, Arbuthnot to Liverpool, 2 September 1814; *Quebec Mercury,* 15 November 1814; Gash, *Lord Liverpool,* 110–111.

81. Henry Adams, *History,* 9: 1–17; Perkins, *Castlereagh and Adams,* 39–50, 59–61.

82. Perkins, *Castlereagh and Adams,* 72–73. For British discussion on the issue, see TNA, FO 5/104, "Papers on Impressment of Seamen."

83. John Quincy Adams, *Memoirs,* 3: 3–12; H. Adams, *History,* 9: 17–20.

84. N. Atcheson, "The Compressed View of the Points to Be Discussed in Treaty with the United States of America . . .," *The Pamphleteer* 5 (1815), 105–139.

85. TNA, CO 42/147, pp. 213–214, Prevost to Bathurst, 5 October 1812.

86. *The Kingston Gazette,* 16 October 1813.

87. TNA, CO 43/23, pp. 150–155, Bathurst to Prevost, 3 June 1814.

88. BL, Liverpool Papers, 38259, pp. 51–53, "Draft of Note to American Emissaries," 24 August 1814; Vane, *Correspondence, Despatches of Castlereagh,* 10: 86–89; Michael F. Schener, "Who Should Own the Lakes? Negotiations Preceding the Treaty of Ghent," *IS* 38 (Winter 1982), 236–244; G. G. Hatheway, "The Neutral Indian Barrier State: A Project in British North American Policy, 1754–1815" (Ph.D. diss., Indiana University, 1957), 424–454.

89. WLC, Goulburn Papers, Castlereagh to Commissioners, 28 July 1814; Vane, *Correspondence, Despatches of Castlereagh,* 10: 67–72, 100–101.

90. WLC, Goulburn Papers, American Commissioners to British Commissioners, 24 August 1814; Burt, *United States, Great Britain, and British North America,* 347–348; Engelman, *The Peace of Christmas Eve,* 87.

91. Perkins, *Castlereagh and Adams,* 81–85.

92. TNA, WO 6/2, p. 12, Bathurst to Ross, 6 September 1814.

93. Hickey, *War of 1812,* 287.

94. Kenneth Ross Nelson, "Socio-Economic Effects of the War of 1812 on Britain" (Ph.D. diss., University of Georgia, 1972), 74–82, 102–107.

95. TNA, CO 42/160, pp. 101–104, 107–110, Letters of Assurance Companies, Petitions of Merchants of Liverpool and Bristol, Glasgow and Newark, published 10 and 13 February 1815.

96. *Morning Chronicle,* 2 November 1814; Hickey, *War of 1812,* 217–218.

97. Coggeshall, *History of American Privateers,* 241.

98. Liverpool to Bathurst, 11 September 1814, in Wellesley, *Despatches, Correspondence and Memoranda,* 9: 247; Bickley, *Report on Manuscripts of Bathurst,* 286–289.

99. Editorial, *NC* 32 (July–December 1814), 419; also 137–144; Hume, "Letters," 293.

100. Yonge, *Life and Administration of Robert Banks,* 6: 62–64; Wilbur H. Siebert, "The Exodus of Loyalists from Penobscot and the Loyalist Settlements of Passamaquoddy," *Collections of the New Brunswick Historical Society* 3 (1907–1914), 485–529.

101. Bickley, *Report on Manuscripts of Bathurst,* 294–295; Perkins, *Castlereagh and Adams,* 87–89.

102. Robert S. Allen, *His Majesty's Indian Allies,* 86; Engelman, *The Peace of Christmas Eve,* 175, 186, 200–203. See also Dwight L. Smith, "A North American Neutral Indian Zone: Persistence of a British Idea," *NOQ* 61 (1989), 46–63.

103. Goulburn to Bathurst, 21 October 1814, in Wellesley, *Despatches, Correspondence and Memoranda,* 9: 366.

104. Liverpool to Wellington, 28 October 1814, ibid., 384.

105. Roosevelt, *Naval War of 1812,* 188–189. Madame Charretton having since died, the privateer was purchased by Ordronaux and two other trustees and issued a new letter of marque. Shortly after next sailing she was sighted on 28 December 1814 by the British frigate HMS *Newcastle* (50) and two others and finally caught after an all-day pursuit in a heavy gale. She was sent to England to be surveyed for purchase into the Royal Navy, but was damaged in dry dock and sold off. Her lines were reportedly later used in the design of a famous opium-smuggler, *Red Rover.*

106. See Rammage, *The Militia Stood Alone.*

107. For a biography see James R. Walters Jr., *Alexander James Dallas.*

108. See Fredrick C. Curry, ed., "A Letter from Ogdensburg in 1814," *OH* 41 (1949), 207–212.

109. H. Adams, *History,* 8: 213–215; Dewey, *Financial History,* 132, 139.

110. H. Adams, *History,* 8: 264–280.

111. See Donald R. Hickey, "New England's Defense Problem and the Genesis of the Hartford Convention," *New England Quarterly* 50 (1977), 587–604.

112. H. Adams, *History,* 8: 225.

113. J. S. Martell, ed., "A Sidelight on Federalist Strategy during the War of 1812," *AHR* 43 (1935), 557.

114. Lovell, *From Trafalgar to the Chesapeake,* 166–167.

115. Henry Adams, *Documents Relating to New-England Federalism,* 398, 400–402, 404–406; Morison, *Life and Letters of Harrison Gray Otis,* 95–108.

116. See Dwight, *History of the Hartford Convention;* Banner, *To the Hartford Convention;* Buel, *America on the Brink;* Hickey, *War of 1812,* chap. 10.

117. Morison, *Life and Letters of Harrison Gray Otis,* 130–155; Hickey, *War of 1812,* 278–279. Recent scholarship has considered the international quality of the convention, and suggests that both Republicans and Federalists regarded it as an attempt to negotiate a place for New England in the newly formed international relations triangle that comprised Britain, France, and the United States. See Alison LaCroix, "A Singular and Awkward War: The Transatlantic Context of the Hartford Convention," *American Nineteenth Century History* 6 (2005), 3–32. For a full analysis of party voting during the war see Harry Fritz, "The Collapse of Party: President, Congress and the Decline of Party Action, 1807–1817" (Ph.D. diss., Washington University, 1970); and Donald R. Hickey, "Federalist Party Unity and the War of 1812," *JAS* 12 (1978), 26–31.

118. Horsman, *War of 1812,* 208–209.

17. New Orleans

Epigraph: Jimmy Driftwood was a high school principal and history teacher who loved to sing, play instruments, and write songs to help his students learn about this battle and other historical events. This song proved so popular that it won the 1959 Grammy Award for "Song of the Year," and Johnny Horton's recording of it won the 1959 Grammy for "Best Country and Western Performance"; it was also successfully recorded by Glasgow skiffle-artist Lonnie Donnegan.

1. Hickey, *War of 1812,* 151.

2. NLS, Cochrane Papers, 2328, Woodbine to Cochrane, 9 August 1814; TNA, ADM 1/505, pp. 152–153, Percy to Cochrane, 9 September 1814; Cotterill, *The Southern Indians,* 188.

3. LC, Jackson Papers, reel 10, Jackson to Thomas Pinckney, 18 May 1814; Jackson to Blount, 18 April 1814, in Brannan, *Official Letters,* 327–328; Andrew Jackson, *Correspondence,* 2: 4, 24.

4. Articles of Agreement and Capitulation, 9 August 1814, in U.S. Congress, *American State Papers, II: Indian Affairs,* 2 vols. (Washington, D.C.: Gales and Seaton, 1832–1834), 1: 326–327: Parton, *Life of Andrew Jackson,* 1: 535, 549–560; Owsley, *Struggle for the Gulf Borderlands,* 86–94: Remini, *Andrew Jackson,* 225–232. It would not be the end of Creek suffering; they would be pushed into western areas of Arkansas and Tennessee and finally, in the 1830s, into Oklahoma in starkly diminished numbers. Their extremely rich former lands were quickly opened to white settlers and became a prime source of cotton, the engine of the southern economy, which helped to revive the flagging institution of slavery; Mary E. Young, "The Creek Frauds: A Study in Conscience and Corruption," *MVHR* 42 (1955–56), 411–437.

5. See Nathaniel Millett, "Britain's 1814 Occupation of Pensacola and America's Response: An Episode of the War of 1812 in the Southeastern Borderlands," *FHQ* 84 (Fall 2005), 229–255.

6. J. S. Bassett, ed., "Major Howell Tatum's Journal While Acting Topographical Engineer (1814) to General Jackson Commanding the Seventh Military District," *Smith College Studies in History* 8 (October 1921), 10–52; A. Jackson, *Correspondence,* 2: 31–34, 40–41, 50–51; Latour, *Historical Memoir,* 34 (Latour says the garrison was 130).

7. For the importance of the city and its attitude to the war see W. F. Galpin, "The Grain Trade of New Orleans, 1804–1814," *MVHR* 14 (1927–28), 496–507; Everett S. Brown, ed., "Letters from Louisiana, 1813–1814," *MVHR* 11 (1924–25), 570–579.

8. NLS, 2574 F.3, Draft by Cochrane, 27–28 April 1812; 2345 F.13, Cochrane to Melville, 17 July 1814. In November 1812 Warren had suggested seizing New Orleans only to be rebuffed through lack of resources; NMM, LBK/2, Warren to Melville, 18 November 1812, and Melville to Warren, 19 February 1813; BL, Liverpool Papers, 38249, pp. 194–198; 38251, pp. 330–335; TNA, WO 1/142, pp. 1–3; Wrottesley, *Life and Correspondence of Burgoyne,* 1: 298.

9. WLC, Barrie Papers, Cockburn to Barrie, 16 July 1814; TNA, WO 1/141, pp. 7–14, Coker to Cochrane, 10 August 1814.

10. Latour, *Historical Memoir,* app., pp. vii–viii.

11. John Sugden, "Jean Lafitte and the British Offer of 1814," *Louisiana History* 20 (1979), 159–167. There have been many biographies of Lafitte, some very colourful and not all worth reading. The most recent and most thorough treatment is William C. Davis, *The Pirates Laffite.* See also Arthur, *Jean Laffite;* Charnley, *Jean Lafitte;* de Grummond, *Baratarians and Battle of New Orleans;* Ramsay, *Jean Laffite;* Saxon, *Lafitte the Pirate;* Tallant, *The Pirate Lafitte and the Battle of New Orleans;* Gaspar Cusachs, "Lafitte, the Louisiana Pirate and Patriot" *LHQ* 2 (1919), 418–438; Robert C. Vogel, "Jean Laffite, the Baratarians, and the Battle of New Orleans: A Reappraisal," *Louisiana History* 41 (Summer 2000), 261–276; idem, "Jean Laffite, the Baratarians, and the Historical Geography of Piracy in the Gulf of Mexico," *Gulf Coast Historical Review* 5 (1990), 63–77; and *DAB,* 10: 540–541. Lafitte's memoirs, *The Journal of Jean Laffite,* supposedly written in the form of several letters to his children, was not published until 107 years after his death at his request. Lafitte has also been the subject of two films, both titled *The Buccaneer.* The first, starring Frederick March as Lafitte, was directed by Cecil B. DeMille in 1938. It is far superior to the better-known 1958 effort of Anthony Quinn (who appeared as "Beluche" in the 1938 film), starring Yul Brynner as Jean Lafitte and Charlton Heston as Andrew Jackson, which is less about the battle than about Brynner being pursued by two beauties, Claire Bloom and Inger Stevens.

12. Wilbur S. Brown, *Amphibious Campaign,* 34–35.

13. Saxon, *Lafitte the Pirate,* 30.

14. Stanley Faye, "Privateers of Guadeloupe and Their Establishment in Barataria," *LHQ* 23 (1940), 428–444.

15. Frank Dobie, "The Mystery of Laffite's Treasure," *Yale Review* 18 (September 1938), 124.

16. Maclay, *History of American Privateers,* 332; William S. Dudley, *Naval War of 1812,* 2: 632–634, 639–640.

17. Gayarré, *History of Louisiana,* 4: 303–308.

18. De Grummond, *Baratarians and Battle of New Orleans,* 18–20; Saxon, *Lafitte the Pirate,* 66; Arthur, *Jean Laffite,* 31–33.

19. Caspar F. Goodrich, "Our Navy and the West Indian Pirates," *USNIP* 42 (1916), 1463–75; Stanley Faye, "Privateersmen of the Gulf and Their Prizes," *LHQ* 22 (1939), 1012–94; idem, "Privateers of Guadeloupe and Barataria."

20. Edward A. Parsons, "Jean Lafitte in the War of 1812, a Narrative based on the Original Documents," *Proceedings of the American Antiquarian Society* 50 (October 1940), 216; Stanley Faye, "The Great Stroke of Pierre Lafitte," *LHQ* 23 (1940), 733–826; W. S. Brown, *Amphibious Campaign,* 29–33.

21. LC, reel 62, Jackson Papers, Proclamation, 21 September 1814; Robert C. Vogel, "The Patterson and Ross Raid on Barataria, September 1814," *Louisiana History* 33 (1992), 157–170; Sugden, "Lafitte and the British Offer"; Latour, *Historical Memoir,* app., pp. ix–xiv. See also James D. Little Jr., "The Navy at the Battle of New Orleans," *LHQ* 54 (1971), 18–29.

22. TNA, ADM 1/505, pp. 156–159, Percy to Cochrane, 16 September 1814; WO 1/144, pp. 420–421, "Nicholls Memorial"; Lawrence to Jackson, 15 and 16 September 1814, in Brannan, *Official Letters,* 424–426.

23. Queen's Lancashire Regiment Museum, Preston, "The Autobiography of Sergeant William Lawrence, 40th Regiment of Foot, 1791–1817," p. 58.

24. Cooke, *Narrative,* 121–122.

25. Philippart, *Royal Military Calendar,* 2: 112–113.

26. TNA, WO 6/2, pp. 24–27, Bathurst to Lambert, 5 October 1814, and Bathurst to Pakenham, 24 October 1814; Liverpool to Castlereagh, 21 October 1814, in Wellesley, *Despatches, Correspondence and Memoranda,* 9: 367. For biographical details see *DNB,* 42: 422–423; Philippart, *Royal Military Calendar,* 2: 55–56.

27. Wellesley, *Dispatches of Wellington,* 6: 434.

28. TNA, WO 1/141, pp. 495–501, Bathurst to Ross, 6 September 1814.

29. W. S. Brown, *Amphibious Campaign,* 74–75.

30. For the most thorough study of the campaign as an amphibious operation by a former U.S. Marine Corps general, see W. S. Brown, *Amphibious Campaign,* and his conclusions, 169–180. See also W. L. Ainsworth, "An Amphibious Operation That Failed: The Battle of New Orleans," *USNIP* 71 (February 1945), 193–201.

31. A. Jackson, *Correspondence,* 2: 79–80, 82–83, 86–87.

32. W. S. Brown, *Amphibious Campaign,* 28; Mahon, *War of 1812,* 351n.

33. Gordon and Gordon, *Letters and Records of Admiral Gordon,* 194–195; Bassett, "Tatum's Journal," 65–83; Brannan, *Official Letters,* 451–453.

34. Ruth A. Fisher, ed., "The Surrender of Pensacola as Told by the British," *AHR* 54 (January 1948), 326–329; W. S. Brown, *Amphibious Campaign,* 50–56; Frank L. Owsley, "Jackson's Capture of Pensacola," *Alabama Review* 19 (1966), 175–185.

35. Mark F. Boyd, "Events at Prospect Bluff on the Apalachiola River," *FHQ* 16 (1937), 55–93; "Documents Relating to Colonel Edward Nicholls and Captain George Woodbine in Pensacola in 1814," *FHQ* 10 (1931), 51–54; James W. Covington, "The Negro Fort," *Gulf Coast Historical Review* 5 (1990), 79–91; Dudley W. Knox, "A Forgotten Fight in Florida," *USNIP* 62 (1936), 507–513; Eugene P. Southall, "Negroes in Florida prior to the Civil War," *Journal of Negro History* 19 (1934), 77–87; James Leitch Wright, "A Note on the First Seminole War as Seen by the Indians, Negroes and Their British Advisors," *Journal of Southern History* 34 (1968), 565–575. For a study of the Seminoles see Coe, *Red Patriots.*

36. TNA, ADM 1/505, pp. 167–170, Percy to Cochrane, 16 September 1814; WO 1/144, p. 197, "Memorial of Edward Nicolls"; Latour, *Historical Memoir,* 36–38; Mahan, *Sea Power,* 2: 387–388; A. Jackson, *Correspondence,* 2: 50–51; W. S. Brown, *Amphibious Campaign,* 55, 57.

37. See Huber, *New Orleans as It Was in 1814–15;* Arthur, *Old New Orleans;* W. S. Brown, *Amphibious Campaign,* 68–72; Reilly, *The British at the Gates,* 178–194, 201–207.

38. New Hampshire Historical Society, Concord, Plumer Papers, Windship to William Plumer Jr., 20 March 1814.

39. TNA, ADM 1/508, p. 222, Cochrane to Croker, 7 December 1814; Brenton, *Naval History,* 4: 525–530.

40. TNA, WO 1/141, p. 249, "Proclamation," 5 December 1814; J. H. Leslie, ed., "Artillery Services in North America in 1814 and 1815, Being Extracts from the Journal of Colonel Sir Alexander Dickson K.C.B., Commanding Royal Artillery," *JSAHR* 8 (1929), 84–85.

41. Codrington, *Memoir,* 1: 329.

42. Parton, *Life of Andrew Jackson,* 2: 25–27, 30; Bassett, "Tatum's Journal," 85–87; A. Jackson, *Correspondence,* 2: 101–107.

43. M. James, *Andrew Jackson,* 221; Mahon, *War of 1812,* 353.

44. USNA, RG 107/M221/R63, Jackson to Monroe, 27 December 1814; Brooks, *Siege of New Orleans,* 73–75, 84–87; W. S. Brown, *Amphibious Campaign,* 63–69; Reilly, *The British at the Gates,* 215–216, 220–221.

45. Bassett, "Tatum's Journal," 96–101; A. Jackson, *Correspondence,* 2: 111–112.

46. Mahon, *War of 1812,* 354–355.

47. William James, *Full Account of Military Occurrences,* 354–355; B. E. Hill, *Recollections,* 1: 303, 333.

48. For biographies, see Gene A. Smith, *Thomas ap Catesby Jones;* and Udolpho Theodore Bradley, "The Contentious Commodore: Thomas ap Catesby Jones of the Old Navy, 1788–1858" (Ph.D. diss., Cornell University, 1933). For a detailed account of the action see La Violette, *Sink or Be Sunk!* See also Edwin N. McLellan, "The Navy at the Battle of New Orleans," *USNIP* 50 (1924), 2041–60.

49. TNA, ADM 1/508, pp. 268–269, 364–367, Lockyer to Cochrane, 16 December 1814, and Cochrane to Croker, 28 December 1814; Ap Catesby Jones to Daniel Patterson, 12 March 1815, in Brannan, *Official Letters,* 487–490; Latour, *Historical Memoir,* 57–62; Brooks, *Siege of New Orleans,* 90–97; W. S. Brown, *Amphibious Campaign,* 79–82; Reilly, *The British at the Gates,* 234–235.

50. For a history of this unit see Holmes, *Honor and Fidelity.* See also Matthew Warshauer, "The Battle of New Orleans Reconsidered: Andrew Jackson and Martial Law," *Louisiana History* 39 (1998), 261–291.

51. Henry P. Dart, ed., "Andrew Jackson and Judge D. A. Hall," *LHQ* 5 (1922), 509–570; idem, "Jackson and the Louisiana Legislature, 1814–15," *LHQ* 9 (1926), 221–280; Grace King, trans. and ed., "Marigny's Reflections on New Orleans Campaign," *LHQ* 22 (January 1939), 65; Reilly, *The British at the Gates,* 244–247.

52. Saxon, *Lafitte the Pirate,* 173–175.

53. Latour, *Historical Memoir,* 79; Gayarré, *History of Louisiana,* 4: 411; Edwin H. Carpenter Jr., "Latour's Report on Spanish American Relations in the Southwest," *LHQ* 30 (July 1947), 716. In February 1815 Madison pardoned the Lafitte brothers, and while some of the gang tried to resume their old lifestyle, increased patrols by both Royal and U.S. Navies meant that the age of piracy was over within ten years; Robert C. Vogel, "Jean Lafitte, the Baratarians, and the Historical Geography of Piracy in the Gulf of Mexico," *Gulf Coast Historical Review* 5 (1990), 63–77.

54. Bassett, "Tatum's Journal," 103–106; A. Jackson, *Correspondence,* 2: 115–116.

55. "Lobscouse" was a form of all-in stew common among sailors and has given its name to the Liverpool dialect of English and to those who speak it, "Scousers." Brown's observation also suggests that some aspects of British Army life have changed little in 200 years.

56. David Brown, "Diary of a Soldier 1805–1827," *Journal of the Royal Highland Fusiliers (Princess Margaret's Own Glasgow and Ayrshire Regiment)* 8 (June 1973), 78–79; John Keane, "A Journal of Operations against New Orleans," in Wellesley, *Despatches, Correspondence and Memoranda,* 10: 395–396; Latour, *Historical Memoir,* 78, 82–87; Cooke, *Narrative,* 187–188; Forrest, *The Battle of New Orleans,* 23–28.

57. Gayarré, *History of Louisiana,* 4: 420–421; Latour, *Historical Memoir,* 86–87; Reilly, *The British at the Gates,* 251–253; Alexander Walker, *Jackson and New Orleans,* 126–127.

58. Surtees, *Twenty-five Years in the Rifle Brigade,* 336–338, 340–341; *PFB,* 1028–29; TNA, ADM 1/508, pp. 376–378, Cochrane to Croker, 18 January 1815; Henry Adams, *History,* 8: 337–338.

59. A number of free black units served in defence of the city. See McConnell, *Negro Troops of Antebellum Louisiana;* and Donald E. Everett, "Emigrés and Militiamen: Free Persons of Color in New Orleans, 1803–1815," *Journal of Negro History* 38 (1953), 377–402.

60. H. Hayman, "Some Notes from New Orleans in 1814–5. From the Private Memoranda of an Eye-witness," *United Service Magazine,* n.s., 2 (1891), 412.

61. TNA, WO 1/141, pp. 149–156, 179–181, Keane to Pakenham, 26 December 1814; Jackson to Monroe, 27 December 1814, in A. Jackson, *Correspondence,* 2: 124; A. P. Hayne to Jackson, 10 January 1815, in Brannan, *Official Letters,* 453–455, 457–458; Cooke, *Narrative,* 189–199; Gleig, *Narrative of the Campaigns,* 289–298; Leslie, "Artillery Services," 89–98; Reilly, *The British at the Gates,* 255–258; Remini, *Battle of New Orleans,* 72–82.

62. Brooks, *Siege of New Orleans,* 162–178; Forrest, *The Battle of New Orleans,* 32–37.

63. Henry B. Hamilton, *Historical Records of the 14th (King's) Hussars,* 178; Oatts, *The Emperor's Chambermaids,* 201; Codrington, *Memoir,* 1: 332; Chesterton, *Peace, War and Adventure,* 191–193; Carson I. A. Richie, "The Louisiana Campaign," *LHQ* 44 (January–April 1961), 13–32.

64. TNA, ADM 1/508, pp. 160–163, Cochrane to Croker, 28 December 1814; B. E. Hill, *Recollections,* 1: 327; Reilly, *The British at the Gates,* 284–286; Remini, *Battle of New Orleans,* 90–94.

65. Philippart, *Royal Military Calendar,* 2: 122–123.

66. Brooks, *Siege of New Orleans,* 180–182, 187–189; Keane, "Journal of Operations," 397.

67. Leslie, "Artillery Services," 101–104; B. E. Hill, *Recollections,* 1: 333–334.

68. Latour, *Historical Memoir,* 165–169; Reilly, *The British at the Gates,* 292–294.

69. W. S. Brown, *Amphibious Campaign,* 126–127; Codrington, *Memoir,* 1: 334; Keane, "Journal of Operations," 398–399.

70. Leslie, "Artillery Services," 109–112; Codrington, *Memoir,* 1: 334; B. E. Hill, *Recollections,* 2: 3–4; Bassett, "Tatum's Journal," 120–122; A. Jackson, *Correspondence,* 2: 130; H. Adams, *History,* 8: 358–366; Reilly, *The British at the Gates,* 297–301, 307; Remini, *Battle of New Orleans,* 106–114.

71. Leslie, "Artillery Services," 148–150. See Robert J. Marrion and I. S. Hyman, "7th Regiment of Foot (The Royal Fusiliers), 1815," *MCH* 20 (Winter 1968), 120–122; idem, "43rd (Monmouthshire) Light Infantry, 1814–1815," *MCH* 21 (Summer 1969), 52–54.

72. Parton, *Life of Andrew Jackson,* 2: 36.

73. Buell, *History of Andrew Jackson,* 1: 423; Reilly, *The British at the Gates,* 304–305.

74. Brooks, *Siege of New Orleans,* 191–201; Parton, *Life of Andrew Jackson,* 2: 152–154; Reed M. Adams, "New Orleans in the War of 1812," *LHQ* 17 (1934), 357; Z. F. Smith, "The Battle of New Orleans," *FCHQ* 19 (1904), 66.

75. TNA, WO 1/141, pp. 137–140, Lambert to Bathurst, 10 January 1815.

76. Wheater, *Historical Record of the Seventh,* 145.

77. Captain Harry Jones RE noted in a report made just after the war that the position was "one of the Strongest possible by nature"; Wrottesley, *Life and Correspondence of Burgoyne,* 1: 302–304.

78. Bassett, "Tatum's Journal," 122–124; A. Jackson, *Correspondence,* 2: 132, 164–170.

79. Reilly, *The British at the Gates,* 309–310.

80. NMM, Codrington Papers, "Attack Order," 7 January 1815.

81. Robert J. Marrion, "93rd Highland Regiment, 1814–1815," *MCH* 21 (Winter 1969), 126–128.

82. TNA, WO 1/141, pp. 137–140, Lambert to Bathurst, 10 January 1815; Willoughby Verner, ed., "Diary of a Private Soldier in the Campaign of New Orleans," *Macmillan's Magazine* 77 (March 1898), 321–333.

83. Harry Smith, *Autobiography*, 235.

84. Nolte, *Fifty Years in Both Hemispheres*, 221. Various other accounts of New Orleans by Americans include Anon., "A Contemporary Account of the Battle of New Orleans by a Soldier in the Ranks," *LHQ* 9 (1926), 11–15; idem, "A Massachusetts Volunteer at the Battle of New Orleans," ibid., 30–31; idem, "Journal of an Officer," *DeBow's Review* 16 (June 1854), 641–646; idem, "New Orleans: From the Manuscript of an Eyewitness," *Graham's Magazine* 27 (July 1845), 40–42; George Allen, "A Letter Concerning the Battle of New Orleans," *PMHB* 19, no. 2 (1895), 268–269; Edward A. Parson, ed., "A Letter from the Battle of New Orleans," *LHQ* 32 (January 1949), 225. See also Robert Simpson, "The Battle of New Orleans," *Blackwood's Magazine* 28 (September 1828), 354–357.

85. John Spencer Cooper, *Rough Notes from Seven Campaigns*, 139.

86. Gleig, *Narrative of the Campaigns*, 330–331; Reilly, *The British at the Gates*, 313–314.

87. They wore not kilts and bonnets but tartan trousers and forage caps.

88. Cavendish, *An Reisimeid Chataich*, 44.

89. Leslie, "Artillery Services," 162; Pakenham, *Pakenham Letters*, 258.

90. Cooke, *Narrative*, 240.

91. J. S. Cooper, *Rough Notes from Seven Campaigns*, 142.

92. Latour, *Historical Memoir*, 160.

93. NAM, 2001-09-36, "A Memoir by Major Joseph Hutchison."

94. T. H. Palmer, *Historical Register*, 4: 292; David B. Morgan, "General David B. Morgan's Defense of the Conduct of the Louisiana Militia in the Battle of New Orleans," *LHQ* 9 (January 1926), 16–29; Remini, *Battle of New Orleans*, 158–162.

95. Thomas Carter, *Historical Record of the Forty-fourth*, 60; Cavendish, *An Reisimeid Chataich*, 46; Levinge, *Historical Records of the Forty-third Regiment*, 222–224; Wheater, *Historical Record of the Seventh*, 145–147; Reilly, *The British at the Gates*, 317–326; Remini, *Battle of New Orleans*, 141–152; Tracy, *The Naval Chronicle*, 273–281.

96. Mahon, *War of 1812*, 368.

97. J. S. Cooper, *Rough Notes from Seven Campaigns*, 142.

98. William P. Lawrence, "An Eyewitness of the Battle of New Orleans," *Boston Public Library Quarterly* 9 (July 1957), 160. See also Joseph G. Tregle Jr., "Andrew Jackson and the Continuing Battle of New Orleans," *JER* 1 (1981), 373–393.

99. James Roberts, *Narrative*, 18; Kai Wright, *Soldiers of Freedom*, 47–49.

100. Overton to Jackson, 19 January 1815, in Brannan, *Official Letters*, 464–465; Ewart, *James Ewart's Journal*, 123–124.

101. Queen's Lancashire Regiment Museum, "Autobiography of Sergeant William Lawrence, 40th Regiment of Foot, 1791–1817."

102. Reilly, *The British at the Gates*, 360.

103. NAM, 2001-09-36, "Memoir by Major Joseph Hutchison"; Gleig, *Narrative of the Campaigns,* 187–188; Reilly, *The British at the Gates,* 331–344.

104. Jackson to Monroe, 25 January 1815, in A. Jackson, *Correspondence,* 2: 151; M. James, *Andrew Jackson,* 274–275, 284–286; Latour, *Historical Memoir,* 187–197.

105. Fortescue, *History of British Army,* 10: 176–177.

106. A. Wellesley, "Letter of the Duke of Wellington on the Battle of New Orleans," *LHQ* 9 (January 1926), 8.

107. TNA, WO 1/141, p. 202, Brooke to Bunbury, 28 March 1815; WO 6/2, pp. 479–508, "America and West Indies, 1814"; Chesterton, *Peace, War and Adventure,* 208; B. E. Hill, *Recollections,* 2: 13; T. Carter, *Historical Record of the Forty-fourth,* 64. See "Court-Martial Held at the Royal Barracks, Dublin, for the Trial of Brevet Lieutenant-Colonel Thomas Mullins," *LHQ* 9 (January 1926), 33–110.

18. The Peace of Christmas Eve

1. Kenneth Ross Nelson, "Socio-Economic Effects of the War of 1812 on Britain" (Ph.D. diss., University of Georgia, 1972), 129–144. For a study of the subject of British war financing see P. K. O'Brien, "Government Revenue, 1793–1815: A Study of the Fiscal and Financial Policy in the Wars against France" (Ph.D. diss., Oxford University, 1968).

2. Yonge, *Life and Administration of Robert Banks,* 2: 75.

3. Henry Adams, *History,* 7: 385; Hickey, *War of 1812,* 303.

4. Duffy, *Captain Blakeley and the Wasp,* 222–224.

5. Charles Petrie, *Lord Liverpool and His Times,* 206–207.

6. Wellesley, *Despatches, Correspondence and Memoranda,* 9: 401–402, 404–407, 424–426.

7. C. Petrie, *Lord Liverpool and His Times,* 209.

8. See Dudley Mills, "The Duke of Wellington and the Peace Negotiations at Ghent in 1814," *CHR* 2 (March 1921), 19–32; Yonge, *Life and Administration of Robert Banks,* 2: 54–64.

9. Yonge, *Life and Administration of Robert Banks,* 2: 73.

10. Gash, *Lord Liverpool,* 113.

11. Yonge, *Life and Administration of Robert Banks,* 2: 75–77.

12. Goulburn to Bathurst, 13 December 1814, in Bickley, *Report on Manuscripts of Bathurst,* 316.

13. H. Adams, *History,* 9: 42–52; Perkins, *Castlereagh and Adams,* 117–127.

14. The treaty is given in full in *ASP: FR,* 3: 745–748.

15. WLC, Castlereagh to Commissioners, 28 July 1814, and Goulburn to Bathurst, 30 December 1814; Worthington C. Ford, ed., "Intended Instructions [to the British commissioners at Ghent]," *PMHS* 48 (1914–15), 161; Engelman, *The Peace of Christmas Eve,* 289; Perkins, *Castlereagh and Adams,* 121.

16. TNA, CO 42/157, pp. 242–243, 341, 360, Prevost to Bathurst, 7 October, 16 and 19 November 1814; ADM 2/1381, p. 68, Croker to Owen, 12 December 1814; ADM 1/2738, pp. 81–82, Yeo to Croker, 23 March and 16 May 1815; Drummond to Prevost, 9 November 1814, and Yeo to Drummond, 14 November 1814, in *SBD,* 3: 245–248, 291–292; Malcomson, *Lords of the Lake,* 315–317, 19–22.

17. Field, *Britain's Sea Soldiers,* 301; Fredriksen, *Green Coats and Glory,* 66–67; Morriss, *Cockburn and British Navy in Transition,* 114–116.

18. Lovell, *From Trafalgar to the Chesapeake,* 174.

19. James Scott, *Recollections,* 3: 356–360; Nicolas, *Historical Record of Royal Marine Forces,* 266–267.

20. T. H. Miller, "The Capture of St. Mary's, Georgia, by Admiral Cockburn," *Publications of the Southern History Association* 7 (July 1903), 235.

21. Robert G. Stewart, "The Battle of the Ice Mound, February 7, 1815," *MHM* 70 (1975), 373–378.

22. TNA, WO 1/141, pp. 259–263, Lambert to Bathurst, 14 February 1815 (also pp. 267–268); ADM 1/508, pp. 527–529, Cochrane to Croker, 14 February 1815; J. H. Leslie, ed., "Artillery Services in North America in 1814 and 1815, Being Extracts from the Journal of Colonel Sir Alexander Dickson K.C.B., Commanding Royal Artillery," *JSAHR* 8 (1929), 225–226; Brannan, *Official Letters,* 471–474; Cowper, *The King's Own,* 22; Field, *Britain's Sea Soldiers,* 304; B. E. Hill, *Recollections,* 2: 51–52; Latour, *Historical Memoir,* 207–215; Lovell, *From Trafalgar to the Chesapeake,* 173–174; Nicolas, *Historical Record of Royal Marine Forces,* 228–229; Wheater, *Historical Record of the Seventh,* 148; Wrottesley, *Life and Correspondence of Burgoyne,* 1: 308–310; William S. Coker, "The Last Battle of the War of 1812: New Orleans. No, Fort Bowyer!" *Alabama Historical Quarterly* 43 (1981), 42–63; Edward A. Mueller, "'Fighting Nicolls' of the British Royal Marines," *Pensacola History Illustrated* 5 (Summer 1996), 10–12; Robert Ricketts, "The Men and the Ships of the British Attack Fort Bowyer—February 1815," *Gulf Coast Historical Review* 5 (1990), 7–17.

23. TNA, WO 1/143, pp. 37–43, 53–63, Cochrane to Lambert, 3 February 1815, and Cochrane to Malcolm, 17 February 1815. See Gene A. Smith, "'Our Flag Was Display'd within Their Works': The Treaty of Ghent and Conquest of Mobile," *AR* 52 (January 1999), 3–21.

24. TNA, ADM 1/509, pp. 163, 178, Ramsey to Cockburn, 28 January 1815, and Phillot to Cockburn, 26 February 1815; Nicolas, *Historical Record of Royal Marine Forces,* 287–288. See Bullard, *Black Liberation on Cumberland Island.*

25. Pack, *Man Who Burned the White House,* 211.

26. C. P. Stacey, ed., "An American Plan for a Canadian Campaign: Secretary James Monroe to Major-General Jacob Brown, February 1815," *AHR* 46 (1940–41), 348–358.

27. TNA, ADM 2/1381, pp. 96–97, 101–102, 109–110, Croker to Cochrane, 27 December 1814, and Croker to senior officers in Chesapeake Bay, 27 and 30 December 1814.

28. Edward Napier, *Life and Correspondence of Admiral Napier,* 91–93.

29. See Alan Conrad Aimone, "The Cruise of the U.S. Sloop *Hornet* in 1815," *MM* 61 (1975), 377–384; Gordon K. Harrington, "The American Naval Challenge to the English East India Company during the War of 1812," in Jack Sweetman et al., *New Interpretations in Naval History,* 144–145; Paullin, "The Cruise of the *Peacock,*" in *American Voyages to the Orient,* 19–23.

30. Long, *Sailor-Diplomat,* 50–52.

31. George N. Hollins, "Autobiography of Commodore George Nicholas Hollins, C.S.A.," *MHM* 34 (1939), 279.

32. TNA, ADM 1/508, pp. 387–390, Hayes to Hotham, 17 January 1815.

33. Hollins, "Autobiography," 280.

34. TNA, ADM 1/508, pp. 390–392, 393–394, Hayes to Hotham, 17 January 1815; Hope to Hayes, 15 January 1815; Hotham to Croker, 28 January 1815; Decatur to Crowinshield, 18 January 1815, in Brannan, *Official Letters,* 481–483; Gardiner, *Naval War of 1812,* 164–166; William James, *Naval History,* 527–530; idem, *Naval Occurrences,* 213–219; Nicolas, *Historical Record of Royal Marine Forces,* 234–235; Roosevelt, *Naval War of 1812,* 221–226; Tracy, *The Naval Chronicle,* 267–272.

35. Kurlansky, *Salt,* 238, 244–245; Richard K. Murdoch, "The Battle of Orleans, Massachusetts (1814) and Associated Events," *AN* 24 (1964), 171–182.

36. TNA, ADM 1/1771 (loose), Griffith to Emsworth, 3 July 1815; Stewart to Jones, May 1815, in Brannan, *Official Letters,* 492–494; W. James, *Naval Occurrences,* 228–230; Roosevelt, *Naval War of 1812,* 230–234; Daphne D. Pouchin-Mold, ed., "What It Was Like to Be Shot Up by 'Old Ironsides,'" *American Heritage* 34 (April–May 1983), 65–67.

37. Whipple, *Letters from Old Ironsides,* 21; Lynn W. Turner, "The Last Cruise of Old Ironsides," *American Heritage* 6 (April 1955), 56–61.

38. W. James, *Naval History,* 558; Roosevelt, *Naval War of 1812,* 234–235.

39. Maclay, *History of American Privateers,* 295–300.

40. Gardiner, *Naval War of 1812,* 75; W. James, *Naval Occurrences,* 239–240.

41. W. James, *Naval Occurrences,* 489, 499.

42. Long, *Sailor-Diplomat,* 52–53.

43. Biddle to Secretary of the Navy, 25 March 1815, in *ASP: NA,* 1: 377; Christine F. Hughes, "Lewis Warrington and the USS *Peacock* in the Sunda Strait, June 1815," in William S. Dudley and Michael J. Crawford, *The Early Republic and the Sea,* 117–118; W. James, *Naval Occurrences,* 242–244; Roosevelt, *Naval War of 1812,* 236–240.

44. Long, *Sailor-Diplomat,* 56–58. See also Alan C. Aimone, ed., "The Cruise of the U.S.S. Sloop *Hornet* in 1815," *MM* 61 (November 1975), 377–384.

45. See Nell, *Services of Colored Americans.* This pamphlet tells the story of Richard Seavers, or "Big Dick," who led his fellow African-American prisoners at Dartmoor. It also highlights the services of African-Americans at New Orleans.

46. Rhodes, *Dartmoor Prison,* 47–82; Tullett, *Inside Dartmoor,* 46. See also Patricia K. Crimmin, "Prisoners of War and British Port Communities, 1793–1815," *NM/MN* 6, no. 4 (1997), 17–27; Ira Dye, "American Maritime Prisoners of War, 1812–1815," in Clark

G. Reynolds, *Proceedings of the North American Society of Oceanic History, March 19–20, 1977, at Peabody Museum* (Salem, Mass.); Robin F. A. Farbel, "The Laws of War in the 1812 Conflict," *JAS* 14 (1980), 389–392; Reginald Horsman, "The Paradox of Dartmoor Prison," *American Heritage* 26 (February 1975), 12–17, 85.

47. Dye, *Fatal Cruise of the Argus,* 291–296.

48. Bunnell, *Travels and Adventures,* 139; TNA, ADM 98/228, pp. 195, 203, Leay to Shortland, 27 February and 16 March 1815; ADM 98/123, pp. 193, 194, Grey et al. to Croker, 31 March and 10 April 1815; ADM 98/291, pp. 236–237, 243, Leay to Beasly, 10 and 19 April 1815; Charles Andrews, *The Prisoners' Memoirs,* 21–24, 127–139, 144–151, 162, 167–206, 222–235; Maclay, *History of American Privateers,* 359–376; Rhodes, *Dartmoor Prison,* 74–81; Tullett, *Inside Dartmoor,* 78–82; Nathaniel Pearce, "Journal of Nathaniel Pearce of Newburyport, Kept at Dartmoor Prison, 1814–1815," *EIHC* 73 (1937), 24–59; Benjamin F. Palmer, *Diary,* 126–127; Melish, *Description of Dartmoor Prison.* See also Uriah Phillips Levy, *Defense of Uriah Phillips Levy,* 6–8; "Reminiscences of a Dartmoor Prisoner," *Knickerbocker Magazine* 23 (February, April, June 1844), 146–158, 356–360, 517–522; 24 (November, December 1844), 457–463, 519–524; Nathaniel Pearce, "Journal of Nathaniel Pearce of Newburyport, Kept at Dartmoor Prison, 1814–15," *EIHC* 73 (January 1937), 24–59. For further accounts see Bates, *Autobiography of Joseph Bates;* B. F. Palmer, *Diary;* Roads, *The Marblehead Manual;* Valpey, *Journal of Joseph Valpey;* [Dr. Amos G. Babcock], *Journal of a Young Man of Massachusetts.*

49. Gardiner, *Naval War of 1812,* 91–93; W. James, *Naval Occurrences,* 249–250; Roosevelt, *Naval War of 1812,* 240–241; Hughes, "Lewis Warrington," 120.

50. Hickey, *War of 1812,* 297; Harry Smith, *Autobiography,* 251.

51. *Morning Chronicle,* 27 December 1814; *The Times,* 27 and 30 December 1814.

52. J. C. A. Stagg, "The Politics of Ending the War of 1812," in Bowler, *War along the Niagara,* 101. See also James A. Carr, "The Battle of New Orleans and the Treaty of Ghent," *Diplomatic History* 3 (1979), 273–282.

53. TNA, CO 42/153, pp. 212–217, Mountain to Bathurst, 3 June 1813.

54. Bowler, *War of 1812,* 75–76. *The Letters of Veritas* were ten letters, comprising some twenty columns of abuse, published within two months of Prevost's departure from Montreal. Although the authorship of *Veritas* has never been absolutely established, some evidence suggests Stephen Sewell, Prevost's solicitor-general; but John Richardson, a Montreal merchant and member of the Executive Council who belonged to the anglophone faction that hated Prevost, also fell under suspicion, and is most widely credited with them. The writing of *Nerva* is attributed to Samuel Gale, another prominent Tory; *DCB,* 5: 697; 6: 268–270, 643, 701. See also *The Canadian Inspector,* published to refute it.

55. Antal, *A Wampum Denied,* 389.

56. Verdict of Trial, 26 August 1814, in *SBD,* 3: 401.

57. TNA, ADM 1/2738, pp. 140–144, Yeo to Croker, 5 September 1815; Fitz-Enz, *The Final Invasion,* 188–193.

58. Turner, *British Generals in the War of 1812,* 56–57. For a defence of Prevost see A. M. J. Hyatt, "The Defence of Upper Canada in 1812" (Master's thesis, Carleton University, 1961). The perverted version of events penned by Prevost's Canadian enemies formed the basis of an inflammatory article published in London, possibly written by Henry Proctor, accusing Prevost of, among other things, "imbecility of judgment"; "Campaigns in the Canadas," *Quarterly Review* 27 (July 1822), 405–449. It was rebutted by Edward Brenton, Prevost's former civil secretary, in *Some Account of the Public Life of the Late Lieutenant-General Sir George Prevost.* Unfortunately this was badly written, and the citing of the wrong issue of the offending publication was merely one factual error among many that undermined its case; Hitsman, *Incredible War,* 276–277, 352–353.

59. John Quincy Adams, *Diary,* 131; Everest, *War in Champlain Valley,* 199–201.

60. Young, *Battle of the Thames,* chap. 8; Stagg, "The Politics of Ending the War," 102; idem, *Mr. Madison's War,* 330n.

61. Engelman, *The Peace of Christmas Eve,* 290; Elting, *Amateurs to Arms!* 327.

62. John H. L. Henderson, *John Strachan,* 54; Michael A. Bellesiles, "Experiencing the War of 1812," in Flavell and Conway, *Britain and America Go to War,* 229–230.

63. Patrick, *Florida Fiasco,* 67–69.

64. Stagg, *Mr. Madison's War,* 371–373, 398–418; Bourne, *Britain and the Balance of Power,* 5–6, 115–116. For a discussion of the war's early historiography, see S. F. Wise, "The War of 1812 in Popular History," in Bowler, *War along the Niagara,* 105–120.

65. *National Aegis* (Worcester, Mass.), 22 February 1815; Hickey, *War of 1812,* 299, 309; Rodger, *Command of the Ocean,* 572.

66. Stephen Jay Gould, "George Canning's Left Buttock," in *Bully for Brontosaurus,* 23.

67. Stuart, *United States Expansionism and British North America,* 76.

68. Agar, *The Price of Union,* 182. Recent writers on the war that style it thus in their titles include Neil Gerson, Don Lawson, and J. W. Hammack.

69. Lambert, *War at Sea in the Age of Sail,* 206.

70. Webster, *Foreign Policy of Castlereagh,* 197.

71. P. J. Cain and A. G. Hopkins, *British Imperialism,* 86–89.

72. Schroeder, *Transformation of European Politics,* 517–582.

73. See Bourne, *Britain and the Balance of Power.*

74. Updyke, *Diplomacy of the War of 1812,* 358–478.

75. Liverpool to Castlereagh, 23 December 1814, in Wellesley, *Despatches, Correspondence and Memoranda,* 9: 495. See Carr, "Battle of New Orleans and Treaty of Ghent."

76. See Frank E. Stevens, *The Black Hawk War,* 48–50; Thwaites, *Wisconsin,* 172–178; John Shaw, "Shaw's Narrative," *WHC* 2 (1853), 197–232. See also Lizzie M. Brown, "The Pacification of the Indians of Illinois after the War of 1812," *Journal of Illinois State Historical Society* 8 (1915–16), 550–558; Charles G. Davis, "The Indian Boundary Line under the Treaty of August 24, 1816," ibid., 28 (1935–36), 26–48; Warrick W. Sheridan, "The American Indian Policy in the Upper Old Northwest Following the War of 1812," *Ethno History* 3 (1956), 109–125.

77. Churchill, *History of the English Speaking Peoples,* 3: 294.

78. LAC, Bulger Papers, 1: 46, Garrison Order, Michilimackinac, 13 October 1814.

79. Reuben G. Thwaites, "The Bulger Papers," *WHC* 13 (1895), 143.

80. Bulger, *Autobiographical Sketch of Captain Andrew Bulger,* 22.

81. Robert L. Fisher, "The Treaties of Portage des Sioux," *MVHR* 19 (1932–33), 495–508. For the situation on the Upper Lakes post-war, see Gough, *Fighting Sail,* chaps. 7 and 8.

82. TNA, WO 1/143, pp. 151, 161, 165–166, Nicolls to Hawkins, 28 April, 12 May, and 12 June 1815; Mahon, *War of 1812,* 383.

83. Hickey, *War of 1812,* 305–306.

84. See Steven Albert Watts, "The Republic Reborn: The War of 1812 and the Making of Liberal America" (Ph.D. diss., University of Missouri–Columbia, 1984); and Arthur P. Wade, "Artillerists and Engineers: The Beginnings of American Seacoast Fortifications, 1794–1815" (Ph.D. diss., Kansas State University, 1977). For recent studies of Jeffersonian politics see Onuf and Sadosky, *Jeffersonian America;* and Owsley and Smith, *Filibusters and Expansionists.*

85. Hickey, *War of 1812,* 308; McMaster, *History,* 4: 229; Leonard D. White, *The Jeffersonians,* 253–255; Perret, *A Country Made by War,* 133. For a study of the demise of the Federalist party see Livermore, *The Twilight of Federalism.*

86. Gallatin, *Writings,* 1: 651.

87. Andrew W. Robertson, "'Look on This Picture . . . and on This!': Nationalism, Localism, and Partisan Images of Otherness in the United States, 1787–1820," *AHR* 106 (2001), 1263–80.

88. Jackson enhanced his reputation in the First Seminole War in 1818 and by his invasion of Spanish West Florida without presidential or congressional authorization, which led to the execution of two British subjects. For a study of Jackson's less than edifying involvement in this epsiode, see Heidler and Heidler, *Old Hickory's War.*

89. William G. Keener, "The Price of Fame: Staffordshire Wins the War of 1812," *Timeline,* April–May 1989, 29–33.

90. It did not completely demilitarize the frontier, however; that would take another fifty years. E. H. Scammell, "The Rush-Bagot Agreement of 1817," *OHSPR* 13 (1915), 58–66; C. P. Stacy, "The Myth of the Unguarded Frontier, 1815–1871," *AHR* 56 (1950–51), 1–18; Stanley L. Falk, "Disarmament on the Great Lakes: Myth or Reality?" *USNIP* 87 (December 1967), 69–73.

91. Joseph Scafer, "The British Attitude to the Oregon Question, 1815–1846," *AHR* 16 (1910–11), 273–299; Robert Fraser, "The New South Wales Corps and Their Occupation of Massachusetts during the Anglo-American War of 1812," *Sabretache* 29 (April–June 1988), 9.

92. Maldwyn A. Jones, *The Limits of Liberty,* 109–111.

93. Brenton, *Naval History,* 5: 199–200, 205; *DCB,* 7: 104–105.

94. See Bigelow, *Breaches of Anglo-American Treaties.*

95. See Piers, *Evolution of Halifax Fortress,* 50–59; Henry Campbell Wilkinson, *Bermuda from Sail to Steam;* Kenneth Bourne, "British Preparations for War with the North," *English Historical Review* 76 (1961), 600–632.

96. Emanuel Raymond Lewis, *Sea Coast Fortifications,* 21–66. See also S. J. Watson, "Knowledge, Interest and the Limits of Military Professionalism: The Discourse on American Coastal Defence, 1815–1860," *War in History* 5 (1998), 280–307.

97. C. J. Bartlett, *Great Britain and Sea Power,* 71, 125, 214–215, 274–276.

98. See Gerald S. Graham, ed., "Views of General Murray on the Defence of Upper Canada, 1815," *CHR* 34 (1953), 158–165; Eric Jarvis, "Military Land Granting in Upper Canada following the War of 1812," *OH* 67 (September 1975), 121–134; Robert England, "Disbanded and Discharged Soldiers in Canada prior to 1914," *CHR* 27 (1946), 9–10; Craig, *Upper Canada,* chaps. 5–13; Dunham, *Political Unrest in Upper Canada.* See also Ryan James Watts, "Two Views of War: A Comparison of Nineteenth Century Central Canadian and American Views of the War of 1812" (Master's thesis, Queen's University, 1990).

99. Thomas B. Akins, "History of Halifax City," *Nova Scotia Historical Society Collections* 8 (1892–94), 163. See John N. Grant, *Immigration and Settlement of Black Refugees;* Boileau, *Half-Hearted Enemies,* 123–143; idem, "Internees, Evacuees and Immigrants," *The Beaver* 84 (2004), 31–35; Arnett G. Lindsay, "Diplomatic Relations between the United States and Great Britain Bearing on the Return of Negro Slaves, 1783–1828," *Journal of Negro History* 5 (1920), 391–419; William R. Riddell, "Slavery in Canada," ibid., 261–377; Matthew Mason, "The Battle of the Slaveholding Liberators: Great Britain, the United States, and Slavery in the Early Nineteenth Century," *WMQ,* 3d ser., 59 (2002), 672–696; Harvey Amani Whitfield, "Black Refugee Communities in Early Nineteenth Century Nova Scotia," *Journal of the Royal Nova Scotia Historical Society* 6 (2003), 92–109.

100. Stuart, *United States Expansionism and British North America,* 84.

101. Young, *Battle of the Thames,* 108.

102. M. A. Jones, *The Limits of Liberty,* 182. Lawrence J. Burpee suggested the war had an influence on Lord Selkirk's Red River settlement, the nucleus of modern Manitoba, and on Astoria; "Influence of the War of 1812 upon the Settlement of the Canadian West," *OHSPR* 12 (1914), 114–120; Katherine B. Judson, "The British Side to the Restoration of Fort Astoria," *Oregon Historical Quarterly* 20 (1919), 305–330; Frederick Mark, "The Genesis of the Oregon Question," *MVHR* 36 (1949–50), 583–612; G. F. G. Stanley, "Documents Relating to the Swiss Immigration to Red River in 1821," *CHR* 22 (March 1941), 42–50.

103. See C. P. Stacy, "The War of 1812 in Canadian History," in Zaslow, *Defended Border,* 315–330, reprinted from *OH* 50 (1958), 153–159; J. Castell Hopkins, "The War of 1812–15," *OHSPR* 12 (1914), 42–57.

104. Mark Russell Shulman, "The Influence of History upon Sea Power: The Navalist Reinterpretation of the War of 1812," *JMilH* 56 (1992), 183–206. See also Robert B. Greene, "Wisdom and Prudence: The Teachings of Admiral A. T. Mahan" (Ph.D. diss., Claremont Graduate School, 1979).

105. Peter Carlson, "Raiding the Icebox," *Washington Post,* 30 December 2005; Shawn McCarthy, "They'd Take Halifax (Then We'd Kill Kenny)," *Globe and Mail,* 31 December 2005; Floyd Rudmin, "Secret War Plans and the Malady of American Militarism," *Counter Punch* 13 (1–15 January 2006).

106. USNA, "Joint Army and Navy Basic War Plan—RED," Joint Board JB 325, serial 435–641 (amended draft), pp. 6–7, 26, 28, 41, 57, 82, 84; Preston, *Defence of the Undefended Border,* 221, 223.

107. USNA, "Joint Army and Navy Basic War Plan—RED," p. 85; Commander A. S. Carpender and Colonel W. Krueger, Memorandum to the Joint Board, 17 October 1934, appended to ibid.

108. Preston, *Defence of the Undefended Border,* 226.

109. M. A. Jones, *The Limits of Liberty,* 394; Meinig, *The Shaping of America,* 50–52.

Select Bibliography

Abbott, John, Graeme S. Mount, and Michael J. Mulloy. *The History of Fort St. Joseph.* Toronto: Dundurn, 2000.

Adair, J. *Letters of General Adair and General Jackson Relative to the Charge of Cowardice Made by the Latter against Kentucky Troops at New Orleans.* Lexington, Ky.: Thomas Smith, 1827.

Adams, Henry. *History of the United States during the Administration of James Madison.* 4 vols. *History of the United States of America during the Administrations of Thomas Jefferson and James Madison,* Nos. 5–9. New York: A. and C. Boni, 1930.

———, ed. *Documents Relating to New-England Federalism, 1800–1815.* New York: B. Franklin, 1969.

Adams, John Quincy. *The Diary of John Quincy Adams, 1794–1845.* Ed. Alan Nevins. New York: Scribner's 1951.

——— *Memoirs of John Quincy Adams: Comprising Portions of His Diary from 1795 to 1848.* Ed. C. F. Adams. 7 vols. Philadelphia: J. B. Lippincott, 1874–1877.

Adams, J. T. *New England in the Republic, 1776–1850.* Boston: Little, Brown, 1926.

———, ed. *Dictionary of American History.* 6 vols. London: Oxford University Press, 1963.

Agar, Herbert. *The Price of Union.* Boston: Houghton Mifflin, 1950.

Air Defense Bases: Hearings before the Committee on Military Affairs, House of Representatives, Seventy-fourth Congress, First Session on H.R. 6621 and H.R. 4130, February 11, 12, 13, 1935. Washington, D.C.: Government Printing Office, 1935.

Albion, Robert G., and Jennie B. Pope. *Sea Lanes in Wartime: The American Experience, 1775–1942.* New York: W. W. Norton, 1942.

Albright, Harry. *New Orleans—The Battle of the Bayous.* New York: Hippocrene Books, 1990.

Alexander, R. S. *Napoleon.* London: Arnold, 2001.

Allen, Gardner W. *Our Naval War with France.* Cranbury, N.J.: Scholars Bookshelf, 2005.

Allen, Harry Cranbrook. *The Anglo-American Relationship since 1783.* London: Adam and Charles Black, 1959.

SELECT BIBLIOGRAPHY

Allen, Joseph. *Battles of the British Navy: From A.D. 1000 to 1840.* 2 vols. London: A. H. Beirly, 1842.

Allen, Robert S. *The Battle of Moraviantown, October 5, 1813.* Ottawa: Canadian War Museum, 1994.

——— *His Majesty's Indian Allies: British Indian Policy in Defense of Canada, 1774–1815.* Toronto: Dundurn, 1992.

Allison, Robert J. *Stephen Decatur: American Naval Hero, 1779–1820.* Amherst: University of Massachusetts Press, 2005.

Altoff, Gerard T. *Amongst My Best Men: African-Americans and the War of 1812.* Put-in-Bay, Ohio: Perry Group, 1996.

——— *Deep Water Sailors, Shallow Water Soldiers.* Put-in-Bay, Ohio: Perry Group, 1993.

Ames, William E. *A History of the National Intelligencer.* Chapel Hill: University of North Carolina Press, 1972.

Ammon, Harry. *James Monroe: The Quest for National Identity.* New York: McGraw-Hill, 1971.

Anderson, John. *A Short History of the Life of John Anderson.* Ed. Richard C. Knopf. Columbus: Anthony Wayne Parkway Board, Ohio Historical Society, 1956.

Andrews, Charles. *The Prisoners' Memoirs; or, Dartmoor Prison; Containing a Complete and Impartial History of the Entire Captivity of the Americans in England, from the Commencement of the Late War between the United States and Great Britain, Until All Prisoners Were Released by the Treaty of Ghent. Also, a Particular Detail of All Occurrences Relative to That Horrid Massacre at Dartmoor, on the Fatal Evening of the 6th April, 1815. The Whole Carefully Compiled from the Journal of Charles Andrews, a Prisoner in England, from the Commencement of the War, until the Release of the Prisoners.* New York: C. Andrews, 1852.

Annals of Congress. See U.S. Congress, *The Debates and Proceedings of the Congress of the United States.*

Anson, Bert. *The Miami Indians.* Norman: University of Oklahoma Press, 1970.

Anson, Walter Vernon. *The Life of Admiral Sir John Borlase Warren, Bart., G.C.B., P.C., Knight of the Guelphic Order; Knight of St. Catherine, D.C.L., &c., &c.* London: Simpkin, Marshall, 1914.

Antal, S. *A Wampum Denied: Proctor's War of 1812.* Ottawa: Carleton University Press, 1997.

Anthony, Katherine S. *Dolley Madison: Her Life and Times.* Garden City, N.Y.: Doubleday, 1949.

Armstrong, John. *Notices of the War of 1812.* 2 vols. New York: Wiley and Putnam, 1840.

Arthur, Stanley C. *Jean Laffite: Gentleman Rover.* New Orleans: Harmanson, 1952.

——— *Old New Orleans.* Gretna, La.: Pelican Publishing, 1990.

Ashton, T. S. *An Economic History of England: The Eighteenth Century.* London: Methuen, 1955.

Askin, John. *The John Askin Papers, 1747–1820.* Ed. Milo M. Quaife. 2 vols. Detroit: Burton Historical Collections, 1928 and 1931.

Askwith, W. H. *List of Officers of the Royal Regiment of Artillery from the Year 1716 to the Year 1899. To Which Are Added the Notes on Officers' Services Collected by General W. H. Askwith.* London: Loudon and Beccles, 1900.

Aspinall, Arthur. *Lord Brougham and the Whig Party.* Manchester: Manchester University Press, 1927.

Atherton, William. *Narrative of the Suffering & Defeat of the North-Western Army under General Winchester: Massacre of the Prisoners, Sixteen Months Imprisonment of the Writer and Others with the Indians and British.* Frankfort, Ky.: A. G. Hodges, 1842.

Atkinson, C. T. *The Dorsetshire Regiment: The Thirty-ninth and Fifty-fourth Foot and the Dorset Militia and Volunteers.* Vol. 1, Part I: *The Thirty-ninth.* Oxford: Printed at the University Press, 1947.

Au, Dennis M. *War on the Raisin: A Narrative Account of the War of 1812 on the River Raisin Settlement, Michigan Territory.* Monroe, Mich.: Monroe County Historical Commission, 1981.

Auchinleck, G. Gilbert. *History of the War between Great Britain and the United States of America during the years 1812, 1813 and 1814.* London: Arms and Armour, 1972.

[Babcock, Amos G.] *Journal of a Young Man of Massachusetts, Late Surgeon on Board an American Privateer, Who Was Captured by the British, in May, Eighteen Hundred and Thirteen, and Was Confined First at Melville Island, Halifax, Then at Chatham, in England, and Last, at Dartmoor Prison; Interspersed with Observations, Anecdotes and Remarks Tending to Illustrate the Moral and Political Characters of Three Nations, to Which Is Added a Correct Engraving of Dartmoor Prison Representing the Massacre of American Prisoners. Written by Himself.* Ed. Benjamin Waterhouse [Amos Babcock]. Boston: Rowe and Hooper, 1816.

Babcock, Louis L. *The Siege of Fort Erie, an Episode in the War of 1812.* Buffalo: Peter Paul Book, 1899.

——— *The War of 1812 on the Niagara Frontier.* Buffalo: Buffalo Historical Society, 1927.

Bagamudré, Ven. *Isaac Brock: Larger than Life.* Montreal: XYZ Publishing, 2000.

Bailey, T. A. *A Diplomatic History of the American People.* Englewood Cliffs, N.J.: Prentice-Hall, 1980.

Bales, John, ed. *America in the Middle Period: Essays in Honor of Bernard Mayo.* Charlottesville: University of Virginia Press, 1973.

Balinky, Alexander. *Albert Gallatin: Fiscal Theories and Policies.* New Brunswick, N.J.: Rutgers University Press, 1958.

Ball, Charles. *A Narrative of the Life and Adventures of Charles Ball, A Black Man.* New York: John S. Taylor, 1837.

Ball, J. V. *A Refutation of the Charges by Sundry Officers of the Late Regiment of Light Dragoon against Brevet Colonel James V. Ball.* Winchester, Va.: J. Heiskell, 1815.

Banner, James M., Jr. *To the Hartford Convention: The Federalists and the Origins of Party Politics in Massachusetts, 1789–1815.* New York: Alfred A. Knopf, 1970.

SELECT BIBLIOGRAPHY

Banning, Lance. *The Jeffersonian Persuasion: Evolution of a Party Ideology.* Ithaca: Cornell University Press, 1980.

Banta, Richard E. *The Ohio.* London: William Hodge, 1951.

Barbuto, Richard V. *Niagara, 1814: America Invades Canada.* Lawrence: University Press of Kansas, 2000.

Barker, Jacob. *Incidents in the Life of Jacob Barker of New Orleans, Louisiana.* Washington, D.C.: n.p., 1855.

Barnes, James. *Naval Actions of the War of 1812.* London: Cornmarket Press, 1969.

Barney, M., ed. *A Biographical Memoir of the Late Commodore Joshua Barney: From Autographical Notes and Journals in Possession of His Family, and Other Authentic Sources.* Boston: Gray and Bowen, 1832.

Barrett, C. R. B. *The 85th King's Light Infantry (Now 2nd Bttn. The King's Shropshire Light Infantry) By "One of Them."* London: Spottiswoode, 1913.

Bartlett, C. J. *Castlereagh.* London: Macmillan, 1966.

——— *Great Britain and Sea Power, 1815–1853.* Oxford: Clarendon Press, 1963.

Bartlett, Irving H. *John C. Calhoun: A Biography.* New York: W. W. Norton, 1993.

Bashkina, Nina N., et al., eds. *The United States and Russia: The Beginning of Relations, 1765–1815.* Washington, D.C.: Government Printing Office, 1980.

Bates, Joseph. *The Autobiography of Joseph Bates, Embracing a Long Life on Shipboard.* Battle Creek, Mich.: Steam Press of the 7th Day Adventist Publishing Association, 1868.

Bauer, Karl Jack. *Zachary Taylor: Soldier, Planter, Statesman of the Old Southwest.* Baton Rouge: Louisiana State University Press, 1985.

Baylies, Nicholas. *Eleazor Wheelock Ripley of the War of 1812, Major-General in the United States Army, Member of Congress etc.* Des Moines: Brewster, 1897.

Beaumont, William. *William Beaumont's Formative Years: Two Early Notebooks, 1811–1821.* Ed. G. Miller. New York: Henry Schulman, 1946.

Beeler, John F. *British Naval Policy in the Gladstone-Disraeli Era, 1865–1880.* Stanford: Stanford University Press, 1997.

Beirne, Francis F. *The War of 1812.* New York: E. P. Dutton, 1949.

Bemis, Samuel F. *Jay's Treaty: A Study in Commerce and Diplomacy.* Westport, Conn.: Greenwood, 1975.

——— *John Quincy Adams and the Foundations of American Foreign Policy.* New York: Alfred A. Knopf, 1969.

Benn, Carl. *The Battle of York.* Belleville, Ont.: Mika Publishing, 1984.

——— *Historic Fort York, 1793–1993.* Toronto: Natural Heritage/Natural History, 1993.

——— *The Iroquois in the War of 1812.* Toronto: University of Toronto Press, 1998.

——— *The War of 1812.* Oxford: Osprey, 2002.

Bentley, William. *The Diary of William Bentley, D.D., Pastor of the East Church, Salem, Massachusetts.* 4 vols. Gloucester, Mass.: Peter Smith, 1962.

Bernard, Daniel D. *A Discourse on the Life, Services and Character of Stephen Van Rensselaer Delivered before the Albany Institute, April 15, 1839.* Albany, N.Y.: Hoffman and White, 1839.

Bernstein, Richard B. *Thomas Jefferson.* London: Oxford University Press, 2003.

Berton, Pierre. *Flames across the Border: The Canadian-American Tragedy, 1813–1814.* Boston: Little, Brown, 1981.

——— *The Invasion of Canada, 1812–1813.* Toronto: McClelland and Stewart, 1980.

Berube, Claude G., and John Rodgaard. *A Call to the Sea: Captain Charles Stewart of the USS Constitution.* Dulles, Va.: Potomac Books, 2005.

Bickley, F., ed. *Report on the Manuscripts of Earl Bathurst Preserved at Cirencester Park.* London: Historical Manuscripts Commission, 1923.

Biddulph, J. *The Nineteenth and Their Times; Being an Account of the Four Cavalry Regiments in the British Army That Have Borne the Number Nineteen and of the Campaigns in Which They Served.* London: John Murray, 1899.

Bigelow, John. *Breaches of Anglo-American Treaties: A Study in History and Diplomacy.* New York: Sturgis and Walton, 1917.

Bilow, John A. *Châteaugay, N.Y., and the War of 1812.* St.-Lambert, Quebec: Payette and Simms, 1984.

Bird, Harrison. *Navies in the Mountains: The Battles on the Waters of Lake Champlain and Lake George, 1609–1814.* New York: Oxford University Press, 1962.

——— *War for the West, 1790–1813.* New York: Oxford University Press, 1971.

Black Hawk. *Life of Black Hawk.* Ed. Milo M. Quaife. Trans. A. LeClair. New York: Dover, 1994.

Blanchard, Rufus. *The Discovery and Conquest of the Northwest.* Chicago: Cushing and Thomas, 1880.

Boileau, John. *Half-Hearted Enemies: Nova Scotia, New England and the War of 1812.* Halifax, N.S.: Formac, 2005.

Bonnel, U. *La France, Les Etats-Unis et la guerre de la course (1797–1815).* Paris: U. Bonnel, 1961.

Bonney, C. V. R. *A Legacy of Historical Gleanings.* 2 vols. Albany, N.Y.: Albert Maunsell, 1875.

Borden, Morton. *The Federalism of James A. Bayard.* New York: Columbia University Press, 1957.

Borneman, Walter R. *1812: The War That Forged a Nation.* New York: HarperCollins, 2004.

Boss, W. *The Stormont, Dundas and Glengarry Highlanders, 1783–1951.* Ottawa: Runge, 1951.

Bourne, Kenneth. *Britain and the Balance of Power in North America, 1815–1908.* London: Longmans, 1967.

Bowers, William. *Naval Adventures during Thirty-five Years' Service.* 2 vols. London: Richard Bentley, 1833.

Bowler, R. Arthur. *The War of 1812.* London: Holt-Blond, 1973.

———, ed. *War along the Niagara: Essays on the War of 1812 and Its Legacy by Carl Benn, R. Arthur Bowler, John C. Fredriksen, Donald E. Graves, John D. Morris, J. C. A. Stagg, Joseph M. Thatcher, Sydney P. Wise.* Youngstown, N.Y.: Old Fort Niagara Association, 1991.

Bowling, Kenneth R. *Creating the Federal City, 1774–1800: Potomac Fever.* Washington, D.C.: American Institute of Architects Press, 1988.

Boyd, John Parker. *Documents and Facts Relative to Military Events during the Late War.* Boston, 1816.

Bradenburg, O. *The Battle of Plattsburgh Bay: The British Navy's View.* Plattsburgh, N.Y.: Clinton County Historical Association, 1978.

Bradford, James C., ed. *Command under Sail: Makers of the American Naval Tradition, 1775–1850.* Annapolis: Naval Institute Press, 1985.

Brands, H. W. *Andrew Jackson: His Life and Times.* New York: Doubleday, 2005.

Brannan, John, ed. *Official Letters of the Military and Naval Officers of the United States, during the War with Great Britain in the Years 1812, 13, 14, & 15. With Some Additional Letters and Documents Elucidating the History of That Period.* Washington, D.C.: Way and Gideon, 1823.

Brannon, Gary. *The Last Voyage of the Tonquin: An Ill Fated Expedition to the Pacific Northwest.* Waterloo, Ont.: Escart Press, 1992.

Brant, Irving. *James Madison: Commander-in-Chief, 1812–1836.* New York: Bobbs-Merrill, 1961.

——— *James Madison: The President, 1809–1812.* New York: Bobbs-Merrill, 1956.

——— *James Madison: Secretary of State, 1800–1809.* New York: Bobbs-Merrill, 1953.

Brenton, E. B. *The Naval History of Great Britain.* 5 vols. London: Henry Colburn, 1825.

——— *Some Account of the Public Life of the Late Lieutenant-General Sir George Prevost Bart: Particularly of His Services in the Canadas Including a Reply to the Strictures of His Military Character in the Quarterly Review for October 1822.* London: T. Cadell and T. Egerton, 1823.

Briggs, Herbert W. *The Doctrine of Continuous Voyage.* Buffalo: W. S. Hein, 2003.

Briggs, John H. *Naval Administrations, 1827–1892.* London: Sampson Low, 1897.

Brightfield, Myron F. *John Wilson Croker.* Berkeley: University of California Press, 1940.

Brighton, John G., ed. *Admiral of the Fleet Sir Provo W. P. Wallis, G.C.B. Etc.: A Memoir.* London: Hutchinson, 1892.

——— *Admiral Sir P. B. V. Broke, Bart: A Memoir.* London: Sampson Low, 1866.

Brinckman, Rowland. *Historical Record of The Eighty-ninth Princess Victoria's Regiment.* Chatham: Gale and Polden, 1888.

Broadley, Alexander M., and Richard G. Bartelot. *Nelson's Hardy: His Life, Letters, and Friends.* London: John Murray, 1909.

Brooks, Charles B. *The Siege of New Orleans.* Seattle: University of Washington Press, 1961.

Brown, Dee. *Bury My Heart at Wounded Knee: An Indian History of the American West.* London: Vintage, 1991.

Brown, Roger H. *The Republic in Peril: 1812.* New York: W. W. Norton, 1971.

Brown, Samuel R. *Views of the Campaigns of the North-Western Army, &c., Comprising Sketches of the Campaigns of Generals Hull and Harrison, &c.* Philadelphia: W. G. Murphy, 1815.

——— *Views on Lake Erie: Comprising a Minute and Interesting Account of the Conflict on Lake Erie, Military Anecdotes, Abuses in the Army, Plan of a Military Settlement, View of the Lake Coast from Buffalo to Detroit.* Troy, N.Y.: Francis Addancourt, 1814.

Brown, Stuart G. *The First Republicans: Political Philosophy and Public Policy in the Party of Jefferson and Madison.* Westport, Conn.: Greenwood, 1977.

Brown, Wilbur S. *The Amphibious Campaign for West Florida and Louisiana, 1814–1815: A Critical Review of Strategy and Tactics at New Orleans.* Tuscaloosa: University of Alabama Press, 1969.

Bruce, William C. *John Randolph of Roanoke, 1773–1833: A Biography.* 2 vols. New York: G. P. Putnam's Sons, 1922.

Brunson, Alfred. *A Western Pioneer; or, Incidents from the Life and Times of Alfred Brunson.* 2 vols. Cincinnati: Hitchcock, Walden, 1872.

Bryant, Arthur. *The Age of Elegance, 1812–1822.* London: Reprint Society, 1954.

Bryon, Gilbert. *St. Michaels, the Town That Fooled the British.* Satern, Md.: Eastern Publishing, 1963.

Buchan, John. *The History of The Royal Scots Fusiliers (1678–1918).* London: Thomas Newton and Sons, 1925.

Buchanan, John. *Jackson's Way: Andrew Jackson and the People of the Western Waters.* New York: John Wiley and Sons, 2001.

Buel, Richard. *America on the Brink: How the Political Struggle over the War of 1812 Almost Destroyed the Young Republic.* New York: Palgrave Macmillan, 2005.

Buell, Augustus C. *History of Andrew Jackson.* 2 vols. London: Bickers and Son, 1904.

Bulger, Andrew H. *An Autobiographical Sketch of the Services of the Late Captain Andrew Bulger of the Royal Newfoundland Fencible Regiment.* Bangalore, India: Regimental Press, 1865.

Bullard, Mary R. *Black Liberation on Cumberland Island in 1815.* South Dartmouth, Mass.: Mary R. Bullard, 1983.

Bunnell, D. C. *The Travels and Adventures of D. C. Bunnell during Twenty-two Years of a Sea-Faring Life.* Palmyra, N.Y.: J. H. Bortles, 1831.

Burdick, Virginia M. *Captain Thomas Macdonough: Delaware Born Hero of the Battle of Lake Champlain.* Wilmington: Delaware Heritage Press, 1991.

Burnett, T. A. J. *The Rise and Fall of a Regency Dandy: The Life and Times of Scrope Berdmore Davies.* London: John Murray, 1981.

Burns, Robert J. *Fort Wellington: A Narrative and Structural History, 1812–1838.* Parks Canada Manuscript Reports, No. 296. Ottawa: Parks Canada, 1979.

Burrows, John W. *The Essex Regiment 1st Battalion (44th) 1741–1919.* Southend-on-Sea: J. H. Burrows, n.d.

Burt, A. L. *The United States, Great Britain, and British North America from the Revolution to the Establishment of Peace after the War of 1812.* New Haven: Yale University Press, 1940.

Burton, Clarence M., William Stocking, and Gordon K. Miller, eds. *The City of Detroit, Michigan, 1701–1922.* 5 vols. Detroit: S. J. Clarke, 1922.

Butler, Lindley S. *Pirates, Privateers, & Rebel Raiders of the Carolina Coast.* Chapel Hill: University of North Carolina Press, 2000.

Butler, Mann. *History of the Commonwealth of Kentucky.* Cincinnati: Wilcox, Dickerson, 1836.

Butler, William F. *Sir Charles James Napier.* London: Macmillan, 1890.

Butterfield, Consul Willshire. *An Historical Account of the Expedition against Sandusky under Col. William Crawford in 1782.* Columbus, Ohio: Long's College Books, 1950.

Byrn, John D. *Crime and Punishment in the Royal Navy: Discipline on the Leeward Islands Station 1784–1812.* Aldershot: Scolar, 1989.

Byron, Gilbert. *The War of 1812 on the Chesapeake Bay.* Baltimore: Maryland Historical Society, 1964.

Caffrey, Kate. *The Lion and the Union: The Anglo-American War 1812–1815.* London: André Deutsch, 1978.

Cain, Emily. *Ghost Ships: Hamilton and Scourge, Historical Treasures from the War of 1812.* New York: Beaufort Books, 1983.

Cain, P. J., and A. G. Hopkins. *British Imperialism: Innovation and Expansion, 1688–1914.* London: Longman, 1993.

Calloway, Colin. *Crown and Calumet: British-Indian Relations, 1783–1815.* Norman: University of Oklahoma Press, 1987.

Campbell, Maria, and James Freeman Clarke. *Revolutionary Services and Civil Life of General William Hull . . . Together with the History of the Campaign of 1812 and Surrender of the Post of Detroit.* New York: G. S. Appleton, 1848.

Campbell, Marjorie W. *The North West Company.* Vancouver: Douglas and McIntyre, 1957.

The Canadian Inspector: No. 1, Containing a Collection of Facts Concerning the Government of Sir George Prevost in the Canadas. Montreal: Nahum Mower, 1815.

Canadian Ministry of Natural Resources. *HMS Nancy and the War of 1812.* Toronto, 1978.

Canney, Donald L. *Sailing Warships of the U.S. Navy.* Annapolis: Naval Institute Press, 2002.

——— *U.S. Coast Guard and Revenue Cutters, 1790–1935.* Annapolis: Naval Institute Press, 1995.

Canning, George. *Some Official Correspondence of George Canning, 1820–1827.* Ed. E. J. Stapleton. 2 vols. London: Longman, 1887.

Carden, J. S. *A Curtail'd Memoir of Incidents and Occurrences in the Life of John Surman Carden. Written by Himself, 1850.* Ed. C. T. Atkinson. Oxford: Clarendon Press, 1912.

Carr, Albert Z. *The Coming of War: An Account of the Remarkable Events Leading to the War of 1812.* Garden City, N.Y.: Doubleday, 1960.

Carroll, Francis M. *A Good and Wise Measure: The Struggle for the Canadian-American Border, 1783–1842.* Toronto: University of Toronto Press, 2001.

Carroll, John D. *My Boy Life. Presented in a Succession of True Stories.* Toronto: William Briggs, 1882.

Carter, Clarence Edwin F., ed. *The Territorial Papers of the United States.* 10 vols. Washington, D.C.: Government Printing Office, 1942.

Carter, Samuel. *Blaze of Glory: The Fight for New Orleans, 1814–15.* London: Macmillan, 1971.

Carter, Thomas. *Historical Record of the Forty-fourth, or The East Essex Regiment of Foot.* London: W. O. Mitchell, 1864.

——— *Historical Record of the Thirteenth, First Somersetshire, or Prince Albert's Regiment of Light Infantry.* London: W. O. Mitchell, 1867.

Casey, Powell A. *Louisiana in the War of 1812.* Baton Rouge: P. A. Casey, 1963.

Cass, Lewis. *Life of General Lewis Cass: Comprising an Account of His Military services in the North-West during the War with Great Britain, His Diplomatic Career and Civil History. To Which Is Appended a Sketch of the Public and Private History of Major-General W. O. Butler, of the Volunteer Service of the United States.* Philadelphia: G. B. Zieber, 1848.

Cassell, Frank A. *Merchant Congressman in the Young Republic: Samuel Smith of Maryland, 1752–1839.* Madison: University of Wisconsin Press, 1971.

Cavendish, A. E. J. *An Reisimeid Chataich: The 93rd Sutherland Highlanders Now 2nd Bn. The Argyll and Sutherland Highlanders (Princess Louise's) 1799–1927.* Privately published, 1928.

Chamier, Frederick. *The Life of a Sailor. By a Captain in the Navy.* 3 vols. London: Richard Bentley, 1832.

Channing, E. *A History of the United States.* 6 vols. New York: Macmillan, 1905–1932.

Chapelle, Howard I. *Fulton's "Steam Battery": Blockship and Catamaran.* Washington, D.C.: Smithsonian Institution, 1964.

——— *The History of the American Sailing Navy: Their Ships and Their Development.* New York: Bonanza, 1949.

Chapin, Cyrenius. *Chapin's Review of Armstrong's Notices of the War of 1812.* Black Rock, N.Y.: D. P. Adams, 1836.

Charnley, Mitchell V. *Jean Lafitte, Gentleman Smuggler.* New York: Grosset and Dunlap, 1934.

Chartrand, René. *British Forces in North America, 1793–1815.* Oxford: Osprey, 1998.

——— *British Forces in the West Indies, 1793–1815.* London: Osprey, 1996.

——— *Émigré and Foreign Troops in British Service (2) 1803–15.* Oxford: Osprey, 2000.

——— *Uniforms and Equipment of the United States Forces in the War of 1812.* Youngstown, N.Y.: Old Fort Niagara Association, 1992.

Chartrand, René, and Jack L. Summers. *Military Uniforms in Canada, 1665–1970.* Ottawa: National Museums, 1981.

Chesterton, George Laval. *Peace, War and Adventure: An Autobiographical Memoir of George Laval Chesterton, Formerly of the Field Train Department of The Royal Artillery, Subsequently a Captain in the Army of Columbia, and at Present Governor of the House of Correction at Cold Bath Fields.* 2 vols. London: Longman, Brown, Green, 1853.

Chidsey, Donald Barr. *The Battle of New Orleans: An Informal History of the War That Nobody Wanted.* New York: Crown, 1961.

Churchill, Winston S. *History of the English Speaking Peoples.* 4 vols. London: Cassell, 1956–1958.

Claiborne, W. C. C. *Official Letter Book of W. C. C. Claiborne, 1801–1816.* Ed. D. Rowland. 6 vols. Jackson, Mich.: State Department of Archives and History, 1917.

Clarke, Allen C. *Life and Letters of Dolley Madison.* Washington, D.C.: W. F. Roberts, 1914.

Clarke, James Freeman. *History of the Campaign of 1812 and the Surrender of the Post of Detroit.* New York: D. Appleton, 1848.

Clauder, Anna C. *American Commerce as Affected by the Wars of the French Revolution and Napoleon, 1793–1812.* Clifton, N.J.: Augustus M. Kelly, 1972.

Clay, Henry. *Papers of Henry Clay.* Vol. 1: *The Rising Statesman, 1797–1814.* Ed. J. F. Hopkins. Lexington: University Press of Kentucky, 1959.

Cleaves, Freeman. *Old Tippecanoe: William Henry Harrison and His Time.* New York: C. Scribner's Sons, 1939.

Clift, Glen G. *Remember the Raisin! Kentucky and Kentuckians in the Battles and Massacres at Frenchtown, Michigan Territory, in the War of 1812.* Frankfort: Kentucky Historical Society, 1961.

Clowes, William Laird. *The Royal Navy: A History from the Earliest Times to the Present.* Vol. 5. London: Sampson Low, Marston, 1897.

Cobbett, William. *The Autobiography of William Cobbett: The Progress of a Plough-Boy to a Seat in Parliament.* Ed. William Reitzel. London: Faber and Faber, 1967.

Cochrane, Alexander. *The Fighting Cochranes: A Scottish Clan over Six Hundred Years of Naval and Military History.* London: Quiller Press, 1983.

Codrington, Edward. *Memoir of the Life of Admiral Sir Edward Codrington: With Selections from His Public and Private Correspondence.* Ed. Lady Bourchier. 2 vols. London: Longmans, Green, 1876.

Coe, Charles H. *Red Patriots: The Story of the Seminoles.* Gainesville: University Presses of Florida, 1974.

Coffin, R. S. *A Concise Narrative of the Barbarous Treatment Experienced by American Prisoners in England and the West Indies, Etc. Written by a Young Man Who Was a Prisoner Nearly Six Months in the Island of Barbadoes, and Five in England. Interspersed with Anecdotes, Remarks, Etc. Etc.* Danville, Vt.: Ebenezer Eaton, 1816.

Coffin, William F. *1812: The War and Its Moral: A Canadian Chronicle.* Montreal: J. Lovell, 1864.

Coffman, Edward M. *The Old Army: A Portrait of the American Army in Peacetime, 1784–1898.* New York: Oxford University Press, 1986.

Cogar, William B., ed. *New Interpretations in Naval History: Selected Papers from the Eighth Naval History Symposium.* Annapolis: Naval Institute Press, 1989.

Coggeshall, George. *History of the American Privateers, and Letters-of-Marque, during Our War with England in the Years 1812, '13 and '14. Interspersed with Several Naval Battles between American and British Ships-of-War.* New York: G. Coggeshall, 1856.

Cohen, Daniel A., ed. *The Female Marine and Related Works: Narratives of Cross-Dressing and Urban Vice in America's Early Republic.* Amherst: University of Massachusetts Press, 1997.

Coit, Margaret L. *John C. Calhoun: American Portrait.* New York: Houghton Mifflin, 1950.

Colden, Cadwallader. *Life of Robert Fulton.* New York: Kirk and Mercein, 1817.

Cole, Cyrenus. *I Am a Man—The Indian Black Hawk.* Iowa City: State Historical Society of Iowa, 1938.

Cole, G. D. H. *The Life of William Cobbett.* London: Collins, 1947.

Coles, H. L. *The War of 1812.* Chicago: University of Chicago Press, 1965.

Coletta, Paolo, ed. *American Secretaries of the Navy.* 2 vols. Annapolis: Naval Institute Press, 1980.

Collins, G. *Guidebook to the Historic Sites of the War of 1812.* Toronto: Dundurn, 1998.

Combs, Jerald A. *The Jay Treaty: Political Battleground of the Founding Fathers.* Berkeley: University of California Press, 1970.

Combs, Leslie. *Colonel William Dudley's Defeat Opposite Fort Meigs, 1813.* Cincinnati: Spiller and Gates, 1869.

Conant, Thomas. *Upper Canada Sketches.* Toronto: William Briggs, 1898.

Congreve, William. *The Details of the Rocket System.* Ottawa: Museum Restoration Service, 1970.

Cooke, John H. *A Narrative of Events in the South of France, and of the Attack on New Orleans, in 1814 and 1815.* London: T. and W. Boone, 1835.

Cookson, J. E. *The British Armed Nation, 1793–1815.* Oxford: Oxford University Press, 1997.

——— *The Friends of Peace: Anti-War Liberalism in England, 1793–1815.* Cambridge: Cambridge University Press, 1982.

Cooper, James Fenimore. *History of the Navy of the United States of America.* London: Richard Bentley, 1839.

——— *Ned Myers; or, A Life before the Mast.* New York: Stringer, Townsend, 1854.

Cooper, John Spencer. *Rough Notes of Seven Campaigns in Portugal, Spain, France and America during the Years 1809–10–11–12–13–14–15.* Carlisle: G. and T. Coward, 1914.

Costello, Frederick H. *Nelson's Yankee Boy: The Adventures of a Plucky Young New Englander at Trafalgar and Elsewhere, and Later in the War of 1812.* London: J. M. Dent, 1904.

Cotterill, Robert Spencer. *The Southern Indians: The Story of the Civilised Tribes before Removal.* Norman: University of Oklahoma Press, 1954.

Coues, Henry, ed. *New Light on the Early History of the Greater Northwest: The Manuscript Journals of Alexander Henry and David Thompson.* 3 vols. New York: Francis A. Harper, 1897.

The Court of Neptune, and The Curse of Liberty, with Other Poems, on Subjects Connected with the Late War. New York: Van Winkel, Wiley, 1817.

Cowper, L. I. *The King's Own: The Story of a Royal Regiment.* Vol. 2: *1814–1914.* Oxford: Printed at the University Press, 1939.

Cox, Isaac J. *The West Florida Controversy, 1798–1813: A Study in American Diplomacy.* Baltimore: Johns Hopkins Press, 1918.

Crackel, Theodore J. *Mr. Jefferson's Army: Political and Social Reform of the Military Establishment, 1801–1809.* New York: New York University Press, 1987.

Craig, Gerald M. *Upper Canada: The Formative Years, 1784–1841.* Toronto: McClelland and Stewart, 1963.

Cranwell, John Philips, and William Bowers Crane. *Men of Marque: A History of Private Armed Vessels out of Baltimore during the War of 1812.* New York: W. W. Norton, 1940.

Crawford, Charles W., ed. *Governors of Tennessee.* Vol. 1: *1790–1835.* Memphis: Memphis State University Press, 1979.

Crawford, Michael J. *The Naval War of 1812: A Documentary History.* Vol. 3: *1814–1815, Chesapeake Bay, Northern Lakes, and Pacfic Ocean.* Washington, D.C.: Naval Historical Center, 2002.

Cress, Lawrence D. *Citizens in Arms: The Army and Militia in American Society to the War of 1812.* Chapel Hill: University of North Carolina Press, 1982.

Crisman, Kevin J. *The Eagle: An American Brig on Lake Champlain during the War of 1812.* Shelburne, Vt.: New England Press, 1987.

——— *The History and Construction of the United States Schooner Ticonderoga.* Alexandria, Va.: Eyrie Publications, 1983.

Crockett, David. *A Narrative of the Life of David Crockett of the State of Tennessee.* Philadelphia: E. L. Carey, A. Hart, 1834.

Croker, John Wilson. *The Croker Papers: The Correspondence and Diaries of the Rt. Hon. John Wilson Croker, Secretary to the Admiralty from 1809 to 1831.* Ed. L. J. Jennings. 3 vols. London: John Murray, 1884.

——— *A Key to the Orders in Council.* London: John Murray, 1812.

Crouzet, François. *L'Economie Britannique et le blocus continental, 1806–1813.* 2 vols. Paris: Economica, 1987.

Crowhurst, Patrick. *The Defence of British Trade, 1689–1815.* Folkestone: Dawson, 1977.

Cruikshank, Ernest A. *The Battle of Fort George.* Niagara-on-the-Lake, Ont.: Niagara Historical Society, 1990.

——— *Drummond's Winter Campaign, 1813.* Welland, Ont.: Lundy's Lane Historical Society, 1895.

——— *The Employment of Indians in the War of 1812.* Washington, D.C.: Government Printing Office, 1896.

——— *The Fight in the Beechwoods: A Study in Canadian History.* Welland, Ont.: W. Sawle, 1889.

——— *The Origin and Official History of the Thirteenth Battalion of Infantry, and a Description of the Work of the Early Militia of the Niagaran Peninsula in the War of 1812 and the Rebellion of 1837.* Hamilton Ont.: E. Ruddy, 1899.

——— *The Political Adventures of John Henry: The Record of an International Imbroglio.* Toronto: Macmillan, 1936.

——— *Record of the Services of Canadian Regiments in the War of 1812—The Glengarry Light Infantry.* Toronto: Canadiana House, 1968.

——— *Record of the Services of Canadian Regiments in the War of 1812—The Militia of the Eastern District.* Toronto: Canadiana House, 1968.

——— *The Siege of Fort Erie, August 1st–September 23rd 1814.* Welland, Ont.: Lundy's Lane Historical Society, 1905.

———, ed. *Documentary History of the Campaigns upon the Niagara Frontier in 1812–1814.* 9 vols. [Titles vary slightly.] Welland, Ont.: Tribune, 1896–1908.

——— *Documents Relating to the Invasion of Canada and the Surrender of Detroit, 1812.* 1896; reprint, Manchester, N.H.: Ayer Company Publishers, 1979.

——— *Documents Relating to the Invasion of the Niagara Peninsula by the United States Army, Commanded by General Jacob Brown, in July and August, 1814.* Niagara-on-the-Lake, Ont.: Niagara Historical Society, 1920.

Cuffe, Paul. *Narrative of the Life and Adventures of Paul Cuffe, a Pequot, during Thirty Years Spent at Sea and Traveling Foreign Lands.* Vernon, N.Y.: H. N. Bill, 1839.

Cullum, George W. *Campaigns of the War of 1812–15, against Great Britain, Sketched and Criticized: With Brief Biographies of the American Engineers.* New York: James Miller, 1879.

Cunliffe, Marcus. *The Royal Irish Fusiliers, 1793–1950.* London: Oxford University Press, 1952.

Cunningham, Noble E. *In Pursuit of Reason: The Life of Thomas Jefferson.* Baton Rouge: Louisiana State University Press, 1987.

——— *The Jeffersonian Republicans in Power: Party Operations, 1801–1809.* Chapel Hill: University of North Carolina Press, 1963.

Cushing, Daniel Lewis. *Captain Cushing in the War of 1812.* Ed. H. Lindley. Columbus: Ohio State Archaeological and Historical Society, 1944.

Cusick, James G. *The Other War of 1812: The Patriot War and the American Invasion of Spanish East Florida.* Gainesville: University Press of Florida, 2003.

Dagg, John L. *Autobiography of John L. Dagg.* Rome, Ga.: J. H. Shanklin, 1878.

Dale, Ronald J. *The Invasion of Canada: Battles of the War of 1812.* Toronto: James Lorimer, 2001.

Dallas, George. *A Biographical Memoir of the Late Sir Peter Parker.* London: Longman Hurst, Rees, Orme and Brown, 1816.

Dalliba, James. *A Narrative of the Battle of Brownstown: Which Was Fought on the 9th of August, 1812, during the Campaign of the North Western Army under the Command of Brigadier General Hull.* New York: D. Longworth, 1816.

Dangerfield, George. *The Era of Good Feelings: A Study of American Politics from 1811 to 1829.* London: Methuen, 1953.

Darnell, Elias. *A Journal, Containing an Accurate and Interesting Account of the Hardships, Sufferings, Battles, Defeat and Captivity, of Those Heroic Kentucky Volunteers and Regulars, Commanded by General Winchester, in the Years 1812–13. Also, Two Narratives, by Men That Were Wounded in the Battles on the River Raisin, and Taken Captive by the Indians.* Philadelphia: Grigg and Elliot, 1834.

David, Saul. *Prince of Pleasure: The Prince of Wales and the Making of the Regency.* London: Little, Brown, 1998.

Davidson, Gordon Charles. *The North West Company.* Berkeley: University of California Press, 1918.

Davis, Curtis Carroll. *Defenders' Dozen: Some Comments along the Way at the Halts during the Cavalcade of the Society of the War of 1812.* Baltimore: Society of the War of 1812 in Maryland, 1974.

Davis, P. M. *An Authentic History of the Late War between the United States and Great Britain. With a Full Account of Every Battle by Sea and Land; the Defection of General Hull, His Trial and Sentence; the Massacre at the River Raisin; the Destruction of the City of Washington; the Treaty of Peace in 1815. To Which Will Be Added, the War with Algiers, and the Treaty of Peace with the Various Tribes of North American Indians and the United States Army Register, and Peace Establishment.* New York: Ebenezer F. Baker, 1836.

——— *The Four Principal Battles of the Late War. Being a Full and Detailed Account of the Battle of Chippeway, Fall and Destruction of the City of Washington, Battles of Baltimore, and New Orleans.* Harrisburg, Pa.: Jacob Baab, 1832.

Davis, William C. *The Pirates Laffite: The Treacherous World of the Corsairs of the Gulf.* New York: Harcourt, 2005.

Dearborn, Henry A. S. *Defense of Gen. Henry Dearborn against the Attack of Gen. William Hull.* Boston: Edgar W. Davies, 1824.

——— *The Life of William Bainbridge, Esq., of the United States Navy.* Ed. J. Barnes. Princeton: Princeton Universtiy Press, 1931.

Debo, Angie. *The Road to Disappearance: A History of the Creek Indians.* Norman: University of Oklahoma Press, 1979.

DeConde, Alexandre. *The Quasi-War: The Politics and Diplomacy of the Undeclared War with France, 1797–1801.* New York: Scribner, 1966.

de Grummond, Jane Lucas. *The Baratarians and the Battle of New Orleans.* Baton Rouge: Louisiana State University Press, 1961.

De Kay, James Tertius. *The Battle of Stonington: Torpedoes, Submarines, and Rockets in the War of 1812.* Annapolis: Naval Institute Press, 1990.

——— *Chronicles of the Frigate "Macedonian," 1809–1922.* New York: W. W. Norton, 1995.

——— *A Rage for Glory: The Life of Commodore Stephen Decatur, USN.* New York: Free Press, 2004.

De Lacey Evans, George. *Facts Relating to the Capture of Washington, in Reply to Some Statements Contained in the Memoirs of Admiral Sir G. Cockburn.* London: Henry Colburn, 1829.

Delafield, Julia. *Biographies of Francis Lewis and Morgan Lewis.* 2 vols. New York: A. D. F. Randolph, 1877.

Denison, Charles Wheeler. *Old Ironsides and Old Adams: Story Leaves from the Logbook of a Man of War's Man.* Boston: W. W. Page, 1846.

Derry, John W. *Castlereagh.* London: Allen Lane, 1976.

Deveau, J. Alphonse, ed. *Diary of a Frenchman: François Lambert Bourneuf's Adventures from France to Acadia, 1787–1871.* Halifax, N.S.: Nimbus, 1990.

Dewar, Donald Keith, and Paul Hutchinson. *The Battle of Beaverdams: The Story of Thorold's Battle in the War of 1812.* St. Catharines, Ont.: Slabtown Press, 1996.

Dewey, Davis R. *Financial History of the United States.* New York: A. M. Kelley, 1968.

Dickinson, Henry W. *Robert Fulton, Engineer and Artist: His Life and Works.* London: John Lane, 1913.

Dictionary of American Biography. 20 vols. London: Oxford University Press, 1928–1937.

Dictionary of Canadian Biography. 13 vols. Toronto: University of Toronto Press, 1966–1994.

Dillon, John Brown. *The History of Indiana, from Its Earliest Exploration by Europeans, to the Close of the Territorial Government, in 1816.* Indianapolis: W. Sheets, 1843.

Dillon, Richard. *We Have Met the Enemy: Oliver Hazard Perry, Wilderness Commodore.* New York, McGraw-Hill, 1978.

Dobbins, W. W. *History of the Battle of Lake Erie (September 10, 1813) and Reminiscences of the Flagships "Lawrence" and "Niagara."* Erie, Pa.: Ashby Printing, 1913.

Donovan, Frank. *The Odyssey of the* Essex. New York: David McKay, 1969.

Doster, James F. *The Creek Indians and the Florida Lands, 1740–1823.* New York: St. Martin's, 1974.

Douglas, Howard A. *A Treatise on Naval Gunnery.* London: John Murray, 1852.

Douglas, John. *Medical Topography of Upper Canada.* London: Burgess and Hill, 1819.

Douglas, W. A. B. *Gunfire on the Lakes: The Naval War of 1812–1814 on the Great Lakes and Lake Champlain.* Ottawa: National Museum of Man, 1977.

Douglass, D. B. *The Campaign of 1814.* Ed. S. W. Jackman. Bala: Cromlech Press, 1957.

Dowd, Gregory Evans. *A Spirited Resistance: The North American Indian Struggle for Unity, 1745–1815.* Baltimore: Johns Hopkins University Press, 1992.

Dudley, Wade G. *Splintering the Wooden Wall: The British Blockade of the United States, 1812–1815.* Annapolis: Naval Institute Press, 2003.

Dudley, William S., ed. *The Naval War of 1812: A Documentary History.* 2 vols. Washington, D.C.: Naval Historical Center, 1985 and 1992.

Dudley, William S., and Michael J. Crawford, eds. *The Early Republic and the Sea: Essays on the Naval and Maritime History of the Early United States.* Washington, D.C.: Brassey's, 2001.

Duffy, Stephen W. H. *Captain Blakeley and the Wasp: The Cruise of 1814*. Annapolis: Naval Institute Press, 2001.

Duncan, Ennis. *The Journal of Ennis Duncan, Junior, Orderly Sergeant, 16th Regiment, Kentucky Militia Detached.* Ed. R. C. Knopf. Columbus: Ohio State Museum, 1958.

Duncan, Francis. *History of the Royal Regiment of Artillery, Compiled from the Original Records.* 2 vols. London: John Murray, 1873.

Dunham, Aileen. *Political Unrest in Upper Canada, 1815–1836.* London: Longmans, Green, 1927.

Dunlop, William. *Recollections of the American War, 1812–14: With a Biographical Sketch of the Author by A. H. U. Colquhoun of the Toronto News.* Toronto: Historical Publishing, 1905.

Dunnigan, Brian L. *The British Army at Mackinac, 1812–1815.* Mackinac, Mich.: Mackinac State Historic Park, 1980.

——— *Forts within a Fort: Niagara's Redoubts.* Lewiston, N.Y.: Old Fort Niagara Association, 1989.

Durand, James. *James Durand: An Able Seaman of 1812. His Adventures on "Old Ironsides" and as An Impressed Sailor in the British Navy.* Ed. G. S. Brooks. New Haven: Yale University Press, 1926.

Durham, Walter T. *James Winchester, Tennessee Pioneer.* Gallatin, Tenn.: Sumner County Library Board, 1979.

Dutton, Charles J. *Oliver Hazard Perry.* New York: Longmans, Green, 1935.

Dwight, Theodore. *History of the Hartford Convention: With a Review of the Policy of the United States Government, Which Led to the War of 1812.* New York: N. and J. White; Boston: Russell, Odiorne, 1833.

Dye, Ira. *The Fatal Cruise of the Argus: Two Captains in the War of 1812.* Annapolis: Naval Institute Press, 1994.

Eckert, Allan W. *A Sorrow in Our Heart: The Life of Tecumseh.* New York: Bantam Books, 1992.

Eckert, Edward K. *The Navy Department in the War of 1812.* Gainesville: University of Florida Press, 1973.

Edgar, Matilda. *General Brock.* Revised by E. A. Cruikshank. London: Oxford University Press, 1926.

——— *Ten Years of Upper Canada in Peace and War, 1805–1815; Being the Ridout Letters with Annotations by M. E. Also an Appendix of the Narrative of the Captivity among the Shawanese Indians, in 1788, of T. Ridout, etc.* London: T. Fisher Unwin, 1891.

Edmunds, R. David. *The Potawatomis, Keepers of the Fire.* Norman: University of Oklahoma Press, 1978.

——— *The Shawnee Prophet.* Lincoln: University of Nebraska Press, 1985.

——— *Tecumseh and the Quest for Indian Unity.* Boston: Little, Brown, 1984.

Edsall, John. *Incidents in the Life of John Edsall.* Catskill, N.Y.: J. Edsall, 1831.

Egan, Clifford L. *Neither Peace nor War: Franco-American Relations, 1803–1812.* Baton Rouge: Louisiana State University Press, 1983.

Egerton, Charles C. *The Journal of an Unfortunate Prisoner on Board the British Prison Ship Loyalist.* Baltimore: C. C. Egerton, 1813.

Eisenhower, John S. D. *Agent of Destiny: The Life and Times of General Winfield Scott.* New York: Free Press, 1997.

Eller, Ernest M., William J. Morgan, and Richard M. Basoco. *Sea Power and the Battle of New Orleans.* New Orleans: Landmark Society, 1965.

Elliot, Charles W. *Winfield Scott: The Soldier and the Man.* New York: Ayer Company Publishing, 1979.

Elliott, James. *Billy Green and the Battle of Stoney Creek, June 6, 1813.* Hamilton, Ont.: Stoney Creek Historical Society, 1994.

Elliott, Jesse D. *Correspondence in Relation to the Capture of the British Brigs, Detroit and Caledonia on the Night of October 8, 1812.* Philadelphia: U.S. Book and Job Printing Office, 1843.

——— *Speech of Commodore Jesse D. Elliott, U.S.N., Delivered in Hagerstown, Maryland, on November 14, 1843.* Philadelphia: G. B. Zieber, 1844.

Ellis, Alfred Burdon. *The History of the First West India Regiment.* London: Chapman and Hall, 1885.

Ellis, James H. *Mad Jack Percival: Legend of the Old Navy.* Annapolis: Naval Institute Press, 2002.

Elting, John R. *Amateurs to Arms! A Military History of the War of 1812.* New York: Da Capo, 1995.

Elze, Carl Friedrich. *Lord Byron: A Biography with a Critical Essay on His Place in Literature.* London: J. Murray, 1872.

Emerson, George D., ed. *The Perry's Victory Centenary—Report of the Perry's Victory Centenary Commission, State of New York.* Albany: J. B. Lyon, 1912.

Emmerson, John C. *The Chesapeake Affair of 1807: An Objective Account of the Attack by HMS Leopard upon the U.S. Frigate Chesapeake off Cape Henry, Va., June 22, 1807, and Its Repercussions.* Portsmouth, Va., 1954.

——— *The War in the Lower Chesapeake and Hampton Roads Areas, 1812–1815, as Reported in Norfolk Newspapers.* Portsmouth, Va., 1946.

Emsley, Clive. *British Society and the French Wars, 1793–1815.* London: Macmillan, 1979.

Engelman, F. L. *The Peace of Christmas Eve.* London: Rupert Hart-Davis, 1962.

Ermatinger, Edward. *Life of Colonel Talbot, and the Talbot Settlement, Its Rise and Progress, with Sketches of the Public Characters, and Career of Some of the Most Conspicuous Men in Upper Canada.* St. Thomas, Ont.: A. McLachlin's Home Journal Office, 1859.

Erney, Richard Alton. *The Public Life of Henry Dearborn.* New York: Arno, 1979.

Estes, Todd. *The Jay Treaty Debate, Public Opinion, and the Evolution of Early American Political Culture.* Amherst: University of Massachusetts Press, 2006.

Everard, Hugh. *History of Thos. Farrington's Regiment Subsequently Designated The 29th (Worcestershire) Foot 1694 to 1891.* Worcester: Littlebury, 1891.

Everest, Allan S. *The Military Career of Alexander Macomb and Alexander Macomb at Plattsburgh.* Plattsburgh, N.Y.: Clinton County Historical Association, 1989.

——— *The War of 1812 in the Champlain Valley.* Syracuse: Syracuse University Press, 1981.

Everett, Henry. *The History of The Somerset Light Infantry (Prince Albert's) 1685–1914.* London: Methuen, 1934.

Ewart, James. *James Ewart's Journal Covering His Stay at the Cape of Good Hope (1811–1814) and His Part in the Expedition to Florida and New Orleans (1814–1815).* Ed. A. Gordon-Brown. Cape Town: C. Struick, 1970.

Ewell, James. *Concise and Important History of the Capture of Washington and the Diseases Which Sprang from That Most Deplorable Disaster.* Philadelphia: J. Ewell, 1817.

Ewing, Frank E. *America's Forgotten Statesman: Albert Gallatin.* New York: Vantage, 1959.

Facey-Crowther, David R. *The New Brunswick Militia, 1787–1867.* Fredericton: New Brunswick History Society and New Ireland Press, 1990.

———, ed. *Better than the Best.* St. Johns: Royal Newfoundland Regiment Advisory Council, 1995.

Facts Relating to the Campaign on the Niagara in 1814. Boston: Patriot Office, 1815.

Fairbanks, Charles. *The Old Soldier's History, Containing an Account of the Movements of the Northwestern Army during the Years 1813–14, under Four Different Generals, Their Encampments, Battles, Executions, and Other Punishments.* Haverhill, N.H.: F. G. Forthingham, 1861.

Fairburn, William Armstrong. *Merchant Sail.* 6 vols. Center Lovell, Maine: Fairburn Marine Educational Foundation, 1945–1955.

Fairchild, George M., ed. *Journal of an American Prisoner at Fort Malden and Quebec in the War of 1812.* Quebec City: Frank Carrell, 1909.

Falconer, William. *A New Universal Dictionary of the Marine, Being a Copious Explanation of the Technical Terms and Phrases Usually Employed in the Construction, Equipment, Machinery, Movements, and Military as Well as Naval, Operations of Ships: with Such Parts of Astronomy, and Navigation, as Will be Useful to Practical Navigators. Illustrated with a Variety of Modern Designs of Shipping, etc. Together with Separate Views of the Masts, Yards, Sails, and Rigging. To Which Is Annexed a Vocabulary of French Sea-phrases and Terms of Art, Collected from the Best Authorities. Originally Compiled by William Falconer, Author of the Shipwreck, &c. Now Modernized and Much Enlarged, by William Burney, LL.D. Master of the Naval Academy.* Gosport: T. Cadell and W. Davies, 1815.

Falwell, Byron. *Eminent Victorian Soldiers: Seekers of Glory.* New York: W. W. Norton, 1988.

Fardy, B. D. *Before Beaumont Hamel: The Royal Newfoundland Regiment 1775–1815,* St. John's, Newf.: Creative Publishers, 1995.

Farragut, David G. *The Life of D. G. F. . . . Embodying His Journal and Letters.* New York: G. Appleton, 1879.

Fenton, Alfred H. *Oliver Hazard Perry.* New York: Farrar and Rinehart, 1944.

Ferling, John. *Adams vs. Jefferson: The Tumultuous Election of 1800.* New York: Oxford University Press, 2004.

Field, Cyril. *Britain's Sea Soldiers: A History of the Royal Marines and Their Predecessors and of Their Services, in Action, Ashore and Afloat, and upon Sundry Other Occasions of Moment.* 2 vols. Liverpool: Lyceum, 1924.

Finan, P. *Journal of a Voyage to Quebec in the Year 1825, with Recollections of Canada during the Late American War in the Years 1812–1813.* Newry, Ire.: A. Peacock, 1828.

Fine, Sidney, and Gerald S. Brown, eds. *The American Past: Conflicting Interpretations of the Great Issues.* Vol. 1. New York: Macmillan, 1976.

Firth, Edith D., ed. *The Town of York: A Collection of Documents of Early Toronto.* Toronto: Champlain Society for the Government of Ontario, 1962.

Fischer, David H. *The Revolution of American Conservatism: The Federalist Party in the Era of Jeffersonian Democracy.* Chicago: University of Chicago Press, 1976.

Fitz-Enz, David G. *The Final Invasion: Plattsburgh, the War of 1812's Most Decisive Battle.* New York: Cooper Square, 2001.

——— *Old Ironsides: Eagle of the Sea.* Boulder: Taylor Trade Publishing, 2005.

FitzGibbon, Mary A. *A Veteran of 1812: A Life of James FitzGibbon.* Toronto: William Briggs, 1894.

Flandrau, Grace. *Astor and the Oregon Country.* St. Paul, Minn.: Great Northern Railway, 1926.

Flavell, Julie, and Stephen Conway, eds. *Britain and America Go to War: The Impact of War and Warfare in Anglo-America, 1754–1815.* Gainesville: University Press of Florida, 2004.

Foley, William E. *Wilderness Journey: The Life of William Clark.* Columbia: University of Missouri Press, 2004.

Footner, Geoffrey M. *Tidewater Triumph: The Development and Worldwide Success of the Chesapeake Bay Pilot Schooner.* Centreville, Md.: Tidewater Publishers, 1998.

Footner, Hulbert. *Sailor of Fortune: The Life and Adventures of Commodore Barney.* New York: Harper Brothers, 1940.

Forester, C. S. *The Naval War of 1812.* London: Landsborough Publications, 1958.

Forrest, Charles Ramus. *The Battle of New Orleans: A British View. The Journal of Major C. R. Forrest, Assist. QM General, 34th Regiment of Foot.* Ed. Hugh F. Rankin. New Orleans: Hauser Press, 1961.

Fortescue, J. W. *British Statesmen of the Great War 1793–1814.* Oxford: Clarendon Press, 1911.

——— *A History of the British Army.* 10 vols. London: Macmillan, 1920.

Foster, Augustus John. *Jeffersonian America: Notes on the United States of America Collected in the Years 1805–6–7 and 11–12 by Sir Augustus John Foster, Bart.* Ed. Richard Beale Davis. San Marino, Calif.: Huntington Library, 1954.

Franchère, Gabriel. *Adventures at Astoria, 1810–1814*. Trans. and ed. Hoyt C. Franchère. Norman: University of Oklahoma Press, 1967.

——— *Journal of a Voyage on the North West Coast of North America during the Years 1811, 1812, 1813 and 1814*. Trans. Wessie Tipping Lamb. Ed. W. Kaye Lamb. Toronto: Champlain Society, 1969.

Fraser, E., and L. G. Carr-Laughton. *The Royal Marine Artillery, 1804–1923*. London: Royal United Services Institution, 1930.

Fredriksen, John C. *Green Coats and Glory: The United States Regiment of Riflemen, 1808–1821*. Youngstown, N.Y.: Old Fort Niagara Association, 2000.

——— *War of 1812 Eyewitness Accounts: An Annotated Bibliography*. Westport, Conn.: Greenwood Press, 1997.

———, ed. *Free Trade and Sailors' Rights: A Bibliography of the War of 1812*. Westport, Conn.: Greenwood, 1985.

——— *Officers of the War of 1812 with Portraits and Anecdotes*. Lewiston, N.Y.: Edgar Mellen, 1989.

——— *Resource Guide for the War of 1812*. Los Angeles: Subia, 1979.

Fry, Michael. *The Dundas Despotism*. Edinburgh: Edinburgh University Press, 1992.

Fryer, Mary Beacock. *Battlefields of Canada*. Toronto: Dundurn, 1986.

——— *Bold, Brave and Born to Lead: Major General Isaac Brock and the Canadas*. Toronto: Dundurn, 2004.

Gaff, Alan D. *Bayonets in the Wilderness: Anthony Wayne's Legion in the Old Northwest*. Norman: University of Oklahoma Press, 2004.

Gaines, Pierce W. *William Cobbett and the United States, 1792–1835; Bibliography with Notes and Extracts*. Worcester, Mass.: American Antiquarian Society, 1971.

Gallatin, Albert. *The Writings of Albert Gallatin*. Ed. Henry Adams. 3 vols. Philadelphia: J. B. Lippincott, 1879.

Gardiner, Robert. *Frigates of the Napoleonic Wars*. London: Chatham, 2000.

———, ed. *The Naval War of 1812*. London, Chatham, 1998.

Gardner, C. K. *Trial by Court-Martial*. Boston, 1816.

Garitee, Jerome R. *The Republic's Private Navy: The American Privateering Business as Practiced by Baltimore during the War of 1812*. Middletown, Conn.: Mystic Seaport for Wesleyan University Press, 1977.

Garratt, Geoffrey. *Lord Brougham*. London: Macmillan, 1935.

Garrison, William Lloyd. *The Loyalty and Devotion of the Colored Americans in the Revolution and War of 1812*. Boston: R. F. Wallcut, 1861.

Gash, Norman. *Lord Liverpool: The Life and Political Career of Robert Banks Jenkinson, Second Earl of Liverpool, 1770–1828*. Cambridge, Mass.: Harvard University Press, 1984.

Gayarré, Charles Étienne. *History of Louisiana*. 4 vols. New Orleans: F. F. Hanswell and Bros., 1903.

Gellner, John, ed. *Recollections of the War of 1812: Three Eyewitness Accounts*. Toronto: Baxter Publishing, 1964.

George, Christopher T. *Terror on the Chesapeake: The War of 1812 on the Bay.* Shippensburg, Pa.: White Mane Books, 2000.

Gerson, Noel B. *Mr. Madison's War. 1812: The Second War for Independence.* New York: Julian Messner, 1967.

Geyl, Pieter. *Napoleon, For and Against.* Trans. O. Renier. Harmondsworth: Penguin, 1976.

Gilbert, Bil. *God Gave Us This Country: Tekamthi and the First American Civil War.* New York: Atheneum, 1989.

Gillen, Mollie. *Assassination of the Prime Minister: The Shocking Death of Spencer Perceval.* London: Sidgwick and Jackson, 1972.

Gillett, Mary C. *The Army Medical Department, 1775–1818.* Washington, D.C.: Center of Military History, United States Army, 1981.

Gillmer, Thomas C. *Old Ironsides: The Rise, Decline, and Resurrection of USS Constitution.* Camden, Maine: International Marine/Ragged Mountain, 1996.

——— *Pride of Baltimore: The Story of the Baltimore Clippers, 1800–1990.* Camden, Maine: International Marine, 1992.

Gilpin, Alec R. *The War of 1812 in the Old North-West.* East Lansing: Michigan State University Press, 1958.

Gleaves, Albert. *James Lawrence.* New York: G. P. Putnam's Sons, 1904.

Gleig, George Robert. *A Narrative of the Campaigns of the British Army at Washington and New Orleans under Generals Ross, Pakenham, and Lambert, in the Years 1814 and 1815: With Some Account of the Countries Visited.* London: John Murray, 1821.

Glover, Richard. *Britain at Bay: Defence against Bonaparte 1803–14.* London: George Allen and Unwin, 1973.

——— *Peninsular Preparation: The Reform of the British Army.* Cambridge: Cambridge University Press, 1963.

Goebel, Dorothy B. *William Henry Harrison: A Political Biography.* 1926; reprint, Philadelphia: Porcupine, 1974.

Goldowsky, Seebert J. *Yankee Surgeon: The Life and Times of Usher Parsons, 1788–1868.* Boston: Francis A. Countway Library of Medicine in Cooperation with Rhode Island Publications Society, 1988.

Gordon, Elizabeth, Adelaide Gordon, and Sophie Gordon, eds. *Letters and Records of Admiral Sir J. A. Gordon, G.C.B., 1782–1869.* London, 1890.

Gore, John Francis. *Nelson's Hardy and His Wife: Some Account of the Lives and Married Life of Vice-Admiral Sir Thomas Masterman Hardy, G.C.B. ("Nelson's Hardy") and of His Wife, Louisa, Lady Hardy (afterwards Lady Seaford), Derived from the Hitherto Unpublished Journals and Correspondence of Lady Seaford, and from the Hardy Papers, 1769–1877.* London: John Murray, 1935.

Gough, Barry M. *Fighting Sail on Lake Huron and Georgian Bay: The War of 1812 and Its Aftermath.* Annapolis: Naval Institute Press, 2002.

——— *The Royal Navy and the Northwest Coast of America, 1810–1914: A Study of British Maritime Ascendancy.* Vancouver: University of British Columbia Press, 1971.

——— *Through Water, Fire and Ice: Schooner Nancy and the War of 1812.* Toronto: Dundurn, 2006.

Gould, Robert. *Mercenaries of the Napoleonic Wars.* Brighton: Tom Donovan Publishing, 1995.

Gould, Stephen Jay. *Bully for Brontosaurus: Further Reflections in Natural History.* Harmondsworth: Penguin, 1992.

Graham, Gerald S. *Sea Power and British North America, 1783–1820: A Study in British Colonial Policy.* Cambridge, Mass.: Harvard University Press, 1941.

Graham, Gerald S., and R. A. Humphreys, eds. *The Navy and South America, 1807–1823.* London: Navy Records Society, 1962.

Graham, William H. *Tiger Dunlop.* London: Hutchinson, 1962.

Grant, Bruce. *Isaac Hull, Captain of Old Ironsides.* Chicago: Pellegrini and Cudahy, 1947.

Grant, John N. *The Immigration and Settlement of the Black Refugees of the War of 1812 in Nova Scotia and New Brunswick.* Dartmouth, N.S.: Black Cultural Centre, 1990.

Grattan, William. *Adventures with the Connaught Rangers.* Ed. C. Oman. London: Greenhill, 2003.

Graves, Donald E. *Field of Glory: The Battle of Crysler's Farm, 1813.* Toronto: Robin Brass Studio, 1999.

——— *Fix Bayonets! A Royal Welch Fusilier at War, 1796–1815.* Toronto: Robin Brass Studio, 2007.

——— *Red Coats and Grey Jackets: The Battle of Chippawa, 5 July 1814.* Toronto: Dundurn, 1994.

——— *Sir William Congreve and the Rocket's Red Glare.* Bloomfield, Ont.: Museum Restoration Service, 1989.

——— *"Where Right and Glory Lead!" The Battle of Lundy's Lane, 1814.* Toronto: Robin Brass Studio, 1997.

———, ed. *Merry Hearts Make Light Days: The War of 1812 Journal of Lieutenant John Le Couteur, 104th Foot.* Ottawa: Carleton University Press, 1993.

——— *Soldiers of 1814: American Enlisted Men's Memoirs of the Niagara Campaign by Jarvis Hanks, Amasiah Ford, and Alexander McMullen.* Youngstown, N.Y.: Old Fort Niagara Association, 1995.

Gray, Denis. *Spencer Perceval: The Evangelical Prime Minister, 1762–1812.* Manchester: Manchester University Press, 1962.

Gray, Elma E. *Wilderness Christians: The Moravian Mission to the Delaware Indians.* Toronto: Macmillan, 1956.

Gray, W. M. *Soldiers of the King: The Upper Canadian Militia, 1812–1815. A Reference Guide.* Erin, Ont.: Boston Mills, 1995.

Green, Constance M. *The Secret City: A History of Race Relations in the Nation's Capital.* Princeton: Princeton University Press, 1967.

Green, Michael D. *The Politics of Indian Removal: Creek Government and Society in Crisis.* Lincoln: University of Nebraska Press, 1982.

Gribbin, William J. *The Churches Militant: The War of 1812 and American Religion.* New Haven: Yale University Press, 1973.

Griffith, Benjamin W., Jr. *McIntosh and Weatherford, Creek Indian Leaders.* Tuscaloosa: University of Alabama Press, 1988.

Groom, Winston. *Patriotic Fire: Andrew Jackson and Jean Lafitte at the Battle of New Orleans.* New York: Alfred A. Knopf, 2006.

Guernsey, Rocellus S. *New York City and Vicinity during the War of 1812–15, Being a Military, Civic and Financial Local History of That Period, with Incidents and Anecdotes Thereof, and a Description of the Forts, Fortifications, Arsenals, Defenses and Camps in and about New York City and Harbor, and Those at Harlem and on East River, and in Brooklyn, and on Long Island, and at Sandy Hook, and Jersey City. With an Account of the Citizens' Movements, and of the Military and Naval Officers, Regiments, Companies, Etc., in Service There.* 2 vols. New York: Charles L. Woodward, 1889 and 1895.

Guitard, Michelle. *The Militia of the Battle of the Chateauguay: A Social History.* Ottawa: Parks Canada, 1983.

Gunckel, John E. *The Early History of the Maumee Valley.* Toledo, Ohio: Hadley Printing, 1902.

Gurney, Russell. *History of the Northamptonshire Regiment 1742–1934.* Aldershot: Gale and Polden, 1935.

Guttridge, Leonard F., and Jay D. Smith. *The Commodores.* Annapolis: Naval Institute Press, 1986.

Gwyn, Julian. *Frigates and Foremasts: The North American Squadron in Nova Scotia Waters, 1745–1815.* Vancouver: University of British Columbia Press, 2003.

Haeger, John Dennis. *John Jacob Astor: Business and Finance in the Early Republic.* Detroit: Wayne State University, 1991.

Hagan, Kenneth J. *In Peace and War: Interpretations of American Naval History, 1775–1984.* Westport, Conn.: Greenwood, 1984.

——— *The People's Navy: The Making of American Seapower.* New York: Free Press, 1991.

Hagan, William T. *The Sac and Fox Indians.* Norman: University of Oklahoma Press, 1958.

Halbert, Henry S., and T. H. Ball. *The Creek War of 1813 and 1814.* Ed. F. L. Owsley Jr. Tuscaloosa: University of Alabama Press, 1977.

Hall, Basil. *Fragments of Voyages and Travels.* London: Edward Moxon, 1841.

Hall, Christopher D. *British Strategy in the Napoleonic War, 1803–15.* Manchester: Manchester University Press, 1992.

Hallahan, John M. *The Battle of Craney Island: A Matter of Credit.* Portsmouth, Va.: St. Michael's, 1986.

Hallaman, E. *The British Invasions of Ohio—1813.* Columbus: Anthony Wayne Parkway Board, Ohio Historical Society, 1958.

Hamilton, Henry B. *Historical Record of the 14th (King's) Hussars from A.D. 1715 to A.D. 1900.* London: Longmans, Green, 1901.

Hamilton, Holman. *Zachary Taylor, Soldier of the Republic.* Hamden, Conn.: Archon Books, 1966.

Hammack, James W. *Kentucky in the Second American Revolution: The War of 1812.* Lexington: University of Kentucky Press, 1976.

Hampton, Celwyn E. *History of the Twenty-first U.S. Infantry, from 1812 to 1863.* Columbus, Ohio: Edward T. Miller, 1911.

Hanna, John S. *History of the Life and Services of Samuel Dewees. A Native of Pennsylvania and Soldier of the Revolutionary and Last War in All of Which He Was Particularly Engaged.* Baltimore: R. Neilson, 1844.

Hannay, James. *History of the War of 1812, between Great Britain and the United States of America.* St. John, N.B.: John A. Bowes, 1901.

Hannon, Leslie F. *Forts of Canada: The Conflicts, Sieges and Battles That Forged a Great Nation.* Toronto: McClelland and Stewart, 1969.

Hansard, T. C., ed. *The Parliamentary Debates from the Year 1803 to the Present Time Forming a Continuation of the Work Entitled "The Parliamentary History of England from the Earliest Period to the Year 1803."* Vols. 1–41. London: T. C. Hansard, 1803–1820.

Hanyan, Craig, and Mary L. Hanyan. *De Witt Clinton and the Rise of the People's Men.* Montreal: McGill–Queen's University Press, 1996.

Harrison, William Henry. *Messages and Letters of William Henry Harrison.* Ed. L. Esarey. 2 vols. New York: Arno, 1975.

Harvey, A. D. *Collision of Empires: Britain in Three World Wars, 1793–1945.* London: Hambledon, 1992.

Hatch, William S. *A Chapter of the History of the War of 1812 in the Northwest, Embracing the Surrender of the Northwestern Army and Fort at Detroit, August 16, 1812, with a Description and Biographical Sketch of the Celebrated Indian Chief Tecumseh.* Cincinnati: Miami Print, 1872.

Hatzenbuehler, Ronald L., and Robert L. Ivie. *Congress Declares War: Rhetoric, Leadership, and Partisanship in the Early Republic.* Kent: Kent State University Press, 1983.

Havighurst, Walter. *Three Flags at the Straits: The Forts of Mackinac.* Englewood Cliffs, N.J.: Prentice-Hall, 1966.

Hawes, Frances. *Henry Brougham.* London: Jonathan Cape, 1957.

Hawkins, Benjamin. *Letters, Journals and Writings of Benjamin Hawkins.* Ed. C. L. Grant. 2 vols. Savannah, Ga.: Bee Hive, 1980.

Hay, Thomas R., and M. R. Werner. *The Admirable Trumpeter: A Biography of General James Wilkinson.* Garden City, N.Y.: Doubleday, Doran, 1941.

Hayden, Frederick A. *Historical Record of the 76th "Hindoostan" Regiment from Its Formation in 1787 to 30 June 1880.* Lichfield: "Johnson's Head," 1909.

Haythornthwaite, Philip J. *Weapons and Equipment of the Napoleonic Wars.* London: Arms and Armour, 1979.

Healey, David. *1812: Rediscovering Chesapeake Bay's Forgotten War.* Rock Hill, S.C.: Bella Rosa, 2005.

Hecksher, Eli F. *The Continental System: An Economic Interpretation.* Oxford: Clarendon Press, 1922.

Heidler, David S., and Jeanne T. Heidler. *Old Hickory's War: Andrew Jackson and the Quest for Empire.* Baton Rouge: Louisiana State University Press, 2003.

———, eds. *Encyclopedia of the War of 1812.* Annapolis: Naval Institute Press, 2004.

Heine, William C. *96 Years in the Royal Navy: The Astonishing Story of Halifax Born Admiral of the Fleet Sir Provo Wallis, Who Joined the Royal Navy at the Age of Four and Served for 96 Years.* Hantsport, N.S.: Lancelot, 1987.

Heitman, F. B., ed. *Historical Register and Dictionary of the United States Army from Its Organization, September 29, 1789, to March 2, 1903.* 2 vols. Washington, D.C.: Government Printing Office, 1903.

Helm, Linai Taliaferro. *The Fort Dearborn Massacre, Written in 1814 by Lieutenant Linai T. Helm, One of the Survivors, with Letters and Narrative of Contemporary Interest.* Ed. N. K. Gordon. Chicago: Rand McNally, 1912.

Henderson, James. *The Frigates: An Account of the Lighter Warships of the Napoleonic Wars, 1793–1815.* London: Leo Cooper, 1994.

——— *Sloops and Brigs: An Account of the Smallest Vessels of the Royal Navy during the Great Wars 1793 to 1815.* London: Adlard Coles, 1972.

Henderson, John H. L., ed. *John Strachan: Documents and Opinions.* Toronto: McClelland and Stewart, 1969.

Hepper, David J. *British Warship Losses in the Age of Sail, 1650–1859.* Rotherfield: Jean Boudriot, 1994.

Hibbert, Christopher. *George IV.* Harmondsworth: Penguin, 2002.

Hickey, Donald R. *Don't Give Up the Ship! Myths of the War of 1812.* Chicago: University of Chicago Press, 2006.

——— *The War of 1812: A Forgotten Conflict.* Chicago: University of Illinois Press, 1990.

Hidy, Ralph W. *The House of Baring in American Trade and Finance: English Merchant Bankers at Work, 1763–1861.* Cambridge, Mass.: Harvard University Press, 1949.

Higginson, T. B., ed. *Major Richardson's: Major-General Sir Isaac Brock and the 41st Regiment.* Burke Falls, Ont.: Old Rectory, 1976.

Hill, B. E. *Recollections of an Artillery Officer: Including Scenes and Adventures in Ireland, America, Flanders, and France.* 2 vols. London: Richard Bentley, 1836.

Hill, Frederic Stanhope. *The "Lucky Little Enterprise" and Her Successors, 1776–1900.* Boston, 1900.

Hinde, Wendy. *George Canning.* London: Collins, 1973.

Hinderaker, Eric. *Elusive Empires: Constructing Colonialism in the Ohio Valley, 1673–1800.* Cambridge: Cambridge University Press, 1997.

Historical Record of The King's Liverpool Regiment of Foot, Containing an Account of the Formation of The Regiment in 1685, and of Its Subsequent Services to 1903; (Including

Affiliated Militia and Volunteer Battalions;) Also, Succession Lists of the Officers Who Served in Each of the Regimental Ranks, with Biographical Notices and Summaries of Their War Services. Enniskillen: William Trimble, 1904.

Hitsman, J. Mackay. *The Incredible War of 1812: A Military History.* Ed. D. E. Graves. Toronto: Robin Brass Studio, 1999.

——— *Safeguarding Canada, 1763–1871.* Toronto: University of Toronto Press, 1969.

Hoard, Gerard C. *Major General Jacob Jennings Brown.* Watertown, N.Y.: Hungerford, Holbrook, 1979.

Holland, James W. *Andrew Jackson and the Creek War: Victory at the Horseshoe.* Tuscaloosa: University of Alabama Press, 1968.

Holliday, Murray. *The Battle of the Mississinewa, 1812.* Marion, Ind.: Grant County Historical Society, 1964.

Hollon, W. Eugene. *The Lost Pathfinder: Zebulon Montgomery Pike.* Norman: University of Oklahoma Press, 1949.

Holmes, Jack D. L. *Honor and Fidelity: The Louisiana Infantry Regiment and the Louisiana Militia Companies, 1766–1821.* Birmingham, Ala.: Jack Holmes, 1965.

Hopkins, Fred W., Jr. *Tom Boyle, Master Privateer.* Cambridge, Mass.: Tidewater Publishers, 1976.

Hopkins, Thomas M. *Reminiscences of Col. John Ketcham of Monroe County, Indiana.* Bloomington, Ind.: Whitaker, Walker, 1860.

Horsman, Reginald. *The Causes of the War of 1812.* Philadelphia: University of Pennsylvania Press, 1962.

——— *Expansion and American Indian Policy, 1783–1812.* Norman: University of Oklahoma Press, 1992.

——— *The Frontier in the Formative Years, 1783–1815.* New York: Holt, Rinehart and Winston, 1970.

——— *Matthew Elliott, British Indian Agent.* Detroit: Wayne State University Press, 1964.

——— *The War of 1812.* London: Eyre and Spottiswoode, 1969.

Hough, Franklin B. *A History of St. Lawrence and Franklin Counties, New York.* Baltimore: Regional Publishing, 1970.

House of Lords Sessional Papers. Microfilm. Dobbs Ferry, N.Y.: Oceana Publications, 1970.

Howard, Martin. *Wellington's Doctors: The British Army Medical Services in the Napoleonic Wars.* Staplehurst: Spellmount, 2002.

Howe, H., ed. *Historical Collections of Ohio.* 2 vols. Cincinnati: Robert Clarke, 1888.

Hoyt, Edwin P. *The Tragic Commodore: The Story of Oliver Hazard Perry.* London: Abelard-Schuman, 1966.

Huber, Leonard V. *New Orleans as It Was in 1814–15.* New Orleans: Louisiana Landmarks Society, Samuel Wilson Jr. Publication Fund, 1989.

Hughes, B. P. *British Smooth-Bore Artillery: The Muzzle-Loading Artillery of the 18th and 19th Centuries.* London: Arms and Armour Press, 1969.

——— *Firepower: Weapons Effectiveness on the Battlefield, 1630–1850.* London: Arms and Armour, 1974.

Hull, Isaac. *Commodore Hull: Papers of Isaac Hull, Commodore, United States Navy.* Ed. G. W. Allen. Boston: Boston Athenaeum, 1929.

Hull, William. *Memoirs of the Campaigns of the North Western Army of the United States, A.D. 1812.* Boston: True and Greene, 1824.

——— *Report of the Trial of Brig. General William Hull; Commanding the North-Western Army of the United States: By a Court Martial Held at Albany, on Monday, 3d January, 1814, and Succeeding days / Taken by Lieut. Col. Forbes, of the Forty-second Regt. U.S. Infantry, and a Supernumerary Member of the Court.* New York: Eastburn and Kirk, 1814.

Hunt, John. *The John Hunt Memoirs.* Ed. R. J. Wright. Maumee, Ohio: Maumee Valley Historical Association, 1977.

Hunter, Alfred T. *History of the 12th Regiment, York Rangers, with Some Account of the Different Raisings of Militia in the County of York, Ontario.* Toronto: Murray Printing, n.d.

Hurd, H. D. *History of Norfolk County, Massachusetts.* Philadelphia: J. W. Lewis, 1884.

Hurt, R. D. *The Ohio Frontier: Crucible of the Old Northwest, 1720–1830.* Bloomington: Indiana University Press, 1998.

Hussey, John A., ed. *The Voyage of the "Racoon": A "Secret" Journal of a Visit to Oregon, California and Hawaii, 1813–1814.* San Francisco: Book Club of California, 1958.

Huston, J. A. *The Sinews of War: Army Logisitics, 1775–1953.* Washington, D.C.: Office of the Chief of Military History, United States Army, 1966.

Hutcheon, Wallace. *Robert Fulton: Pioneer of Undersea Warfare.* Annapolis: Naval Institute Press, 1981.

Ilisevich, Robert D. *Daniel Dobbins, Frontier Mariner.* Erie, Pa.: Erie County Historical Society, 1993.

An Impartial and Correct History of the War between the United States of America and Great Britain; Comprising a Particular Detail of the Naval and Military Operations and a Faithful Record of the Events Produced during the Contest. From Its Commencement, June 18, 1812 to the Treaty of Peace, Ratified at the City of Washington, February 17, 1815. New York: John Law, 1816.

Ingersoll, Charles Jared. *Historical Sketch of the Second War between the United States of America, and Great Britain, Declared by Act of Congress, the 18th of June, 1812, and Concluded by Peace, the 15th of February, 1815. Embracing the Events of 1812–13.* 2 vols. Philadelphia: Lea and Blanchard, 1845 and 1849.

——— *History of the Second War between the United States of America, and Great Britain, Declared by Act of Congress, the 18th of June, 1812, and Concluded by Peace, the 15th of February, 1815. Embracing the Events of 1814 and 1815.* 2 vols. Philadelphia: Lippincott, Grambo, 1852.

Ingraham, E. D. *A Sketch of the Events Which Preceded the Capture of Washington by the British, on the Twenty-fourth of August, 1814.* Philadelphia: Carey, Hart, 1849.

Ingrams, Richard. *The Life and Adventures of William Cobbett.* London: HarperCollins, 2005.

Ireland, Bernard. *Naval Warfare in the Age of Sail: War at Sea, 1756–1815.* London: HarperCollins, 2000.

Irving, H. L. *Officers of the British Forces in Canada during the War of 1812–1815.* Welland, Ont.: Canadian Military Institute, 1908.

Irwin, Ray W. *Daniel D. Tompkins: Governor of New York and Vice President of the United States.* New York: New York Historical Society, 1968.

Izard, George. *Official Correspondence with the Department of War, Relative to the Military Operations of the American Army under the Command of Major-General Izard on the Northern Frontier of the United States, in the Years 1814 and 1815.* Philadelphia: Thomas Dobson, 1816.

Jackson, Andrew. *The Correspondence of Andrew Jackson.* Ed. J. S. Bassett. 7 vols. Washington, D.C.: Carnegie Institution of Washington, 1926–1935.

——— *The Papers of Andrew Jackson.* Vol. 2: *1804–1813.* Eds. H. D. Moser and S. Macpherson. Knoxville: University of Tennessee Press, 1985.

Jackson, George. *The Bath Archives: A Further Selection from the Letters and Diaries of Sir George Jackson, K.C.H., from 1809 to 1816.* Ed. Lady Jackson. 2 vols. London: Richard Bentley and Son, 1873.

Jacobs, J. G. *The Life and Times of Patrick Gass.* Wellburg, Va.: Jacobs, Smith, 1859.

Jacobs, James R. *The Beginning of the U.S. Army, 1783–1812.* Princeton: Princeton University Press, 1947.

——— *Tarnished Warrior: Major-General James Wilkinson.* New York: Macmillan, 1938.

Jacobs, James R., and Glenn Tucker. *The War of 1812: A Compact History.* New York: Hawthorn Books, 1969.

James, Marquis. *Andrew Jackson, the Border Captain.* New York: Literary Guild, 1933.

James, William. *A Full and Correct Account of the Military Occurrences in the Late War between Great Britain and the United States.* 2 vols. London: W. James, 1818.

——— *The Naval History of Great Britain: During the French Revolutionary and Napoleonic Wars.* Vol. 6: *1811–1827.* 1837; reprint, London: Conway Maritime Press, 2002.

——— *Naval Occurrences of the War of 1812: A Full and Correct Account of the Naval War between Great Britain and the United States of America, 1812–1815.* 1817; reprint, London: Conway Maritime Press, 2004.

Jarvis, Samuel Parker. *Historical Record of the Eighty-second Regiment, or Prince of Wales's Volunteers.* London: W. O. Mitchell, 1866.

Jefferson, Thomas. *The Writings of Thomas Jefferson.* Ed. P. L. Ford. 10 vols. New York: G. P. Putnam's Sons, 1892–1899.

Jenkins, Brian. *Henry Goulburn, 1784–1856: A Political Biography.* Liverpool: Liverpool University Press, 1996.

Jennings, Walter W. *The American Embargo, 1807–1809, with Particular Reference to Its Effect on Industry.* Iowa City: University of Iowa Press, 1921.

Johnson, Charles M. *The Battle for the Heartland: Stoney Creek, June 6, 1813*. Stoney Creek, Ont.: Pennel Printing, 1963.

———, ed. *The Valley of the Six Nations: A Collection of Documents on the Indian Lands of the Grand River.* Toronto: Champlain Society, 1964.

Johnson, Ida Amanda. *The Michigan Fur Trade.* Grand Rapids, Mich.: Black Letter Press, 1971.

Johnson, Timothy D. *Winfield Scott: The Quest for Military Glory.* Lawrence: University Press of Kansas, 1998.

Johnston, H. Winston. *The Glengarry Light Infantry, 1812–1816: Who Were They and What Did They Do in the War?* Charlottetown, P.E.I.: Benson Publishing, 2003.

Johnston, Samuel B. *Letters Written during a Residence of Three Years in Chili, Containing an Account of the Most Remarkable Events in the Revolutionary Struggles of That Province. With an Interesting Account of the Loss of a Chilian Ship, and Brig of War, by Mutiny, and the Consequent Imprisonment and Sufferings of Several Citizens of the United States, for Six Months, in the Dungeons of Callao.* Erie, Pa.: R. I. Custis, 1816.

Johnston, S. H. F. *The History of The Cameronians (Scottish Rifles).* Vol. 1: *1689–1910.* Aldershot: Gale and Polden, 1957.

Johnstone, Robert M., Jr. *Jefferson and the Presidency: Leadership in the Young Republic.* Ithaca: Cornell University Press, 1978.

Jonasson, E., ed. *Canadian Veterans of the War of 1812.* Winnipeg, Man.: Wheatfield Press, 1981.

Jones, Maldwyn A. *The Limits of Liberty: American History, 1607–1980.* Oxford: Oxford University Press, 1983.

Jones, Noah. *Journals of Two Cruises aboard the American Privateer Yankee, by a Wanderer.* Ed. E. M. Eller. New York: Macmillan, 1967.

Jordan, Weymouth T. *George Washington Campbell of Tennessee: Western Statesman.* Tallahassee: Florida State University, 1955.

Kaiser, D. *Politics and War: European Conflict from Philip II to Hitler.* London: Tauris, 1990.

Kappler, Charles J., ed. *Indian Affairs: Laws and Treaties.* 2 vols. Washington, D.C.: Government Printing Office, 1903.

Katcher, Philip, and Bryan Fosten. *The American War, 1812–14.* London: Osprey, 1990.

Keefer, F. H. *Beaver Dams.* Thorold, Ont.: Thorold Post Printers, 1914.

Kellogg, Louise P. *The British Régime in Wisconsin and the Northwest.* Madison: State Historical Society of Wisconsin, 1935.

Kennedy, Paul M. *The Rise and Fall of the Great Powers: Economic Change and Military Conflict from 1500 to 2000.* London: Unwin Hyman, 1988.

Kenrick, N. C. E. *The Story of The Wiltshire Regiment (Duke of Edinburgh's), The 62nd and 99th Foot (1756–1959), The Militia and The Territorials, The Service Battalions and All Those Others Who Have Served or Been Affiliated with The Moonrakers.* Aldershot: Gale and Polden, 1963.

Kent, Charles Deane. *Norfolk Spies in 1812.* Ottawa: Westboro Printers, 1989.

Kerber, Linda. *Federalists in Dissent: Imagery and Ideology in Jeffersonian America.* Ithaca: Cornell University Press, 1970.

Kert, Faye M. *Prize and Prejudice: Privateering and Naval Prizes in Atlantic Canada in the War of 1812.* St. John's, Newf.: International Maritime Economic History Association, 1997.

——— *Trimming Yankee Sails: Pirates and Privateers of New Brunswick.* Fredericton, N.B.: Goose Lane Editions, 2005.

Ketcham, Ralph. *James Madison: A Biography.* Charlottesville: University of Virginia Press, 1990.

Kieffer, Chester L. *Maligned General: The Biography of Thomas Sidney Jesup.* San Rafael, Calif.: Presidio, 1979.

King, Dean, with John B. Hattendorf, eds. *Every Man Will Do His Duty: An Anthology of First Hand Accounts from the Age of Nelson, 1793–1815.* New York: Henry Holt, 1997.

Kingsford, Charles Lethbridge. *The Story of the Royal Warwickshire Regiment (Formerly the Sixth Foot).* London: Country Life, 1921.

Kingsford, William. *The History of Canada.* 10 vols. Toronto: Rowell and Hutchison, 1887–1898.

Kirby, T. *The Life and Times and Wonderful Achievements of the Adventurous and Renowned Capt. Kirby, the Hero of the War of 1812.* Cincinnati: T. Kirby, 1865.

Kirby, William. *Annals of Niagara.* Toronto: MacMillan of Canada, 1927.

Kirk, Russell. *Randolph of Roanoke: A Study in Conservative Thought.* Chicago: University of Chicago Press, 1951.

Knapp, Horace S. *History of the Maumee Valley.* Toledo: Black Mammoth Printing, 1872.

Knight, C. R. B. *Historical Records of The Buffs East Kent Regiment (3rd Foot) Formerly Designated The Holland Regiment And Prince George of Denmark's Regiment 1704–1914.* Vol. 2. London: Medici Society, 1935.

Knoll, Denys W. *Battle of Lake Erie: Building the Fleet in the Wilderness.* Washington, D.C.: Naval Historical Foundation, 1979.

Knopf, Richard C., ed. *Document Transcriptions of the War of 1812 in the Northwest.* 10 vols. Columbus: Ohio Historical Society, 1961–1962.

——— *Return Johnathan Meigs and the War of 1812.* Columbus: Anthony Wayne Board, Ohio Historical Society, 1957.

Kochan, James L., and David Rickman. *The United States Army 1812–1815.* Oxford: Osprey, 2000.

Kohn, Richard L. *Eagle and Sword: The Federalists and the Creation of the Military Establishment in America, 1783–1802.* New York: Free Press, 1975.

Kreidberg, Marvin A., and Merton G. Henry. *The History of Military Mobilization in the United States Army.* Washington, D.C.: Department of the Army, 1955.

Kroll, Steven. *By the Dawn's Early Light: The Story of the Star-Spangled Banner.* New York: Scholastic, 1994.

Kurlansky, Mark. *Salt: A World History.* London: Vintage, 2003.

Laffite, J. *The Journal of Jean Laffite: The Privateer-Patriot's Own Story.* New York: Vantage, 1958.

Lambert, Andrew. *War at Sea in the Age of Sail.* London: Cassell, 2000.

Landon, Harry F. *Bugles on the Border: The Story of the War of 1812 in Northern New York.* Watertown, N.Y.: Watertown Daily Times, 1954.

——— *Western Ontario and the American Frontier.* Toronto: Ryerson Press, 1941.

Langguth, A. J. *Union 1812: The Americans Who Fought the Second War of Independence.* London: Simon and Schuster, 2006.

Langley, Harold D. *Social Reform in the United States Navy, 1798–1862.* Urbana: University of Illinois Press, 1967.

Lardas, Mark, and Tony Bryan. *American Heavy Frigates 1794–1826.* Oxford: Osprey, 2003.

Latham, Frank B. *Jacob Brown and the War of 1812.* New York: Cowles, 1971.

Latham, Jean Lee. *Anchors Aweigh: The Story of David Glasgow Farragut.* New York: Harper and Row, 1968.

Latour, A. L. *Historical Memoir of the War in West Florida and Louisiana in 1814–15: With an Atlas.* Ed. G. A. Smith. Gainesville: University Press of Florida, 1999.

Latrobe, Benjamin Henry. *The Correspondence and Miscellaneous Papers of Benjamin Henry Latrobe.* Ed. J. C. Van Horne. 3 vols. New Haven: Yale University Press, 1988.

Laughton, J. K., ed. *Letters and Papers of Charles, Lord Barham, Admiral of the Red Squadron, 1758–1813.* 3 vols. London: Navy Records Society, 1907–1911.

Lavery, Brian. *Shipboard Life and Organization, 1731–1815.* London: Ashgate, 1999.

———, ed. *Nelson's Navy: Ships, Men and Organization, 1793–1815.* London: Conway Maritime Press, 2004.

La Violette, Paul Estronza. *Sink or Be Sunk! The Naval Battle in the Mississippi Sound That Preceded the Battle of New Orleans.* Waveland, Miss.: Annabelle Publishing, 2002.

Lawler, W. R. *Index of the Civilian Loss Claims for the Western District from the War of 1812–14.* Chatham, Ont.: Ontario Genealogical Society, 1997.

Laws, M. E. S. *Battery Records of the Royal Artillery, 1716–1859.* Woolwich: Royal Artillery Institution, 1952.

Lawson, Don. *The War of 1812: America's Second War for Independence.* London: Abelard-Schuman, 1966.

Leask, J. C., and H. M. McCance. *The Regimental Records of the Royal Scots.* Dublin: A. Thom, 1915.

Leavitt, Henry Howe. *Autobiography of the Hon. Henry Howe Leavitt, Written for His Family.* New York, 1893.

Leavitt, T. W. *History of Leeds and Grenville, Ontario, from 1749 to 1879: With Illustrations and Biographical Sketches of Some of Its Prominent Men and Pioneers.* Brockville, Ont.: Recorder Press, 1879.

Lee, James. *The Masting and Rigging of English Ships of War, 1625–1860.* London: Conway Maritime Press, 1984.

Leech, Samuel. *Thirty Years from Home; or, A Voice from the Main Deck.* London: John Neale, 1844.

Lehmann, Joseph. *Remember You Are an Englishman: A Biography of Sir Harry Smith 1787–1860.* London: Jonathan Cape, 1977.

Leland, Sherman. *An Oration Pronounced at Dorchester, Massachusetts, in Commemoration of the Independence of the United States, etc.* Boston, 1815.

Lemmon, Sarah McCulloh. *Frustrated Patriots: North Carolina and the War of 1812.* Chapel Hill: University of North Carolina Press, 1973.

Le Roy, Perry. *The Weakness of Discipline and Its Consequent Results in the Northwest during the War of 1812.* Columbus: Anthony Wayne Parkway Board, Ohio Historical Society, 1958.

Lerwill, L. *The Personnel Replacement System in the United States Army.* Washington, D.C.: Department of the Army, 1951.

Lessem, Harold I., and George C. Mackenzie. *Fort McHenry: National Monument and Historic Shrine, Maryland.* Washington, D.C.: National Park Service, 1954.

Lester, Malcolm. *Anthony Merry Redivivus: A Reappraisal of the British Minister to the United States, 1803–6.* Charlottesville: University of Virginia Press, 1978.

The Letters of Veritas, Re-Published from the Montreal Herald; Containing a Succinct Narrative of the Military Administration of Sir G. Prevost, during His Command in the Canadas; Whereby It Will Appear . . . That the Merit of Preserving Them from Conquest, Belongs Not to Him. Montreal: W. Gray, 1815.

Levinge, R. G. A. *Historical Records of The Forty-third Regiment, Monmouthshire Light Infantry, with a Roll of Officers and Their Services from the Period of Embodiment to the Close of 1867.* London: William Clowes, 1868.

Levy, Leonard W. *Jefferson and Civil Liberties: The Darker Side.* Chicago: Ivan R. Dee, 1989.

Levy, Uriah Phillips. *Defense of Uriah Phillips Levy before the Court of Inquiry Held at Washington City, November and December, 1857.* New York: W. C. Bryant, 1857.

Lewis, Charles L. *David Glasgow Farragut, Admiral in the Making.* Annapolis: United States Naval Institute, 1941.

——— *The Romantic Decatur.* Philadelphia: University of Pennsylvania Press, 1937.

Lewis, Dennis M. *British Naval Activity on Lake Champlain during the War of 1812.* Plattsburgh and Elizabethtown, N.Y.: Clinton and Essex County Historical Societies, 1994.

Lewis, Emanuel Raymond. *Sea Coast Fortifications of the United States.* Annapolis: Naval Institute Press, 1970.

Lewis, Jon E., ed. *The Mammoth Book of Life before the Mast: An Anthology of Eye-Witness Accounts from the Age of Fighting Sail.* London: Robinson, 2001.

Lewis, Michael A. *A Social History of the Navy, 1793–1815.* London: George Allen and Unwin, 1960.

Lighthall, William D. *An Account of the Battle of Chateauguay Being a Lecture Delivered at Ormstown, March 8th, 1889 by W. D. Lighthall, M.A. With some Local and Personal Notes by W. Patterson, M.A.* Montreal: W. Drysdale, 1889.

Linder, Adolphe. *The Swiss Regiment Meuron at the Cape and Afterwards, 1781–1816.* Cape Town: Castle Military Museum, 2000.

Linn, John Blair. *Annals of Buffalo Valley, Pennsylvania, 1755–1855.* Harrisburg, Pa.: Lane S. Hart, 1877.

Litt, Paul, Ronald F. Williamson, and Joseph W. A. Whitehorne. *Death at Snake Hill: Secrets from a War of 1812 Cemetery.* Toronto: Dundurn, 1993.

Little, George. *Life on the Ocean; or, Twenty Years at Sea: Being the Personal Adventures of the Author.* Boston: Watts, Pierce, 1843.

Livermore, Shaw, Jr. *The Twilight of Federalism: The Disintegration of the Federalist Party, 1815–1830.* Princeton: Princeton University Press, 1962.

Livingston, John. *Portraits of Eminent Americans.* New York: Craighead, 1854.

Lloyd, Alan R. *The Scorching of Washington: The War of 1812.* Newton Abbott: David and Charles, 1974.

Lloyd, Christopher. *Captain Marryat and the Old Navy.* London: Longmans, Green, 1939.

Loftus, Charles. *My Youth by Sea and Land from 1809–1816.* 2 vols. London: Hurst and Blackett, 1876.

Lomax, D. A. N. *A History of the Services of the 41st (the Welch) Regiment, Now 1st Battalion The Welch Regiment, from Its Formation, in 1719, to 1895.* Devonport: Hiorns and Miller, 1899.

London, Joshua E. *Victory in Tripoli: How America's War with the Barbary Pirates Established the U.S. Navy and Shaped a Nation.* New York: John Wiley and Sons, 2005.

Long, David F. *"Mad Jack": The Biography of Captain John Percival, USN, 1779–1862.* Westport, Conn.: Greenwood, 1993.

——— *Nothing Too Daring: A Biography of Commodore David Porter, 1780–1843.* Annapolis: Naval Institute Press, 1970.

——— *Ready to Hazard: A Biography of Commodore William Bainbridge, 1774–1833.* Hanover, N.H.: University Press of New England, 1981.

——— *Sailor-Diplomat: A Biography of James Biddle, 1783–1848.* Boston: Northeastern University Press, 1983.

Lord, Walter. *The Dawn's Early Light.* New York: W. W. Norton, 1972.

Lorrain, Alfred M. *The Helm, the Cross and the Sword: A Life Narrative.* Cincinnati: Poe, Hitchcock, 1862.

Lossing, Benson J. *The Pictorial Field-Book of the War of 1812; or, Illustrations, by Pen and Pencil, of the History, Biography, Scenery, Relics, and Traditions of the Last War for American Independence. With Several Hundred Engravings on Wood, by Lossing and Barritt, Chiefly from Original Sketches by the Author.* New York: Harper Brothers, 1869.

Lovell, William Stanhope. *From Trafalgar to the Chesapeake: Adventures of an Officer in Nelson's Navy.* Ed. R. F. Mackay. Annapolis: Naval Institute Press, 2003.

Lucas, Charles Prestwood. *The Canadian War of 1812.* Oxford: Clarendon Press, 1906.

Lucas, Robert. *The Robert Lucas Journal of the War of 1812 during the Campaign under General William Hull.* Ed. J. C. Parish. Iowa City: State Historical Society of Iowa, 1906.

Luxon, Norval. *Niles' Weekly Register: News Magazine of the Nineteenth Century.* Baton Rouge: Louisiana State University Press, 1947.

MacCarthy, Fiona. *Byron: Life and Legend.* London: John Murray, 2002.

MacDonald, Janet, *Feeding Nelson's Navy: The True Story of Food at Sea in the Georgian Era.* London: Chatham, 2004.

Macdonough, Rodney. *The Life of Commodore Thomas Macdonough, U.S. Navy.* Boston: Fort Hill, S. Usher, 1909.

Mackay, Charles. *Memoirs of Extraordinary Popular Delusions.* 2 vols. London, 1841.

Mackenzie, Alexander Slidell. *The Life of Commodore Oliver Hazard Perry.* 2 vols. New York: Harper and Brothers, 1840–1841.

——— *Life of Stephen Decatur, a Commodore in the Navy of the United States.* Boston: C. C. Little and J. Brown, 1846.

Mackenzie, Robert Holden. *The Trafalgar Roll: Containing the Names and Services of All Officers of the Royal Navy and Royal Marines Who Participated in the Glorious Victory of the 21st October 1805, Together with a History of the Ships Engaged in the Battle.* London: George Allen, 1913.

Mackenzie, Ruth. *James FitzGibbon: Defender of Upper Canada.* Toronto: Dundurn, 1983.

——— *Laura Secord: The Legend and the Lady.* Toronto: McClelland and Stewart, 1971.

Mackesy, Piers. *War without Victory: The Downfall of Pitt, 1799–1802.* Oxford: Clarendon Press, 1984.

Maclay, E. S. *A History of American Privateers.* New York: D. Appleton, 1899.

——— *A History of the United States Navy from 1775 to 1884.* 2 vols. New York: D. Appleton, 1894 and 1897.

Macomb, Alexander. *Memoir of Alexander Macomb, the Major General Commanding the Army of the United States.* Ed. George H. Richards. 1835; reprint, Ann Arbor: University Microfilms International, 1979.

Madison, James. *Letters and Other Writings of James Madison.* Ed. P. R. Fendall. 4 vols. Philadelphia: J. B. Lippincott, 1865.

——— *The Writings of James Madison.* Ed. Gaillard Hunt. 9 vols. New York: G. P. Putnam's Sons, 1908.

Mahan, Alfred T. *The Influence of Sea Power upon the French Revolution and Empire: 1793–1812.* 2 vols. London: Sampson Low, Marston, 1891.

——— *Sea Power in Its Relations to the War of 1812.* 2 vols. Boston: Little, Brown, 1905.

Mahon, John K. *The War of 1812.* Gainesville: University of Florida Press, 1972.

Mahon, John K., and Romana Danysh. *Army Lineage Series, Infantry Part I: Regular Army.* Washington, D.C.: Office of the Chief of Military History, United States Army, 1972.

Malcomson, Robert. *Historical Dictionary of the War of 1812.* Lanham, Md.: Scarecrow, 2006.

——— *Lords of the Lake: The Naval War on Lake Ontario, 1812–1814.* Toronto: Robin Brass Studio, 1998.

——— *A Very Brilliant Affair: The Battle of Queenston Heights, 1812.* Annapolis: Naval Institute Press, 2003.

——— *Warships of the Great Lakes 1754–1834.* London: Chatham, 2001.

———, ed. *Sailors of 1812: Memoirs and Letters of Naval Officers on Lake Ontario.* Youngstown, N.Y.: Old Fort Niagara Association, 1997.

Malcomson, Robert, and Tom Malcomson. *H.M.S. Detroit: The Battle for Lake Erie.* St. Catharines, Ont.: Vanwell Publishing, 1990.

Mallory, Enid L. *The Green Tiger: James Fitzgibbon, a Hero of the War of 1812.* Toronto: McClelland and Stewart, 1976.

Malone, Dumas. *Jefferson and His Time.* 6 vols. Charlottesville: University of Virginia Press, 2006.

——— *Jefferson the President: Second Term, 1805–1809.* Boston: Little, Brown, 1974.

Maloney, Linda M. *The Captain from Connecticut: The Life and Naval Times of Isaac Hull.* Boston: Northeastern University Press, 1986.

Mann, Butler. *History of the Commonwealth of Kentucky.* Cincinnati: Wilcox, Dickerman, 1836.

Mann, James. *Medical Sketches of the Campaigns of 1812, 13, 14. To Which Are Added, Surgical Cases; Observations on Military Hospitals and Flying Hospitals Attached to a Moving Army. Also, an Appendix, Comprising a Dissertation on Dysentery Which Obtained the Boylstonial Prize Medal for the Year 1806 and Observations on the Winter Epidemic of 1815–16, Denominated Peripneumonia Notha, as It Appeared at Sharon and Rochester, State of Massachusetts.* Dedham, Mass.: H. Mann, 1816.

Mapp, Alf J., Jr. *Thomas Jefferson: Passionate Pilgrim.* Lanham, Md.: Madison Books, 1991.

Marcus, Geoffrey J. *Heart of Oak: A Survey of British Sea Power in the Georgian Era.* London: Oxford University Press, 1975.

Marcus, J. R., ed. *Memoirs of American Jews, 1775–1865.* 3 vols. Philadelphia: Jewish Publication Society, 1955.

Marine, W. M. *The British Invasion of Maryland, 1812–1815.* Hatboro, Pa.: Tradition Press, 1965.

Marriott, John A. R. *George Canning and His Times: A Political Study.* London: John Murray, 1907.

Marshall, John. *Royal Naval Biography; or, Memoirs of the Services of All the Flag-Officers, Superannuated Rear-Admirals, Retired-Captains, Post-Captains and Commanders: Whose Names Appeared on the Admiralty List of Sea Officers at the Commencement of the Present Year, or Who Have Since Been Promoted: Illustrated by a Series of Historical and Explanatory Notes, Which Will Be Found to Contain an Account of All the Naval Actions, and Other Important Events, from the Commencement of the Late Reign, in 1760 to the Present Period: With Copious Addenda.* 12 vols. London: Longman, Hurst, Rees, Ormen and Brown, 1823–1835.

Marsters, Roger. *Bold Privateers: Terror, Plunder and Profit on Canada's Atlantic Coast.* Halifax, N.S.: Formac, 2004.

Martin, Arthur Patchett. *Life and Letters of the Right Honourable Robert Lowe, Viscount Sherbrooke, G.C.B., D.C.L., etc.: With a Memoir of Sir John Coape Sherbrooke, G.C.B., Sometime Governor-General of Canada.* London: Longmans, Green 1893.

Martin, Christopher. *Damn the Torpedoes! The Story of America's First Admiral: David Glasgow Farragut.* London: Abelard-Schuman, 1970.

Martin, Joel W. *Sacred Revolt: The Muskogees' Struggle for a New World.* Boston: Beacon, 1991.

Martin, Tyrone G. *A Most Fortunate Ship: Narrative History of Old Ironsides.* Shrewsbury: Airlife, 1997.

——— *Undefeated: Old Ironsides in the War of 1812.* Chapel Hill, N.C.: Tryon Publishing, 1997.

Masefield, John. *Sea Life in Nelson's Time.* London: Sphere Books, 1972.

Mason, Philip P., ed. *After Tippecanoe: Some Aspects of the War of 1812.* East Lansing: Michigan State University Press, 1963.

May, George S. *War 1812: The United States and Great Britain at Mackinac, 1812–1815.* Mackinac Island, Mich.: Mackinac Island State Park Commission, 2004.

Mayo, Bernard. *Henry Clay: Spokesman of the New West.* New Haven, Conn.: Shoe String, 1966.

McAfee, Robert B. *History of the Late War in the Western Country: Comprising a Full Account of All the Transactions in That Quarter, from the Commencement of Hostilities at Tippecanoe, to the Termination of the Contest at New Orleans on the Return of Peace.* Westminster, Md.: Heritage Books, 1994.

McClellan, James. *Joseph Story and the American Constitution: A Study in Political and Legal Thought with Selected Writings.* Norman: University of Oklahoma Press, 1971.

McClure, George. *Causes of the Destruction of the American Towns on the Niagara Frontier and the Failure of the Campaign of the Fall of 1813.* Bath, N.Y.: Benjamin Snead, 1817.

McConnell, Roland C. *Negro Troops of Antebellum Louisiana: A History of the Battalion of Free Men of Color.* Baton Rouge: Louisiana State University Press, 1968.

McCoy, Drew R. *The Elusive Republic: Political Economy in Jeffersonian America.* Chapel Hill: University of North Carolina Press, 1996.

——— *The Last of the Fathers: James Madison and the Republican Legacy.* Cambridge: Cambridge University Press, 1991.

McCullough, David. *John Adams.* New York: Simon and Schuster, 2001.

McKee, Christopher. *A Gentlemanly and Honorable Profession: The Creation of the U.S. Naval Officer Corps, 1794–1815.* Annapolis: Naval Institute Press, 1991.

McKenney, T. L. *Memoirs, Official and Personal, with Sketches of Travels among Northern and Southern Indians, Embracing a War Excursion, and Descriptions of Scenes along the Western Borders.* 2 vols. New York: Paine and Burgess, 1846.

McLeod, Donald. *A Brief Review of the Settlement of Upper Canada by the U. E.Loyalists and Scotch Highlanders, in 1783: and of the Grievances Which Compelled the Canadas to Have Recourse to Arms in Defence of Their Rights and Liberties, in the Years 1837 and 1838: Together with a Brief Sketch of the Campaigns of 1812, '13, '14: With an Account of the Military Executions, Burnings, and Sackings of Towns and Villages, by the British, in the Upper and Lower Provinces, during the Commotion of 1837 and '38.* Cleveland: Printed for the author by F. B. Penniman, 1841.

McMaster, John Bach. *A History of the People of the United States, from the Revolution to the Civil War.* 4 vols. New York: D. Appleton, 1911–1914.

McNutt, W. S. *The Atlantic Provinces: The Emergence of Colonial Society, 1712–1857.* Toronto: McClelland and Stewart, 1965.

Meddert, P. F. *Raw Recruits and Bullish Prisoners: Ohio's Capital in the War of 1812.* Jackson, Ohio: Ross County Historical Society, 1992.

Meigs, William M. *The Life of Charles Jared Ingersoll.* Philadelphia: J. B. Lippincott, 1897.

Meinig, D. W. *The Shaping of America: A Geographical Perspective on 500 Years of History.* New Haven: Yale University Press, 1993.

Melish, John. *A Description of Dartmoor Prison, with an Account of the Massacre of the Prisoners; Designed as an Accompaniment to the View of Dartmoor Prison, Drawn by J. J. Taylor, One of the Prisoners.* Philadelphia: J. Melish, 1815.

Merritt, Jebediah. *Biography of the Honourable William H. Merritt, M.P., of Lincoln, District of Niagara.* St. Catharines, Ont.: E. S. Leavenworth, 1875.

Merritt, William Hamilton. *Journal of Events Principally on the Detroit and Niagara Frontiers during the War of 1812.* St. Catharines, Ont.: Historical Society B. N. A., 1863.

Meuron, Guy de. *Le Régiment Meuron 1781–1816.* Lausanne: Le Forum Historique, 1982.

Meyer, Leland M. *The Life and Times of Colonel Richard M. Johnson of Kentucky.* New York: AMS Press, 1967.

Meyer, Sam. *Paradoxes of Fame: The Francis Scott Key Story.* Annapolis: Eastwind Publishing, 1995.

Miller, Nathan. *Broadsides: The Age of Fighting Sail, 1775–1815.* New York: John Wiley and Sons, 2000.

Miller, Stephen F., ed. *Memoir of General David Blackshear.* Philadelphia: J. B. Lippincott, 1858.

Mills, James C. *Oliver Hazard Perry and the Battle of Lake Erie.* Detroit: John Phelps, 1913.

Morgan, Henry J. *Sketches of Celebrated Canadians and Persons Connected with Canada: From the Earliest Period in the History of the Province down to the Present Time.* Montreal: R. Worthington, 1865.

Morgan, J. C. *The Emigrant's Note Book and Guide; With Recollections of Upper and Lower Canada, during the Late War.* London: Longman, Hurst, Rees, Orme, and Brown, 1824.

Morison, Samuel Eliot. *By Land and by Sea: Essays and Addresses.* New York: Alfred A. Knopf, 1953.

——— *The Life and Letters of Harrison Gray Otis, Federalist, 1765–1848.* 2 vols. Boston: Houghton Mifflin, 1913.

——— *The Maritime History of Massachusetts, 1783–1860.* Boston: Houghton Mifflin, 1941.

Morison, Samuel Eliot, and Henry Steele Commager. *The Growth of the American Republic.* 2 vols. New York: Oxford University Press, 1962.

Morison, Samuel Eliot, Frederick Merk, and Frank Friedel, eds. *Dissent in Three American Wars.* Cambridge, Mass.: Harvard University Press, 1970.

Morris, Charles. *The Autobiography of Commodore Charles Morris, USN.* Annapolis: Naval Institute Press, 2002.

Morris, John D. *Sword of the Border: Major General Jacob Jennings Brown, 1775–1828.* Kent: Kent State University Press, 2000.

Morrison, Jean. *Superior Rendez-vous Place: Fort William in the Canadian Fur Trade.* Toronto: Natural Heritage/Natural History, 2001.

Morriss, Roger. *Cockburn and the British Navy in Transition: Admiral Sir George Cockburn 1772–1853.* Exeter: University of Exeter Press, 1997.

Mouzon, Harold A. *Privateers of Charleston in the War of 1812.* Charleston: Historical Commission of Charleston, South Carolina, 1954.

Muir, Rory. *Salamanca 1812.* New Haven: Yale University Press, 2001.

——— *Tactics and the Experience of Battle in the Age of Napoleon.* New Haven: Yale University Press, 2000.

Mullaly, B. R. *The South Lancashire Regiment The Prince of Wales's Volunteers.* Bristol: White Swan Press, n.d.

Muller, Charles G. *The Darkest Day: 1814; The Washington-Baltimore Campaign.* Philadelphia: J. B. Lippincott, 1963.

——— *The Proudest Day: Macdonough on Lake Champlain.* New York: John Day, 1960.

Myer, Jesse S. *Life and Letters of Dr. William Beaumont, Including Hitherto Unpublished Data concerning the Case of Alexis St. Martin.* St. Louis, Mo.: C. V. Mosby, 1912.

Myers, H. L. *Pennsylvania and the War of 1812.* Hamburg, Pa.: Pennsylvania Historical and Museum Commission, 1964.

Myers, M. *Reminiscences, 1780–1814, Including Incidents in the War of 1812.* Washington, D.C.: Crane, 1900.

Nagel, Paul F. *John Quincy Adams: A Public Life, A Private Life.* New York: Alfred A. Knopf, 1997.

Napier, Edward. *The Life and Correspondence of Admiral Sir Charles Napier, K.C.B., from Personal Recollections, Letters, and Official Documents.* 2 vols. London: Hurst and Blackett, 1862.

Napier, W. F. P. *The Life and Opinions of General Sir Charles Napier, G.C.B.* 4 vols. London: John Murray, 1857.

Narrative of the Capture of the U.S. Brig Vixen, 14 Guns, by the British Frigate Southampton and the Subsequent Loss of Both Vessels on a Reef off Conception Island. New York: "The War," 1813.

Narrative of the Life of General Leslie Combs: Embracing Incidents in the Early History of the Northwestern Territory. Washington, D.C.: J. T. and Lem Towers, 1855.

Neal, David A. *East by Sea and West by Rail: The Journal of David Augustus Neal of Salem, Massachusetts, 1793–1861.* Toronto: Eldridge Printing, 1979.

Nell, William Cooper. *Services of Colored Americans in the Wars of 1776 and 1812.* Boston: Prentiss and Sawyer, 1851.

Nelson, Larry L. *Men of Patriotism, Courage and Enterprise! Fort Meigs in the War of 1812.* Westminster, Md.: Heritage Books, 2003.

Nelson, Rodney B. *Beaumont: America's First Physiologist.* Geneva, Ill.: Grant House, 1990.

Neptune, W. J. *The Life and Adventures of W. J. Neptune, Commonly Called General Jarvis, Written by Himself.* Kingston upon Hull: Peck, Smith, 1832.

Nerva; or, A Collection of Papers Published in the Montreal Herald. Montreal: William Gray, 1814.

Nettels, C. P. *The Emergence of a National Economy, 1775–1815.* New York: Harper and Row, 1969.

New, Chester W. *The Life of Henry Brougham to 1830.* Oxford: Clarendon Press, 1961.

Nicholas, Isaac P. *Twenty Years before the Mast; or, Life in the Forecastle.* New York: J. P. Beckwith, 1845.

Nichols, Roger L. *Black Hawk and the Warrior's Path.* Wheeling, Ill.: Harlan Davidson, 1992.

Nicholson, G. W. L. *The Fighting Newfoundlander: A History of The Royal Newfoundland Regiment.* London: Thomas Nelson for the Government of Newfoundland, 1964.

——— *The Gunners of Canada: The History of the Royal Regiment of Canadian Artillery.* Toronto: McClelland and Stewart, 1967.

Nicolas, Paul Harris. *Historical Record of the Royal Marine Forces.* Vol. 2. London: Thomas and William Boone, 1845.

Nielson, Peter Raymond. *Financial History of the United States, 1811–1816.* Washington, D.C.: Catholic University of America Press, 1926.

Niven, John. *John C. Calhoun and the Price of Union.* Baton Rouge: Louisiana State University Press, 1988.

Nolte, Vincent. *Fifty Years in Both Hemispheres; or, Reminiscences of the Life of a Former Merchant.* New York: Redfield, 1856.

Norton, John. *The Journal of Major John Norton, 1816.* Ed. C. F. Klinck and J. J. Talman. Toronto: Champlain Society, 1970.

Norton, Louis A. *Joshua Barney: Hero of the Revolution and 1812.* Annapolis: Naval Institute Press, 2000.

Norway, Arthur S. *History of the Post Office Packet Service, between the Years of 1783 and 1815.* London: Macmillan, 1895.

Nosworthy, Brent. *Battle Tactics of Napoleon and His Enemies.* London: Constable and Robinson, 1997.

Nursey, Walter R. *The Story of Isaac Brock, Hero, Defender and Savior of Upper Canada, 1812.* Toronto: McClelland and Stewart, 1923.

Oatts, Lewis Balfour. *The Emperor's Chambermaids: The Story of the 14th/20th King's Hussars.* London: Ward Lock, 1973.

O'Brien, Sean Michael. *In Bitterness and in Tears: Andrew Jackson's Destruction of the Creeks and Seminoles.* Westport, Conn.: Praeger, 2003.

Onuf, Peter S., and Leonard J. Sadosky. *Jeffersonian America.* Malden, Mass.: Blackwell Publishers, 2002.

Osborne, John W. *William Cobbett: His Thought and His Times.* New Brunswick, N.J.: Rutgers University Press, 1966.

Ouellet, Fernand. *Economic and Social History of Quebec, 1760–1850: Structures and Conjectures.* Toronto: Gage, 1983.

Owsley, Frank L., Jr. *Struggle for the Gulf Borderlands: The Creek War and the Battle of New Orleans, 1812–1815.* Gainesville: University Presses of Florida, 1981.

Owsley, Frank L., Jr., and Gene A. Smith. *Filibusters and Expansionists: Jeffersonian Manifest Destiny, 1800–1821.* Tuscaloosa: University of Alabama Press, 2004.

Oxford Dictionary of National Biography. 60 vols. Oxford: Oxford University Press, 2004.

Pack, A. J. *The Man Who Burned the White House: Admiral Sir George Cockburn, 1772–1853.* Emsworth: Kenneth Mason, 1987.

Padfield, Peter. *Broke and the Shannon.* London: Hodder and Stoughton, 1968.

Paine, R. D. *The Fight for a Free Sea: A Chronicle of the War of 1812.* New Haven: Yale University Press, 1920.

Pakenham, Thomas. *Pakenham Letters, 1800 to 1815.* London: John and Edward Bumpus, 1914.

Palmer, Benjamin F. *The Diary of Benjamin F. Palmer, Privateersman.* New Haven: Tuttle, Moorehouse, Taylor, 1914.

Palmer, F. *Early Days in Detroit.* Detroit: Richmond and Blacker, 1906.

Palmer, Michael A. *Stoddert's War: Naval Operations during the Quasi-War with France, 1798–1801.* Columbia: University of South Carolina Press, 1987.

Palmer, T. H., ed. *The Historical Register of the United States: From the Declaration of War in 1812, to January 1, 1814.* 4 vols. Philadelphia: G. Palmer, 1814.

Pancake, John S. *Samuel Smith and the Politics of Business, 1752–1839.* Tuscaloosa: University of Alabama Press, 1970.

Parissien, Steven. *George IV.* London: St. Martin's, 2002.

Parkinson, C. N., ed. *The Trade Winds: A Study of British Overseas Trade during the French Wars, 1793–1815.* London: George Allen and Unwin, 1948.

Parks, Joseph Howard. *Felix Grundy: Champion of Democracy.* Baton Rouge: Louisiana State University Press, 1940.

Parsons, Usher. *Battle of Lake Erie: A Discourse Delivered before the Rhode Island Historical Society . . . Delivered Feb. 16, 1852.* Providence: Benjamin T. Albro, 1853.

——— *Surgeon of the Lakes: The Diary of Dr. Usher Parsons.* Ed. John C. Fredriksen. Erie, Pa.: Erie County Historical Society, 2000.

Parsons, William Barclay. *Robert Fulton and the Submarine.* New York: Columbia University Press, 1922.

Parton, James. *Life of Andrew Jackson.* 3 vols. Boston: Houghton Mifflin, 1883.

Patrick, Rembert Wallace. *Florida Fiasco: Rampant Rebels on the Georgia-Florida Border, 1810–1815.* Athens: University of Georgia Press, 1954.

Patton, Charles. *Chalmette: The Battle for New Orleans and How the British Nearly Stole the Louisiana Territory.* Bowling Green, Ky.: Hickory Tales Publishing, 2001.

Paullin, Charles O. *American Voyages to the Orient, 1690–1865.* Annapolis: Naval Institute Press, 1991.

——— *Commodore John Rodgers, 1773–1838.* Annapolis: Naval Institute Press, 1967.

———, ed. *The Battle of Lake Erie: A Collection of Documents, Chiefly by Commodore Perry; Including the Court-Martial of Commander Barclay and the Court of Inquiry on Captain Elliott.* Cleveland: Rowfant Club, 1918.

Pearse, H. W. *History of The 31st Foot Huntingdonshire Regt. and 70th Foot Surrey Regt. Subsequently 1st and 2nd Battalions The East Surrey Regiment.* Vol. 1: *1702–1914.* London: Spottiswoode, Ballantyne, 1916.

Pemberton, Charles Reece. *The Autobiography of Pel. Verjuice.* London: Scholartis, 1929.

Penley, J. *A Narrative. A Short and Thrilling Narrative of a Few of the Scenes and Incidents That Occurred in the Sanguinary and Cruel War of 1812–14 between England and the United States.* Norway, Maine: J. Penley, 1853.

Penny, Joshua. *Life and Adventures of Joshua Penny. A Native of South Old, Long Island, Suffolk County, New York, Who Was Impressed into British Service.* Brooklyn, N.Y.: Alden Spooner, 1815.

Perkins, Bradford. *Castlereagh and Adams: England and the United States, 1812–1823.* Berkeley: University of California Press, 1964.

——— *The First Rapprochement: England and the United States, 1795–1805.* Philadelphia: University of Pennsylvania Press, 1955.

——— *Prologue to War: England and the United States, 1805–1812.* Berkeley: University of California Press, 1961.

———, ed. *The Causes of the War of 1812: National Honor or National Interest?* New York: Holt, Rinehart and Winston, 1962.

Perret, Geoffrey. *A Country Made by War: From the Revolution to Vietnam—The Story of America's Rise to Power.* New York: Random House, 1989.

Perrett, Bryan. *The Real Hornblower: The Life of Admiral Sir James Gordon, GCB.* Annapolis: Naval Institute Press, 1997.

Perrin, W. G., and C. Lloyd, eds. *The Keith Papers.* Naval Records Society, vols. 62, 90, and 96. London, 1927–1955.

Peters, R., G. Mont, and G. P. Sanders, eds. *The Public Statutes at Large (The Statutes at Large, Treaties and Proclamations) of the United States of America from the Organization of Government in 1789 to March 3, 1845. With References to the Matter of Each Act and to the Subsequent Acts on the Same Subject, and Copious Notes of the Decisions of the Courts of the United States.* 8 vols. Boston: Little, Brown, 1845.

Peters, Virginia B. *The Florida Wars.* Hamden, Conn.: Archon Books, 1979.

Peterson, Merrill D. *Thomas Jefferson and the New Nation: A Biography.* Norwalk, Conn.: Easton, 1987.

Petre, F. L. *The Royal Berkshire Regiment (Princess Charlotte of Wales's).* Vol. 1: *1743–1914.* Reading: The Barracks, 1925.

Petrie, Charles. *George Canning.* London: Eyre and Spottiswoode, 1946.

——— *Lord Liverpool and His Times.* London: James Barrie, 1954.

Petrie, Donald A. *The Prize Game: Lawful Looting on the High Seas in the Days of Fighting Sail.* Annapolis: Naval Institute Press, 1999.

Phelan, M. K. *The Burning of Washington: August 1814.* New York: Thomas Y. Crowell, 1975.

Philip, Cynthia Owen. *Robert Fulton: A Biography.* New York: Franklin Watts, 1985.

Philippart, John. *The Royal Military Calendar. Containing the Services of Every General Officer, Lieutenant-General and Major-General, in the British Army. From the Date of the First Commission, and the Services of Colonels and Lieutenant-Colonels; with Appendices, Containing Accounts of the Operations of the Army under Lieutenant-General Sir John Murray on the Eastern Coast of Spain in 1812–13.* 3 vols. London: A. J. Valpy, 1815.

Phillips, Walter Alison, and Arthur H. Reede. *Neutrality: Its History, Economics, and Law.* Vol. 2: *The Napoleonic Period.* New York: University of Columbia Press, 1936.

Picking, Sherwood. *Sea Fight off Monhegan: Enterprise and Boxer.* Portland, Maine: Machigionne, 1941.

Piers, Harry. *The Evolution of Halifax Fortress, 1749–1928.* Halifax: Public Archives of Nova Scotia, 1947.

Pierson, Marion John Bennett. *Louisiana Soldiers in the War of 1812.* Baton Rouge: Louisiana Genealogical and Historical Society, 1963.

Pirtle, Alfred. *The Battle of Tippecanoe.* Louisville, Ky.: Filson Club Publications, 1900.

Pitch, Anthony S. *The Burning of Washington: The British Invasion of 1814.* Annapolis: Naval Institute Press, 1998.

Pocock, Tom. *Captain Marryat, Seaman, Writer and Adventurer.* London: Chatham, 2000.

Poolman, Kenneth. *Guns off Cape Ann: The Story of the Shannon and the Chesapeake.* London: Evans Bros., 1961.

Pope, Dudley. *Life in Nelson's Navy.* London: Chatham, 1997.

Porter, David. *Journal of a Cruise Made to the Pacific Ocean, by Captain David Porter, in the United States Frigate Essex, in the Years 1812, 1813, and 1814.* 2 vols. New York: Wiley and Halstead, 1815.

Porter, Kenneth W. *John Jacob Astor, Businessman.* 2 vols. Cambridge, Mass.: Harvard University Press, 1931.

Pound, Merritt B. *Benjamin Hawkins: Indian Agent.* Athens: University of Georgia Press, 1951.

Pratt, Fletcher. *Preble's Boys: Commodore Preble and the Birth of American Sea Power.* New York: W. Sloane, 1950.

Pratt, Julius W. *Expansionists of 1812.* New York: Macmillan, 1925.

Preston, Richard A. *The Defence of the Undefended Border: Planning for War in North America, 1867–1939.* Montreal: McGill–Queen's University Press, 1977.

Pringle, J. F. *Lunenburgh, or the Old East District.* Cornwall, Ont.: Standard Printing House, 1890.

Proceedings of a Court Martial Holden at Quebec for the Trial of Lieutenant Benoit Bender of the 41st Regiment of Foot, in July, 1815. Montreal: J. Lane, 1817.

[Proctor, G.] *The Lucubrations of Humphrey Ravelin, Esq., Late Major in the ** Regiment of Infantry.* London: G. B. Whitaker, 1823.

Proctor, H. A. *Defence of Major General Proctor Tried at Montreal by a General Court Martial upon Charges Reflecting His Character as a Soldier.* Montreal: John Lovell, 1842.

Pryke, K. G., and L. L. Kusilek, eds. *The Western District: Papers from the Western District Conference.* Windsor, Ont.: Essex Historical Society, 1983.

Pullen, H. F. *The Shannon and the Chesapeake.* Toronto: McClelland and Stewart, 1970.

Purdon, H. G. *Memoirs of the Services of The 64th Regiment (Second Staffordshire) 1758 to 1881.* London: W. H. Allen, n.d.

Quaife, Milo M. *Chicago and the Old Northwest, 1673–1835: A Study of the Evolution of the Northwestern Frontier, Together with a History of Fort Dearborn.* Urbana: University of Illinois Press, 2001.

——— *The Yankees Capture York.* Detroit: Wayne University Press, 1955.

Quimby, Robert S. *The U.S. Army in the War of 1812: An Operational and Command Study.* 2 vols. East Lansing: Michigan State University Press, 1997.

Quisenberry, A. C. *Kentucky in the War of 1812.* Frankfort: Kentucky Historical Society, 1915.

Raddall, T. H. *The Path of Destiny.* Toronto: Doubleday, 1958.

Raise the Flag, and Other Patriotic Canadian Songs and Poems. Toronto: Rose Publishing, 1891.

Rakove, Jack. *James Madison and the Creation of the American Republic.* New York: HarperCollins, 1990.

Ralfe, James J., ed. *The Naval Biography of Great Britain: Consisting of Historical Memoirs of Those Officers of the British Navy Who Distinguished Themselves during the Reign of His Majesty George III.* 4 vols. London, 1828.

——— *The Naval Chronology of Great Britain: An Historical Account of Naval and Maritime Events, from the Commencement of the War in 1803, to the End of the Year 1816; Also Particulars of the Most Important Courts-Martial, Votes of Parliament, Lists of Flag-Officers . . .* 3 vols. London: Whitmore and Fenn, 1820.

Rammage, Stuart A. *The Militia Stood Alone: Malcolm's Mills, 6 November 1814.* Summerland, B.C.: Valley Publishing, 2000.

Ramsay, Jack C., Jr. *Jean Laffite, Prince of Pirates.* Austin, Tex.: Eakin, 1996.

Ratner, Lorman A. *Andrew Jackson and His Tennessee Lieutenants: A Study in Political Culture.* Westport, Conn.: Greenwood, 1997.

Read, David B. *The Life and Times of Major-General Isaac Brock, K.B.* Toronto: William Briggs, 1894.

Reader, Red. *The Story of the War of 1812.* New York: Duell, Sloan and Pearce, 1960.

Reid, Stuart. *British Redcoat (2) 1793–1815.* Oxford: Osprey, 1997.

Reilly, Robin. *The British at the Gates: The New Orleans Campaign in the War of 1812.* Toronto: Robin Brass Studio, 2002.

Remini, Robert V. *Andrew Jackson and His Indian Wars.* New York: Viking, 2001.

——— *Andrew Jackson and the Course of American Empire, 1767–1821.* New York: Harper and Row, 1977.

——— *The Battle of New Orleans: Andrew Jackson and America's First Military Victory.* London: Pimlico, 2001.

——— *Henry Clay: Statesman for the Union.* New York: W. W. Norton, 1993.

The Report of the Loyal and Patriotic Society of Upper Canada. Montreal: William Gray, 1817.

Reynolds, John. *My Own Times, Embracing Also the History of My Life.* Chicago: Fergus Print, 1879.

Rhodes, Albert John. *Dartmoor Prison: A Record of 126 Years of Prisoner of War and Convict Life, 1806–1932.* London: John Lane/The Bodley Head, 1933.

Ribbe, Claude. *Le Crime de Napoléon.* Paris: Editions Privés, 2005.

Richardson, James D., ed. *A Compilation of the Messages and Papers of the Presidents, 1789–1897.* 10 vols. Washington, D.C.: Government Printing Office, 1909.

Richardson, John. *Richardson's War of 1812, with Notes and a Life of the Author by A. C. Casselman.* Toronto: Historical Publishing, 1902.

Richardson, John D. *Defense of Craney Island on the 22nd of June, 1813.* Richmond, Va., 1849.

Richter, Daniel K. *Facing East from Indian Country: A Native History of Early America.* Cambridge, Mass.: Harvard University Press, 2001.

Risch, Erna. *Quartermaster Support of the Army: The History of the Corps, 1775–1939.* Washington, D.C.: Office of the Quartermaster General, 1962.

Risjord, Norman K. *The Old Republicans. Southern Conservatism in the Age of Jefferson.* New York: Columbia University Press, 1965.

Rives, G. L., ed. *Selections from the Correspondence of Thomas Barclay, Formerly British Consul-General at New York.* New York: Harper and Brothers, 1894.

Roads, Samuel. *The Marblehead Manual.* Marblehead, Mass.: Statesman Publishing, 1883.

Roberts, James. *The Narrative of James Roberts, Soldier in the Revolution and the Battle of New Orleans.* Chicago: J. Roberts, n.d.

Robertson, Thomas B. *The Fighting Bishop: John Strachan—The First Bishop of Toronto, and Other Essays in His Times.* Ottawa: Graphic Publishers, 1926.

Robinson, C. W. *Canada and Canadian Defence: The Defensive Policy of the Dominion in Relation to the Character of Her Frontier, the Events of the War of 1812–14, and Her Position Today.* London: Hugh Rees, 1910.

——— *Life of Sir John Beverley Robinson, Bart, C.B., D.C.L., Chief Justice of Upper Canada.* Toronto: Morgan, 1904.

Rodger, N. A. M. *The Command of the Ocean: A Naval History of Britain 1649–1815*. London: Allen Lane, 2004.

Rogers, Robert Louis. *History of the Lincoln and Welland Regiment.* Ottawa: The Regiment, 1954.

Rogers, Samuel. *Autobiography of Elder Samuel Rogers.* Cincinnati: Standard Publishing, 1880.

Rogin, Michael Paul. *Fathers and Children: Andrew Jackson and the Subjugation of the American Indian.* New York: Alfred A. Knopf, 1975.

Rolo, Paul J. V. *George Canning: Three Biographical Studies.* London: Macmillan, 1965.

Ronda, James. *Astoria and Empire.* Lincoln: University of Nebraska Press, 1990.

Roosevelt, Theodore. *The Naval War of 1812.* New York: Modern Library, 1999.

Rosenberg, Max. *The Building of Perry's Fleet on Lake Erie, 1812–1813.* Harrisburg: Pennsylvania Historical and Museum Commission, 1950.

Ross, Alexander. *Adventures of the First Settlers on the Oregon or Columbia River.* London: Smith Elder, 1849.

Rowe, Mary Ellen. *Bulwark of the Republic: The American Militia in Antebellum West.* Westport, Conn.: Praeger, 2003.

Rowland, D. *Andrew Jackson's Campaign against the British, or the Mississippi Territory in the War of 1812, Concerning the Military Operations of the Americans, Creek Indians, British and Spanish, 1813–1815.* New York: Macmillan, 1926.

The Royal Inniskilling Fusiliers: Being the History of the Regiment from December 1689 to July 1914. London: Constable, 1928.

Royall, Anne. *Letters from Alabama, 1817–1822.* Ed. L. Griffith. Tuscaloosa: University of Alabama Press, 2003.

Royster, Charles. *Light Horse Harry Lee and the Legacy of the American Revolution.* New York: Alfred A. Knopf, 1981.

Russell, J., Jr., comp. *The History of the War.* Hartford: G. and J. Russell, 1815.

Rutland, Robert A. *James Madison: Founding Father.* New York: Macmillan, 1987.

——— *Madison's Alternatives: The Jeffersonian Republicans and the Coming of War, 1805–1812.* Philadelphia: J. B. Lippincott, 1975.

———, ed. *James Madison and the American Nation, 1751–1836.* New York: Simon and Schuster, 1994.

Ryerson, Egerton. *The Loyalists of America and Their Times, from 1620 to 1816.* 2 vols. Toronto: Briggs, 1880.

Sale, Kirkpatrick. *The Fire of His Genius: Robert Fulton and the American Dream.* New York: Free Press, 2001.

Sapio, Victor A. *Pennsylvania and the War of 1812.* Lexington: University of Kentucky Press, 1970.

Saunt, Claudio. *A New Order of Things: Property, Power, and the Transformation of the Creek Indians, 1773–1816.* New York: Cambridge University Press, 1999.

Savage, Carlton. *Policy of the United States toward Maritime Commerce in War.* Washington, D.C.: Government Printing Office, 1934.

Saxon, Lyle. *Lafitte the Pirate.* New York: Century, 1930.

Scanlan, Peter Lawrence. *Prairie du Chien: French, British, American.* Menasha, Wis.: George Banta, 1937.

Schlesinger, Arthur M., Fred L. Israel, and William P. Hansen, eds. *History of American Presidential Elections: 1789–1968.* 4 vols. New York: Chelsea House Publishers in Association with McGraw-Hill, 1971.

Schmidt, Philip R. *Hezekiah Niles and American Economic Nationalism: A Political Biography.* New York: Arno, 1982.

Schom, Alan. *Trafalgar: Countdown to Battle, 1803–1805.* Harmondsworth: Penguin, 1992.

Schroeder, Paul W. *The Transformation of European Politics, 1763–1848.* Oxford: Oxford University Press, 1994.

Scott, James. *Recollections of a Naval Life.* 3 vols. London: Richard Bentley, 1834.

Scott, Winfield. *Memoirs of Lieut.-General Scott, LL.D. Written by Himself.* 2 vols. New York: Sheldon, 1864.

Sears, Alfred Byron. *Thomas Worthington: Father of Ohio Statehood.* Columbus: Ohio State University Press, 1998.

Sears, Louis M. *Jefferson and the Embargo.* Durham, N.C.: Duke University Press, 1927.

Sellar, Robert. *The U.S. Campaign of 1813 to Capture Montreal: Crysler, the Decisive Battle of the War of 1812.* Huntington, Quebec: Gleaner Office, 1913.

Sellers, Charles Grier. *The Market Revolution: Jacksonian America, 1815–1846.* New York: Oxford University Press, 1991.

Shaler, N. S. *Kentucky: A Pioneer Commonwealth.* Boston: Houghton Mifflin, 1885.

Sharp, Solomon P. *Sharp's Motion. Relating to the Conduct of Martin Chrittenden, Governor of Vermont, in . . . Ordering the Militia of That State, Engaged in the Service of the United States, to Withdraw from Their Service.* Washington, D.C.: A. and G. Way, 1814.

Shaw, Elijah. *Short Sketch of the Life of Elijah Shaw, Who Served Twenty One Years in the United States Navy, Taking Part in Four Different Wars.* Rochester, N.Y.: Strong, Dawson, 1843.

Sheads, Scott S. *Guardian of the Star-Spangled Banner: Lt. Colonel George Armistead and the Fort McHenry Flag.* Baltimore: Toomey, 1999.

——— *The Rockets' Red Glare: The Maritime Defense of Baltimore in 1814.* Centreville, Md.: Tidewater Publishers, 1986.

Sheads, Scott S., and Merle T. Cole. *Fort McHenry and Baltimore's Harbor Defenses.* Charleston, S.C.: Arcadia Publishing, 2001.

Sheldon, E. M. *The Early History of Michigan from the First Settlement to 1815.* New York: A. S. Barnes, 1856.

Shepard, Elihu H. *The Autobiography of Elihu H. Shepard, Formerly Professor of Languages in St. Louis College.* St. Louis, Mo.: George Knapp, 1869.

Sheppard, George. *Plunder, Profit, and Paroles: A Social History of the War of 1812 in Upper Canada.* Montreal: McGill–Queen's University Press, 1994.

Shomette, Donald G. *Flotilla: Battle for the Patuxent.* Solomons, Md.: Calvert Marine Museum Press, 1981.

——— *Ships on the Chesapeake: Maritime Disasters on Chesapeake Bay and Its Tributaries, 1608–1978.* Centreville, Md.: Tidewater Publications, 1982.

——— *Tidewater Time Capsule: History beneath the Patuxent.* Centreville, Md.: Tidewater Publications, 1995.

Silver, James W. *Edmund Pendleton Gaines: Frontier General.* Baton Rouge: Louisiana State University Press, 1949.

Silverstone, Scott A. *Divided Union: The Politics of War in the Early American Republic.* Ithaca: Cornell University Press, 2004.

Siry, Steven E. *De Witt Clinton and the American Political Economy: Sectionalism, Politics, and Republican Ideology, 1787–1828.* New York: Peter Lang, 1990.

Sistler, Byron, and Samuel Sistler, comps. *Tennesseans in the War of 1812.* Nashville: Bryon Sistler and Associates, 1992.

Skaggs, David Curtis. *Thomas Macdonough: Master of Command in the Early U.S. Navy.* Annapolis: Naval Institute Press, 2003.

Skaggs, David Curtis, and Gerard T. Altoff. *A Signal Victory: The Lake Erie Campaign, 1812–1813.* Annapolis: Naval Institute Press, 1997.

Skeen, Carl Edward. *Citizen Soldiers in the War of 1812.* Lexington: University Press of Kentucky, 1999.

——— *John Armstrong Jr., 1758–1843: A Biography.* Syracuse, N.Y.: Syracuse University Press, 1981.

Sketch of the Life of General Nathan Towson, United States Army. Baltimore: N. Hickman, 1842.

Skirven, Percy Granger. *Kent's Part in the War, 1812–1814: "The Battle of Caulk's Field."* Sykesville, Md.: Springfield State Hospital Press, 1914.

Slosek, Anthony M. *Oswego and the War of 1812.* Ed. H. M. Breitbeck. Oswego, N.Y.: Heritage Foundation of Oswego, 1989.

Smelser, Marshall. *The Congress Founds the Navy, 1787–1798.* Notre Dame, Ind.: University of Notre Dame Press, 1959.

——— *The Democratic Republic, 1801–1815.* New York: Harper and Row, 1968.

Smith, Adam. *An Inquiry into the Nature and Causes of the Wealth of Nations* (1776). Ed. Edwin Cannan. 2 vols. London: Methuen, 1904.

Smith, Dwight L. *The War of 1812: An Annotated Bibliography.* New York: Garland, 1985.

Smith, Gene A. *"For the Purposes of Defense": The Politics of the Jeffersonian Gunboat Program.* London: Associated Presses, 1995.

——— *Thomas ap Catesby Jones: Commodore of Manifest Destiny.* Annapolis: Naval Institute Press, 2000.

Smith, Harry. *The Autobiography of Lieutenant-General Sir Harry Smith Baronet of Aliwal on the Sutlej G.C.B.* Ed. G. C. Moore-Smith. London: John Murray, 1902.

Smith, John Cotton. *The Correspondence and Miscellanies of the Hon. John Cotton Smith. With an Eulogy Pronounced before the Connecticut Historical Society at New Haven, May 27th, 1846, by the Rev. William W. Andrews.* New York: Harper, 1847.

Smith, Joseph Burkholder. *The Plot to Steal Florida: James Madison's Phony War.* New York: Arbor House, 1983.

Smith, Joshua M. *Borderland Smuggling: Patriots, Loyalists, and Illicit Trade in the Northeast, 1783–1820.* Gainesville: University Press of Florida, 2006.

Smith, Margaret B. *Forty Years of Washington Society Portrayed by the Family Letters of Mrs. Samuel Harrison Smith (Margaret Bayard) from the Collection of Her Grandson J. Henley Smith.* Ed. G. Hunt. London: T. Fisher Unwin, 1906.

Smith, Moses. *Naval Scenes of the Last War; or, Three Years aboard the Frigates Constitution and the Adams, Including the Capture of the Guerrière.* Boston: Gleason's Publishing House, 1846.

Smith, Philip Chadwick Foster. *The Frigate Essex Papers: Building the Salem Frigate, 1798–1799.* Salem, Mass.: Peabody Museum of Salem, 1974.

Smyth, Benjamin. *History of the XX Regiment 1688–1888.* London: Simkin, Marshall, 1889.

Smyth, Carter J. *The Story of Dundas, Being a History of the County of Dundas from 1784 to 1903.* Iroqouis, Ont.: St. Lawrence News, 1905.

Snelling, Josiah. *Remarks on "General Hull's Memoir of the Northwestern Army, 1812."* Detroit: Sheldon, Wells, 1825.

Snider, C. H. J. *The Glorious "Shannon's" Old Blue Duster and Other Faded Flags of Fadeless Fame.* Toronto: McClelland and Stewart, 1923.

——— *In the Wake of the Eighteen-Twelvers. Fights and Flights of Frigates and Fore-'n'-Afters in the War of 1812–15 on the Great Lakes.* London: John Lane, 1913.

——— *Leaves from the War Log of the Nancy: Eighteen Hundred and Thirteen.* Toronto: Rous and Mann, 1936.

——— *The Story of the Nancy and Other Eighteen-Twelvers.* Toronto: McClelland and Stewart, 1928.

——— *Under the Red Jack: Privateers of the Maritime Provinces of Canada in the War of 1812.* London: M. Hopkinson, 1928.

Sonneck, Oscar G. T. *Report on "The Star-Spangled Banner," "Hail Columbia," "America," "Yankee Doodle."* Washington, D.C.: Government Printing Office, 1909.

Spater, George. *William Cobbett: The Poor Man's Friend.* 2 vols. Cambridge: Cambridge University Press, 1982.

Spiller, Roger I., Joseph G. Dawson, and T. Harry Williams, eds. *Dictionary of American Military Biography.* 3 vols. Westport, Conn.: Greenwood, 1984.

Spivak, Burton. *Jefferson's English Crisis: Commerce, Embargo, and the Republican Revolution.* Charlottesville: University of Virginia Press, 1979.

Sprout, Harold, and Margaret Sprout. *The Rise of American Naval Power, 1776–1918.* Annapolis: Naval Institute Press, 1990.

Squires, W. A. *The 104th Regiment of Foot (The New Brunswick Regiment) 1803–1817*. Fredericton, N.B.: Brunswick Press, 1962.

Stacey, C. P. *The Battle of Little York*. Toronto: Toronto Historical Board, 1963.

——— *The Military Problems of Canada: A Survey of Defence Policies and Strategic Conditions Past and Present*. Toronto: P. Ryerson for Canadian Institute of International Affairs, 1940.

Stagg, J. C. A. *Mr. Madison's War: Politics, Diplomacy, and Warfare in the Early American Republic, 1783–1830*. Princeton: Princeton University Press, 1983.

Stahl, John Meloy. *The Battle of Plattsburg: A Study in and of the War of 1812*. Argos, Ind.: Van Trump, 1918.

Stanley, G. F. G. *Battle in the Dark: Stoney Creek, 6 June, 1813*. Toronto: Balmuir Publishing, 1991.

——— *Canada Invaded: 1775–1776*. Candian War Museum Series, Historical Publications No. 8. Toronto: Samuel Stevens Hakkert, 1977.

——— *The War of 1812: Land Operations*. Toronto: Macmillan, 1983.

Starkey, David J., E. S. van Eyck van Heslinga, and J. A. de Moor, eds. *Pirates and Privateers: New Perspectives on the War on Trade in the Eighteenth and Nineteenth Centuries*. Exeter: Exeter University Press, 1997.

Steele, Ian K. *Betrayals: Fort William Henry and the Massacre*. New York: Oxford University Press, 1990.

Steffen, Jerome O. *William Clark: Jeffersonian Man on the Frontier*. Norman: University of Oklahoma Press, 1977.

Stephen, James. *War in Disguise; or, The Frauds of the Neutral Flags*. London: University of London Press, 1917.

Stevens, Frank E. *The Black Hawk War, Including a Review of Black Hawk's Life*. Chicago: Frank E. Stevens, 1903.

Stevens, William Oliver. *An Affair of Honor: The Biography of Commodore James Barron, U.S.N.* Norfolk, Va.: Norfolk County Historical Society of Chesapeake, Virginia, in Cooperation with the Earl Gregg Swemm Library of the College of William and Mary, 1969.

——— *David Glasgow Farragut: Our First Admiral*. New York: Dodd, Mead, 1942.

Stevenson, James. *War of 1812 in Connection with the Army Bill Act*. Montreal: W. Foster Brown, 1892.

Stinchcomb, William. *The XYZ Affair*. Westport, Conn.: Greenwood, 1980.

Stockell, William. *The Eventful Narrative of Capt. William Stockell, of His Travels, of His Various and Signal Engagements in the Land and Naval Service of His Britannic Majesty, and of the United States and of His Adventures and Achievements in the Whale Fishery*. Cincinnati: S. Ward, 1840.

Stone, William L. *The Life and Times of Red Jacket*. New York: Wiley, Putnam, 1841.

Story, Joseph. *Joseph Story: A Collection of Writings by and about an Eminent American Jurist*. Ed. Mortimar D. Schwartz and John C. Hogan. New York: Oceana Publications, 1959.

Stott, Glenn. *Greater Evils: The War of 1812 in Southwestern Ontario.* Arkona, Ont.: G. Stott Publishing, 2001.

Strachan, John. *The John Strachan Letterbook, 1812–1834.* Ed. George W. Spragge. Toronto: Ontario Historical Society, 1946.

——— *Memoir of the Right Reverend John Strachan, D.D., L.L.D: First Bishop of Toronto.* Ed. Alexander D. Bethune. Toronto: H. Rowsell, 1870.

Stuart, Reginald C. *The Half-Way Pacifist: Thomas Jefferson's View of War.* Toronto: University of Toronto Press, 1978.

——— *United States Expansionism and British North America, 1775–1871.* Chapel Hill: University of North Carolina Press, 1988.

Studenski, Paul, and Herman E. Krooss. *Financial History of the United States: Fiscal, Monetary, Banking, and Tariff, Including Financial Administration and State and Local Finance.* New York: McGraw-Hill, 1952.

Sugden, John. *Tecumseh: A Life.* London: Pimlico, 1999.

——— *Tecumseh's Last Stand.* Norman: University of Oklahoma Press, 1985.

Sulte, Benjamin. *La Bataille de Châteauguay.* Quebec City: R. Renault, 1899.

Surtees, William. *Twenty-five Years in The Rifle Brigade.* London: Frederick Mueller, 1973.

Sutcliffe, Alice Crary. *Robert Fulton and the "Clermont": The Authoritative Story of Robert Fulton's Early Experiments, Persistent Efforts, and Historic Achievements, Containing Many of Fulton's Hitherto Unpublished Letters, Drawings, and Pictures.* New York: Century, 1909.

Sutherland, Stuart. *His Majesty's Gentlemen: A Directory of Regular British Army Officers of the War of 1812.* Toronto: Iser Publications, 2000.

———, ed. *Two British Soldiers in the War of 1812.* Toronto: Iser Publications, 2002.

Suthren, Victor. *The War of 1812.* Toronto: Canadian Publishers, 1999.

Swanton, John R. *Social Organization and Social Usages of the Indians of the Creek Confederacy—Religious Beliefs and Medical Practices of the Creek Indians.—Aboriginal Culture of the Southeast.* Forty-second Annual Report, U.S. Bureau of American Ethnology, Smithsonian Institution. Washington, D.C.: Government Printing Office, 1928.

Swayze, Fred. *The Rowboat War on the Great Lakes.* London: Macmillan, 1965.

Sweetman, Jack, Douglas C. Meister, Sharon Pfeiffer, and Brian Van De Mark, eds. *New Interpretations in Naval History: 10th Naval History Symposium.* Annapolis: Naval Institute Press, 1993.

Swift, Joseph Gardner. *The Memoirs of Gen. Joseph Gardner Swift, LL.D., U.S.A., First Graduate of the United States Military Academy, West Point, Chief Engineer U.S.A. from 1812 to 1818: 1800–1865: to Which Is Added a Genealogy of the Family of Thomas Swift of Dorchester, Mass., 1634.* Ed. Ellery Harrison. Worcester, Mass.: F. S. Blanchard, 1890.

Symonds, Craig L. *Navalists and Anti-Navalists: The Naval Policy Debate in the United States, 1785–1827.* Newark: University of Delaware Press, 1980.

Symons, J., ed. *The Battle of Queenston Heights, Being a Narrative of the Opening of the War of 1812, with Notices of the Life of Major-General Isaac Brock K.B., and Description of the Monument Erected to His Memory.* Toronto: Thompson and Sons, 1859.

Tallant, Robert. *The Pirate Lafitte and the Battle of New Orleans.* Gretna, La.: Pelican Publishing, 1998.

Talman, J. J., ed. *Loyalist Narratives from Upper Canada.* Toronto: Champlain Society, 1946.

Taylor, George Rogers, ed. *The War of 1812: Past Justifications and Present Interpretations.* Boston: D. C. Heath, 1963.

Temperly, Howard., ed. *New Brunswick Journals of 1811 and 1813 by Lieutenant-Colonel Joseph Gubbins, Inspecting Officer of Militia.* Fredericton, N.B.: New Brunswick Heritage, 1980.

Tennyson, Brian D., ed. *Canada and the Commonwealth Caribbean.* London: University Press of America, 1988.

Testimony Taken before the Committee of Grievances and Courts of Justice: Relative to the Late Riots and Mobs in the City of Baltimore. Annapolis: Jonas Green, 1813.

Thacher, James. *American Medical Biography.* Vol. 2. New York: Milford House, 1967.

Thompson, Neville. *Earl Bathurst and the British Empire.* Barnsley: Leo Cooper, 1999.

Thwaites, Reuben G. *Wisconsin: The Americanization of a French Settlement.* Boston: Houghton Mifflin, 1908.

Todd, Charles S., and Benjamin Drake. *Sketches of the Civil and Military Services of William Henry Harrison.* Cinncinati: U. P. James, 1840.

Toll, Ian W. *Six Frigates: The Epic History of the Founding of the U.S. Navy.* New York: W. W. Norton, 2006.

Tompkins, Daniel D. *The Public Papers of Daniel D. Tompkins, Governor of New York.* Ed. H. Hastings. 3 vols. New York: J. B. Lyon, 1898–1902.

Townsend, Robert B. *The Story of HMS St. Lawrence: The Canadian Built Ship That Won the War of 1812.* Carrying Place, Ont.: Odyssey, 1998.

Tracy, Nicholas, ed. *The Naval Chronicle: Contemporary Views of the War at Sea.* Vol. 5. London: Chatham, 2003.

Treat, Joseph. *The Vindication of Captain Joseph Treat, Late of Twenty-first Regiment United States Infantry, against the Atrocious Calumny Comprehended in Major General Brown's Official Report of the Battle of Chippeway.* Boston, 1815.

Trowbridge, Francis Bacon. *The Trowbridge Genealogy.* New Haven: Tuttle, More, Taylor, 1908.

Tucker, Glenn. *Poltroons and Patriots: A Popular Account of the War of 1812.* 2 vols. Indianapolis: Bobbs-Merrill, 1954.

——— *Tecumseh: Vision of Glory.* Indianapolis: Bobbs-Merrill, 1956.

Tucker, Spencer C. *Arming the Fleet: United States Navy Ordnance in the Muzzle-Laoding Era.* Annapolis: Naval Institute Press, 1989.

——— *The Jeffersonian Gunboat Navy.* Columbia: University of South Carolina Press, 1993.

——— *Stephen Decatur: A Life Most Bold and Daring.* Annapolis: Naval Institute Press, 2004.

Tucker, Spencer C., and Frank T. Reuter. *Injured Honor: The Chesapeake-Leopard Affair, June 22, 1807.* Annapolis: Naval Institute Press, 1996.

Tuckerman, Henry Theodore. *The Life of John Pendleton Kennedy.* New York: G. P. Putnam and Sons, 1871.

Tulchinsky, Gerald, ed. *To Preserve and Defend: Essays on Kingston in the Nineteenth Century.* Montreal: McGill–Queen's University Press, 1976.

Tullett, Eric. *Inside Dartmoor.* London: Frederick Muller, 1966.

Tunstall, Brian. *Naval Warfare in the Age of Sail: The Evolution of Fighting Tactics, 1650–1815.* Annapolis: Naval Institute Press, 1990.

Tupper, Ferdinand Broele, ed. *The Life and Correspondence of Major-General Sir Isaac Brock, K.B.: Interspersed with Notices of the Celebrated Indian Chief Tecumseh, and Comprising Brief Memoirs of Daniel De Lisle Brock Esq, Lieutenant E. W. Tupper R.N., and Colonel W. De Vic Tupper.* London: Simpkin, Marshall, 1847.

Turner, Wesley B. *British Generals in the War of 1812: High Command in the Canadas.* Montreal: McGill–Queen's University Press, 1999.

——— *The War of 1812: The War That Both Sides Won.* Toronto: Dundurn, 1990.

———, ed. *The Military in the Niagara Peninsula.* St. Catharines, Ont.: Vanwell Publishing, 1990.

Tyler, Samuel. *Memoir of Roger Brooke Taney, L.L.D.* Baltimore: John Murphy, 1872.

U.S. Congress. *American State Papers, I: Foreign Relations.* 6 vols. Washington, D.C.: Gales and Seaton, 1832–1859.

——— *American State Papers, II: Indian Affairs.* 2 vols. Washington, D.C.: Gales and Seaton, 1832–1834.

——— *American State Papers, III: Finance.* 5 vols. Washington, D.C.: Gales and Seaton, 1832–1859.

——— *American State Papers, V: Military Affairs.* 7 vols. Washington, D.C.: Gales and Seaton, 1832–1861.

——— *American State Papers, VI: Naval Affairs.* 4 vols. Washington, D.C.: Gales and Seaton, 1834–1861.

——— *The Debates and Proceedings of the Congress of the United States* [*Annals of Congress*]. 42 vols. Washington, D.C.: Gales and Seaton, 1834–1856.

Updyke, F. A. *The Diplomacy of the War of 1812.* Baltimore: Johns Hopkins Press, 1915.

Up the Glens: Stormont, Dundas and Glengarry Highlanders, 1783–1994. Cornwall, Ont.: Old Bookstore, 1995.

Valpey, Joseph, Jr. *Journal of Joseph Valpey, Jr., of Salem, November 1813–April, 1815. With Other Papers Relating to His Experience in Dartmoor Prison.* Ed. E. G. Valpey. Detroit: Michigan Society of Colonial Wars, 1922.

Vandal, Albert. *Napoléon et Alexandre 1er: L'Alliance russe sous le premier empire.* 2 vols. Paris: Plon, 1891 and 1896.

Van der Voort, P. J. *The Pen and the Quarter-deck: A Study of the Life and Works of Captain Frederick Chamier.* Leiden: Leiden University Press, 1972.

Vane, C. W., ed. *Memoirs and Correspondence of Viscount Castlereagh, Second Marquess of Londonderry.* Vols. 1–4. London: H. Colburn, 1848–1849.

——— *Correspondence, Despatches and Other Papers of Viscount Castlereagh, Second Marquess of Londonderry.* Vols. 5–12. London: H. Colburn, 1850–1853.

Van Horne, James. *Narrative of James Van Horne . . . on the Plains of Michigan.* Middleboro, Miss.: Lawrence B. Romaine, n.d.

Van Rensselaer, Stephen. *A Narrative of the Affair of Queenstown: In the War of 1812. With a Review of the Strictures on That Event in a Book Entitled, "Notices of the War of 1812" (by J. Armstrong).* Boston: Leavitt, Lord, 1836.

Verchères de Boucherville, Thomas. *War on the Detroit: The Chronicles of Thomas Verchères de Boucherville and the Capitulation, by an Ohio Volunteer.* Ed. Milo M. Quaife. Chicago: R. R. Donnelley and Sons, 1940.

Vernon, B. J. *Early Recollections of Jamaica with Particulars of an Eventful Passage Home via New York and Halifax at the Commencement of the American War of 1812.* London: Whittaker, 1848.

Viger, Jacques. *Reminiscences of the War of 1812–14: Being Portions of the Diary of a Captain of the "Voltigeurs Canadiens" While in Garrison at Kingston, etc.* Trans. J. L. H. Neilson. Kingston, Ont.: News Printing, 1895.

Waddell, I. H. *Horrid Massacre at Dartmoor Prison, England, Where the Unarmed American Prisoners of War Were Wantonly Fired upon by the Guard, under the Command of the Prison Turn-Key, the Bloodthirsty Shortland. Seven Were Killed, and about Fifty Wounded (Several Mortally) . . .* Boston: Nathaniel Conerly, 1815.

Wade, Richard C. *The Urban Frontier: The Rise of Western Cities, 1790–1830.* Cambridge, Mass.: Harvard University Press, 1959.

Wailes, B. L. C. *Memoir of Leonard Covington by B. L. C. Wailes, Also Some of General Covington's Letters Edited by Nellie Wailes Brandon and W. M. Drake.* Natchez, Miss.: Natchez Printing and Stationery, 1928.

Walker, Adam. *A Journal of Two Campaigns of the Fourth Regiment of U.S. Infantry: In the Michigan and Indiana Territories, under the Command of Col. John P. Boyd, and Lt. Col. James Miller, during the Years 1811 & 12.* Keene, N.H.: Privately published at Sentinel Press, 1816.

Walker, Alexander. *Jackson and New Orleans: An Authentic Narrative of the Achievements of the American Army under Andrew Jackson before New Orleans.* Cranbury, N.J.: Scholars Bookshelf, 2005.

Walker, H. M. *A History of The Northumberland Fusiliers 1674–1902.* London: John Murray, 1919.

Wallace, W. S. *The Story of Laura Secord: A Study in Historical Evidence.* Toronto: Macmillan, 1932.

Walters, James R., Jr. *Alexander James Dallas: Lawyer, Politician, Financier, 1759–1817.* New York: Da Capo, 1969.

Walters, Ray. *Albert Gallatin, Jeffersonian Financier and Diplomat.* New York: Macmillan, 1957.

Walton, E. P., ed. *Records of the Governor and Council of the State of Vermont.* Vol 6: *Vermont in the War of 1812.* Montpelier, Vt.: J. and J. M. Poland, 1878.

Warden, David Bailie. *A Chorographical and Statistical Description of the District of Columbia: The Seat of the General Government of the United States.* Paris: Smith, 1816.

Watkins, Walter Kendall. *The Defence of Boston in the War of 1812–15. Prepared for the Bostonian Society and United States Daughters of the War of 1812, with an Appendix Containing a Bibliography of the War, and a List of the Officers of the Massachusetts Militia Engaged in the Defence.* Boston: W. K. Watkins, 1899.

Watson, J. S. *The Reign of George III, 1760–1815.* Oxford: Oxford University Press, 1960.

Watts, Steven. *The Republic Reborn: War and the Making of Liberal America, 1790–1820.* Baltimore: Johns Hopkins Unviersity Press, 1989.

Webster, Charles K. *The Foreign Policy of Castlereagh, 1812–1815.* London: Bell, 1931.

———, ed. *British Diplomacy, 1813–1815: Select Documents Dealing with the Reconstruction of Europe.* London: G. Bell and Sons, 1921.

Weigley, R. F. *History of the U.S. Army.* New York: Macmillan, 1967.

Weiss, J. M. *The Merikens: Free Black American Settlers in Trinidad, 1815–16.* London: McNish and Weiss, 2002.

Wellesley, Arthur, Duke of Wellington. *Despatches, Correspondence and Memoranda of Field Marshal Arthur, Duke of Wellington.* Ed. A. R. Wellesley. 15 vols. London: John Murray, 1858–1872.

——— *The Dispatches of Field Marshal the Duke of Wellington, during His Various Campaigns in India, Denmark, Portugal, Spain, the Low Countries, and France from 1799–1818.* Ed. J. Gurwood. 13 vols. London: John Murray, 1837–1839.

Welsh, William Jeffrey, and David Curtis Skaggs, eds. *War on the Great Lakes: Essays Commemorating the 175th Anniversary of the Battle of Lake Erie.* Kent, Ohio: Kent State University Press, 1991.

Weybright, Victor. *Spangled Banner: The Story of Francis Scott Key.* New York: Farrar and Rinehart, 1935.

Wheater, W. *Historical Record of The Seventh or Royal Regiment of Fusiliers Compiled at the Request and with the Assistance of the Officers of the Regiment.* Leeds: Privately printed, 1875.

Wheelan, Joseph. *Jefferson's War: America's First War on Terror, 1801–1805.* New York: Carroll and Graf, 2004.

Whipple, Pardon Mawney. *Letters from Old Ironsides, 1813–15, Written by Pardon Mawney Whipple.* Ed. Norma Adams Price. Tempe, Ariz.: Beverly-Merriam, 1984.

White, Leonard D. *The Jeffersonians: A Study in Administrative History, 1801–1829.* New York: Macmillan, 1951.

White, Patrick C. T. *A Nation on Trial: America and the War of 1812.* New York: John Wiley and Sons, 1965.

White, Samuel. *A History of American Troops during the Late War under the Command of Cols. Fenton and Campbell.* Baltimore: S. White, 1829.

Whitehill, Walter Muir, ed. *New England Blockaded in 1814: The Journal of Henry Edward Napier, Lieutenant in H.M.S. Nymphe.* Salem, Mass.: Peabody Museum, 1939.

Whitehorne, A. C. *The History of The Welch Regiment, Part I: 1719–1914.* Cardiff: Western Mail and Echo, 1932.

Whitehorne, Joseph A. *The Battle for Baltimore, 1814.* Baltimore: Nautical and Aviation Publishing Company of America, 1997.

——— *While Washington Burned: The Battle of Fort Erie, 1814.* Baltimore: Nautical and Aviation Publishing Company of America, 1992.

Whitelaw, Ralph W. *Virginia's Eastern Shore: A History of Northampton and Accomack Counties.* 2 vols. Richmond: Virginia Historical Society, 1951.

Whitton, Frederick Ernest. *The History of the Prince of Wales's Leinster Regiment (Royal Canadians) Late the 100th Prince of Wales's Royal Canadian Regiment Descended from The 100th Prince Regent's County of Dublin Regiment of Foot Disbanded in 1818: And The 109th Foot Formerly the Honorable East India Company's 3rd Bombay European Regiment: To Which Were Added Respectively The King's County Militia: The Queen's County Militia and The Royal Meath Militia: and 6th and 7th Service Battalions Raised in 1914 on the Outbreak of the Great War: Part One, The Old Army.* Aldershot: Gale and Polden, 1924.

Wilder, Patrick A. *The Battle of Sackett's Harbour: 1813.* Baltimore: Nautical and Aviation Publishing Company of America, 1994.

Wilkinson, Henry Campbell. *Bermuda from Sail to Steam: The History of the Island from 1784 to 1901.* 2 vols. Oxford: Oxford University Press, 1973.

Wilkinson, James. *Memoirs of My Own Times.* 3 vols. Philadelphia: Reprint Services Corporation, 1816.

Williams, Hugh Neel. *The Life and Letters of Admiral Sir Charles Napier, K.C.B.* London: Hutchinson, 1917.

Williams, J. S. *History of the Invasion and Capture of Washington and of the Events Which Preceded and Followed.* New York: Harper and Brothers, 1857.

Williams, Samuel. *Two Western Campaigns in the War of 1812–13.* Cincinnati: R. Clarke, 1871.

Williamson, William D. *The History of the State of Maine: From Its First Discovery, A.D. 1602, to the Separation, A.D. 1820, Inclusive.* 2 vols. Hallowell, Maine: Glazier, Masters, 1832.

Wills, Garry. *Henry Adams and the Making of America.* Boston: Houghton Mifflin, 2005.

Wilmer, James Jones. *A Narrative Respecting the Conduct of the British from Their First Landing at Spetsutia Island till Their Progress to Havre de Grace . . . by a Citizen of Havre de Grace.* Baltimore: P. Mauro, 1813.

Wilson, George. *Stephen Girard: America's First Tycoon.* Conshohocken, Pa.: Combined Books, 1995.

Wilson, Joseph T. *The Black Phalanx: A History of the Negro Soldiers of the United States in the Wars of 1775, 1812, 1861–'65.* Hartford: American Publishing, 1888.

Wiltse, Charles M. *John C. Calhoun: Nationalist, 1782–1828.* Indianapolis: Bobbs-Merrill, 1944.

Winslow, Richard E. *Wealth and Honour: Portsmouth during the Golden Age of Privateering.* Portsmouth, N.H.: P. E. Randall, 1988.

Winstock, Lewis. *Songs and Music of the Redcoats: A History of the War Music of the British Army, 1642–1902.* Harrisburg, Pa.: Stackpole, 1970.

Wohler, J. Patrick. *Charles Michel de Salaberry, Soldier of the Empire, Defender of Quebec.* Toronto: Dundurn, 1984.

Wood, William. *The War with the United States.* Toronto: University of Toronto Press, 1967.

Wood, W. C. H., ed. *Select British Documents of the Canadian War of 1812.* 3 vols. Toronto: Champlain Society, 1920–1928.

Woodford, Frank B. *Mr. Jefferson's Disciple: A Life of Justice Woodward.* East Lansing: Michigan State College Press, 1953.

Wright, J. Leitch, Jr. *Britain and the American Frontier, 1783–1815.* Athens: University of Georgia Press, 1975.

——— *Creeks and Seminoles: The Destruction and Regeneration of the Muscogulge People.* Lincoln: University of Nebraska Press, 1986.

Wright, Kai. *Soldiers of Freedom: An Illustrated History of African Americans in the Armed Forces.* New York: Black Dog and Levanthal Publishers, 2002.

Wrobel, Sylvia, and George Grider. *Isaac Shelby: Kentucky's First Governor and Hero of Three Wars.* Danville, Ky.: Cumberland Press, 1974.

Wrottesley, G. *Life and Correspondence of Field Marshal Sir J. Burgoyne, Bart.* 2 vols. London: Richard Bentley, 1873.

Wybourn, T. Marmaduke. *Sea Soldier. An Officer of Marines with Duncan, Nelson, Collingwood and Cockburn: The Letters and Journal of Major T. Marmaduke Wybourn, RM, 1797–1813.* Ed. Anne Petrides and Jonathan Downs. Tunbridge Wells: Parapress, 2000.

Wylly, H. C. *History of the Manchester Regiment (Late the 63rd and 96th Foot).* Vol. 1: *1758–1883.* London: Forster, Green, 1923.

Yonge, Charles D. *The Life and Administration of Robert Banks, Second Earl of Liverpool, K.G., Late First Lord of the Treasury.* 3 vols. London: Macmillan, 1868.

Young, Bennett Henderson. *The Battle of the Thames in Which Kentuckians Defeated the British, French, and Indians, October 5, 1813 with a List of the Officers and Privates Who Won the Victory.* Louisville, Ky.: Filson Club Publications, 1903.

Zacks, Richard. *The Pirate Coast: Thomas Jefferson, the First Marines, and the Secret Mission of 1805.* New York: Hyperion, 2005.

Zaslow, Morris, ed. *The Defended Border: Upper Canada and the War of 1812. A Collection of Writings Giving a Comprehensive Picture of the War of 1812 in Upper Canada:*

The Military Struggle, the Effects of the War on the People, and the Legacies of the War. Toronto: Macmillan, 1964.

Zimmerman, James F. *Impressment of American Seamen.* New York: Columbia University Press, 1925.

Zuehlke, Mark. *For Honour's Sake: The War of 1812 and the Brokering of an Uneasy Peace.* Toronto: Alfred A. Knopf, 2006.

Index

INDEX

INDEX

INDEX

INDEX

INDEX

INDEX

INDEX